IN DEFENSE OF

AMERICAN LIBERTIES

A History of the ACLU

SAMUEL WALKER

New York   Oxford
OXFORD UNIVERSITY PRESS
1990

Oxford University Press

Oxford   New York   Toronto
Delhi   Bombay   Calcutta   Madras   Karachi
Petaling Jaya   Singapore   Hong Kong   Tokyo
Nairobi   Dar es Salaam   Cape Town
Melbourne   Auckland

and associated companies in
Berlin   Ibadan

Published by Oxford University Press, Inc.,
200 Madison Avenue, New York, New York 10016

Oxford is a registered trademark of Oxford University Press

Library of Congress Cataloging-in-Publication Data
Walker, Samuel, 1942–
In defense of American liberties:
a history of the ACLU/ Samuel Walker.
p.   cm.   Bibliography: p.   Includes index.
ISBN 0–19–504539–4   I. Title.
JC599.U5W28   1990   323'.0973—dc20   89–32843   CIP

246897531

Printed in the United States of America
on acid-free paper

This book is dedicated to the thousands of civil libertarians who, over the years, contributed—some at great personal sacrifice, others in small but nonetheless important ways—to the struggle for a freer society. It is also dedicated to the generations of civil libertarians to come. No battle, after all, ever stays won.

Preface

At the outset, this book calls for a personal comment on the relationship between scholarship and political commitment. Readers have a right to know that I am an active member of the American Civil Liberties Union (ACLU). I have served on the board of directors of the ACLU since 1983 and on the board of the Nebraska Civil Liberties Union for over a decade, including two years as president of the affiliate. Thus, I can be fairly described as committed to the goals of the organization whose history I have written. In addition, I have participated in some of the events covered in the last two chapters—voting on particular ACLU policies, for example. Moreover, I was a civil rights worker in Mississippi from 1964 through 1966, an experience that is covered in Chapter Twelve, and was an active opponent of the Vietnam War, the subject of Chapter Thirteen.

These activities inevitably raise questions about scholarly objectivity. Readers might well ask how someone so deeply committed to an organization could purport to write an objective, scholarly account of its history. The answer consists of two parts. First, simply disclosing the facts of my commitments constitutes a form of "truth in labeling." Readers can make their own judgment about whether the pages that follow are biased in a way that distorts the historical record. I have not shied away from covering in detail the less attractive episodes in ACLU history—particularly the controversial events of 1940 and the cold war years. Whether I have been sufficiently critical of all aspects of the ACLU's history is for readers, reviewers, and subsequent scholars to determine. Freedom of inquiry is an important principle for civil libertarians, and so I invite critics and historians to inquire freely into my guiding assumptions, my handling of the evidence, and my conclusions.

There is, however, a second and more complex aspect to the question of how one's commitments affect scholarly objectivity. All scholarship inevitably reflects the values of the author. In fact, it is impossible for anyone to view history free of values. If you believe that people have the right to criticize the government, even in wartime, then you have made a judgment that will affect your view of the history of the ACLU. If you believe that the courts should enforce the equal protection clause of the Fourteenth Amendment, your attitude also will influence how you view ACLU history. If you believe that the Constitution does or does not protect the right to an abortion, that opinion will help determine how you think about the ACLU and its activities. We cannot free ourselves from our views on these social and political issues, and, I believe, no historian can dissociate himself or herself from them. Some of our most prominent historians and political scientists, who have written extensively on public affairs, have in fact been friends, advisers, and in some cases paid staff members of the figures they have written about. These associations, which inevitably affect how they view issues and events, have not always been disclosed to readers of their books. My only claim is that I have disclosed the nature and extent of my commitments.

Scholarly objectivity in this context means examining ACLU history with an impartial eye, fairly presenting the different sides of particular controversies and fully examining the embarrassing episodes in ACLU history—of which there are many. Still, selecting those episodes and placing them in the context of ACLU history and in the larger context of American history are inevitably a matter of judgment that reflects one's values. In the words of the sociologist C. Wright Mills: "I have tried to be objective, I cannot claim to be detached."

Omaha, Nebr.   S. W.
June 1989

Acknowledgments

At an early stage in the research for this book, I met a senior ACLU staff member near the elevator at the ACLU office in New York. When I told her I needed to interview her for a history of the ACLU, she inquired, "What part are you doing?" I replied, "The whole thing, 1917 to the present." She burst out laughing, clearly indicating she thought I was crazy to undertake such a task. There have been times over the past five years when I felt she may have been right.

Nobody can write a book of this size without incurring considerable debts, and I would like to acknowledge some of the many people who helped me along the way. Nancy Lane, my editor at Oxford University Press, was excited about this book from the moment I proposed it, just as she was enthusiastic about the first book we did together more than ten years ago. It has been an enormous joy to work with an editor who has an appreciation for the subject and who is, at the appropriate moments, supportive and protective of her authors.

My agent, John Wright, was also excited about this book from the start and demonstrated that a good agent does far more than negotiate a contract. An author himself and a former editor at Oxford University Press, Wright understands what writing involves and, at crucial moments, provided needed encouragement and advice.

The University of Nebraska at Omaha University Committee on Research provided a summer fellowship that supported several months' residence in Princeton, New Jersey, where I conducted a major portion of the research. Vince Webb, chair of the Department of Criminal Justice, along with Dave Hinton, dean of the College of Public Affairs and Community Service, were extremely supportive, granting my requests for leaves of absence so that I could devote myself full time to my research. At Princeton, Professor Stanley Katz introduced me to the ACLU's archives, Dean Douglas Greenberg helped with other arrangements that made life easier, and Dean Donald Stokes arranged an appointment as visiting fellow at the Woodrow Wilson School. Professor Jameson Doig of the Wilson School provided a small grant to help with photo duplication costs.

At Princeton's Mudd Library, where I spent six months in the ACLU archives, Nancy Bresler, director of the Library, Jean Holliday, and the other members of their staff were extraordinarily helpful. I made many daily requests for material, which I was promptly given. The service was, without question, the best I have received at any research library. My profound thanks to all the staff of the Mudd Library.

Several people read early drafts of the manuscript and made comments that improved it enormously. The greatest contribution was from Norman Dorsen, who diligently read all but the last two chapters (in which he is a principal figure) and spotted innumerable points that needed correction or clarification. George Cole's comments on the first draft alerted me to major problems with my approach. Cassie Spohn and Jerry Cederblom read many chapters and offered extremely valuable comments on both their strengths and weaknesses. Nadine Strossen also patiently read different drafts of most of the chapters. Others who read and commented were Phillippa Strum, Paul L. Murphy, Jerold Simmons, Gara LaMarche, David Rabban, and Richard Flamer. Finally, Janet Bryne edited the entire final draft of the manuscript and made many suggestions that strengthened the book. To all of these readers I owe an enormous debt. As always, the errors of commission and omission are entirely my responsibility. At Oxford University Press, Associate Editor Marion Osmun performed heroic labors in bringing out this book on time under a very tight schedule.

Many friends offered encouragement along the way. They include numerous members of the ACLU community—colleagues in the Nebraska Civil Liberties Union, of which I have been an officer for many years, and on the national board of directors, on which I have served since 1983, as well as the various affiliates' members and staff whom I have met in the course of my research. The interest and at times excitement that everyone expressed in the project helped sustain my energies along the way. One of the great pleasures of my research has been the opportunity to meet many of the people who have given their lives to the cause of civil liberties; some of them have helped change American society. To all of them, my appreciation.

My greatest debt is to Mary Ann, who has been a constant companion, best friend, fellow film addict, and more. To her, my deepest thanks.

Contents

Part IV   American Inquisition: The Cold War

Part V   The Great Years, 1954–1964

In Defense of American Liberties

Introduction

The ACLU, Civil Liberties, and American Life

A Revolution in American Life

The history of the American Civil Liberties Union is the story of America in this century. Born out of the fight to defend free speech during World War I, the ACLU has been at the storm center of controversy ever since then. Its part in some of the most famous events in American history—the Scopes "monkey trial," the internment of the Japanese-Americans in World War II, the cold war anti-Communist witch hunt, the fight for abortion rights, and many others—has made it one of the most important and, at times, unpopular organizations in the country.

In the 1988 presidential election campaign, Republican candidate George Bush attacked his opponent, Michael Dukakis, for being a "card-carrying member of the ACLU." Citing the organization's stand on pornography and the separation of church and state, Bush accused the ACLU of being out of the "mainstream" of American life. But as well as casting aspersions on Dukakis, Bush's attack raised more fundamental questions about the nature of American values and the place of the Bill of Rights in American society.

With some justification, the ACLU can claim to have shaped contemporary values. Principles of individual freedom, protection against arbitrary government action, equal protection, and privacy have pervaded our society. When the ACLU was founded in 1920, the promises of the Bill of Rights had little practical meaning for ordinary people. Today, there is a substantial body of law in all the major areas of civil liberties: freedom of speech and press, separation of church and state, free exercise of religion, due process of law, equal protection, and privacy. The growth of civil liberties since World War I represents one of the most important long-term developments in modern American history, a revolution in the law and public attitudes toward individual liberty. Some have called it the "rights revolution"; we prefer to call it the civil liberties revolution. This change forms one of the great themes in twentieth-century American history. Although scarcely mentioned in standard history textbooks, it equals in significance the commonly cited themes of industrialization, urbanization, and American involvement in the world economy.

The ACLU can legitimately claim much of the credit—or be assigned the blame, if you prefer—for the growth of modern constitutional law. Consult a standard constitutional law textbook and note the cases deemed important enough to be listed in the table of contents—the proverbial "landmark" cases. The ACLU was involved in over 80 percent of them; in several critical cases, the Supreme Court's opinion was drawn directly from the ACLU brief. As even its critics have charged, the ACLU has exerted "an influence out of all proportion to its size."

Despite the evident acceptance of many once-unpopular concepts, such as the right to criticize the government during wartime, the ACLU itself remains controversial. Americans have always had a curiously ambivalent attitude toward the Constitution and the Bill of Rights. It has often been a self-centered approach: my freedom, yes; your freedom, no. The majority has not hesitated to impose its views on the minority and to suppress ideas it did not like. The history of the ACLU lays bare some of the least attractive aspects of American society: ugly strands of religious intolerance and racism and a habit of falling prey to hysteria over alleged threats from foreigners or "foreign ideas." But that same history illuminates a parallel countertheme: the growth of tolerance for different, even obnoxious ideas; the end of some of the worst forms of racial discrimination; and a new sense of privacy that, in myriad ways, limits government intrusion into our lives. These more hopeful changes, rooted in the Bill of Rights, comprise the civil liberties revolution. This book, therefore, is as much about the broader changes in American society as it is about the ACLU.

What Is the ACLU?

Although its name is widely known, the ACLU is little understood. In the 1988 presidential campaign, George Bush invoked the ACLU as a symbol. But a symbol of what? Why does the very mention of its name arouse such intense passion? Who are the civil libertarians, and what drives them?

In a formal sense, the ACLU is a private voluntary organization dedicated to defending the Bill of Rights. Officially established in 1920, the ACLU now claims over 270,000 members. In addition to a national office in New York and a large legislative office in Washington, D.C., it maintains staffed affiliates in forty-six states. The often feisty and independent affiliates handle 80 percent of the ACLU's legal cases. With some justification, the ACLU calls itself "the nation's largest law firm." At any given moment it is involved in an estimated one thousand cases, and it appears before the Supreme Court more often than does any other organization except the federal government. The four thousand to five thousand volunteer "cooperating attorneys," the traditional backbone of ACLU litigation, are joined by over sixty paid staff attorneys—in the national office, the eleven "special projects," and the larger affiliates. The ACLU Washington office, with eleven full-time lobbyists, dwarfs other civil rights groups.

The essential feature of the ACLU is its professed commitment to the non-partisan defense of the Bill of Rights. This means defending the civil liberties of everyone, including the free speech rights of Communists, Nazis, and Ku Klux Klan members. It means defending the due process rights of even the most despicable criminals. Defense of the unpopular has always been the ACLU's touchstone, its proudest principle, and the cause of the most bitter attacks on it. The ACLU's "absolutist" position on freedom from censorship and separation of church and state has led it to oppose censorship of pornography and, every winter at holiday time, to fight religious displays on government property.

It is precisely this absolutist approach that arouses the hatred of its opponents, causes despair among many would-be friends, and inspires its members. The powerless and the despised have been the ACLU's most frequent clients, for the simple reason that they have been the most frequent victims of intolerance and repression. As a result, most ACLU members have historically been liberals or people with leftist sympathies. What distinguishes ACLU members from mainstream liberals, however, is their skepticism of government power and a willingness to challenge extensions of that power justified in the name of social betterment. What distinguishes the ACLU from the left has been its running war with Marxists over their habit of denying that their opponents (Fascists, racists, and such) are entitled to the same freedoms they claim for themselves. And finally, the ACLU differs from most professed conservatives by its commitment to give flesh and blood to traditional Fourth of July rhetoric about liberty, to afford the protections of the Bill of Rights to everyone.

The ACLU is a unique organization, without parallel in other democratic countries. True, there are civil liberties organizations elsewhere—for instance, the National Council on Civil Liberties (NCCL) in England and the Japanese Civil Liberties Union (JCLU) in Japan. None of them, however, plays such a large and controversial role in its country as the ACLU does in the United States. The NCCL, for example, has long taken an explicitly partisan stance on behalf of labor and has neglected to defend the rights of employers or racists. The JCLU has a grand total of seven hundred members and a few court cases: Even most of the affiliates of the ACLU are larger and more active.

The uniqueness of the ACLU is a consequence of several important features of American life: a written Constitution with a Bill of Rights, a cultural heritage that places a premium on individual liberty, and a legal and political tradition in which the Supreme Court plays a prominent role in resolving conflict in terms of constitutional law. Thus, understanding the ACLU's history provides important insight into these basic aspects of American history and culture. Critics who accuse the ACLU of taking the Bill of Rights to extremes are, in effect, voicing a more fundamental complaint about the Constitution, the courts, and some of the deepest impulses in American society.

Yet to say that the ACLU defends civil liberties only raises another question: What is a civil liberty?

What Is a Civil Liberty?

The Encyclopedia of the Constitution defines civil liberties as those rights that individual citizens may assert against the government.[1] In the United States, such liberties are enumerated in the Bill of Rights. The encyclopedia definition, however, begs all the important questions. What does freedom of speech encompass? Is picketing or wearing an armband a form of speech? What exactly does the phrase "due process of law" mean? What is an unreasonable search? What constitutes cruel and unusual punishment? Is there a constitutional right of privacy? More fundamentally, what standard should we use in trying to answer these questions?

The text of the Bill of Rights provides no definitive answers to these questions. Although advocates of the "original intent" school of constitutional law argue that we should adhere strictly to the specific language of the Bill of Rights, our history suggests that the genius of the Constitution is its flexibility and capacity to adapt to changing circumstances. Seventy years ago, in one of his most famous opinions, Justice Oliver Wendell Holmes wrote that our constitutional form of government is "an experiment, as all life is an experiment." The history of civil liberties is the story of that experiment. It is the story of an ongoing effort to redefine the nature of freedom within the framework of the Bill of Rights.

The ACLU is itself an ongoing experiment, with an agenda that constantly changes. Many ACLU members will be surprised to learn that the organization did not always take an "absolutist" position on censorship or the separation of church and state. They will be equally surprised to learn that for a time the ACLU took a strong stand against corporate monopolies in the field of communications. How and why the ACLU's agenda has changed is one of the most important subjects of this book. When and why, for example, did the ACLU adopt an "absolutist" position on the separation of church and state? How did the ACLU determine that the right to an abortion was a civil liberty? The argument in this book is that the ACLU has generally been not just an agent but also a symptom of change—an avenue through which emerging ideas about liberty have been able to express themselves and gain force in the marketplace of ideas.

Critics often charge the ACLU with arrogance. Who, they ask, gave it license to say what a civil liberty is? Who gave it authority to impose its will on the rest of the country? The answers to these questions are, respectively, that no one gave the ACLU any special license and that it has not imposed its will on the country. The ACLU has had no greater authority than any other advocacy group has had. It has argued its point of view in the courts and the arena of public opinion along with every other group. And finally, the remarkable fact is that it has succeeded in persuading many courts, including the U.S. Supreme Court, and a broad spectrum of the public that its views are right.

The ACLU's very success in this regard illuminates some of the most important developments in American history: the changing public attitudes toward individual liberty and the role of the Constitution as a framework for achieving individual freedom in the context of a pluralistic and bureaucratic society. The great controversies over ACLU policies—pornography, separation of church and state, the rights of suspected criminals—go to the heart of the matter: What is the nature of freedom in a democratic society? Where should the lines be drawn in determining the boundaries of individual rights? The pages that follow examine the history of a small but remarkable organization that has contributed much to answering these questions.

I

Origins,
1917-1919

One

War, Repression,
and the Origins
of the Free Speech Fight,
1917-1918

"Jails Are Waiting for Them"

"Jails are waiting for them," warned the *New York Times*. The July 4, 1917, editorial advised the new Civil Liberties Bureau that "freedom of speech" is a fine thing, "well worth fighting for," but there were limits. Liberty did not mean license. In wartime, "good citizens willingly submit" to measures "essential to the national existence and welfare." That is, the Civil Liberties Bureau was going too far in defending opponents of the war.[1]

The United States had entered World War I three months earlier, and already the government was suppressing criticism. A frenzy of patriotic zeal was sweeping the country. World War I was a watershed in American history. The wholesale suppression of civil liberties forced the country to confront the meaning of the Bill of Rights. Did critics of the war have an unlimited right of free speech? Did young men have a constitutional right to refuse to serve in the military because of religious conscience? Did the Civil Liberties Bureau have a right to defend their rights? What, in short, was the meaning of the First Amendment?[2]

The *Times* dismissed the Civil Liberties Bureau as a "little group of malcontents," "troublesome folk," "an unimportant and minute minority—noisy out of all proportion to their numbers." Organized by Crystal Eastman and Roger Baldwin, the bureau was an offshoot of the American Union Against Militarism (AUAM), which since 1914 had led the opposition to America's entry into war. The *Times* expressed amazement that "they have found lawyers willing to aid them in the attainment of these preposterous ends." Most Americans in the summer of 1917 probably agreed that criticizing the government during wartime was indeed preposterous. Because the most vocal of the war critics were socialists, anarchists, labor radicals, and recent immigrants, the public saw free speech as a cloak for everything "un-American."

President Woodrow Wilson led the attack on free speech. The "authority to exercise censorship is absolutely necessary to the public safety," he announced. He told Max Eastman, editor of *The Masses,* that wartime was a "wholly exceptional" situation and that "it is legitimate to regard things which would in ordinary circumstances be innocent as very dangerous to the public welfare."[3] Wilson held a majoritarian theory of democracy. Once the people had spoken, through a congressional declaration of war, there no longer was room for dissent. All national resources, intellectual as well as material, had to be mobilized for service in the war. This war, moreover, was a noble crusade to "make the world safe for democracy."

The Civil Liberties Bureau learned what Wilson meant when in mid-July the U.S. Postal Service banned twelve of its pamphlets. One of these, *War's Heretics,* by Norman Thomas, offered a different view of democracy and dissent. Then a young Presbyterian minister, Thomas argued that although government had a responsibility to promote the general welfare, the power of the state should never "grow to a control over men's convictions." There was a zone of individual conscience over which majority rule had no dominion. Even more important, dissenters were vital to the survival of democracy. Thomas asked "for recognition of the social value of heresy," noting that "every movement worth while began with a minority." The central problem of democracy was the potential tyranny of the majority: "Democracy degenerates into mobocracy unless the rights of the minority are respected."[4]

War's Heretics articulated the principle that became the guiding star of the fight for civil liberties: The First Amendment was the foundation of democracy. Self-government meant that everyone had a right to speak freely, because all ideas must be heard, and thus the government could not rule certain ideas unacceptable. Tolerance for all ideas, no matter how offensive, provided a mechanism for orderly progress. But Thomas and his colleagues in the Civil Liberties Bureau quickly learned that in 1917 this idea was heresy.

War and Repression

"It is a terrible thing to lead this great and peaceful people into war," President Wilson told Congress in his April 2 war message. He had no idea just how terrible it would be. The war unleashed an unprecedented wave of intolerance, repression, and violence. Free speech and due process were swept aside as government officials and private citizens led a national crusade to enforce patriotism and political conformity.

Vocal opposition to the war sprang up immediately after Congress declared war on April 6. Indeed, it was the second most unpopular war in American history, rivaled only by the Vietnam War. Its critics were diverse: Socialists, religious pacifists, German-Americans and Irish-Americans, recent Eastern

European immigrants, and isolationists. The American Socialist party was the center of the organized opposition. In an emergency meeting on April 7, it attacked the war as the work of "predatory capitalists" who profited "from the manufacture and sale of munitions and war supplies." The Socialists pledged "continuous, active and public opposition to the war" and called on "the workers of all countries to refuse to support their governments in their wars." In 1917, the Socialists were a political force to be reckoned with. Presidential candidate Eugene Debs had won 6 percent of their vote in 1912, and over twelve hundred Socialists held state and local political office. In the fall of 1917 Morris Hillquit, campaigning on an antiwar platform, drew 22 percent of the votes in the New York City mayoral election.[5]

Reformer Leonard D. Abbott spoke for many liberal idealists when he denounced the war as "immoral, un-American, and unconstitutional," contrary to the principles of American democracy. The draft was "the entering wedge of military despotism" that would "Prussianize" American society. Max Eastman told the president that he simply did "not recognize the right of a government to draft me to a war whose purposes I do not believe in." Isolationist sentiment also ran deep in the South and the Midwest, where Senators Tom Watson and Robert LaFollette opposed the war. German-Americans had obvious ethnic ties to the enemy, and many Irish-Americans resented the alliance with the English. Likewise, numerous recent Russian immigrants had fled conscription into the czar's army.[6]

From the White House, Wilson fanned the flames of intolerance, warning that disloyalty would be met with "a firm hand of stern repression." Other political leaders joined the campaign to compel loyalty. Former President Theodore Roosevelt attacked pacifists as "a whole raft of sexless creatures."[7]

The war effort unleashed pent-up conflicts in American society. In the previous twenty years American society had changed completely as a result of industrialization, urbanization, and immigration; and the United States was now the world's leading industrial power. The labor movement grew apace, and radical groups challenged the economic status quo. The addition of immigrants made a turbulent brew of ethnic and religious conflict. A million people a year entered the country, most of them Italians, Jews, and other Eastern Europeans. Patriots eagerly exploited the popular fear of foreigners. Roosevelt warned that "the Hun within our gates is the worst of the foes of our own household. . . . Whether he is pro-German or poses as a pacifist . . . matters little." He recommended that "every disloyal native-born American should be disenfranchised and interned. It is time to strike our enemies at home heavily and quickly."[8]

The Machinery of Repression

Anarchists Emma Goldman and Alexander Berkman organized the No Conscription League and were two of the first victims of official repression. The league's first public rally drew a boisterous crowd of eight thousand, including several Justice Department agents. Fights broke out among the crowd. After two more stormy rallies, the government cracked down and indicted, under the Espionage Act, Goldman and Berkman for obstructing the draft. They were eventually convicted, imprisoned, and deported to the Soviet Union.[9]

The Espionage Act was only one of the weapons in the government's arsenal. Enacted in June 1917, the law made it a crime to "willfully obstruct the recruiting or enlistment service of the United States." The Justice Department held that any criticism of the war would influence young men not to enlist. The 1918 amendments, popularly known as the Sedition Act, went even further, outlawing "any disloyal . . . scurrilous, or abusive language about the form of government of the United States, . . . or any language intended to bring the form of government of the United States . . . into contempt, scorn, contumely, or disrepute." The law recalled the notorious Alien and Sedition Act of 1798, which was used to suppress criticism of the government. For example, Socialist party leader Eugene V. Debs was sentenced to ten years in prison for a speech opposing the general idea of war. Socialist Rose Pastor Stokes was convicted for declaring, "I am for the people and the government is for the profiteers." Even the wrong kind of patriotism was risky: Filmmaker Robert Goldstein was prosecuted because his film about the American Revolution, *The Spirit of '76,* cast the British in an unfavorable light.[10]

The immigration laws institutionalized the attack on "foreign" ideas. A 1903 law barred anarchists from entering the country, and a 1917 law allowed the government to denaturalize them. An even broader 1918 law permitted the country to deport those aliens who joined an anarchist organization. This law was often used against radical labor leaders.[11]

The U.S. Postal Service led the most concerted attack on freedom of speech and press. Under existing law, it could deny second-class mailing privileges to any magazine or newspaper. On June 16, 1917, Postmaster General Albert S. Burleson notified all postmasters to "keep a close eye on" all publications that might "embarrass or hamper the government in conducting the war." A few weeks later he banned virtually the entire antiwar and Socialist press: *The Masses, Appeal to Reason, International Socialist Review,* the *Milwaukee Leader,* and a dozen Civil Liberties Bureau pamphlets. Some publications were suppressed by informal pressure. Publisher Ben Huebsch, founder of the Viking Press and later a longtime ACLU board member, withdrew circulars for three books after the local U.S. attorney advised him that the books were "objectionable."[12]

Max Eastman's antiwar magazine, *The Masses,* brought the first important court test of censorship. After the U.S. Postal Service banned the August issue, Eastman sought an injunction to overturn the ban. The August issue contained several antiwar items. One cartoon depicted a naked woman labeled *Democracy* lashed to a wheel. Another showed two naked men, *Labor* and *Youth,* chained to a cannon. There were, however, no calls to resist the draft or otherwise break the law.[13]

District Court Judge Learned Hand granted the injunction with an opinion affirming broad protection for free speech. The government could impose prior restraint on the press only in cases of direct incitement to illegal action. This left much room for criticism of the government and political agitation. Hand argued that "tolerance of all methods of political agitation" was "a safeguard of free government." But the circuit court of appeals reversed him, relying on the prevailing "bad tendency" test. That is, speech could be punished "if the natural and reasonable effect of what is said is to encourage resistance to law, and the words are used in an endeavor to persuade resistance." The *Masses* decision thus gave the government a virtual free hand to suppress political dissent.[14]

Private vigilantes, led by prominent businessmen, joined the effort to enforce loyalty. The American Protective League (APL), the largest and most important such organization, was sponsored by the Justice Department, and its agents carried government-issued badges. APL volunteers rounded up suspected draft evaders in a series of massive "slacker raids." On July 3, 1917, they descended on boardinghouses, theaters, and saloons and indiscriminately arrested over six thousand men. Anyone who could not adequately explain why he was not registered with the draft was seized. The slacker raids continued through the war years, with the APL seizing over twenty thousand men in New York City alone in a series of raids in September 1918.[15]

Mobs tarred, feathered, and even lynched suspected war critics. In one of the most famous incidents, a Cincinnati mob kidnapped Rev. Herbert S. Bigelow on October 28, 1917, tied him to a tree, and brutally whipped him, "in the name of the women and children of Belgium and France." Anti-German hysteria went to absurd lengths. All signs of German culture were banished: Sauerkraut became "liberty cabbage." Hamburgers were renamed "liberty burgers." The works of German composers vanished from the repertoires of symphony orchestras. Nebraska even outlawed the teaching of any foreign language in public or private schools.

Schools and universities joined the drive to compel political conformity. Columbia University President Nicholas Murray Butler told his faculty that "what had been tolerated before becomes intolerable now" and then fired two prominent faculty members for opposing the war. Scott Nearing, having earlier been fired by the University of Pennsylvania for his work on child labor, was dismissed by the University of Toledo and never again held an academic position. The University of Virginia fired journalism professor Leon Whipple for being a pacifist. New York Commissioner of Education John Finley announced that "if a teacher cannot give that unquestioning support to the country that makes his own individual freedom in time of peace possible, his place is not in the schools." The American Association of University Professors (AAUP) abandoned its principles of academic freedom, adopted only two years before. In the heat of war-induced patriotism, the AAUP advised faculty to conform to "the necessities of the grave and perilous business immediately in hand." Faculty of "Teutonic extraction" should completely "refrain from public discussion of the war."[16]

Creating the National Security State

The suppression of civil liberties was not a wartime aberration, as many historians have suggested, nor could it be blamed on a few overzealous cabinet officials. Rather, it marked the birth of a new phenomenon in American society: the apparatus of the national security state. For the first time in American history, the federal government created machinery to punish unorthodox political opinion.[17]

The new machinery included political spying. A young clerk in the Federal Bureau of Investigation named J. Edgar Hoover was given the task of identifying political heretics. With a passionate hatred for anything different from his own view of Americanism, he quickly established secret files on over 200,000 people, with detailed profiles of about 60,000. The files were based entirely on guilt by association. Pacifists, Socialists, labor radicals, black activists, and civil libertarians were swept into Hoover's net. Most, like pacifist and feminist Jane Addams, simply opposed the war. The bureau then used these files to harass dissenters. For example, agents pressured the (later) Civil Liberties Bureau's landlord into evicting the organization in August 1918.[18]

Congress and state legislatures began to investigate political ideas and groups as well. The U.S. Senate's Overman Committee investigated German and Bolshevik propaganda. But far more important for its impact on public opinion was the New York legislature's Lusk Committee. Led by its chief investigator, Archibald Stevenson, it published a four-volume report, *Revolutionary Radicalism,* that smeared liberals, pacifists, and civil libertarians as agents of international Communism. For the next twenty years it was the primary source of right-wing attacks on the ACLU. The Overman and Lusk committees provided the intellectual bridge between the anti-German sentiment of the war years and postwar anti-Communism.[19]

The attack on political dissent was an integral part of the mobilization for war. Conscription of opinion was the logical—and, to some, a necessary—complement to the conscription of soldiers. A successful war effort left no room for doubts about the national purpose: The war had accelerated the centralization of government control in all industrial countries, thereby fostering the drift toward totalitarianism.[20] Indeed, the suppression of dissent in World War I took the United States to the brink of totalitarianism. Freedom of speech ultimately survived, but only because the wartime crisis galvanized a small group of Americans into fighting for it. That group was the Civil Liberties Bureau.

Birth of the Civil Liberties Bureau

While Wilson delivered his war message to Congress, Crystal Eastman convened an emergency meeting of the AUAM Executive Committee in New York. Since 1914 the committee had led the fight against the United States' entry into the war, and it was devastated by the prospect of war. Rev. John Haynes Holmes recalled the shock of discovering "that America is no longer, probably never was, the country that we loved." Many felt personally betrayed by Wilson, whom they had supported for reelection in 1916 because he had "kept the country out of war." He had encouraged their efforts and even met with them in the White House. Ben Huebsch recalled a debonair Wilson "smiling and greeting everybody" in the AUAM delegation. Max Eastman led a desperate last-minute effort on February 28, 1917, when they again met with Wilson in the Oval Office. But all their efforts were for naught, as Congress subsequently declared war.[21]

But Crystal Eastman was undaunted. The energetic AUAM executive secretary already had an ambitious "war time program" of opposition to the draft, assistance to conscientious objectors, and support for "A Just and Lasting Peace." Her hopes of success, furthermore, were not unreasonable. The AUAM was a respected organization, with many friends in the Wilson administration. Cochairs Lillian Wald and Paul U. Kellogg were prominent Progressive reformers with a substantial record of influencing national policy. Wald's settlement house on Henry Street was a nerve center of Progressive-Era social reform, and Kellogg was the editor of *The Survey,* virtually a house organ for social work reformers. They had successfully lobbied two presidents to create the federal Industrial Relations Commission, a broad-ranging government inquiry into labor–management conflict. The previous summer Eastman had organized a bold "people's diplomacy" campaign that helped stop American intervention in Mexico.[22]

Eastman was joined by Roger Baldwin, who had just arrived from St. Louis. The two were remarkably similar in outlook, talent, and temperament. They shared a broad vision of social reform, believing that the promise of democracy could be achieved only if good people put their talents to the task. Both had boundless energy and a particular genius for organization building. Eastman had written a detailed investigation, *Work Accidents and the Law,* in 1910, and Baldwin had coauthored the leading book on the juvenile court. Both charmed nearly everyone they met. Eastman was as strikingly beautiful as her brother Max was handsome: Poet Claude McKay called her the most beautiful white woman he ever met. And Baldwin maintained a twinkle in his eye until he died at age ninety-seven. Their energy, charm, and infectious enthusiasm helped give birth to the ACLU.[23]

Baldwin's and Eastman's immediate task was to stop Congress from creating a military draft. They regarded conscription as a violation of democratic principles: If people would not volunteer to fight, the country should not go to war. England, they pointed out, had fought for two years without a draft. Over 2.5 million of the 4.6 million eligible men had voluntarily enlisted. Conscription was also contrary to the Christian principles on which American society was based and violated the "sacred liberty of conscience" implicit in the Bill of Rights. This was a novel and untested legal argument, for no one knew for sure whether the First Amendment's guarantee of religious freedom included exemption from military service. But the AUAM's arguments fell on deaf ears, and on May 18 Congress overwhelmingly passed the Selective Service Act.

The law created serious problems for prospective conscientious objectors (COs). The only men eligible for CO status were certain government officials, ministers, divinity students, and members of "well recognized religious sects or organizations whose creed or principles are opposed to participation in war." In practice this meant only the three "historic peace churches": Quakers, Mennonites, and the Brethren. There was no provision for the "absolutists" who refused to cooperate with the war in any way, even by registering or accepting alternative service. The administration of the draft aggravated the COs' problems. Local draft boards had complete discretion to decide CO cases, and they freely vented their hostility toward suspected draft evaders.[24]

As the June 5 draft registration day approached, inquiries from young men poured into the AUAM office. Eastman and Baldwin established the Bureau of Conscientious Objectors and advised draft-age men to comply with the law: "Don't try to evade registration. Obedience to law, to the utmost limits of conscience, is the basis of good citizenship." They were confident that a satisfactory arrangement would be worked out with the government. Even Wilson himself had said that the draft was "by no means a conscription of the unwilling." The War Department, moreover, was filled with Progressive reformers they knew personally. Secretary of War Newton D. Baker, Third Assistant Secretary Frederick Keppel, and Walter Lippmann were men of high ideals whom they knew opposed war in principle. AUAM leaders and government officials came from the Ivy League elite. Surely, they could quietly work out a compromise together.[25]

Baldwin told Secretary of War Baker, "We are entirely at the service of the War Department" and sent him a detailed list of suggesions. He told Keppel, his primary contact in the administration, "We don't want to make a move without consulting you." As a gesture of good faith, he also sent them advance copies of all AUAM publications.[26] He also met with Army Provost Marshall General E. H. Crowder and remained optimistic that "the administration will do what was necessary."[27]

Anticipating a court test, Baldwin asked attorney Harry Weinberger to prepare a legal memorandum on the constitutionality of the draft. Weinberger produced a "kitchen sink" memo raising every imaginable objection. He argued that Congress did not have the "constitutional power to raise an army by draft to send overseas to engage in offensive war in foreign lands"; the law unconstitutionally delegated to the executive branch the authority to raise a militia; and granting CO status to only certain religious groups violated the establishment clause of the First Amendment. Weinberger incorporated all of these arguments into his brief in the cases that eventually reached the Supreme Court. Walter Nelles contributed a Civil Liberties Bureau *amicus* brief focusing on the establishment of religion issue. But on January 7, 1918, the Court dismissed all the objections and summarily upheld the constitutionality of the draft.[28]

By mid-June Eastman and Baldwin realized they faced a far more serious crisis than the draft. The mounting wartime furor threatened fundamental rights of freedom of speech, press, and assembly. They warned President Wilson that the proposed Espionage Act "may easily lend itself to the suppression of free speech, free assemblage, [and] popular discussion and criticism." They begged him "to make an impressive statement" about upholding "our constitutional rights and liberties." Wilson said nothing. AUAM Washington lobbyists Charles T. Hallinan, Harry Weinberger, and Jane Addams lobbied against the Espionage bill, but without success. Congress enacted the law on June 15 by an overwhelming majority.[29]

The Test of Principle

The AUAM was suddenly uncertain about its own legal status. Did the Espionage Act's prohibition of "willfully obstruct[ing]" the draft include advising young men about conscientious objection? An AUAM pamphlet warned prophetically that "a district attorney or court might construe almost any activity in favor of peace or in criticism of the Government's war policies as coming within its provision." The AUAM's Executive Committee anxiously asked Weinberger for his opinion about "the legality of our present and proposed activities."[30]

AUAM cochairs Wald and Kellogg were particularly upset by Eastman's and Baldwin's activities. Although staunch pacifists, they accepted Wilson's argument that the declaration of war settled the issue. They had hoped to influence the eventual peace settlement of this war to end all wars, but such influence required credibility in Washington, which in turn meant avoiding even the appearance of opposition. Wald and Kellogg and their allies in the AUAM faced a crucial choice: Would they defend civil liberties principles, regardless of the cost to their influence, or would they ignore them in the hope of gaining influence on other issues? They chose the latter course, and the resulting split with Eastman and Baldwin marked the birth of the civil liberties fight.

Wald first proposed reorganizing Eastman's and Baldwin's work as "a separate enterprise." But three days later, at a heated meeting, Wald threatened to resign: "We cannot plan continuance of our program which entails friendly governmental relations, and at the same time drift into being a *party of opposition* to the government."[31] Eastman and Baldwin replied that their work was an important defense of principle. They had assumed an obligation as the national clearinghouse for information about COs. Eastman felt that the defense of free speech would actually increase their stature in Washington. The presence of men like Baker, Keppel, and Lippmann in the War Department was a "guarantee of good faith." Events in the next few months, however, rudely shattered this naive assumption.[32]

Eastman pleaded that "time for parting is not yet" and proposed a compromise. The AUAM's work would be divided among three subcommittees devoted to civil liberties, wartime labor conditions, and international peace. The Executive Committee accepted this idea, and on July 1 the Civil Liberties Bureau (CLB) was born. But the arrangement fell apart almost immediately. Eastman and Baldwin had decided to participate in the People's Council, a new coalition of radical organizations. Wald denounced it as "impulsive radicalism" rather than "the organized reflective thought of those opposed to war." Thus when the AUAM Executive Committee stood by its original decision, Wald resigned. With obvious regret she told them that "perhaps all of us may reassemble again for this high purpose" of peace. Most of the Executive Committee stood by Eastman and Baldwin, and on October 1, 1917, they established the National Civil Liberties Bureau (NCLB) as a separate organization. The AUAM, which by then had virtually no program apart from Eastman's and Baldwin's work, quietly faded away.[33]

Liberalism and Civil Liberties

The dispute that had produced the Civil Liberties Bureau defined the basic terms of the free speech fight. The principled defense of civil liberties was a two-sided struggle: It fought the suppression of free speech by government officials and conservative superpatriots, but at the same time, it rejected liberal pragmatism. The temptation to ignore violations of civil liberties in the name of pursuing some other worthy social objective was a constant theme in ACLU history.

Wald's and Kellogg's position was a product of their reformist ideals. They were instinctively attracted to Wilson's rhetoric about making the world safe for democracy and his call for an international peacekeeping agency. Like many other prewar reformers, they were seduced by the opportunities for social change created by the enormous expansion of government regulation in the war effort. The National War Labor Board recognized collective bargaining, imposed a minimum wage and the eight-hour workday, and improved working conditions for women and children. The Shipping Board and the Department of Labor sponsored the first public housing units. Mary Van Kleeck, a major ACLU figure in the 1930s, drafted War Labor Board standards for women. And the 1917 Military and Naval Insurance Act included an experimental social security program.[34]

The opportunity to wield power was an intoxicating experience. As some historians have argued, the war represented not a contradiction but the fulfillment of Progressive reform. Prewar reformers implicitly assumed that the welfare of the individual and the interests of the state were synonymous. They saw no fundamental conflict between state intervention and individual rights.

Liberal intellectuals offered elaborate rationalizations for the war effort. A *New Republic* editorial welcomed it as a historic opportunity for the "remaking of the life of the world" and "the creation of a united America." Philosopher John Dewey wrote that "some surrenders and abandonments of the liberties of peace time are inevitable." Many of these liberals were swept up by the wartime patriotic fervor and welcomed the common national purpose.[35] Randolph Bourne, a maverick Progressive, answered Dewey with a devastating attack on liberal pragmatism. "It has been a bitter experience," he wrote, "to see the unanimity with which the American intellectuals have thrown their support to the use of war-technique." Like their European counterparts, they willingly put their talents in the service of the most undemocratic forces and ceased to think critically. In a stinging indictment of Wald, Kellogg, and the *New Republic* editors, Bourne argued that their "pragmatism" came to this: "If we obstruct, we surrender all power for influence. If we responsibly approve, we then retain our power for guiding." The price of responsible approval meant overlooking the systematic suppression of all political dissent. Bourne's essay, "The War and the Intellectuals," became an American classic and reappeared during World War II and the Vietnam War when the question of the responsibility of intellectuals in wartime arose again.[36]

The Civil Libertarians

The members of the NCLB's Executive Committee came from three groups: Eastman and Baldwin were social workers who saw the free speech fight as a logical extension of prewar social reform activities. Largely oblivious to civil liberties considerations before the war, the wartime crisis forced them to abandon both their faith in the inevitability of social progress and their majoritarian view of democracy. They now began to see that majority rule and liberty were not necessarily synonymous and thus discovered the First Amendment as a new principle for advancing human freedom.[37]

The second group were Protestant clergy, inspired by the reform ideas of the social gospel. Norman Thomas served a Presbyterian church in a poor section of New York City, and John Haynes Holmes led a Unitarian church. Harry F. Ward taught social ethics at Union Theological Seminary and was a prolific writer on social questions. The wartime crisis shattered their old faith and pushed them toward a secular, civil libertarian outlook: Thomas abandoned religion for the Socialist party. Holmes severed his formal ties with Unitarianism, renamed his church the Community church, and transformed it into a nonsectarian community center. Ward eventually became a Marxist.[38]

Conservative lawyers comprised the third group. They idealized the Constitution and were outraged by the violations of free speech and due process. L. Hollingsworth Wood, a successful New York attorney, was also moved by Quaker pacifism. Albert DeSilver, an outspoken, prowar patriot, declared that "my law-abiding neck gets very warm under its law-abiding collar these days at the extraordinary violations of fundamental laws which are being put over." Independently wealthy, he dropped his private law practice, assisted Morris Hillquit in the *Masses* case, and then worked nearly full time with the NCLB, using his war bonds to post bail for defendants in free speech cases.[39]

Over the next seventy years, this mixture of liberal social reformism and conservative faith in the promises of the Constitution remained the basic ingredient in the ACLU.

Conspicuously absent from the NCLB was Theodore Schroeder, leader of the Free Speech League. Established in 1902, the league was the first organized effort to defend free speech in American history. It was largely the personal vehicle of the eccentric Schroeder. A brilliant lawyer and indefatigable writer, he opposed all forms of censorship, and his views anticipated better-known First Amendment theorists by many decades. He argued that the First Amendment protected all speech except for direct incitements to lawbreaking. Alone among prewar legal scholars, Schroeder responded to the emerging sexual revolution and the need for freer discussions of sexuality. Early on, he articulated the point that censorship inevitably led to intrusive government surveillance. In 1910 he denounced "Government by Spies." At a time when most Progressive reformers welcomed the expansion of government intervention, in the interests of social reform, Schroeder argued passionately for freedom from government encroachment.[40]

While Schroeder produced a steady stream of articles, other Free Speech League members—writers Lincoln Steffens and Hutchins Hapgood and attorneys Gilbert Roe and Harry Weinberger—took up the fight on different fronts. For instance, Steffens intervened in a 1914 incident in which New York City police brutally dispersed a meeting of unemployed men. He persuaded Police Commissioner Arthur Woods to keep the police away from the next rally and jubilantly called this "a victory and a precedent for free speech." The league also represented Unitarian minister Michael X. Mockus, prosecuted in Connecticut for blasphemy after questioning the literal truth of the biblical story of Jonah and the whale. The league also defended William Sanger, arrested by Anthony Comstock for distributing one of his wife Margaret's birth control pamphlets. Schroeder also testified before the U.S. Industrial Commission in regard to the violations of the workers' free speech rights.[41] Nonetheless, despite his advanced position on the First Amendment, Schroeder declined to challenge the suppression of free speech during the war. He joined a July 1917 Madison Square Garden rally protesting mail censorship but refused to speak in 1918. He told Baldwin that the wartime issues had little to do with "problems of the more personal liberties." He then withdrew into the study of psychology that preoccupied him for the rest of his life. Consequently, the Free Speech League, which had never developed a cohesive national program, vanished from the scene.[42]

The league's disappearance highlights the pivotal role of Roger Baldwin in creating the ACLU. Schroeder and Baldwin were polar opposites in talent and temperament: Schroeder was absorbed in his own intellectual pursuits, with little interest in or talent for organizational work. His prickly personality, moreover, offended many potential allies. Baldwin, meanwhile, was the consummate organization builder. Never an original thinker, he was best at publicizing other people's ideas. He had a special talent for creating and maintaining an organization—producing pamphlets, recruiting committee members, setting agendas, running meetings, and raising funds. Indeed, without Baldwin's unique combination of purely administrative talents, the NCLB would not have survived the war years and evolved into the ACLU.

The Fight for Civil Liberty, 1917–1918

From the moment it was born, the AUAM Civil Liberties Bureau was overwhelmed by the assault on dissent. The first crisis in early July was the U.S. Postal Service's suppression of the antiwar press. Baldwin convened an emergency meeting of nearly one hundred editors and journalists and urged his AUAM contacts around the country to send protests to the president. He led a delegation to Washington to seek a meeting with Wilson "in order to bring to his personal attention this violation of one of America's most precious rights."[43] On July 16, he, Oswald Garrison Villard, Clarence Darrow, and Amos Pinchot met with Postmaster General Burleson. Darrow used "all his folksy talents of persuasion," but to no avail. Neither Postal Service nor Justice Department officials would define the limits of permissible discussion of the war. One even bluntly told them to "cut out war criticism."[44]

The Postal Service seized all the Civil Liberties Bureau's mail in mid-July. Baldwin met with postal officials and fired off another protest to the president. But eventually, over twelve pamphlets were banned as "unmailable," including *War's Heretics, The Truth About the IWW,* and an account of the near-lynching of Rev. Bigelow.[45] Such an action was unexpected, as Baldwin had taken great pains to clear in advance his publications with the government, sending the Justice Department copies of all AUAM pamphlets in June and explaining that "we are exceedingly careful not to print anything which is likely to be questioned in the slightest." He also had asked postal officials whether *War's Heretics* "might lawfully be transmitted through the United States mails." Despite initial assurances, the post office seized all 3,500 copies. Quiet negotiations failed, and the NCLB eventually sued to obtain release of their material. The case dragged on for over a year until another suit secured release of all the seized mail.[46]

Faced with mounting pressure, Baldwin concentrated on influencing public opinion. A stream of leaflets and memos poured forth from the NCLB office, stressing the American tradition of free speech, the importance of respecting religious conscience, and the need to respect fundamental principles of due process. Zechariah Chafee credited one of Walter Nelles's pamphlets on wartime prosecutions with influencing his thinking about the First Amendment.[47] Chafee's articles, in turn, may have influenced Supreme Court Justice Oliver Wendell Holmes's pivotal dissent in the 1919 *Abrams* case. Baldwin tried to organize a series of mass meetings to rally public opinion but soon gave up because auditorium managers were reluctant to rent to him, and many of the prominent liberals he tried to recruit backed away.

The lawyers—Nelles, DeSilver, and Weinberger—meanwhile tried to cope with the flood of legal inquiries. They answered the queries of draft-age men, referring them to sympathetic lawyers. By the fall of 1917 the NCLB's co-operating attorneys were handling about 125 conscientious objector cases a week.[48]

When the first draftees began reaching military training camps in September, even the War Department had not settled on a clear policy toward the COs. Baldwin continued to lobby behind the scenes. He met with Provost Marshall John Henry Wigmore and Judge Advocate General Felix Frankfurter and sent them a list of proposals that included offering noncombatant duty or alternative government service to all men claiming CO status. Absolutists were to be court-martialed. Baldwin was thus particularly concerned about due process in the courts-martial and advised the War Department to establish written procedures to ensure their uniformity. He also proposed that no sentence be for a term longer than the duration of the war. The War Department rejected all his suggestions.[49]

By mid-September a major crisis had developed in the military camps. Through a quirk in the law, men who registered but then refused to take the physical examination were tried in civilian courts and faced a maximum sentence of one year in jail. But the absolutists who refused to register were sent to military camps for court-martial, faced much longer sentences, and were physically beaten by draftees. Some commanders put the COs on a diet of bread and water and subjected them to forced labor and various indignities. Baldwin did not at first realize the extent of the brutality. Late in the fall, however, he discovered that the Postal Service was intercepting letters from the COs in the camps. By November the situation was clearly out of hand, and Baldwin reported an "alarming increase" in brutality.[50]

The situation in the camps put Baldwin in an extremely awkward position. He tried simultaneously to maintain his cordial relations with the War Department and to be candid with prospective COs. Frankfurter advised him to "just continue your attitude of cooperation. I am full of confidence the thing will work out all right." Baldwin reciprocated by promising not to embarrass the administration with any unfavorable publicity. He assured Secretary of War Baker that "we are equally anxious that the whole problem of the conscientious objector be not made a controversial public issue." He sent his NCLB contacts a deliberately ambiguous letter in the hope of "forestalling any organized public agitation at this time."[51]

Baldwin still assumed that he could have it both ways: that he could challenge the government in public and also work closely with administration officials behind the scenes. As events soon proved, however, it was an untenable position.

Government figures eventually showed a total of 3,989 COs out of the 2.8 million draftees, a figure that omitted those tried in civilian courts. Most COs either accepted noncombatant status in the military or were furloughed for argicultural work or to the Friends Reconstruction Unit run by the Quakers. A total of 450 absolutists were court-martialed,[52] 27 of which belonged to an obscure sect known as the International Bible Students Association. Twenty years later, this sect, now called the Jehovah's Witnesses, took over fifty cases to the Supreme Court and, with ACLU assistance, helped esatblish an important body of First Amendment law.[53]

The government's assault on dissent also included gross violations of due process of law. Federal agents—often private citizens working through the American Protective League—descended, without warrants, on private homes and the offices of political groups, seizing records and arresting virtually everyone in sight. The government seized and eventually burned all of the records of the Industrial Workers of the World (IWW). There were seven raids on the International Bible Students' Association in March 1918 alone, with officials seizing nearly 100,000 of the sect's pamphlets. The NCLB called for fair trials for all Espionage Act defendants, but with little effect: Virtually all war critics were convicted and sentenced to long prison terms.[54]

The government directed its heaviest attacks against the Socialist party and the IWW, neither of which regained its prewar strength. The Socialist party was crippled through the Postal Service's ban on virtually all of its publications and the prosecution of many of its top leaders. The government's attack on the IWW was even more systematic. Prompted by business interests and government officials who feared the Wobblies' radical brand of unionism, the Justice Department staged a coordinated series of raids on every IWW office in the country on September 5, 1917. Hundreds of suspected members were indiscriminately arrested. Eventually 169 of the top leaders, including Big Bill Haywood, were indicted under the Espionage Act.[55]

Baldwin sprang to the IWW's defense, writing to President Wilson, Secretary of Labor William B. Wilson, and Frankfurter to demand the indictments be dropped. In private meetings he suggested to Justice Department attorney John Lord O'Brian and presidential adviser Joseph Tumulty that "wholesale prosecutions were about the most unfortunate methods which could be devised of dealing with radical organizations in America." The NCLB demanded a fair trial and helped raise legal defense funds for the IWW. Baldwin began a long and stormy relationship with IWW member Elizabeth Gurley Flynn, whose own indictment had been dropped. (Flynn helped found the ACLU in 1920 but was expelled from the ACLU board in 1940 in one of the most controversial episodes in ACLU history.)[56]

The NCLB's defense of the IWW finally brought down the wrath of the government. Administration hard-liners saw this as conclusive proof that the rhetoric of free speech was merely a smoke screen for revolutionary radicalism. Both military intelligence and the federal Bureau of Investigation began spying on the NCLB.[57] Prominent liberals drew back in fear. As a result, the *New Republic,* the *Atlantic Monthly,* and the *Outlook* refused to publish NCLB ads defending the rights of the IWW. Max and Crystal Eastman also were cowed. The *Liberator,* which they founded in 1918 to replace the suppressed *Masses,* deliberately refrained from criticizing the government. Max explained that they "would have to temper [their] speech to the taste of the Postmaster General." In this political climate the outcome of the IWW trials was a foregone conclusion. Big Bill Haywood and thirteen other defendants received twenty-year prison sentences; thirty-three others were sentenced to ten years. Judge Kenesaw Mountain Landis explained bluntly, "You have a legal right to oppose, by free speech, preparations for war. But once war is declared, that right ceases."[58]

Free Speech in the Supreme Court

In 1919, the Supreme Court finally addressed the question of free speech in wartime, four months after the war had ended. The result was a devastating defeat for civil liberties.[59]

The first of the three major 1919 decisions involved Socialist party General Secretary Charles T. Schenck, convicted for mailing antiwar and antidraft leaflets to draft-age men. The leaflets denounced conscription as slavery and urged young men to resist: "Do not submit to intimidation. . . . Assert your rights." At issue was whether these words represented obstruction of the draft under the Espionage Act or were constitutionally protected speech. On March 3, 1919, the Court unanimously upheld Schenck's conviction. Justice Oliver Wendell Holmes held that "in many places and in ordinary times the defendants . . . would have been within their constitutional rights" to express these views. "But," he went on, "the character of every act depends upon the circumstances in which it is done." He explained his point in a passage that immediately became one of the most famous in American law: "The most stringent protection of free speech would not protect a man in falsely shouting fire in a theater and causing a panic." Holmes wrote that "the question in every case is whether the words used in such circumstances are of such a nature as to create a clear and present danger that they will bring about the substantive evils that Congress has a right to prevent."[60]

Over the next fifty years, the "clear and present danger" test became the standard for First Amendment cases. As applied, it offered little protection for unpopular speech, as it allowed legislative majorities to decide what kind of speech might be "dangerous."

The implications of *Schenck* became clear a week later when the Court unanimously upheld the conviction of Eugene Debs. In a June 16, 1918, speech to a Socialist party convention in Canton, Ohio, Debs had condemned war and capitalism but had carefully refrained from advocating any illegal conduct. "I abhor war," he declared. "I would oppose the war if I stood alone." While government agents took notes, he asserted that the courts, the press, and the entire political system were controlled by the rich. Acutely aware of possible prosecution, he commented, "I realize that, in speaking to you this afternoon there are certain limitations placed upon the right of free speech. I must be exceedingly careful, prudent, as to what I say, and even more careful and prudent as to how I say it." He stressed the importance of political activity and labor organization: "Political action and industrial action must supplement and sustain each other. . . . Vote as you strike and strike as you vote." Despite his disclaimer, the Court upheld his conviction. *Debs* was a shocking indication of how elastic the clear and present danger test could be. Schenck's pamphlets urged resistance to the draft and might be interpreted as counseling illegal action, but Debs's Canton speech was an abstract discussion of war and politics.[61]

The *Abrams* decision five months later marked an important change on the Court. Jacob Abrams and his five codefendants were convicted under the 1918 Sedition Act for distributing leaflets attacking American military intervention in Russia. In this little-known episode, the United States sent 7,500 troops to help overthrow the Bolshevik revolution. Abrams's leaflets denounced the intervention and advocated solidarity with Russian workers: "The Russian Revolution calls to the workers of the world for help. . . . Awake! Awake!, you workers of the World!" Abrams even added a disclaimer: "It is absurd to call us Pro-German. We hate and despise German militarism." The key point was the fact that the United States was not officially at war with the Soviet Union, and so the leaflet could hardly be held to interfere with the war against Germany. It did not advocate any illegal action but only called on American workers to "Awake!" and "Rise!" Nonetheless, the Court upheld the convictions in a seven-to-two decision.[62]

In a sharp and unexpected break with their position in *Schenck* and *Debs,* Justices Holmes and Louis Brandeis dissented. Holmes wrote an impassioned defense of the "sweeping command" of the First Amendment. History, he argued, taught the importance of tolerance for unpopular ideas. Truth was best "reached by free trade in ideas," and "the best test of truth is the power of the thought to get itself accepted in the competition of the market." Freedom of speech, he concluded, "is the theory of our Constitution. It is an experiment, as all life is an experiment. . . . While that experiment is part of our system I think that we should be eternally vigilant against attempts to check the expression of opinions that we loathe." Holmes revised his own clear and present danger test to add the element of imminent harm. Speech could be punished only in case of an "emergency that makes it immediately dangerous to leave the correction of evil counsel to time."[63]

Holmes's *Abrams* dissent marks the beginning of modern First Amendment theory. He gave judicial notice to the idea, expressed two years earlier by Norman Thomas, that free speech was the basis of democratic self-government. The distinguished legal scholar John Henry Wigmore replied by restating the majoritarian view that "the moral right of the majority to enter upon the war imports the moral right to secure success by suppressing public agitation against completion of the struggle." There was no right to dissent from a democratically determined goal.[64] Holmes's change of heart between *Schenck* and *Abrams* may have been stimulated by a summer meeting with Harvard law professor Zechariah Chafee, author of two important articles on free speech in wartime in the *New Republic* and the *Harvard Law Review.*[65]

Chafee elaborated his views in a 1920 book, *Freedom of Speech,* which celebrated Holmes's *Abrams* dissent. A classic in legal literature, Chafee's book shaped the development of First Amendment law for nearly two generations, reappearing in a greatly revised and expanded version on the eve of World War II when the country again faced the question of free speech during wartime. His view of the history of the First Amendment, however, was more polemical than scholarly. As historian Leonard Levy later argued, the founding fathers did not intend to abolish the law of seditious libel, which made it a crime to criticize the government. *Schenck* and *Debs,* in other words, were consistent with the history of the First Amendment.[66] Nonetheless, Chafee's powerful defense of free speech influenced the law's course in the years ahead, and conservative Harvard alumni responded to his advocacy of free speech by pressuring the university to fire him. Using material secretly supplied by the Federal Bureau of Investigation, they forced an informal "trial" of Chafee at the Harvard Club. But Harvard President A. Lawrence Lowell, in one of the few courageous defenses of academic freedom in those years, refused to fire Chafee.[67]

With his *Abrams* dissent, Holmes broke with his own well-developed views on the First Amendment, including *Schenck,* and the entire body of prewar First Amendment case law. In the twenty years before the war, the Supreme Court exhibited what one historian called a "pervasive hostility" to free speech.[68] Holmes himself accepted the "bad tendency" test to justify the suppression of speech, press, and assembly. In the important 1907 *Patterson v. Colorado* decision, the Court upheld the contempt conviction of an editor who had criticized a judge. Holmes conceded that the First Amendment prevented prior restraint but allowed the "subsequent punishment of such as may be deemed contrary to the public welfare." Nor was truth a defense; even valid criticism of judicial behavior would "tend to obstruct the administration of justice."[69] Holmes was also the source of the Supreme Court's restrictive view of freedom of assembly. In its 1897 *Davis v. Massachusetts* case, the Court sustained his lower court decision, holding that an ordinance restricting meetings on Boston Common was "no more an infringement" of the right of a public assembly than was an individual's refusing use of his house for the same reason. The decision sanctioned the power of mayors and police chiefs to ban public meetings.[70]

With Justice John Marshall Harlan usually in lonely dissent, the Court consistently rejected the idea that the due process clause of the Fourteenth Amendment incorporated the protections of the Bill of Rights. It left the question "undecided" in *Patterson v. Colorado* and, eight years later, rejected the incorporation doctrine in a decision upholding Ohio's system of film censorship. The 1915 *Mutual* decision held that motion pictures were merely an item of commerce and not a form of expression entitled to First Amendment protection.[71]

Civil Liberties in American Life

The prewar posture of the Supreme Court on free speech was consistent with long-standing American practice. Roger Baldwin and others in the NCLB attacked the wartime suppression of free speech as a violation of "old fashioned American liberties," but this was a highly romanticized view of American history. There was no tradition of free speech before World War I, in either legal doctrine or public tolerance for unpopular views. The glittering phrases of the First Amendment were an empty promise to the labor movement, immigrants, unorthodox religious sects, and political radicals. Intolerance began with the first English settlers who attempted to suppress religious heresy. The Puritans may have come to the new world seeking religious freedom for themselves, but they had no intention of granting it to others in their own communities. Through the end of the nineteenth century, American society was a set of "island communities," each a "closed enclave," intolerant of the ideas or behavior it disliked. For most, liberty meant economic freedom, the right to engage in economic pursuits free from government restraint. The geographic expanse of the country allowed dissident religious groups to set themselves apart, effectively postponing the question of tolerance in a pluralistic community.[72]

Democratic theory justified the suppression of unpopular ideas and groups. Majority rule meant the right to suppress anything threatening or distasteful. Throughout the nineteenth century, the courts scarcely functioned in many frontier communities. The majority imposed swift and certain justice through vigilante action. The anti-Catholic mob that burned the Charlestown Convent in 1834 was led by pillars of the community. The northern mobs that attacked and, in some cases, killed abolitionists were composed of "gentlemen of property and standing." In 1856, the San Francisco Vigilance Committee, representing powerful business interests, staged a political coup d'état in city government.[73]

The new aspect of the World War I assault on unpopular ideas was its national scope and the role of the federal government. Vigilantism had previously been a local and ad hoc phenomenon. But the war then nationalized the repression of unpopular ideas and institutionalized the machinery of the national security state. This in turn spurred an organized movement to defend free speech. Most of the wartime advocates of free speech—Baldwin, DeSilver, Nelles, Thomas, and Chafee—were from wealthy families or comfortably respectable Protestant backgrounds. They had no personal experience of the intolerance and suppression visited upon immigrants, labor unions, Catholics, minor religious sects, black Americans, and political radicals, and the wartime violations of free speech shattered their comfortable illusions about American liberty. The trauma of the war years exposed the First Amendment as an empty promise and galvanized this small group into the defense of free speech. In 1920 the old National Civil Liberties Bureau became the American Civil Liberties Union.

Two

Roger Baldwin and the Founding of the ACLU

Baldwin to the Fore

By late 1918 Roger Baldwin dominated the free speech fight. Crystal Eastman had withdrawn because of ill health. Through sheer force of energy, personal charm, and a remarkable talent for organizing, Baldwin pulled into his orbit Fanny Witherspoon's Bureau of Legal First Aid, Harry Weinberger's Legal Defense League, and the Liberty Defense Union. With Baldwin as secretary, the Liberty Defense Union aided all the major victims of government prosecution: *Masses* editors, Socialist Kate Richards O'Hare, Scott Nearing, Jacob Abrams, and the IWW (Industrial Workers of the World). Weinberger represented Emma Goldman and Alexander Berkman and handled Abrams's Supreme Court appeal. He appeared in court so often that Judge Learned Hand began calling him "Harry Habeas Corpus" Weinberger. By November, Baldwin was coordinating all of the legal efforts.[1]

In the course of his long and active life, Roger Baldwin left a lasting imprint on American society. He was responsible for the distinctive flavor of first the NCLB (National Civil Liberties Bureau) and then the ACLU: a complex mixture of liberal social reform impulses and conservative reverence for the Bill of Rights—the latter no less an expression of idealism than the former. Without Baldwin, the ACLU would not have survived its early years, and as a consequence, the law of civil liberties probably would have developed differently. In his thirty years as director of the ACLU he created something that transcended his own efforts—both an organization that carried on long after he retired and, more important, an idea that inspired countless other people over the years. The defense of the rights of everyone, the downtrodden and even the advocates of the most hateful ideas, became the guiding principle of Baldwin's life and that of the ACLU. The development of civil liberties in the first half of this century cannot be understood apart from the life of Roger Baldwin. He did not, however, begin as a civil libertarian. Before World War I, he was indifferent to the Bill of Rights, discovering civil liberties only in the trauma of wartime repression.

Boston: The Roots of Reform

With family ties reaching back to the *Mayflower,* Roger Baldwin inherited a Puritan conscience and an elitist view of his role in society. He was born in Wellesley, Massachusetts, in 1884, was raised in the Unitarian church, and was educated at Harvard. Inspiration for a life of public service came not from his father, a conservative businessman, but from his Uncle William and Aunt Ruth. A prominent railroad executive, William Baldwin was deeply involved in civil rights, child labor, and urban reform crusades. He helped found the National Urban League, was a leader of the National Child Labor Committee, and chaired the Committee of Fifteen which investigated prostitution in New York City. He met Booker T. Washington while vice president of the Southern Railroad and became a leading patron of Tuskegee Institute. At the family dinner table, Roger acquired the habit of moving comfortably among society's leaders. Booker T. Washington was "a guest in our house," and his Aunt Ruth introduced him to reformers Lillian Wald, Jacob Riis, Felix Adler, Owen Lovejoy, and Paul U. Kellogg. These contacts served him well: Kellogg's *Survey* published his accounts of his work in St. Louis and introduced him to the AUAM circle.[2]

Baldwin's background insulated him from the growing problems of industrial America. He was a political moderate who saw nothing basically wrong with society's institutions. The promise of democracy could be fulfilled through minor adjustments, engineered by well-intentioned people. As his friend Norman Thomas later explained, "The pre-war reformer generally held to a beautiful, romantic and uncritical faith in the wisdom of political democracy and the power of moral sentiments." The New England tradition of reform was, in fact, drifting off into amiable respectability. Baldwin later recalled that although "the unconventional, the dissenters, the 'different' seemed to flourish in the Boston atmosphere," nonconformity had definite limits: "Three subjects were never mentioned—sex, money, and age." Socialism was a forbidden subject. Baldwin had no contact with working-class or immigrant life and was always a bit of a snob. Even in his most radical phase he preferred the "best people" and pursued prominent conservative lawyers to take ACLU cases. Although he worked closely with many Jews in the ACLU, he harbored some anti-Semitic attitudes. Late in life, he nearly severed relations with his daughter when she married an Italian. But his Boston abolitionist heritage gave him a deep, if paternalistic, concern for black Americans, and he continued his uncle's work with the Urban League and the National Association for the Advancement of Colored People (NAACP).[3]

The puritanical Baldwin also had a highly ambivalent attitude toward sex. His private life was unconventional, entering into an egalitarian marriage to Madeline Doty in 1919 in which they split the housework and finances.

Nudism was a regular part of weekends at his New Jersey farm and vacations on Martha's Vineyard. In his public life, however, Baldwin was always squeamish about sex, and partly as a result, the ACLU avoided in its early years challenging the censorship of material with sexual themes.[4]

When he graduated from Harvard in 1905 Baldwin was, by his own estimation, "a not unconventional Boston product." Although active in social service projects at Harvard, he had no clear sense of direction. After a family trip to Europe, he consulted his father's lawyer for advice about a career. This lawyer happened to be Louis D. Brandeis, then a successful corporate attorney. "I was debating between a business career against a career of public service," Baldwin recalled. "Mr. Brandeis promptly, gently and firmly turned my mind completely away from the somewhat alluring business prospects held out before me." With the nudge from Brandeis, Baldwin took a social work job in St. Louis. At the time that Baldwin met with Brandeis in 1906, neither had thought about civil liberties or had any idea that Baldwin was destined to be a pioneer in the field. Indeed, later as a Supreme Court justice, Brandeis wrote some of the Court's most eloquent opinions on free speech, some in regard to cases brought by Baldwin's ACLU.[5]

St. Louis: Social Work and Social Reform

Baldwin was a smashing success in St. Louis. Nine years after arriving, unknown and inexperienced, he was named one of the ten most influential people in the city. After quickly earning a master's degree as Harvard, he took two jobs in St. Louis, directing a social settlement house and teaching the first courses on sociology at Washington University. He also threw himself "into the thick of reform" and soon became a civic leader. He was appointed chief probation officer of the St. Louis juvenile court in 1908 and then secretary of the St. Louis Civic League in 1910. Sponsored by business and professional men, the league was a typical Progressive Era urban reform agency, supporting a variety of civic causes. Baldwin led the fight for a revised city charter, helped introduce civil service to municipal government, lobbied for controls over billboards and air pollution, and worked for improvements in the conditions of children and blacks. He established the life-style he would lead for the next seventy years. For all practical purposes, he had no private life, and every meal was the occasion for a meeting. While continuing to teach, Baldwin organized the City Club to discuss good government issues and the Joint Committee for Social Service Among Colored People. Articles in *The Survey* won him national recognition, and in 1908 he helped organize the National Probation Association.[6]

The Juvenile Court and Progressive Reform

Baldwin's views on the juvenile court provide a revealing glimpse into his social philosophy. First established in Chicago in 1899, the juvenile court was one of the great achievements of prewar Progressivism. In a burst of reform, by 1910, thirty-three states had established juvenile courts and juvenile probation. Most of the remaining states soon followed suit. A mixture of humanitarian uplift and coercive social control, the juvenile court represented both the best and the worst of Progressivism. Designed to help young offenders rather than punish them as criminals, it adopted a therapeutic-rehabilitative approach that dispensed with both the formal legal procedures and the terminology of criminal courts. Juvenile court judges were to act as kindly parents with broad discretion to determine "the best interests of the child." Court proceedings were enveloped in a fog of humanitarian rhetoric: "Clients" were "referred" for a "hearing" that resulted in a "disposition." Such terminology, however, masked the coercive nature of the proceedings. Judges had enormous discretion, unchecked by standards of due process. Furthermore, the new delinquency statutes extended their social control, by criminalizing a broad range of behavior that would not have been illegal if committed by an adult.[7]

With Bernard Flexner, secretary of the National Probation Association, Baldwin coauthored the first text on the juvenile court. Financed by the Rosenwald Foundation, *Juvenile Courts and Probation* was the closest thing to an official statement of professional standards. Flexner and Baldwin argued that the formalities of due process had no place in the juvenile court. "The position of counsel in the hearing," they wrote, "is quite different from that in the trial of a criminal case. It is rarely necessary or desirable for counsel to appear in the interest of children." The young offender did not need a lawyer because "the judge and the probation officer . . . represent his interests and welfare." Formal legal procedures were "relics" of an older era and intruded in a "contentious way." The professional judgment of trained experts would protect the interests of the child.[8] Like most Progressive reformers, Baldwin and Flexner were convinced that good training and good intentions would produce good results.

The philosophy articulated by Baldwin and Flexner guided American juvenile justice until the late 1960s. Convinced that they were creating a humane and effective instrument for uplifting the disadvantaged, they were oblivious to potential due process problems. A later generation discovered how bureaucratic exigencies could distort the worthy objectives of the juvenile court. Only then did civil libertarians seriously begin to question the essentially coercive nature of many social welfare measures. In the words of ACLU director Ira Glasser, welfare bureaucracy clients were in fact "prisoners of benevolence." Ironically, when the Supreme Court overthrew the philosophy of the juvenile court in 1967, ruling that due process guarantees were required in the juvenile court, it did so in an ACLU case (*In re Gault*) argued by the future ACLU president Norman Dorsen.[9]

Free Speech in St. Louis

While he lived in St. Louis, Baldwin was little interested in free speech. In later years he credited a speech by Emma Goldman with introducing him to

free speech concerns: "That Sunday afternoon's lecture was a turning point
in my intellectual life. . . . Here was a vision of the end of poverty and
injustice."[10] His memory was clouded by his subsequent friendship with Goldman. The contemporary record reveals a hesitant attitude when she made the
first of several appearances in St. Louis. Later in 1909 when she wrote him
requesting use of the Self-Culture Hall, he replied apologetically that "we are
slaves to public opinion and the good-will of our subscribers," adding, "I
hardly think the Board would consent to its use for such subjects as you
would desire to speak on, altho [sic] many of us personally are very much
interested." He was, nevertheless, "anxious to meet you privately."[11]

A year later, when Goldman was denied permission to speak at Washington University, Baldwin intervened quietly on her behalf, assuring the university that "I have been to a number of her lectures, and the audiences she gets
in St. Louis are distinctly high class. I have never seen anything approximat-
ing a disturbance at any one of her meetings."[12] Margaret Sanger provoked
Baldwin's first defense of free speech. When the police shut down her birth
control lecture in 1912, he led a protest. "She and I got up on the hall
steps . . . and we made a speech. It was my first free speech meeting." It
reflected a generalized sense of civic duty ("I felt that my duties as guardian
of good government somehow required me to act") rather than a commitment
to free speech per se.[13]

First Doubts: Race and Reform

Racism posed the first serious challenge to Baldwin's assumptions about social
reform. As an advocate for black Americans, he was in a distinct minority
among white Americans, especially in southern-influenced St. Louis. He provoked a controversy at Washington University in 1909 by inviting two black
school principals to speak to his social work class. Two years later he quietly
protested when the university refused to admit black women to his course.
Anxious to train black social workers, he persuaded Chancellor David F.
Houston "to establish a special course for colored people . . . so that no
embarrassing questions would arise as to the presence of colored people in
the same class as whites."[14]

Baldwin was no civil rights militant, however. By temperament and family
tradition he identified with the accommodationist views of Booker T. Washington and the new Urban League, which were that black Americans would
rise in society through self-help, not civil rights agitation. Baldwin also was
an active member of the Special Committee on the Housing of Negroes and
contributed to the Investigation of Industrial Conditions Among Negroes in
St. Louis, whose subsequent report did not mention racial discrimination in
its conclusion but advised that "progress must come through the Negro himself. Recognition will come with merit."[15]

One of Baldwin's greatest accomplishments, however, did bring him face
to face with the problem of racism: As secretary of the Civic League he led
a campaign to adopt intiative, referendum, and recall, three Progressive Era

reforms designed to give citizens a more direct voice in government. Nothing better reflected the Progressives' profound faith in "the people" than did these instruments of direct democracy, but events in St. Louis quickly deflated Baldwin's high hopes. The first initiative placed on the ballot was an ordinance to segregate neighborhoods by race. For six years white property owners and real estate agents had tried unsuccessfully to get a segregation ordinance through the city council. Direct democracy proved to be the answer. Segregation proponents, in fact, "were among the foremost supporters of the initiative and referendum amendment." The segregation initiative passed overwhelmingly in March 1916. Similar ordinances were enacted in Baltimore, Richmond, Louisville, and other cities. In one of its first cases, the NAACP took a challenge to the Supreme Court. The Court ruled the segregation ordinance to be unconstitutional in *Buchanan v. Warley* (1917), holding that under the due process clause of the Fourteenth Amendment, it violated the right of property owners to buy and sell their assets.[16]

Although the segregation ordinance was a rude shock, Baldwin still did not see the problem as a fundamental conflict between majority will and minority rights. Nor did the NAACP's success in *Buchanan* convince him that litigation was an effective strategy for protecting those rights. Although disturbed by the course of events in St. Louis, he had no alternative framework for his reformist energies.

Growing Doubts

Other events between 1914 and the spring of 1917 drove Baldwin toward a more radical perspective. The outbreak of war in Europe in 1914 was a profound shock that challenged his assumption that progress was only a matter of goodwill. He began to look at the social work field with a fresh and critical eye. Then rapidly becoming professionalized, the field was losing the broad reform outlook of Jane Addams and other pioneers, in favor of a preoccupation with individual cases. Baldwin contributed to this movement. He established the School of Social Economy at Washington University to give social workers expertise in counseling, and his book on the juvenile court was essentially a manual on administrative technique. By temperament, however, he was attracted to the old reform tradition and felt increasingly alienated from the new breed. "Most were preoccupied with techniques which I minimized or accepted as routine. The 'art of case work,' the goal of so many social workers, left me cold or scoffing."[17]

Baldwin's growing awareness of the problems of industrial society was reinforced by the 1916 report of the U.S. Industrial Commission. A detailed investigation of American labor–management problems, the commission's hearings included Theodore Schroeder's testimony on the systematic violations of workers' free speech rights. Baldwin wrote the commission chair Frank P. Walsh, "I cannot refrain from saying to you what a deep impression the report . . . has made on me. . . . [It] will do more to educate public opinion to the truth of existing conditions than any other one in existence."

Taking his first tentative step toward a more radical view of America's economic problems, Baldwin observed, "It is so easy for those who do not want to see the real struggle to suggest all the petty remedies which are being offered to bridge a gulf that never can be bridged." He confessed to a "feeling of impotence before the great problem of poverty . . . and the need of tying up fundamental reform."[18] Baldwin had shown little interest in socialism until then and usually ignored speeches by Eugene V. Debs and other radicals in St. Louis. On one of her visits, Emma Goldman found him "rather confused in his social views, . . . a very pleasant person, though not very vital, rather a social lion surrounded by society girls, whose interests in the attractive young man was apparently greater than in his uplift work."[19]

Inspired by the Industrial Commission, Baldwin organized the Division on Industrial and Economic Problems at the 1916 meeting of the National Conference of Social Work (NCSW), and he wrote the division's report calling for "a complete reorganization of the ownership and use of land," the organization of labor, and the replacement of the competitive system with "cooperative systems of production and distribution." Social workers, moreover, should actively identify with "those labor and political movements" seeking fundamental changes in the economic system. In a separate statement, "Social Work and Radical Economic Movements," he delivered a stinging indictment of the profession: "We social workers often delude ourselves into a belief that we are important factors in the remaking of society. . . . [But] our work is essentially for the existing economic order—not against it." Social workers dealt with only the symptoms of industrial capitalism, and Baldwin challenged his colleagues to "fearlessly examine these radical programs." The NCSW published his report in 1917 with the caveat that not all its members subscribed to it. But by then Baldwin had already abandoned social work for the free speech fight.[20]

The Break

The approach of war in early 1917 precipitated Baldwin's final break with his social work career. Horrified by the carnage in Europe and convinced that American intervention would destroy all hopes of social reform, he organized an emergency peace committee in conjunction with the Socialist party, the Women's Peace party, and the American Union Against Militarism (AUAM). A rally in early February drew over six hundred people, and he wrote the AUAM in New York to suggest similar mass meetings across the country. "I am with you to the finish on this and only wish I could be in on your counsels in New York." Two years earlier, Baldwin had been offered the job of executive secretary, which Crystal Eastman now held, but had declined, indicating that he was "skeptical" of the AUAM's likely effectiveness.[21] By March 1917 he felt a new sense of urgency. He wrote Eastman that "the time is rapidly coming now when I feel that I can no longer carry on the local work. . . . If war is actually declared I should cut loose at once from this local work."

He offered to come to New York without promise of pay: "How ⟨
in your judgment could you best use me?" When he arrived at tⁱ
office in New York ten days later, the founder of the ACLU embarkeᵤ ᵤᵤ
lifelong crusade.[22]

The Making of a Radical

Despite the worsening repression in late 1917, Baldwin remained supremely
confident that he could persuade the administration to stop its suppression of
free speech. It responded by turning him into a criminal, and in November
1918, Baldwin went to prison. By force of circumstance, he became an outcast and a radical.

The government's attack began when Colonel Ralph Van Denman of the
Military Intelligence Division prepared a report accusing the NCLB of violating the Espionage Act. Assistance to conscientious objectors was bad enough,
but defense of the IWW was clear proof that the NCLB was a criminal organization. Caught in an awkward situation, Third Assistant Secretary of War
Fred Keppel warned Baldwin that he "may before long decline to have any
communication with the Civil Liberties Bureau." Keppel secretly sent Baldwin a copy of the report and tried to reassure him that Colonel Van Denman
was "himself a Harvard graduate, and an open-minded and partiotic officer."
Perhaps the Ivy League connection would ease the government's suspicions.
Baldwin told Keppel that "we are entirely willing to discontinue any [illegal]
practices." He then sent the Justice Department the most sensitive NCLB
files: the names of financial contributors and cooperating attorneys, the mailing list, and copies of all its publications. This extraordinary disclosure of
presumably confidential information exposed many NCLB supporters to prosecution for aiding draft resisters, and it also reflected Baldwin's still-unshaken
belief that he and the government were united in a common purpose.[23]

Despite Baldwin's trust, the government's covert assault escalated. The
federal Bureau of Investigation began spying on the NCLB in late 1917, but
even when the investigations became overt, NCLB leaders did not grasp their
implications. In November 1917 Crystal Eastman let a Bureau of Investigation agent examine the NCLB files on five Los Angeles pacifist ministers.
Agents from the American Protective League visited the office in February,
and a Bureau of Investigation agent stopped by to talk with Norman Thomas
in April. No one objected to these inquiries, much less suspected that more
insidious investigations were under way.[24] For the moment, the Justice Department was divided over whether to prosecute. There were still several
voices of moderation in the department, notably staff attorneys John Lord
O'Brian and Frances Fisher Kane. Indeed, one official reviewed the military
intelligence report and concluded that the NCLB "has carefully avoided
crossing the line which separates lawfulness and unlawfulness." Moreover,
"the purpose of this Bureau . . . strikes me as not only lawful but a good

one." He even suggested that the Justice Department "keep in close touch with" the NCLB "so that it may continue to feel that it must carefully avoid any anti-war or obstructive propaganda."[25]

The reprieve lasted only a few weeks, however. In May Keppel caved in to the mounting pressure and severed relations with Baldwin. "I have had a talk with the Secretary of War," he explained, and they had decided that "it would not be in the public interest for us . . . to cooperate in any way with the Civil Liberties Bureau."[26] Baldwin was stunned and requested a personal meeting. After the meeting he complained that they wouldn't say "what activities of ours are considered improper." Keppel refused NCLB chair L. Hollingsworth Wood's request for a meeting, explaining that "I happen to know you men all personally and like you" but that under the circumstances he could no longer have any official contact. Baldwin suggested that Keppel circumvent official policy by corresponding with him as a private individual. Unable to believe that his friends would treat him as a pariah, Baldwin's pleas became increasingly pathetic. "Won't you be good enough to let me have a definite word which will settle my difficulties?" he asked. Wood finally met with Keppel but found the situation hopeless. "Keppel seemed a good deal wrought up," he reported, "and remarked again and again that the Military Intelligence had put us down as a suspect organization." Moreover, the NCLB's "activities were very embarrassing to him." Keppel claimed to be working quietly "to develop the liberal policies of the Secretary of War" with regard to the conscientious objector (CO) problem and said that he considered the NCLB protests to be counterproductive.[27]

Outlaw

The Justice Department finally struck in August. It tapped the NCLB's phone and pressured their landlord to evict them. On Saturday morning, August 31, federal agents burst into the office. Leading the raid was Archibald Stevenson, a wealthy attorney and full-time radical hunter. Walter Nelles challenged the search warrant but backed off when an agent drew his gun. Baldwin appeared completely unhinged. Agent R. H. Finch reported that he "told us that he 'did not give a damn about anything—go ahead, lock him up, shoot him, hang him, or anything else.'" However, "Mr. Baldwin appeared sincerely agreeable to the search, in fact he stated that we were at liberty to come in at any time and that it was not necessary to have secured a search warrant at all." Baldwin "rendered every assistance he could in helping us make the search of his office." Stevenson's men began carting off the NCLB files, many of which the Lusk Committee used in its report entitled *Revolutionary Radicalism*.[28]

After the raid, Nelles warned members of the NCLB Executive Committee that "all or most" of them might be indicted. Their fears were heightened by the massive "slacker" raid in New York beginning on September 3. For three days American Protective League volunteers indiscriminately rounded up over twenty thousand young men. "Civil Liberty Dead," pronounced *The Nation*.[29] Baldwin continued to cooperate with the Justice Department and made a formal agreement allowing them to "remove all the files from the office for one week" and "keep anything . . . required for prosecution." He told Finch that "plenty of indictments could be secured from the minute book itself."

On October 7 the NCLB was spared, as the Justice Department recommended against prosecution. The NCLB's personal contacts with President Woodrow Wilson probably helped. Executive committee member John Nevin Sayre wired his brother Francis, the president's son-in-law, to ask if Attorney General Thomas Gregory would meet with him and Norman Thomas. No record of any meeting remains, but the attorney general undoubtedly understood the implications of prosecuting people with such close ties to the president. Just a few weeks after the raid, Nevin Sayre talked with Wilson over dinner about the U.S. Postal Service's ban on Norman Thomas's pacifist magazine, *The World Tomorrow*. In one of the few times he intervened to protect civil liberties, Wilson had Burleson lift the ban. Meanwhile, Hollingsworth Wood reported to the NCLB's friends that their work had "not been interrupted" by the raid. The Justice Department, however, publicly warned people not to contribute to "so-called 'civil liberties,' 'liberty defense' " or similar organizations because they sought only to "hinder the prosecution of the war."[30]

As this drama unfolded, Baldwin faced a personal crisis: Congress extended the draft to men up to age thirty-five, leaving him, at age thirty-four, eligible. Up to this point his defense of conscientious objectors had been a fight for an abstract principle, a defense of other people's rights. He now faced a test of his principles. But he did not agonize over the decision and notified his draft board that he would refuse induction. Facing a year in jail, he began putting his own affairs in order. He resigned as director of the NCLB and agreed with Madeline Doty to postpone their marriage.[31] On September 12 he registered with Local Board 129 and gave them a statement of his position: "I am opposed to the use of force to accomplish any end, however good. I am therefore opposed to participation in this or any other war. My opposition is not only to direct military service, but to any service whatsoever designed to help prosecute the war." Three weeks later he advised the U.S. attorney that he would "respectfully decline to appear" for his physical and was "presenting myself to you for prosecution." He would appear without counsel, plead guilty, and refuse bail. Bail was "one of the many devices by which the courts operate for the benefit of the well-to-do and against the poor." This was Baldwin's first step toward identifying with the outcasts of society.[32]

Under arrest, the irrepressible Baldwin promptly took charge of his own detention. The U.S. attorneys were mostly Ivy League graduates and regarded him as a celebrity. He assured his mother that "my guardian [is] a fine young Yale man." Spending little time in jail—the infamous New York "Tombs"—

he agreed to help the Bureau of Investigation sort out the NCLB files, which had been thoroughly disorganized in the raid. In the evening he and his U.S. marshal dined at a fine restaurant. His daily routine had hardly changed.[33]

"The Legend of Roger Baldwin"

At his October 30 trial Baldwin delivered to the court an eloquent statement of his principles: "All my good friends were there," he recalled. At this point, his friends included the core of the antiwar community in New York: prominent social worker Florence Kelley, radical socialists Helen and Scott Nearing, labor writer John Graham Brooks, Socialist Rose Pastor Stokes, Jewish leader and antiwar activist Judah Magnes, Norman Thomas, and Crystal Eastman.

"The compelling motive for refusing to comply with the draft act," Baldwin told Judge Julius Mayer, "is my uncompromising opposition to the principle of conscription of life by the State for any purpose whatsoever, in time of war or peace." Conscription was "a flat contradiction of all our cherished ideals of individual freedom, democratic liberty and Christian teaching." He refused to accept any form of alternative service: "I can make no moral distinction between the various services which assist in prosecuting the war— whether rendered in the trenches, in the purchase of bonds or thrift stamps at home, or in raising farm products under the lash of the draft act." Rather than protest his innocence as the other radicals had done, Baldwin chose to confront directly the machinery of the state: "I scorn evasion, compromise and gambling with moral issues, . . . I understand full well the penalty of my heresy, and am prepared to pay it."[34]

Judge Mayer was evidently impressed. Looking down from the bench he told Baldwin that "out of a considerable number of cases that are of familiar character, you do stand out in that you have retained your self-respect." He had presided over the trials of Emma Goldman, Alexander Berkman, Scott Nearing, Max Eastman, and countless draft law violators, but Baldwin prompted him to debate fundamental principles. "In all that you have said," Judge Mayer continued, "I think you have lost sight of one very fundamental and essential thing for the preservation of that American liberty of which by tradition you feel that you are a genuine upholder." No matter how conscientious one's motives might be, "a Republic can last only so long as its laws are obeyed." Mayer conceded that dissenters played an important role: "It might be that in the history of things, he, who seems to be wrong today, may be right tomorrow." But this was not for him to judge. Mayer did his duty under the law, saying, "You ask for no compromise. You will get no compromise." He then sentenced Baldwin to the maximum term of eleven months and ten days in prison, granting him credit for his twenty days in jail.[35]

The trial was widely covered in the press. Crystal Eastman wrote Madeline Doty: "I am desperately sorry that you missed Roger's wonderful appearance in court this morning. It was a beautiful and moving and at the same time brief and logical statement. Altogether we all felt it was a historic occasion."[36] Although Baldwin told Judge Mayer he sought "no martyrdom, no publicity," he quietly arranged for his statement to the court to be published in *The Nation* and *The Survey,* and his friends distributed a privately printed copy. It proved to be an enduring statement of uncompromising resistance to the machinery of war and was republished during World War II and the Vietnam War.[37]

Baldwin's performance was not entirely original, however, as it had been inspired by Eugene V. Debs's stirring address to the jury at his Cleveland trial only a month before. "Gentlemen, I do not fear you in this hour of accusation," Debs told the jury. "Nor do I shrink from the consequences of my utterances or my acts." Then after a motion for a new trial was denied, he delivered one of the most famous speeches in American political history: "I said then, and I say now, that while there is a lower class, I am in it, while there is a criminal element I am of it, and while there is a soul in prison, I am not free." Debs's speech came at a turning point in Baldwin's life. Cut off by his friends in the administration and facing a year in jail, he was casting about for a new self-image. Debs provided a model of the Outsider, the uncompromising opponent of authority. Years later he acknowledged the debt: "Such bold language and uncompromising a stand as Debs's found an instant echo in me."[38]

"My Vacation on the Government"

No prison could contain Baldwin. Calling it his "vacation on the government," he immediately began an extensive reading and writing program, arranged to tend the prison garden, and conducted classes for other inmates. After two weeks he told his mother, "I have seventeen jobs listed on my pad to do—three of them being books to write, and 10 of them magazine articles. I have enough to fill the whole year, if I do nothing else. Besides, I have 20 or 30 books on my list to read." Initially committed to the Essex County, New Jersey, jail in Newark (ironically on November 11, Armistice Day), he later was transferred to the county penitentiary in Caldwell, New Jersey, "in order to get outdoor farm work." Once again, he hardly seemed to be in custody at all. He established a friendly relationship with the warden (who as an Irish-American admired Baldwin's refusal to fight alongside the English). His cell door remained unlocked, and during the day he was free to take a walk whenever he pleased. The transfer to Caldwell was not entirely voluntary. Always an organizer, Baldwin established at the Essex County jail a chapter of the Mutual Welfare League, a Progressive Era prisoner self-help group. The prospect of a prisoners' organization alarmed the sheriff, who then arranged the transfer. Baldwin also wrote detailed accounts of prison life that were mimeographed and sent to his family and friends. He now considered his private life an important public matter.[39]

The prison sabbatical gave him time to reflect on the traumatic events of the past year. The Harvard graduate and former confidant of high government officials now rubbed shoulders with common criminals. From the vantage point of prison, he thus was able to broaden his critique of American society. Convinced now that the entire machinery of the state served only the interests of the business class, that the Constitution meant nothing in a time of crisis, and that the working class could get power only by organizing, Baldwin decided to join the radical IWW, and he emerged from prison on July 19, 1919, committed to the cause of radical though peaceful social change.[40]

The Red Scare

While Baldwin sat in jail, the political hysteria gripping the country escalated even further. If anything, the attack on everything "un-American" worsened after the war ended in November 1918. The following year was one of the most violent in American history, marked by an unprecedented wave of strikes, race riots, terrorist bombings, and even more flagrant violations of civil liberties by the federal government.

Postwar economic dislocation produced more strikes than there had been in any previous year, with major walkouts in the steel and coal industries, a general strike in Seattle, and a police strike in Boston. The Seattle and Boston strikes terrified millions of Americans, who saw law and order collapsing. Racial tensions exploded into riots in Chicago, Knoxville, and Omaha. The Chicago riot paralyzed the city for a week, and federal troops were called out to restore order in Omaha.[41]

The formation of the first American Communist parties and a series of terrorist bombings inflamed public fears of a Bolshevik revolution. The bombings began after the collapse of the Seattle general strike when Mayor Ole Hanson received a bomb in the mail. The next day another bomb exploded at the home of former Georgia Senator Thomas Hardwick, injuring his maid. When a New York postal clerk heard the news, he remembered some suspicious packages and, rechecking, found thirty-four bombs addressed to prominent Americans: John D. Rockefeller, J. P. Morgan, Justice Oliver Wendell Holmes, Attorney General A. Mitchell Palmer, and Postmaster General Albert Burleson, On June 2, bombs exploded in eight cities, one killing its deliverer on the doorstep of Attorney General Palmer's house.[42]

The bombings spurred a new government crackdown on suspected radicals. Under heavy pressure from Congress and with an eye to the Democratic presidential nomination, Palmer moved swiftly. He ordered the new head of the Bureau of Investigation, William J. Flynn, to coordinate all antiradical work. Flynn, in turn, instructed J. Edgar Hoover to create the General Intelligence Division. Hoover systematized the existing files, added new ones, and soon had index cards on 200,000 people. The files included virtually anyone who had ever criticized the government.[43] Because the 1918 Sedition Act was scheduled to expire in 1921, Montana Senator Tom Walsh introduced a bill for a peacetime sedition law. By early 1920 it seemed assured of passage.

Congress and the New York legislature, meanwhile, perfected the technique of legislative investigations into political activities. In February the U.S. Senate authorized a subcommittee chaired by Senator Overman to extend to domestic Communism its investigation of German propaganda. The New York legislature's Lusk Committee investigation was even more sensational: Committee counsel Archibald Stevenson drew heavily on the seized NCLB files and smeared all pacifists and war critics as subversives. Although the NCLB material mainly documented quiet negotiations with government officials, such fine points were lost in the antiradical atmosphere. Published in 1920, *Revolutionary Radicalism* condemned the new ACLU as "a supporter of all subversive movements, . . . its propaganda is detrimental to the interests of the State. It attempts not only to protect crime but to encourage attacks upon our institutions in every form." The Lusk Report established the standard right-wing attack on the ACLU and free speech: that the defense of free speech was the same as advocating violent revolution itself.[44]

Many state legislatures institutionalized the attack on political dissent with a series of criminal syndicalism and "red flag" laws. By 1921 thirty-three states had outlawed the possession or display of red or black flags, the symbols of, respectively, communism and anarchism. New York made it a misdemeanor to display any "symbol or emblem of any organization or association, or in furtherance of any political, social or economic principle, doctrine or propaganda." Thirty-five states passed criminal syndicalism, criminal anarchy, or sedition laws. The California criminal syndicalism statute outlawed "advocating, teaching or aiding and abetting the commission of crime, sabotage . . . or unlawful acts of force or violence or unlawful methods of terrorism as a means of accomplishing a change in industrial ownership or control, or effecting any political change."[45] Between 1919 and 1921 over five hundred people were arrested in California under the new law; another thousand suspected radicals were arrested in other states. Prosecutions went even further than the Supreme Court's "clear and present danger" test and were based on mere membership in a radical group. The arrests of two Communists in November 1919—Benjamin Gitlow in New York and Charlotte Whitney in California—eventually reached the Supreme Court as major First Amendment cases.[46]

The Palmer Raids

In November, the Bureau of Investigation staged the first of the notorious "Palmer Raids." Named after the attorney general, they were one of the worst violations of civil liberties in American history. The November raid targeted the Union of Russian Workers (URW), most of whose members were vulnerable to deportation under the Immigration Act. On November 7 the bureau made coordinated raids on the URW in twelve cities. Over 250 men were arrested. Agents broke into the Russian People's House in New York, smashing furniture and beating everyone in sight. The next day the New York Lusk Committee, led by the relentless Archibald Stevenson, arrested 500 people in its own raids. But the November raids were only a trial run for an even more massive roundup planned for January. Acting Secretary of Labor John W.

Abercrombie facilitated the plan by revising the rules on deportation arrests. Instead of immediately advising suspects of their right to counsel, Justice Department agents could now delay until the case had "proceeded sufficiently in the development of the facts to protect the Government's interests."[47] On December 21 the Justice Department deported 249 aliens to the Soviet Union. The *Buford,* dubbed the "Red Ark," carried the recently denaturalized Emma Goldman and Alexander Berkman.

On the night of January 2, 1920, the Justice Department conducted a second and even larger series of raids. Agents swooped down on suspected radicals in thirty-three cities, arresting over four thousand people. The raids involved wholesale abuses of the law: arrests without a warrant, unreasonable searches and seizures, wanton destruction of property, physical brutality, and prolonged detention. Anyone who looked vaguely "foreign" was likely to be arrested. In Hartford, Connecticut, ninety-seven suspects were held in solitary confinement, "practically buried alive for five months, being denied the privilege of seeing their relatives or friends." In Detroit, eight hundred suspects were confined for up to six days in a narrow, windowless corridor and denied all contact with family or counsel. The initial public reaction was very favorable. The *Washington Post* cheered on the government: "There is no time to waste on hairsplitting over infringement of liberty."[48]

Five days later the red scare reached its climax when the New York legislature refused to seat five Socialists elected to the lower house, with the speaker of the assembly denouncing the Socialist platform as "absolutely inimical to the best interests of the state of New York." The drive to purify legislatures had begun two months earlier when Congress refused to seat Socialist party leader Victor Berger, and when he was reelected, he was denied his seat again. The NCLB's Walter Nelles joined other attorneys in a brief defending the New York Socialists at a formal legislative hearing, but to no avail. These attacks on the democratic process, effectively disenfranchising tens of thousands of voters, finally provoked some prominent conservatives to speak out: Republican Party leader Charles Evans Hughes denounced the ban on the New York Socialists as "absolutely opposed to the fundamental principles of our government."[49]

Adverse public reaction to the Palmer Raids then began to set in. The recently organized ACLU and the National Popular Government League published the blistering *Report upon the Illegal Practices of the United States Department of Justice.* Signed by twelve prominent lawyers, including Zechariah Chafee, Felix Frankfurter, Swinburne Hale, and Frank P. Walsh, the *Report* condemned the "utterly illegal acts which have been committed by those charged with the highest duty of enforcing the laws." The abuses "struck at the foundation of American free institutions, and have brought the name of our country into disrepute."[50] Attorney General Palmer suddenly found himself on the defensive and had to answer sharp criticisms from Senator Walsh. In a few other isolated instances, common sense returned. Federal Judge George W. Anderson in Boston asked Frankfurter and Chafee to participate in the deportation hearings of William and Amy Colyer, an English couple arrested in the January Palmer Raids. The two Harvard law professors drafted an *amicus* brief that helped Anderson cancel the deportation orders. In his *Colyer* opinion Anderson also denounced the "terrorizing" actions of the Justice Department.[51]

Birth of the ACLU

While the red scare was climbing to its climax, the NCLB debated its future. Although the war was over, the free speech fight clearly needed to continue. The NCLB leaders regarded Roger Baldwin as the obvious choice to head the organization, but Baldwin himself was uncertain about accepting the position. He left prison planning to join the radical IWW, though his friend Scott Nearing advised against it: "You cannot get into a labor organization on a level with the others. No Harvard graduate can." Elizabeth Gurley Flynn agreed, telling Baldwin that he couldn't expect "to go into the I.W.W. . . . on a level with the other boys." "Excuse me if I seem to lecture," Nearing apologized, but "you did great work with the NCLB—that is the kind of thing for which you are fitted by training and temperament."[52] Many people, it seemed, had an investment in Baldwin's future. The *New York Tribune* and the *St. Louis Post-Dispatch* reported his release from prison (three months early because of a clerical error in computing his time served), and his friends welcomed him back with a party at Norman Thomas's apartment. IWW official L. S. Chumley jokingly attended in order to "protect our prospective Fellow Worker Baldwin from the insidious bourgeois influence that such a meeting, held in the home of a reverend, germinates."[53]

Baldwin had some personal matters to attend to first: He and Madeline Doty were married in August. The ceremony was essentially a political statement. Norman Thomas presided over their exchange of self-composed vows that linked the personal and the political: "To us who passionately cherish the vision of a free society, the present institution of marriage among us is a grim mockery of essential freedom. Here we have the most intimate, the most sacred, the most creative relationship shackled in the deadening grip of private property and essentially holding the woman subservient to the man." Baldwin vowed that "whether my course may lead me again to prison, or to distant travel and to long separation, our union will be no barrier to freedom of action, but rather a source of added strength and keener purpose." Doty described their marriage as a "foundation for the new free brotherhood of which we strive where all men shall live together in love and harmony."[54]

Doty's stature as a reformer matched Baldwin's. Lawyer, feminist, pacifist, and prison reformer, she had been Crystal Eastman's roommate when Baldwin arrived in New York in 1917. Under the pseudonym of Maggie Martin she had spent a week in the New York state prison at Auburn in 1913, an act that undoubtedly won Baldwin's admiration and strengthened his own commitment to go to jail.[55] News of their egalitarian marriage made headlines, with one paper declaring, "Hubby Pays Wife for Doing Housework in Happy

Doty–Baldwin 50–50 Marriage." When Doty did more than half of the cleaning, Baldwin paid her 50 cents an hour. Indeed, they embarked on marriage with the same crusading zeal they brought to their political work. At age thirty-five, instead of settling into middle-age respectability, Baldwin challenged social and political convention with the energetic idealism of a recent college graduate.[56]

After a camping-trip honeymoon, Baldwin took off on a three-month journey through the Midwest as a laborer, "to study the psychology and conditions of labor at first hand."[57] Arriving in Pittsburgh in the midst of the great steel strike, Baldwin worked in a mill at the request of strike organizer (and future Communist party leader) William Z. Foster to investigate the productivity of the strikebreakers. When management discovered his true role a week later, they fired him. Undercover agents, meanwhile, ransacked his hotel room and stole his reports. Baldwin then moved on to Chicago where he joined the IWW and the waiters' union. A few weeks later he returned to St. Louis where, he wrote his mother, "I was just a common day laborer in blue overalls . . . with a pick and shovel. It was a great experience." The Harvard graduate was proud of his firsthand experience with manual labor. He sent IWW leader Bill Haywood "the first dollar I ever earned at productive labor. I earned it at 37¢ per hour working in a brick yard." He claimed he had gotten "more knowledge of the conditions and point of view of labor in these two months . . . than I have got in years of observation and reading." But then the St. Louis police, claiming they were acting under federal orders, also raided his room and seized his personal papers.[58]

Founding the ACLU

Returning to New York in mid-November, Baldwin acceded to the pleas of his friends and agreed to head a reorganized NCLB. He had few other options. He was disillusioned with social work and, given his notoriety, would probably have had trouble finding a job. Indeed, while Baldwin was in prison, even the mention of his name at the annual National Council of Social Work convention brought forth a storm of protest. He finally agreed to head the new civil liberties organization, but only on his own terms. He would work half time and devote the rest of his energy to other projects. And in 1920 alone Baldwin created three other organizations. The NCLB would have to be "reorganized and enlarged to cope more adequately with the invasions of civil liberty incident to the industrial struggle which has followed the war." He was disappointed in DeSilver's management of the NCLB during his stay in prison, feeling that it had done little more than sponsor, with English civil libertarians, a conference in October 1919 on Anglo-American civil liberties. But Baldwin's criticism was unfair. DeSilver had organized campaigns to repeal the Espionage Act and to secure amnesty for imprisoned dissenters as soon as the war ended. Rather, Baldwin's complaints were characteristic of a lifelong trait: He never felt he could trust anyone else to direct the civil liberties cause.[59]

Baldwin's vision of the civil liberties struggle called for militant and direct action. "The cause we now serve is labor"; he wanted "no detachment from the struggle in the field." "Our place is in the fight." They should "take the risks of conflict with the authorities and even of mob violence." Direct action meant sending "a few well known liberals" into the Pennsylvania coalfields, where their arrests "would dramatize the situation effectively." Almost as an afterthought, he added that "of course, we should retain our cooperating attorneys and such legal aid as is necessary." He put little stock in litigation as a means of securing civil liberties. Walter Nelles, having lost virtually every one of his wartime cases, agreed. Further litigation before hostile courts was futile, and Nelles proposed to edit a magazine publicizing free speech violations. The battle for civil liberties, they all agreed, was in the arena of public opinion, not in the courts.[60]

Casting about for a name for the new organization, Baldwin considered the National Civil Rights League (or Union) and the American Civil Liberties League, before settling on the American Civil Liberties Union. On January 12, 1920, ten days after the Palmer Raids, the NCLB Executive Committee accepted his plan, and a week later, on January 19, the ACLU was born.[61]

The ACLU was a unique organization. A small group of civil rights organizations already existed: the NAACP (1909), the Anti-Defamation League (1913), and the American Jewish Congress (1916), but each served a specific interest group. In contrast, the ACLU adopted the policy of impartially defending civil liberties, including the principle of free speech, without reference to the content of that speech. It was an inauspicious time, however, to launch a permanent civil liberties defense organization. When the twelve members of the ACLU Executive Committee met for lunch on West Sixteenth Street that afternoon, the country was still full of suspicion, and free speech was a suspect idea. The Supreme Court had soundly rejected all First Amendment claims. Congress was at that moment debating a peacetime sedition law, and similar laws were either in place or under consideration in a majority of the states. The executive branch, fresh from the Palmer Raids, was even more aggressively anti–civil libertarian. The labor movement had lost all of the major 1919 strikes and was tainted with the label of Bolshevism. The old centers of opposition, the Socialist party and the IWW, had been crushed. If free speech was everywhere in retreat and under a cloud of suspicion, the war years had at least accomplished one important thing: It had dramatized the issue of civil liberties and placed it, for the first time, on the national political agenda.[62]

II

Lean Years, 1920-1932

Three

Civil Liberties
in the Wilderness,
1920-1924

Launching the Fight for Free Speech

Passaic, New Jersey, police officers charged into a meeting of the Amalgamated Textile Workers union and shut off the lights. But the intrepid ACLU leaders Harry F. Ward, Norman Thomas, and Albert DeSilver were undeterred and continued reading aloud the New Jersey Constitution by candlelight. It was a symbolic gesture, designed to protest the ban on all textile workers' meetings in Passaic. The Passaic confrontation in April 1920 was typical of the ACLU's initial fight for free speech, in every respect except one: It succeeded. The mayor relented and allowed the Amalgamated Textile Workers to continue its organizing drive.[1]

It was a rare victory. The antiradical crusade of the war years left what historian Paul Murphy described as "a new permanent dimension of intolerance" in American society. Right-wing superpatriots, heavily financed by business interests, attacked free speech as a dangerous idea. When the ACLU defended union organizers and Communists, these so-called patriots labeled it "un-American." New York City school authorities even refused to allow the ACLU to conduct a forum on "old fashioned American liberties."[2]

Roger Baldwin began each ACLU Executive Committee meeting with the "Report on the Civil Liberty Situation for the Week," listing police raids on union meetings, denial of speaking permits, and mob violence against blacks, union organizers, and Socialists. The August 15, 1921, summary included a post office ban on the Italian anarchist newspaper *Il Martello,* denial of a permit to hold a Sacco and Vanzetti Defense Committee rally on the Boston Common—on the grounds that it "might lead to disorder"—and an American Legion mob attack on a Socialist meeting in Shenandoah, Iowa.[3]

"Never before in American history were the forces of reaction so completely in control of our political and economic life," began the ACLU's first *Annual Report*. In May 1920 an ACLU-sponsored demonstration in support of steel workers in Duquesne, Pennsylvania, produced a sweeping injunction prohibiting all union meetings.[4] Philadelphia police banned meetings by Italian workers in 1920. The police commissioner of Newark laughed when Communist party leader William Z. Foster sought a permit to speak. "You can't talk in Newark," he told Foster, "not while we run this town." Near Los Angeles, author Upton Sinclair was arrested in 1923 for trying to read the First Amendment at an IWW (Industrial Workers of the World) rally. Two years later Los Angeles police dragged ACLU attorney Leo Gallagher from a podium near city hall. The police chief swore he would "not allow any man to deny the existence of God down there on the plaza." A New York City cop closed down a 1923 birth control speech by Margaret Sanger on order, he explained, from "the Cardinal."[5]

The ACLU claimed a network of one thousand "correspondents" and eight hundred cooperating attorneys in 1920—figures that were probably exaggerated.[6] In truth, there was little the ACLU could do in the face of massive public hostility. Baldwin concentrated on influencing public opinion and produced a steady stream of pamphlets. One of the first and most successful, the *Report upon the Illegal Practices of the United States Department of Justice,* condemned the government's "illegal acts" and helped persuade the Senate to hold hearings on the Palmer Raids.[7] The peacetime sedition bill, which earlier seemed certain to pass, died in committee. The worst of the wartime hysteria ended, and ACLU Washington lobbyist Charles T. Hallinan reported excitedly that "we have them on the run."[8]

Few other efforts proved effective as the *Illegal Practices* report. Baldwin sent journalists John L. Spivak and Winthrop Lane to investigate the near–civil war conditions in the West Virginia coalfields, issued a report documenting police suppression of political meetings in one hundred cities, and published a pamphlet called *The Gag on Teachers,* but these had no discernible impact on public opinion or the courts.[9]

"How to Get Civil Liberty"

In the face of a seemingly hopeless situation, the ACLU was divided over the best strategy for advancing civil liberties. One group, led by Baldwin, Norman Thomas, and Scott Nearing, favored direct action in support of the labor movement. They disdained litigation. Baldwin argued that "standards of civil liberty cannot be attained as abstract principles or as constitutional guarantees" because rights "are not granted" by those in power. They could be won only by militant action. Baldwin's rhetoric in these years had a class-conscious tinge, but he never became a Marxist. Rather, he always described himself as a "philosophical anarchist," once advising students at the New School to "trust your emotions, your instincts . . . as against your intellectual convictions. It seems to me highly undesirable for any of us to seek intellectual consistency."[10] His approach to civil liberties was more a matter of temperament than ideology, a gut-level passion for justice, and a bottomless "capacity for indignation."[11]

Arthur Garfield Hays, a successful New York attorney with a lucrative corporate and show business practice, who also was in the forefront of many ACLU battles between 1920 and 1954, shared the same outlook: "I hate to see people pushed around."[12] In 1923 he and Rev. John A. Ryan defied a ban on meetings by mine workers in Logan County, West Virginia. In another West Virginia confrontation ten years later he was warned that "they'll tar and feather you and castrate you." Hays admitted, with characteristic good humor, that this was "a new and decidedly disturbing idea." In any case, he practiced the provocative speech he so often defended: Addressing a 1934 Communist party rally, he told them they could not get a fair trial in the United States. But their cheers turned to boos when he said the bourgeoisie couldn't get a fair trial in the Soviet Union either.[13]

Hays was cynical about the legal process and saw court proceedings as a platform for broad political and philosophical statements, an opportunity to educate both the judges and the public. He was simultaneously idealistic about the Bill of Rights and cynical about the courts. He once told Alexander Meikeljohn that "if one can persuade a judge to think he is right, then the judge is likely to be able to find some way to come to that conclusion on legal grounds." His obituary in the *New York Times* described him as "the lawyer who grew rich representing corporations and who became famous defending civil liberties without pay."[14] He established a long ACLU tradition of successful lawyers who abandoned their private practice out of boredom for the politically and intellectually challenging ACLU cases.

Attorneys Walter Nelles and Walter Pollak represented a different element in the ACLU leadership. They believed in the legal process and patiently carried test cases to the Supreme Court, establishing the ACLU tradition of legal craftsmanship. They scored their first breakthrough in the 1925 *Gitlow* decision but won no clear-cut victories until 1931.[15]

These two groups in the ACLU maintained a laissez-faire attitude toward each other, managing to avoid the debilitating factionalism that beset left-wing political groups. Whatever their differences, all the ACLU leaders shared a belief in the Constitution and the Bill of Rights that bordered on religious faith. Though Baldwin wore his contempt for the legal process like a badge, he and the others repeatedly invoked the imagery of "old fashioned American liberties." Their tactic of reading the Declaration of Independence, the Constitution, or the Bill of Rights in free speech fights was a calculated appeal to patriotic sentiment. It was an exercise in mythmaking, an effort to capture the symbols of Americanism for the cause of civil liberties. In the long run the strategy worked. First the Supreme Court and then other Americans came to accept the promises of the Bill of Rights as the touchstone of freedom. Appeal to conservative impulses remained an important element of the ACLU's efforts.[16]

ACLU leaders escaped the profound disillusionment that overtook most prewar reformers in the twenties. The war was a shattering experience for most American liberals, destroying their faith in progress, if not democracy itself. But Baldwin and his ACLU colleagues emerged from the war with a new vision of democracy rooted in the principle of free speech. Their faith in the Bill of Rights sustained them through the following decade of steady defeats.[17]

Civil Liberties Campaigns

"The Cause We Now Serve Is Labor"

The antiunion crusade of the 1920s was led by a well-financed network of self-styled patriotic groups.[18] The National Security League, the American Defense Society, the Better America Federation, and others kept up a barrage of propaganda equating unionism, liberalism, and free speech with foreign radicalism. The National Security League, funded by John D. Rockefeller, J. P. Morgan, a Du Pont, and a Vanderbilt, attacked unionism and called for an "AMERICAN AMERICA." The assault was highly successful: Union membership dropped from 5,047,800 in 1920 to 3,622,000 in 1923, and by 1929 the labor movement was weaker than it had been since the 1890s.[19]

The ACLU tried to counter these attacks with its own publicity. Baldwin sent journalists Winthrop Lane and John Spivak to West Virginia after the Matewan "massacre" in which the mayor, a detective, and three union officials were killed in a bloody shoot-out. Lane found a virtual civil war. Mine operators controlled local police and maintained near-feudal conditions in company-owned towns. A federal court injunction prohibited union leaders from even mentioning the strike. Arthur Garfield Hays and Rev. John A. Ryan led an ACLU confrontation with Sheriff Don Chafin, himself a coal operator, who had announced that "no meeting would be permitted." Zechariah Chafee chaired the Committee of Inquiry on Coal and Civil Liberties, cosponsored by the ACLU and the League for Industrial Democracy, and gave its findings to the U.S. Coal Commission. But violations of freedom of speech and assembly continued, and union membership steadily declined.[20]

A 1923 Los Angeles free speech fight led to the founding of the ACLU's first permanent affiliate when marine transport workers went out on strike in Los Angeles's port of San Pedro. Strikers filled the jails, and the remnants of the IWW joined the fight, demanding the release of members imprisoned from the war years. When the police banned all public meetings, a wealthy sympathizer, Minnie Davis, offered her property for a rally. When author Upton Sinclair and five friends marched up "Liberty Hill" to read the First Amendment, the police chief warned them to "cut out that Constitution stuff." Before they could finish they were arrested and charged with criminal syndicalism. The charges were eventually dropped, but the aroused Sinclair helped organize the Southern California ACLU.[21]

The injunction became a devastating antiunion weapon. Employers persuaded state and federal courts that all union organizing involved coercion and intimidation. A typical injunction banned "any picketing which is annoying, harassing, or intimidating to the plaintiff's customers or his present employees," "any system of organized picketing," and visiting workers at home to persuade them "to leave their employment." Courts routinely granted employers' requests for *ex parte* injunctions that broke strikes before the union could contest the court order. In 1921 the Supreme Court upheld restrictions on peaceful picketing because such tactics "inevitably lead to intimidation and violence."[22]

Baldwin convened a national conference on the injunction problem in late 1920, confessing to Felix Frankfurter that the ACLU was completely at a loss.[23] Frankfurter, emerging as the leading expert on injunctions, outlined a campaign for a federal law restricting the scope of the injunctions. This was consistent with his general view that civil liberties were best protected by legislation rather than through the courts. The ACLU and the American Federation of Labor (AFL) began lobbying in 1925 and secured the first congressional hearings two years later.[24]

Baldwin's prolabor rhetoric frequently led to misunderstandings about the ACLU's relationship to organized labor. Although it often appeared that the ACLU was part of the labor movement, in fact it supported labor only on freedom of speech and assembly issues. The ACLU and labor thus eventually parted company in the 1930s when the Wagner Act established labor's right to organize.[25]

Ending the Wartime Hysteria

The ACLU's second priority in the 1920s was to undo the damage of the war years, including ending censorship of the mails, amnesty for political prisoners, and repeal of state sedition laws.

Freeing the mails proved to be the easiest task. Although the Supreme Court upheld the power of the postmaster general, Will Hays, to suspend second-class mailing privileges, he announced that he had no intention of being a censor. Hays thereupon restored the mailing privileges of the Socialist *Milwaukee Leader* and ended the ban on all but four political books. Hays even sought the ACLU's advice on how the postal laws might be amended so as to curtail censorship.[26] The U.S. Postal Service continued to censor sexually related books, however, and subsequent postmasters general were less tolerant than Hays was. In 1928 the Postal Service refused to mail letters carrying an Anti-Imperialist League sticker reading "Protest Against Marine Rule in Nicaragua." The ACLU sued, but a federal judge upheld the ban, ruling that "this court will not aid the perpetuation of falsehoods" and that the stickers were part of a campaign to "encourage desertion of United States marines to the forces of Sandino." The ACLU's Art Hays suggested printing new stickers, "Protest Against the Marines in Nicaragua," which contained no allegations of marine "rule." The Postal Service, afraid of losing the case, allowed them to be mailed, but the arbitrary power of the postmaster general remained intact.[27]

The amnesty campaign began as soon as the war ended. Many COs received incredibly harsh prison terms of thirty years or longer, whereas those convicted under the Espionage Act generally got the maximum term of ten years. Seeking their release created a dispute over strategy, with the ACLU and many prisoners making crucial distinctions among amnesty, pardon, and commutation. The most common form of release, commutation, simply shortened a sentence to allow immediate release. Pardon represented forgiveness for wrongdoing but sustained the original conviction in principle. Some prisoners refused even to apply for a pardon. Amnesty implied that the person had done nothing wrong and, from the ACLU's perspective, legitimized the original political dissent.[28]

An embittered President Wilson refused to make any concessions to political prisoners, though after the 1920 elections, some administration officials released imprisoned COs through commutation. Amnesty for the Espionage Act cases was far more difficult, and the campaign dragged on for years. Republican President Warren G. Harding expressed sympathy and met with ACLU representatives Norman Thomas and Albert DeSilver in April 1921. It was the only occasion in that decade when the ACLU gained access to the White House. Harding suggested that they could free his hand by mobilizing public opinion. The strategy of "persistent if quiet agitation" did produce some results. On Christmas Day, 1921, Harding commuted the sentences of Eugene Debs and twenty-four other prisoners, releasing all of them. Adverse public reaction, however, halted further releases.[29]

Access to the White House raised anew the tactical question of how to relate to government officials. Baldwin now favored vigorous public pressure on the president. He proposed "making life a burden" for Harding by picketing the White House and his golf course. Anticipating the direct-action tactics of the 1960s, Baldwin suggested picketing even inside the White House and the attorney general's office. But the Joint Amnesty Committee insisted on a low-key approach, and so Baldwin withdrew his support in protest.[30] President Calvin Coolidge released more prisoners in 1923, but the issue lingered on for another decade. Finally, on Christmas Day, 1933, President Franklin D. Roosevelt restored the citizenship of the remaining fifteen hundred former prisoners.[31]

The campaign to repeal the state criminal syndicalism laws failed completely. Although most states stopped enforcing them by 1921, California continued to use its law aggressively. Then the arrest of Communist Labor party member Charlotte Anita Whitney set the stage for a major Supreme Court test of the California law. The ACLU scored its lone victory in 1921 when New York Governor Al Smith vetoed a package of antiradical laws, one of which would have dismissed any teacher who advocated "a form of government other than the government of the United States." Another, directed at the left-wing Rand School, would have allowed the state to close any private school advocating the overthrow of the government. In a politically courageous act, Smith vetoed both laws, arguing that they struck "at the very foundation of one of the most cardinal institutions of our nation—the fundamental right of the people to enjoy full liberty in the domain of idea and speech."

He also halted further prosecutions under the state Criminal Anarchy law and pardoned Communist Benjamin Gitlow after the Supreme Court upheld his conviction in 1925.[32]

The "Heresy" of Free Speech

Right-wing groups leveled a steady stream of attacks on the ACLU, with the Industrial Defense Association calling it "the legal agency of the Communist Party of Russia," and the Allied Patriotic Societies demanding a congressional investigation. An American Legion official swore out an arrest warrant for Baldwin after a 1921 speech in Cincinnati, charging him with criminal syndicalism. The National Civic Federation called free speech a "nuisance," and its head, Ralph Easley, told J. Edgar Hoover that the ACLU "crowd" got its funds from Moscow. War Department librarian Lucia Maxwell produced a "spider-web chart" purporting to illustrate the connections among various liberals and radicals. The chart implicated, among others, Elizabeth Gurley Flynn, William Z. Foster, and Jane Addams in a purported IWW-Communist-pacifist-ACLU plot to subvert America.[33]

Even some of the ACLU's labor movement allies joined the attacks. In 1923 AFL head Samuel Gompers accused the ACLU of aiding "revolutionary" organizations, and United Mine Workers leader John L. Lewis attacked the ACLU as "communistic." Ideological and organizational motives prompted these attacks. Gompers was always eager to dissociate the AFL from any radical taint. Moreover, both he and Lewis were being challenged by rival unions, some led by radicals the ACLU had defended. Gompers and Lewis gave the ACLU an early taste of one of its most frustrating experiences. Powerless groups repeatedly sought the ACLU's assistance when their own rights were violated but then turned anti–civil libertarian in the face of groups or ideas they did not like.[34]

The ACLU responded to these attacks with its own publicity campaign. Baldwin sponsored Norman Hapgood's *Professional Patriots* which documented the corporate funding of right-wing groups. (The president and chief financial backer of the Better America Federation was a wealthy Los Angeles businessman named H. M. Haldeman. His grandson, H. R. Haldeman, was convicted for his role in the Watergate scandal fifty years later. Ironically, the elder Haldeman made his fortune in the plumbing supply business.)[35] The ACLU also struck back in the courts, suing the *Chicago Tribune* for libel in 1924 after being accused of taking the proverbial "Moscow gold." The *Tribune* published a retraction. The *Boston Transcript* repeated the accusation, but the ACLU decided not to sue, on the advice of the ever-cautious Frankfurter. Arthur Garfield Hays had an active libel practice on behalf of private individuals. He won a major suit against the American Defense Society's Fred Marvin, who accused him of advocating criminal anarchy. The award was overturned on appeal. As these suits indicated, the ACLU did not at this point regard libel actions as violations of free speech.[36]

The Bureau of Investigation, relying heavily on private "red hunters," continued to spy on the ACLU. Frequently the agents were comically incompetent and prone to the wildest delusions. The financially pressed ACLU would have been amused to read the March 1920 bureau report that it, the ACLU, had "unlimited financial backing," and a 1921 memo warning that "fifty-two persons control U.S." A report on Baldwin incorrectly identified his parents and place of birth. The bureau's spying on the Southern California ACLU was particularly intense, and it even obtained the affiliate's membership list.[37]

Freedom in the Schools

The right-wing campaign to impose its view of Americanism on the country inevitably focused on schools and colleges. New York City's school board hardly needed persuading, holding that "the most virile motive of the school is the advancement of Americanism." In the prevailing climate, this meant inculcating patriotism, Protestantism, and reverence for the free enterprise system—in equal measure. The ACLU's protests forced the withdrawal of materials prepared for the U.S. Bureau of Education's American Education Week in 1923. Dictated by the American Legion, these materials were filled with praise for militarism and attacks on organized labor. The War Department agitated for compulsory military training, and by 1925 eighty-three colleges required all male students to enroll in Reserve Officer Training Corp (ROTC) courses. Baldwin thereupon organized the special Committee on Militarism in Education. The ACLU then brought to the Supreme Court a challenge to compulsory ROTC at the University of California at Los Angeles (UCLA), arguing that it violated religious freedom. The Court, however, rejected this argument in 1934.[38]

The most direct confrontation over forced patriotism in the schools involved the Jehovah's Witnesses. In 1926 the Denver schools suspended fifty children who refused to participate in patriotic exercises on the grounds that it violated their religious beliefs. The ACLU wanted to take a challenge to the Supreme Court, but the cases died when school officials readmitted the students. The compulsory flag salute controversy disappeared for over a decade, only to return as a national crisis in the years just before World War II.[39]

Discrimination against Catholic teachers was a serious problem in the 1920s, and the Ku Klux Klan (KKK) was nearly as anti-Catholic and anti-Semitic in those years as it was antiblack. After the 1928 presidential election in which Democratic party candidate Al Smith encountered vicious anti-Catholic attacks, the editor of the Catholic journal *America* lamented, "We are strangers in our own land." The Oregon Klan sponsored an initiative effectively closing all private schools. In many of the small and medium-sized towns of the Midwest and Far West, the politically powerful Klan dominated local school boards. When KKK members captured control of the Akron, Ohio, school board in 1923 and tried to fire the Catholic teachers, Baldwin tried to help but could do little from his office in New York. The incident illustrated the weakness of the ACLU in responding effectively to problems outside the major cities.[40]

In 1921 the ACLU began its own fight with the New York City schools. The school board barred John Haynes Holmes from speaking and, five years later, banned anyone from the ACLU from "talking in school buildings under any auspices." The board's regulations required all speakers to "be loyal to American Institutions," refrain from speaking in a foreign language, and discuss only "subjects that will tend toward active support of American ideas, institutions and ideals." In denying an ACLU request to hold a forum on "old fashioned free speech" at Stuyvesant High School, the board accused the ACLU of advocating a student "revolt against regulations." The ACLU sued and won a court order directing the school board to grant it a hearing. The board finally relented and approved an ACLU-sponsored meeting on the innocuous topic "The Growth of New York Since 1900."[41]

"Dangerous Foreign Ideas"

The government continued its efforts to keep allegedly dangerous ideas and individuals from entering the country. The U.S. Customs Service banned many literary classics and new books on sexuality. Its list of 739 books included Boccaccio's *Decameron,* Balzac's *Droll Stories,* and Rabelais's works. It banned Marie Stopes's *Married Love,* a discussion of female sexuality, and Radclyffe Hall's novel about lesbianism, *The Well of Loneliness.* The most famous banned book was James Joyce's *Ulysses,* already recognized as one of the greatest novels in the English language. Customs clerks had unfettered discretion to seize books, usually just informing a returning traveler that "sorry, Madam, this book is banned by the Treasury Department. You'll have to leave it with me." American tourists nonetheless continued to smuggle literary classics into the country until the late 1950s.[42]

Foreign-born individuals deemed too radical were either deported or denied visas. The secretary of labor had complete discretion to determine who was "undesirable." In one of the more celebrated cases, the Harding administration bowed to pressure from Italy and suppressed the anti-Fascist Carlo Tresca. The Postal Service banned his paper, *Il Martello,* and when the ACLU helped lift the ban, the government prosecuted Tresca for publishing a birth control ad in it. The State Department at first tried to deny a visa to Count Michael Karolyi, the first president of the Hungarian Republic, but then finally issued one on the condition that he not discuss politics. Roger Baldwin was subject to similar conditions when he visited England in 1927.[43]

The Fight Against Racism

During the 1920s, KKK violence was an ever-present reality throughout the entire United States. There were sixty-four reported lynchings in 1921 and an untold number of unreported assaults on black Americans. The Klan had enormous national strength during this decade, particularly in the Midwest. The 1924 Democratic party's national convention deadlocked over the question of whether to condemn the KKK by name.

The ACLU was virtually the only predominately white organization to champion racial justice in the twenties, as the modern civil rights movement, in the form of a broad-based coalition, did not coalesce until the 1940s. At the outset the ACLU established a close working relationship with the NAACP (National Association for the Advancement of Colored People), allowing it to take most court cases: "In cases involving Negroes' rights it is our policy to refer them first to the N.A.A.C.P., offering to cooperate, and if they do not assume the responsibility we go into it ourselves." Beginning with James Weldon Johnson, Baldwin always made sure a high-ranking NAACP official sat on the ACLU Executive Committee.

The ACLU was particularly weak in the South. In early 1920 Baldwin asked NAACP leader Mary White Ovington for the names of sympathetic southerners. She replied apologetically that "I take it that you mean white men, and I confess that I do not know of any names to send you. . . . There is so little liberty in the South in times of peace as well as in times of war."[44]

The ACLU concentrated on publicizing civil liberties violations and repeatedly condemned KKK violence. Although the lynching of blacks continued, the total number steadily dropped from more than sixty in 1922 to eleven in 1928. In 1931, the ACLU published *Black Justice,* a comprehensive report on the denial of rights to black Americans.[45] But the ACLU's relations with the NAACP were not without difficulty, as the ACLU also defended the right of the KKK to march peaceably.

Free Speech for Everyone? The Test of Principle

At an early ACLU Executive Committee meeting, Scott Nearing lamented the "growing intolerance of the radicals and workers themselves, and their disbelief in civil liberty in principle."[46] Not all the attacks on free speech came from right-wing conservatives. Many of the ACLU's liberal and left-wing friends also tried to suppress ideas they thought were dangerous. Although the Ku Klux Klan was riding high during the twenties and anti-Semitic views were promulgated by such prominent individuals as Henry Ford, the liberals fought back and in a number of instances won restrictions on racist speech. These efforts forced the ACLU to define its stand on free speech. Did the First Amendment mean free speech for racists? Where did you draw the line between racist speech and Klan violence? Was the Klan a political organization or a secret criminal conspiracy? Right-wingers attacked the Communist party on the same grounds. Did the First Amendment protect the KKK, the Communists, and all antidemocratic groups?

The ACLU's answer was not a foregone conclusion in these early years. During World War I the NCLB (National Civil Liberties Bureau) had defended conscientious objectors and antiwar protesters, but they had stood for ideas the NCLB supported. Thus defending free speech in regard to ideas the ACLU found abhorrent posed a more serious test. There was also pressure from the ACLU's friends to limit the rights of some extremist groups. It was difficult for the ACLU to tell its beleaguered allies in the NAACP that it supported the rights of the Klan. Jewish friends objected to the ACLU's defense of anti-Semites. The radical left was especially anti–civil libertarian; the Communists aggressively opposed free speech for "reactionaries." It was in the context of these disputes with its friends and frequent clients that the ACLU sharpened its position on free speech.

The Rights of the Klan

The issue of free speech for the Ku Klux Klan arose in 1923 when Boston Mayor James Curley banned their meetings. One Klan rally attracted over three hundred sympathetic Harvard students. The ACLU sprang to the Klan's defense, offering to defend them in court.[47] An exchange of letters between Boston ACLU leader John Codman and Mayor Curley became a lively debate over the meaning of the First Amendment. Curley proclaimed himself a "stout stickler for freedom of meeting, speech and press" but challenged the ACLU's position. That is, he contended that the Constitution did not protect a group "whose avowed purpose is to persecute and restrict the liberties of other citizens, which fosters race and religious hatreds, foments civic dissension, disturbs the peace [and] places itself clearly outside the constitution and the law." Curley argued that the Klan was not a legitimate political party but a "secret conspiracy," not entitled to First Amendment protection. A democracy had a duty to preserve itself, and an antidemocratic organization "cannot expect to shelter itself behind the rights it denies and the guarantees it repudiates."[48] A similar argument was later used against the Communists during the cold war.

The ACLU replied by questioning Curley's power to be the "sole judge" of who could hold meetings. Such power was "not authorized by our Constitution and law." If his view prevailed, "there would be considerable parts of this country in which religious intolerance would prohibit Catholics, Jews, and indeed, the representatives of some Protestant sects, from holding meetings or speaking at all." In fact, that was the case throughout most of the country in those years. Furthermore, the ACLU drew the line "between word and deed," not between "one kind of speech and another." Rather, violent acts, not words or political associations, could be prohibited. While maintaining that "we detest its secrecy, its bullying, its masked anarchy," the ACLU argued that the proper remedy for the Klan was "exposure and ridicule."[49]

Curley's professed support for the right "to discuss any and all laws" was hypocritical. Earlier he had banned Margaret Sanger from speaking on the grounds that birth control was a "crime against civilization" and that the term *birth control* was nothing more than a "euphemism" for murder. Yet Curley had permitted an anti-Sanger speech in Boston.[50]

The Klan faced restrictions in other areas. The mayor of Cudahy, Wisconsin, banned KKK meetings in 1924, and a year later, a Kansas court prohibited all KKK marches. The ACLU offered legal assistance wherever "the Klan's civil rights are at stake," but no test cases developed. The ACLU did not oppose all restrictions on the Klan, however. It endorsed a 1923 New York law outlawing parading in masks on the grounds that this was a form of intimidation. The ACLU did oppose the provisions of the New York law requiring registration and disclosure of the Klan's membership list. The Supreme Court, under the "bad tendency" rationale, upheld the New York law in 1928. Experience, the Court held, had demonstrated that there were "two classes of associations" and that the KKK's tendency toward antisocial acts placed it outside the protection of the Constitution.[51]

The ACLU clashed with the NAACP over the Klan. In 1920, when the NAACP asked the Postal Service to ban KKK literature from the mails, the ACLU's Albert DeSilver told the NAACP's James Weldon Johnson that this was "a great mistake." "We do not think that it is ever a good policy for an organization interested in human liberty to invoke repressive measures against any of its antagonists. By doing so it creates a danger of making a precedent against itself." The ACLU knew from bitter firsthand experience how the Postal Service could arbitrarily suppress unpopular ideas. Johnson replied with the argument that the KKK was a criminal conspiracy. The NAACP also made repeated efforts to suppress the film *Birth of a Nation.* One of the greatest films of all time, it presented a viciously racist view of the Reconstruction Era. The NAACP's Walter White told Baldwin that it was "the very excellence of the film [that] makes it one of the most potent evils." The ACLU protested bans on the film in Newark, Philadelphia, Jersey City, and Detroit.[52]

Henry Ford: Anti-Semite

The famous automaker Henry Ford presented the ACLU with another test when his newspaper, the *Dearborn Independent,* published a series of wildly anti-Semitic articles. "The International Jew: The World's Foremost Problem" described a Jewish plot to take over the United States by undermining the basic values of Christianity, country, and family. Jews were guilty of fostering intellectual relativism—the "poison of liberalism"— and stimulating "calculation, greed, and the insatiable desires of men. An anthology of these articles sold over 500,000 copies.[53] Cleveland and Toledo officials banned the *Independent,* and Columbus, Ohio, banned the sale of both the *Independent* and an opposing paper, *Facts.* The ACLU protested and asserted that "every view, no matter how ignorant or harmful we may regard it, has a legal and moral right to be heard." That is, the proper response to hateful speech was more speech. While denouncing "propaganda against Jews," the ACLU argued that "the way to combat such views is by argument, not by prosecution." The Ford episode presaged later controversies over the ACLU's defense of Nazi groups.[54]

The ACLU and the Communists

The Communists posed an even more difficult problem. Because of government repression, they were the ACLU's most frequent clients. Communists Benjamin Gitlow and Charlotte Whitney were the plaintiffs in the two most important ACLU Supreme Court cases in the 1920s. Baldwin and others in the ACLU were also deeply sympathetic to the Soviet Union, which, in the pre-Stalinist years captured the imagination of many disaffected Americans as a bold experiment in economic democracy. Baldwin spent two months there in 1927 and wrote an informative book entitled *Liberty Under the Soviets.* He also organized support for the Kuzbas, an American industrial colony in Russia—an activity that right-wingers took as conclusive proof of his Communist affiliation. In one embarrassing incident, Baldwin was indicted for fraud on charges brought by a disillusioned Kuzbas recruit. The charges were eventually dropped.[55]

All the ACLU leaders were repelled by Communist ideology and tactics, the result being a stormy relationship that formed some of the most important and controversial chapters in the organization's history. The ACLU objected to the Communists' secrecy (until 1924 the two competing Communist parties were officially underground) and their tactic of denying their party membership under oath, which left them open to perjury charges. The Communists also sought to control cooperating attorneys, dictating legal strategy and limiting public statements. ACLU lawyers always refused to submit. (Hays and Darrow withdrew from the Scottsboro case in 1932 for this reason.) Finally, the Communists took a completely cynical view of the First Amendment, arguing that reactionaries were not entitled to free speech. On several occasions they disrupted speeches by Russian émigrés or other critics of the Soviet Union, including one by Roger Baldwin. The ACLU sent the party two formal protests in 1925, but party leader Earl Browder replied by heaping contempt on liberals and the whole notion of civil liberties. The Communists' newspaper, the *Daily Worker,* joined in, denouncing the ACLU and liberals in general for supporting "the advocates and practitioners of assassination of Soviet leaders . . . in the name of 'freedom' and 'opposition to violence.' "[56]

These fundamental differences put the ACLU in an awkward position. Afraid that public criticism would appear to endorse government repression, in 1921 the ACLU Executive Committee issued a formal statement on its relationship with the Communists—the first of many over the next thirty years. The carefully worded statement asserted that the ACLU did not support secrecy and perjury as tactics but quickly added a stronger attack on the political repression, which "prompted these tactics." If the Communists were "left free to express their political views in the open, there will be no longer any reason for underground methods." On the crucial question of whether the First Amendment protected the right to advocate revolution, the ACLU hedged. Southern California ACLU director Clinton J. Taft asked

Baldwin if the ACLU supported the Communists, "in view of their avowed goal of taking power by means of an armed revolution." Baldwin replied that "we make no distinctions whatever as to whose rights are involved. We will defend the Ku Klux Klan and the Communists, both of whom are opposed to free speech." But he admitted that the Executive Committee was not unanimous on this question: "There are some within our own organization who dissent from this view of 100% free speech, and who are a little timid advocating it in extreme cases." The ACLU's position on the limits of free speech was still in flux. Baldwin was firmly committed to an absolutist position: "The only test of our integrity of purpose is our willingness to defend persons with whom we totally disagree."[57]

Baldwin nonetheless had few illusions about either the Communist party or the Soviet Union. He founded the International Committee for Political Prisoners (ICPP) to attack repression abroad and edited a collection entitled *Letters from Russian Prisons*. In the introduction, Baldwin rejected the Soviet argument that suppression of dissent was "an issue of minor importance," maintaining that "we cannot withhold the material for fear of misuse."[58] Publication of the *Letters* brought down the wrath of the Communists on Baldwin. Party members disrupted an ICPP meeting at Town Hall where Baldwin tried to discuss repression in Russia. Six years later, in 1931, the Communists deposed him as chair of the League Against Imperialism. He explained to India's Jawaharlal Nehru, with whom he corresponded, that the Communists objected to his support for the "bourgeoise" Indian National Congress. Baldwin had earlier expressed his reservations about "the extent of Communist control" of the international office of the League Against Imperialism.[59]

These early conflicts with the Communists were significant because of the long controversy over Baldwin's subsequent relationship with the Communist party. In the mid-1930s he set aside his reservations and cooperated with the Communists in the Popular Front. He then abruptly reversed course again in the late 1930s and became a strong anti-Communist. These reversals baffled observers, leaving some wondering whether he had any firm political principles at all or simply bent with the political wind.[60] Throughout his career Baldwin adhered to a pragmatism in the defense of civil liberties that resulted in a number of reversals on particular issues. This in turn led to his close relationship with the Communists in the mid-1930s but a strong anti-Communist posture after 1940. Baldwin was a complex person, at once an idealist and a crafty pragmatist.

Baldwin, the Communists, and the FBI

The ACLU's most vigorous defense of the Communists in the early 1920s culminated in an improbably friendly relationship with J. Edgar Hoover and the federal Bureau of Investigation. This began on August 21, 1922, when federal agents and local police raided a secret Communist meeting in the little town of Bridgeman, Michigan. Party leaders, including Charles Ruthenberg and William Z. Foster, were arrested and indicted under the Michigan Criminal Syndicalism law. The ACLU protested the use of federal agents and offered to aid the Communists, pointing out in a letter to Attorney General Harry Daugherty that "there is no federal law . . . which makes it unlawful for anyone to advocate a soviet form of government for the United States, or to advocate the overthrow of government by force or violence." It demanded to know "under what authority and under whose direction" the federal agents had acted.[61]

To aid the Bridgeman defendants, Baldwin helped establish the Labor Defense Council. Conflicts with the party quickly surfaced. Baldwin objected to their attempt to control the defense committee and the fact that some Communists were working "under alias." Exposure of this would result in "fatal" publicity. Moreover, the Communists had made "injudicious" attacks on other leftists and liberals supporting their political rights. The ACLU Executive Committee thus threatened to withdraw its support "unless a complete readjustment is made." In another of its periodic statements on relations with the Communists, it announced that "while we thoroughly disagree with the Communist attitude toward free speech . . . we shall defend their right to meet and to speak as they choose."[62] Baldwin negotiated a compromise, but problems persisted.

The person most upset with the Communists was Elizabeth Gurley Flynn, whose speaking tours were a principal source of publicity and funds. In the midst of a 1924 tour she angrily resigned from the Labor Defense Council, accusing the Communists of manipulating her appearances to their advantage. Baldwin tried to smooth over the conflict.[63] Twelve years later, Flynn joined the Communist party, and in 1940 Baldwin helped purge her from the ACLU board because of her membership. The Bridgeman cases ended inconclusively. Ruthenberg was convicted in 1923, but his sudden death made moot a Supreme Court test of the Michigan criminal syndicalism law. The state eventually dropped the other cases.

The ACLU used the Bridgeman arrests to mount a campaign against the Justice Department's spying, oblivious to the fact that it was one of the department's major targets. The campaign fortuitously coincided with the Teapot Dome scandal, which forced the resignation of Attorney General Daugherty. President Coolidge then appointed Harlan Fiske Stone to clean up the Justice Department, and he immediately fired federal Bureau of Investigation Director William J. Burns. Stone appointed J. Edgar Hoover acting director of the bureau and ordered an end to political surveillance.[64]

Baldwin had met Stone during the war and now sensed an opportunity. He sent him a copy of the ACLU's pamphlet *The Nationwide Spy System Centering in the Department of Justice* and began lobbying hard but quietly. Hoover answered the ACLU's criticisms by denying any illegal activity by the bureau and asserting that most of the information on political groups in its files came from private organizations—a disingenuous defense, as the bureau had created and encouraged many of these red-hunting groups. Baldwin argued his case in personal meetings with Stone and Hoover. After meeting Hoover, he told Stone that he was extremely impressed: "I think I owe it to him and to you to say that I think we were wrong in our estimate of his attitude." The reform of the bureau "meets every suggestion which any of us could possibly make." Hoover, meanwhile, reported to Stone that Baldwin "seemed to be fully satisfied . . . and I believe that the Bureau of Investigation will no longer be the subject of attack by either himself or his organization."[65]

Baldwin was so pleased that he spread the word among his friends that the bureau was in good hands and that criticisms of it should be toned down. In January 1925 when Hoover complained to him that some radical publications were repeating the old charges about political spying, Baldwin told him to bring these items to his attention "so that we may correct them." As he had during the first months of the war, Baldwin was confident he could establish a close working relationship with top government officials. An elitist at heart, he jumped at this chance to be a Washington insider, virtually the only opportunity that arose during the twenties.[66]

This curious chapter in the long and usually antagonistic relationship between the ACLU and the FBI soon ended. For the next ten years, Hoover generally complied with Stone's prohibition of political spying, and consequently the bureau's files on the ACLU contain only a few items for those years. In one notable exception to this pattern, the FBI burglarized the ACLU office on February 26, 1929, in response to a direct request by Hoover, and examined its files for the previous year.[67] The FBI seems to have ignored Baldwin during his most explicitly radical phase in the mid-1930s, while the ACLU stopped worrying about the bureau. In 1933 Baldwin told an ACLU member that Hoover's anti-Communist obsession was "pretty nearly exhausted." But not everyone was convinced that the bureau had changed. In 1924 Frank Walsh warned Baldwin about whether Stone, "earnest as his aspirations may be, is powerful enough . . . to make any radical changes in the department." It was a prophetic warning, as Hoover renewed political spying on an even larger scale in the late 1930s.[68]

Inside the ACLU

"I'm in the civil liberties union for a reason that has made some thousands of people become members," confessed Ben Huebsch, "because of Roger Baldwin."[69] Baldwin kept the ACLU alive through the lean years of the 1920s. His infectious enthusiasm was the magnet that attracted the members of the Executive Committee, recruited the "correspondents" across the country, and raised the funds. His great contribution lay in creating a vehicle for the enormous talents of others. Walter Pollak wrote the briefs that influenced the Supreme Court. Felix Frankfurter was the leading expert on labor injunctions. Arthur Garfield Hays was the first to espouse a truly absolutist position on free speech. Morris Ernst pushed the ACLU into the fight against censorship of literary works. Baldwin held together the vehicle that gave their efforts greater force than if they had acted independently.

Codirector Albert DeSilver was also critical to the ACLU's survival in the first five years. Until his death in a freak accident in 1924 he volunteered his time in the office, coordinated its legal affairs, and kept the ACLU afloat financially. His own contributions ranged between $1,000 and $1,500 a month—more than half the entire ACLU budget at some points. Wealthy Quakers provided much of the rest, as they had during the war. The ACLU had only 1,000 members the first year and only 2,500 ten years later. Their $2.00-a-year dues thus hardly covered the budget, which began at $20,000 in 1920 and rose to $25,000 by 1930.[70]

By all accounts the weekly Executive Committee meetings were a "lively, social affair," with a vigorous discussion of the latest civil liberties issues.[71] Members fondly recalled the meetings as the most exciting part of their lives. Arthur Garfield Hays called his ACLU work the "salt" that livened up the otherwise mundane practice of law. The Scopes case gave him an education "on questions of evolution and the Bible" and introduced him to the person he admired even more than Baldwin, Clarence Darrow. The ACLU "brought me into contact with a variety of circles, usually the poor, defenseless, and unpopular, always the dissenters and persecuted. It has shielded me from the corroding influence of the particular groups who would normally be my associates." The noted playwright Elmer Rice recalled that at ACLU meetings "week after week, year after year, there is a panoramic revelation of America's political and economic life." The sheer excitement of being on the frontier of social change, combating intolerance, fighting for ideals, and eventually creating new law was one of the keys to the ACLU's longevity and its ability to attract new talent with each passing generation. For many, civil liberties became the equivalent of a secular religion—a set of core principles that gave meaning to their lives.[72]

For an organization committed to democratic principles, the ACLU was itself remarkably undemocratic. The Executive Committee was a self-perpetuating group of New York City residents. The sixty-member National Committee had nominal authority in all policy matters but rarely exercised it. It was essentially a letterhead group, created to give the ACLU an air of respectability. In 1920 the National Committee included Jane Addams, Felix Frankfurter, Helen Keller, and Morris Hillquit. With the exception of Frankfurter, few took an active role in the ACLU's affairs. Baldwin was very much an autocrat, reluctant to share control. He usually got his way with the Executive Committee, but of course he had personally recruited most of them in the first place. He later confessed that he often manipulated the agenda by holding back a pet issue if he knew strong opponents planned to attend. Because attendance was very irregular, this gave him considerable room to maneuver. Occasionally, however, the Executive Committee overruled him: Three times, for example, it rejected his efforts to involve the ACLU in international human rights issues.[73]

Making Civil Liberties Policy

A surprising consensus on basic civil liberties policy prevailed in the early years. The ACLU's agenda was extremely limited, primarily emphasizing labor and political speech issues and giving little attention to censorship in the arts. Equally surprising was its virtual silence about the rampant search-and-seizure violations accompanying the enforcement of Prohibition. Given the outrage it expressed about similar violations in the *Illegal Practices* report, this oversight is inexplicable. The ACLU also played no role in the 1928 *Olmstead* case challenging wiretapping as a violation of the Fourth Amendment. Justice Louis Brandeis's dissenting opinion is the classic statement on the right to privacy ("the right to be let alone—the most comprehensive of rights and the right most valued by civilized man"). The ACLU's failure to take up these issues in the twenties raises an intriguing historical question. Might the law of due process or the concept of privacy have developed earlier if the ACLU had challenged Prohibition enforcement violations and if Walter Pollak had contributed a strong brief in *Olmstead?* If the ACLU did influence the law and public opinion in areas where it did act, then its failure to act in other areas must be weighed in the balance.

The ACLU's agenda grew slowly and haltingly, with new issues adopted through a process of consensus making. Initially there was some ambivalence on the organization's part about whether the First Amendment protected advocacy of violent revolution or whether the Constitution barred religious activities in schools. Members of the Executive Committee had their own special concerns and were often little interested in other civil liberties issues. For example, Norman Thomas was mainly interested in labor issues and cared little about censorship in the arts or about church–state questions. Morris Ernst took an advanced position against literary censorship but was often out of step with the ACLU's position on political speech. Aside from Baldwin himself, Art Hays came closest to being a civil liberties "generalist," with a concern for virtually all issues.

Baldwin's fellow pacifists constituted the core of the ACLU's early leadership: Norman Thomas, John Haynes Holmes, L. Hollingsworth Wood, and John Nevin Sayre. Thomas had particular influence because of his close personal friendship with Baldwin. "He was my most faithful colleague," Baldwin recalled. In the first years, "we telephoned each other almost every day."[74] Despite his original plan of creating a broadly representative group, Baldwin had difficulty recruiting conservatives and labor leaders. The original Executive Committee included Henry R. Linville, president of the New York teachers' union, and independent radicals Elizabeth Gurley Flynn and Scott Nearing. Wood and DeSilver were the only conservatives. Baldwin always reserved a seat for the NAACP, and all of the top NAACP leaders eventually served on the ACLU board: James Weldon Johnson, Charles H. Houston, Thurgood Marshall, Roy Wilkins, and Robert L. Carter. But despite Baldwin's efforts to recruit conservatives, the ACLU's political complexion remained decidedly left of center. An internal survey of the National Committee in

1935 found twenty-eight Socialists, twenty-two Democrats, four Communist sympathizers, and only three Republicans.[75]

Lawyers were not a strong presence at first, numbering only three of the twenty Executive Committee members in 1920. This reflected the fact that there were few courtroom victories in the first years. The civil liberties–civil rights bar, which had become such an important feature of American life by the 1960s, did not exist in the 1920s. The lawyers' influence, however, grew as the courts became more receptive to civil liberties. Success fed upon itself, and more lawyers were attracted with each new victory. The appointment of Hays and Ernst as co–general counsels in 1929 signaled a decisive shift in the ACLU's priorities: From that point on lawyers were a major force.

Baldwin personally recruited most of the ACLU's "correspondents" on his annual trip across the country. Some were the only people willing to speak out for civil liberties in their community. Others represented organizations or ad hoc committees. Baldwin initially established working relationships with the New England Civil Liberties Committee and the Youngstown [Ohio] Workers Defense League, among others. There were fifteen such affiliates at first, most fading away in the hostile climate of the 1920s. But Baldwin was not entirely sorry to see them go, because he had deep reservations about a large ACLU membership and a network of formal affiliates. Ever the elitist, he doubted whether there were very many genuine civil libertarians in the country. Better, he thought, to organize a small cadre of true believers. He also instinctively sensed that strong affiliates would want a voice in the ACLU's policymaking, something he was extremely reluctant to grant. "Autocracy tempered by advice" remained his philosophy on ACLU governance.[76]

Some of Baldwin's personal quirks were the source of problems for the ACLU. He was a terrible employer who treated his staff shabbily. He paid very low wages and, never able to delegate authority, rewrote the material produced by the publicity directors. Several of them—Louis Budenz, Eugene Lyons—took their revenge when they eventually became prominent anti-Communists and accused the ACLU of being a Communist "front." Forrest Bailey, who served as codirector from 1926 to 1932, earned Baldwin's contempt for lacking sufficient "capacity for indignation."[77] In the fall of 1921 the staff threatened to strike when he refused to give them Columbus Day off. Unhappy but afraid of public embarrassment, the great friend of labor gave in.[78]

Baldwin had a profound ambivalence about the responsibilities of running a national organization. Although he legitimately regarded the ACLU as his personal creation, he disdained the mundane administrative chores of answering correspondence, maintaining membership files, and the like. Such tasks were beneath his dignity. Forced to run the office full time after Albert De-Silver's death in late 1924, he became terribly unhappy and nearly quit. In one outburst, he complained to Chairperson Harry F. Ward that he "couldn't go on indefinitely at a desk." He took three leaves of absence—in 1923, 1925, and all of 1927. He then returned in 1928 with the understanding that he would work only half time.[79]

Baldwin's curiously puritanical attitude toward money was another problem. Money was probably the closest thing to sin he could imagine. He adopted an ascetic life-style and tales of his penny pinching were legendary. He wore ill-fitting hand-me-down clothes for years and wrote memos on scraps of paper to save money. In the early 1920s he wrote a soul-searching article on the problem of how to live honorably in a materialistic society. Scott Nearing claimed that he and Baldwin refused to accept a $100,000 bequest from a wealthy widow to avoid the "real threat of riches." (Oswald Garrison Villard accepted the money.)[80] Because the ACLU was a noble calling demanding personal sacrifice, Baldwin paid himself a subsistence salary. Although this kept the ACLU budget low, it also meant that other staff salaries were unconscionably low, even by the standards of public-interest groups. In 1936, after divorcing Madeline Doty, however, Baldwin married Standard Oil heiress Evelyn Preston, whose money allowed them to maintain a brownstone in Manhattan, a farm in New Jersey for weekends, and a cottage on Martha's Vineyard for an August vacation. Norman Thomas also relied on his wife's inheritance.[81] Like many other liberal and radical causes, the ACLU depended on inherited wealth.

"Garland's Millions"

One of the major sources of financial support for ACLU projects was a private foundation, the American Fund for Public Service. Known as the Garland Fund, it was another of the many organizations Baldwin created and directed. In 1919 a young Bostonian named Charles Garland, who happened to oppose the possession of great wealth, inherited nearly a million dollars. Words of his unusual dilemma reached Baldwin, who proposed establishing a private foundation to support social reform. Garland agreed, and Baldwin put together the fund, bringing onto its board of directors all of his ACLU colleagues—Nelles, Ernst, Flynn, Ward, Thomas—and a few non-ACLU people, such as Sidney Hillman. Baldwin's continual ability to tap people for such projects earned him the title of "the pope of the liberals." Over the next ten years the Garland Fund was the major source of financial support for left-wing literary, educational, and legal defense projects. It founded the Vanguard Press, which published books on radicalism and Russia (including Baldwin's own *Liberty Under the Soviets*), the Federated Press, a labor and left-wing press service that distributed the ACLU's releases, and such magazines as the radical *New Masses,* Norman Thomas's pacifist *The World Tomorrow,* and *Labor Age.* Grants supported radical educational experiments such as the Brookwood Labor College, the Rand School, and Commonwealth College.[82]

Baldwin's dominant influence actually worked to the ACLU's disadvantage as he bent over backwards to avoid giving it direct assistance. Instead, the fund supported the ACLU indirectly with grants to legal defense committees (such as Sacco and Vanzetti) and an ACLU-administered bail fund. Through a marvelous quirk of American capitalism, the fund's assets increased faster than they could be given away. As the stock market boomed, the value of the fund's stocks in the First National Bank more than doubled. While Baldwin and his colleagues doled out small grants to groups fighting capitalism, that very system generated ever more money to give away. But this all came to an end with the stock market crash in 1929, and the fund virtually ceased operation by 1930.

Civil Liberties at Mid-Decade

By mid-decade, the prospects for civil liberties seemed as bleak as they had five years before. Baldwin reported in 1926 that "the reason for the decrease in repression is that there is little to repress." The ACLU had almost nothing to show for its efforts. The courts remained hostile to civil liberties, and direct-action tactics had made little impression on public opinion. In January 1925 Baldwin asked for a leave of absence. The future of the ACLU was very much in doubt.[83]

Four

The First Victories,
1925-1932

Just when everything seemed hopeless, the ACLU scored its first great victories. Two events in 1925 signaled a shift in national attitudes toward civil liberties. The sensational Scopes "monkey trial" thrust the ACLU into the national spotlight as the defender of the freedom to learn. Then, in *Gitlow v. New York* the Supreme Court accepted the principle that the Fourteenth Amendment incorporated the protections of the Bill of Rights. By the mid-1920s, new social and political forces were encouraging respect for civil liberties principles.[1]

Scopes: The Great "Monkey Trial"

While routinely clipping the newspapers for civil liberties news in the spring of 1925, ACLU secretary Lucille Milner noticed an intriguing item. Tennessee had just passed a law forbidding the teaching of evolution. She brought the clipping to Roger Baldwin and said, "Here's something that ought to have our attention." Baldwin agreed and, in a newspaper article, offered ACLU assistance to anyone willing to challenge the law.[2] This set in motion one of the most famous courtroom battles in American history. The Scopes "monkey trial" became a fight over the freedom to learn and specifically the freedom from state-imposed religious dogma. The ACLU rarely provided counsel at the trial level, and so Baldwin's offer reflected his growing concern over political restraints on teachers. Indeed, he had recently created the ACLU Academic Freedom Committee.[3]

The Tennessee law prohibited teachers in state-supported schools and universities from teaching "any theory that denies the story of the Divine Creation of man as taught in the Bible." It was symptomatic of a wave of Protestant fundamentalism sweeping the country. This movement was a rearguard action, protesting the advance of science, secularism, cultural plural-

72

ism, and changing sexual mores. Although the public schools had always been permeated with Protestant dogma, it had never been imposed by state law. Nor had any state ever prohibited the teaching of a new scientific idea. The real significance of the Scopes case lay in the fact that the forces of science and secular education were strong enough to oppose the fundamentalists. *Scopes* introduced a new chapter in American politics, a long-running struggle over the place of religion in American life in general and in the public schools in particular.[4]

Dayton, Tennessee, businessman George Rappelyea, whose interest lay less in academic freedom than in boosting the local economy, instigated the case as a scheme to promote Dayton, by persuading a young science teacher, John Thomas Scopes, to violate the law. Angling for publicity, they sent a telegram to William Jennings Bryan, asking him to enter the case. The three-time Democratic presidential candidate was the most widely known fundamentalist in the country. Bryan, already in Tennessee to address the national convention of the World Christian Fundamentals Association, accepted, and Clarence Darrow offered to represent Scopes. The flamboyant sixty-eight-year-old lawyer was at least as famous as Bryan was, notorious as a self-proclaimed atheist, opponent of capital punishment, and defender of unpopular cases. Only a year before, the famous "attorney for the damned" had saved the young murderers Nathan Leopold and Richard Loeb from the death penalty in a sensational trial. Scopes accepted Darrow's offer, and the case suddenly became a confrontation over the literal interpretation of the Bible.[5]

The case was a publicity bonanza for the ACLU. "Our office was filled with all the top journalists," Baldwin recalled.[6] Never before had the ACLU received such favorable attention. For the first time it defended a cause with which the national press and its readers could identify. That is, they had little interest in the rights of Communists but saw science and education as the key to progress.

Privately, most ACLU leaders were disturbed about the direction the case was taking. Walter Nelles eagerly anticipated a Supreme Court test of whether the law represented an establishment of religion, by making the Bible the test of truth. Baldwin wanted to use the case to publicize the larger academic freedom issue. Darrow's flamboyant style was not sufficiently "respectable," however, and so Nelles and Baldwin tried to ease him out, sending feelers out to John W. Davis—himself a former Democratic presidential candidate and a noted Supreme Court litigator—and Charles Evans Hughes. Only Arthur Garfield Hays, who served as cocounsel at the trial, rose to Darrow's defense: "I never yet have found any conservative lawyer who, at the beginning, wants to undertake a case which *might* reflect discredit upon him." At a tense luncheon meeting in New York, Nelles, Frankfurter, and their allies tried unsuccessfully to persuade Scopes to reject Darrow. Scopes finally said, "I want Darrow," and the stage was set for a confrontation between Genesis and Darwin in Dayton, Tennessee, beginning on July 10.[7]

The eight-day trial was a circus. Reporters from the *New York Herald Tribune, New York Times, Brooklyn Eagle, St. Louis Post Dispatch, The*

Nation, and even the London *Times* poured into Dayton. Chicago radio station WGN provided live coverage—a first in the history of the young radio industry. The town was plastered with signs admonishing everyone to "Read Your Bible Daily," "Come to Jesus," and "Prepare to Meet Thy Maker." H. L. Mencken, one of five *Baltimore Sun* reporters, fashioned the stereotypes associated with the "monkey trial" ever since. Mocking the "morons" and "hillbillies" of Dayton, he implied that all southerners and fundamentalists were ignorant and bigoted fanatics, opposed to modern science and education, whereas he cast the ACLU in a favorable light as the defender of enlightened common sense. In one of several famous speeches during the trial, Darrow, with Hays assisting, framed the issue in terms of a broad tolerance for new ideas: "If today you can take a thing like evolution and make it a crime to teach it in the public school, tomorrow you can make it a crime to teach it in the private school. . . . At the next session you may ban books and the newspapers. Soon you may set Catholic against Protestant and Protestant against Protestant, and try to foist your own religion upon the minds of men." Far from a prophecy, this was a reasonably accurate description of the prevailing spirit of religion and ethnic intolerance in America in the mid-1920s.[8]

The trial immediately went badly for Darrow, whom the prosecution outwitted, by persuading Judge John Raulston to confine the case to the narrow question of the right of the legislature to control public school curricula and to exclude all the expert testimony about science and religion that the ACLU had patiently assembled from noted scientists and theologians. The former were prepared to testify that the Tennessee law was unreasonable in light of modern science, whereas the latter would argue that even sincere Christians disagreed over the meaning of the Genesis story. At a stroke, therefore, Judge Raulston virtually destroyed the ACLU's entire case.[9]

With his case in shambles, Darrow spent the weekend devising a scheme to get the evolution issue into court by trapping Bryan himself into testifying. Bryan could not resist the opportunity to proclaim his religious faith from the witness stand and fell headlong into the snare. Under Darrow's merciless questioning, he made a fool of himself. For instance, Darrow got him to say, "I do not think about things I don't think about" and, in a crucial exchange over Genesis, admitted that he did not believe the earth was created in "six days of twenty-four hours." Audible gasps could be heard in the courtroom as Bryan undermined his own case for a literal interpretation of the Bible. He sputtered on desperately, dimly aware that something had gone wrong. Mercifully, Judge Raulston adjourned the trial, and the next day a clearly embarrassed prosecutor ended the trial. The jury took just nine minutes to find John T. Scopes guilty. Judge Raulston then made a serious mistake by incorrectly instructing the jury: Under Tennessee law fines over $50 had to be set by the jury, but the misinstructed jury allowed Raulston himself to impose a $100 fine.[10]

A devastated Bryan died a week after the trial. In New York, ACLU leaders were appalled by Darrow's conduct and sought to remove him from the appeal. Hays again defended his partner. "The Strategy of the Scopes Defense" was to raise the political question of "whether among civilized people ignorance and intolerance, even when indulged in by the majority and made into law, should be permitted to stifle education." The trial was a platform for raising broad issues of human freedom.[11] Darrow and Hays forged a warm friendship and went on to collaborate on other celebrated cases. Immediately after the trial they went to Detroit where they defended the black doctor Ossian Sweet, charged with murder, in one of the most famous civil rights cases of the 1920s. A year later they challenged censorship in Boston by personally selling a banned magazine on Boston Common.[12]

In 1927 the Tennessee Supreme Court reversed Scopes's conviction because of Judge Raulston's error. Expressing its embarrassment over the entire affair, the court said it saw "nothing to be gained by prolonging the life of this bizarre case."[13]

The Impact of Scopes

The Scopes case reverberated through American history. Mencken's stereotypes lived on and were even exaggerated in the 1955 play *Inherit the Wind* and a 1960 film version. In the wake of the trial it was difficult to determine who really won. By successfully dramatizing the issue of academic freedom, the ACLU scored an important public opinion victory. The trial also took the steam out of the antievolution law movement. Similar laws were defeated in Georgia, Florida, and North Carolina in 1925, in Texas and Louisiana the following year, and in seventeen state legislatures in 1927. A Mississippi antievolution law went unenforced. The ACLU tried to find a client but finally gave up and declared the law a "dead letter." Mainstream Protestant churches began to distance themselves from fundamentalism. In 1928 the General Conference of the Methodist Church voted ten to one against forming a committee to investigate "modernistic" theories.[14]

The trial also spurred American Bar Association (ABA) president Charles Evans Hughes to speak out. He warned fellow ABA members that "the most ominous sign of our time is the growth of an intolerant spirit." Although the majority should prevail in a democracy, they should not try to impose their religious views on everyone. Such attempts constituted the "saddest pages of history." Hughes added that "freedom of learning is the vital breath of democracy and progress." These views, from the future chief justice of the Supreme Court, marked an important shift in thinking among the American elite.[15]

The case transformed the image of the ACLU, with the *St. Louis Post-Dispatch* hailing it as "the only organization of its kind in the United States, if not in the world"—the first endorsement the ACLU had ever received from a major American newspaper.[16] A single mailing to the American Academy for the Advancement of Science raised enough funds to cover the trial's expenses and left an unprecedented surplus of $2,429.32. The ACLU had struck a responsive chord in an influential segment of the public, and consequently Baldwin began thinking about broadening the ACLU's program.[17]

The underlying issue of legislative control over public education, however, remained unresolved. The ACLU's new friends who made fun of southern fundamentalists did not always support academic freedom in their own schools. As Howard K. Beale perceptively noted in a report on academic freedom, "Try teaching communism in the schools of a community that denounced Tennessee intolerance." "Fundamentalism is to the Tennessean what the profit system is to a Northern middle-class business man—the thing each believes in with all his heart." When the ACLU was denied the use of Stuyvesant High School in 1926, *The Nation* commented sardonically, "Rural papers please note, and be not too unkind."[18]

The battle over evolution had far-reaching social and political ramifications. It accelerated the split among Protestants, with mainstream denominations accommodating themselves to science and the new sexual morality, while fundamentalists steadily gravitated to other sects. In certain respects, the fundamentalists won the battle over the curriculum. Under pressure from state and local school authorities, publishers eliminated or downplayed evolution. The American Book Company deleted all references to evolution in *A Civic Biology,* the text used by Scopes. The result was lasting damage to American science education. Indeed, a survey in 1941 found that only half of high school biology teachers taught the theory of evolution. Full treatment of evolution did not return to the textbooks until the early 1960s, as a result of national alarm over the quality of American science education in the wake of the Soviets' first space satellite in 1957.[19]

The evolution question finally reached the Supreme Court in 1968 in a case challenging a 1928 Arkansas antievolution law. In *Epperson v. Arkansas* the pro–civil libertarian Warren Court declared the law to be unconstitutional on the grounds that it violated the establishment clause of the First Amendment. In the 1980s, fundamentalists pushed a new theory of "scientific creationism," and the Supreme Court again sustained the ACLU in 1987 by declaring unconstitutional a Louisiana law requiring its teaching. On the day of that decision, a reporter asked ACLU Executive Director Ira Glasser how long the ACLU had been fighting the case. "Sixty-two years," he replied.[20]

The ACLU and Religion in the Schools

The ACLU was ambivalent about other religious issues in the schools. In 1926 an uncertain Northern California ACLU asked Baldwin for guidance on a proposed amendment to the California constitution requiring in-school Bible reading.[21] He polled the ACLU National Committee and found a deep division of opinion. Socialist leader Morris Hillquit and literary critic Robert Morss Lovett dismissed it as an unimportant issue. Norman Thomas was personally opposed to compulsory Bible reading but thought any ACLU action would alienate "that large body of liberals or potential liberals" sympathetic to other ACLU issues. Sociologist Edward A. Ross favored teaching religion in the schools in order to foster assimilation and social reform. He was afraid that without some religious instruction, Catholic parents would abandon the public schools for parochial schools, which would only accentuate the religious divisions that stood in the way of liberal reform. Only Baldwin and labor radicals A. J. Muste and Robert Dunn favored the strict separation of church and state. With the National Committee so sharply divided, Baldwin advised the Northern California ACLU to maintain a "cautious neutrality" on the issue. California voters eventually rejected the Bible-reading initiative.[22]

The following year, the Northern California ACLU decided that the practice of releasing students from school for religious instruction did not infringe on civil liberties. North Dakota passed a law requiring the Ten Commandments to be posted in all classrooms. Although Baldwin wanted to take "this fool law into the courts," Arthur Hays and Morris Ernst convinced him that a challenge based on the Fourteenth Amendment was certain to lose. In 1930 the ACLU offered to represent anyone willing to challenge the laws in the eleven states that required or permitted Bible reading in public schools. Apparently it found no takers. Gradually, a consensus on a strong separationist position emerged in the ACLU, and in 1932 the Academic Freedom Committee declared that separation of church and state was "fundamental" to academic freedom.[23]

Two other incidents in the mid-1920s portended a somewhat different controversy over religion and education. Denver school authorities suspended fifty students who, as Jehovah's Witnesses, had refused to salute the flag on the grounds that it violated their religious beliefs. Meanwhile, in Bellingham, Washington, authorities removed a child named Russell Tremain from his parents' custody and placed him up for adoption—in a suitably "patriotic and Christian family"—because his parents refused to allow him to salute the flag. The ACLU offered assistance in both cases, but no test case developed because the authorities relented. Nonetheless, these episodes were a harbinger of a national controversy involving the Jehovah's Witnesses, beginning in the late 1930s.[24]

Victory in Paterson

Hard on the heels of Scopes, the ACLU won its first free speech victory in court—appropriately in a case involving Roger Baldwin. The case began in 1924 when eight thousand silk workers went out on strike in Paterson, New Jersey. The mill owners obtained an injunction banning picketing and forbidding strikers from congregating in crowds. By October, fifteen separate injunctions had shut down virtually all union activity. The silk workers then turned to the ACLU for help. Baldwin organized a free speech demonstration and led to City Hall thirty protestors carrying American flags. Union leader John C. Butterworth began to read the First Amendment, but police arrested him before he could finish. Baldwin turned himself in the next day, explaining his role in organizing the demonstration. The publicity had the desired effect, and the police permitted several rallies over the next few weeks.[25]

Baldwin was subsequently convicted under a 1796 unlawful assembly law. His appeal touched off a bitter fight among ACLU lawyers which brought to the surface the underlying differences over legal strategy. Hays and Samuel Untermyer (who had advised the prosecution in the Scopes case) drafted a political brief discussing Anglo-American traditions of free speech. Felix Frankfurter objected strenuously: "I have no sympathy at all with the aim of counsel who shape their briefs with a view to securing a 'landmark' opinion rather than securing a favorable decision." He advised arguing the case on the narrow factual question of whether Baldwin's behavior fell within the scope of the law's prohibition of "assaults, batteries, false imprisonment, affrays, riots, unlawful assemblies, nuisances, cheats, [and] deceits" and whether any of the demonstrators were armed as charged. Hays, fresh from the theatrical Scopes trial, replied that it was important to make the court "see that there is more involved in this case than the facts of this meeting." Frankfurter told Baldwin he didn't have "much confidence" in the lawyers who seemed to be "indulging in the dramatic love of a fight."[26]

Baldwin remained supremely indifferent to his fate. He didn't think the brief would make any difference in either event. Although conceding that Frankfurter had made some valid points, he pointed out that "my own inclinations are usually in the direction of Hays' line of tactics" and endorsed his brief. Frankfurter's "careful, lawyer-like work" was "just what the courts should never hear." He told Ernst he didn't want "a reversal on narrow or technical grounds. I want it squarely on the issue of what is unlawful assembly, and I'd like to couple with it a denunciation by the court of police lawlessness."[27] He soon left for a year's sabbatical in Europe and was out of the country when the intermediate court of appeals sustained his conviction.

The appeal to the state's high court intensified the dispute among the lawyers. Acting ACLU Director Forrest Bailey eased out Hays and Untermyer on the pretext that New Jersey judges did not like to be "lectured" by New York lawyers. He replaced them with Arthur T. Vanderbilt, one of the most distinguished lawyers in New Jersey and the future chief justice of its supreme court.[28] Baldwin, returning from Europe in time for the final arguments, told a New Jersey audience that "my homecoming would have lost some of the zest of American life if it had been not to keep a date with a prosecutor and judge and to hear again the familiar voice of law and order."[29] Privately, he told Vanderbilt he was "not over-sanguine about the approaching decision" and inquired about arranging a sentence to the state prison instead of the Passaic County Jail. An equally pessimistic Vanderbilt replied that "it is a distinct relief to have a client who . . . does not expect his lawyers to perform miracles."[30]

To everyone's astonishment, the New Jersey Court of Errors and Appeals unanimously reversed Baldwin's conviction in a decision that was a ringing affirmation of freedom of speech and assembly. The decision held that the guarantees of both the New Jersey and the U.S. Constitutions, "being in favor of liberty of the people, must be given the most liberal and comprehensive construction." The purpose of Baldwin's rally "was per se not an unlawful one," and there was no proof that it constituted a threat to public order.[31] Citing the Magna Carta, the Petition of Right, and other ancient documents, the Court's opinion was filled with the very historical and philosophical arguments Frankfurter had tried to eliminate. Baldwin, who had always dismissed the courts as effective protectors of civil liberties, won the most sweeping First Amendment victory of the entire decade. The decision was yet another sign that the tide of public and judicial opinion was slowly beginning to turn in favor of civil liberties.

Breakthrough in the Supreme Court

Just as the ACLU was preparing for the Scopes trial, it scored its first significant breakthrough in the Supreme Court. The decision in *Gitlow v. United States* offered the hope of judicial protection of civil liberties in the future.

The case involved Benjamin Gitlow, a founder of the Communist party, who had been convicted under the 1902 New York Criminal Anarchy law. At issue in his appeal was the question of whether his pamphlet, *The Left-Wing Manifesto,* was constitutionally protected speech. The revolutionary *Manifesto* declared, "The old order is in decay. Civilization is in collapse. The proletarian revolution and the commuist reconstruction of society—*the struggle for these*—is now indispensable." That is, though it advocated revolution in the abstract, it did not urge any immediate illegal action.[32]

Walter Pollak, a New York attorney with a corporate law practice, handled the appeal for the ACLU, with Nelles and DeSilver assisting. "The case," Pollak argued, "brings to this Court for the first time the question of the constitutionality of making advocacy per se, and without regard to consequences, a crime." Exploring the scope of the First Amendment, Pollak distinguished between *public* and *private* speech. In private matters a person could be punished for libel, obscenity, or fraudulent promises. In the public realm, however, "the citizen's liberty to take part in public affairs stands on another and broader footing." Following Oliver Wendell Holmes's *Abrams* dissent, Pollak contended that the right of free speech was "in the interest of the whole community. The citizen has a right to express, for the State may have an interest in hearing, any doctrine," no matter how foolish or unpopular. Because Gitlow was prosecuted under state law, Pollak argued that he was protected by the First Amendment because the due process clause of the Fourteenth Amendment incorporated its guarantees. The Court had never accepted the incorporation idea.[33]

The Court affirmed Gitlow's conviction and upheld the constitutionality of the New York Criminal Anarchy Act. But in a crucial passage, conservative Justice Edward T. Sanford held that "for the present purposes we may and do assume that freedom of speech and of the press—which are protected by the First Amendment from abridgment by Congress—are among the fundamental personal rights and 'liberties' protected by the due process clause of the Fourteenth Amendment from impairment by the states." Although cold comfort to Gitlow, this dictum was a major breakthrough, holding out the promise of future judicial protection of civil liberties.[34]

Several legal scholars grasped the implications of this dictum. Charles Warren, a conservative professor at the Harvard Law School, saw that the Court had created a "new 'liberty,'" with enormous potential for protecting the rights enunciated in the Bill of Rights. His colleague Zechariah Chaffee, Jr., called it a "victory out of defeat."[35] But ACLU leaders were divided over the decision. Baldwin, as skeptical of the courts as ever, saw it as a crushing defeat. In the ACLU *Annual Report* he concluded that "the repressive measures passed during and since the war were strengthened by the U.S. Supreme Court in the *Gitlow* case."[36] Pollak and Nelles, on the other hand, saw it as a near miss and turned with renewed enthusiasm to the Charlotte Whitney appeal which loomed as the Court's next important First Amendment case.

Charlotte Anita Whitney's political odyssey resembled Baldwin's. She came from old New England stock, had graduated from Wellesley, and had become a Progressive reformer. She had been radicalized by the war and so had joined the Communist Labor party. Her conviction struck even more deeply at freedom of political association, as she had been convicted for simply organizing a political party: She had neither given an incendiary speech nor distributed any revolutionary pamphlet.[37] In 1927 the Court dashed the hopes raised by *Gitlow* and unanimously sustained her conviction. It held that California had a legitimate right to "punish those who abuse" freedom of speech "by utterances inimical to the public welfare, tending to incite to crime, disturb the public peace, or endanger the foundations of organized government and threaten its overthrow by unlawful means."[38]

Despite the defeat, Justice Louis Brandeis wrote a concurring opinion that became one of the most eloquent statements on freedom of speech. "Those who won our independence by revolution," Brandeis observed, "were not cowards. They did not fear political change. They did not exalt order at the cost of liberty." Revising Justice Oliver Wendell Holmes's "clear and present danger" test, he held that "no danger flowing from speech can be deemed clear and present, unless the incidence of the evil apprehended is so imminent that it may befall before there is opportunity for full discussion." Proximity and danger were the crucial elements. If there were time to discuss the ideas involved, no matter how false or foolish, "the remedy to be applied is more speech, not enforced silence."[39]

A second 1927 case, little noted then and forgotten today, was actually the first free speech victory in the Supreme Court. IWW (Industrial Workers of the World) organizer Harold Fiske had been convicted under the Kansas Criminal Syndicalism law, but the only evidence against him was his possession of the preamble to the IWW's constitution. Thus, with the ACLU financing the appeal, the Court overturned his conviction on the grounds of insufficient evidence. Because the IWW's preamble did not mention violence, no inference could be made that his activities fell within the scope of the Kansas law. The decision did not touch on the constitutionality of the law and contained no eloquent opinions, but Harold Fiske was the first person to have his First Amendment rights upheld by the Supreme Court. As Chafee observed, "In *Fiske,* the Supreme Court for the first time made freedom of speech mean something."[40]

The Court and Civil Liberties

ACLU leaders were sharply divided over the Court's role in protecting civil liberties. If Baldwin thought the Supreme Court wouldn't defend them, Felix Frankfurter thought it shouldn't. Two decisions involving education stimulated Frankfurter's thoughts on the matter. In 1923 the Court struck down a 1919 Nebraska law prohibiting teaching in any language other than English. A product of wartime paranoia, the law was designed primarily to ban German. In *Meyer v. Nebraska* the Court held that it infringed on the right of parents to educate their children as they saw fit. Two years later the Court invalidated an Oregon law requiring all children to attend public schools. This KKK-sponsored law was designed mainly to close Catholic parochial schools. Then in *Pierce v. Society of Sisters* the Court ruled that the law violated the schools' property rights and interfered with parents' rights to control their children's education. The ACLU did not participate in either *Meyer* or *Pierce* (although it denounced the Oregon law) and apparently did not see civil liberties implications in them. *Meyer* and *Pierce* thus languished in doctrinal obscurity for forty years but suddenly resurfaced in the 1960s as important precedents for a constitutional right of privacy.[41]

Frankfurter liked the results in *Meyer* and *Pierce* but voiced strong reservations about the Supreme Court as a protector of civil liberties, warning that "a heavy price has to be paid for these occasional services to liberalism." In the long run the Court could not "guarantee toleration" and should not assume the role of a national legislature. What it gave it could just as easily take away. Legislative protection of civil liberties—such as his proposed law curbing labor injunctions—was both more democratic and a more secure foundation for individual liberty. In his role as ACLU adviser during the 1920s Frankfurter enunciated the philosophy of judicial restraint that he later applied as a Supreme Court justice.[42]

Pollak, Nelles, and Ernst, on the other hand, believed that the Court not only should, but eventually would, give substantive meaning to the Bill of Rights. The Court evenutally confirmed their faith, and they were responsible for launching the influential Supreme Court litigation program for which the ACLU became famous.

Walter Pollak's role in the development of American constitutional law cannot be underestimated. Between 1925 and 1935 he argued four landmark cases before the Supreme Court: *Gitlow* (1925), *Whitney* (1927), *Powell* (1932), and *Patterson* (1935). The later two cases arose out of the celebrated Scottsboro case, the defense of the nine black Alabama youths, which marked the first stirrings of a national civil rights movement. In *Powell,* the Court held that the Sixth Amendment required that persons charged with a capital crime be provided legal counsel at trial. It became the cornerstone of an eventual "due process revolution," by means of which the Court applied constitutional standards to virtually the entire criminal process. The Court remanded Patterson's case on the grounds that the exclusion of blacks from Alabama juries had denied him equal protection of the law. Pollak's role in influencing the Court was an awesome personal achievement and a monument in the history of the ACLU.[43]

By the late 1920s, change was clearly in the wind. The antiradical hysteria was fading, and the courts were more receptive to protecting freedom of speech and assembly. Sensing the change, the ACLU shifted its priorities and began to pay more attention to litigation.[44]

New Horizons in Freedom of Expression

"The Boston Massacre"

With thousands of people milling around the Boston Common on April 5, 1926, Arthur Garfield Hays and H. L. Mencken sold copies of Mencken's *American Mercury,* banned that month by the Boston Watch and Ward Society because Herbert Asbury's article, "Hatrack," made fun of fundamentalists. Hays and Mencken went to Boston, obtained a peddler's license, and provoked an arrest. Hays won an acquittal for Mencken and a court order restraining the Watch and Ward Society. The society, an odd coalition of Protestant Brahmins and puritanical Catholics, retaliated with an even more energetic crusade against indecency. The ensuing "Boston Massacre" popularized the phrase "Banned in Boston" and launched the ACLU's first serious attack on censorship in the arts.[45]

The sixty-five books banned in Boston included Theodore Dreiser's *An American Tragedy,* Sinclair Lewis's *Elmer Gantry,* Ernest Hemingway's *The Sun Also Rises,* and John Dos Passos's *Manhattan Transfer.* Boston readers were also denied books by Bertrand Russell, William Faulkner, Upton Sinclair, Babette Deutsch, and Olive Schreiner and productions of Eugene O'Neill's *Desire Under the Elms* and *Strange Interlude.* The official city censor, John Michael Casey, explained that his test was "whether he would want his mother, wife, daughter or sister to see such a play." He banned *Strange Interlude* because it mentioned abortion. Most booksellers and theater owners voluntarily withdrew works in the face of veiled threats.[46]

Until the Boston crisis, the ACLU had taken little interest in censorship of the arts. Following the dominant school of First Amendment theory articulated by Zechariah Chafee (and later Alexander Meikeljohn), it had focused on political speech. Other forms of expression were not central to the process of self-government and so did not deserve the same protection.[47] Baldwin and his closest ACLU friends, Norman Thomas and John Haynes Holmes, were extremely puritanical: Holmes thought local communities could restrict "indecent" material and expressed shock at "all those four-letter words" in *Lady Chatterly's Lover*. In 1931 Thomas approved a ban on *Birth of a Nation* because it might stir up mob violence. In March 1927, the ACLU's acting director, Forrest Bailey, told a Massachusetts librarian that "I hope you will not be too greatly disappointed when I tell you we cannot go into the 'anti-obscenity' campaign in Boston. That is a phase of free speech which we have kept clear of . . . to avoid complicating our main issues."[48]

Consequently, Hays and Ernst led the fight for a broader ACLU attack on censorship. Thoroughly secularized Jews, they shared none of the puritanism of the ACLU Protestants. They were not embarrassed by sex and believed that personal freedom extended into the realm of private sexual relations. Hays even proposed an early version of no-fault divorce and was the first ACLU leader to articulate a rudimentary "absolutist" position of no restrictions on "the expression of opinion of any kind, at any time, by anyone or anywhere."[49]

Ernst was a more complex figure. From the 1920s onward he litigated the most important anticensorship cases, including the famous victory over the ban on *Ulysses* in 1933, and wrote a series of popular books on freedom of expression. His 1928 book, *To the Pure,* framed the main ideas of the anticensorship campaign for the next forty years. Rather than attempt to define obscenity, Ernst argued the futility of the attempt and focused on the irrational psychology of the censors. As the long-time general counsel for Planned Parenthood, he also led the first attacks on federal and state laws restricting the dissemination of birth control information and devices. Yet he was not a First Amendment absolutist and in the late 1930s advocated restrictions on the Communist party and other totalitarian groups.[50]

The turning point for the ACLU in the Boston controversy came when the mayor, again having allowed an anti–birth control speech, banned a speech by Margaret Sanger. Baldwin charged that the action "raise[d] a square issue of discrimination."[51] The Civil Liberties Union of Massachusetts (CLUM) mobilized some of the most noted scholars in the Boston area: Mary E. Wooley, president of Mount Holyoke College; Harvard law professors Chafee, Frankfurter, and James M. Landis; and Harvard historians Arthur M. Schlesinger, Sr., and Samuel Eliot Morison. The highlight of its campaign was a hilarious spoof of censorship at Ford Hall. In one skit, a gagged Sanger stood by while Schlesinger read her suppressed speech. CLUM immediately launched a campaign to repeal the Blasphemy Act, end the censorship of plays and meetings, and allow unrestricted meetings on the Boston Common.[52]

The ACLU pamphlet *Censorship in Boston* (signed by Chafee but actually written by Baldwin) was a benchmark in its evolving view of the First Amendment. While opposing all prior restraints, it approved subsequent criminal proceedings against indecent books and plays. The ACLU, operating on the assumption that ordinary citizens were more tolerant than government bureaucrats were, sought at this point to transfer the power to determine what was indecent from public officials to juries. The juries, however, should "take

into consideration the entire book at issue and not isloated parts." The ACLU
was not yet ready to defend "indecency," much less obscenity. Also, the
pamphlet made a significant concession on political speech: "If a speaker
in a Boston public hall utters indecencies, or advocates crimes such as the
overthrow of the government by violence, he can be punished after conviction
by a jury." Not as broad a protection of political speech as the ACLU had
argued elsewhere, *Censorship in Boston* may have been tailored to avoid
offending potential allies.[53]

But the ACLU's efforts did not end censorship in Boston, for *Strange Interlude, An American Tragedy,* and birth control meetings were still banned in
the 1930s. The campaign, however, had a profound effect on the ACLU.
Coming hard on the heels of the Scopes case, it reinforced the growing sense
that the public was ready for a broader anticensorship campaign.

"Talking" Pictures and Free Speech

At the height of the Boston campaign, the introduction of sound in motion
pictures forced the ACLU to reconsider the issue of movie censorship. Before
1929 the ACLU had ignored the widespread censorship of films by state and
local authorities. The Supreme Court's 1915 *Mutual* ruling held that movies
were an item of commerce not entitled to First Amendment protection, and
formal censorship mechanisms existed in eight states and several cities. The
licensing boards were generally dominated by the most prudish individuals.
For example, the Chicago film board was composed of widows of police
officers. In addition, apart from these formal mechanisms, police in all cities
routinely banned any film they deemed offensive. In one incident, the Newark, New Jersey, police commissioner banned *The Naked Truth,* a sex education drama with male and female nudity. The police commissioner was
William J. Brennan, Sr., father of the future Supreme Court Justice who
became a staunch opponent of censorship.[54]

The ACLU also had regarded silent films as mere pictures, not protected
by the First Amendment. "Talkies," however, did involve speech, and in
early 1929 the ACLU announced that it was "wholly opposed to any censorship whatever of films accompanied by speech." Ernst led the way, coauthor-
ing a 1930 book, *Censored: The Private Life of the Movie,* a survey of film
censorship practices. A 1933 ACLU pamphlet, *What Shocked the Censors,*
ridiculed the cuts made by the New York censors.[55] The crusade for freedom
of expression in the movies achieved little success until the 1950s, but the
battle had begun.

Mary Ware Dennett and The Sex Side of Life

Mary Ware Dennett's pamphlet *The Sex Side of Life* finally forced the ACLU
to come to terms with sex. A long-time ACLU activist, Dennett had been
secretary of the National American Women's Suffrage Association and had
worked closely with Baldwin during World War I. Although forgotten in

later years, in the 1920s she was Margaret Sanger's chief rival as the leader of the birth control movement. Unable in 1915 to find any adequate sex education materials for her children, she wrote her own. Friends began borrowing copies, and soon *The Sex Side of Life* had a large audience. The *Medical Review of Reviews* published it in 1918, and a reprint eventually sold over 35,000 copies through only one small advertisement.[56]

Dennett's short pamphlet contained an elementary description of male and female anatomy and a discussion of sexual intercourse, masturbation, and sexually transmitted diseases, concluding with a moralistic tribute to married love. The U.S. Postal Service declared it obscene in 1922 but never tried to stop its circulation. In 1928 Dennett was entrapped by a member of the Daughters of the American Revolution who requested a copy under a fictitious name. But the prosecution backfired as influential members of the medical community and conservative Republican clubwomen rose to Dennett's defense. The response was a revealing index of changing public mores. In just twenty years birth control had moved from being a radical idea—the property of Emma Goldman and Elizabeth Gurley Flynn—to an eminently respectable cause in wealthy and conservative circles.[57]

Ernst represented Dennett at trial, and the ACLU coordinated publicity and fund-raising. The jury took only forty minutes to convict her, agreeing with the government that the pamphlet was "pure and simple smut." The judge fined her $300. The ACLU reported that the conviction "aroused wider interest than [had] any censorship case in years." Publisher Roy Howard and Mrs. Marshall Field of Chicago lent their names to the defense committee, along with John Dewey and many eminent doctors and social workers. Dewey found it "almost incredible" that anyone should object to this fine pamphlet. Ernst won reversal of the conviction on appeal. Augustus Hand, cousin of Learned Hand, ruled that Dennett's pamphlet did not fall within the scope of the Comstock law's ban on "obscene, lewd or lascivious" material. Rather, it should be judged in terms of its "main effect," which, in this case, was to "promote understanding and self-control." Hand also remarked that adolescents should not be left without any alternative but "the casual gossip of ignorant playmates."[58]

Even before the case was over, the Dennett Defense Committee called for a "permanent agency" to fight restrictions on birth control information, turning over to the ACLU its $1,265 surplus. Baldwin thereupon organized the Committee Against Stage Censorship in early 1931, with Ernst, Harry Elmer Barnes, Walter Lippmann, H. L. Mencken, Eugene O'Neill, Lewis Mumford, and Elmer Rice as members. All agreed that the problem was much broader than just the theater and proposed a national effort to fight censorship in the "literary arts, the press, motion and talking pictures, the radio, and the scientific discussion of sex." The new National Committee on Freedom from Censorship (NCFC) marked the beginning of the ACLU's frontal assault on all forms of censorship.[59]

The Dennett case was an indication of changing public attitudes toward sexuality and the coming revolution in sex roles. Birth control pioneers Emma

Goldman, Margaret Sanger, and Dennett understood that control of reproduction was one of the keys to changing the power and status of women in society generally. This, in turn, required readily available information. Hays and Ernst were the first in the ACLU to understand the link between censorship and sex roles.[60]

A year after the Dennett decision, Ernst successfully challenged a U.S. Customs Service ban on Marie Stopes's *Married Love,* a discussion of female sexuality. Three months later he won another victory, defeating the U.S. Customs Service's ban on Stopes's *Contraception.* With characteristic hyperbole, Ernst proclaimed: "Sex wins in America."[61] Judge John M. Woolsey's opinion, however, applied only to literature imported by a doctor and said nothing about contraceptive devices.[62]

Finally, in 1933 Ernst won one of American history's greatest victories over censorship. On behalf of the Random House publishing firm, he defeated the Customs ban on James Joyce's *Ulysses.* Taking into account the work as a whole, Judge Woolsey held that *Ulysses* was not obscene. The defeat was such an embarrassment to the Customs Service that it promptly hired Huntington Cairns as a special advisory on obscenity matters and greatly reduced the number of books it banned.[63] By the early 1930s, the tide was running against censorship.

The ACLU Expands

Baldwin sensed the changes in public opinion and the courts: The public response to the *Scopes* and *Dennett* cases clearly suggested untapped sources of support for civil liberties. With a new self-confidence he decided it was time to broaden the ACLU's horizons. Outlining an ambitious ten-point expansion plan, Baldwin announced that "our program as defined heretofore is too narrow."[64]

Civil rights topped the agenda as Baldwin proposed "aid to Negroes in their fight for civil rights" and a new campaign on behalf of Native Americans. He further advised a vigorous campaign against police misconduct, a more vigorous defense of aliens in naturalization and deportation proceedings, opposition to compulsory military training in schools, and a broad-based fight against the censorship of "books, plays, radio, movies and talking movies." Finally, he wanted the ACLU to address international civil liberties issues, including "opposition to the control of weaker nations" by the American military and a more general campaign of protest against repression in other countries "where American interests are involved."[65]

The ACLU also needed to expand organizationally: "We have too long operated as a committee centralized here in New York." He proposed creating more subject matter committees similar to the Academic Freedom Committee, and a larger network of affiliates. "The time has come to decentralize our work; to build up local organizations all over the country."

Most on the ACLU National Committee enthusiastically endorsed Baldwin's plan, with Felix Frankfurter the strongest dissenter. Worried about di-luting the ACLU's slender resources, he thought the ACLU should not try to take on "the whole load of free spirited liberal aims." But the ACLU rejected Frankfurter's pessimistic outlook and adopted Baldwin's proposal, with one significant change: It omitted his call for involvement in international civil liberties issues. This was neither the first nor the last time they would rebuff Baldwin on this point.[66]

Shaping Public Policy

Baldwin had accurately gauged the changing political climate. His program was a huge success, and over the next five years the ACLU exerted a signifi-cant influence over public policy. The 1929 expansion was one of several piv-otal moments in ACLU history. On this and other occasions it took a daring leap in the face of limited resources and an unknown public response. In ev-ery instance, the gamble proved correct.

Their greatest victory during these years was the 1932 Norris–La Guardia Act restricting labor injunctions. Baldwin organized the National Committee on Labor Injunctions in 1930 to spearhead the lobbying effort, and Frank-furter and Nathan Greene published their classic study, *The Labor Injunc-tion*. Frankfurter also helped draft the Norris–La Guardia bill. The law rep-resented a historic reversal of public policy, declaring that workers had a right to "full freedom of association, self-organization, . . . [and] to be free from the interference, restraint, or coercion of employers." It required the courts to find evidence of actual violence or substantial harm to the employer before issuing injunctions. The law did not, however, solve all of labor's prob-lems; employers still did not have to negotiate with nascent unions, but it was a historic step toward ending the wholesale denial of the right of freedom of speech and assembly for millions of American workers.[67]

The ACLU also played a pivotal role in creating a national debate on the problem of police misconduct. Ernst had suggested that "a good broadside at-tack on invasion of civil liberties in connection with the prohibition law would help our general standing in the community," but few agreed.[68] A new oppor-tunity arose in 1929 when President Herbert Hoover established the Wicker-sham Commission to conduct the first federal study of American criminal justice. Baldwin successfully lobbied the commission to hire Walter Pollak, Zechariah Chafee, and Carl Stern to write the report on police practices. Chafee had already assisted in a similar ACLU investigation in Boston, and Baldwin supplied the Wickersham Commission with material from the ACLU files.[69]

The ensuing report, *Lawlessness in Law Enforcement,* created a national sensation, overshadowing all the other ten commission reports. It concluded that "the third degree—the inflicting of pain, physical or mental, to extract confessions or statements—is widespread throughout the country." It also persuasively documented the beating of suspects with fists and rubber hoses, protracted questioning (including keeping the suspect "standing for hours . . .

deprived of food or sleep" or with bright lights shining directly in his or her face) and "prolonged illegal detention." Philadelphia police commonly put suspects in "cold storage" for a week so they could "think it over." Detroit police moved suspects "around the loop" to hide them from family, friends, or counsel. Finally, the Buffalo police commissioner brazenly announced, "If I have to violate the Constitution . . . I'll violate the Constitution. . . . Shysters have turned the Constitution into a refuge for the criminal."[70]

To implement the report's recommendations, the ACLU drafted a model statute requiring the immediate arraignment of all arrested persons, detention by an agency other than the police, and the right of all suspects to consult an attorney. Eventually, the courts embraced most of these ideas. Hays and Ernst, meanwhile, served on New York City Mayor Fiorello La Guardia's committee to investigate the 1935 Harlem race riot, and they offered a novel suggestion for reviewing complaints against the police by a committee of citizens.

Although police reform was painfully slow in coming, *Lawlessness in Law Enforcement* was a watershed. It strengthened the hand of reform-minded police chiefs, creating a political constituency for change and advancing the idea that the police should be held accountable to the law through formal procedures.[71]

A fundamental reversal of public policy toward Native Americans was a third major ACLU achievement during the early 1930s. Since 1887 the federal government policy had tried to dissolve tribal autonomy and assimilate Native Americans into society as individuals. In 1930 Baldwin organized the ACLU Committee on Indian Civil Rights which lobbied for restoring the Native Americans' tribal autonomy and control over their land. "As an experiment in getting tribes out of the jurisdiction" of the Bureau of Indian Affairs, the committee proposed incorporating one tribe, the Klamaths. Other reforms included criminal penalties for kidnapping Native American children and taking them to federal boarding schools and repeal of an old espionage act that allowed reservation superintendents to restrict communication by Native Americans with one another or with outside sympathizers. In January 1933 the ACLU committee sponsored an all-day conference on Native American rights in Washington and lobbied for the 1934 Indian Reorganization Act. Interior Secretary Harold Ickes, an ACLU member, implemented the law, which some described as "a New Deal for the American Indian."[72]

Civil Rights: The Margold Report and the Road to Brown

The ACLU was one of the few predominantly white organizations to champion the cause of racial equality in the late 1920s and early 1930s. It continued to defer civil rights cases to the NAACP and instead concentrated on public education. In 1931 the ACLU published *Black Justice,* a comprehensive survey of institutionalized racism. As an example, in the ten states of the Deep South, "the Negro may not vote. The Negro may not marry according to his choice. The Negro must accept separate accommodations in public schools and on public conveyances." In addition, the entire machinery of criminal justice served the racist status quo.[73] The American Bar Association did not admit blacks, and virtually all of the top ACLU lawyers—Hays, Ernst, Fraenkel—refused to join it on that account.

The overriding question was how to attack segregation, and the boldest proposal came from Morris Ernst, chair of the Garland Fund's Committee on Negro Work. The Margold Report, as it became known, laid the foundation for the subsequent legal assault on segregation and was, arguably, the single most important report ever sponsored by a private foundation.[74]

Committee members Ernst, journalist Lewis Gannett, and NAACP Secretary James Weldon Johnson conceived a legal attack on segregation. Their initial 1929 memo called for "a dramatic, large-scale campaign to win equal rights [for southern blacks] in the public schools, in the voting booths, on the railroad, and on juries."[75] The committee's vision went far beyond mere legal equality and pointed toward a social, political, and economic transformation of the South, if not the entire country. Blacks constituted "the largest group of unorganized workers in America," and winning their civil rights would invigorate the labor movement and revolutionize southern politics. The committee argued that the proposed campaign could be "the largest single contribution to social change the Garland Fund could make" and suggested allocating "the remainder of its fund" to this effort. Bold as it was, the plan represented some notable compromises: It proposed challenging the inequality of public school funding and not segregation per se. Because the courts seemed unlikely to strike down segregation, the "but equal" prong of the prevailing *Plessy* doctrine might be an opening wedge for short-term improvements in black education.[76]

Not everyone in the ACLU shared the committee's faith in litigation. Baldwin advised against the grant, arguing that the "legalistic" approach would not be effective: "The Negro will succeed . . . only by his union with white workers on the field of common struggle against their economic masters." Not even his recent victory in the New Jersey Supreme Court altered his view of litigation. In a 1934 article for the Urban League Baldwin contended that "history supports the contention that law is the weakest of instruments for overcoming the power of a privileged class." KKK vigilantes would simply nullify any court order by means of force and violence.[77] Other ACLU liberals were uneasy about a direct assault on segregation: Hollingsworth Wood warned that it "would stir up a great amount of bitterness," trigger lynch mobs, and seriously set back the cause of interracial understanding. Sociologist Howard W. Odum, one of the few southern liberals in regard to race relations, also thought the NAACP's militancy was counterproductive.[78]

The Margold Report provoked one of the rare open debates over ACLU strategy. In the context of 1929, neither side had a monopoly on wisdom. Baldwin spoke boldly about direct action but had few victories to show for it. Organized labor was weaker in 1930 than it had been ten years earlier. The advocates of litigation thus could offer little more than hope for their case. With rare exception, the courts were as hostile to civil rights for black Ameri-

cans as they were to civil liberties generally. The committee's report cited the
1917 Supreme Court decision outlawing a residential segregation ordinance,
but no other decisions. The wisdom of the strategy used by the Committee on
Negro Work became apparent only in retrospect. In 1929, however, neither
strategy appeared certain of success.

The Garland Fund compromised by giving the NAACP a $10,000 plan-
ning grant and pledging another $90,000 for subsequent implementation. The
NAACP hired Frankfurter protégé Nathan Margold to develop the final plan,
and he made a number of important changes, including a more direct attack
on unequal public school funding. But Margold's final report was a bit too
daring even for the NAACP, and so its legal director, Charles Houston,
shelved it. In any event, the depression wiped out the Garland Fund, and
the NAACP never received the remaining $90,000. Nonetheless, the Margold
Report played a historic role in expanding the horizons of the civil rights
movement. In the long run, according to one historian, it helped "open up
vistas" that had not been imagined before and eventually set the NAACP on
the road that led to *Brown*.[79]

Vindication

In 1931 the Supreme Court vindicated the ACLU's efforts with two landmark
decisions affirming First Amendment protection of freedom of speech and
press. The first involved Communist party member Yetta Stromberg, convicted under the California law outlawing display of "a red flag, banner or
badge . . . as a sign, symbol or emblem of opposition to organized government." Stromberg was a counselor at a Communist summer camp for children. Although the children saluted the Soviet flag every morning, Stromberg
was not charged with inciting revolutionary violence. The ACLU, sharing the
appeal to the Supreme Court with the International Labor Defense, was optimistic about the case. As attorney John Beardsley said, "We have a fighting
chance."[80]

The Court justified this optimism, overturning Stromberg's conviction and
invalidating the red flag section of the California law. Chief Justice Charles
Evans Hughes's opinion affirmed a broad principle of freedom of association:
"The maintenance of the opportunity for free political discussion . . . is a
fundamental principle of our constitutional system." The ban on red flags was
"vague and indefinite" and "repugnant to the guaranty of liberty contained in
the Fourteenth Amendment." *Stromberg* was a dramatic break from the entire line of Court decisions reaching back to the 1919 *Schenck* case. It affirmed the ideas expressed in Holmes's *Abrams* dissent and vindicated the
ACLU's eleven-year fight for free speech.[81]

Stromberg was no fluke, as the Court immediately followed it with another
ground-breaking First Amendment decision. *Near v. Minnesota* affirmed the
principle that the First Amendment protected the press against prior restraint.
As was true of so many landmark cases, this basic freedom was won by a

thoroughly disreputable plaintiff. In his scurrilous weekly, *The Saturday Press,* Jay Near indulged his anti-Catholic, anti-Semitic, antiblack, and antilabor prejudices in a long scandal-mongering career in Minneapolis. In the episode that provoked his Court case, he leveled sweeping charges of corruption and nonfeasance against the mayor, the police chief, the county attorney, and the major daily newspapers in Minneapolis. The authorities closed down *The Saturday Press* under a 1925 public nuisance abatement law. The ACLU offered to defend Near but, to its chagrin, was maneuvered out of the case by Colonel Robert McCormick, publisher of the *Chicago Tribune.* Having recently faced a costly libel suit by Henry Ford, the conservative McCormick had developed an interest in freedom of the press.[82]

On June 1, 1931, the Supreme Court ruled the Minnesota law to be unconstitutional, in a decision that firmly established the freedom of the press against prior restraint, with Chief Justice Hughes holding that "it is no longer open to doubt that the liberty of the press and of speech is within the liberties safeguarded by the due process clause of the Fourteenth Amendment from invasion by state action." The incorporation of the freedom of the press clause fulfilled the promise of *Gitlow* six years before and vindicated Walter Pollak's ground-breaking arguments on the Fourteenth Amendment.[83]

Stromberg and *Near* marked a historic turn for the Supreme Court on the First Amendment and, in a broader sense, indicated a deeper change in public attitudes. Historian Paul Murphy noted "the singular lack of broad-scale criticism." That is, the public was apparently not alarmed at the Court's protection of Communists and publishers of scandal sheets. Broad changes in public attitudes are difficult to measure, but it appears that by the early 1930s, support for freedom of expression had gained ground. The Scopes case, the birth control movement, and the new currents in American literature had helped bring about a new spirit of tolerance for unpopular ideas.[84]

The Court's new attitude was not confined to the First Amendment. A year later it opened another important avenue of constitutional rights in *Powell v. Alabama,* the first of the Scottsboro cases. Nine young black men were charged with raping two white women near the small town of Scottsboro, Alabama, in March 1931. The case instantly became a major cause célèbre, a focal point of national outrage over southern racism that laid the foundations for the national civil rights coalition. Although the ACLU was not initially involved in the case (Hays and Darrow refused to submit to the restrictions imposed by the International Labor Defense lawyers), the ILD eventually asked the ACLU's Walter Pollak to handle the Supreme Court appeal. The Court reversed Powell's conviction on the grounds that he had been denied adequate counsel. It was a limited victory, applying only to capital cases. As Ernst pointed out, the Court also ignored the two other points raised by the defense: the fairness of the trial itself and the exclusion of blacks from the jury. Nonetheless, it was a historic breakthrough, as the Court extended the process of selectively incorporating the protections of the Bill of Rights into the Fourteenth Amendment by including the Sixth Amendment guarantee of a fair trial. *Powell* represented the third appearance by Pollak in a major Supreme Court argument and his first victory. The decision vindicated his arguments in *Gitlow,* seven years earlier, and began a more extensive constitutional scrutiny of the criminal process.[85]

Out of the Wilderness

By 1932 the ACLU was out of the wilderness. After twelve years of lonely effort, civil liberties principles had established a small but significant beachhead. Perhaps even more important than the Supreme Court decisions was the change in public attitudes: Freedom of speech was no longer a heretical idea, and key opinion makers had begun to speak out on behalf of tolerance for the new and the unpopular.[86] The country had changed in the years since World War I, and the ACLU could claim much of the credit for the new attitudes toward the Bill of Rights.

III

Advances and Retreats, 1933-1945

Five

The New Deal Revolution
in Civil Liberties

Civil Liberties in a Decade of Crisis

"For the first time in a long time," observed John Haynes Holmes, "we found ourselves face to face with fundamentals."[1] The ACLU did come face to face with fundamentals in the 1930s. The depression and President Franklin D. Roosevelt's New Deal effected a social and political revolution in American life, with profound ramifications for civil liberties. The enormous expansion of government under the New Deal brought new protections for individual rights and, at the same time, posed new threats to liberty. Toward the end of the decade, the Supreme Court emerged as an active defender of individual rights. At the same time, the rise of totalitarian movements abroad and at home raised serious questions about the survival of constitutional democracy. The combination of these powerful forces presented the ACLU and the country with basic questions about the meaning of civil liberties.

As the Great Depression descended on the country, assaults on freedom of speech and assembly increased dramatically. Roger Baldwin called 1930 "the worst year since the war for free speech prosecutions and for meetings broken up or prohibited." His correspondents across the country reported a fivefold increase in mob violence and free speech prosecutions. The number of lynchings doubled. In California's Imperial Valley, vigilantes kidnapped and savagely beat Southern California ACLU attorney A. L. Wirin and assaulted Ernest Besig, director of the Northern California ACLU. The Philadelphia and Cleveland police banned all meetings of the unemployed. The ACLU condemned the New York City police as "the most conspicuous offender among police departments . . . with the long record of meetings and picket-lines broken up." The head of the Los Angeles "red squad," Captain William F. Hynes, brazenly assaulted Clinton J. Taft, director of the Southern California ACLU, in the city council chambers, saying that lawyers who represented Communists should be "thrown out of ten story windows."[2]

95

The federal government renewed its attack on foreign ideas. Deportations of alien radicals rose from one each in 1928 and 1929 to fifty-one in 1932. Customs seized Russian posters and art reproductions in 1932 belonging to Corliss Lamont. A few weeks later it seized posters belonging to seminary student James Dombrowski. The ACLU negotiated release of all the posters. Both Lamont and Dombrowski won important First Amendment cases in the same term of the Supreme Court thirty-five years later.[3]

The economic collapse and the increase in repression drove Roger Baldwin further to the left. "As I read history," he wrote, "all progress has been made by the struggle of oppressed economic classes for a greater share of political and economic power." The 1931 Supreme Court decisions in *Stromberg* and *Near* did not impress him: "Power preserves rights. Pieces of paper do not. Free speech is not an issue of law. It is an issue of power. . . . Rarely do results come through court decisions." Politics was a "sideshow," and Baldwin did not think the 1932 presidential election would "make much difference to the cause of civil liberties."[4] He was not the only one to misjudge Franklin D. Roosevelt.

The ACLU was deeply divided over Roosevelt's New Deal. Whereas Hays and Ernst were enthusiastic supporters, Baldwin was dubious, warning that "the enormous increase of the power of the federal government under New Deal policies carries with it inevitable fears of inroads on the right of agitation." Wedded to a traditional view of civil liberties as freedom from government, Baldwin could not imagine it as a positive instrument for protecting individual rights. Besides, Roosevelt was too closely tied to business interests. The principal New Deal economic recovery program, the National Recovery Administration (NRA), suspended antitrust laws and established collaborative agreements between business and labor. To Baldwin it bore an uncomfortable resemblance to the Fascist policies of Benito Mussolini's Italy.[5]

Labor issues dominated Baldwin's thinking. At a December 1934 ACLU conference, Civil Liberties Under the New Deal, he and other ACLU leftists attacked the NRA's labor provisions. Section 7(a) guaranteed labor the right to organize, but Mary Van Kleeck argued that in practice the law "gravely jeopardized" the rights of working people. Businessmen either ignored it or created compliant company unions. NRA boards discouraged strikes in the hope of promoting economic recovery. A conference resolution declared that the NRA constituted a "violation of the interests of workers' rights to organize and strike—their only resources of power and liberty."[6]

Roosevelt was little interested in civil liberties himself but appointed many civil libertarians to New Deal agencies. In December 1933 the administration pardoned the remaining World War I Espionage and Sedition Act victims. Determined to end the U.S. Customs Service censorship, Treasury Secretary Henry Morgantheau allegedly ordered his staff to "find me a lawyer who has read a book." The U.S. Postal Service, meanwhile, reduced its censorship of the mails. Baldwin successfully lobbied for the appointment of Daniel Mac-Cormack as commissioner of immigration. Receptive to the ACLU argument that aliens should not be excluded because of their political views, MacCormack reduced deportations from seventy-four in 1933 to only twenty in 1934.[7]

The ACLU's staunchest friend was Interior Secretary Harold Ickes, a member of the ACLU. Two agencies of the Interior Department were hotbeds of civil liberties activity: The Bureau of Indian Affairs implemented the 1934 Indian Reorganization Act, which the ACLU had championed, and Commissioner of Education John W. Studebaker instituted a civil liberties education program for schoolteachers. He even retained Baldwin to help with a weekly CBS radio program, "Let Freedom Ring."[8]

Anti–New Deal conservatives offered backhanded tributes to the extent of the ACLU's influence. Representative Hamilton Fish listed twelve New Deal officials "tutored" by Felix Frankfurter and associated with the ACLU. Anti-Communist fanatic Elizabeth Dilling, the Phyllis Schlafly of her day, called the ACLU the " 'pulse' of the Roosevelt regime." By 1938 Baldwin had shed his doubts about the New Deal, finding that civil liberties had "advanced tremendously within the last three years."[9]

The New Deal was not, however, an unalloyed triumph for the ACLU; by any means. The political revolution that realigned American politics for a generation brought to power a coalition of organized labor and urban political machines, rooted in Catholic and Jewish communities, and the white South. Many of the groups that were liberal on economic issues, moreover, were very conservative on social questions. The political upheaval began in 1930 as many civil libertarian liberals won state and local offices. The new mayor of Detroit, Frank Murphy, ended police harassment of the unemployed and established a "free speech forum." Patrick H. O'Brien, former chair of the Detroit ACLU Legal Committee, was elected Michigan's attorney general in 1932. The mayor of Cleveland also established a free speech zone on Public Square. Governor George Earle of Pennsylvania created a state bureau of civil liberties in 1937, the first of its kind in the country (although it was abolished two years later in an economy move). The Chicago Corporation's counsel, Barnet Hodes, temporarily reversed the long-standing anti–civil libertarian policies of city government and proudly claimed that he had issued more opinions "affirmatively insisting upon adherence to the American Bill of Rights" than had all of his predecessors.[10]

But for every Frank Murphy, however, the New Deal also strengthened the power of anti–civil libertarian politicians. Mayor Frank Hague, boss of the Jersey City political machine, waged an all-out war against the labor movement. Fiorello La Guardia, one of the ACLU's few friends as a member of Congress in the 1920s, established a terrible civil liberties record as mayor of New York, condoning police brutality (once ordering the police to "muss em up") and suppressing magazines and plays he regarded as indecent. In 1940 he banned all picketing of foreign offices and churches on the grounds that "you can't picket.God." Ernst called him "our worst best mayor." ACLU attorney Osmond Fraenkel arranged a three-hour "frank off the record talk" with him, but to no avail. When Baldwin confronted him privately, La Guardia confessed, "When I was outside I could talk to you. . . . Now I'm on the inside, it's all different."[11]

Because of the power of southern Democrats, the Roosevelt administration did nothing in the area of civil rights. Indeed, the ACLU confronted the ugly fact of segregation in the nation's capital at its 1934 conference. The Hotel Arlington refused to serve the black delegates—who included Walter White from the NAACP and Robert Weaver from the Interior Department—in the main dining room. Baldwin rejected the offer of a private dining room and moved the conference to Howard University. The conference produced an ACLU-supported coalition to press for a federal antilynching law and other civil rights issues.[12]

Cultural Politics and Civil Liberties

Cultural issues became the flash point of important civil liberties conflicts in the 1930s. In the new configuration of American politics, the Catholic community used its new power and status to impose its moral views on the country, particularly regarding censorship and birth control. Militant Catholic moralism was an international phenomenon. The Vatican proscribed birth control for the first time in a 1930 encyclical and endorsed film censorship in 1936. Catholics moved into the void left by the mainstream Protestant denominations, which developed a more tolerant attitude toward sexuality.[13]

As the ACLU stepped up its anticensorship efforts, it came into increasing conflict with the Catholic church. The resignation of Rev. John A. Ryan from the ACLU's National Committee in 1934 severed the two groups' last link. As director of the National Catholic Welfare Conference, Ryan had worked closely with Roger Baldwin in defense of conscientious objectors and on labor issues. In the thirties he became the leading Catholic lobbyist, earning the title "The Right Reverend New Dealer." After he resigned, no Catholic cleric held a position in the ACLU until Rev. Robert F. Drinan joined the National Committee in the 1970s.[14]

Sexuality was the crux of ACLU–Catholic conflict. Birth control continued to gain public acceptance, and between 1930 and 1940 the number of clinics in the country increased from 34 to 549. Yet under the federal Comstock law, contraceptives were still obscene. The initial battle in Congress involved the Customs ban on contraceptives. The ACLU supported Mary Ware Dennett's bill to end all restrictions, whereas Margaret Sanger's proposal allowed only doctors to import contraceptives. Dennett and the ACLU attacked her "doctors only" approach, which the medical profession supported, as an unacceptable concession. Rev. Ryan led the opposition.[15]

Morris Ernst, in his multiple roles as a private attorney, author, and general counsel for both the ACLU and Planned Parenthood, proved to be the most effective opponent of censorship. In 1936 he won a case that allowed doctors to import contraceptives (Margaret Sanger hailed it as the "greatest legal victory" ever), and he turned his attention to the Massachusetts and Connecticut laws restricting the distribution of contraceptives. The Massachusetts Supreme Court rejected a suit on behalf of doctors on the grounds that they were not exempt from the general prohibition. The U.S. Supreme Court did not find a substantial federal question and refused to hear an appeal. A 1940 challenge to the Connecticut law also failed. Two years later Ernst lost another Connecticut suit arguing that doctors could prescribe contraceptives when "pregnancy would jeopardize life." In 1944 he again lost, this time arguing that the law unconstitutionally deprived a woman of her right to life and liberty. Reproductive rights litigation finally succeeded in the 1960s.[16]

The ACLU also fought efforts to censor public discussion of sexuality. The April 11, 1938, issue of *Life* magazine was banned across the country because it published thirty-five pictures from the public health film *The Birth of a Baby*. Given *Life*'s circulation of over two million, the article itself was an indication of changing public attitudes. Boston Police Commissioner Joseph F. Timilty organized an attack on the issue. The 1931 *Near* decision notwithstanding, Timilty persuaded New England magazine distributors not to handle any publication not approved by his board of censors. When Pennsylvania Governor Earle and local officials in St. Louis, Memphis, Chicago, and New Orleans also banned the April 11 issue of *Life,* Ernst helped arrange an obscenity prosecution in New York of publisher Roy Larsen, winning an acquittal. The film *Birth of a Baby* was banned in New York, although the courts allowed it to be shown to private audiences for scientific purposes. In Chicago the police banned a U.S. Public Health Service film, *The Fight for Life,* on the grounds that any discussion of pregnancy and birth was "indecent." The Chicago ACLU challenged the ban but lost.[17]

Increased Censorship of the Movies

The slow but steady gains against censorship of books were offset by increased censorship of the movies. The new repression, institutionalized in the 1934 Hollywood Production Code, was the result of a public reaction against the nudity and racy language that was common in films. The uninhibited style was epitomized by Mae West, who delivered lines such as "Is that a gun you're carrying, or are you just glad to see me?" Religious leaders complained about a decline in morality, and social workers expressed concern about the impact of films on children. The 1933 Payne Fund report, *Our Movie Made Children,* concluded that the movies' celebration of sex and crime had "social consequences highly undesirable." In 1932 Iowa Senator Smith Brookhart threatened a congressional investigation of Hollywood morality.[18]

Although state and local film restrictions were widespread, the censorship forces were not well organized at the national level. The film industry issued a list of "Don'ts and Be Carefuls" in 1927 but had no enforcement mechanism. This dramatically changed when Catholics organized the Leigon of Decency in 1933. Three years later, a Vatican encyclical, *Vigilanti Cura,* denounced immorality in films.[19] Industry leaders were terrified by a series of

Catholic-led boycotts in 1933 and 1934. The Philadelphia boycott reportedly reduced movie attendance by 40 percent. Already hard hit by the depression, Hollywood moved quickly to accommodate the Catholics. In cooperation with the archbishop of Cincinnati, the industry established a new Production Code Administration (PCA). Under the code, no studio-controlled theater could show a film without a PCA seal of approval. And because the studios controlled most of the theaters, the code had real teeth.[20]

Martin Quigley drafted the code with the covert assistance of Jesuit priest Father Daniel A. Lord. Joseph I. Breen, a Catholic seminary dropout, was hired to run the code office. The code imposed a repressive, Victorian-era sexual morality, championing a simplistic respect for God, family, and authority. It banned nudity, vulgar language, the treatment of sex outside marriage, and the use of narcotics: "The sympathy of the audience shall never be thrown to the side of crime, wrong-doing, evil or sin," and "the sanctity of the institution of marriage and the home shall be upheld. No film shall infer that casual or promiscuous sex relationships are the accepted or common thing." Nor could any film "throw ridicule on any religious faith."[21] The ACLU found the code particularly difficult to attack, for as a private voluntary action, it was beyond the reach of court tests based on state action.[22]

The Legion of Decency also posed a serious dilemma for the ACLU. It conceded that protests of film immorality were a legitimate exercise of First Amendment rights. At the same time, however, this pressure clearly prevented free expression in the movies. Forced to draw the line between two competing civil liberties principles, the ACLU issued the first of several statements on private pressure groups. It argued that private, voluntary boycotts by the Legion of Decency were protected by the First Amendment. But any attempt "to use the legal processes of government to impose their will on other people" was an impermissible form of censorship.[23]

Catholic censorship took a more political turn after the outbreak of the Spanish Civil War in 1936. The pro-Loyalist films *Spain in Flames* and *Spanish Earth* were banned by state authorities in Pennsylvania and Ohio and several cities. Catholic pressure was also responsible for Mayor La Guardia's attempt to ban picketing of churches. Powerful pro-German forces in Chicago, meanwhile, attacked anti-Nazi films. A *March of Time* feature, "Inside Nazi Germany," and *Concentration Camp* were banned until ACLU protests won their release.[24]

The film censorship campaign encouraged Catholic bishops to create the National Organization for Decent Literature (NODL) in 1938 to fight indecent books and magazines. Inevitably, literary classics and political works came under attack. John Steinbeck's *The Grapes of Wrath* was banned by public libraries in San Jose, Kansas City, and other cities. The library board in East St. Louis ordered its three copies burned. Hemingway's novels were also banned because of his support for the Loyalists in the Spanish Civil War. A twenty-year fight for the rights of the nudist movement began when the U.S. Postal Service banned Maurice Parmelee's *Nudism in Modern Life* in 1934. The New York Civil Liberties Committee fought a running battle with

Mayor La Guardia's periodic crusades against "indecent" magazines and books.[25]

The Wagner Act Revolution

The ACLU was forced to rethink its basic philosophy about the relationship of the individual and the state in a case involving the free speech rights of antiunion automaker Henry Ford.[26] The controversy arose out of an order issued by the National Labor Relations Board (NLRB), created by the 1935 Wagner Act. The law had a near-revolutionary impact on American life, guaranteeing workers the right to organize unions "of their own choosing." Giving power and dignity to millions of American workers, it was arguably the greatest civil rights law in American history. This historic reversal of public policy ended one hundred years of industrial relations violence and established organized labor as a powerful force in American life. Labor became the backbone of the dominant Democratic party coalition.[27]

The ACLU did not endorse the Wagner Act. Clinging to its traditional fear of governmental power, Roger Baldwin advised New York Senator Robert Wagner that no "federal agency intervening in the conflicts between employers and employees can be expected to fairly determine the issues of labor's rights." Then in his most leftist period, Baldwin was convinced that labor would have to gain power entirely on its own. The pro–New Deal liberals in the ACLU eagerly supported Wagner's bill. Hays argued that it would protect the rights of workers without denying "civil rights to any individual or union." Finding the ACLU board sharply divided, Baldwin reluctantly notified Wagner that the ACLU "withdraws its opposition to the bill, and takes no position whatsoever as an organization." In any event, the ACLU's position made little difference, as Congress overwhelmingly passed the Wagner Act.[28]

It was ironic that after fifteen years of championing the rights of labor, the ACLU took no position on the law that finally guaranteed the workers' right to organize. The law, however, introduced several new and troubling civil liberties issues. The first and most important involved the powers of the new National Labor Relations Board, which forced the ACLU to reconsider the entire question of the scope of governmental regulation.

Free Speech for Employers?

Even before the Ford controversy arose, the ACLU was deeply split over the question of employers' rights. A deep ideological gulf appeared within the ACLU, pitting a left-wing, prolabor faction against a centrist group. Led by board chairman Harry Ward, Mary Van Kleeck, Nathan Greene, Elizabeth Gurley Flynn, Robert Dunn, and Abraham Isserman, the leftists decided civil liberties issues in terms of what was best for labor. The centrists became increasingly alarmed about this partisan tendency among the leftists. Accentuating the split was the fact of Flynn's membership in the Communist party. Norman Thomas and John Haynes Holmes were already strongly anti-Communist, and they began to raise questions about Flynn's motives. For the first time in its fifteen-year history, the ACLU was torn by mistrust arising from ideological differences.

The sit-down strikes in the automobile industry in late 1936 brought these ideological differences to the surface. The ACLU leftists saw them as a legitimate form of protest, whereas others thought they were criminal trespass. The New York Civil Liberties Committee said it would not support employees who "enter or remain in any building and refuse to leave after being requested to do so." The ACLU board, led by Van Kleeck and Flynn, adopted a statement that carefully avoided condemning sit-downs: "The Civil Liberties Union is not organized to protect the rights of property." Rather, its sole concern is the "maintenance of democratic processes."[29] The sit-down strikes passed without the ACLU's having to resolve the issue, but the battle lines were clearly drawn.

By 1937 free speech controversies began to arise under the administrative machinery of the National Labor Relations Act created by the Wagner Act. In the first, the ACLU endorsed an NLRB inquiry into the authorship of an antiunion editorial in the St. Mary's, Pennsylvania, *Daily Press*. Drafted by the prolabor faction, the ACLU statement asserted that "freedom of the press is not a real issue" and that the NLRB's inquiry was entirely proper. ACLU moderates were horrified at this threat to freedom of the press, and their suspicions about the leftists accordingly increased.[30]

Free Speech for Henry Ford?

The Ford case brought the conflict into the open. Henry Ford's hostility to unions was notorious. He employed a gang of thugs to fight the United Auto Workers, and the picture of his men beating Walter Reuther is one of the famous images of the decade. In late 1937 the NLRB issued a sweeping cease-and-desist order directing Ford to stop circulating antiunion literature. One of his pieces called unions "the worst thing that ever struck the earth, because they take away a man's independence." His "Fordism" repeatedly denounced unions as corrupt rackets. The NLRB ruled that such statements had to be considered in their context: "No employee could fail to understand that if he disregarded the warning he might find himself in difficulties with his employer." "Freedom of speech," it concluded, "is a qualified, not an absolute right."[31]

The ACLU's leftist-dominated Committee on Labor's Rights supported the NLRB. Citing the clear and present danger test, it distinguished between antiunion statements addressed to a general audience and threatening remarks to employees: "Utterances may properly be punishable if they are part of an illegal act," and in the context of a labor-organizing drive, Ford's antiunion diatribes were coercive acts.[32]

The ACLU moderates fought back. Roger Riis, son of the famous urban reformer Jacob Riis, accused the leftists of a "serious departure from principle." The ACLU, he argued, had always sought "the freeing of speech" and had never endorsed any restriction. Furthermore, the NLRB's rationale could return to haunt labor through restrictions on union statements about employers. The issue involved fundamental free speech principles: "We, of all organizations," he concluded, "must not attempt to control speech, even in the interests of social betterment."[33] In a *Reader's Digest* article, Riis placed the controversy in an international context. The rise of dictatorships around the world dramatized the urgency of an evenhanded defense of free speech. With Hitler and Stalin on his mind, Riis subtly questioned the integrity of the ACLU leftists and Communist party member Flynn in particular.[34]

John Haynes Holmes agreed with Riis and wrote ACLU Chairperson Harry Ward that "for the first time in a long time we found ourselves face to face with fundamentals. I have a feeling that little by little, step by step, almost without realizing it, under the impact of our real sympathy for labor's cause, we are allowing ourselves to become mere advocates of the rights of labor." Holmes asked for a special ACLU meeting to discuss these "fundamentals."[35]

Arthur Garfield Hays dominated the meeting by drafting a statement that substantially revised the ACLU's position on government regulation. The Ford case, he contended, was not an either–or proposition. Instead, the ACLU should support the main thrust of the NLRB's cease-and-desist order but oppose those sections restricting noncoercive speech. This meant that Ford had a First Amendment right to express his antiunion views but could not directly threaten individual workers. The ACLU board accepted Hays's logic and submitted a memo to the NLRB asking it to "clarify that part of the order" involving Ford's expressions of opinion. Ultimately, Hays's reasoning prevailed and a 1940 decision by the Sixth Circuit Court of Appeals followed his logic.[36]

New Directions for the ACLU

By endorsing in principle the power of the NLRB, the ACLU accepted the idea of government as a positive instrument for protecting individual liberty. Government power was not unlimited, however, but was confined by the guarantees of the Bill of Rights. The ACLU's role became that of defining the precise scope of those guarantees in the modern administrative state. On this issue, the ACLU reaffirmed its role as a persistent critic of mainstream liberalism which, under the sway of New Deal gains, was less critical of government power than ever. In a parallel development, the new field of administrative law developed also to define the limits of government regulatory power. In the middle of the Ford case debate, Morris Ernst announced, with some justification, "We are on the threshold of developing a new body of law."[37]

The ACLU's support for Ford provoked sharp criticism from the labor movement and the political left. Some even accused the ACLU of becoming "antilabor." Baldwin "categorically" denied any change in ACLU philosophy, stating that the ACLU had "never been pro-labor or anti-labor."[38] This, of course, was not entirely true. There were twenty years of prolabor rhetoric on the record—most of it Baldwin's own. Baldwin simply was trying to paper over a major change in ACLU policy by denying that it had happened. In fact, he was busily cutting his ties with the left and moving the ACLU toward a more centrist position.

At this critical juncture, several ACLU leaders proposed basic changes in the ACLU's mission. Some leftists wanted the ACLU to become a general legal aid society. The Chicago and New York chapters of the National Lawyers Guild had experimented with neighborhood offices in low-income areas. The ACLU's Chicago affiliate planned to follow suit until overruled by the ACLU board. The majority felt that the Ford case dramatized the need to maintain the ACLU's special mission of guarding basic civil liberties principles.[39]

Morris Ernst, meanwhile, wanted the ACLU to become more active as a liberal lobbying group and urged the board to develop a "positive" legislative program. Ernst had several objectives. By the late 1930s he saw himself as a Washington power broker. A 1944 *Life* magazine article described him as "the censor's enemy, the president's friend." He was also obsessed with Communism, which he saw as a serious threat to democracy. Ernst's "positive" program included a disclosure law requiring political groups using the mails to reveal their officers and sources of funds. He thought the exposure of Communist fronts would head off the coming "avalanche" of laws even more damaging to civil liberties. But the ACLU rejected the disclosure idea on the grounds that it would inhibit minority political parties of all sorts.[40]

Underlying his specific proposal was Ernst's belief that the ACLU should abandon its "doctrinaire" approach to civil liberties. Rather, it should become more pragmatic and willing to compromise in the political arena. This proposal, coming from one of the most influential voices in the organization, would have greatly altered the ACLU's course, but it was soundly rebuffed. Art Hays led the opposition and argued that the ACLU had to stand above the political fray and focus on fundamental civil liberties issues, which would require a rigorously nonpartisan stance. The ACLU should no more be seduced by the opportunities for advancing liberalism, as Ernst's proposal suggested, than it should become the uncritical friend of the labor movement— the issue at hand in the Ford case.[41]

Storm over the Supreme Court

Until 1937, the Supreme Court had been only an occasional defender of civil liberties. That year it dramatically reversed direction and created the first significant protections of individual rights. This change arose from a major political crisis arising from its hostility to the New Deal. There was little celebration of the one hundred fiftieth anniversary of the Constitution in 1937. The country was embroiled in a profound political crisis over the Constitution itself. The Supreme Court had invalidated all of the major New

Deal economic measures. The University of Wisconsin's law school dean, Lloyd K. Garrison, warned that it was no longer a question of "how government functions, but whether we shall govern at all." Alabama Senator Hugo Black complained that "120,000,000 are ruled by five men." Norman Thomas accused the Court of operating as "a sort of permanent constitutional convention." Liberal and left-wing critics proposed eliminating the Court's power of judicial review.[42]

Reelected by a landslide in November 1936, Roosevelt decided to take on the Court. In February 1937 he announced a "court reorganization" plan that would allow presidents to appoint an additional federal judge for every one currently over the age of seventy. The plan also would allow him to appoint six new Supreme Court justices, giving him a ten-to-five majority. "We cannot yield our constitutional destiny," FDR declared, "to the personal judgment of a few men who, fearful of the future, would deny us the necessary means of dealing with the present." But Roosevelt misread the temper of the country, and his plan provoked strong opposition. Conservatives denounced it as an arrogant power grab, and many liberals and moderates were disturbed by the threat to an independent judiciary.[43]

Roger Baldwin polled the ACLU's top lawyers about the court-packing plan, and their discussions offered a revealing glimpse into the ACLU's attitudes toward the Court and civil liberties. The panel represented a galaxy of legal talent: Ernst, Hays, Fraenkel, Frankfurter, Lloyd Garrison, Whitney North Seymour, Walter Gellhorn, Edward M. Borchard, and John Finerty. Although all supported the New Deal and knew that the Court had done little to protect civil liberties, they were concerned about maintaining an independent judiciary. Some argued that the plan would not affect civil liberties one way or the other. Gellhorn felt that "there has been a tendency to exaggerate the importance of the courts as safeguards of our liberties." A long debate left everyone "in hopeless conflict," and so the ACLU took no position on Roosevelt's plan.[44]

The lawyers also discussed proposals to limit the power of judicial review. Several favored giving Congress the power to override Court decisions by a two-thirds vote. Fraenkel recommended a constitutional amendment allowing the voters to overrule specific court decisions: "In this way the people could promptly pass upon the action of the Supreme Court and could rewrite the Constitution step by step." Surprisingly, Norman Thomas, who normally had little faith in the Supreme Court, warned that restricting the Court would unleash a flood of anti–civil liberties legislation in the South.[45] Twenty years later, attitudes toward the Court had completely reversed, with conservatives proposing stripping the powers of an activist Court. Many repeated Hugo Black's 1937 complaint about five men running the country—ironically, in response to then-Justice Black's decisions. The ACLU, meanwhile, had become a staunch defender of an independent and activist Court.

In the midst of the debate over the court-packing plan, the Court executed a dramatic about-face, upholding the constitutionality of a state minimum wage law in *West Coast Hotel v. Parrish* and, two weeks later, sustaining the

Wagner Act. Overnight, the constitutional crisis passed. The "switch in time that saved nine" marked the end of an era in American law: The Court withdrew from its strict scrutiny of economic measures and began to protect political and civil liberties.[46]

A Judicial Rationale for Civil Liberties

The *DeJonge* decision on January 4, 1937, was the first indication of the Court's new direction. Communist party organizer Dirk DeJonge had been convicted under the Oregon criminal syndicalism law for organizing a meeting to support a longshoremen's strike. Because none of the speakers had advocated violence, the prosecution was based entirely on DeJonge's Communist party membership. Overturning his conviction, the Court held that "peaceable assembly for lawful discussion cannot be made a crime."[47]

Jointly sponsored by the ACLU and the International Labor Defense (ILD), *DeJonge* marked the first Supreme Court oral argument by Osmond Fraenkel, who had replaced Pollak as the ACLU's premier litigator. Fraenkel became one of the great Supreme Court lawyers of all time, appearing before the Court 103 times and giving twenty-six oral arguments, twelve of which he won.[48]

Three months after *DeJonge* the Court extended even further the First Amendment protection of Communists: A black Communist party organizer named Angelo Herndon was convicted of inciting insurrection, under an old Georgia law. The pamphlets in his possession demanded federal unemployment insurance, social security, emergency relief for farmers, and equal rights for Negroes but contained no references to violent revolution. Conservative New York attorney Whitney North Seymour handled the ACLU's brief, in cooperation with the ILD. The Court overturned Herndon's conviction, holding that "to make membership in the party and solicitation of members for the party a criminal offense, punishable by death . . . is an unwarranted invasion of the right of freedom of speech."[49] Coming so soon after *DeJonge, Herndon* clearly suggested a new attitude on the part of the Court.

The so-called Roosevelt Court (1937 to 1949) created the first significant body of civil liberties law in American history. Roosevelt replaced eight justices, appointing some of the greatest civil libertarians ever to sit on the Court: Hugo Black, William O. Douglas, and Frank Murphy. Ironically, the ACLU voiced some reservations about Black because of his anti–civil libertarian tactics as chair of a Senate investigating committee.[50] Felix Frankfurther, on the other hand, was a great disappointment to the ACLU. Nominated in 1939, he was attacked during his confirmation hearings for his connections to the ACLU. Baldwin held his breath, afraid that this would doom the nomination. Once on the bench, however, Frankfurter became the leading advocate of judicial restraint. Indeed, a distressed Baldwin approached him on Martha's Vineyard and gingerly expressed the hope that he was "still carrying on his traditions with us." Frankfurter quickly replied that he now had "different responsibilities in the Court. I'm not an advocate."[51]

Justices Benjamin Cardozo and Harlan Fiske Stone provided the Court with a coherent rationale for its simultaneous withdrawal from scrutiny of economic regulation and activism regarding political and civil liberties. In *Palko v. Connecticut* (1937), Cardozo argued that the Constitution contained a hierarchy of rights. At the top were those that represented "the very essence of a scheme of ordered liberty" and those principles of justice "so rooted in the traditions and conscience of our people as to be ranked as fundamental." The Fifth Amendment occupied a low position in his view, and the Court ruled against Palko in this case. Freedom of speech and press, however, represented "the indispensible condition, of nearly every other form of freedom." This statement vindicated the ACLU's seventeen-year fight for free speech. After *Palko* the Court embarked on a selective incorporation of parts of the Bill of Rights into the Fourteenth Amendment's due process clause. Debate over constitutional doctrine shifted to the question of which parts met Cardozo's definition of "fundamental."[52]

Justice Stone elaborated further on the Court's role in political and civil liberties. Curiously, it appeared in a footnote in an otherwise obscure 1938 case, *Carolene Products*. In what may be the most famous footnote in Court history, Stone argued that the Court would approach economic regulation with a presumption of constitutionality: "There may be a narrower scope for operation of the presumption of constitutionality [however], when legislation appears on its face to be within a specific prohibition of the Constitution, such as those of the first ten amendments." Stone added, "It is not necessary to consider now" whether the Court would examine "with more exacting judicial scrutiny" laws that restrict the political process, or laws "directed at particular religious, or national, or racial minorities; [or the question of] whether prejudice against discrete and insular minorities may be a special condition" that "may call for a correspondingly more searching judicial inquiry." But it was clear that Stone felt the Court should adopt a more activist role on these civil liberties issues.[53]

The Jehovah's Witnesses and Civil Liberties

It has been unpopular ideas and groups that have brought the cases that have produced landmark Court decisions establishing new protections for civil liberties. For example, the Jehovah's Witnesses, ably represented by their attorney, Hayden Covington, took forty-five cases to the Supreme Court between 1938 and 1955, winning thirty-six. It was a record rivaled only by Thurgood Marshall of the NAACP Legal Defense Fund, who won twenty-nine of thirty-two Court cases. The ACLU filed *amicus* briefs in most of the major cases and, in the area of public education, urged tolerance of their views.[54]

The Court cases were part of a national crisis over the Witnesses, provoked in part by their aggressive and often offensive tactics. In the mid-1930s a new leader, Joseph Franklin ("Judge") Rutherford, reorganized the sect and promulgated a wildly paranoid vision of the world controlled by big business, organized religion, and political parties, with the most vicious attacks directed at the Catholic church. Witnesses descended on communities en masse, in a "locust" tactic, accosting people in "street-corner witnessing" and door-to-door canvassing. Local communities responded by restricting leafleting, canvassing, and the sale of literature. Vigilante mobs attacked the Witnesses with tar and feathers. The result was a national crisis over tolerance for unpopular religious minorities.

In the first important Witness case, *Lovell v. Griffin,* the Court unanimously invalidated an ordinance prohibiting the distribution of "literature of any kind" without a permit, on the grounds that it restricted freedom of the press. With Osmond Fraenkel handling the ACLU *amicus* brief, assisted by future Attorney General Francis Biddle, *Lovell* was a breakthrough in defining streets and parks as a public forum.[55] The Court struck down another set of antilittering ordinances in 1939 (*Schneider v. Irvington*)[56] and invalidated an ordinance restricting door-to-door canvassing in 1943 (*Martin v. Struthers.*)[57] But the Witnesses did not always win. In the 1941 *Cox v. New Hampshire* case the Court upheld "time, place and manner" restrictions on public demonstrations. And in the *Chaplinsky* case it held that certain "fighting words" were not protected by the First Amendment. The decision was a serious setback for free speech and an exception to the Court's evolving position on the First Amendment.[58]

The 1940 *Cantwell* decision established another important precedent. In a typical Witness confrontation, Newton Cantwell had gone to a predominantly Catholic neighborhood and played the virulently anti-Catholic record "Enemies" on a portable record player. The police arrested him for breach of the peace and soliciting without a permit. The Supreme Court reversed the conviction, holding that his proselytizing, however offensive, was protected by the free exercise clause of the First Amendment. Thus the Court incorporated the free exercise clause into the Fourteenth Amendment and created a legal framework for judicial protection of the numerous small and often unpopular religious groups in America.[59]

The Flag Salute Controversy

The most explosive controversy involved the refusal of Witness schoolchildren to participate in compulsory flag salute exercises. The Witnesses believed that saluting the flag violated the biblical command "You shall have no other gods before me . . . you shall not bow down to them or serve them" (Exod. 20:3–5). The confrontation came to a head in the late 1930s as a result of both increased Witness militance and a new wave of school requirements. In an atmosphere of rising international tensions, local authorities sought to instill "Americanism" through compulsory flag salutes and prayer. Art Hays observed that the New York flag salute requirement reminded him of Nazi Germany, "where people are penalized because of failure to 'Heil' Hitler on required occasions."[60]

War had already broken out by the time the flag salute controversy reached the Supreme Court, and this seemed to influence the justices. School authorities in Minersville, Pennsylvania, expelled Lillian and William Gobitis, age twelve and ten respectively, for refusing to salute the flag. The lower federal courts supported their parents' claim that the requirement violated their religious beliefs. The Supreme Court, however, upheld the flag salute requirement in an eight-to-one decision. In a militantly patriotic opinion Felix Frankfurter held that "we live by symbols" and the "flag is the symbol of our national unity, transcending all internal differences, however large, within the framework of government." Frankfurter was apparently influenced by his feelings about the need for national unity in a time of war and his own status as a foreign-born Jew. The lone dissenter was Justice Stone, whose concern for conscientious objectors reached back to World War I. The essence of liberty, he argued, involved "the freedom of the individual from compulsion as to what he shall think and what he shall say, at least where the compulsion is to bear false witness to his religion."[61]

Gobitis unleashed a new wave of violence against the Witnesses. In Litchfield, Connecticut, virtually the entire adult population assaulted a group of sixty Witnesses. An American Legion mob in Louisiana attacked Witnesses gathering for a regional convention and drove them into Texas. A Nebraska mob castrated a Witness. An ACLU report documented violent incidents in over 355 local communities in forty-four states. To stem the violence, Art Hays urged the mayors of eighteen cities to protect Witness conventions scheduled for July. Baldwin urged the Justice Department to prosecute vigilantes. FBI Director J. Edgar Hoover called on the public to "outlaw the vigilante." In a popular magazine article, later reprinted by the ACLU, he declared that "vigilante methods have no place in America today."[62]

Gobitis also produced more flag salute requirements, and conflict with the Witnesses escalated. By 1943 over two thousand of their children had been expelled from schools. Then, in an unprecedented confession of error, Justices Black, Douglas, and Murphy announced that *Gobitis* had been "wrongly decided," thereby setting the stage for a second flag salute case.[63]

West Virginia v. Barnette reached the Court in the midst of World War II. In a dramatic reversal, the Court upheld the rights of the Witnesses, with Justice Robert Jackson's opinion one of the greatest affirmations of the supremacy of individual conscience: "If there in any fixed star in our constitutional constellation," he wrote, "it is that no official, high or petty, can prescribe what shall be orthodox in politics, nationalism or other matter of opinion or force citizens to confess by word or act their faith therein." Undoubtedly aware of the symbolic effect, the Court rendered its decision on June 14—Flag Day.[64] The Court's willingness to protect the right of an extremely unpopular group to refuse to salute the flag in the midst of wartime was the most striking evidence of how much the country had changed since the last great war. The public response to *Barnette* was also revealing: Whereas the *Gobitis* decision had unleashed a wave of vigilante attacks on the Witnesses, the second flag salute decision was greeted with apparent public acceptance. Through its many decisions protecting the rights of the Witnesses, the Court had assumed the role of great teacher, advancing the principle of religious tolerance.

The Battle Against Boss Hague

One of the most significant ACLU victories of the late 1930s occurred in the struggle against the regime of Jersey City Mayor Frank Hague, who ran one of the most autocratic political machines in the country. Conservative on social and economic issues, he decided to attract businesses to Jersey City by suppressing labor unions, particularly the militant new Congress of Industrial Organizations (CIO). His tactics—the arbitrary denial of meeting permits and police harassment of pickets—had once been common practices but, as a result of the Wagner Act, were increasingly anachronisms.[65]

The ACLU's clash with Hague began in 1934 when board member Corliss Lamont was arrested for picketing. Educated at Harvard and the heir to a banking fortune, Lamont remarked that he had "learned more about the American legal system in one day . . . than in one year at Harvard Law School." The Jersey City struggle escalated over the next three years and eventually involved a coalition of the ACLU, the CIO, the Communists, and the Socialists. On the night of April 30, 1938, the police bodily evicted Norman Thomas from the city. A month later Arthur Garfield Hays climbed atop a car and gave an impromptu speech in defiance of Mayor Hague's ban on meetings. Hague stated his views bluntly: "We hear about constitutional rights, free speech and free press," he said. But "everytime I hear these words, I say to myself, 'that man is a Red, that man is a Communist.' " Alan Reitman, later an ACLU staff member, recalled Hague's police padlocking his parents' synagogue after a union meeting was held there.[66]

The battle against Boss Hague brought the ACLU an enormous amount of favorable publicity. With European Fascism on people's minds, Hague appeared as un-American. Norman Thomas wrote a pamphlet entitled *Hague-ism Is Fascism*. Editorial cartoons portrayed him as a homegrown Mussolini, out of step with American values of respect for law. "Mayor Hague's conception of Americanism . . . is essentially un-American," commented the Baton Rouge, Louisiana, *Advocate*. The Providence, Rhode Island, *Bulletin* argued that "Adolph Hitler has used the same logic as Mayor Hague." As Bryan and the fundamentalists had done in the 1920s, Hague served as a foil for the broader acceptance of civil liberties values.[67]

With Morris Ernst directing the legal strategy, the CIO launched another Jersey City campaign in late 1937. Hague banned all CIO leaflets and turned down meeting requests by the ACLU and the Socialist party. Instead of provoking arrests, Ernst decided to seek an immediate injunction against Hague's systematic denial of First Amendment rights. The strategy worked. In late 1938 District Court Judge William Clark ordered the city to stop evicting the union organizers from the city, end illegal searches and seizures, and cease interfering with meetings and the distribution of literature. The CIO and the

ACLU, he ruled, were lawful organizations, and there was no evidence that their meetings would produce a breach of the peace.[68]

The Supreme Court upheld the injunction in *Hague v. CIO* and defined streets and parks as a "public forum" protected by the First Amendment. Justice Owen Roberts wrote that "wherever the title of streets and parks may rest, they have immemorially been held in trust for the use of the public and, time out of mind, have been used for purposes of assembly, communicating thoughts between citizens, and discussing public questions." In fact, public areas had never been "held in trust" for discussions of public issues. Repression, by the very techniques used by Mayor Hague, was the grand American tradition. Free public discussion of ideas, no matter what the subject, was a new and hard-won right.[69]

A year later the Court further bolstered the rights of labor, holding in *Thornhill* that the First Amendment protected picketing as a form of speech. (Earlier it had refused to hear an ACLU challenge to a ban on picketing foreign embassies in Washington.) In a 1941 ACLU case, the Court struck down a California law prohibiting indigent persons from entering the state, with the majority finding the law to be an infringement on interstate commerce.[70]

The Court, the ACLU, and the Public-Interest Bar

The Supreme Court's growing support for civil liberties had a profound effect on the ACLU, the bar, and American politics. Roger Baldwin quickly shed his skepticism of the courts and strengthened the ACLU's litigation program. A permanent staff counsel was hired in 1941, and Whitney North Seymour organized the first ACLU lawyers' panel in 1942 to help with the increased volume of cases. Additional help came from Walter Gellhorn, who devoted his Columbia law school clinical practice course to civil liberties and civil rights cases referred by the ACLU, the NAACP, and the American Jewish Congress. Some ACLU leaders, having tasted a few victories in the Supreme Court, now wanted it all. Raymond Wise drafted a constitutional amendment explicitly incorporating into the Fourteenth Amendment all of the provisions of the Bill of Rights. Representative Emmanuel Celler introduced a bill to that effect in the House. Although it did not receive serious attention, it was indicative of the soaring expectations of carrying the Roosevelt Court's protection of civil liberties to its logical conclusion.[71]

Other organizations responded to the Court's initiatives. The NAACP established its Legal Defense Fund in 1938 and stepped up its legal assault on segregation. The American Bar Association (ABA) established its Committee on the Bill of Rights in 1938. And in 1945 the American Jewish Congress created its Commission on Law and Social Action, with several full-time lawyers and an ambitious program of social change through litigation. In short, the Court stimulated the growth of the public interest bar.[72]

Constitutional litigation became a new force in American politics. Minority groups now had an important avenue for redress and for influencing public policy. In the process, the *amicus* brief acquired a new and important role. Historically an impartial voice (literally a "friend of the court"), it now became an instrument of advocacy.[73]

This, in turn, stimulated the process of shaping social policy questions in terms of constitutional law. A broad range of social problems—the place of religion in American life, civil rights, the conduct of criminal justice agencies—were eventually defined in constitutional terms. The Bill of Rights became a set of secular principles for governing American society. As the Court assumed a larger role in the following decades, the ACLU's ability to shape public policy increased along with it.

Public Opinion and Civil Liberties, 1937–1940

The Court did not act in a social and political vacuum; a number of forces encouraged support for civil liberties principles in the late 1930s. The New Deal coalition represented acceptance of the pluralism of American life. Working people, Catholic, and Jews were no longer outcasts from the American mainstream. Toleration of diversity was becoming part of the unofficial American creed. The Supreme Court functioned as a great teacher, with *DeJonge, Hague, Cantwell,* and *Barnette* affirming the idea of tolerance for Communists, labor unions, and fringe religious groups. A survey of civil liberties in the South, long the great backwater, found that even there "indisputable progress" had been made.[74]

Finally, American attitudes toward civil liberties were influenced by international events. In the final paragraphs of his *Hague* opinion, District Court Judge William Clark contrasted American constitutionalism with Soviet and Nazi totalitarianism. "Ultimately," he wrote, "Russia will not be judged by how much bread it has given its people . . . but by how much freedom, self-respect, equality, truth and human kindness it has brought into the world."[75] The special quality of America was its capacity to guarantee liberty to all, including even the most unpopular groups.

Hague coincided with the one hundred fiftieth anniversary of the Bill of Rights. From the president on down, national leaders hailed the principles of the Bill of Rights, particularly tolerance for minorities, as the essence of American democracy. Several important professional organizations sought to embody these principles in concrete action: When the ABA created its Committee on the Bill of Rights, it modeled it on the ACLU. ABA leaders who had expressed no previous concern for civil liberties were now motivated by fear and opportunism. The new National Lawyers Guild posed a threat to the ABA's leadership of the bar. Grenville Clark, a prominent New York corporation attorney, warned that "the time has come for the conservative elements of the United States to join the fight for the defense of civil liberties." The struggle for justice had been "allowed to drift very largely into the hands of elements of the Left." A leader of the Junior Bar, Lewis Powell, also warned that "the existing agencies defending civil liberties are considerably left of center." According to Clark, "true conservatism" meant recognizing the "inviolability" of "fundamental personal rights."[76] Roosevelt's court-packing plan also alarmed conservatives. ABA leader William J. Donovan (later the founder of the Office of Strategic Services, forerunner of the Central Intelligence Agency) lectured his fellow members on the importance of an independent judiciary. The Supreme Court had always "acted in defense of the oppressed citizen." At this point, in early 1937, Donovan could cite only a handful of Court cases. Nonetheless, his message was clear: Out of self-interest, conservatives should take up the defense of civil liberties.[77]

Clark contacted the ACLU and expressed a "keen" interest in formal "contact and consultation." He confessed to Art Hays: "You are a veteran in this subject and I am a comparative newcomer and amateur." Baldwin welcomed the ABA to the struggle and even suggested that the ACLU might "step aside" if Clark's committee wanted to assume responsibility for a case.[78] The ABA's committee filed an *amicus* brief in *Hague* and joined in several of the Jehovah's Witnesses cases. A Carnegie Corporation grant funded the *Bill of Rights Review,* which in its short existence was an important forum for civil liberties.[79] Even more important was the committee's network of local chapters in twenty-three states and fifty-three cities which gave many lawyers their first taste of civil rights and civil liberties litigation.[80]

The American Library Association, meanwhile, adopted the Library Bill of Rights in 1939. Originating the year before with the Des Moines, Iowa, Public Library, this statement of professional principles opposed all forms of censorship and called on libraries to select books without reference to "the race or nationality, or the political or religious views of the writers." The library itself should be a public forum, available to all groups "as an institution to educate for democratic living." The opening reference to "growing intolerance, suppression of free speech, and censorship, affecting the rights of minorities and individuals" in other countries was another indication of the impact of foreign events on American thinking.[81]

In higher education the Association of American Universities (AAU) and the American Association of University Professors (AAUP), representing administrators and faculty, respectively, reached an agreement on academic freedom and tenure. After many years of negotiation, the AAU finally accepted the AAUP's statement in 1939. Formally ratified the following year, the AAUP's "1940 Statement" remains the basic charter of academic freedom in higher education.[82]

The Justice Department also joined the fight for individual rights, at long last. In February 1939 Attorney General Frank Murphy created the Civil Liberties Unit, forerunner of the present Civil Rights Division. This was the first affirmative effort by the Justice Department to protect the rights of individual citizens. Baldwin referred civil rights complaints to the new unit, but it did little more than investigate. Nonetheless it represented an important first step in federal enforcement of civil rights.[83]

The End of an Era

The growth of civil liberties in the late 1930s marked the end of an era in American history. The ACLU could look back with justifiable pride on an impressive achievement. Principles that it had championed virtually alone for twenty years were now the law of the land and part of the American credo. With their characteristic lack of a sense of history, however, most Americans had little appreciation for what a long and bitter struggle it had been. Nothing better illustrated this than a 1944 address, "The Spirit of Liberty," by Judge Learned Hand. Speaking on "I Am an American Day" at the height of World War II, Hand declared that "liberty lies in the hearts of men and women; when it dies there, no constitution, no law, no court can save it. . . . While it lies there it needs no constitution, no law, no court to save it." But the increasingly conservative Hand had misread recent history: Commitment to liberty was not an inborn virtue but the product of a long struggle. Constitutions, courts, and laws did play a critical role in promoting the principles of liberty and shaping the attitudes and behavior of millions of Americans. Justice Louis Brandeis was closer to the mark when he wrote that the law was a "great teacher." Nor did Hand appreciate the role of the ACLU—making, in an earlier 1930 version of his speech, a sneering reference to "civil liberties unions." Yet, the triumph of civil liberties principles was to a great extent the result of the ACLU's tireless efforts to educate the public, bring the cases before the courts, and adhere to the core principle that the Bill of Rights protected all Americans.[84]

Six

International Currents:
Origins of the Cold War

The fate of American civil liberties in the 1930s was profoundly affected by totalitarianism, at home and abroad. The effect was contradictory. The rise of Hitler and Stalin gave Americans a new appreciation for the unique virtues of constitutional democracy. At the same time, fear of Communism imposed new restrictions on political freedom. Even the ACLU was affected by the anti-Communist hysteria and, in 1940, momentarily abandoned its own principles and imposed a political test on its own leaders.

Free Speech for Nazis?

The rise of domestic Fascist groups posed the most serious test yet of the ACLU's commitment to free speech. After Hitler's 1933 triumph, a host of groups sprang up: Silver Shirts, White Shirts, Khaki Shirts, the White Legion, the Order of '76, and the Friends of New Germany. Most were tiny groups led by eccentrics, but the German-American Bund staged pro-Nazi demonstrations in New York, New Jersey, Cleveland, and Chicago that drew thousands of people. In the summer of 1937 over eighteen thousand attended the Bund's Camp Nordland in New Jersey, marching in Nazi uniforms, saluting the Nazi flag and singing "Deutschland über Alles."[1]

Anxious Americans asked themselves whether it could happen here. Hitler's victory demonstrated how vulnerable democratic governments were to disciplined, paramilitary groups, and many liberals and leftists argued that democracies had a right of self-preservation and urged the suppression of Fascist groups. ACLU leaders Baldwin, Thomas, and Hays were among the relatively few Americans to grasp the horror of Nazism in 1933 and 1934. Baldwin saw the Nazis firsthand on his 1927 European trip. Hays, in one of the more remarkable chapters of an already fabulous life, helped represent Georgi Dimitrov, one of the defendants in the 1933 Reichstag fire trial.[2] But the vast majority of Americans, isolationist and anti-Semitic, remained indifferent. Walter Lippmann, dean of American political columnists, spoke for them when he wrote that Jews were often responsible for their own problems. In another column in 1933 he praised Hitler as "the authentic voice of a genuinely civilized people."[3]

The internationalist-minded Baldwin tried to involve the ACLU in anti-Nazi efforts but was rebuffed by the board. With evident regret, ACLU secretary Lucille Milner informed the National Committee to Aid Victims of German Fascism that "the work of the Civil Liberties Union is confined entirely to the United States."[4]

A number of ACLU members and friends urged the suppression of domestic Fascists. Margaret DeSilver, widow of the ACLU cofounder and a major financial contributor, opposed allowing Nazis "the liberty to destroy liberty."[5] Many Jewish leaders criticized the ACLU's defense of Nazi groups. The Communists reiterated their long-standing opposition to free speech for Fascists. In 1934 ACLU staff counsel A. L. Wirin urged the temporary House Un-American Activities Committee to investigate Fascist groups: "May we suggest an examination of such groups as the Silver Shirts, the White Shirts, the White Legion, the Gray Shirts." His suggestion was apparently unauthorized, but it revealed the power of anti-Fascist sentiment even within the ACLU.[6]

In the face of these pressures, the ACLU underwent an agonizing soul-searching. Baldwin confessed that "our Board has been considerably exercised as to what to do." A special committee examined the issue and produced a statement entitled *Shall We Defend Free Speech for Nazis in America?* With periodic modification, this 1934 document remained the ACLU's basic policy on the issue of the rights of totalitarian groups.[7] *Shall We Defend* acknowledged that "some of our members have sharply criticized the Union for championing the right of German-American Nazis to hold meetings and to conduct their propaganda." It replied that abridging their rights was wrong in principle and dangerous in practice. If the ACLU "condoned the denial of rights to Nazi propagandists, in what position would it be to champion the rights of others?" Proposed restrictions were vague and open to abuse. The category of "political enemies" was extremely elastic and had always been used to suppress left-wing movements. Nor was there a consensus on what "race or religious hatred" encompassed. It could include atheist attacks on established religion or even Jewish attacks on pro-German groups. Finally, suppression only created martyrs and brought Fascist groups "hundreds of sympathizers." Rather, the best response to Nazi propaganda was open discussion, protest, and counterpropaganda—in short, more, not less, speech.[8]

Baldwin commissioned two studies of Fascist movements. Travis Hoke's exposé of extremist groups, *Shirts!*, concluded that "none of the movements can yet be regarded as serious in size or significance." Their "propaganda can best be combatted in the open, not by suppressing it into underground conspiracies."[9] Political scientist Karl Loewenstein, meanwhile, produced a scholarly study of European anti-Fascist laws. These included prohibitions on antidemocratic propaganda, offensive racial and religious speech, and parades by paramilitary groups. A 1936 French law allowed the president to dissolve "fighting groups and private militias." Under the 1936 Public Order Act, British police could control the routes of political parades or ban them altogether. But the ACLU rejected these measures, contending that they were particularly "dangerous in the hands of administrative officials who may apply them not only to Fascists but to labor and progressive groups as well." Lucille Milner reported in *The Nation* that British authorities had used the Public Order Act to restrict "the legitimate activities of democratic and left-wing organizations." Loewenstein supported restrictions on the grounds that the current world crisis required a "militant democracy." Just as it was necessary to subordinate "free [economic] competition to state interventionism," so "preventive methods in government" were necessary to combat totalitarian forces.[10]

The ACLU endorsed a few limited restrictions on paramilitary groups, reiterating its view that masked parades could be banned, and endorsed police routing of provocative parades into "safe districts, as in the case of Klan demonstrations in Negro districts." Baldwin drafted a bill to outlaw military drills and the possession of firearms by "political groups" and got his old nemesis. Representative Hamilton Fish, to introduce it. But the bill did not define "political groups," and Baldwin was flirting with a restriction on freedom of assembly that diverged from ACLU policy.[11]

The most popular anti-Fascist measure was the "race hate" or "group libel" law. A 1935 New Jersey law prohibited speech "advocating hatred, abuse, violence, or hostility against any group or groups of persons by reason of race, color, religion, or manner of worship." Group libel laws were another consequence of the New Deal political realignment. Catholics and Jews, the main targets of religious bigotry, now commanded sufficient political power to enact such laws.[12] The ACLU's worst fears were confirmed when the first person arrested under the New Jersey law was a Jehovah's Witness accused of distributing anti-Catholic and anti-Jewish leaflets. Newark attorney Abraham Isserman took the case for ACLU, and the charges were later dropped.[13] The ACLU then successfully lobbied against a similar New York law in 1937, joining the American Jewish Congress in arguing that "intolerance thrives in suppression." A test case in New Jersey was introduced when ten Bund leaders were indicted for possession of anti-Semitic literature. One of the defendants had shouted that "the real Fifth Column is Roosevelt and his Jewish bosses." The New Jersey Supreme Court declared the law unconstitutional in late 1941 under both the First Amendment and the New Jersey Constitution, citing the "excellent brief of the amicus curiae" filed by the ACLU's Art Hays.[14]

Over the years, the defense of Nazis became one of the touchstones of the ACLU's commitment to defend free speech for everyone—and the source of repeated controversies. It also distinguished the ACLU from its English counterpart, the National Council for Civil Liberties (NCCL). Organized in 1934 (a similar organization had existed briefly during World War I), the NCCL was always closely allied with the British Labour party and, under left-wing influence, countenanced restrictions on extreme right-wing political groups. Conversely, ACLU leaders prided themselves on their nonpartisan stand and willingness to defend even the hated Nazis.[15]

The ACLU and the Popular Front

The ACLU's relationship with the Communist party became particularly tangled in the 1930s. The economic collapse pushed Roger Baldwin further to the left, and his rhetoric became more explicitly Marxist. The Communists dropped their revolutionary rhetoric in 1935 and began organizing the Popular Front, a coalition with liberals. They won broad support by aggressively championing civil rights and leading the anit-Fascist efforts in the Spanish Civil War.[16]

An instinctive coalition builder, Roger Baldwin threw himself into the Popular Front, organizing a seemingly endless list of groups: the American League for Peace and Democracy, the American Committee for the Protection of the Foreign Born, the North American Committee to Aid Spanish Democracy, the American Student Union, the National Committee to Aid Striking Miners, and numerous legal defense committees. Relations between the ACLU and the Communists had ruptured completely in 1930 when five Communists facing criminal charges from the Gastonia, North Carolina, textile strike jumped bail and fled to the Soviet Union. The ACLU Bail Fund lost $28,500, and the board ruled that henceforth it would cooperate with the Communists only in special circumstances.[17] In 1935, the combination of the party's new moderate policy and the specter of international Fascism produced a reconciliation. Like many other liberals, Baldwin took the Communists at face value. He pressed party attorney Joseph Brodsky for a suit to get a "judicial determination" of the party's disavowal of violent revolution. Brodsky refused, probably because he knew that the party's current policy was only a tactical maneuver.[18]

The ACLU benefited enormously from the Popular Front. It cooperated with Communists in the Scottsboro Defense Committee after 1935 and in the important *DeJonge* and *Herndon* cases. The ACLU also helped subsidize the International Juridical Association's *Bulletin,* edited by Carol Weiss King, which was an important forum for civil liberties legal strategy.[19] The Popular Front's vision of a mass civil rights–civil liberties movement inspired Baldwin to expand the network of ACLU affiliates. Between 1935 and 1939, ACLU affiliates appeared in St. Louis, San Francisco, Seattle, Cleveland, Philadelphia, and even in Iowa, Indiana, and Texas, where the ACLU had never before had a presence. By 1939 five affiliates had full-time paid staffs.[20]

The affiliates were especially valuable, as they could fight local censorship or police misconduct far more effectively than Baldwin could from New York. For example, the Chicago Civil Liberties Committee waged a running battle with the police film censorship board and was the first predominately white organization to push for a state antidiscrimination law. The New York and

Chicago committees fought proposals for released time for religious instruction of public school students. By 1941 the St. Louis Civil Liberties Committee had subcommittees on academic freedom, freedom of the press, labor, federal legislation, and conscientious objectors. The fledgling Iowa Civil Liberties Union conceded that it had "little influence" on anti-Communist legislation, but the mere presence of a state civil liberties voice was a significant advance for the ACLU. By 1938, Baldwin had to publish a supplemental *Annual Report* to cover the affiliates' activities.[21]

The ACLU's ties with the Popular Front brought new charges that the ACLU was a Communist "front." The fact that Harry Ward chaired both the ACLU and the American League for Peace and Democracy, the largest Popular Front group, caused much misunderstanding. Baldwin then created his own problems with some careless rhetoric. In a 1934 *Soviet Russia Today* article, he declared that "when that power of the working class is once achieved [as in Russia] I am for maintaining it by any means whatever." This seemed to endorse the suppression of civil liberties after the revolution. In his thirtieth-anniversary Harvard yearbook, he wrote, "I seek social ownership of property, the abolition of the propertied class and sole control by those who produce wealth. Communism is the goal." Conservatives seized on these statements as evidence of Baldwin's Communist views. Both statements were atypical (he made no others like them) and were apparently a product of the desperate conditions of 1934—the depression and the rise of Hitler. But they were on the public record, and for decades right-wing critics hounded him over them.[22]

If anything, the ACLU influenced the Communists in the American League for Peace and Democracy (ALPD) rather than vice versa. The ALPD did not advocate suppressing domestic Fascists; Communist ALPD members evidently acquiesced on this issue in order to placate Baldwin, Ward, and the other ACLU members who were crucial to the league's appeal to liberals.[23]

One 1934 incident sowed the seeds of anti-Communism in the ACLU: Communists disrupted a Socialist party rally at Madison Square Garden called to protest the Nazi coup in Vienna. The Socialists tried to evict them and in the process assaulted *Daily Worker* editor Clarence Hathaway. The incident threatened to destroy any chance of an anti-Nazi coalition. Baldwin tried to heal the breach by appointing a special ACLU Commission of Inquiry. Its report criticized both sides: "The immediate responsibility for breaking up the meeting rests . . . squarely upon the Communist Party," whereas the Socialists were guilty of "disgraceful and wholly unnecessary" conduct. Norman Thomas was outraged and began a campaign to purge Communists from the ACLU. He told Corliss Lamont that some people were "more interested in Communism than in Civil Liberties." John Haynes Holmes first broached the idea of barring Communists from ACLU leadership. Baldwin talked him out of it by assuring him that there currently were no Communists on the board or the national committee. But Holmes was only temporarily placated, and he and Thomas later revived their anti-Communist campaign.[24]

The Cold War Begins

The popularity of the American Communist party sparked a new anti-Communist movement. Fear of foreign radicalism was nothing new, but it now acquired a single-minded focus on the Communist party. What later was called the cold war began in the late 1930s and produced the House Un-American Activities Committee, a federal peacetime sedition law, loyalty oaths for teachers, and renewed FBI spying. Freedom of political expression suffered its worst setback since World War I.

Origins of HUAC

After a lapse of ten years, congressional investigations of political groups returned in 1930. The House created a Special Committee to Investigate Communist Activities, chaired by Hamilton Fish, which leveled a broad indictment of the Communist party, radical labor leaders, and the ACLU. Fish claimed the ACLU was "closely affiliated with the Communist movement in the United States, and fully 90 per cent of its efforts are on behalf of communists." Roger Baldwin testified voluntarily and explained that Communists were "the chief victims of attack." In a sharp exchange with Fish, Baldwin argued that the First Amendment protected the advocacy of violence in general but not "the overt act, or attempted act." Fish pressed him further. Was it all right to advocate murder? Yes, replied Baldwin, if it were merely advocacy of an idea. What about assassination? Baldwin cited the law of Hyde Park, London, according to which it was legal to advocate the assassination of kings, but not "the assassination of the king; you may not advocate the direct incitement or commit the specific act." The exchange received considerable publicity and forced the ACLU to issue its clearest statement to date on the outer limits of free speech.[25]

After the Fish Committee lapsed, the House created a second temporary committee in 1935 to investigate alleged incitement to disaffection in the military. The ACLU protested the MacCormack Committee's mandate, expressing "unqualified opposition" to any federal laws "to suppress any kind of propaganda." There was "no emergency" to justify any of the existing proposals. Liberal Representative Samuel Dickstein campaigned tirelessly for a permanent committee to investigate Fascist and anti-Semitic groups. State legislative committees, meanwhile, investigated alleged subversion in Illinois, Wisconsin, and Massachusetts. Finally, in 1938, the House created a Special Committee on Un-American Activities (HUAC).[26]

Known as the Dies Committee, after its chair, Martin Dies, HUAC raised the fear of Communism to a fever pitch. Its sensational public hearings were a platform for wild allegations of Communist influence, particularly in the Congress of Industrial Organizations (CIO) and New Deal agencies. Witnesses indulged in personal or political vendettas. American Federation of Labor (AFL) official John P. Frey charged Communist influence in the rival

CIO. A disgruntled Native American accused the ACLU of running the Bureau of Indian Affairs. Walter Steele of the American Coalition Committee on National Security named the ACLU, the Campfire Girls, and hundreds of other groups as Communist fronts. Ex-Communists J. B. Matthews, Louis Budenz, Benjamin Gitlow—all former ACLU clients or employees—provided inside accounts of Communist machinations and the party's subservience to Moscow.[27]

The initial 1938–1939 hearings established the methods that HUAC used throughout its thirty-eight-year history. Persons named as Communists could not cross-examine their accusers or rebut the charges. Naming involved indiscriminate guilt by association. That is, being associated with Communists in a lawful activity—a legal defense committee, for example—was the same as being an avowed Communist. The hearings had a profound effect on public opinion, helping defeat several prominent liberals in the 1938 elections, including Michigan Governor Frank Murphy. Roosevelt accused the committee of anti-Democratic bias, but to no avail. Witnesses mentioned the ACLU six different times in the initial round of hearings, and the committee's January 1939 report concluded equivocally that it could not "definitely state whether or not" the ACLU was "a Communist organization." The ACLU's image was severely damaged. One survey found that its approval rating had dropped from 34 percent to 30 percent, and its disapproval rating had risen dramatically, from 5 percent to 38 percent. Alarmed ACLU leaders failed to notice that a 30 percent approval rating would have been unimaginable only a few years earlier. The survey was clear evidence of the ACLU's new stature.[28]

The ACLU mounted a threefold response to the Dies Committee: lobbying for its abolition, advocating reform of its procedures, and attempting to clear the ACLU's name. As it had been one of the principal targets of the old Lusk Committee, the ACLU had always opposed legislative investigations of political activities on the grounds that they violated freedom of speech and association. After the 1938 hearings, however, HUAC was politically untouchable, and the ACLU did not press abolition vigorously.[29]

The Dies Committee's tactics forced the ACLU to examine the First Amendment and due process questions involved in legislative investigations. Were all inquiries into political beliefs and associations unconstitutional? Could a witness refuse to testify on First Amendment grounds? Could witnesses invoke the Fifth Amendment? Baldwin asked board member Abraham Isserman to prepare a memorandum on these questions. Isserman summarized the small body of case law and recommended that witnesses consult an attorney before testifying. The memo was perhaps the first systematic discussion of the rights of witnesses before legislative committees. Unfortunately, it became entangled in ACLU factionalism. Isserman was a leader of the left-wing group (he was actually a secret Communist party member, along with Mary Van Kleeck and Robert Dunn), and Baldwin never distributed the memo. "What have you done with my memorandum?" Isserman complained at one point. He eventually quit the ACLU, and the National Federation for Constitutional Liberties (NFCL), a new Communist party–affiliated group, published his memo.[30]

HUAC caught the ACLU and most liberals off guard. In the 1930s, legislative investigations had become a major instrument for advancing liberal social policies. For example, the Senate Banking and Currency Committee's sensational investigation of the stock market in 1933 produced the Securities Act, the Securities Exchange Act, and the Public Utility Holding Company Act. Alabama Senator Hugo Black investigated lobbying by the utilities industries, and Burton K. Wheeler examined railroad financing. The Nye Committee investigated the influence of munitions manufacturers on the United States' entry into World War I. The La Follette Committee's investigation of the violations of labor's rights was, in fact, one of the ACLU's great successes. Baldwin's lobbying helped create the committee, and he fed it investigative leads from the ACLU files.[31] Enthusiastic about the goals, few liberals questioned the methods. Felix Frankfurter spoke for them in 1924 when he advised the courts to keep "hands off the investigations." The fact-finding powers of legislatures should not be constrained by "artificial and technical limitations." Hugo Black, under fire for some questionable tactics by his committee, quoted Woodrow Wilson: "If there is nothing to conceal, then why conceal it?" It was "a fair presumption that secrecy meant impropriety."[32]

The liberal-dominated committees of the 1930s perfected the techniques later used by HUAC: exposure for the sake of exposure, scapegoating, and conspiracy mongering. To wit: The Banking Committee in effect blamed the Morgan banking interests for the stock market crash, and the Nye Committee blamed World War I on the munitions makers. The Banking Committee's primary target was Thomas W. Lamont, and twenty years later Wisconsin Senator Joseph McCarthy used the same techniques against Lamont's son Corliss, a friend of the Soviet Union (although not a Communist) and an ACLU board member.

The ACLU protested the more outrageous abuses: the subpoenas of telegraph traffic issued by Hugo Black's committee, Senator Sherman Minton's request for income tax returns, Senator Joseph O'Mahoney's subpoena of all the Jones and Laughlin Steel Company's correspondence, and the La Follette Committee's request for income tax records. These were ad hoc responses, however, and the ACLU remained unprepared for HUAC's sweeping assault on political beliefs and associations.[33]

The HUAC hearings reached a peak of sensationalism after the August 1939 Nazi–Soviet Pact, with Communist party leader Earl Browder belligerently claiming that the party used other groups as "transmission belts" for Communist ideas—specifically mentioning the ACLU. The ACLU demanded an apology, but the damage had been done. Dies had earlier accused the ACLU of being Communist influenced, and he reiterated the attack in October. The committee then called Harry Ward, whose dual role as chair of both the ACLU and the American League for Peace and Democracy threw an even larger shadow over the ACLU.[34]

HUAC investigators, meanwhile, staged surprise raids on left-wing groups in Chicago, Philadelphia, and Washington, D.C. The ACLU condemned the raids as "lawless" and "without precedent," but Dies, undeterred, first published the membership list of the ALPD's Washington, D.C., chapter, exposing them to reprisals, and then demanded the Communist party's membership list. Party leaders refused and were cited for contempt. The ACLU, hoping for a court test of HUAC's powers, offered to represent them, but the party gave the case to another group.[35] In February 1940 the Justice Department arrested eleven Abraham Lincoln Brigade supporters in a midnight raid in Detroit. Attorney General Frank Murphy, normally a staunch civil libertarian, apparently approved the arrests to ensure his appointment to the Supreme Court. His successor, Robert Jackson, dismissed the indictments, but the raid stood as testimony to the power of anti-Communist hysteria in 1940.[36]

A Peacetime Sedition Law: The Smith Act

The hysteria whipped up by HUAC assured passage of the first peacetime sedition law in American history. Dozens of bills flooded Congress in early 1939. The ACLU was one of only three organizations (along with the CIO and the AFL) to testify in opposition at the House hearings in April. Osmond Fraenkel recalled the violations of free speech under the 1798 Sedition Act and during World War I. The pending bill, he warned, would "encourage informers, . . . persecution, . . . [and] hysteria." Curiously, neither the Communists nor any other left-wing political parties testified. At the Senate hearings in May 1940 ACLU representative John Finerty, while stressing his own anti-Communist credentials, argued that the bill was unconstitutional under the Supreme Court's clear and present danger test. But the stunning German conquest of the Netherlands, Belgium, and France had inflamed public fears about national security, and Congress overwhelmingly passed the Smith Act, officially the Alien Registration Act, on June 28.[37]

The key provision of the Smith Act was Section 2(a), which made it illegal to "advocate, abet, advise, or teach the duty, necessity, desirability, or propriety of overthrowing or destroying any government in the United States by force or violence." Other provisions outlawed membership in any organization advocating the overthrow of the government or publishing or distributing literature advocating its overthrow. Baldwin warned that the Smith Act was "the most sweeping assault on civil liberty by federal law in years." Given the Supreme Court's decisions in *DeJonge* and *Herndon,* there was some reason to think it might find the Smith Act unconstitutional. For the moment, however, the Justice Department sought no indictments.[38]

Purging the Ballot

In the most direct attack on the Communist party, ten states barred their candidates from the ballot in 1940. The movement to purge the electoral process began in 1932 when eleven states barred either the Communist or Socialist parties or both. These initial attacks relied primarily on complex filing requirements that inhibited small parties. The 1940 assault on the Communist party, however, was a national, though uncoordinated, movement. Pennsylvania election officials rejected the Communist party candidates' petitions on the grounds that signatures were obtained by fraud, and then they indicted thirty-two petition circulators on conspiracy and perjury charges. The Washington secretary of state refused to accept the party's petitions altogether. A California law specifically banned the Communists from the ballot. In the charged atmosphere of 1940, officials held that Communists were inherently deceitful.[39]

Rising to the Communists' defense, the ACLU called on Attorney General Robert Jackson to investigate the "general conspiracy to interfere with the right of minority parties on the ballot."[40] It eventually assisted the party in court challenges in ten states. Fraenkel lost a New York case, but Hays, after losing in Pennsylvania and Illinois, had the California law declared unconstitutional in 1942. The ACLU participated in Communist party cases in seven states in 1942, successfully getting them on the ballot in California and New York but losing in Illinois, Ohio, Pennsylvania, Indiana, and Wisconsin.[41]

In another move reminiscent of World War I, the Washington legislature refused to seat Senator Lemus Westman because he allegedly was a Communist. Baldwin fired off a protest, but the ACLU leader in Seattle, State Senator Mary Farquharson, voted to bar Westman. Baldwin demanded an explanation. Farquharson replied that Westman had lied about his party membership. "I have never felt that 'free speech' included unlimited lying," she told Baldwin. Nonetheless, a year later Farquharson organized the ACLU's defense of Gordon Hirabayashi's challenge to the internment of Japanese-Americans. Her contradictory stand on two fundamental civil liberties issues indicated the impact of anti-Communist fever even within the ACLU.[42]

Cleansing the Academy

Anti-Communists stepped up their efforts to purge Communists from schools and colleges, producing between 1931 and 1936 special loyalty oaths for teachers in twenty-one states and the District of Columbia. The initial oaths were affirmative, involving a pledge to obey the laws and uphold the Constitution that was little different from the oaths required of most public officials. But the ACLU opposed them on the grounds that they singled out teachers as an occupational group and tended to chill the free discussion of political ideas. ACLU lobbying helped persuade Governor Herbert H. Lehman to veto a New York teachers' oath in 1934, but a year later he signed a similar bill into law. Gradually, the affirmative oaths were replaced with the far more chilling disclaimer oaths requiring teachers to swear they were not members of any group advocating the violent overthrow of the government. Although primarily directed at Communists, they were used against all left-wing groups. The ACLU was uncertain about bringing constitutional tests of the teachers' oaths, as some ACLU leaders feared that the courts would uphold them on the grounds that school authorities had a right to set qualifications for teachers.[43]

The assault on academic freedom reached its height in New York. In 1940 when City College offered a position to English philosopher Bertrand Russell,

Protestant and Catholic clergy led a storm of protest over his well-known atheism and unconventional views on sex and marriage. The Catholic diocese denounced him as the "professor of paganism," while a legislative resolution attacked him as "an advocate of barnyard morality." Mrs. Jean Kay of Brooklyn filed a taxpayer's suit asking the court to void the appointment on the grounds that public funds should not be used to support atheism. Mayor Fiorello La Guardia, meanwhile, quietly deleted the position from the City College budget. With the ACLU coordinating the publicity, the American Association of University Professors (AAUP) and many prominent educators rose to Russell's defense. Judge John McGeehan ruled the appointment "an insult to the people of the City of New York" and "in direct violation of the public health, safety, and the morals of the people." Russell was not a party to the suit, but he did retain the ACLU's Osmond Fraenkel to file a brief on his behalf in the appeal. The appellate court refused to hear the case.[44]

An aroused legislature began a broader inquiry into the "extent to which, if any, subversive activities have been permitted to be carried out in the schools and colleges" in New York City. The Rapp–Coudert investigation used all the techniques of the Dies Committee: the parade of ex-Communist witnesses, indiscriminate naming of names, guilt by association, exposure for the sake of exposure, and demands for membership lists. State Senator Frederick Coudert stated that Communist teachers should be "shot like dogs," and Brooklyn College President Harry D. Gideonse promised they would be "cleaned out." Teachers named as Communists faced an impossible legal situation. The Board of Higher Education announced it would fire anyone who was a member of a "Communist, Fascist or Nazi group" or who refused to cooperate with a legislative investigation. Party members faced the alternative of automatic dismissal if they admitted their membership or perjury if they denied it. In the end, the Board of Education's internal investigation produced twenty dismissals and eleven resignations.[45]

While many liberals rationalized the investigation and Communists engaged in fatally self-destructive tactics, the ACLU remained divided. Its two Academic Freedom Committees—one national and one local—included a galaxy of distinguished scholars: Robert S. Lynd, Sidney Hook, Karl Llewellyn, Walter Gellhorn, Wesley C. Mitchell, and Reinhold Niebuhr. Disillusioned ex-Communists, Hook and Niebuhr were rapidly moving to the right and contended that Communists were unfit to teach. Committee member James O'Neill produced a "credo" regarding academic freedom, arguing that "no Communist can or does believe in academic freedom or civil liberties" and, therefore, that "no Communist or 'fellow-traveller' " could "possibly be a good teacher or a good influence," as they were enslaved to a totalitarian dogma and subservient to a foreign power.[46] The majority of the ACLU Academic Freedom Committee disagreed and reaffirmed the ACLU's "established policy that no teachers should be dismissed for their opinions or associations." The ACLU was still ambivalent about legislative investigations, however, and informed Senator Coudert that it was "not opposed to your inquiry" but objected only to certain procedures.[47]

The ACLU opposed the Board of Education's policy of automatically firing anyone who was a member of a totalitarian group, but it made one significant concession: It held that membership in a political group could be taken into account if the teacher were accused of "disruptive activities as a disciplined unit within the educational institution."[48] Osmond Fraenkel handled several cases for the New York Civil Liberties Committee: a challenge to the subpoena of Teachers Union records, a challenge to a ban on Communist party meetings at Public School 11, and an *amicus* brief for six Brooklyn College teachers fired on the basis of accusations by ex-Communist witnesses.

The Morris Schappes case illustrated the difficulty of defending Communists: Schappes, who made the preposterous claim that he was the only remaining party member at City College, was indicted for perjury. The ACLU chose not to defend the perjury charge. Instead, Fraenkel argued—unsuccessfully—for an *amicus* brief, charging jury prejudice against Communists. Then the ACLU tried to challenge a 1939 New York law barring public employment to anyone who advocated the violent overthrow of the government. The case dissolved, however, when Nancy Reed, an acknowledged Communist, dropped her suit.[49] Although the ACLU opposed the worst aspects of the Rapp–Coudert investigation, there were clear signs of uncertainty in its responses.

The FBI Resurgent

FBI spying resumed in 1936—at the initiative of President Roosevelt rather than J. Edgar Hoover. Since 1924 Hoover had largely complied with Attorney General Harlan Fiske Stone's ban on political surveillance. The New Deal gave him a new opportunity, however, with Attorney General Homer Cummings promoting a "war on crime" that encouraged Hoover to build a bureaucratic empire. Then Roosevelt asked him to investigate domestic Fascists and Communists. Roosevelt expanded Hoover's authority after war broke out in September 1939, by ordering the FBI to "take charge of investigative work in matters relating to espionage, sabotage, and violations of the neutrality regulations." Another paragraph of Roosevelt's request added the phrase "subversive activities" to the bureau's mandate. The distinction was crucial. Espionage, sabotage, and neutrality violations involved clear-cut lawbreaking, whereas "subversive activities" opened the door to the surveillance of political groups. Hoover had mastered the technique of stretching presidential directives far beyond their original intent.[50]

Fearing a return to repressive World War I policies, the ACLU demanded that Attorney General Jackson define "subversive activities." But Jackson did not reply. In one of the last speeches of his forty-year political career, Nebraska Senator George Norris warned of an FBI-led police state, but in the fearful climate of 1940, his warning fell on deaf ears.[51] On December 17, 1940, Hoover ordered bureau field offices to make "thorough, discreet and complete investigations" of thirty-three political groups, including the American Youth Congress, the American Student Union, Veterans of the Abraham

Lincoln Brigade, the American Committee for the Protection of the Foreign Born, and the National Negro Congress. Agents were to obtain membership lists, publications, lists of sponsors, and personal histories of officers.[52]

Although Hoover told several agents he was "not interested" in the ACLU and did not include it in his 1940 memo, in fact that year he resumed with a vengeance spying on the organization. Military intelligence had already begun indexing the names of ACLU leaders in 1936 and negotiated a joint arrangement with the FBI in 1938. When the ACLU publicly opposed a special $100,000 appropriation for the bureau in early 1940, an enraged Hoover ordered a new spying campaign.[53] One agent took out an ACLU membership under a fictitious name, and others began spying on affiliate offices. A West Coast agent found the Northern California ACLU director Ernest Besig "not a Communist [but] enough of a troublemaker not to be left alone." But "every person" in the Southern California ACLU office "is a Communist." Then in its most outrageous act, the FBI secretly labeled Baldwin a Communist and designated him for custodial detention in case of a national emergency. Hoover's secret detention program was completely unauthorized; when Attorney General Francis Biddle discovered it in 1943 and ordered it abolished, Hoover simply changed the name and continued it. The FBI placed Baldwin in Group A, which included "individuals believed to be the most dangerous and who in all probability should be interned in event of war." Far from being a Communist, however, Baldwin was then staunchly and openly anti-Communist. But in Hoover's eyes, anyone who dared criticize the bureau was a target for attack.[54]

Hoover was not entirely a rogue elephant, as the federal government had begun an official loyalty program in 1939. The Hatch Act barred federal employment to anyone belonging to an organization advocating the violent overthrow of the government, and in 1940, the U.S. Civil Service Commission authorized the dismissal of suspected subversives. These measures laid the foundation for the far more extensive federal loyalty program of 1947.

Crisis in the ACLU

The anti-Communist fever swept through the ACLU and produced the one great deviation from principle in its history: A 1940 ACLU policy barred from official positions anyone who supported totalitarian movements. Under the policy the board purged Elizabeth Gurley Flynn from its ranks, introducing into its own affairs the kind of political test it had always opposed.

Baldwin Moves to the Center

Domestic and international events in 1937 began pushing Roger Baldwin toward the center. The Wagner Act, his friends in New Deal agencies, and the victories in the Supreme Court gave him a new appreciation of the vitality of

American democracy. Simultaneously, the bizarre spectacle of the Moscow trials, in which Stalin's former colleagues abjectly confessed their "crimes" before being executed, renewed his old doubts about the Communists. He thus cut his ties with Popular Front groups and began to remold the ACLU board, recruiting conservatives to balance the left-wing faction. He candidly told Chairman Ward that he wanted "some strong conservatives . . . provided they did not attempt to inject their political or economic beliefs." His most important catch was Whitney North Seymour, who had written the *Herndon* brief. After two years as an informal member of the board, Seymour told Baldwin that "the dreamers of the Union do not frighten me any more," and he became an official member in 1939. Forceful and articulate, he was a major conservative influence in the ACLU over the next fifteen years. Baldwin unsuccessfully courted Henry R. Luce of the *Time/Life* publishing empire and William J. Donovan of the American Bar Association (ABA).[55]

Baldwin also became more sensitive to right-wing charges of Communist influence in the ACLU. A 1936 *American Mercury* article, "Liberalism à la Moscow," accused the ACLU of supporting Communist "revolution" and "class war," and in return, the ACLU sued for libel. In an out-of-court settlement, the *American Mercury* published another article on the ACLU by H. L. Mencken. But this "retraction" did as much harm as good. While praising the ACLU's "public usefulness"—he no doubt had fond memories of the great *Scopes* case and his Boston arrest with Art Hays—the now-conservative Mencken advised the ACLU to cut its ties with Communist-front organizations, thus reinforcing the original charge that the ACLU was Communist influenced.[56]

The divisions on the ACLU board escalated into a bitter ideological and personal feud. Norman Thomas, John Haynes Holmes, and Morris Ernst were determined to get the ACLU to adopt an unequivocally anti-Communist policy. Revision of the 1934 statement *Shall We Defend Free Speech for Nazis in America?* provoked the first open conflict. After much infighting, it reappeared in early 1939 under the title *Why We Defend Free Speech for Nazis, Fascists—and Communists,* reaffirming the ACLU's defense of free speech for antidemocratic political movements. Nonetheless, the equation of Communists with Nazis in the title outraged the leftists. Mary Van Kleeck accused Thomas of seeking "Socialist scores against Communists." Elmer Rice retorted that "if a disruptive force exists [in the ACLU], it consists of those members of a tiny bloc who are Communists first and civil libertarians second."[57] In fact, the major disputes within the ACLU—such as the Ford–NLRB (National Labor Relations Board) controversy—were legitimate disagreements over how to apply civil liberties principles to new circumstances. Both sides caucused and kept raising their pet issues. Whereas the leftists were overly sympathetic to organized labor, their opponent Morris Ernst sought to trim the ACLU's policy to suit the Roosevelt administration. If anything, the anti-Communists were the devious ones. Norman Thomas aired the ACLU's internal disputes in the press and engaged in vicious personal attacks on Lamont and Ward. The Moscow trials had convinced them that Communists were beyond the pale of democracy and had to be removed in order to save the ACLU. For them, it was an ideological holy war.

Baldwin, Hays, and Ernst, meanwhile, sought to clear the ACLU's name with the Dies Committee. After the first HUAC attacks, Hays fired off a telegram demanding the right to testify on behalf of the ACLU, and in a January 1939 radio talk, he stated that the ACLU had "begged" Congress "to investigate our books and records." He claimed there were no Communists or Fascists among the ACLU leaders, but he knew that Elizabeth Gurley Flynn was a Communist party member. In late December 1938, Baldwin, John Haynes Holmes, and Ben Huebsch submitted affidavits to HUAC investigators that the ACLU was not a "Communist front."[58] Baldwin and others met privately with the HUAC staff, and Baldwin told them that the ACLU's old files were available at the New York Public Library and that they were welcome to examine the recent records at the ACLU office.[59] This offer was consistent with Baldwin's attitude toward self-disclosure dating back to 1917. Neither he nor the others talking with HUAC, however, believed that self-disclosure legitimized the principle of congressional investigations. Trumpeting the ACLU's non-Communist credentials, unfortunately, only fed the anti-Communist fervor.[60]

The Nazi–Soviet Pact in August 1939 pushed Baldwin solidly into the anti-Communist camp. Vacationing on Martha's Vineyard when he heard the news, he called it "the biggest shock of my life. I was never so shaken by anything as I was by that pact." Overwhelmed with disgust and embarrassment about his deep involvement in the Popular Front, Baldwin agreed to remove any Communists from the ACLU board.[61]

Ernst, meanwhile, arranged two informal meetings with Hays, Adolph Berle, Representative Dies, and himself. Rumors of a secret "deal" soon appeared in both the conservative and the Communist press. Some ACLU members were also suspicious. Gardner Jackson, the ACLU's chief anti-HUAC lobbyist, demanded "a complete and detailed report of Mr. Ernst's discussions and possible agreements with Mr. Dies."[62] These meetings remain a bitter controversy fifty years later. None of the participants ever gave a detailed explanation, but subsequent events clearly suggest some informal understanding.

Dies issued a public statement on October 23, "clearing" the ACLU of Communist connections, and the ACLU took several important steps favorable to Dies. Baldwin continued to sit on Isserman's memo about legislative investigations and appointed a special committee on HUAC that initially praised its objectives. Finally, the ACLU barred Communists from leadership positions and so purged Elizabeth Gurley Flynn.[63]

A deal with Dies was fully consistent with Ernst's style. By 1938 Ernst had become a rabid anti-Communist, having just led a noisy exodus from the National Lawyers Guild over Communist participation. He aspired to be a behind-the-scenes adviser to top government officials. He wrote obsequious letters to FDR, offering to handle little political chores, and eventually established an intimate relationship with J. Edgar Hoover. Dissociating the ACLU from Communism was part of his strategy to establish his credibility.

At the same time, however, a deal with Dies was inconsistent with Art Hays's record. Although long opposed to Communism, he always preferred public confrontation to behind-the-scenes negotiation and compromise. His participation in the negotiations with HUAC therefore remains a mystery.[64]

For a report on the HUAC, Baldwin stacked the committee with fervent anti-Communists (Ernst, Florina Lasker, and Roger Riis, with Raymond Wise as chair). The initial draft condemned the committee's procedures but concluded that "the Dies Committee has performed a useful and important service" in exposing Communist propaganda. The report then recommended replacing the HUAC with a new committee with a more clearly defined mandate, procedural safeguards for witnesses, and a balanced membership. Fraenkel, Jackson, and others were outraged by the draft and demanded changes. The final version toned down the favorable comments but still held that legislative inquiries into political beliefs and associations were legitimate.[65]

A Self-inflicted Wound: The 1940 Resolution

The crisis in the ACLU reached its climax in 1940. Thomas, Ernst, and Holmes were implacable and demanded an ACLU statement denouncing Communism, the removal of Harry Ward as chair, and the expulsion of Elizabeth Gurley Flynn from the board. With good reason, Baldwin was afraid that these men would quit the ACLU and create a rival organization if they did not get their way. And also feeling betrayed himself by the Communists, Baldwin acceded to their demands. Although this accession was a deviation from ACLU principles, he rationalized it on the grounds that it would allow the ACLU to defend Communists with "clean hands." If in his heart he knew it was a betrayal, he never said so publicly.[66]

The battle raged through 1939, with the outcome often hinging on the vagaries of attendance at board meetings. The anti-Communists finally pushed through a statement that the ACLU was "opposed to all totalitarian governments—Fascist, Nazi or Communist—as the antithesis of civil liberties." A few weeks later, however, a different majority in attendance rescinded it. Thomas demanded that Ward repudiate "the crimes against civil liberty committed in Russia."[67] The board then supported Ward with a resolution that "members of the Union differ sharply in their economic and political views, and are all free to express them without involving the Union." Thomas then published a vicious attack on Ward in the Socialist *Call*. An outraged Osmond Fraenkel reprimanded Thomas for making personal attacks and asked him whether he would also bar Catholics from the ACLU because they belonged to an authoritarian organization. Thomas, by this point, was a pathetic figure: The Socialist party had collapsed under him, and he was obsessed with his old Communist rivals.[68]

With Baldwin's apparent approval, the board's nominating committee barred any nominee "who is a Communist, Fascist, or an advocate or supporter of any form of totalitarian government, or will not disavow such." But the board repudiated this requirement, saying that now was "no occasion to adopt a resolution setting up standards of qualification" for ACLU leadership positions. Trying to avert a showdown, Baldwin offered a complex proposal that chairs of committees could not serve on the board. Designed to remove the leaders of both factions, his scheme won no support, which set the stage for the ACLU's climactic annual meeting. On February 5, 1940, the board and the National Committee adopted a resolution barring from ACLU leadership positions anyone supporting totalitarianism.[69]

The 1940 Resolution, as it came to be known, declared that "while the American Civil Liberties Union does not make any test of opinion on political or economic questions a condition of membership . . . the personnel of its governing committees and staff is properly subject to the test of consistency in the defense of civil liberties in all aspects and all places." The last three words were crucial, for they would include anyone who spoke favorably of the Soviet Union. Support for civil liberties "is inevitably compromised by persons who champion civil liberties in the United States and yet who justify or tolerate the denial of civil liberties by dictatorships abroad." Finally, it was "inappropriate for any person to serve on the governing committees of the Union or on its staff, who is a member of any political organization which supports totalitarian dictatorship in any country or who by his public declarations indicates his support of such a principle. And, within this category we include organizations in the United States supporting totalitarian governments of the Soviet Union and of the Fascist and Nazi countries (such as the Communist Party, the German-American Bund and others); as well as native organizations with obvious anti-democratic objectives or practices."[70]

The 1940 Resolution provoked an immediate upheaval. Harry Ward resigned and was replaced as chair by the fervently anti-Communist John Haynes Holmes. For twenty years Ward had conducted board meetings in a fair and evenhanded manner. Contrary to the charges against him, there was no evidence that he tried to manipulate board meetings or circumvent its will. Although he remained active in left-wing politics for another twenty years, Ward vanished from the ACLU's institutional memory.

Dissidents led by Alexander Meikeljohn, Robert S. Lynd, Theodore Dreiser, I. F. Stone, Carey McWilliams, and James Wechsler condemned the resolution "as unworthy of [the ACLU's] traditions and incompatible with its principles." It only "encourages the very tendencies it was intended to fight." Citing the ACLU's long-standing opposition to political tests, they asked the obvious questions: What did "support" for totalitarianism mean? What constituted a "totalitarian" government? What about "those faithful Catholics who, following the policy laid down by their Church, approve the Fascist regimes in Spain and Italy?" The two California affiliates, along with Chicago and Massachusetts, led a move to rescind the resolution, dramatizing the fact that they had had no formal voice in setting ACLU policy. Baldwin tried to explain away the resolution, claiming that it represented no change in policy:

"The present resolution merely states what has been always the unwritten policy of the Union in elections and appointments." But this was just not true, and his dissembling persuaded no one.[71]

The Purge of Elizabeth Gurley Flynn

With the resolution in place, the anti-Communists moved against its real target: Elizabeth Gurley Flynn, a colorful radical and a living legend to the American left. Flynn had made her first political speech, on women and Socialism, at age sixteen. A few months later she was arrested for the first of many times. Her striking beauty and powerful voice made her a charismatic presence. She joined the Industrial Workers of the World (IWW) in 1906 and participated in the historic strikes in Lawrence, Massachusetts, in 1912 and Paterson, New Jersey, in 1913. She helped found the ACLU in 1920 and was one of Baldwin's closest allies. Health problems had forced her to withdraw from politics in 1929. But she reappeared in the mid-1930s, joining the Communist party in 1936, being elected to the ACLU board in 1936, and becoming a member of the Communist party's National Committee the following year.[72]

When the ACLU board asked her to resign, she refused, publishing angry replies in the Communist press. She asserted that the ACLU board had no right to bar her for her "political beliefs and affiliations" and pointed out that she had been reelected in 1939, with her party membership a matter of public record. She also accused the ACLU of making a deal with Dies, of cooperating with the Justice Department, and of becoming obsessed with its public image. Faced with her refusal, the board scheduled a formal "trial" over her qualifications. Baldwin got Dorothy Bromley to file the actual charges, apparently in the belief that it might appear unchivalrous for a man to do the job. Flynn's press attacks on the ACLU became two of the three formal charges against her, whereas Norman Thomas's equally public attacks on Ward a few months earlier had simply been overlooked.[73]

The trial took place at a special May 7 board meeting at the City Club of New York. It was a bizarre evening as the ACLU, long opposed to political tests, conducted its own heresy trial. The confrontation was filled with uncertainty. The ACLU bylaws empowered the board to remove members, but there were many unanswered questions about procedure. Could Flynn submit evidence on her own behalf or vote on her own case? In any event, procedural fine points—which everyone attending would insist be answered in any state-initiated criminal trial—were irrelevant. This was a political trial, and most board members arrived with their minds made up. Curiously, some of the leading partisans on both sides failed to attend: Norman Thomas was absent, as was Flynn ally Mary Van Kleeck, who stayed away in protest.[74]

Flynn took the initiative and immediately moved to dismiss all three charges. The first, that she was disqualified from the ACLU board because of her Communist party membership, was the only important one. She objected in principle to any qualification based on ideas and associations: "This charge violates every principle we fought for in the past." Why not expel Roger Baldwin as a self-proclaimed anarchist? she asked. Osmond Fraenkel quietly assumed the role of her counsel, but Chair John Haynes Holmes ruled against her on every point. (Holmes himself had been expelled from Norman Thomas's Socialist party for "un-Socialist conduct" three years before.)[75] As the long evening wore on, it was clear that the Soviet Union was the real defendant. Flynn defended Stalin, which only diverted attention from the issue of an ACLU political test. Art Hays gave the most curious performance of the night. Although he ultimately voted for her, he conducted a long and hostile interrogation regarding the relationship between the Communist party and the Soviet Union. Torn between his commitment to principle and his antipathy to Communism, Hays epitomized the divided soul of the ACLU on this fateful night.[76]

At 2:20 A.M., after a bitter and exhausting six-hour debate, the board finally voted. Fraenkel moved to dismiss the first charge, and William L. Nunn countered with a substitute motion to sustain it. Incredibly, the vote ended in a nine-to-nine tie. Holmes then cast the tiebreaking vote against Flynn. There thus remained only the formalities of approving two lesser charges and officially removing Flynn from the board.[77]

By every conceivable measure, the purge of Elizabeth Gurley Flynn was a disaster for the ACLU. A breach of principle, it both failed to placate right-wing critics, who continued to vilify the ACLU as a Communist front, and outraged the left, many of whom never let the ACLU live down the "trial." Criticism of the 1940 events dogged the ACLU for decades. Critics cited them as evidence of the ACLU's failure in the cold war, often going so far as to accuse the ACLU of "causing" the cold war, a view that certainly exaggerated the ACLU's influence.[78] Nonetheless, the 1940 Resolution and the Flynn purge had an important symbolic value, legitimizing the idea that Communists were not entitled to constitutional protections—a point that became one of the cornerstones of the cold war. From a public relations standpoint, the 1940 events obscured the ACLU's actions in defense of the rights of Communists. Indeed, in 1940 the ACLU led the opposition to the Smith Act and represented the Communist party in several states where it had been barred from the ballot. It also defended left-wing labor leader Harry Bridges in the course of the government's long campaign to deport him. During the worst of the cold war the ACLU challenged virtually all anti-Communist measures, but these actions were obscured by the continuing controversy over the 1940 events.

Flynn was ultimately vindicated: The antitotalitarian resolution was abolished in 1968, and her supporters, led by Corliss Lamont, won her posthumous reinstatement to the board in 1976.[79]

Civil Liberties After Twenty Years

The 1940 Resolution and the Flynn purge dramatized the uncertain state of civil liberties on the eve of World War II. The gains since the last war were a remarkable achievement. The Supreme Court, the Congress, and a host of federal agencies had begun to defend freedom of speech, press, and assembly and the protection of unpopular viewpoints. Influential opinion makers—the ABA Committee on the Bill of Rights, for example—saw civil liberties as basic to American democracy. The ACLU could legitimately claim much of the credit for these changes: Ideas that it had championed virtually alone in 1920 were now established law and public policy. The ACLU itself enjoyed unprecedented prestige and influence. Twenty years after his release from prison, Roger Baldwin had friends in nearly every federal agency who welcomed the ACLU's advice. Eleanor Roosevelt was the featured speaker at the 1939 Chicago ACLU banquet and Attorney General Frank Murphy addressed the October 1939 ACLU Conference on Civil Liberties in the Present Emergency.[80]

On the eve of World War II, national leaders professed their support for civil liberties principles. Opening the one hundred fiftieth anniversary celebration of the Bill of Rights on March 4, 1939, Roosevelt declared that "not for freedom of religion alone does this nation contend by every peaceful means. We believe in the other freedoms of the Bill of Rights, the other freedoms that are inherent in the right of free choice by free men and women." In 1941 he designated December 15 as Bill of Rights Day, directing Archibald MacLeish, head of the Office of Civilian Defense, to coordinate a "nation-wide program." MacLeish, in turn, asked Baldwin and the ACLU to help. Other public officials joined the celebration. The Chicago City Council declared the week of March 7, 1940, "Civil Liberties Week," and the New York Board of Regents designated a Bill of Rights Week for the state's public schools. The chair of the Baltimore ABA Bill of Rights Committee reported that "the Bill of Rights in our community has long since ceased to be news. It is an accepted and integral part of everyday and ordinary use."[81]

This celebration of the Bill of Rights, however, had another, more ominous side. "Americanism" inevitably implied its opposite: "un-American" ideas and forces. It was hardly accidental that the House Un-American Activities Committee appeared and flourished at the same time the country celebrated the one hundred fiftieth anniversary of the Bill of Rights. As before in American history, fear of foreign ideas and groups swept the country. Many Americans, including some civil libertarians, were persuaded that foreign totalitarism seriously threatened American values. To preserve democracy, it was necessary to exclude Communists and Fascists from the democratic process—or at least to restrict their political activities. Therefore, despite the enormous growth of support for civil liberties in the years just before the war, Americans were still uncertain about the real meaning of the Bill of Rights. Another world war, followed by a new "cold" war, would pose serious tests for civil liberties.

Seven

Civil Liberties in the Age of World War, 1941-1945

Preparing for War

"We will not, under any threat, or in the face of any danger, surrender the guarantees of liberty our forefathers framed for us in our Bill of Rights."[1] Eight days after the Japanese attack on Pearl Harbor, President Franklin D. Roosevelt promised not to repeat the terrible mistakes of the last war. To a great extent Roosevelt kept his promise. Instead of whipping up public hysteria as President Woodrow Wilson had done during World War I, Roosevelt and his cabinet admonished the country to preserve constitutional freedoms. But it was a popular war, with little dissent to suppress in any event. Virtually all Americans—including the Communists—supported the war against the Nazis and the Japanese. The one major exception to Roosevelt's otherwise impressive record was the internment of 120,000 Japanese-Americans. Such a shameful action, supported by nearly everyone, provided the ACLU with a shining moment. Almost alone it challenged this wholesale violation of individual rights.

Along with the rest of the country, the ACLU began preparing for war after the outbreak of hostilities in 1939. To prevent another wave of wartime repression, Baldwin organized a public education campaign to remind the country of the civil liberties violations during the last war. In October 1939 he convened the Conference on Civil Liberties in the National Emergency. Keynote speaker Attorney General Frank Murphy pledged to respect civil liberties: "An emergency does not abrogate the Constitution or dissolve the Bill of Rights."[2] ACLU secretary Lucille Milner published a series of articles on the rights of conscientious objectors and freedom of speech in wartime in *Harper's, The American Mercury,* and *The New Republic.* James R. Mock wrote the first scholarly account of the wartime abuses, *Censorship 1917.* Zechariah Chafee, alarmed by the Smith Act, revised and expanded his now-classic book, *Free Speech in the United States.*[3]

The Roosevelt administration also joined the campaign. Three days after Pearl Harbor, Attorney General Francis Biddle told the country, "It is essential at such a time as this that we keep our heads, keep our tempers,—above all, that we keep clearly in mind what we are defending." The country should guard freedom "most zealously at home." Finally, in a display of wartime unity, defeated Republican presidential candidate Wendell Willkie, who later volunteered to represent a prominent Communist before the Supreme Court, declared, "In the courtroom and from the public rostrum I will fight for the preservation of civil liberties, no matter how unpopular the cause may be in any given instance. We must preserve civil liberties for all or else our sacrifices in winning this war may be in vain."[4]

America's Concentration Camps

Despite its assurances, however, the Roosevelt administration perpetrated one of the worst civil liberties violations in all of American history: evacuating 120,000 Japanese-Americans from the West Coast and holding them in concentration camps. The surprise Japanese attack on Pearl Harbor on December 7, 1941, nearly wiped out the United States' Pacific fleet and left the West Coast vulnerable to attack. The presence of the large Japanese-American community on the coast, including nearly 40,000 aliens, inevitably aroused fears of sabotage. Nonetheless, the initial public reaction to Pearl Harbor was remarkably restrained, with no vigilante violence. The government quickly arrested 736 Japanese nationals on December 7 and another 600 over the next three days. Roosevelt imposed a curfew on Japanese, German, and Italian aliens. For the moment, the situation seemed well in hand.[5]

The campaign to remove Japanese-Americans from the West Coast developed slowly over the next few weeks. Although carried out in the name of military necessity, the evacuation was largely the product of long-standing racism. Pressure for evacuation came from the military and West Coast politicians steeped in anti-Asian prejudice. General John DeWitt argued relentlessly that the coast was vulnerable to attack and that the Japanese-American communities were, by accident or design, located close to critical military establishments. He regarded Japanese-Americans as inherently loyal to Japan. Unlike the case of Americans of German or Italian descent, it was impossible to distinguish the loyal from the disloyal Japanese-Americans. In addition, DeWitt suppressed the military's own evidence that wholesale evacuation was not necessary, hiding it from the Justice Department's lawyers. California politicians were even more vocal in demanding evacuation; Attorney General Earl Warren argued that "every alien Japanese should be considered in the light of a potential fifth columnist" and, in a grotesque bit of logic, suggested that the absence of any sabotage (by early February) was proof of sabotage to come. Warren mobilized the California sheriffs and police chiefs and testified at state and congressional hearings in favor of the mass evacuation of Americans of Japanese descent. By contrast, the removal of German and Italian nationals would be "disruptive of national unity." Political columnist Walter Lippman, after talking with Warren, added his influential voice to the evacuation campaign.[6]

DeWitt finally convinced the administration. Justice Department lawyers Ed Ennis and James Rowe, arriving at the climactic February 17 meeting anticipating a proposal to remove only enemy aliens, were stunned to find a plan to evacuate citizens as well. Attorney General Biddle, already fighting heavy pressure to restrict free speech, voiced token objection and then approved DeWitt's plan. Ennis, in tears, almost resigned in protest. Rowe persuaded him to stay, however, and over the next four years, he fought the program from within the Justice Department.[7]

Two days later, on February 19, Roosevelt issued Executive Order 9066, authorizing the secretary of war to designate military zones "from which any or all persons may be excluded." This was a sweeping delegation to the military of power over American citizens. Although there was no reference to Japanese-Americans, everyone knew they were the real target. Nor did the president's order authorize or even refer to detention, but when the government found itself with 120,000 evacuees on its hands, concentration camps were the inevitable result.[8]

The military proceeded to implement the order with a series of directives. Public Proclamation 1 designated as Military Area no. 1 a broad strip of land, including the western halves of California, Oregon, and Washington. On March 19, Congress enacted Public Law 503, providing for criminal penalties for refusing to obey any command issued under Executive Order 9066. Public Proclamation 3 imposed an 8 P.M. to 6 A.M. curfew on enemy aliens and all Japanese-Americans. On the same day, March 24, DeWitt issued the first of 108 "exclusion orders" directing Japanese-Americans to report to assembly centers. Between late spring and early summer, over 100,000 Japanese-Americans were placed in assembly centers and then evacuated to ten hastily constructed relocation centers. When the governors of other western states refused to accept the resettled evacuees, the War Relocation Authority converted the centers into permanent detention facilities. A series of administrative orders by the military and the War Relocation Authority (WRA) imposed criminal penalties for leaving the camps without permission. Willy-nilly, the United States government created concentration camps.

The ACLU Responds

Executive Order 9066 raised the most fundamental constitutional questions about the limits of presidential power. At its next board meeting, on March 2, the ACLU issued a public statement denouncing the order and calling for "an immediate court test." A letter to Roosevelt attacked this "unprecedented order," finding it "open to grave question on constitutional grounds by depriving American citizens of their liberty and use of their property without due process of law." Moreover, the order was unnecessary because "the protection of our country in war time can be assured without such a wholesale invasion of civil rights and without creating a precedent so opposed to democratic principle." As an alternative, the ACLU proposed individual hearings, similar to those used by the Selective Service, to determine which Japanese-Americans were security risks. Even enemy aliens should be removed only on the basis of conduct clearly indicating disloyalty. In a second and stronger letter to Roosevelt the ACLU pointedly compared the evacuation with that of Nazi Germany: "Enforcing this on the Japanese alone approximates the totalitarian theory of justice practiced by the Nazis in their treatment of the Jews." It was a strong statement that appeared to set the stage for a major confrontation with the government.[9]

Baldwin told the ACLU's West Coast affiliates to look for potential test cases. Fortuitously, two of the ACLU's strongest affiliates were in Los Angeles and San Francisco, but they encountered a serious problem: a lack of plaintiffs. That is, with only a handful of exceptions, the Japanese-Americans dutifully obeyed the order. Even before Pearl Harbor, Japanese-American Citizens League (JACL) leaders had made strenuous efforts to establish their partiotism. In March 1941 they met with military intelligence officials and offered "to put all of the facilities of the J.A.C.L. at the disposal of the authorities." Immediately following the evacuation order, Assistant Attorney General Tom Clark and Assistant Secretary of War John J. McCloy assured them their property would be protected and warned of "drastic measures" if they resisted. The JACL leaders faced a terrible dilemma, for which there may have been no honorable solution. They knew too well the depth of West Coast racism and feared the consequences of organized resistance. Therefore, justifying it as a patriotic move, they urged their members to cooperate: "We are going into exile as our duty to our country." At that point neither they nor the administration foresaw prolonged detention. The JACL accurately gauged the temper of its membership: Of the 120,000 people ordered to evacuate, no more than 12 openly resisted, and 4 of these cases eventually reached the U.S. Supreme Court. A disgusted Ernest Besig wrote Baldwin that the Japanese-Americans were "in favor of acquiescence . . . even at the cost of their inherited liberties."[10]

The four test cases began as isolated acts of resistance. Min Yasui walked into a Portland, Oregon, police station at 11:00 P.M. on March 28 and demanded to be arrested for violating the curfew. Six weeks later Gordon Hirabayashi, a Quaker and a student at the University of Washington, went to the Seattle FBI office asking to be arrested for violating the curfew and refusing to report for evacuation. His case was the first to reach the Supreme Court. On May 30, Fred Korematsu was arrested in San Leandro, California. Korematsu was very different from the others. Because he was planning to marry a Caucasian, he had undergone plastic surgery to alter his appearance. And unlike Yasui and Hirabayashi, he did not voluntarily turn himself in. Finally, Mitsuye Endo tried a different legal strategy. She reported to the Tanforan assembly center near San Francisco and then filed a habeas corpus petition challenging her detention.[11]

The ACLU assumed responsibility for two of the four cases. Mary Farquharson organized Hirabayashi's defense committee in Seattle, and Baldwin raised funds from wealthy easterners. In San Francisco, Besig and attorney Wayne Collins agreed to take Korematsu's case. Yasui and Endo, meanwhile, retained independent counsel. The ACLU was nervous about Yasui's case because his previous connections with the Japanese consulate might leave him open to charges of being an enemy agent. The ACLU first voted not to enter the case but reversed itself after Besig decided to file an *amicus* for the Northern California affiliate.[12] Endo's attorney told the ACLU to quit "meddling" in her case. Southern California ACLU attorney A. L. Wirin felt utterly frustrated. Outraged by the evacuation order and eager to take a challenge to the Supreme Court, he was unable to secure a viable case. Ernest and Toki Wakayama were interested in a habeas corpus challenge, but their case became clouded after they were arrested for holding an illegal meeting at the assembly center. They eventually dropped their case and sought repatriation to Japan.[13]

Split in the ACLU

While Baldwin assembled the test cases, an improbable coalition on the ACLU board questioned the ACLU's stance.[14] With somewhat different motives, conservatives, liberals, and leftists opposed challenging the president's order. The conservatives, led by Whitney North Seymour, instinctively deferred to presidential authority in wartime. The liberals—Morris Ernst, Roger Riis, Elmer Rice, and Raymond Wise—were swayed by political loyalty to Roosevelt and their horror regarding Hitler. Successful prosecution of the war was the nation's top priority, and they did not want even to appear to question the judgment of the commander in chief. Alexander Meikeljohn saw no violation of fundamental civil liberties: "For us to say that they are taking away civil rights, would have as much sense as protesting because a 'measles' house is isolated. The Japanese citizens, as a group, are dangerous both to themselves and to their fellow-citizens." He had already voted against the Northern California affiliate's challenging the curfew order. Ernst did not see "any possible constitutional question if there is military necessity," adding sarcastically, "and I assume the ACLU does not pretend to know anything about military necessities." Leftists Corliss Lamont and William Spofford, moved by their sympathy for the Soviet Union which was then carrying virtually all of the burden of the war against Germany, also emphasized the urgency of the war effort. The ACLU's position, Lamont charged, was "obstructionist" and gave "aid and comfort" to the enemy.[15]

The strongest opposition to the president's order came from the old pacifists—Baldwin, Norman Thomas, and John Haynes Holmes—and Art Hays. The pacifists instinctively recoiled at any infringement on individual liberty in the name of military necessity. Hays and Evan Thomas, Norman's brother, understood better than the others did that the current situation was very different from that of the last war; the principal threat to freedom was the enormous centralization of government power in the democracies as well as overtly totalitarian societies. Evan Thomas wrote, "The struggle of the future is not the old one of Democratic individualism vs. collectivism but of a vicious oppressive totalitarianism vs. cooperation." The president's order was all the more seductive because it was issued in the name of a war to preserve democracy and defeat totalitarianism.[16]

The debate within the ACLU board turned on the same issues that had split the American Union Against Militarism (AUAM) in the summer of 1917. What were the limits of governmental power during wartime? More to the point, what were the responsibilities of civil libertarians in the midst of a national crisis? Was the defense of freedom best served by supporting what they believed to be the government of the freest country in the world, then engaged in a war to preserve democracy? Or was it best served by defending principles to the utmost, even if it meant a direct confrontation with the government over a major policy? As it had twenty-five years earlier, the crucible of war forced the civil libertarians to define the exact nature of their commitment.

As the evacuations began on the West Coast, the conservative–liberal–left coalition forced a referendum on the ACLU's policy. Hays drafted Resolution 1 opposing the president's order in principle: "The Civil Liberties Union," it declared, "is of the opinion that in the absence of any conditions justifying a declaration of martial law, any order . . . investing either military or civil authorities with power to remove any *citizen* or *group of citizens* from any zone established by such authorities . . . constitutes a violation of civil liberties." The italicized words highlighted what Hays saw as the two main issues. That is, the internment program violated the rights of bona fide American citizens and did so because of their race. His statement was even stronger than the earlier letters to Roosevelt, opposing any system of individual loyalty hearings: "No system of civilian hearing boards to determine what citizens should be removed can cure the fundamental violation of constitutional rights." Hays concluded that the president's order, if "pushed to its logical conclusion would justify even the adoption of Fascism in the United States to beat the Fascism of our enemies."[17]

Resolution 2, put forward by the conservative–liberal–left coalition, was a compromise. Although many undoubtedly wanted the ACLU to take no action at all, they realized that the ACLU majority would not agree. Thus they offered a statement accepting the president's order in principle but hedging it with procedural constraints. It began by conceding that "the government has the right in the present war to establish military zones and to remove persons, either citizens or aliens, from such zones when their presence may endanger national security, even in the absence of a declaration of martial law." Any action, however, had to be "directly necessary to the prosecution of the war or the defense of national security." The wording implied that the government had not met this burden of proof. The removal of individuals, moreover, must be carried out by civilian rather than military authorities and "should be based on a classification, having a reasonable relationship to the danger intended to be met." This seemed to imply that a racial classification was unacceptable. Every person was entitled to a separate hearing before being removed. Finally, there could be no prolonged detention, and evacuees "should be allowed full liberty in the United States outside of such military zones."[18]

By a decisive fifty-two-to-twenty-six vote, the ACLU National Committee approved Resolution 2.[19] Although it was a retreat from the earlier statements, the new ACLU policy still offered four grounds for legal challenges to the government's program: the absence of a clear military necessity, racial discrimination, the lack of individual hearings, and detention. Considerable misunderstanding arose in later years over the ACLU's role in the Japanese-American cases. Because it represented a step back from the initial statements, the new policy gave rise to the widespread impression that the ACLU had "approved" the government's program and "did nothing." Indeed, over the years, several ACLU leaders in San Francisco, angry over the board's change, perpetuated this view. But although the ACLU's stand did approve the president's order in principle, it also provided the basis for the ACLU's involvement in the cases that eventually reached the Supreme Court. Baldwin, however, was dismayed by the new policy and fought to keep the minority view alive. The ACLU's pamphlet *Military Power and Civil Rights* reprinted the rejected Resolution 1—the only time the ACLU ever published the losing argument in a major policy debate.[20]

The new policy had serious ramifications for the cases already under way. Farquharson and Besig had made commitments to Hirabayashi and Korematsu with no restrictions on what issues could be raised in court. Besig in particular was intent on challenging the president's order on its face. Baldwin agreed with him in principle but felt duty bound to carry out the board's mandate. He therefore tried to finesse the problem by proposing to transfer the cases to nominally independent defense committees. The ACLU could still help indirectly through fund-raising and the use of staff time. The ACLU's name would not appear on any brief raising an issue that went beyond official policy. Farquharson was amenable to this solution for Hirabayashi, but an incensed Besig refused to accept it. Feeling honor bound by his earlier commitment to Korematsu, he fired off a note to Baldwin saying, "We don't intend to trim our sails to suit the Board's vacillating policy."[21] At this moment, however, he had problems with his own affiliate. The Northern California ACLU voted (119 to 65) to approve the president's order and (100 to 91) not to challenge its constitutionality. Even more an autocrat than Baldwin was, Besig simply disregarded the vote until he could arrange a reconsideration. He told Baldwin flatly, "I favor testing constitutional issues."[22]

The dispute over the *Korematsu* case aggravated other ACLU internal conflicts. Besig still resented Baldwin's "meddling" in his affiliate's affairs in 1935, the 1940 Resolution, and the absence of the affiliates' voices in ACLU policymaking, and so he now dug in his heels, more convinced than ever that he and Northern California represented the true voice of civil liberties. In October a new ACLU policy on sedition cases deepened the split. Besig's abrasive style only made matters worse as he fired off vituperative letters to the ACLU's national office. The Northern California affiliate nearly severed its ties with the ACLU in 1944 and hostile feelings remained for the next thirty years, until Besig's retirement in the early 1970s.[23]

In the midst of the war, the ACLU stood alone in bringing court tests of the government's evacuation and internment policy. The American Bar Association (ABA)'s Bill of Rights Committee blandly said it would keep an eye on the program. Left-wing groups abandoned civil liberties. The National Lawyers Guild pledged its "wholehearted support to the war effort" and uttered not a word of protest over the internment program. It even offered to supply lawyers to assist local draft boards and "other war operations." The now aggressively patriotic Communist party also looked the other way. Ironically, in just a few years both the Guild and the Communist party would be crushed by cold war measures based on an identical national security rationale.[24]

Carey McWilliams, a leading authority on racism, illustrated the extent to which many on the left rationalized the internment program when he contended in a 1942 article that it would break up the exploitative labor conditions in Japanese-American businesses and help integrate Japanese-Americans into American society by redistributing them across the country. The article contained not one word critical of the evacuation and internment. McWilliams resembled the prowar liberals of World War I who found in the war effort a chance to advance social reform. Even the JACL did not recover its footing until early 1943 when, under new leadership, it filed an *amicus* brief in the *Hirabayashi* case. The only Americans to protest the internment were members of religious groups, notably the Quakers. They denounced the government's action and provided humanitarian relief to individual evacuees (for some, the boldest step was to provide box lunches for the evacuees).[25]

A. L. Wirin paid the highest price of any Caucasian for his defense of the Japanese-Americans. Although he never found a viable test case, he was punished for trying. His private law practice was based largely on retainers with Congress of Industrial Organizations (CIO) unions in Southern California, and he rented office space in a CIO-owned building. But CIO leaders told him to choose between their all-out support for the war effort and the ACLU. When he stuck by his principles, they canceled their retainers and evicted him from his office. This was not the only time Wirin paid a price for his defense of unpopular cases: As Dan Pollitt later observed, Wirin lost his American Federation of Labor (AFL) accounts in the late 1930s for representing the CIO's Harry Bridges, lost his CIO retainers in the 1940s because of the Japanese-Americans, and lost the Japanese-Americans in the 1950s for defending Communists.[26]

Baldwin's Dilemma

By late 1942 Roger Baldwin found himself in an extraordinary situation. The ACLU was the only organization challenging the internment program, but he was besieged by attacks from two sides within his own organization. The conservative–liberal–left coalition on the board thought he was doing too much, whereas his most vocal affiliate attacked him for not doing enough. In another bizarre twist he found one of his strongest allies in, of all places, the Justice Department.

As the Court cases slowly developed through late 1942 and early 1943, Baldwin lobbied intensively in Washington. There he found the sympathetic ear of Ed Ennis, director of the Enemy Alien Control Unit, who was quietly but determinedly fighting the very program he was charged with administering.[27] Baldwin successfully lobbied him on a number of issues: He helped convince Ennis to go to Hawaii and look into problems arising from the martial law imposed on Hawaii on December 7, 1941. Ennis mooted an ACLU case challenging the suspension of habeas corpus for enemy aliens, by ordering Hans Zimmerman released. He refused to end martial law, however, and the Supreme Court finally declared it unconstitutional in an ACLU case argued by Osmond Fraenkel.[28]

Baldwin's lobbying dramatized the perils of the ACLU's new respectability. Enjoying again the status of Washington insider he had held during the early months of World War I, he regularly met with top administration officials, returning to New York to give the ACLU board "confidential" memoranda on his discussions. Other ACLU leaders enjoyed the same access, meeting with Biddle, Ennis, J. Edgar Hoover, John J. McCloy, and Paul V. McNutt, chair of the War Manpower Commission. Ernest Angell, chair of the ACLU's National Committee on Conscientious Objectors, met with Roosevelt himself.[29]

Access to the corridors of power was extremely seductive and tested the ACLU's principles. In his August 26, 1942, "Confidential Memorandum," Baldwin reported that virtually all top government officials "are about as much troubled as we ourselves" by the evacuation program. Justice Department officials conceded that the one major sedition indictment was prompted by political pressure but that "no other [indictment] of the sort is being contemplated." The attitude of administration officials thus produced strong pressures in the ACLU to moderate its opposition. Whitney North Seymour argued forcefully that the ACLU should not push free speech issues too far, that it would alienate the Justice Department and lead to more sweeping repression. Baldwin was tempted and commented in his August 26 memo that perhaps the ACLU might combat censorship "in ways more effective than court proceedings."[30]

Baldwin's effort to cultivate his administration allies led to occasional lapses of judgment. In November 1942 he sent General DeWitt a letter congratulating him on completing the evacuation "with a minimum of hardship," noting the "comparatively few complaints of injustice and mismanagement." Considering the fact that it referred to putting eighty thousand American citizens in concentration camps, it was an utterly incredible statement. Norman Thomas exploded and sent Baldwin a sarcastic letter suggesting that "since the ACLU is going in for congratulating the army on being humane, may I inquire whether you have yet practiced on a letter to Colonel Lanser who . . . is an officer of the German Army of occupation in Norway. He also tried to be humane." It was a telling point, and Thomas was virtually alone in questioning the wisdom of intimate contacts with government officials.[31] But John Haynes Holmes rose to Baldwin's defense: "I see perfectly the danger . . . but I favor working with the government to the accomplishment of our ends and aims to the furthest extent possible." Then, in an outburst that captured the sentiments of many in the ACLU, Holmes declared, "Thank God we have a government with which we can thus work."[32]

A sense of their own history weighed heavily on the minds of these ACLU leaders. Veterans of the terrible World War I years, they inevitably judged the government's performance by that standard. They felt enormous pressure to accept the gains they had won over the past twenty-five years and not to try to press civil liberties to extremes.[33]

Baldwin may have committed a more serious breach of principle in his negotiations with the War Relocation Authority (WRA) where he worked closely with director Dillon Myer to improve conditions in the camps. In one 1945 incident, five young men were sentenced to the camp stockade for violating regulations—in this case nothing more than blowing bugles and wearing certain forbidden clothing. Besig and Collins wanted to bring an immediate habeas corpus proceeding on their behalf, but Baldwin urged them to hold off and give the government more time. These and similar incidents led Besig and Collins to conclude that Baldwin had completely sold out. One historian, accepting their viewpoint, accused Baldwin of being a WRA "agent."[34]

The Japanese-Americans in the Supreme Court

As the four test cases headed toward the Supreme Court, ACLU infighting over the *Korematsu* case took a new twist. Virtually everyone close to the case concluded that Northern California ACLU attorney Wayne Collins was incompetent. His "kitchen-sink" brief raised every imaginable issue and was filled with gratuitous and potentially counterproductive attacks on the courts. Even Besig recognized the problem and, putting aside his hostility toward Baldwin, suggested that the ACLU national office handle the Supreme Court appeal. There were also questions about the ability of Hirabayashi's attorney, Frank Walters. Wirin sensed an opportunity and jumped in to suggest that because the Justice Department was coordinating its arguments in the four cases, the ACLU should do the same. That is, the ACLU's national office should take charge of all the cases, with Fraenkel assuming general responsibility for the briefs. Wirin was candid about his own ambitions: "I must confess a personal and selfish interest in the matter, for I am quite desirous of . . . playing a part in the oral arguments before the Supreme Court."[35]

But the circuit court of appeals rudely disrupted everyone's plans on March 27, 1943, when it certified the cases directly to the Supreme Court. The cases would now reach the Court almost a year earlier than expected. With only six weeks to prepare, Fraenkel completely rewrote Walters's *Hirabayashi* brief. Because of ACLU policy, he was unable to challenge directly the constitutionality of Roosevelt's order, and so he concentrated on two points. First,

Public Law 503 exceeded the scope of the president's order because it was not required by military necessity. Second, the entire curfew–evacuation–internment program was an unconstitutional form of racial discrimination. Fraenkel was, however, on thin legal ice on this point. The equal protection clause of the Fourteenth Amendment applied to the states, not the federal government. Fraenkel argued that it violated the due process clause of the Fifth Amendment but could cite few legal precedents.[36]

To share the oral argument with Walters, Baldwin lined up Harold Evans, a Philadelphia Quaker and an old ally from World War I days. Collins submitted an *amicus* on behalf of the Northern California ACLU, while a revived JACL submitted its own *amicus*. Ernst, meanwhile, was busy maneuvering behind the scenes. Afraid that the Supreme Court would rule the government's program unconstitutional, he wrote to FDR offering to help revise the evacuation order to distinguish between citizens and aliens in a way that would moot the pending cases. FDR told him to go ahead, but nothing came of it.[37]

The Supreme Court heard the oral arguments in *Hirabayashi, Korematsu* and *Yasui* on May 10 and 11, 1943. The cases raised the most basic questions of constitutional government. What were the limits of war powers in the Constitution? How far could the president or the Congress go in suspending the rights of citizens to prosecute a war? Was the judgment of the executive branch or the military subject to judicial review? The major precedent was President Abraham Lincoln's suspension of habeas corpus during the Civil War. In *Ex Parte Milligan* the Supreme Court had rebuked Lincoln and affirmed the primacy of the Constitution. The most relevant section of *Milligan* held that claims of military necessity were not self-justifying, and were subject to review by civilian courts. The government was not completely powerless in the face of invasion or civil war, but "martial law cannot arise from a threatened invasion. The necessity must be actual and present; the invasion real, such as effectually closes the courts and deposes the civil administration." *Milligan* seemed to bode ill for the government, as there had been no invasion or even serious threat of invasion of the continental United States.[38]

On June 21, 1943, the Court sustained the government and unanimously upheld Gordon Hirabayashi's conviction for violating the curfew order. Justice Harlan Fiske Stone addressed the war powers question directly: The power to wage war was "power to wage war successfully," extending "to every matter and activity so related to war as substantially to affect its conduct and progress." The Court should defer to the commander in chief's need for broad discretion in conducting the war. Inevitably war involved "some infringement on individual liberty," but the measures in question here were not different from "the police establishment of fire lines during a fire." Turning to the issue of racial discrimination. Stone conceded that "distinctions between citizens solely because of their ancestry are by their very nature odious to a free people." But, he continued, "we cannot close our eyes to the fact . . . that in a time of war residents having ethnic affiliations with an invading enemy may be a greater source of danger than those of a different ancestry." He stopped short of upholding the entire government program and evaded the far more serious constitutional question of evacuation: "We need not now attempt to define the ultimate boundaries of the war power." This would have to wait for *Korematsu,* which the Court remanded to the lower courts.[39]

All of the Court's civil libertarians concurred in *Hirabayashi.* Displaying an extraordinary deference to military authorities, Justice William O. Douglas wrote, "We must credit the military with as much good faith in that belief as we would any other public official acting pursuant to his duties." Yet as subsequent scholarship has established, the military had acted in bad faith, suppressing its own reports that sabotage was not likely to be a problem among the Japanese-Americans.[40] Murphy, horrified by the program's racial aspects, nearly dissented but was persuaded by other justices not to. But his concurrence read like a dissent: He argued that the case went "to the very brink of constitutional power," pointing out that the curfew "bears a melancholy resemblance to the treatment accorded to members of the Jewish race in Germany and in other parts of Europe."

The Korematsu *Case*

Although *Hirabayashi* was a devastating blow, the Court had not ruled on the far more serious evacuation issue raised by *Korematsu* or Endo's challenge to detention. As these cases worked their way to the Court between June 1943 and December 1944, the infighting on both sides escalated.

The ACLU's national office ordered the Northern California affiliate to remove its name from any *Korematsu* brief challenging the president's order per se. But Besig held his ground, and the dispute became hopelessly intertwined with conflicts over other policies. When Northern California threatened to disavow publicly the official ACLU policy, the board warned that such a step would be "regarded as compromising the Branch's affiliation with the Union." For a moment it appeared that the ACLU would be torn apart. The dispute dragged on through 1944, with more threats and counterthreats, but in the end both sides backed away from a showdown.[41]

In later years, the myth arose that Northern California "disaffiliated" from the ACLU. In fact, at that time, none of the affiliates had integrated memberships with the national ACLU. Then when the ACLU began to integrate affiliates into a national structure in the 1950s, Besig's staunch refusal perpetuated the myth. The Chicago Civil Liberties Committee (CCLC), however, did sever its relations with the ACLU in 1945. Dominated by CIO leaders and other leftists, it openly supported Roosevelt for reelection in 1944, in violation of the ACLU's nonpartisan policy, and endorsed a number of non–civil liberties economic issues. The ACLU demanded changes, and so the CCLC disaffiliated.[42]

The government's lawyers were nearly as divided as the ACLU's. Ed Ennis fought his colleagues in the Justice and War departments and, for all practical purposes, began coaching Baldwin on how the ACLU should argue *Korematsu.* He too believed that Wayne Collins was incompetent, pointing out his failure in his *Korematsu* brief to link evacuation with detention—the government's most vulnerable point. The evacuation order presented Fred Korematsu with two alternatives: He could refuse to report to the assembly center and be arrested, or he could report and be detained in a relocation center. Either way he would lose his liberty. Ennis urged Charles Horsky, an attorney with the prestigious Washington law firm of Covington and Burling who was handling the ACLU's *amicus,* to emphasize this point. Historian Peter Irons suggested that Ennis may have breached legal ethics by coaching the ACLU, although Ennis denied the charge. The situation was fraught with irony. Norman Thomas accused Baldwin of collaborating with the government, even though in fact Ennis was collaborating with him. With respect to *Endo,* the lawyers on both sides were virtually certain that the Court would rule her continued detention to be unconstitutional.[43]

In late 1942, a new crisis erupted in the relocation centers as the WRA began selectively releasing internees. To determine eligibility, it devised a questionnaire containing two particularly offensive questions. Question 27 asked males, "Are you willing to serve in the armed forces of the United States, in combat duty, or wherever ordered?" Question 28 asked everyone, "Will you swear unqualified allegiance to the United States . . . and foreswear any form of allegiance or obedience to the Japanese emperor?" The inherent offensiveness of a loyalty test was aggravated by the peculiar legal status of many internees, the Japanese cultural tradition of strong family loyalty, and the conditions in the camps. Those born in Japan, the Issei, were by law ineligible for American citizenship, and they understandably feared that an affirmative answer to Question 28 would leave them stateless. And many American-born internees joined their parents in answering no to Question 28, in effect renouncing their citizenship.

Meanwhile, Japanese nationalists organized into paramilitary gangs and assumed de facto control of the camps. Through language and physical education classes, these militants pressured others into public displays of loyalty to Japan. The WRA responded by segregating suspected troublemakers in the Tule Lake camp, creating a particularly volatile situation. Riots broke out in late 1943, and Tule Lake was placed under martial law. An angry Congress responded with a law facilitating the renunciation of citizenship, and soon nearly 5,700 Japanese-Americans had renounced their American citizenship, including many children and adults who clearly made the decision under duress.[44]

On December 18, 1944, the Supreme Court decided *Korematsu* and *Endo.* The Court upheld Korematsu's conviction and sustained the constitutionality of the president's order by a six-to-three vote. Hugo Black's majority opinion in *Korematsu* went even further than *Hirabayashi* in deferring to the military. He accepted the government's argument that mass evacuation was necessary because "it was impossible to bring about an immediate segregation of the disloyal from the loyal." "Hardships are part of war," he wrote, "and war is an aggregation of hardships." Black evaded the crucial linkage between evacuation and detention, and brushed aside the charge that the relocation centers were concentration camps: "We deem it unjustifiable to call them concentration camps with all the ugly connotations that term implies." Finally, he rejected the racial discrimination issue, arguing that "to cast this case into outlines of racial prejudice, without reference to the real military dangers which were presented merely confuses the issue." It was an extraordinarily cavalier dismissal of violations of individual rights by a judge who later became one of the great civil libertarians in the history of the Court.[45]

Justices Frank Murphy, Owen Roberts, and Robert Jackson broke ranks and delivered vigorous dissents. Murphy was the most outspoken on the question of race: The evacuation program went "over 'the brink of constitutional power' and falls into the ugly abyss of racism." He also argued that "there was no adequate proof that the FBI and the military naval intelligence services did not have the espionage and sabotage situation well in hand."[46] The conservative Owen Roberts called the evacuation "a clear violation of Constitutional rights." And Jackson warned that the majority opinion set a dangerous precedent with regard to the president's war powers: "A judicial construction of the due process clause that will sustain this order is a far more subtle blow to liberty than the promulgation of the order itself." Once validated, this principle "lies about like a loaded weapon ready for the hand of any authority that can bring forward a plausible claim of an urgent need." Jackson's warning was prophetic, as the Vietnam War eventually thrust the war powers questions to the forefront of national politics.

The same day, the Court unanimously upheld Endo's challenge, ruling that the government had no right to detain a "concededly loyal" individual. This victory came rather late, as Endo and ninety thousand other citizens had already spent two and a half years in detention. In addition, anticipating defeat in the Supreme Court, the government had already begun to dismantle the internment program. The day before, in fact, the administration had issued Public Proclamation 21, officially ending mass exclusion. Everyone except those identified by name would be free on January 20, 1945.[47]

Aftermath of a Tragedy

The reaction to *Korematsu* was swift and strong. With the war coming to an end, public opinion turned against the internment program. Prominent members of the legal community led the attack. Yale Law Professor Eugene V. Rostow denounced, in scholarly and popular magazine articles, the government's action as a "disaster" and "our worst wartime mistake." He also urged new court tests to overturn the dangerous precedents set by *Hirabayashi* and *Korematsu* and suggested reparations to compensate the interned Japanese-Americans for their losses. Nanette Dembitz, Ennis's assistant in the Justice Department, published a lengthy law review article attacking the Court's reasoning in *Korematsu*. Ultimately, the cases became orphans in legal scholarship. No one published a defense of either the government's program or the Court's decisions.[48] Both Ennis and Dembitz soon resigned from the Justice Department and joined the ACLU. Ennis eventually became chair of the board in 1969 and, in that capacity, oversaw the ACLU's challenges to violations of civil liberties during the Vietnam War.

The public opinion backlash had an important effect on other issues involving Japanese-Americans. The most urgent problem involved the so-called renunciants whom the government had begun to deport. Many changed their minds and sought to regain their American citizenship. The JACL, however, still leery of any taint of disloyalty, refused to touch their cases.[49] The ACLU offered to represent them, but this only precipitated another bitter internal dispute. Wayne Collins, angry over being shoved aside by the ACLU's national office in *Korematsu,* grabbed as a private attorney the main case, involving 2,300 renunciants. Wirin later managed to salvage an ACLU role by representing three clients in a separate case. The courts halted immediate deportation and, in a series of cases that dragged on until 1951, ordered citizenship restored to the renunciants. A decision in late 1947 ruled that Nisei under age twenty-one could not renounce their citizenship and, in a companion case, that the renunciation by three of the adults was "not a result of their free and intelligent choice but rather because of fear, intimidation, and coercions." The following year Judge Louis E. Goodman restored citizenship to 2,300 renunciants. The repeated denunciation of the government by several federal judges also indicated the rising national shame over the internment.[50]

Reaction to the racism of the internment program spurred an attack on other forms of discrimination against Japanese-Americans. Wirin finally got his day in the Supreme Court in a Southern California ACLU suit challenging the 1913 California Alien Land Law, which prohibited alien Japanese-Americans from owning land. California attempted to strip American-born Fred Oyama of the six acres of farmland he had purchased in 1934, on the grounds that he was actually buying it for his ineligible father. With Dean Acheson assisting on the ACLU brief, the Supreme Court threw out the law. Justice Murphy called the law "nothing more than an outright racial discrimination [that] deserves constitutional condemnation." The next year, Wirin and Acheson won another victory in the Supreme Court, overturning a 1943 California law denying fishing licenses to resident alien Japanese.[51]

In 1988, forty-six years after event, the nation sought to atone for the disgrace of the evacuation and internment: Congress approved an official apology on behalf of the government and authorized $20,000 in reparations to each surviving victim.

The Draft and Conscientious Objectors

In the summer of 1940, as German troops occupied virtually all of Europe, Congress debated a draft. The ACLU confronted the issue of conscientious objection that had created the Civil Liberties Bureau in 1917. Because the United States was not yet at war, this meant a peacetime draft. Reversing a long-standing policy, and with apparently little debate, the ACLU announced that it would not oppose the draft, though it had explicitly condemned peacetime conscription only three years before. The Spanish Civil War had already eroded the commitment of many pacifists; in 1937 Roger Baldwin had stated, "My pacifism goes completely under when it comes to defense of democracy against Fascism. What way out have you other than arms?" In 1940 he apparently concluded that opposing the draft was futile and might split the already-divided ACLU. Instead, the ACLU concentrated on obtaining adequate protections in the law for conscientious objectors.[52]

Historian Howard K. Beale, a pacifist and member of the ACLU's Academic Freedom Committee, spearheaded the ACLU's lobbying. Working with the other pacifist groups—the Fellowship of Reconciliation, the Women's International League for Peace and Freedom—he sought exemption for "absolutists" (men "unable in good conscience to accept any form of compulsory service") and a definition of "conscience" including political as well as religious views. Beale testified before Congress, lobbied quietly behind the scenes, and wrote speeches for antidraft senators. Other pacifists later credited him with being primarily responsible for the relatively generous provisions of the 1940 Selective Service Act.[53]

Compared with its World War I predecessor, the law signed by Roosevelt on September 16 was remarkably tolerant of conscientious objectors: It allowed CO status on the basis of "religious training and belief" (rather than membership in particular denominations) and created a system of alternative service. It did not, however, include either total exemption for absolutists or exemption for nonreligious objectors. Shortly after Congress passed the law, Baldwin convened a meeting of all the leading pacifist groups. This evolved into the National Committee on Conscientious Objectors (NCCO), which essentially functioned as an ACLU national committee, coordinating legal strategy, publicity, and fund-raising. Baldwin tapped the prominent New York lawyer Ernest Angell as chair, evidently hoping that Angell's membership in the American Legion would ensure his credentials as a patriotic American and blunt conservative attacks.[54]

Baldwin opened a September 26 NCCO meeting by announcing that the ACLU would not challenge the constitutionality of the peacetime draft. The ACLU's lawyers had decided that the World War I cases settled the issue and that further challenges were "doomed to failure." This was not quite true, however, as the Selective Draft Cases involved a wartime draft. ACLU Chair John Haynes Holmes was furious at the ACLU's retreat and considered resigning on the grounds that "it is not possible altogether to divorce my pacifism from my position as Chairman." The October 16 draft registration day was only three weeks away, and twenty Union Theological Seminary students planned to refuse to register. Eventually eight of the students refused and were sentenced to a year in prison.[55]

The draft raised an unexpected issue before the United States' entry into the war. In the spring of 1941, workers in several war production plants, apparently inspired by the Communists, staged wildcat strikes. Selective Service Director Major Lewis Hershey issued a "work or fight" order directing local boards to induct strikers. The ACLU protested this restriction on the right to strike, and Hershey quickly rescinded the order. Once the war began, strikes were no problem (with the notable exception of John L. Lewis's mine workers) because both the AFL and the CIO adopted no-strike pledges for the duration.[56]

The language of the selective service law left a number of important questions unanswered, most important of which was the definition of "religious training and belief." Hershey promised Beale that he would make every effort to see that no COs went to prison, while Baldwin had an encouraging discussion with Justice Department officials. But these hopes were soon dashed once the draft began, as Selective Service refused to recognize political grounds for objection, and "absolutists" were convicted and sent to prison. The NCCO/ ACLU's lobbying effort continued throughout the war. Angell met with Attorney General Biddle and President Roosevelt, but with little success. A distracted Biddle seemed little concerned with the problems of COs. FDR expressed sympathy but offered no help. Access to the Oval Office was another indication of the more tolerant atmosphere in Washington, compared with that of World War I.[57]

To the surprise of everyone, in World War II there were far more conscientious objectors than there had been in World War I. Eventually, 42,973 men were classified as COs. Based on the number of draftees, four times as many absolutists went to prison as in the previous war. Jehovah's Witnesses claiming ministerial status accounted for nearly two-thirds of the 6,086 imprisoned "absolutists."[58] The surprising increase in conscientious objection reflected an important new current in American pacifism and the advent of a new force in American politics. The idea of personally confronting government power through nonviolent direct action was born during World War II. Ironically, actions of the old-line pacifist denominations spawned this new militance. The three historic "peace churches"—the Quakers, the Mennonites, and the Brethren—arranged with the government to manage the Civilian Public Service (CPS) camps for COs. Eventually, 12,000 COs worked in the camps run by the National Service Board for Religious Objectors (NSBRO). This well-intentioned effort placed the churches in the role of quasi-official government bureaucrats—collaborators in the eyes of CO militants. Norman Thomas observed that "despite many good intentions—perhaps partly on account of the good intentions," the NSBRO "has been maneuvered into a position where it is the religious arm for dealing with the state's heretics."[59]

Militant COs fought back with nonviolent resistance, organizing work strikes and walking out of the camps in a direct challenge to government authority. Despite being convicted of criminal violations, they continued their protests in prison, leading a long strike over racial segregation in the Danbury, Connecticut, penitentiary.

Although a relatively minor phenomenon during the war, the tactic of nonviolent direct action burst upon the country as a major political force in the 1960s. Indeed, a number of civil rights and anti–Vietnam War activists—

David Dellinger, James Peck—had formed their political views in World War II. The first civil rights sit-in occurred in Chicago in 1942, organized by members of the pacifist Fellowship of Reconciliation.[60]

As the war progressed, Baldwin began to realize that the administration would not accommodate the COs as he wanted, and so he grew more willing to go to court. But as with so many issues in this popular war, there was a notable shortage of plaintiffs. Baldwin finally found Socialist party member Herman Berman willing to claim CO status on political grounds (although it was not entirely clear whether the ACLU board had formally authorized arguing this point; Baldwin may have been stretching his authority in the Berman case). Angell and Fraenkel handled the case but lost in the lower courts and were unable to obtain a Supreme Court hearing.[61]

The rebellion of the militant COs in the CPS camps, meanwhile, forced the ACLU to consider the question of the constitutionality of the camps themselves. Pacifist A. J. Muste argued that because the COs worked without pay (religious groups or family provided subsistence money), it was a form of involuntary servitude. But moderate pacifists resisted a court test on the grounds that a successful challenge would close down the camps and leave the COs with no choice but prison. Two cases raising Thirteenth Amendment issues reached the Second Circuit Court of Appeals, but the Supreme Court refused to hear the cases, and with the end of the war, the issue died.[62]

In one of its most inexplicable actions, the ACLU endorsed the idea of a civilian labor draft. When severe labor shortages developed in 1942, the administration floated the idea of registration and compulsory service for all adult men and women. Several bills to authorize the conscription of the entire adult civilian population were introduced in Congress. Incredibly, given its long-standing opposition to conscription, the ACLU endorsed the idea. It concluded that "the United States has a right to mobilize all persons subject to its jurisdiction for the purposes of the prosecution of a war, whether for combatant or civilian service."[63] This was perhaps the best example of its often contradictory position during the war. Although it approved a peacetime draft, it was also the only organization to challenge the racially segregated draft. And it broke new ground on the question of the political rights of soldiers. These contradictions were the result of the deep difference of opinion within the ACLU board.

New Issues

The question of a postwar draft arose before the war was over, and again the ACLU found itself divided. NCCO chair Ernest Angell opposed any public statement by the ACLU. The question thus went to a referendum, and by a decisive vote of fifty-four to eleven the National Committee adopted a strong statement that "universal military service inevitably is an infringement upon the liberties of the individual and since it is impossible to determine [the postwar situation] at the present time . . . we oppose the present adoption of proposals for such conscription." The qualifying phrase "at the present time" indicated the ACLU's ambivalence regarding the peacetime draft.[64]

New questions about the rights of military personnel also surfaced, initially as a free speech question: Did soldiers have a right to communicate with the president and members of Congress, either in writing or as witnesses before congressional committees? Many feared that airing the grievances of discontented soldiers could disrupt the war effort or be used by Republicans to attack the Roosevelt administration. The ACLU argued that military personnel were entitled to "exercise their democratic rights as citizens" and that "compulsory silence is hostile to the interest of a democracy and of the morale essential to its armed forces." It also endorsed the right of soldiers to vote, extending civil liberties to a previously neglected area. The ACLU's initial foray into the area of soldiers' rights anticipated a far more extensive inquiry into military justice during the Vietnam War.[65]

The most ominous defeat on a conscientious objector issue came in the case of Clyde Summers, who had been denied admission to the Illinois bar because he had been a CO. When the Supreme Court upheld the denial, the ACLU expressed its alarm at the "far-reaching implications" of this penalty for a person's political or religious beliefs. The decision was a harbinger of the Court's subsequent approval of loyalty oaths during the cold war. Summers was later admitted to the New York bar, began a long and distinguished teaching career, and became the leading ACLU expert on labor questions. A year after *Summers,* however, the Court ruled that an alien could not be denied citizenship on the grounds of pacifist beliefs. Overturning its 1929 *Schwimmer* decision, the Court upheld the right to citizenship of James Girouard, a Seventh Day Adventist. Justice Douglas observed that "it is hard to believe that one need foresake his religious scruples to become a citizen." *Girouard* was a historic step forward in removing political considerations as barriers to citizenship.[66]

Freedom of Speech in Wartime

Attorney General Francis Biddle deserved much of the credit for the administration's relative tolerance of free speech during the war. A committed civil libertarian and former ACLU cooperating attorney (he assisted Fraenkel in the *Herndon* case), Biddle set a standard for tolerance of free speech in wartime unmatched by any attorney general before or since. He resisted strong pressure from Roosevelt and segments of the public to take more repressive measures, although he eventually authorized a series of admittedly token prosecutions.[67]

The most serious blot on Biddle's otherwise fine record was the first use of the Smith Act. Five months before Pearl Harbor, the Justice Department indicted twenty-nine Minneapolis teamsters who belonged to the Trotskyist Socialist Workers party. The prosecution was a shabby political deal, brought at the request of the Teamsters president Dan Tobin, who wanted to be rid of his critics. The Communists, meanwhile, cheered on the prosecution, in a cynical and shortsighted vendetta against the rival Trotskyists: Seven years later they would be destroyed by Smith Act prosecutions.

The ACLU demanded that Biddle drop the indictments on the grounds that none of the defendant's speeches or publications met the clear and present danger test. The Trotskyists provided their own legal defense team, and the ACLU handled publicity and fund-raising and assisted in the appeals. Osmond Fraenkel filed an *amicus* brief challenging the constitutionality of the Smith Act and argued the case in the Eighth Circuit Court of Appeals. Fraenkel was reasonably optimistic, and even Biddle authorized the case because he "hoped and believed" the Supreme Court would declare the Smith Act unconstitutional. Given the trend of Court decisions since 1937, these hopes were not entirely unrealistic. But no Supreme Court test of the Smith Act materialized. The eighth circuit court upheld the convictions, and the Supreme Court refused to hear an appeal.[68]

After Pearl Harbor, President Roosevelt gave conflicting signals regarding his attitude toward freedom of speech and press. On December 14, he warned that "some degree of censorship is essential in war time, and we are at war," but the next day, Bill of Rights Day, he asserted, "We will not, under any threat, or in the face of any danger, surrender the guarantees of liberty our forefathers framed for us in our Bill of Rights." On January 21 he told J. Edgar Hoover this might be the time to "clean up a number of these vile publications." Roosevelt had a vindictive streak, with special grievances against the conservative *Chicago Tribune* and Henry Luce's *Time* and *Life*.[69]

Biddle asserted himself and advised Roosevelt against attacks on the press. He had dismissed the first three Espionage Act indictments in December 1941 and instructed all U.S. attorneys to obtain his approval of future indictments. Political pressure for some action against domestic Fascists began to build in early 1942, and Roosevelt put more pressure on Biddle. At a March 20 cabinet meeting the rest of the cabinet unanimously supported FDR's demand for "vigorous action" against seditious speech and publications, at which point Biddle gave in and authorized Espionage Act indictments of several domestic Fascists.

The most noteworthy case involved George W. Christians, leader of the anti-Semitic White Shirts, who was prosecuted for sending antiwar leaflets to soldiers at Fort Oglethorpe, Georgia. The government also reindicted Robert Noble and Ellis O. Jones, leaders of the Friends of Progress in Los Angeles, for speeches opposing the war and criticizing military officers. Jones had publicly declared, "I am for Germany." This case was enormously embarrassing to the Southern California ACLU, as the eccentric Jones was a member of its board of directors. They immediately expelled him from the board and as a member. The conspiracy indictment of twenty-eight right-wing extremists in July 1942 generated the most controversy. The defendants included Elizabeth Dilling (who had long attacked the ACLU as a Communist front), Silver

Shirts leader William Dudley Pelley, and Lawrence Dennis, the most prominent American Fascist. The defendants had no significant following and posed
no threat to the war effort. The conspiracy charge was even more questionable, as there was serious doubt about whether the defendants had conspired
as a group, much less in Washington, D.C., where they were indicted. Many
observers saw the indictment was a ploy to take the political pressure off the
administration.[70]

The conspiracy case provoked another split within the ACLU. It first attacked the indictments as an "ominous" reversion to World War I practices
and chastised Biddle for abandoning his original policy of restraint. The ACLU
saw Christians as "an obvious crank" with "virtually no influence." Jones and
Noble exhibited "mental instability" and had engaged only in "expressions of
opinion." Furthermore, the wild ravings of Dilling and the other defendants
did not meet the standard of "direct and dangerous interference with the conduct of the war" that Biddle had earlier established.[71]

The same conservative–liberal–left coalition that had forced a limitation of
the ACLU's defense of the Japanese-Americans now sought to block ACLU
participation in this case.[72] The conservative Whitney North Seymour approved suppressing speech with "dangerous" tendencies. The liberal Ernst
wanted to curry favor with Roosevelt, and playwright Elmer Rice, head of
the National Council of Freedom from Censorship, was emotionally caught
up in the war against the Nazis. When democracy is threatened, he argued,
"the first business of the individual becomes the preservation of the democratic society itself."[73] The most articulate proponent of the self-preservationist
view was David Riesman, then a professor of law and later famous as a sociologist and author of *The Lonely Crowd*. In a series of influential articles he
endorsed the idea of "administrative control of propaganda." The major threat
to freedom was not the state but private Fascist groups; liberals should abandon the "negative" approach to protecting freedom, with its emphasis on freedom from state intervention, and support affirmative efforts to curb antidemocratic tendencies. The example of Nazi Germany had taught him that a negative
stance "plays directly into the hands of the groups whom supporters of democracy need most to fear." Riesman did not, however, specify where he
would draw the line between protected free speech and "dangerous and
suppressible speech."[74]

Corliss Lamont led the ACLU left-wing faction (substantially reduced by
the departures of Elizabeth Gurley Flynn, Harry Ward, Mary Van Kleeck,
Robert Dunn, and Abraham Isserman) in opposing any ACLU role in the
sedition cases, arguing that the exigencies of war took precedence over an absolute right of free speech. At a May 11 board meeting Lamont charged that
"the *objective results* of certain actions on the part of the Civil Liberties
Union would be to give aid and comfort to those who do not wish to see
the United States successfully prosecute this war," leading board chair Holmes
to reprimand him for questioning the patriotism of fellow board members. Lamont had also opposed ACLU involvement in the Japanese-American internment cases. His credibility with his fellow board members was then greatly

reduced because of his sudden reversals, which paralleled those of the Communist party. Ernst, although now an ally on wartime issues, sneeringly recalled "some of the positions you took, Corliss, before Hitler attacked Stalin." Lamont was never a Communist party member, but his sympathy for the Soviet Union influenced his position on particular issues at times.[75]

Most of the pressure on the ACLU to support suppression of domestic Fascists came from the left. *The Nation* issued a belligerent call to "curb the Fascist press," and editor Freda Kirchwey resigned from the ACLU National Committee in protest. The Communists said, "Lock them up, Mr. Biddle." The Lawyers Guild published a lengthy report demanding suppression of Father Charles Coughlin's *Social Justice.* Apart from its anti-Semitic rhetoric, the magazine published the same criticisms of war voiced by Baldwin, Thomas, and the Socialists during World War I—that it was un-Christian and served only the interests of the rich. The leftist Chicago Civil Liberties Committee also objected to the ACLU's support for Fascists. Finally, Lucille Milner, Baldwin's longtime secretary, resigned over the ACLU's defense of right-wingers, whom she labeled "foreign agents."[76]

Art Hays argued the case for an "absolutist" defense of free speech in wartime. Replying to *The Nation,* he restated the ACLU's traditional view that speech could be restricted only in cases of direct incitement to break the law. The advocates of censorship, Hays contended, lacked faith in the capacity of the majority to weigh different arguments and make a wise choice. Stating his own faith in unequivocal terms, he observed, "I believe that democracy works."[77]

The dispute over the sedition cases finally erupted at a special board meeting on October 12. Osmond Fraenkel opened the meeting at Walter Frank's Greenwich Village apartment with a motion that the ACLU would defend anyone except when his or her utterances interfered with the war effort. Although this represented the traditional ACLU distinction between speech and action, Fraenkel was shocked when "no one appeared to agree." Many were caught up in the spirit of the war effort. In an emotional outburst Elmer Rice declared that "he was for America and against anyone who opposed the American way." Ernst warned that "we are losing our influence" because of criticisms of the administration. Baldwin, Hays, and Holmes were stunned. Hays said he was "astonished to hear so much talk against civil liberties." Baldwin, already deeply upset over the board's position on the Japanese-American cases, made a thinly veiled threat to resign. "There might be situations," he warned, in which "he would be unable to act in carrying out the Board's orders and in which he might, independently, feel he must take contrary action." Holmes accused the majority of being "actuated by other considerations than devotion to civil liberties."[78]

The factions in this dispute represented a significant realignment since 1940. Thomas and Holmes, who had led the fight for the 1940 anti-Communist measures, were now among the staunchest defenders of freedom for extreme political groups. Lamont had moved in the opposite direction. Hays and Fraenkel maintained the consistent position that the ACLU should defend all speech, whereas Ernst and Seymour just as consistently endorsed limiting dangerous speech. The meeting ended with bad feelings all around, and a vote on an official policy statement was postponed for a week.

On October 19, the board adopted what became known as the "Seymour resolution." In convoluted and ambiguous language it stated that the ACLU would not automatically defend everyone charged with sedition. "Our military enemies are now using techniques of propaganda which may involve an attempt to pervert the Bill of Rights to serve the enemy," it began. Consequently, the ACLU "will not participate—except where the fundamentals of due process are denied,—in cases where, after investigation, there are grounds for a belief that the defendant is cooperating with or acting on behalf of the enemy, even though the particular charge against the defendant might otherwise be appropriate for intervention" by the ACLU. But the statement did not define the key phrase, "fundamentals of due process," leaving the ACLU's position unclear. The ACLU would think twice before defending during wartime the First Amendment claims of accused Fascists.[79]

Baldwin, Hays, Thomas, and Holmes were near despair. The majority had forced through compromises on the two most important wartime issues, the Japanese-American internment and the sedition cases. A worried Fraenkel stated, "The all-out for the war group is getting out of hand, it seems to me." Baldwin confessed "regretfully" that "the caution of our majority of the Board pretty accurately reflects our membership." Ernst, feeling momentarily triumphant, taunted Holmes: "You, and Roger, and Art . . . don't represent the Board any more." Thomas again threatened to resign but was talked out of it by Baldwin and Holmes, who invoked the memory of their twenty-five-year fight together for civil liberties.[80]

The two California affiliates, already angry over the 1940 events and the Japanese-American cases, were near revolt. Wirin labeled the Seymour resolution an "emasculation" of ACLU principles. The ACLU board rejected their demand for a referendum on the questionable grounds that it was out of order because there had been no change in policy. The Northern California ACLU threatened to repudiate the Seymour resolution and was warned that if it did so it would "be regarded as compromising the Branch's affiliation with the Union."[81] In the midst of war, with a historic test of the war powers clause of the Constitution only a few weeks away, the ACLU was on the verge of flying apart at the seams. Founding members were threatening to resign, and one of the largest affiliates was on the verge of breaking away. Baldwin desperately tried to hold the ACLU together, unsure whether he could faithfully carry out the board's official policies.[82]

In one case Baldwin did carry out his threat to act independently of the ACLU—and only exacerbated the crisis. A Detroit restauranteur named Max Stephan was convicted and sentenced to death for aiding an escaped German pilot. Baldwin, Thomas, and Hays, long active in the campaign to abolish the death penalty, were horrified at the sentence, as Stephen had provided only temporary food and shelter. When the ACLU board refused to join the appeal for clemency, Baldwin organized an independent defense committee and worked out of his ACLU office, something he had done all through his career with the ACLU. But he inadvertently used the ACLU letterhead stationery for one mailing. Lamont jumped at the opportunity to settle some old scores and submitted a long list of charges against Baldwin's leadership. He accused him of deviating from ACLU policies, manipulating board minutes, and a host of other sins. Some of the charges were valid. Baldwin had always been highly independent and, on occasion, had drafted the minutes or the wording of press releases to suit his personal views. Lamont had few friends at this point, however, and the viciousness of his attack alienated what little support he might have had. Baldwin survived, but the enmity between him and Lamont continued for years.[83]

Applying the Seymour resolution only deepened the dispute. The conservative Seymour replaced the absolutist Hays as chair of the Sedition Committee which reviewed individual cases,[84] and the board reversed an earlier decision and voted not to send Biddle a letter protesting the conspiracy indictments. A referendum widened the division. Seymour argued for no ACLU role in the conspiracy case, believing that "all of the defendants were cooperating with, or acting on behalf of, the enemy." Without embarrassment, he admitted his political motives. The Justice Department had exercised "comparative restraint and wisdom," and so criticism by the ACLU would "shake public confidence in the Department's good faith" and weaken its ability to resist pressure for more repressive actions. Fraenkel urged the ACLU to send Biddle the letter. The "drag net conspiracy" indictments were outrageous because the defendants were largely unconnected and were not being prosecuted in "the places where the utterances were made." Seymour carried the day, and the ACLU National Committee voted forty-four to thirty-five against sending the letter.[85]

Ultimately, the conspiracy trial degenerated into an embarrassing circus, and the government was spared further humiliation when the judge's death by heart attack produced a mistrial. Nonetheless, the ACLU's uncertain posture represented a significant blot on its record.

Battling the Post Office

On other censorship issues, the ACLU acquitted itself rather well, rising to the defense of both Father Coughlin and the Trotskyists. Postmaster General Frank Walker barred Coughlin's *Social Justice* from the mails in April 1942, and the Justice Department contemplated prosecution under the Espionage Act. The ACLU, raising a long-standing issue, protested the U.S. Postal Service's arbitrary power to determine what items could legally be mailed. To avoid a risky court case, Biddle silenced Coughlin through behind-the-scenes political maneuvering. An FDR supporter spoke to the archbishop of Detroit, who, already embarrassed by Coughlin's ravings, shut down *Social Justice*.[86] When the Postal Service banned the Social Workers party's *The Militant,* Osmon Fraenkel won back its mailing privileges in an administrative hearing.[87]

The black press narrowly escaped repression. As the war dramatized the contradiction between the American ideal of equality and the reality of segregation, black leaders escalated their demands for equal employment in the defense industries, the abolition of poll taxes, and the enactment of a federal antilynching law. In late 1943 J. Edgar Hoover, always aroused by any sign of black militancy, produced a 714-page report charging that many black leaders had "reportedly acted or have exhibited sentiments in a manner inimical to the Nation's war effort." He urged Biddle to prosecute, but the attorney general refused.[88]

Postmaster General Frank Walker was more concerned about sex than politics and restricted by 1942 nearly sixty publications, either denying them second-class mailing privileges or banning them altogether. The ACLU challenged the ban on the American Institute of Family Relations' *Preparing for Marriage,* and Osmond Fraenkel defended the banned Consumers Union pamphlet on birth control. In both cases the District of Columbia Court of Appeals overruled the Postal Service. Postmaster General Walker made his greatest blunder in 1944 when he revoked the second-class mailing privileges of *Esquire* magazine, making the sweeping claim that *Esquire* was not of "a public character contributing to the arts, literature and sciences." No previous postmaster general had ever suggested that a publication had to prove itself worthy to qualify for a second-class permit. The ACLU joined the case and, in 1946, won a resounding victory when the Supreme Court rejected Walker's idea that a second-class mailing permit was a privilege issued only at his discretion.[89]

The Velvet Glove of Censorship

The most serious threat to freedom of speech and press during World War II was far more subtle and dangerous than overt government censorship: the media's willing compliance with government requests for voluntary censorship. On December 18, 1941, Congress authorized the president to create the Office of Censorship. The director had unlimited power to control the flow of news to and from other countries. The Code of Wartime Practices advised editors to "exercise discretion" in publishing news about either the war or home front problems. Over ACLU protests, the administration suppressed news of domestic racial disturbances, afraid that it might provoke unrest among black troops overseas; military authorities also heavily censored news from the battlefronts.[90]

The film industry eagerly collaborated with the government. Roosevelt said he wanted "no censorship of the motion picture," but it was hardly necessary. With Warner Brothers taking the lead, the Hollywood studios produced numerous films glamorizing combat and promoting the war effort—many also promoted ethnic tolerance by depicting integrated combat units. The industry proved to be acutely sensitive to political currents and enlisted just as eagerly in the anti-Communist crusade during the cold war.[91]

Norman Thomas was one of the few who saw the insidious effects of the "tendency in the United States to set up an unofficial censorship" through self-restraint by writers, editors, and publishers.[92] The habit of deference to government claims of national security, which began in the climate of this popular war, left a dangerous legacy. When the advent of nuclear weapons in 1945 raised the stakes in international conflict, the press became even more compliant. The media's uncritical posture also corrupted government officials. Democratic and Republican administrations alike learned that a claim of "national security" was sufficient to bring to an end virtually all serious questioning. For example, during the cold war, serious criticism could easily be discredited with a subtle or not-so-subtle accusation that it followed the Communist "line." Government officials became steadily more arrogant through the 1950s and 1960s, finding that they could simply lie when necessary. The collaborative relationship between the government and the media came to a bitter end in the Vietnam War when the contradiction between official pronouncements and obvious facts became too great. Like the "imperial presidency," the "credibility gap" had its roots in World War II.

The Simmering Cold War

The Communists escaped repression during the war because of the administration's alliance with the Soviet Union, but it was a narrow escape. The fear of Communists led to the conviction of several party leaders between 1938 and mid-1941. When Hitler invaded the Soviet Union on June 22, 1941, the Communist party did an about-face—literally overnight. It later pledged full support to the war effort, opposed all strikes, and refused to criticize the evacuation and internment of the Japanese-Americans. The administration, for its part, abruptly halted further prosecutions of party leaders and, in a show of goodwill toward the Soviet Union, pardoned Earl Browder, who had been convicted of fraudulently obtaining a passport.[93]

The anti-Communist crusade, however, had a momentum of its own that could not be completely stopped. The most important pending case was the attempt to denaturalize party leader William Schneidermann, charged in 1939 with not believing in the principles of the Constitution because of his party membership. Yet at his 1927 naturalization hearing he had not been asked about Communist party membership, and the prosecution entered no evidence that he had advocated the violent overthrow of the government. As the case headed for the Supreme Court, it was clear that it would have direct implications for the Smith Act. Baldwin arranged for former Republican presidential candidate Wendell Willkie to handle the Supreme Court appeal. In a momentous civil liberties victory, the Court restored Schneidermann's citizenship. Justice Murphy repudiated the idea of guilt by association, writing that "under our traditions beliefs are personal and not a matter of mere association." The government had the burden of proving that an individual personally advocated the illegal doctrines in question. "There is a material difference between agitation and exhortation calling for present violent action which creates a clear and present danger of public disorder . . . and mere doctrinal justification or prediction of the use of force under hypothetical conditions at some indefinite future time." The decision seemed to suggest that the Court might rule the Smith Act unconstitutional.[94]

In Congress, meanwhile, the Dies Committee kept up its relentless attack on alleged subversives in the Roosevelt administration. Attorney General Biddle submitted a confidential report on the FBI loyalty investigations, which Dies then read into the *Congressional Record*. The report named twelve organizations as subversive and referred extensively to former ACLU board members Harry Ward, Elizabeth Gurley Flynn, and Abraham J. Isserman. Even Roger Baldwin was mentioned in connection with the Robert Marshall Fund which supported several ACLU projects.[95] Although little noticed in the midst of the war, Biddle's list set a precedent for the 1947 Attorney General's List of Subversive Organizations. But Dies was still not satisfied and, in an effort to embarrass the administration, succeeded in attaching to a 1943 appropriations bill a rider specifically barring payment of salaries to three federal employees. One was Robert Morss Lovett, secretary of the Virgin Islands and a long-time ACLU activist. In 1946 the Supreme Court restored their salaries, ruling that the congressional action was a bill of attainder punishing individuals without benefit of a judicial proceeding. *Schneidermann* and *Lovett* seemed to indicate that the Supreme Court would strike down the Smith Act and other antisubversive measures.[96]

When Roger Baldwin queried J. Edgar Hoover about the federal loyalty program, the director assured him the bureau would not ask any improper questions about political beliefs or associations. The ACLU, moreover, should immediately notify him of any complaints. Baldwin was deeply impressed and told Hoover he appreciated the commitment to "observe with scrupulous care the civil rights of everybody." The ACLU leader was completely fooled; just a few weeks before, Hoover had secretly designated him for custodial detention and was spying on the ACLU. Baldwin was the victim of his own eagerness to think the best of Hoover. The FBI director played a masterful game, condemning both brutality by local police and vigilante attacks on Jehovah's Witnesses. And the ACLU distributed his article "Outlaw the Vigilante."[97]

Baldwin was so taken in by Hoover that he muted his public comments on the FBI. In 1942 the *New Republic* asked him to write an article on FBI civil rights enforcement. He submitted a carefully balanced assessment, warning that "certain of the FBI's activities are dangerous to our democracy" but generally praising the bureau for its restraint. Baldwin naively concluded that Hoover's personal views were "a matter of little concern, since he is the subordinate of the Attorney-General." Hoover's nominal superior, however, had no knowledge of the extent of the FBI's spying or of the custodial detention program. After meeting with Hoover, however, Baldwin withdrew the manuscript, feeling "it would be unwise to publish it during the war or perhaps at any time." In a covering memo he explained that Hoover had "changed his views on the dangers from labor and the left" and was now "violently anti-

Dies and all the witch-hunting for reds." From 1941 onward Baldwin (along with many other ACLU leaders) had a blind spot regarding Hoover and the FBI.[98]

New Horizons in Civil Rights

"New World a Coming":
Birth of the Civil Rights Movement

The case was too explosive for the NAACP, and so they passed it on to Art Hays and the ACLU. Winfred Lynn, a black landscape gardener, announced that he would challenge the segregated draft. A successful challenge could disrupt the entire war effort. Yet it exposed the blatant contradiction between American ideals of equality and the stark facts of racism and discrimination. Nazi racism, however, had heightened the consciousness of many Americans, black and white, and gave birth to the modern civil rights movement as a broad-based interracial coalition.[99]

The first expression of the new black militancy was A. Philip Randolph's 1941 March on Washington Movement (MOWM). Randolph, president of the Brotherhood of Sleeping Car Porters and one of the few black leaders not dependent on a white constituency, proposed a massive march on the nation's capital to demand a federal fair employment practices act. Although the country was not yet at war, economic mobilization had already begun and had finally ended the long depression. Black leaders moved to get a fair share of expanding job opportunities. In the context of this period, the very idea of an assertive black demand was electrifying. Less than fifteen years before, the Ku Klux Klan had marched en masse through the nation's capital. The blacks' threat of militant action worked. Roosevelt issued Executive Order 8802 on June 25, 1941, establishing a Fair Employment Practices Committee (FEPC). Although it was a weak agency with little enforcement power, the president's concession did persuade Randolph to cancel the march. But local civil rights leaders, unwilling to compromise, organized rallies in New York and Chicago. The FEPC was a disappointment, and southern racists in Congress inhibited its vigorous implementation. The ACLU thus joined the NAACP and other members of the new civil rights coalition in lobbying for a tough federal fair employment law.[100]

Rising black expectations and the social dislocations accompanying mobilization aggravated racial tensions in the South and the North. In the military bases throughout the South, northern black recruits ran headlong into both a segregated army and institutionalized Jim Crow laws in the surrounding towns. In the industrial cities in the North and West, meanwhile, prosperity lured tens of thousands of white and black job seekers. Detroit gained 400,000 white and 60,000 black residents between 1940 and 1943. The flood of migrants produced a severe housing shortage, heightened the competition for good jobs, and led to violent incidents on buses and in parks. The accumulating tensions finally exploded in a bloody race riot in the summer of 1943. Like the World War I–era riots, the Detroit riot involved attacks on the black community by marauding bands of whites. In the summer of 1943 riots broke out in New York and Los Angeles (the so-called zoot-suit riots), with violence narrowly averted in Washington, D.C., and other cities. The Detroit riot lasted nearly a week, shut down production in the critical weapons plants, and required the mobilization of federal troops.[101]

The riots spurred a national effort to promote racial harmony. Civic leaders quickly established state and local human relations commissions and made the first organized effort to improve police–community relations. Fear that the Germans and the Japanese would exploit racial discontent to weaken the American war effort prompted these efforts. For the first time since Reconstruction, civil rights advocates had significant political leverage. Innumerable religious, business, and political leaders who had never before given any thought to racial equality joined the emerging coalition.[102]

The ACLU threw itself into the civil rights effort. In early 1942 Baldwin created the national Committee Against Racial Discrimination (CARD), chaired by the noted author Pearl Buck. CARD called for equal employment opportunity, a federal antilynching law, abolition of the poll tax, and an end to discrimination in the military. Baldwin conferred with NAACP leader Roy Wilkins about how best to continue their traditional working relationship. Wilkins thought that the ACLU, with its extensive contacts in the Roosevelt administration, could be most effective in lobbying behind the scenes. He recommended stressing the importance of civil rights gains to maintain the morale of black soldiers. The ACLU lobbied the chair of the new Fair Employment Practices Committee, but with little success; nor was Baldwin able to persuade Attorney General Biddle to take positive steps on behalf of black Americans. The FBI, meanwhile, noted that the ACLU's civil rights program "closely follows the Communist Party line."[103]

The attack on race discrimination deepened the split between the ACLU and some of its old labor allies: The ACLU National Committee included A. F. Whitney, president of the Brotherhood of Railroad Trainmen, whose constitution barred blacks from membership. When John Haynes Holmes pointed this out, an angry Whitney replied that it was none of the ACLU's business and thereupon resigned. A. L. Wirin filed an *amicus* brief in an FEPC order against the Brotherhood of Boilermakers, Local A92, which confined black members to a separate local without a vote in union affairs. In 1945 Baldwin recruited economist Herbert Northrup, an expert on union race discrimination, for the ACLU board and distributed reprints of his articles.[104]

The civil rights coalition was also active at the state level. Together with Will Maslow of the American Jewish Congress (AJC), the ACLU developed a model state civil rights law to outlaw discrimination in public accommodations, employment, and labor unions. In New York City, the ACLU, AJC, and other groups began a campaign to desegregate the Stuyvesant Town housing project on the Lower East Side.[105] The St. Louis Civil Liberties Committee protested the refusal of Washington University to admit black students and tried to defend black victims of police abuse. But few of these victims would sign affidavits in the face of police threats of reprisal; the police told one man that they would "shoot you and claim you were robbing the store," if he swore out an affidavit against them.[106]

The war years redefined the problem of police misconduct from a labor to a civil rights issue. The Wagner Act had largely established labor's right to organize—except for isolated pockets of resistance—and police attacks on union organizers had become a thing of the past. With the vast migration of blacks to industrial centers in the North and West, the victims of police abuse were increasingly black men. The Supreme Court then indicated its willingness to scrutinize police behavior in the 1943 *McNabb* decision, in which the Court overturned the conviction of a Tennessee moonshiner because his confession had been obtained during an unlawfully long detention. Justice Felix Frankfurter wrote that "the history of liberty has largely been the history of observance of procedural safeguards." In a portent of things to come, conservative Representative Sam Hobbs introduced legislation to overturn the decision and curb the activist Court. The ACLU drafted model legislation to compensate people erroneously convicted of crimes. The Chicago and Los Angeles ACLU affiliates created standing committees on police problems.[107]

The Supreme Court gave additional signals that it was willing to hear a constitutional challenge to institutionalized racial segregation. Particularly important was the Court's 1941 *Classic* decision, which asserted the right of Congress to regulate primary elections and seemed to overrule the Court's earlier decision that primary elections were private functions. Thurgood Marshall, director of the NAACP Legal Defense Fund, organized a new case, and the Supreme Court ruled the white primary to be unconstitutional in the 1944 *Smith v. Allwright* decision. Whitney North Seymour handled the ACLU's *amicus* brief, and other religious groups joined in what was the first real expression of the new civil rights coalition.[108]

The ACLU's attention then turned to discrimination in housing. On September 11, 1945, Mr. and Mrs. J. D. Shelley (who were black) bought a house at 4600 Labadie Avenue in St. Louis. Their purchase, made through a straw buyer because of a restrictive racial covenant, set in motion a case that reached the Supreme Court in 1947. In *Shelley v. Kraemer* the Court unanimously invalidated restrictive covenants in the sale of private housing. According to one analyst, "one of the most important factors in the case" was the *amicus* brief filed by twenty national organizations (including the ACLU). This testified to the new national consensus on civil rights. By the mid-1940s the stage was set for what everyone recognized would be the most important case of all: the constitutional challenge to segregated public schools.[109]

The emerging national consensus on racial equality during the war years was, of course, selective. For example, the same civic leaders who discovered the issue of justice for blacks countenanced the internment of the Japanese-Americans, their response in both cases being motivated by pragmatic considerations in regard to winning the war.[110]

Challenging the Segregated Military

The segregated military was the most explosive civil rights issue of all; it could disrupt the military in the midst of war, whereas the ACLU's challenge to the internment of the Japanese-Americans did not directly affect military operations. The NAACP, divided over whether to challenge the segregated military, finally decided against it. For the ACLU, Ernest Angell delicately raised the issue with War Department officials but then dropped it. The ACLU publicly called for an end to segregation but could find no plaintiffs for a test case.[111] Like most of the Japanese-Americans, blacks were genuinely patriotic and feared the potentially adverse consequences of a test case. Finally a plaintiff appeared in the person of Winfred Lynn, brother of civil rights attorney Conrad Lynn. When he got his draft notice in June 1942 he defiantly wrote his draft board that he was "ready to serve in any unit of the armed forces of my country which is not segregated by race." Unless "assured that I can serve in a mixed regiment," however, "I will refuse to report for induction." The NAACP passed the case to the ACLU (although it later filed an *amicus* brief). Conrad Lynn handled the initial proceedings, and Art Hays took over when he was drafted. Throughout the case, government officials and the courts went to extraordinary lengths to avoid confronting the basic issue. Early on, a very nervous War Department dispatched a black colonel, Campbell Johnson, to try to talk Lynn into dropping his case. The news media virtually ignored it. The case eventually was forgotten and is rarely mentioned in standard accounts of black history or World War II.[112]

At first glance, Lynn had a strong case: Section 4(a) of the Selective Service Act ruled that "in the selection and training of men under this act . . . there shall be no discrimination against any person on account of race or color." Yet the War Department established separate black units, and the Selective Service maintained separate black and white draft quotas to fill them. Lynn refused to report, was arrested, and then filed a writ of habeas corpus. The judge, too, avoided the race issue and dismissed Lynn's petition on the grounds that he could not challenge the law because he had not actually been drafted. To remedy this problem, Lynn's brother and Hays persuaded Lynn to submit to induction. Lynn entered the army in December 1942, and then Hays filed a suit charging discrimination. Both the district court and the circuit court of appeals ruled against Lynn, and a Supreme Court test of segregation in the military loomed. The Supreme Court, however, refused to hear the appeal on a technicality: Because Lynn had been transferred overseas, the Court held that he was no longer in the custody of the respondent named in the suit—a ruling that overlooked the established procedure of substituting respondents in such situations.[113]

One aspect of the case revealed the new militant currents stirring in civil rights and pacifist circles. Hays's handling of the case was sharply criticized by Dwight MacDonald who, along with his wife Nancy, handled the publicity. MacDonald attacked Hays for arguing the case on the "narrowest legalistic grounds": Although the law prohibited discrimination in both selection and training, Hays challenged only the selection process. MacDonald contended that the main issue was not how blacks got into the military but the discrimination in training and promotional opportunities once they were in. (Thurgood Marshall raised the larger issues in an *amicus* brief for the NAACP, which had shed its initial reluctance to be associated with the case.) Hays replied with a defense of incremental change: "The law moves step by step and . . . if we can get the decision we contend for, it will be a step toward a future case to be brought in peace time which will directly raise the question of segregation." It was a curious role reversal. For over twenty years Hays had always disdained narrow legalistic challenges and sought to use his briefs and oral arguments as occasions for raising the broadest questions of individual liberty. Now he was the voice of moderation, attacked by a new and more militant generation of activists for the very tactics he had always criticized.[114]

A Bill of Rights for Union Members

The ACLU opened up a new civil liberties issue in 1941 by championing the rights of labor union members. In the newly powerful unions, union bureaucrats often proved to be as autocratic and high-handed as their employers were.[115] In a 1941 case the ACLU represented Samuel Keller, who had been fired from his job under the union's contract clause prohibiting criticism of the local union. Baldwin now argued that "beyond all other private associations, trade unions have a public obligation to practice democracy in their internal affairs." The law had accorded them their democratic rights of free association; they now had a "moral obligation" to avoid autocratic tendencies.[116] The ACLU's deliberations culminated in a ground-breaking "bill of rights for union members," published in a 1944 pamphlet entitled *Democracy in Trade Unions*. Union members had "the right to criticize union officials; the right to inform fellow members of their opposition; the right to organize groups within the union to oppose the administration."[117] The new ACLU policy also included opposition to racial discrimination in union membership, a position that further alienated the organization from its former allies in the labor movement.

The ACLU was the first, and for many years virtually the only, organization to raise the issue of union democracy. Liberal Democrats, beholden to organized labor, refused to touch the issue, whereas conservative Republicans were interested in curbing unions per se but cared little about individual union members. The campaign finally culminated in the 1959 Landrum–Griffin Act which drew heavily from the ACLU's statement on union democracy.[118]

The "Unequal Rights Amendment"

Women's rights also emerged as a new issue during the war. The increased employment of women in war industries focused attention on the questions of equal pay and barriers to women in various occupations. The equal rights amendment (ERA), first introduced in 1923, suddenly gained new life. Along with virtually every major feminist organization, the ACLU took a strong stand against what it called the "unequal rights amendment." Baldwin and all of the women in the ACLU were heirs to the old social work tradition that had campaigned for protective legislation for women, and felt the ERA would wipe out their hard-won gains. Some feminists attacked Alice Paul and the Women's party, who initiated the ERA, because of their upper-class background, arguing they were indifferent to the problems of working women.[119]

In 1944 Baldwin created the ACLU Committee on Discrimination Against Women, chaired by New York lawyer Dorothy Kenyon. One of the first women admitted to the New York City bar association, Kenyon had served a brief term as a municipal court judge and had spent many years on the ACLU board. In 1950 she had the distinction of being the first person named as a Communist by Senator Joseph McCarthy, and in 1956, she raised the first lonely voice in the ACLU in support of women's right to an abortion.[120] Kenyon's committee lobbied for a federal equal pay for equal work bill and led the fight against the ERA. The ACLU's support for equal pay had its roots in a handful of scattered sex discrimination cases in the 1930s. The most common case involved discrimination against married female teachers. For example, in 1937 ACLU represented thirteen New Haven, Connecticut, schoolteachers who were denied reinstatement after being granted maternity leaves. (Unfortunately, this case ended abruptly when the teachers withdrew their complaints because their husbands claimed that the ACLU was a Communist-front organization.)[121] In 1943 the ACLU adopted a policy opposing employment discrimination against married women, and the Massachusetts affiliate won a state supreme court ruling ending a Boston school board ban on hiring married women as teachers.

The ERA found a surprising amount of support in Congress. In the first Senate floor vote in 1946, it passed by a vote of thirty-eight to thirty-five. In the House, Representative Emanuel Celler simply refused even to hold any hearings. The ACLU was a leading member of the National Committee to Oppose the Unequal Rights Amendment which continued to fight the ERA through the late 1950s. It finally died in the early 1960s but revived in the very different political context of the late 1960s, with the rebirth of the women's movement.[122]

The ACLU at Age Twenty-Five

The end of the war coincided with the ACLU's twenty-fifth anniversary, and it was an occasion to reflect on the organization's achievements. The contrast between the fate of civil liberties in the two world wars was eloquent testimony to the ACLU's impact on American law and life. With the glaring exception of the Japanese-American internment, individual freedom had fared rather well in the most recent war. The president and the attorney general had promised to respect freedom at home and, for the most part, had honored the pledge. Prosecutions for political speech and censorship of the mails had been relatively minor events. Perhaps even more important, the Supreme Court had, in the 1943 flag salute case, strongly affirmed the principle of freedom of conscience, not only in the midst of war but also in a controversy surrounding the emotionally charged symbol of the American flag. The idea that American ideals meant tolerance for unpopular minorities was a striking contrast with the situation in World War I when the entire machinery of government set out to compel conformity. The internment of the Japanese-Americans, however, was a somber reminder of the extent to which racism and considerations of national security could lead to wholesale violations of individual rights.

The performance of the ACLU itself was evidence of the contradictory American attitudes toward civil liberties. On the one hand, the ACLU could claim much of the credit, since World War I, for the growing respect for the Bill of Rights. During this war it had acquitted itself well, with its lonely defense of the Japanese-Americans one of the crown jewels in its long record of defending the unpopular. At the same time, however, there were signs that even within the ACLU there were strong pressures to approve limits on civil liberties during times of crisis. If the ACLU was now a respected organization, gaining the ear of top government officials, there also were some leaders who were ready to trim the defense of civil liberties in order to maintain that respect.

To mark the ACLU's anniversary, Baldwin organized a lavish conference and dinner at the Biltmore Hotel in New York. Evidence of the ACLU's status was everywhere. President Harry S. Truman sent a telegram saluting the ACLU's "outstanding service to the cause of true freedom. The integrity of the American Civil Liberties Union has never been, and I feel, never will be questioned." New York Governor Thomas Dewey was equally lavish in his praise: "You have established . . . beyond all possible doubt, proof that the American Civil Liberties Union is an essential part of American life. The war for freedom is an endless one. Without the [ACLU] there would be no organization to take up the cudgels for lone, oppressed individuals."[123]

This was a far cry from the lonely days of 1920 when free speech was a suspect idea. Only Art Hays was troubled by this new respectability and was not impressed that ACLU meetings were now "addressed by the Attorney General, with district attorneys, Senators, mayors, and other important dignitaries at the speakers' table." He longed for the old days "when no one sat on the dais who had not shown his devotion to civil liberties by having served at least a short time in jail." These "old days" were actually less than a decade in the past—a fact that testified to the rapid changes in support for civil liberties.[124]

The conference participants wasted little time reflecting on past accomplishments but turned to the ACLU's future. The momentum of the emerging civil rights movement dominated the conference, with five of the eight "immediate tasks" for the ACLU involving some aspect of racial discrimination. The ACLU called for federal and state fair employment practices laws, federal legislation to outlaw the poll tax, and an end to housing discrimination. Two other items dealt with discrimination against Asian-Americans.[125]

Separation of church and state emerged as another priority. The ACLU was already involved in a challenge to a New Jersey law providing public funds for busing parochial school students. Two years later, the Supreme Court's decision in that case, *Everson v. Board of Education,* opened four decades of litigation over the establishment clause of the First Amendment. The ACLU emerged as one of the leading advocates of a strong position on separation of church and state and, as a result, was increasingly attacked by Christian groups as the agent of "godlessness."[126]

The conference also reflected the special concerns of certain ACLU leaders: For instance, an entire session was devoted to international civil liberties. Once again Roger Baldwin attempted to take the ACLU into international human rights issues, but as it had at least twice before, the ACLU board soundly rejected this idea. The ACLU's mandate thus remained focused on civil liberties issues within the United States.

The ACLU conference was also remarkable for what it did not foresee. There was no awareness of the impending cold war. Not a single session was devoted to the issue of loyalty and security questions or the rights of unpopular political groups. These were serious oversights, as the most serious assaults on civil liberties since World War I lay just ahead. As they deliberated the future of civil liberties at the Biltmore, the ACLU's leaders could take great satisfaction in an extraordinary record of accomplishment. But they completely underestimated the impending threats.

IV

American Inquisition:
The Cold War

Eight

The Anti-Communist Crusade
Begins, 1947-1950

An Age of Suspicion

Called before the State Department's Security Hearing Board to testify on behalf of John Paton Davies, journalist Theodore White suddenly found himself on trial. Hadn't he tried to incite black troops in Burma to revolt during World War II? "Is it true, Mr. White, that your wife is a member of the Communist Party?"[1]

Decca Treuhaft was abruptly fired as a classified ad salesperson for the *San Francisco Chronicle* because she didn't have "the personality for this type of work." The truth was that FBI agents had informed the *Chronicle* that she and her husband were Communist party members. Out of work, she turned to writing and began a highly successful career under her maiden name of Jessica Mitford.[2]

When the Academy Awards announced that Robert Rich had won the 1957 Oscar for best screenplay, no one came forward. "Robert Rich" was the pseudonym for Dalton Trumbo, blacklisted by Hollywood as a suspected Communist.[3]

President John F. Kennedy took Martin Luther King, Jr., into the White House rose garden for a private chat in June 1963. Kennedy warned King that the FBI believed his closest adviser, Stanley Levison, was a Communist. The president thereupon urged King to drop Levison, even though Levison had abandoned Communism years before. Meanwhile, the FBI was systematically spying on King's own private life.[4]

White, Mitford, Trumbo, and King were only a few of the more prominent victims of the cold war's anti-Communist crusade. The lives of untold thousands of others were ruined during this age of suspicion and guilt by association. People were "named" because they had attended a lawful political meeting twenty years before or had subscribed to a magazine now deemed "subversive." But they could not confront their faceless accusers. Even ideas became suspect, and the ensuing suspicion warped American political dialogue. Representative Albert Canwell, chair of the Washington State Un-American Activities Committee, charged that "if a person says that in this country Negroes are discriminated against and there is inequality of wealth, there is every reason to believe that person is a Communist."[5] If the Communists were for civil rights, then civil rights was suspect; if the Communists were for "peace," then anyone who advocated peace (or disarmament, or criticized American foreign policy) must be a Communist. Even the Bill of Rights was suspect: On Bill of Rights Day in 1957, Attorney General Tom Clark advised the country to "ferret out those who cloak themselves under the Bill of Rights and who would undermine our form of government." The cold war thus developed into the greatest assault on the freedom to think, to speak, and to join political groups in American history.[6]

The United States' alliance with the Soviet Union had begun to unravel even before World War II was over, as both sides competed for control over Eastern Europe. Then British Prime Minister Winston Churchill's famous "Iron Curtain" speech on March 5, 1946, finally ended the alliance with the Soviet Union. The cold war officially began in March 1947 when President Harry Truman promised American aid to fight the Communist insurgency in the Greek Civil War. Under a policy of "containment," the United States would fight Communism anywhere in the world. Nine days later Truman launched an attack on Communism at home, creating a federal loyalty program to eliminate subversives from the federal government.[7]

The cold war was an irrational outburst, one of the many episodes of popular hysteria that punctuate American history. The fear of Communism, however, bore little relationship to the facts. The American Communist party was pathetically weak and lost the goodwill it had won with its patriotic stance during the war when, in 1945, it again adopted a revolutionary stance. The Soviet Union was devastated by the war, whereas the United States reached its peak of military and economic superiority. Nonetheless, several new factors aroused popular anxieties: Nuclear weapons were a new and terrifying force. Together with long-range bombers (and then missiles) they posed the threat of a direct attack on the continental United States. The very idea of a cold war, of "containment" without a clear-cut victory, was frustrating to Americans accustomed to victory. Finally, there was actual Soviet espionage—confirmed by the 1946 confession of scientist Klaus Fuchs in Britain. The sensational American cases that followed—the Alger Hiss perjury case, the Rosenbergs' trial—convinced Americans that there was massive Soviet espionage.

To a later generation, "McCarthyism" became a convenient synonym for the cold war. The anti-Communist crusade, however, began long before Wisconsin Senator Joseph McCarthy burst on the scene in 1950. Rather, it was a genuinely bipartisan effort. Although Republicans McCarthy and California Senator Richard M. Nixon are remembered as symbols of the witch hunt, Democrats also were instrumental in launching it, with Truman's loyalty program and congressional liberals' sponsorship of such legislation as Minnesota

Senator Hubert H. Humphrey's detention-camp provision of the 1950 Internal Security Act. Truman thought he could preempt the anti-Communist issue in 1947, but the Republicans quickly upped the ante to their advantage. Once Truman conceded the threat of Communists' being employed in the government, Nixon and McCarthy did not hesitate to accuse him of failing to root them out. Who, they asked, "gave away" Eastern Europe at Yalta? Who "lost" China? Who allowed the Russians to "steal" the secrets of the atomic bomb? In a new era of international conflict, the anti-Communist rhetoric spun out of control.[8]

Arthur Schlesinger, Jr., the unofficial theoretician of the Democratic party, provided an intellectual rationale for liberal anti-Communism: Preserving the "vital center" of American democracy meant excluding Communists from the political process. He popularized the idea among liberals that Communists both were inherently treacherous and served a foreign power. This idea, that Communists were beyond the pale of constitutional protection, set the stage for a sweeping assault on civil liberties.[9]

Virtually all of the apparatus for a witch hunt was already in place: the House Un-American Activities Committee (HUAC), the Smith Act, loyalty oaths, FBI spying. The technique of smearing people because of their political associations had been established between 1938 and 1941. The anti-Communist crusade simply picked up where it had left off in June 1941.

The ACLU and the Cold War

The ACLU entered the cold war deeply divided. The 1940 Resolution and the Flynn purge had already set a precedent for anti-Communism. Norman Thomas and Morris Ernst were more determined than ever to keep the ACLU free of any taint of Communism, which meant not opposing most of the cold war measures and being very cautious about joining cases involving Communists or suspected Communists. They also believed, along with many other anti-Communist liberals, that Communists could be isolated with surgical precision, without any larger damage to political freedoms. On the other side in the ACLU stood a group of First Amendment absolutists: Arthur Hays, Osmond Fraenkel, and Walter Gellhorn. They opposed on principle all restrictions based on political beliefs and associations, arguing that any attempt to restrict the freedom of Communists would inevitably spill over into a broader assault on the freedom of others, with enormous damage to civil liberties generally.

The balance of power in the ACLU was held by a group of liberal centrists. They were genuinely confused and uncertain about both Communism and the escalating anti-Communist witch hunt. Roger Baldwin epitomized their ambivalence, torn between his commitment to free speech principles and his hostility toward Communism. Members of this group were not fanatic anti-Communists, but they were unwilling to defend civil liberties in absolutist terms. They accepted the federal loyalty program in principle, for example, but objected to its lack of procedural protections, failing to calculate the damage that would result from trying to limit only Communists' rights. It was a miscalculation that many other well-meaning liberals made as well.

Because of his own uncertainty, Baldwin provided weak leadership at this critical moment in the history of the ACLU. Between 1947 and 1954 a cold war also raged inside the ACLU as the three factions struggled for the soul of the organization. Torn by its internal disputes, the ACLU at times appeared hesitant during the cold war. While the American Legion relentlessly attacked it as a Communist front (and demanded a congressional investigation), critics on the left attacked the ACLU for failing to take a more vigorous stance.[10]

Public Opinion, Civil Liberties, and the Court

The division of opinion within the ACLU reflected the national thinking on the Communist question. At issue were fundamental questions about the scope of civil liberties in an age of international conflict. Was the Communist party a legitimate political group or a criminal conspiracy? What were the rights of the accused individual in the face of official inquiry into political beliefs and associations? Like other Americans, many in the ACLU succeeded in placing all Communist-related issues into a single category. On other issues—civil rights, censorship, separation of church and state, police misconduct—they vigorously supported an expanding civil liberties agenda. Morris Ernst dramatized the contradiction: One of the ACLU's leading anti-Communists, who collaborated with the FBI, he was also the foremost opponent of literary censorship and virtually alone in challenging restrictions on birth control. The Supreme Court also distinguished between Communist and non-Communist issues. After the Court's civil libertarian bloc was decimated by the deaths of Justices Frank Murphy and Wiley Rutledge in 1949, the Court upheld virtually all cold war measures, retreating from earlier decisions protecting unpopular speech. At the same time, however, it forged an important new body of law in civil rights, freedom from censorship, separation of church and state, and due process of law.[11]

The Federal Loyalty Program

On March 21, 1947, President Truman issued Executive Order 9835, creating the Federal Loyalty Program. An enormously enlarged version of programs dating back to 1939, this program allowed the government to deny employment to anyone when "reasonable grounds exist for belief that the person involved is disloyal to the Government of the United States." Evidence of disloyalty included "membership in, affiliation with or sympathetic association with any foreign or domestic organization, communist, or subversive, or as having adopted a policy of advocating or approving the commission of acts of force or violence to deny other persons their rights." Truman then directed the attorney general to draw up an official list of subversive organizations.[12]

Truman completely misjudged the dynamics of anti-Communism, and he was not able to keep the program within reasonable bounds. The loyalty program legitimized the idea of judging people on the basis of political beliefs and associations rather than overt criminal acts. And by not defining "subversive" or "sympathetic association," it invited abuse. Any contact with a named organization, no matter how brief or informal or how long ago, was sufficient evidence of disloyalty. Nor were there standards for determining which organizations would be placed on the attorney general's list. People were labeled as "Communist sympathizers" for advocating ideas the Communists happened to support. Indeed, both the ACLU and the Lawyers Guild were attacked as "Communist fronts" for defending the rights of suspected Communists.[13]

The ACLU also misjudged the potential impact of the loyalty program. In its first official response it accepted its basic purpose as legitimate and focused on procedural shortcomings. The ACLU held that "a test of loyalty to the United States may properly be required of persons seeking employment in the Federal service" and that "persons found to be disloyal . . . may be properly denied employment or dismissed from it." There was, however, "grave danger to civil liberties" in certain aspects of the program. The worst was the attorney general's list which it condemned as an official "blacklist." The power to designate organizations was "without limit," as there were no standards to determine the meaning of *subversive* and no opportunity for listed organizations to rebut charges against them at a formal hearing. The procedural protections for individual government employees were also "insufficient." That is, accused persons did not have a right to confront their accusers or to subpoena witnesses on their own behalf. Although membership in an organization on the attorney general's list was supposed to be only one factor in determining loyalty, the ACLU prophetically warned that inevitably the government would "automatically discharge any one definitely associated with a blacklisted organization."[14]

The federal loyalty program reopened a debate in the ACLU that turned on two underlying questions: the nature of the Communist party and whether members of a totalitarian organization should hold public office. Ernst and Thomas argued that the Communist party was a criminal conspiracy rather than a conventional political party, a point that had direct relevance to the scope of the First Amendment: "Since secret advocacy by its very nature precludes public discussion, it does not come within the First Amendment." Osmond Fraenkel replied by citing the traditional ACLU distinction between advocacy and incitement. Belonging to a political party and teaching Marxist theory were forms of protected speech. Following Louis Brandeis's *Whitney* test, only incitement to imminent illegal action could be punished. After a long and bitter debate, Fraenkel's view prevailed. The ACLU's anti-Communists refused to give up, however, and the internal feud intensified.[15]

On the question of whether members of totalitarian groups should hold public office, Roger Baldwin reflected the ambivalence of the centrist liberals. While he opposed any restriction based on membership in a political group, at the same time he stated that the "obligations" of totalitarian organizations were "fundamentally incompatible with the obligations of government employment." A KKK (Ku Klux Klan) member, he suggested, could be barred from serving as a chief of police because he could not be expected to enforce the law fairly. This was a serious concession to political tests for employment, inconsistent with his long-held view and thus a revealing index of the impact of anti-Communism on Baldwin's thinking. Ernie Besig of the Northern California ACLU protested that "it doesn't make any difference whether a Chief of Police is a member of the Ku Klux Klan or the Fellowship of Reconciliation. The test is how he performs his job." The two California ACLU affiliates took strong exception to the official ACLU position on the federal loyalty program. A. A. Heist, director of the Southern California ACLU, charged that it "makes all talk of opposition to 'witch-hunting' a mockery. We are joining those who are out to get Communists out of government employment and labor union leadership." The California affiliates, however, represented a minority position in the ACLU, and when they forced a referendum on the policy statement regarding the loyalty program, they were outvoted, forty-five to ten.[16]

Despite these internal divisions, the ACLU challenged the loyalty program privately and publicly, continuing the two-pronged strategy of quiet lobbying and court tests that had been used during World War II. Board members James L. Fly and Raymond L. Wise met with Attorney General Tom Clark in April 1947 and proposed strengthening the program's procedural protections. Fly had recently resigned as chair of the Federal Communications Commission (FCC) and enjoyed considerable respect within the Truman administration.[17] Publicly, the ACLU announced that it would offer free legal assistance to federal employees charged with being disloyal. Washington attorneys Abe Fortas and Victor Rotnem coordinated the ACLU's effort. But as the first cases developed, Rotnem found the entire process to be "really quite shocking." By the end of the first year the FBI had investigated over 2 million federal employees, conducting full investigations of over 6,000. Of these, 86 had been fired and 619 had resigned; still, these figures did not fully reflect the full impact of the program in creating a climate of suspicion and fear.[18]

The case of Abraham Chasanow, fired in 1953 as a navy hydrographer, was typical of the fate of employees faced with vague innuendos from unidentified informants. The accusations against him included having attended a social gathering in 1941 at the home of someone suspected of being subversive, assisting the Spanish Civil War relief, belonging to the Lawyers Guild for one year in 1939, and advocating economic cooperatives. Chasanow never had an opportunity to confront the sources of these allegations. The Navy Security Appeal Board unanimously ruled his employment "not clearly consistent with the interests of national security." Chasanow fought back and had the benefit of being the subject of a series of prize-winning stories by journalist Anthony Lewis. And by the time Chasanow's story broke in the press in 1953, public opinion had begun to react against the more outrageous abuses of the cold war.

In another celebrated 1953 case, the air force dismissed Milo Radulovich because of his "close and continuing contact" with certain suspect individuals—his father and his sister. His father was an immigrant who regularly read Serbian-language newspapers that the Air force deemed pro-Tito. Then Edward R. Murrow devoted an entire thirty-minute "See It Now" program to Radulovich and helped him win reinstatement.[19]

Dr. Eric Berne, later famous as the author of a best-selling psychology book, was abruptly fired by the Veterans Administration. In addition to "knowingly" associating with a suspected Communist, Berne was accused of being a member of the Northern California ACLU, "which reportedly is heavily affiliated with Communists and fellow travellers."[20]

An Official Blacklist: The Attorney General's List

Attorney General Tom Clark issued the first official list of subversive organizations on December 4, 1947. The eighty-two groups included the Communist party and a host of 1930s Popular Front groups: the American Committee for the Protection of the Foreign Born, the International Labor Defense, the Joint Anti-Fascist Refugee Committee, the National Negro Congress, and others. But no standards guided the designation of "subversive," nor did any organization have the opportunity to challenge the listing. As the ACLU had predicted, it immediately became an official blacklist and was widely adopted by state and local governments. New York City's mayor, William O'Dwyer, for example, banned any listed organization from soliciting funds on the streets. Roger Baldwin was one of many liberals embarrassed by his previous association with many of the listed organizations. To protect his image, he frequently denounced Communism, a tactic that only fed the anti-Communist fervor and weakened his image as a defender of free speech for unpopular political views.[21]

The ACLU denounced the list but was deeply divided over challenging it in court. After a long debate the board decided, by a one-vote margin, to file a brief on behalf of the Joint Anti-Fascist Refugee Committee (JAFRC) in the first important court test. Fraenkel's brief charged that the entire loyalty program "creates a procedural monster antithetical to fundamental principles of American democratic justice." It put the government in the position of prescribing which beliefs were "true" and which were "false." The attorney general's list violated both procedural and substantive rights. The JAFRC had "never received any notice or hearing concerning such designation" and it had had no opportunity to rebut the charges against it. The listing had caused substantive material harm through loss of tax-exempt status and licenses to solicit funds, denial of meeting places, and a decline in contributions and members. But in a concession to the anti-Communist faction, the brief did not challenge the attorney general's list per se.[22]

The Supreme Court was also deeply divided over the attorney general's list. With six different opinions, the Court upheld the JAFRC on the narrow procedural point that the attorney general had listed the organization without any factual basis. The Court never ruled, however, on the constitutionality of the list, which was eventually abolished in 1974.[23]

The Case of the Legless Veteran

The "case of the legless veteran" dramatized the abuse of the attorney general's list and the steadily expanding cold war hysteria. James Kutcher, who had lost both legs in combat during World War II, was dismissed from his job at the Veterans Administration (VA) in 1948 because he belonged to the Socialist Workers party—which was on the attorney general's list. Making "no secret of my views or those of the Socialist Workers Party," Kutcher organized a national defense committee and, with ACLU assistance, sued to get his job back. Then, in yet another unprincipled and self-destructive act, the Communist party tried to undermine Kutcher's efforts because he was a Trotskyist. Party leaders asked rhetorically, "Would [you] ask Negroes to give freedom of speech to the KKK? Would you give civil rights to Jefferson Davis?" The circuit court of appeals in 1952 ordered the government to give Kutcher a hearing. But he lost the hearing, on the grounds that his employment was not "clearly consistent" with national security, and so he had to sue again.[24]

The legless veteran's woes were only just beginning. First, the Veterans Administration cut off his pension, and Kutcher worried publicly whether the order denying him "all" benefits meant that he would have to give back his artificial legs. Public outrage at this vindictive action forced the VA to retreat and restore his pension pending a hearing; he finally won it back in 1956. Meanwhile, in 1952 Congress passed the Gwinn amendment denying public housing to any member of one of the 203 organizations on the attorney general's current list, along with a loyalty oath for all residents. Kutcher and his seventy-three-year-old parents thus faced eviction from their Newark housing project. The New Jersey ACLU filed a suit challenging the Gwinn amendment (as did the ACLU affiliates in New York, California, Michigan, and Washington). The government lost all of the Gwinn cases in the lower courts and so abandoned any attempt to enforce the law. The circuit court ordered Kutcher reinstated in his job, and he returned to work on June 26, 1956. In a final vindictive act, the government refused to pay him because he belonged to an organization advocating the overthrow of the government. President Dwight D. Eisenhower finally ordered him paid, and ten years after he was fired, Kutcher's ordeal ended. The case of the legless veteran dramatized the absurd logic and vindictive dynamic behind the federal loyalty program.[25]

HUAC Resurgent

The Hollywood Ten

The confrontation between the House Un-American Activities Committee (HUAC) and the "Hollywood Ten" in October 1947 catapulted HUAC back into the headlines after many years of relative obscurity. Having heard several "friendly" witnesses who testified to Communist influence, the committee called nineteen writers and directors believed to be Communists. They included some of the most successful figures in the industry: Dalton Trumbo, perhaps the highest paid screenwriter; writer Alvah Bessie, who had fought in the Spanish Civil War; and writer John Howard Lawson, the most prominent Communist in Hollywood. They arrived in Washington accompanied by movie stars Humphrey Bogart and Lauren Bacall, who joined other famous personalities as members of the Committee for the First Amendment.[26]

At that point, the legal questions regarding the rights of witnesses were still unresolved. The Hollywood Ten refused to answer the committee's questions because that would legitimize inquiry into political beliefs and associations. They also rejected their lawyers' advice to take the Fifth Amendment, because this would imply guilt. Instead, they chose to refuse to answer any questions on the grounds that the First Amendment prohibited inquiry into political beliefs and associations. The hearings were an utter disaster. The Ten (the other nine were never called) adopted a belligerent posture and tried to read statements denouncing the committee. One by one, they were removed and eventually cited for contempt. Worse, their public support evaporated. Film industry leaders panicked and, a month later, fired all members of the Ten currently employed and blacklisted all suspected leftists.[27]

The Hollywood Ten contempt cases joined others challenging HUAC. The ACLU was divided over whether to enter the first cases reaching the Supreme Court. After a referendum—the first of many on cold war issues—it filed briefs on behalf of Leon Josephson, Dr. Edward Barsky, and the Hollywood Ten. Fraenkel's brief for Barsky argued that under the First Amendment, "no general inquiry into matters relating to opinion or affecting freedom of association is permissible." The Court had already established that freedom of speech was a "preferred" right that limited the power of the legislature. Going further, Fraenkel challenged HUAC's legality: "The mere existence of such a committee" poses a threat to "the expression of opinion and the conduct of wholly legal activities." Finally, the vagueness of the terms *subversive* and *un-American* violated the Fifth Amendment guarantee of due process.[28]

The challenges to HUAC failed. The circuit court upheld the Josephson and Barsky contempt citations by two-to-one margins, and the Supreme Court refused to hear the appeals, also refusing in 1949 to hear those of Hollywood Ten members Lawson and Trumbo. All went to prison. In one bizarre twist, writer Ring Lardner, Jr. (later to win an Academy Award for the movie *M.A.S.H.*) met his HUAC nemesis in prison; former committee chair J. Parnell Thomas was then serving time in the Danbury, Connecticut, penitentiary for receiving kickbacks. Both the national ACLU office and the Southern California affiliate assisted in later suits challenging the film industry blacklist, but the last of these failed in 1958.[29]

Naming Names: A Nation of Informers

With these victories in the Court, HUAC's power was unrestrained. The Alger Hiss case in 1948 catapulted Richard Nixon to national prominence as a relentless red hunter and convinced the public there were indeed Communist spies in the government. HUAC went on the road and, over the next decade, held public hearings in Los Angeles, Detroit, Chicago, Philadelphia, Gary, Indiana, and, fatefully, San Francisco in 1960. The pattern was the same everywhere. Teachers, union organizers, musicians, and others were subpoenaed to appear. They usually were preceded by testimony from ex-Communist witnesses who named various people as Communists. The hearings brought a reign of fear. Merely being subpoenaed was tantamount to being labeled a Communist, and those who took the Fifth Amendment were labeled "Fifth Amendment Communists."[30]

Other investigating committees followed HUAC's lead: The Senate created the Subcommittee on Internal Security in 1950. The California Fact-Finding Committee on Un-American Activities, chaired by the liberal state Senator Jack Tenney, was the only committee ever to declare officially the ACLU to be a Communist front. Its 1949 report concluded that the ACLU was "heavily infiltrated with Communists and fellow-travelers and frequently following the Communist line and defending Communists." Similar witch hunts were conducted by the Canwell Committee in Washington State and the Broyles Committee in Illinois.[31]

The most disgraceful aspect of HUAC's crusade was the requirement that witnesses name names. In fact, this willingness to name names was HUAC's "ultimate test" of credibility. Many ex-Communists were quite willing to testify about their own activities, but the committee demanded a humiliating ritual of identifying other persons. At the second round of the Hollywood investigations in 1951, actor Larry Parks tried to object: "I would prefer, if you would allow me, not to mention other people's names. . . . This is not the American way." His protest was in vain. Parks capitulated, named names in executive session and was then humiliated when HUAC leaked the information to the press. Witnesses had their careers and, often, their self-respect destroyed. Playwright Lillian Hellman was one of the few who salvaged her honor. She took the Fifth in 1952 but delivered one of the most memorable statements of principle of the entire period. Admitting that the technicalities of the Fifth were "very difficult for a layman to understand," she declared that hurting innocent people by naming them was "inhumane and indecent and dishonorable." "I cannot and will not cut my conscience to fit this year's fashions."[32]

One incident dramatized how well-meaning people thought they were doing the right thing by naming names: In his critical book on Senator Joseph McCarthy, *New Yorker* magazine correspondent Richard H. Rovere casually revealed how he had caused one federal employee to lose his job. A friend told him that a certain "Mr. X" had passed his federal loyalty test despite previous Communist party membership. They worried that if McCarthy discovered this, it would give credence to all of his wild charges about Communists in government. When Rovere finally guessed who Mr. X was, he "reluctantly" told the man's supervisor, and Mr. X promptly resigned. Rovere, the good liberal, prided himself on having deprived McCarthy of this "potential triumph." He conceded that he might have violated journalistic ethics but expressed no qualms about having informed on someone's past political associations and forced his resignation.[33]

Blacklisting

Blacklisting spread from Hollywood to the radio and television industries. Although whispered about, it remained secret and unknown to the general public until it burst into public view in 1950 over the Jean Muir incident. NBC abruptly dropped Muir from the popular television series *The Aldrich Family* because American Business Consultants, a professional red-hunting organization, had accused her of Communist ties.[34]

The Muir incident exposed all of the insidious guilt-by-association elements of the anti-Communist crusade. Muir lost her job because of vague and undocumented charges, completely unrelated to her job performance and brought by informers she could not confront. American Business Consultants was one of many private firms trafficking in anti-Communism. It published *Red Channels,* a list of 151 alleged subversives, and contracted with broadcasters and sponsors to "clear" employees. *Red Channels* listed anyone who had briefly belonged to the Communist party or some Popular Front group in the 1930s. American Business Consultants then "cleared" the ACLU in 1949 with the statement that "we certainly are of the opinion that at present you are not a Communist or even a Communist sympathizer in spite of your former affiliations."[35]

The ACLU responded immediately to the Muir incident in one of its most vigorous actions of the cold war period. The day after Muir was fired, the ACLU board denounced blacklisting and directed the staff to take "immediate and strong action." They hired writer Merle Miller to prepare a detailed report on blacklisting. Published in 1952, *The Judges and the Judged* was a huge success. It sold well and received many favorable reviews. Miller condemned the blacklisting, the tactics of the red hunters, and the moral cowardice of the entertainment industry. *Red Channels* had "wrecked, probably forever, the careers of many talented anti-Communist Americans, not to mention the spiritual pain and humiliation suffered by all of the 151" people it had mentioned. In a series of rhetorical questions, Miller attacked the logic of guilt by association. "Does a man have 'leftist leanings' if . . . he attended a 'spring ball' for the *New Masses* in March 1938? . . . Does one affiliation suffice? Will a dozen do? Are forty-one necessary? Who can say? Who is to judge?" Should people be deprived of their livelihood because they had contributed to an unpopular political cause? Miller concluded with the unequivocal statement that "those who would do the suppressing are a greater threat to the democratic idea than those who would be suppressed."[36] The favorable response to *The Judges and the Judged* indicated that by 1952, public opinion was beginning to turn against the worst of the witch hunt.

The ACLU's prompt and aggressive response to the Muir incident was surprising for several reasons. Not only was the ACLU equivocal on some other cold war issues, but blacklisting involved private-sector employment. That is, the ACLU could easily have ducked the issue on the grounds that it involved no state action. This was one of many contradictions surrounding the ACLU's response to the cold war. The ACLU's anti-Communists tried to block publication of *The Judges and the Judged*. Merlyn Pitzele accused Miller of numerous factual errors and, worse, of failing to condemn left-wing blacklisting of anti-Communists. Then Pitzele went public and published his criticisms in the *New Leader,* setting off an uproar in the ACLU. The board condemned Pitzele's public attack as "grossly improper" and established a special committee to investigate his charges. The committee found only a few minor errors in Miller's report and recommended that it be published.[37]

Fighting HUAC

The ACLU's continued call for the abolition of HUAC proved to be a futile gesture. Instead, more effort went into Morris Ernst's proposal for procedures to protect the rights of witnesses. It would preserve much of the power of investigating committees: Witnesses would have a right to an attorney and to file additional statements but no right to cross-examine accusers. Lobbying privately with Richard Nixon, Ernst disavowed the ACLU's policy, telling him, "I have no use for these silly attacks on the constitutional capacity of the Committee."[38] The ACLU chair, John Haynes Holmes, requested an "off the record discussion" with Nixon, and Roger Baldwin had a "strong meeting of the minds" with HUAC chair J. Parnell Thomas. No one in the ACLU regarded these contacts as sinister or irregular; rather, they continued the pattern of high-level negotiations established during World War II. Indeed, the ACLU's Washington office director, Irving Ferman, claimed that his close contacts with HUAC and the FBI helped quash a 1955 HUAC report attacking the ACLU.[39]

Ernst, believing the democratic process was best served by more information, pressed for a federal law requiring political groups using the mails to disclose their leaders and finances. He persuaded President Truman's Civil Rights Committee, of which he was a member, to endorse the concept. But the ACLU consistently rejected the idea. Art Hays warned that compulsory disclosure would result in the "destruction" of minority political groups.[40] The ACLU also remained ambivalent about voluntary disclosure. When HUAC counsel Ernie Adamson demanded access to ACLU records in 1945, the board voted to send copies of certain correspondence, but not all of its records. In 1952 the organization expressed its willingness to cooperate "fully with governmental agencies in any investigation of its activities," a reflection of the lingering belief that a certain degree of cooperation with the government was the best way to defend civil liberties.[41]

By 1955 reaction to the abuses of HUAC hearings prompted the House to adopt a set of rules of procedure for all committees: Witnesses were to be advised in advance of the subjects to be covered, and persons named by others were allowed to testify in their own defense—a small step forward but still far short of any reasonable standard of due process. The House significantly rejected the ACLU's recommendation that persons named in testimony be allowed to confront and cross-examine their accusers.[42]

Smashing the Communist Party: The Smith Act Cases

The government struck directly at the Communist party in July 1948 when the Justice Department indicted twelve top party leaders under the Smith Act. Charging them with advocating the overthrow of the government and conspiring to organize the Communist party for that purpose, the case presented the most serious test during the cold war of the scope of the First Amendment. Was Communist party doctrine simply theory or direct incitement to illegal action? Was mere membership in the party the same as advocating the violent overthrow of the government?[43]

The ACLU demanded that Attorney General Tom Clark drop the indictments and filed an *amicus* brief in a motion by the party seeking dismissal.[44] The Communist party reeled under the attack, uncertain how to respond. It considered a legalistic strategy based on narrow First Amendment grounds but finally settled on a "political" strategy of using the trial as a platform for a challenge to the witch hunt. The party's own long-standing cynical attitude toward the First Amendment did not help in this regard. In fact, it had helped establish a dangerous precedent for its own case in 1941 by cheering on the Smith Act's prosecution of the Minneapolis Trotskyists. And in 1945 it launched a national campaign to deny free speech to the racist and anti-Semitic Gerald L. K. Smith. The latter affair provoked an embarrassing conflict in the ACLU. While defending Smith's right to speak, Carey McWilliams, a member of the board of the Southern California ACLU and the ACLU's National Committee, joined the campaign against Smith. He told the Los Angeles school board that taxpayers were not "required to provide a platform for native Fascist spokesmen." Baldwin and the Southern California affiliate agonized over what to do about this serious deviation by such a prominent spokesperson. Baldwin later arranged to have him not renominated to the National Committee.[45]

Given the atmosphere of the cold war, the Communist party was probably doomed, in any event. The nine-month trial at the Foley Square courthouse in New York City was one of the stormiest political trials in American history. The lawyers for the defendants engaged in lengthy disputes with Judge Harold Medina, who many thought was blatantly biased against the defendants. The government rested its case on Communist party doctrine and, as its first witness, called former *Daily Worker* editor Louis Budenz to explain Communism and party actions (Budenz, who had become a fanatic anti-Communist in the late 1930s, had succeeded Roger Baldwin as director of the St. Louis Civic Club in 1917 and had become the ACLU's first publicity director in 1920). Defense tactics included imaginative challenges to racial discrimination in jury selection, which delayed the trial but did not change the outcome. In October, the jury found all the defendants guilty, and Medina sentenced them to prison terms ranging from three to five years.

The Smith Act trial had a number of repercussions damaging civil liberties. Judge Medina cited all of the defense attorneys for contempt, and eventually, they all went to prison and were disbarred. Not surprisingly, Medina's action sent a deep chill through the legal profession. The most tragic case involved Abraham Isserman, a former ACLU board member, who did not regain his law license until the early 1960s.[46] Consequently, all but a handful of courageous lawyers fled from Communist party cases. In Maryland, the Communists indicted in the "second tier" of Smith Act cases could not find an attorney, even though they had money available. The local ACLU finally helped them secure counsel. The problem of legal representation for unpopular clients became a national crisis as the organized bar abandoned its obligation to provide counsel for all defendants.[47]

The Smith Act case also led to the destruction of the International Workers Order (IWO), a fraternal insurance society with over 150,000 members (most of them Eastern European blue-collar workers) and $91 million worth of insurance policies. The IWO was closely tied to the Communist party and provided bail for Communist defendants. Even though its finances were sound, the New York State commissioner of insurance dissolved the IWO in 1950 on the grounds that its actions posed a hazard to its policyholders, thereby also denying the Communist defendants an important source of bail bonds.[48]

The ACLU was also shaken by the Smith Act prosecution. Although it maintained its vocal opposition to the law, it grew nervous about being identified with the Communist party. In 1948 it began including in its briefs the disclaimer that the ACLU "is opposed to any governmental or economic system which denies fundamental civil liberties and human rights. It is therefore opposed to any form of the police state or the single-party state, or any movement in support of them whether fascist, Communist, or known by any other name." It also adopted a policy of not allowing other organizations to join ACLU briefs. Thurgood Marshall, director of the NAACP's Legal Defense Fund and then an ACLU board member, protested loudly. He called the policy "unreasonable" in light of the long cooperation between the two organizations. In fact, the ACLU had a double standard, eagerly joining briefs with the NAACP, the American Jewish Congress, and other national groups in civil rights and church–state cases. The non-Communist disclaimer finally died a quiet death in the early 1960s when the ACLU's legal director, Mel Wulf, on his own initiative, "just dropped it."[49]

Finally, the Smith Act trial threatened to bring about an additional restriction on the freedom of assembly. After the Communists organized massive picketing outside the Foley Square courthouse, a bill to prohibit the picketing of federal courts was introduced in Congress. The ACLU, in another cold war–induced retreat from a strong First Amendment stand, endorsed the bill. Disruptive picketing, it held, interfered with the right to a fair trial.[50]

Dennis: *The Supreme Court and Civil Liberties*

The appeal by Communist party leaders set the stage for a Supreme Court test of the Smith Act. The ACLU filed an *amicus* brief in the circuit court of appeals, with Fraenkel and Hays arguing that the Smith Act violated the First Amendment on its face and was invalid as applied in the absence of a jury finding of a clear and present danger. Several factors frustrated the ACLU's attempt to file an *amicus* before the Supreme Court, however. When it tried to recruit a "respectable" conservative attorney for the brief, Whitney North Seymour, John W. Davis, and William J. Donovan all declined. The Communists insisted on the right to reject any attorney. And, in the end, the Justice Department refused to allow the ACLU to file a brief, anyway. The Court had recently adopted a very restrictive rule regarding *amici* briefs. This rule, too, was a reaction to Communist party tactics, as it had flooded the Court with petitions in the Hollywood Ten cases.[51]

The Supreme Court's decision in *Dennis v. United States* was, according to Roger Baldwin, "the worst single blow to civil liberties in all our history."[52] The Court sustained the convictions and upheld the constitutionality of the Smith Act, with the majority opinion marking a substantial retreat from the clear and present danger test. Quoting Learned Hand's circuit court opinion, the Supreme Court held that "we must ask whether the gravity of the evil, discounted by its improbability, justifies such invasion of speech as is necessary to avoid the danger." Thus a "grave and probable" standard replaced the previous clear and present danger test. There was considerable irony that this retreat originated with Learned Hand who, in the 1917 *Masses* case, developed a test far more protective of free speech than Holmes's later one.[53]

Dennis evoked forceful dissents from Justices Hugo Black and William O. Douglas. Black argued that it watered down the First Amendment to the point that it would protect only "those 'safe' or orthodox views which rarely need its protection." He expressed the hope that "in calmer times, when present pressures, passions and fears subside, this or some later Court will restore the First Amendment liberties to the high preferred place where they belong in a free society." It was a prophetic observation, but it would be many years before the calmer times would arrive.

The decision appeared to sanction prosecution of the entire Communist party, including ordinary members. Foreign-born members could be deported immediately, and all members who were teachers might be fired. Patrick Malin, the ACLU's new executive director, asked the board's top lawyers for guidance on these questions. The ACLU thereupon issued a public statement condemning *Dennis* on First Amendment grounds and outlined a three-pronged response. This included another test case designed to overturn *Dennis,* a renewed effort to repeal the Smith Act, and a public education campaign regarding the First Amendment. Privately, Malin and Ernest Angell, the new chair of the ACLU board, tried to limit the damage, by asking Attorney General Howard McGrath to "strictly limit its arrests to those leaders against whom it has evidence of personal participation in the illegal conspiracy." The ACLU board, however, voted eight to seven against asking the attorney general to bring no more indictments.[54]

The Justice Department brushed aside the ACLU's advice and began indicting the second tier of the Communist party leadership in New York, Los Angeles, Baltimore, Cleveland, Detroit, and Philadelphia. By late 1956, 145 party leaders had been indicted, with 108 convicted and only 10 acquitted (with the other cases still pending). As the second-tier prosecutions developed, the ACLU and a few members of the bar regained their nerve about representing Communists. In Los Angeles, A. L. Wirin represented several Communists as a private attorney, and the ACLU affiliate filed an *amicus* urging acquittal. (Ever shortsighted, the Communists sought an injunction against the *Los Angeles Times,* seeking to limit coverage of the trial. The ACLU affiliate supported the *Times*'s freedom of the press claim.) In Maryland, Buffalo, and Cleveland the local ACLUs were instrumental in persuading the local bars to provide counsel at trial. In Cleveland the trial court judge appointed seven prominent attorneys, including local ACLU chair Ralph Rudd. The jury acquitted four of the ten defendants, the first time this had occurred in any Smith Act case. By 1956 the ACLU and its affiliates were filing briefs in all of the appeals of the second-tier cases as they headed for the Supreme Court.[55]

Dennis led to the creation of the Emergency Civil Liberties Committee (ECLC), organized largely by Corliss Lamont, who was convinced the ACLU was not responding effectively to the cold war. With Leonard Boudin as general counsel, the ECLC promised to provide legal counsel at the trial level, rather than waiting for the appeal, as was the ACLU's practice. Over the years the ECLC fought and won a number of important civil liberties cases in the Supreme Court, but it never developed into a national organization with a broad agenda. In part, it was too dependent on Lamont's money and allies. The appearance of the ECLC, however, prodded the ACLU into more vigorous activity, and by 1956, several of the ACLU affiliates were raising more serious challenges to cold war measures than was either the ECLC or the ACLU national office.[56]

Compelling Conformity: The Loyalty Oath Mania

To compel political conformity, a mania for loyalty oaths swept the country. Fifteen states enacted loyalty oaths for public employees in 1949 alone. Four years later there were oaths in thirty-nine states, the federal government, and many local governments. Most resembled the 1947 Taft–Hartley Act, which required labor union officials to swear "I am not a member of the Communist Party or affiliated with such party," and "I do not believe in, and I am not a member of nor do I support any organization that believes in or teaches the overthrow of the United States government by force or by any illegal or unconstitutional methods."[57]

The ACLU affiliates led the opposition to the oaths in Maryland, Pennsylvania, New York, Michigan, Illinois, and California. The Maryland Civil Liberties Committee coordinated the coalition of fourteen groups (including the Americans for Democratic Action (ADA), the Johns Hopkins University American Association of University Professors (AAUP), the Young Women's Christian Association (YWCA), and the West Baltimore Friends Meeting) opposing the 1949 Ober law which provided a model for most other state anti-Communist legislation.[58] In 1951 the new Greater Philadelphia Branch of the ACLU lobbied against the Pechan Act loyalty oath. But oaths became law in almost every state. One of the ACLU's few victories came in Illinois where Governor Adlai Stevenson courageously vetoed the Broyles bill in 1951. Two years later, however, it became law.[59]

The courts consistently upheld the loyalty oaths. The first important Supreme Court test involved the Taft–Hartley Act oath, denying protection of the National Labor Relations Board (NLRB) to any union whose leaders failed to file a non-Communist affidavit—a penalty that would effectively destroy a union. In a five-to-four decision, the Court rejected the First Amendment considerations (raised by the ACLU in an *amicus* brief) and ruled that "Congress might reasonably find that Communists, unlike members of other political parties . . . represent a continuing danger of disruptive political strikes when they hold positions of union leadership."[60]

Douds v. American Communications Association was a combination of guilty by association and the old bad tendency test. That is, mere membership in the Communist party presumed advocacy of disruptive political strikes, and such strikes were deemed illegitimate. A year later the Court upheld the Los Angeles loyalty oath in *Garner v. Board of Public Works,* ruling that "past loyalty may have a reasonable relationship to present and future trust" and thus was an appropriate qualification for employment.[61]

There were only occasional court victories: The Court overturned an Oklahoma loyalty oath on narrow grounds in 1952,[62] and the New Jersey Supreme Court upheld an ACLU challenge to a state loyalty oath for political candidates.[63]

Teachers were singled out for special loyalty oaths. National attention focused on the loyalty oath crisis at the University of California. In 1949 the university's regents voted to require all faculty to swear "I am not a member of the Communist Party, . . . or under any commitment that is in conflict with my obligations under this oath." By the spring of 1950 more than 300 faculty had refused to sign, including 20 percent of the faculty at the flagship Berkeley campus. The faculty senate voted overwhelmingly against the oath (1,154 to 136) but simultaneously approved a statement that "proved members of the Communist Party . . . are not acceptable as members of the faculty." Thus, even the Berkeley faculty accepted the main thrust of the anti-Communist assault on academic freedom. The California regents, led by Governor Earl Warren, then adopted a requirement that each faculty member swear that he or she was not a member of the Communist party. About 240 faculty initially refused to sign, but the outbreak of the Korean War cast an additional chill over dissent and reduced the number to just over 30. In addition to the 26 faculty members eventually fired for refusing to sign the oath, another 37 resigned in protest, and 47 prospective faculty declined job offers.[64]

The anti-Communist hysteria in California continued to escalate. Governor Warren sponsored a loyalty oath for all state employees, the so-called Levering oath, which superseded the one applying just to university faculty. (Among those fired for refusing to sign was San Francisco State University professor Eason Monroe, who became the new director of the Southern California ACLU.) In 1953 Warren signed into law seven anti-Communist measures, including requirements that teachers and other public employees answer questions before legislative investigating committees. Others required loyalty oaths of any individual or organization receiving a property tax exemption, including veterans and churches. These oaths were eventually overturned by the Supreme Court in challenges brought by the two California ACLU affiliates.[65] Ohio, Maryland, and New York, meanwhile, either required an oath for unemployment compensation or denied benefits to witnesses who took the Fifth Amendment before investigating committees. ACLU affiliates in all three states eventually won cases eliminating these requirements.[66]

Professional associations collapsed in the face of the anti-Communist hysteria. The National Education Association (NEA), representing public school teachers, adopted a policy, by a vote of 2,995 to 5, that Communist party membership "and the accompanying surrender of intellectual integrity, render an individual unfit to discharge the duties of a teacher in this county." Four years later, the nation's university presidents, speaking as the Association of American Universities, declared that "present membership in the Communist Party extinguishes the right to a university position." Meanwhile, the AAUP, representing university faculty, was overwhelmed by the flood of academic freedom cases. It eventually began to recover its footing in the mid-1950s, in part through the assistance of ACLU assistant director Louis Joughin, who then became the AAUP's executive director.[67]

The question of whether Communists should be allowed to teach had arisen in the 1940–1941 Rapp–Coudert investigation, and the vote of the Berkeley faculty indicated the extent to which the majority of even the best faculty accepted the anti-Communist argument. In the ACLU, Norman Thomas argued there was "absolutely no case for allowing Communists any more than Ku Klux Klanners or Fascists to teach in the public schools." First Amendment absolutists asked whether Roman Catholics were also not members of an organization controlled by a foreign power: "How can Catholic teachers possibly be free?" asked Margaret DeSilver. Thomas brushed aside the idea of academic freedom as a constitutionally protected civil liberty: "The right to teach in public schools is not a necessary or logical deduction from the Bill of Rights or the right to free speech."[68] The ACLU rejected Thomas's view and, in a 1949 statement, *Civil Liberties of Teachers and Students,* opposed "any ban or regulation" that would bar the employment of a teacher based solely on "political views or associations, even when characterized as Fascist or Communist."[69]

The damage to intellectual freedom extended far beyond the number of teachers who lost their jobs. More serious was the stifling of free inquiry into social and political subjects. For example, searching questions were not raised about the purpose and conduct of American foreign policy, and on domestic issues, historians and social scientists ignored the persistent problem of poverty. Instead, political scientists celebrated the flexibility and pragmatism of the American political system. One index of the benign view of the American economy was the shock that greeted Michael Harrington's "discovery" of poverty in his 1960 book, *The Other America*.

The FBI and the ACLU

Illegal activity by the FBI steadily escalated during the cold war. By the late 1940s, J. Edgar Hoover was politically untouchable, as Washington insiders believed he had files "on everyone." Many had good reason to know, because several presidents asked him to undertake political surveillance for them. Presidents Lyndon B. Johnson and Richard M. Nixon allegedly enjoyed reading the FBI files' derogatory information about their political opponents. Subsequent Freedom of Information Act revelations proved that the bureau had spied on writers, lawyers, and even Supreme Court justices.[70]

The ACLU's greatest failure during the cold war was turning a blind eye on the FBI. At best, it simply refused to pursue allegations of FBI abuses. At worst, it was an active apologist. For example, the ACLU's 1953 *Annual Report* found "a heartening expression of principle" in J. Edgar Hoover's recent article, "Civil Liberties and Law Enforcement." It assured ACLU members that the FBI's violation of civil liberties "seems to be happily infrequent." Two years later ACLU staff counsel Herbert Monte Levy rejected a demand for an investigation of the FBI on the grounds that "we have no evidence that the FBI or any other executive agency . . . is spying into the thought and the associations of every citizen in the land." Morris Ernst was the FBI's advocate in the ACLU, but Roger Baldwin bears much of the responsibility for the ACLU's failure: After his 1942 meeting with Hoover, he refused to believe any of the persistent complaints about FBI misconduct.[71]

Such complaints were abundant. Yale law professor Thomas Emerson and student David Helfeld cited several instances of FBI harassment in a carefully documented 1948 article: In one letter the FBI advised the chair of the NLRB that an employee "is known to have radical tendencies leading toward Communism." Emerson and Helfeld also reported the story, known to them personally, of an FBI report incorporating a landlady's statement that a tenant of hers "kept a number of books on Russia next to his easy chair." Such use of unverified gossip, guilt by association based on nothing more than a person's reading matter, was typical. J. Edgar Hoover regarded all criticisms of the bureau as a personal attack, if not an act of disloyalty, and responded with direct harassment. For example, shortly before Max Lowenthal's critical book on the bureau was published in 1950, he was summoned before the HUAC, and the FBI leaked derogatory information about him to sympathetic reporters.[72]

The Wiretapping Controversy

A highly publicized revelation of FBI misconduct arose in the Judith Coplon case. In 1949 FBI agents arrested Coplon, a low-level Justice Department employee, on charges of delivering FBI reports to a Soviet United Nations official. In the course of her two trials, defense attorneys successfully exposed a pattern of FBI wiretapping. The first conviction was overturned in part because the trial court failed to allow the defense to inspect the records of the FBI's wiretaps on Coplon's telephone and did not allow the defense to pursue the question of whether Coplon was originally targeted for surveillance through information obtained by other wiretaps. The appeals court overturned a second conviction and ordered a determination of whether wiretaps of conversations between Coplon and her attorneys had deprived her of effective assistance of counsel. The revelations were an enormous embarrassment to the bureau and also gave credence to other allegations about its misconduct.[73]

ACLU board member James L. Fly responded to the Coplon revelations with a vigorous attack on FBI wiretapping. As chair of the FCC he had seen bureau reports on government employees that were filled with unverified smears. He thus prodded the ACLU to call for a congressional investigation of FBI wiretapping and lobbied for a federal law outlawing it. Fly raised pointed questions about other possible FBI misconduct: "It would also be of interest," he wrote the chair of the House Appropriations Committee, "to know in how many instances over the past year has the FBI rifled the private mails." Although Fly offered no evidence to support this charge, subsequent revelations proved him correct. He noted an FBI admission that it systematically destroyed records of its own activities in violation of federal law, which suggested other misdeeds. Fly also called on New York Governor Thomas Dewey to investigate the allegedly "widespread" illegal wiretapping by local police.[74]

Fly's charges touched off a heated ACLU debate. Hays and Malin joined his call for a federal law banning all wiretapping, whereas Ernst argued that wiretapping was justified in certain national security cases. Even Fly conceded that Congress could approve it in cases of treason, sabotage, espionage, and kidnapping. Curiously, Fly did not pursue his suspicions about the FBI. The wiretapping issue thus faded away, and the ACLU resumed its benign attitude toward the bureau.[75]

Several ACLU leaders maintained close relations with the FBI. None of these contacts was secret at the time. Ernst talked openly about his relationship with Hoover. His December 1950 *Reader's Digest* article, "Why I No Longer Fear the FBI," was practically written by the bureau. Despite his chummy relationship, Ernst never passed confidential ACLU material to the FBI or named any individuals as subversives. The FBI had other sources and received copies of internal memos and records of some of the affiliates. Irving Ferman, director of the ACLU's Washington office from 1952 to 1959, committed the most serious breach of ACLU confidentiality, providing the FBI with both internal documents and the names of individuals he suspected of being Communists. At one point he admitted to the FBI that "perhaps he was violating his trust." Ferman later denied that he was an "informer." The ACLU's 1940 Resolution, he argued, established anti-Communism as official ACLU policy. Moreover, he claimed to have done good work behind the scenes, helping to "clear" people falsely accused. He also used his FBI contacts to block publication of a HUAC report attacking the ACLU.[76]

Ferman had an arguable point about the 1940 Resolution: Having adopted a political test for its own leaders, the ACLU was inevitably forced into the position of inquiring into political associations. Other ACLU leaders made no secret of their contacts with the FBI. The ACLU's executive director Malin told the board about his talks with Hoover, although these remarks were discreetly not recorded in the minutes. Even Roger Baldwin engaged in the dirty business of naming names. In 1947 he advised Illinois Congressman Arnold Sabath that Ira Latimer, former director of the Chicago ACLU affiliate, was allied with the Communists. Several months later he "cleared" Latimer by writing the Justice Department that he had broken with the Communists. Baldwin's behavior sprang from his antagonism toward the Communists and his felt need to establish his anti-Communist credentials, both products of his ties with the Communists in the 1930s.[77]

The supreme irony of the situation was that while ACLU leaders continued to reassure the country that the FBI was doing a fine job, the bureau was spying on the ACLU. Indeed, the more than forty thousand documents in the FBI files on the ACLU reveal both Hoover's increasing fanaticism and the ACLU's role in fighting the cold war. Before 1947, Hoover was only moderately suspicious of the ACLU; after 1947 he became somewhat hostile; and by 1954 he had targeted the ACLU for massive surveillance. With each passing year the FBI files grew larger, reflecting both Hoover's growing paranoia and the spread of ACLU affiliates, which gave the FBI more targets.[78]

Several ACLU affiliates were deeply suspicious of the FBI. The Southern California ACLU acidly commented in 1950 that "while J. Edgar Hoover and President Truman keep on assuring us that 'We are not going to transform our fine FBI into a Gestapo-like secret police' . . . evidence to the contrary is multiplying."[79] University of Washington historian Max Savelle told staff counsel Herbert Monte Levy of his disappointment at "the apparent disposition of the ACLU to excuse and support the police-state activities of the FBI."[80] In 1955 the Philadelphia affiliate proposed drafting an ACLU pamphlet advising citizens of their rights when questioned by the FBI. Citing widespread reports of FBI abuses in his area, affiliate director Spencer Coxe saw this as a positive form of public education. The proposed pamphlet was moderate in tone, advising people that they had a right to decline to be interviewed by the FBI—a fact not generally appreciated by most people—that if they agreed to be questioned they could have an attorney present, but that if they did refuse the FBI would record that in their files (and that an employer who might obtain that file might draw unfavorable conclusions from such a refusal).[81]

The Philadelphia proposal sent the national ACLU office into apoplexy. Levy conferred with FBI deputy director Louis B. Nichols and brought back a favorable account of FBI procedures. He told Coxe that Hoover had personally assured him that he regarded the ACLU as a "very worthwhile organization." Levy objected to the Philadelphia pamphlet on the grounds that "by constantly warning people to report practices in violation of FBI rules, the implication is that they are frequently violated, whereas the number of complaints that we receive are astonishingly few." ACLU assistant director Louis Joughin called the pamphlet "unjustified," "unwise," and "not comprehensive," thereby sidetracking it on the pretext that it did not cover all federal agencies. Why single out the FBI? he asked, and assigned it to a committee where it quietly died.[82]

Public Opinion and the ACLU

Years later, after the worst of the cold war had abated, many Americans looked back and wondered how it could have happened. The ferocity and irrationality of the witch hunt almost defied explanation.

The truth is that the cold war brought together many deeply ingrained strands in American culture. Intolerance had a much stronger tradition than did tolerance of unpopular views. Furthermore, the body of First Amendment law that developed in the 1930s was planted in extremely thin soil. In times of crisis, particularly national emergency, the American people were still capable of irrational panic. The cold war thus revived their habit of seeking scapegoats in the form of "foreign" people or "un-American" ideas. Americans were also prone to conspiracy mongering and had long seen conspiracies in the Catholic church, the Mormons, Wall Street, or the media: The Communist party fit the bill perfectly. Moreover, there was no shortage of politicians eager to manipulate public fears to their own partisan advantage. Truman and the liberal Democrats were almost as much to blame as were conservative Republicans in conjuring up frightening images of the Communist threat.[83]

Social scientists have measured the devastating impact on public attitudes. For example, Samuel Stouffer's report, *Communism, Conformity and Civil Liberties,* found that 91 percent of the public thought that an admitted Communist should not be allowed to teach in a public high school; 54 percent would not let a Socialist teach; and 84 percent would not let an atheist teach at the college level. An astounding 68 percent thought a Communist should be fired as a store clerk, whereas 77 percent thought he should be stripped of his American citizenship. The only hopeful notes were the findings that community leaders and people with more education were somewhat more tolerant of political nonconformity than was the general public. Stouffer desperately tried to draw an optimistic conclusion from his depressing data. Rising levels of education, increased mobility, and urbanization—factors that correlated with support for civil liberties—did seem to offer hope for the future.[84]

Stouffer's research told only part of the story, however. Focusing exclusively on the question of Communism, he failed to explore public attitudes toward other civil liberties issues such as civil rights, censorship, and separation of church and state. Other research found a growing commitment to racial equality, while events suggested growing public hostility to censorship and government-imposed religion. In short, trends in public attitudes toward civil liberties were extremely complex during the cold war years.[85]

The Supreme Court retreated substantially on the protection of unpopular political speech, particularly after the deaths of Frank Murphy and Wiley Rutledge, two of the most devout civil libertarians, in 1949. While the Court upheld virtually all cold war measures, Black and Douglas remained as lonely civil libertarian dissenters, theirs resembling the role of Holmes and Brandeis in the 1920s.[86]

The ACLU's overall performance was mixed. Its defense of civil liberties was, on balance, stronger than that of any other organization but weaker than what some critics expected. Some people never let the ACLU forget about the 1940 Resolution, the Flynn purge, the compromises on certain cold war issues, and, when the full story became known in the 1970s, its close relations with the FBI. Furthermore, such criticisms often had a bitter, unforgiving tone. For example, in the 1970s Ira Glasser, then director of the New York Civil Liberties Union (NYCLU), asked actor Zero Mostel to appear at a benefit. But Mostel refused, saying he could not forgive the ACLU for its conduct during the cold war. The unflattering version of the ACLU's performance persisted in part because the ACLU never told its own story very well; Corliss Lamont's highly critical account became the version on which the succeeding generation relied. Some of the harshest critics were the ACLU's own affiliates, especially Northern and Southern California. From the time of the 1940 Resolution, both regarded themselves as the true bearer of the civil liberties torch. The World War II controversies over the Japanese-Americans and the sedition policy only strengthened their self-righteous posture. They did not have anti-Communist factions and did not hesitate to criticize the national office for its compromises on the loyalty program or its insensitivity to FBI abuses. The Southern California ACLU, with A. L. Wirin as its feisty counsel, also had an extremely vigorous litigation program. When the ACLU finally agreed to give the affiliates a formal voice in policymaking, Southern California shot back: "Naturally, there are some not unlike 'the old man' [Baldwin] who cannot think of 'the boys' as grown up." The affiliate pointed out that it had "initiated more court cases and carried more of them to the Supreme Court of the United States than did the Board whose representatives talked about 'sharing responsibility.' "[87]

The behavior of the FBI, the American Legion, HUAC, and Senator McCarthy place the criticisms of the ACLU in perspective. All of them regarded the ACLU as a formidable opponent of cold war measures. Hoover conducted a massive spying campaign that escalated in intensity with each passing year—one agent joined the Massachusetts affiliate, finding "many Communists" in it.[88] From 1952 onward, the American Legion annually demanded a congressional investigation of the ACLU. HUAC prepared a report that was never released,[89] and McCarthy repeatedly attacked ACLU leaders as Communists or Communist dupes. In 1950, Dorothy Kenyon became the first person that McCarthy mentioned by name, and in 1953 he subpoenaed Corliss Lamont because of his books on the Soviet Union. Lamont refused to appear, was cited for contempt, and in 1955 won one of the first First Amendment challenges to legislative investigations of political beliefs.[90] The ACLU responded to McCarthy's attacks by defending his civil liberties, criticizing a Seattle radio station that tried to censor his remarks in 1952, and, when the Senate finally decided to investigate McCarthy's conduct, reminding it to respect his due process rights. The ACLU prided itself on "defending our enemy" and honored that commitment in McCarthy's case.[91]

The ACLU was the subject of one of Edward R. Murrow's "See It Now" programs that helped turn the tide of public opinion against the witch hunt. The entire November 24, 1953, segment, "Argument in Indianapolis," was devoted to ACLU's difficulties in securing a meeting place to organize a local affiliate. The War Memorial Auditorium had canceled an agreement four days before the meeting, as a result of pressure from the American Legion and the Minutewomen of Indiana. The Claypool Hotel also canceled a contract. No other hotel or church was willing to allow the meeting. At the last minute, Father Victor Goosens, pastor of St. Mary's Roman Catholic Church, offered his church. This most unlikely host felt that "something more basic" was at stake than a routine meeting. He told Murrow's audience that it was important to stand up for the rights of unpopular groups because "we are all going to be members of a minority group someday." He not only invited the ACLU to use St. Mary's but stated that "we should *insist* they use it." This courageous action by a Catholic parish priest in Indiana indicated that by late 1953 the anti-Communist storm had finally provoked a reaction and had begun to generate new support for fundamental liberties.[92]

Nine

McCarthyism and Recovery, 1950-1954

McCarthyism

"I have here in my hand a list of two-hundred and five [employees] known to the Secretary of State as being members of the Communist Party and who nevertheless are still working and shaping the policy of the State Department." With this February 9, 1950, speech in Wheeling, West Virginia, Wisconsin Senator Joseph McCarthy stepped onto the national scene. Within months the term *McCarthyism* entered the American political vocabulary. McCarthy never produced his list, and the number kept changing: 205, 57, then 87. When a Senate committee investigated his charges a month later, he began by naming ACLU board member Dorothy Kenyon. A former municipal judge and longtime liberal activist, Kenyon was not a Communist, but this kind of reckless smear defined McCarthyism.[1]

Events in the spring of 1950 brought the cold war to a new peak. On June 25, North Korean troops invaded South Korea, and so the cold war became a shooting war. On July 17 the FBI arrested Julius and Ethel Rosenberg for stealing nuclear bomb secrets for the Soviet Union. Russia had exploded its first bomb the previous September, and the confession of British scientist Klaus Fuchs confirmed the existence of an American spy ring. The sequence of events inflamed public fear of Communist spies. Congress responded by enacting the McCarran Act which virtually outlawed the Communist party.

Nothing better illustrated the hysteria of 1950 than the burning of the April 1950 issue of *Scientific American*. After the Soviet Union exploded its first atomic bomb in 1949, the Truman administration began debating whether to develop a hydrogen bomb. The *Scientific American* then published a series of articles on the H-bomb. An April 1950 article by the noted physicist Hans Bethe contained only declassified information, but government agents descended on the magazine's offices on March 31 and seized all three thousand copies. They were burned, and the original plates were destroyed. The April issue was then reprinted with several passages deleted from Bethe's article.[2]

Almost as remarkable as the government's action was the virtual absence of any outcry. The ACLU protested and *Scientific American* publisher Gerard Piel attacked the suppression of scientific information in a speech to the American Society of Newspaper Editors. But Bethe himself, then a contract employee with the Atomic Energy Commission, did not complain, and the incident was quickly forgotten. In the tense atmosphere of 1950, few were willing to question the government on a sensitive national security issue.[3]

The McCarran Act, 1950

The Korean War and McCarthy's rampage assured passage of the 1950 Internal Security Act. Popularly known as the McCarran Act, it required Communist and "Communist-action" organizations to register with the new Subversive Activities Control Board (SACB) and to disclose their officers, finances, and membership. In addition, their mail had to carry the label *Communist organization*. Individual members were ineligible for passports, were barred from government employment, and were required to register with the SACB—which raised a Fifth Amendment issue, as registration would expose individuals to other penalties under this and other laws. Finally, the law authorized American concentration camps. The emergency detention section empowered the president to declare an internal security emergency in case of invasion, declaration of war, or domestic insurrection, after which the attorney general could detain any person for whom there was "reasonable ground to believe that such person probably will engage in, or probably will conspire with others to engage in, acts of espionage or sabotage." This section was sponsored by liberal senators Hubert Humphrey, Paul Douglas, and Estes Kefauver, who were anxious to prove their anti-Communist credentials.[4] The ACLU was evidently affected by the McCarthyite venom and the Korean War. The board thus voted to oppose the emergency detention provision only by a narrow eleven-to-nine margin.[5]

The ACLU had opposed the 1948 Nixon–Mundt bill, predecessor to the McCarran Act, but the testimony revealed the ACLU's divided soul. Art Hays warned that the idea of outlawing the Communist party altogether was constitutionally "indefensible." Morris Ernst, testifying on his own behalf, favored some restraints on the Communists. Staff counsel Clifford Forster, an anti-Communist fanatic, was convinced that the Communist party was actually promoting the bill in order to manipulate liberals into "fronting" for them.[6] One part of Hays's testimony dramatized the untenable position that the ACLU had created for itself with the 1940 Resolution: Nixon interrupted Hays to ask whether it weren't true that the ACLU had barred Communists from leadership positions. Yes it was, replied Hays. Nixon laughed and then asked why the ACLU would deny the government the same power. Hays had no answer. The Nixon–Mundt bill stalled in 1948, but Congress revived it in 1950 and passed it over Truman's veto.[7]

The McCarran Act never achieved its stated goals. The Communist party predictably did not register voluntarily, and so Attorney General Howard McGrath directed the Subversive Activities Control Board to compel it to do so, setting in motion complex litigation that was not settled by the Supreme Court until 1961. Frustrated by the failure of the McCarran Act, Congress passed in 1954 the even more repressive Communist Control Act. This law declared that the Communist party was "in fact an instrumentality of a conspiracy to overthrow the Government of the United States. . . . Therefore, the Communist Party should be outlawed." Liberals, led by Hubert Humphrey, sponsored the new law in another effort to prove their anti-Communist credentials. This law proved to be even less effective than the McCarran Act was and so remained a virtual dead letter. Two years earlier Congress had passed the McCarran–Walter Immigration Act, which strengthened the government's discretionary power to bar foreign visitors for ideological reasons and to deport suspect aliens.

The Right to Travel

The McCarran Act's provision denying passports to Communists was hardly necessary, because the State Department had already assumed unlimited authority to do so. Passport Director Ruth Shipley ran her office like a private fiefdom, arbitrarily denying passport applications to prominent leftists. The question of a constitutional right to travel first arose in 1950 when the State Department ordered the noted black singer Paul Robeson to surrender his passport. Robeson was scheduled to give a European concert tour, and because he was extensively blacklisted in this country, such an order was tantamount to denying him a livelihood. Although Robeson was a well-known Communist sympathizer, there were no allegations of any illegal acts on his part. The ACLU, however, voted not to support Robeson on the grounds that there was "no absolute legal or moral right to a passport."[8]

The ACLU's rationale was similar to its policy regarding the Federal Loyalty Program. While conceding that travel was a "basic right," the government also had a countervailing interest in restricting the movement of people whose activities might be damaging to the national interest. In short, the First Amendment did not guarantee an unrestricted right to travel. Instead, the ACLU focused on the procedural aspects of the passport office's decision making. Anyone denied a passport was entitled to formal notice and a hearing. Lobbying quietly, the ACLU's executive director Pat Malin and chairman Ernest Angell met privately with Shipley and appealed for help from Secretary of State Dean Acheson in a letter gently reminding him of his previous work as an ACLU cooperating attorney. None of these efforts succeeded.[9]

Several ACLU officials themselves ran into passport difficulties: The State Department barred both Chairman John Haynes Holmes and A. L. Wirin from visiting Japan and, in 1951, denied a passport to board member Corliss Lamont.[10] And even Roger Baldwin received a passport validated for only six months for a trip to Europe in 1951. Suspecting "something behind appearances which requires explanation," Baldwin asked former Attorney General Francis Biddle to make a "discreet inquiry." Biddle subsequently reported that Shipley had nothing against the ACLU and that Baldwin ought to talk with her in person to clear the air. Meanwhile, congressional hearings on the State Department's 1952 budget aired a House Un-American Activities Committee (HUAC) report on Baldwin's left-wing associations in the 1930s. Baldwin answered by citing his more recent anti-Communist statements. He also offered a glowing tribute from General Douglas MacArthur, testifying that "Roger Baldwin's crusade for civil liberties has had a profound effect and beneficial influence upon the course of American progress." A *New York Times* headline announced Baldwin's "clearance."[11]

The MacArthur testimonial was typical of the period: Individuals with the right connections could be "cleared" through high-level tributes to their loyalty. Baldwin's relationship with MacArthur was another curious episode in the ACLU founder's long career. In 1947 some old New Dealers in the American Occupation of Japan arranged for Baldwin to visit Japan and advise MacArthur on civil liberties issues. Baldwin enjoyed himself immensely and struck up a warm friendship with MacArthur—clearly envious of his power to impose democracy by fiat. During his 1947 trip Baldwin also helped found the Japanese Civil Liberties Union. Years later, Baldwin dismayed his liberal friends by continuing to praise the general.[12]

In 1956, after an internal upheaval, the ACLU reversed itself and asserted a broad freedom to travel. The William Worthy case precipitated this change: When the State Department canceled the journalist's passport after he had made an unauthorized trip to mainland China in 1956, the ACLU saw this as a freedom of the press issue, which they felt had a stronger claim than did the right to travel. Once into the case, the board decided that it reopened "the whole question" of passports and so unanimously voted to represent Worthy. The ACLU then issued a new policy asserting a constitutional right to travel and the consequent right to a passport.

The reinvigorated ACLU also filed an *amicus* brief on behalf of Rockwell Kent, who had been denied a passport on the grounds that he was a Communist. The issue was resolved in 1958 when the Supreme Court ordered the State Department to issue Kent a passport, declaring that "the right to travel is a part of the 'liberty' of which the citizen cannot be deprived without due process of law under the Fifth Amendment."[13]

Other controversies illustrated how the ACLU's civil liberties horizons began to change in the mid-1950s. In regard to legislative investigations, the public mood began to change when both HUAC and McCarthy attacked prominent religious leaders. In 1953 HUAC subpoenaed Methodist Bishop G. Bromley Oxnam, a longtime member of the ACLU National Committee and leader on church–state questions. One of McCarthy's staff, J. B. Matthews, had accused the mainstream Protestant denominations of being Communist influenced. Both incidents alarmed the public as an assault on freedom of religion. Attacking Communists was one thing, but questioning the loyalty of the Methodist church was another matter altogether. The public uproar thus forced McCarthy to dismiss Matthews.

Later, McCarthy's subpoena of James Wechsler, editor of the then-liberal *New York Post,* aroused widespread concern about freedom of the press. In this way, McCarthy eventually destroyed himself when he began attacking pillars of the Establishment, notably the U.S. Army and the Eisenhower administration. Widespread reaction against the excesses of the cold war began only in the mid-1950s, when established values and institutions appeared threatened. The attack on the Fifth Amendment was an important turning point.[14]

"Fifth Amendment Communists"

The problem, charged Attorney General Herbert Brownell in October 1955, was "those fourteen magic words: I refuse to answer on the grounds that it might tend to incriminate me." Brownell's speech to the National Press Club opened an attack on the Fifth Amendment. Acknowledging the historic importance of the constitutional protection against "unfounded and tyrannical prosecution," he argued that it had been abused by uncooperative witnesses. Citizens had a "duty" to cooperate with investigating committees, and so Brownell asked for legislation to compel testimony.[15]

The threat to the historic right not to incriminate oneself was the final and logical outcome of the anti-Communist witch hunt. With the courts refusing to place First Amendment limits on legislative investigations, witnesses resorted to the Fifth. Thus under the prevailing rules, witnesses had to refuse to answer even the most trivial questions, as answering any question meant waiving one's Fifth Amendment privilege. Enraged anti-Communists therefore began labeling those who invoked the privilege as "Fifth Amendment Communists." People victimized for exercising this most fundamental constitutional right included Joseph Papp, later one of the most important figures in American theater, who was fired by CBS television for invoking the Fifth before HUAC. The *New York Times* fired staff members Robert Shelton, later a prominent music critic, and Alden Whitman for taking the Fifth. A number of New York City schoolteachers also were fired under a policy requiring automatic dismissal for taking the Fifth. The New York Civil Liberties Union represented Papp, Shelton, and the teachers, and the two California affiliates helped defeat a bill that would have revoked the occupational license of anyone taking the Fifth.[16]

The debate within the American Bar Association (ABA) over the Fifth Amendment revealed the logic of the witch hunting. In 1950 the ABA voted to bar any new member who failed to sign an anti-Communist oath. Because real Communists would lie, many contended, it was necessary to identify them through legislative investigations. When witnesses began invoking the Fifth, the anti-Communists argued that they should be disqualified for doing so—a step that the ABA's Special Committee on Communist Tactics and Objectives had proposed in 1953 but the ABA had rejected.[17] The California state bar debated but rejected a proposal to keep out lawyers who took the Fifth. The relatively few in the profession who protested included Ralph Brown of Yale Law School (and later of the ACLU board) and the Association of the Bar of New York City. The strength of the attack on the Fifth within the organized bar served as both eloquent testimony to the power of the anti-Communist crusade and evidence of the dismal performance of the legal profession during this period.[18]

The controversy provoked a national debate over the meaning of the Fifth Amendment. Sidney Hook, a former Marxist and former ACLU member, was the leading advocate of the view that use of the privilege established a "presumption of guilt or unfitness" that could be legitimately used "in a non-legal or moral context." The privilege applied only to criminal investigations. Hook turned the Fifth Amendment inside out, arguing that "what the defendant *fails* to say sometimes counts as evidence against him." In short, taking the Fifth created a presumption of guilt (that is, of membership in the Communist party) and thus became valid grounds for firing an employee. Alan Westin, speaking for many anti-Communist liberals, argued in *Commentary* magazine that witnesses had an obligation to cooperate with investigators and only hurt themselves and society by not doing so. Even Zechariah Chafee agreed that witnesses had a "duty" to cooperate. All this was typical of so much cold war reasoning: Fundamental constitutional rights should be revered but not used.[19]

Torn apart by its own internal cold war, the ACLU nearly faltered on the Fifth Amendment issue. Board member C. Dickerman Williams embraced Hook's view and asserted that "matters of utmost privacy [should be] properly investigated if they appear to have relevance to subjects of public concern" (for example, Communists as teachers). When confronted with the 1953 case of the New York teachers fired for not taking the oath, the board argued until midnight and ended with a tie vote. The New York affiliate filed an *amicus* in the *Slochower* case (one of many examples of the more vigorous stand taken by some affiliates). And in 1956 the Supreme Court held that Harry Slochower could not be fired for pleading the Fifth, without being given a hearing.[20]

The issue became part of a bitterly contested ACLU referendum in late 1953. The ACLU's anti-Communist hard-liners proposed a policy stating that there was no "protection against any consequence of having exercised [the Fifth Amendment privilege] except the imputation of criminal guilt." This and the other two items in the referendum provoked a final showdown in the ACLU, and in 1954, after fighting for a year and a half, the absolutists were victorious, winning approval of a policy stating that "no person, whether public or private employee, should lose a job . . . solely because of his claim" of the Fifth Amendment.[21]

The "Fifth Amendment Communist" issue ultimately led to the 1954 Immunity Act, which allowed federal prosecutors and congressional investigators to compel testimony from witnesses by conferring immunity from prosecution. The ACLU unsuccessfully protested the idea of compelled testimony on the grounds that "there should be some recognition of the right to privacy, especially where it concerns beliefs and associations." The law eventually became a major weapon in the hands of federal prosecutors.[22]

The crisis over the Fifth Amendment helped provoke a reaction against the excesses of the anti-Communist crusade, which set in motion a broader reconsideration of the meaning of the Bill of Rights. In a short 1955 book of lectures entitled *The Fifth Amendment Today,* Dean Erwin Griswold of Harvard Law School explored the various aspects of the Fifth Amendment. In the third and final lecture he argued that the real meaning of the Fifth went far beyond black-letter doctrine and its application to specific cases. The Fifth was a symbol, "a reminder of the necessity of maintaining constant vigilance for the protection of individual rights." Griswold saw the Fifth as "a guide to a number of things which we should be doing better" and cited the old problem of police abuse of individual rights, inflammatory press coverage of criminal cases that impinged on the right to a fair trial, and the right of the defendant to have an attorney at trial. Griswold's thinking went beyond the Fifth Amendment to other neglected constitutional rights. "Is it not shocking," he asked, "that a person can be charged and tried for burglary or robbery or rape without having the assistance of counsel to advise him?" The question answered itself. In this prophetic lecture, Griswold anticipated the Supreme Court's due process revolution in the next ten years.[23]

The abuses of the cold war thus led Griswold and many other Americans, including justices of the Supreme Court, to think anew about basic American liberties. Indeed, the only saving grace of the anti-Communist crusade was that it ultimately discredited itself and dramatized the need for more concrete guarantees of American liberty.

Upheaval in the ACLU

End of the Baldwin Era

Roger Baldwin knew what was coming and desperately tried to filibuster. Herbert Northrup, one of the ACLU board's new members, finally interrupted and reminded everyone why they were meeting. Baldwin sank back into the corner, looking rejected and unwanted. Key members of the board had gathered in Walter Frank's apartment to discuss the recommendation that Baldwin be "elevated" from executive director to "ambassadorial status."[24] In short, the ACLU should kick upstairs its founder and thirty-year executive director. This was only one of a series of organizational changes between 1949 and 1951 that transformed the ACLU in ways that no one had anticipated.

The ACLU board created in late 1948 a special Committee on Policy Planning "to review ACLU policies, activities and organization," setting in motion a series of important changes. Chaired by Walter Gellhorn, the committee produced several recommendations that were surprising in light of subsequent developments. Most notably, it suggested deemphasizing litigation in favor of public education: Other civil rights groups could take more responsibility for litigation, with the ACLU assuming the role of national "coordinator" of civil liberties and civil rights efforts. Given the ACLU's substantial success in the Supreme Court since 1937—to say nothing of even greater influence in the years to come—it was a curious recommendation and probably reflected Gellhorn's view that the Court would be a weak reed in the cold war and that the crucial battle was in the arena of public opinion.[25]

On substantive civil liberties issues, the committee confessed that it was "not in present agreement" over the emerging restrictions on Communists and put the defense of minority political parties low on its list of priorities. Civil rights and the fight against censorship were given first and second priority. Church–state issues also ranked very low (number ten), despite the ACLU's prominent role as an advocate of the separationist view.

The crucial part of Gellhorn's report dealt with the ACLU's membership and finances. The committee conceded that the current membership of just over nine thousand prevented developing a larger program. Nonetheless, it rejected the idea of recruiting a large membership. In a judgment that eventually proved to be astonishingly inaccurate, it observed that "the ACLU cannot itself become a mass organization, with membership in the hundreds of thousands, or even a moderately large organization with, say, fifty thousand members." The position revealed the smug elitism of Baldwin and the board, who felt that the ACLU had "nothing to give its members in the form of services, tangible rewards, or prestige." Other organizations represented special-interest groups: union members, blacks, Jews, and so on. Alas, the ACLU was a *dis*interested group. "Public spirited citizens who are willing to fight for a principle are limited in number," Baldwin advised. He saw the ACLU standing above passions of political life, a small, self-appointed elite, committed to abstract principles.[26]

The discussion ignored the highly critical and prescient observations of Yale law student Norman Redlich. His *Yale Law Journal* article, entitled "Private Attorneys General," was the first assessment of the emerging public-interest bar. Redlich surveyed the accomplishments of the ACLU, the NAACP, and the Commission on Law and Social Action of the American Jewish Congress, noting the accomplishments of each. He drew pessimistic conclusions about the future of the ACLU: "As presently constituted the ACLU is structurally incapable of being an effective force for positive advance in the fields of free expression and thought." The problem was its size: "It is difficult to believe that a contributing membership of 8,000 is the limit of the ACLU's potential following." A larger membership would generate enough funds and volunteers to support a broader and more effective program. But the failure to adjust, he warned, would represent "a serious danger to the future of American civil liberties." Events soon proved Redlich right, but for the moment the ACLU ignored his advice.[27]

Gellhorn's report then turned to the delicate question of the ACLU staff.

Choosing its words carefully, it recommended that "Roger Baldwin . . . be entirely relieved from . . . executive responsibilities" and be given an "ambassadorial" role of speaking, writing, and maintaining relations with other organizations. Despite assurance that this was "no reflection on our devoted and able executives," the message was clear: Baldwin had to go. It was a tough but correct judgment; Baldwin had never liked mundane administrative work but was now the victim of his own success. As long as the ACLU was a lonely voice in the wilderness, he was ideally suited for the job. But as civil liberties had achieved greater acceptance, the ACLU's task became one of extending the fight around the country, and the ACLU needed someone capable of administering a large organization.[28]

In any case, since 1947 Baldwin had become increasingly unhappy as executive director and was especially weary of the endless infighting over cold war issues (at one point he apologized to the National Committee for yet another referendum). As he had during the 1920s, he sought refuge in travel abroad, spending three months in Japan in 1947 and visiting the American zone of Germany the next year.

Baldwin's trip to Japan was a curious but revealing chapter in his career. In a series of letters to his friends, he called it the "most stirring months of my life in years." The United States had "a fair chance to work an historic miracle," by imposing democracy on Japan. His experience brought out all his latent authoritarian impulses; that is, he liked the idea of democracy "applied here without the hindrances of U.S. politics." Baldwin also reported on MacArthur's suppression of civil liberties—the movies were heavily censored, and the rights of the Communist party, the labor unions, and other left-wing groups were restricted—but he expressed no great outrage over it. Paraphrasing the traditional rationale of revolutionary totalitarian movements, Baldwin commented that repression was a necessary stage in the evolution toward democracy—yet another contradiction in Baldwin's long and often contradictory defense of civil liberties.[29]

Removing Baldwin as ACLU director was no easy task, however. The older board members, veterans of the grim World War I years and the lonely battles of the 1920s, could not bring themselves to do it. But newer members such as Gellhorn and Northrup could look at the ACLU's needs with an unsentimental eye. Northrup thus broke Baldwin's filibuster, and the deed was done.[30] It was the end of one of the most remarkable careers in American history.

For years, Baldwin had been the personification of civil liberties, keeping the ACLU alive almost single-handedly during its early years. When he retired in 1950, he left both an organization and a contribution to American life that would continue to grow in the years ahead. In the long history of American reform, few individuals had left as enduring a legacy. For someone of his energy, "retirement" was unthinkable, and so Baldwin carried on, devoting himself to international issues.

Finding a successor, meanwhile, created a financial problem. Baldwin had always taken only a token salary ($3,600 in 1949), and therefore the board

was forced to increase the budget significantly so as to make a competitive offer. Their first choice, Cleveland attorney Jack G. Day, claimed that a salary
of $7,200 was not enough, and so they had to raise it further to recruit Patrick
Murphy Malin. Malin, an economics professor at Swarthmore College, shared
many of Baldwin's elitist credentials: an Ivy League education, experience in
international human rights work, a commitment to pacifism, and an independent income, thanks to his in-laws, the Philadelphia Biddles.[31]

The board's concern with maintaining an image of establishment respectability revealed an offensive criterion: Gellhorn's search committee specified
that "other things being equal, . . . the ACLU director should not be one
whose interest in civil liberties might be mistakenly ascribed to his being a
member of an oppressed minority group."[32] In short: No Jews need apply.
This specification reflected the anti-Semitism prevalent in establishment America at the time: Through the early 1960s no Jew was appointed as head of
a major American university or as dean of a major law school. In this respect,
the ACLU resembled the motion picture industry, which always took great
pains to appoint a very WASP-ish Republican to head the Motion Picture
Producers Association (first Will Hays and then Eric Johnston). Finally the
barriers to Jews' being appointed as heads of major organizations, including
the ACLU, collapsed in the mid-1960s. Concern about respectability also dictated the choice of Ernest Angell as the new ACLU chair. His American Legion membership and service as chair of the regional Federal Loyalty Board
were seen as a shield against the persistent charges that the ACLU was a
Communist front.[33]

Malin could not hope to match the charismatic Baldwin as spokesperson
for civil liberties. An uninspiring speaker and clumsy writer, his performance
gave credence to all the hoary jokes about the literary talents of economists.
Few ACLU veterans of the period remember him with respect, and many held
him in contempt. On civil liberties issues Malin was solidly anti-Communist
and indulged in the ritualistic denunciations of the Communist menace. As a
result, he failed to project an inspiring vision of civil liberties during his tenure from 1950 to 1962. Hired to be an administrator, he functioned well in
that capacity, emerging, improbably, as the hero of the ACLU's subsequent
growth.

Expansion and Activism

Continuing Baldwin's traditional annual tour, Malin immediately sensed what
Baldwin and the board refused to see: The potential for a greatly expanded
ACLU membership. In city after city he found rising concern about the cold
war, a demand for an all-out attack on censorship, a strong desire for stricter
separation of church and state, and a commitment to civil rights. Beneath the
surface of the so-called "silent fifties" percolated a new spirit of political activism. Acting on his instincts, in early 1951 Malin proposed an ambitious
membership recruitment campaign. Because the board had already rejected
this idea, Malin presented it as an "experimental program," funded by a

$25,000 grant from the estate of Florina Lasker, a longtime activist on the New York City Committee. Malin hired George Rundquist in the dual role of executive director of the newly autonomous New York affiliate and national field director for membership and affiliate development.[34]

The results quickly confirmed Malin's judgment: The ACLU's membership tripled to 30,000 by 1955. In January 1955 alone, 1,500 new members joined, the largest one-month increase ever. By 1960 the membership had doubled again, to over 60,000. The increase in the national ACLU figures was partly the result of integrating the affiliates' members, but the affiliates themselves experienced extraordinary growth. For example, the Northern California ACLU grew from 1,564 members in 1950 to 3,550 in 1956. The New York Civil Liberties Union added 230 new members in November 1953, more than double the increase for the previous November.[35]

Because the ACLU did not survey its members, we cannot know precisely who these new members were or why they joined. If the board of directors is any guide, however, it is likely that most began as single-issue people, primarily concerned about censorship, separation of church and state, or civil rights. Probably many knew little about other civil liberties issues. Once in the ACLU, however, their horizons expanded as they learned about other issues.

Baldwin and the board had seriously misjudged the temper of the country; there was far more support for civil liberties than they had ever suspected. The decisions of 1949–1951 were, in retrospect, a crucial turning point for the ACLU. Had Baldwin remained, or had the board rejected Malin's membership plan, the subsequent history of the ACLU would undoubtedly have been very different. It might well have drifted off into amiable respectability, filing briefs in occasional cases, while other organizations tapped the rising tide of political activism. (In fact, the ACLU's new rival, the Emergency Civil Liberties Committee, or ECLC, never developed into a strong national organization because the controlling clique in New York refused to recruit members, develop semiautonomous affiliates, and share decision making.) Malin's program inaugurated a twenty-four-year period of almost uninterrupted growth that brought the ACLU up to 275,000 members by 1974.

The 1950 reorganization included a decision to establish more staffed affiliates. With full-time offices in only Boston, Chicago, San Francisco, and Los Angeles, the ACLU had a weak presence in most big cities; even New York City was served only by a committee of the national ACLU. The South and the Great Plains (with the exception of Iowa) had almost no organized civil liberties activity. Malin thus promptly went to work, with spectacular results: Staffed affiliates appeared in New York, Philadelphia, and Cleveland in 1951, and there were active and growing affiliates in sixteen states by 1954. Ohio had local chapters in nine cities. Colorado and Connecticut each had two local chapters. The New Haven, Connecticut, chapter included the formidable voice of Thomas Emerson, emerging as a leading authority on the First Amendment and a strong critic of the ACLU's cold war policies. With the addition of affiliates in Miami, Kentucky, and New Orleans in 1955–1956, the ACLU established a foothold in the South. In addition, members of both old and new affiliates were integrated into a single ACLU membership. In short, the ACLU began to create a truly national organizational structure.[36]

Growth transformed the ACLU in ways no one could foresee. Ideologically and institutionally the balance of power shifted to a new generation of activists in the affiliates, who were far more willing to challenge cold war orthodoxies, more absolutist regarding the separation of church and state, and far less concerned with maintaining a "respectable" image. In another important move, in 1951 the board revised the ACLU's constitution and bylaws to give the affiliates a voice in policymaking. This concession to internal democracy also had ramifications that no one anticipated. The new bylaws also established the Biennial Conference, a national meeting of the lay membership. Over the next three decades the Biennial Conference became a forum for activists who took the ACLU into new issues, such as capital punishment, abortion, and the rights of the poor.[37]

Struggle for the Soul of the ACLU

The split within the ACLU over cold war issues finally reached its climax in 1953 and 1954 in a bitterly fought referendum. Norman Thomas began by proposing an ACLU statement that "the Communist Party in the United States is an organization operating conspiratorially in the service of a foreign government and is a real danger to civil liberties. An organization of this character can obviously not be simply an organization of 'advocates' and 'teachers.' " Consumed by anti-Communism and steeped in the tradition of left-wing sectarianism, Thomas was obsessed with having the ACLU adopt a "correct" statement.[38]

Eventually, three issues were put to a vote in the ACLU referendum. The first proposal condemned the Communist party as antidemocratic and subservient to the Soviet Union. In addition, it was not "a violation of civil liberties to take into account a person's voluntary choice of association" in determining fitness for employment. Employers could legitimately take into account "the time and circumstances" of Communist party membership, "its duration and, if terminated, the sincerity of its termination." This was guilt by association at its worst. Once "tainted," one would never be free; others were entitled to judge the "sincerity" of one's quitting the party.[39]

The second statement, on academic freedom, reiterated the earlier ACLU position that no one should be barred from teaching solely on the grounds of one's political belief or association. This was undermined somewhat by the view that anything interfering with a teacher's "free and unbiased pursuit of truth" was "incompatible with the objectives of academic freedom," which implied that Communists were not fit to teach. The statement then endorsed a loyalty and security program for United Nations (UN) employees, an issue that was a particular obsession with the anti-Communist hard-liners.

The third statement gutted the Fifth Amendment, with the declaration that "any authority legally responsible for employment to which information concerning Communist or other totalitarian associations is relevant may ask questions concerning such associations." Moreover, using the Fifth did not "carry protection against any consequence" of having done so. In other words, a person could be fired for taking the Fifth.

The three proposals touched off angry protests. Howard K. Beale, an ACLU member for thirty years and longtime leader of the Academic Freedom Committee, bluntly told Malin, "I am for the first time ashamed of the organization." He had just organized an ACLU chapter at the University of Wisconsin and now wondered "whether we made a mistake to affiliate." Yale Law School professors Tom Emerson and Ralph Brown pointed out that if the ACLU adopted the three statements, a newspaper could properly headline the story, "ACLU Denounces Reds, Use of Fifth Amendment." Corliss Lamont charged that the first and third statements "actually give encouragement to the forces in the United States which are engaged in throwing overboard the Bill of Rights." With Statement 1 the ACLU "itself joins the great American witch-hunt and seriously undermines its opposition to both the Smith Act and the Internal Security Act (McCarran Act) of 1950." Statement 3 regarding the Fifth Amendment was "vague, verbose, meandering, inconsistent, [and] incredible." "Losing one's job," Lamont pointed out, "is surely one of the most severe penalties that can be imposed upon an individual." The two California affiliates also objected, and Northern California offered alternative statements that were uncompromising affirmations of the First and Fifth amendments.[40]

The referendum on these statements was the first under the new ACLU constitution that gave the affiliates a vote, and it was immediately embroiled in controversy. The office did not send out the usual pro and con arguments until Lamont complained. In another departure from precedent, Chairperson Angell included a personal letter that expressed his weariness of the continued factionalism: "If these statements are rejected, I despair of the Board being able to reach any more generally satisfactory substitute." An outraged Lamont fired off a telegram to all voters saying that it was "unfair, undemocratic and violative [of] traditional procedures" for the chair to intervene on one side of a referendum, adding a snide remark that the board had adopted the three statements only because of "fatigue, boredom and feeling on part of many Directors this [*sic*] only way to make non-stop talkers cease and desist." The board ignored Angell's violation of procedure and censured Lamont—who had alienated them over the years by his criticisms—for "grossly improper" action.[41]

The results of the referendum stunned everyone. All three statements were rejected, as the affiliates outvoted the board and the National Committee. Democratization of the ACLU made the difference on this crucial issue. The anti-Communists, convinced that Armageddon had arrived, then attempted a virtual coup. James Fly moved to reject the referendum results, but the board opposed this maneuver by only a one-vote margin. Malin then polled the Chicago affiliate by phone, on the grounds that few had voted, and produced a new set of returns that reversed the outcome. Lamont counterattacked by leaking the story to *I. F. Stone's Weekly,* which headlined it "The ACLU's Directors Prepare to Jettison Its Principles." The Chicago affiliate then reversed itself again, restoring the original result. The anti-Communists retaliated by invoking a little-noticed clause in the new bylaws that allowed the board not to accept referenda results when "it believes there are vitally important reasons for not doing so—which it shall explain to the corporation members." They persuaded the board to repudiate the referendum and to adopt the original three statements by a vote of fourteen to four. They apparently felt no embarrassment about using the very undemocratic methods they always attributed to Communists.[42]

With the ACLU about to dissolve in an irreconcilable dispute, the question of the referendum was taken up by the first Biennial Conference on February 15, 1954. The board sought to placate the affiliate representatives by instructing Malin to reformulate "the form, but not . . . the substance, of the three statements." Frank Graham, president of the University of North Carolina, drafted a far stronger affirmation of civil liberties principles that opened with an unequivocal declaration that the ACLU "stand[s] against guilt by association, judgment by accusation, the invasion of privacy of personal opinions and beliefs and the confusion of dissent with disloyalty." The ACLU would act "vigorously to defend the civil liberties of any person, however unpopular that person or his views may be." Graham's draft repudiated the original three policy statements.[43]

But the anti-Communist hard-liners refused to give up. Threatening to resign, Norman Thomas and his allies got the board to repudiate the Biennial's action. Fraenkel confided to his diary that he was tired of the continual resignation threats and felt that "the Board would be better off without some . . . of those involved," naming Thomas, Fly, and Fitelson. Repudiation of the Biennial decision angered the affiliates even more. New Haven wrote that it "deplores the apparent repudiation . . . of the spirit and results" of the Biennial.[44] Strong protests also came, predictably, from the California affiliates. To resolve the seemingly endless and debilitating dispute, Malin put together a "tripartite" committee, consisting of representatives of the affiliates, the board, and the National Committee, to draft an acceptable statement.

The ACLU's internal warfare finally came to an end in August, with a new compromise statement. Adopting much of Graham's language, it opened with a strong denunciation of guilt by association. In a concession to Thomas and his group, it then incorporated a statement on the "dual nature" of the Communist party. The section on the Fifth Amendment was hopelessly muddled, stating that the ACLU was opposed to firing anyone for refusing to answer questions but that it approved of dismissing someone for refusing to disclose to an employer any facts relating to possible unfitness. The statement did conclude with a new and stronger affirmation of the right to refuse to answer questions on First Amendment grounds.[45]

Finally, it was all over. The anti-Communists departed, convinced they had lost the struggle for the soul of the ACLU. Whitney North Seymour resigned to pursue the presidency of the ABA. Merlyn Pitzele was not renominated in 1954, in a trade for not renominating Lamont. C. Dickerman Williams and William Fitelson were not reelected in 1955. Age and a sense of defeat finally caught up with Thomas and Ernst, and both slid into comparative inactivity. Staff counsel Herbert Monte Levy resigned in the summer of 1955, leaving Irving Ferman, director of the Washington office, as the only aggressive anti-Communist on the staff. The anti-Communist bloc was decimated, and the bitter ideological split that had divided the ACLU since 1947 evaporated. The following year Fraenkel commented on how peaceful board meetings had become.[46]

Lamont left when the board rescinded his renomination in late 1953. Friends urged him to run by petition, but he declined, saying, "I am tired of all this. I believe that I can be more helpful to the cause of civil liberties by giving over my energies directly to the fight against McCarthy and McCarthyism." He added that "I shall leave this Board where I have served for 21 years with many regrets . . . I remain glad for the victories we have all won together in the supremely significant and eternally valid cause of civil liberties." Although Lamont remained an ACLU member and generous financial contributor, he gave much of his attention (and considerable wealth) to the rival ECLC, giving it $25,000 in 1954 and always being its primary source of funds.[47]

The ACLU had not heard the last from Lamont, however. In a book and other writings he single-handedly shaped the public reputation of the ACLU's performance in the fifteen years from 1940 to 1954, accusing the organization of abandoning its principles, beginning with the 1940 Resolution and the Flynn purge, and doing virtually nothing in the cold war. It was a highly distorted interpretation, with no mention of the ACLU's fight against loyalty oaths, HUAC, blacklisting, other anti-Communist measures, or its prominent role in the areas of censorship, separation of church and state, and civil rights. In this respect he was the heir to the old Chafee–Meikeljohn tradition that emphasized political speech to the near exclusion of other civil liberties issues. Lamont also maintained a discreet silence concerning the years between 1941 and 1947 and his opposition to the ACLU's defense of Japanese-Americans and right-wing war critics. If some of his criticisms of the ACLU in the cold war were well taken, his own record was not without its lapses as well.[48]

With the departure of the anti-Communists, the character of the ACLU changed almost overnight. Gone were the endless acrimonious disputes over cold war issues. Instead, the new consensus called for a steadily more vigorous attack on cold war measures. Hays retired as general counsel in 1954, marking the end of an era for the ACLU. He died in December, and his obituary appeared in the *New York Times,* appropriately, on December 15, Bill of Rights Day.[49]

1954: The Beginning of the End

The climactic struggle in the ACLU coincided with several events in 1954 that marked the beginning of the end of the cold war and the dawn of a new era in American politics.

On March 9, 1954, CBS television broadcast Edward R. Murrow's "See It Now" program on Senator Joseph McCarthy. Now widely recognized as one of the most famous programs in television history, Murrow's report on the Wisconsin senator was an act of enormous courage. McCarthy had been untouchable for four years; to criticize him was to be called a "Communist dupe." The news media had supinely repeated his wildest charges without checking the facts. And Murrow was particularly vulnerable as a television journalist, given the enormous power of his advertisers. Nevertheless, Murrow built a case against McCarthy by relying on the senator's own words, showing him badgering Reed Harris of the Federal International Information Administration: McCarthy charged that when Harris had been suspended from Columbia University in 1934, he had turned to the "Communist-influenced" ACLU for help. Although Murrow never actually accused McCarthy of acting like a thug, the program led to that inescapable conclusion. Murrow ended with a little sermon: "We will not be driven by fear into an age of unreason, if we dig deep into our own history and our doctrine and remember that we are not descended from fearful men, not from men who feared to write, to speak, to associate, and to defend causes which were for the moment unpopular." It was "no time for men who oppose Senator McCarthy's methods to keep silent."[50]

The program galvanized the nation. Murrow's closing words expressed what many concerned people had been thinking but were afraid to say, and he therefore made it possible for others to act on their revulsion against McCarthy and the excesses of the witch hunt. A few weeks after the Murrow program, McCarthy launched a reckless attack on the United States Army. Televised hearings helped further turn public opinion against him, and in December 1954 the Senate censured McCarthy—not, significantly, for ruining peoples' lives or poisoning the political discourse but for bringing the Senate into disrepute. When the Senate began its inquiry into McCarthy, the ACLU reminded it that even he was entitled to fair procedure in its investigation. Like a balloon that has been punctured, McCarthy collapsed almost immediately. He lost his influence and within three years was dead.[51]

Other elements of the American establishment also moved to reaffirm the values of tolerance and fair play. With a grant of $15 million, the Ford Foundation created the Fund for the Republic, which sponsored a series of books, articles, and programs defending civil liberties and made several highly publicized awards to individuals who had fought the cold war. The *Denver Post* published a series of articles entitled "Faceless Informers and Our Schools," which described six Colorado teachers accused of being loyalty risks, on the basis of "information whose source is hidden behind official secrecy." This article—in one of the first attacks on the FBI in a major newspaper—also accused agents of giving derogatory information to local school officials while piously claiming that the bureau could not verify the information. The *Post* concluded that preservation of standards of due process, particularly the right to confront one's accuser, was fundamental to the "survival and security of the American way of life" and "our continued greatness and freedom as a nation."[52]

The rhetoric of the cold war had shifted in a subtle but important way. Its excesses had produced a backlash: Defense of the American way of life depended not on rooting out every suspected red but on preserving civil liberties. The House of Representatives adopted rules of procedure for its committees in 1955. Though they left much to be desired in regard to protecting the rights of witnesses, they were at least a small step in the direction of curbing HUAC's abuses.

The Supreme Court's decision in *Brown v. Board of Education* on May 17, 1954, ushered in a new era in both civil rights and Supreme Court history. The unanimous decision declaring segregated schools to be unconstitutional was as much a turning point as was the censure of McCarthy. By striking at the entrenched *de jure* segregation in the South, *Brown* promised judicial protection for the rights of minorities and dramatically reshaped the national political agenda. Griswold's 1955 book on the Fifth Amendment meanwhile prophetically charted new horizons in due process of law. New currents were stirring in the legal community, provoked in large part by the crisis of the Bill of Rights in the cold war.[53]

Another 1954 incident raised a new civil liberties issue, one that became a central controversy in national politics by the 1970s. On March 1 the United States detonated a nuclear bomb over the Bikini atoll in the Pacific. The wind unexpectedly shifted and carried fallout from the blast to the east, dropping it on a Japanese fishing boat. By the time the *Lucky Dragon* returned to Japan, all twenty-three members of the crew were suffering from radiation sickness, and six months later one of them died. The Atomic Energy Commission had continually insisted that there was no danger from the fallout. But the fate of the *Lucky Dragon* crew exposed this as a lie and simultaneously stimulated a grass-roots ban-the-bomb movement and raised the whole question of government lying. This was the first significant crack in the cold war consensus. The ban-the-bomb movement represented a new generation of activists, independent of the old left-wing politics inherited from the 1930s, and was a forerunner of the 1960s' protests. Since World War II the news media had been largely uncritical of official versions of American foreign policy, but the doubts raised by the *Lucky Dragon* culminated in the "credibility gap" controversy during the Vietnam War.[54]

The ACLU moved quickly to raise the civil liberties aspects of government lying. Democratic control over foreign policy required informed decision making, which in turn depended on access to information—about nuclear energy and weapons, as well as the precise activities of government agencies. Gerard Piel had voiced a lonely protest in the *Scientific American* incident in 1950. The ACLU itself had been trapped by the distorted political dialogue of the cold war, applauding the 1946 Atomic Energy Act as a civil liberties victory because it provided civilian rather than military control over nuclear energy. But despite some cautionary words about restrictions on scientific inquiry, the ACLU did not object to the law's central aim, to make information about nuclear weapons "classified at birth."[55]

The ACLU commissioned a report by journalist Allen Raymond entitled *The People's Right to Know: A Report on Government News Suppression*. As an index of the changing political climate, Raymond cited the complaints of numerous journalists—Marquis Childs, Joseph Alsop, editors of the *Washington Post* and *Aviation Week*—about government secrecy. Nor was the problem confined to matters of national security. The Agriculture Department, the Federal Trade Commission (FTC), and the Securities and Exchange Commission (SEC) all were guilty of suppressing news. Reporter Clark Mollenhoff named the SEC's secrecy as "the major cause of corruption" in government. Raymond's report concluded with a recommendation for "greater legal sanction to the public's right of information about what the Federal government is doing." Eleven years later this bore fruit in the Freedom of Information Act.[56]

The ACLU noticed the turning of the tide. "Suddenly in the spring and summer of 1955, the current began to run the other way," it reported. "A general awakening of the public conscience to the harm done to the constitutional rights of the people" helped throw "a clear light on the danger in which we stood." Although anti-Communist paranoia had not been played out, the beginning of the end had arrived.[57]

Crystal Eastman (center), co-founder
of the Civil Liberties Bureau, which
was the predecessor of the ACLU.
Feminist, lawyer, and Progressive Era
reformer, Eastman is shown here attending the unveiling of a memorial
to the suffrage movement, with Mrs.
Sinclair Lewis (left) and Mrs. Florence
Bockel (right). Eastman dropped out
of the civil liberties fight in mid-1917
because of poor health; the organizational structure she created as secretary of the American Union Against
Militarism in 1915 remained un-
changed in the ACLU until the mid-
1960s. (UPI/Bettmann Newsphotos)

Roger Baldwin on the campus of
Washington University, St. Louis,
Missouri, 1906. A Progressive Era
social reformer, Baldwin did not discover civil liberties until the United
States entered World War I in April
1917. (Mudd Library, Princeton University)

Mary Ware Dennett during her trial, New York City, 1929. The federal government's prosecution of Dennett under the Comstock Law for mailing her sex education pamphlet, *The Sex Side of Life,* helped launch a more vigorous ACLU campaign against censorship of literary and scientific works. Dennett's subsequent conviction was, with Morris Ernst's help as her attorney, reversed on appeal. (UPI/Bettmann Newsphotos)

Left page

Top. Clarence Darrow in action at the Scopes "monkey trial," Dayton, Tennessee, 1925. (UPI/Bettmann Newsphotos)

Bottom. The ACLU's Scopes trial team reunited in 1934. Left to right: Clarence Darrow, Arthur Garfield Hays, Dudley Malone, and Roger Baldwin. Hays, ACLU general counsel from 1929 to 1954, assisted Darrow in the Scopes trial and was the first one in the ACLU to articulate an "absolutist" position on freedom of speech. Malone also assisted in the Scopes trial. The four are shown here testifying at an unofficial "trial" of Nazi Germany. Baldwin tried unsuccessfully on several occasions to involve the ACLU in international human rights issues. (UPI/Bettmann Newsphotos)

Morris Ernst delivering a radio address denouncing Frank Hague, mayor of Jersey City, New Jersey, January 7, 1938. ACLU general counsel (1929–1954), Ernst won the landmark Supreme Court case *Hague v. CIO,* which established broad protection for freedom of assembly. He was also the most prominent and successful opponent of censorship, winning the famous *Ulysses* case in 1933, and was the first attorney to litigate reproductive freedom issues systematically. In the late 1930s he became a vigorous anti-Communist and developed an intimate relationship with J. Edgar Hoover, director of the FBI. (AP/Wide World)

Seated, front row, left to right: Madeline Z. Doty, official of the Women's International League for Peace and Freedom, Annie Gray, and Roger Baldwin, New York City, 1935. Doty, Baldwin's first wife (1919–1936), reads the newspaper of the American League Against War and Fascism, later the American League for Peace and Democracy (ALPD). Baldwin's close ties with the ALPD and other Popular Front groups between 1935 and 1939 were the source of charges that the ACLU was a "Communist front." (Mudd Library, Princeton University)

Norman Thomas, founding member of the ACLU, being struck by eggs as he attempted to speak in Jersey City, June 4, 1938. Like Roger Baldwin, Thomas disdained litigation in the 1920s and 1930s, arguing that civil liberties could only be secured through direct action. (AP/Wide World)

Ed Ennis in the 1940s. As director of the Justice Department's Enemy Alien Control Unit during World War II, Ennis was nominally responsible for administering the evacuation and internment of Japanese-Americans. He fought the program from within, however, even to the point of virtually advising the ACLU on how to frame its court briefs against the program. After the war, Ennis joined the ACLU, wrote briefs in many important Supreme Court cases during the 1950s and 1960s, and served as chairman of the ACLU board of directors, 1969–1976. (Photo courtesy of Ed Ennis)

Corporal George Bushy supervises evacuation of Mrs. Shigeho Kitamoto and her four children, March 30, 1942, Bainbridge Island, Washington. The ACLU was the only national organization to oppose the evacuation of Japanese-Americans in the courts. (AP/Wide World)

Right page

Top. Elizabeth Gurley Flynn, Communist party leader, commenting on the conviction of eleven top party officials under the Smith Act, December 14, 1949. A founding member of the ACLU, Flynn was removed from its board of directors in May 1940 because of her Communist party membership. The ACLU was influenced by a strong anti-Communist group between 1940 and 1954. The 1949 conviction of the Communist party officials was upheld by the U.S. Supreme Court in 1951 in *Dennis v. United States*. Until 1957, the court upheld virtually all measures restricting the rights of Communists. (UPI/Bettmann Newsphotos)

Bottom. Left to right: Patrick Malin, Rev. John Haynes Holmes, and Roger Baldwin, on the occasion of Baldwin's retirement after thirty years as ACLU executive director, February 22, 1950. Malin served as executive director from 1950 to 1962. Rev. Holmes, a founding member of the ACLU, served as chairman of the board of directors from 1940 to 1950. A Unitarian minister and staunch pacifist, Holmes was one of the most prominent social activists in New York City from the 1920s through the 1950s. (AP/Wide World)

Osmond Fraenkel, at age seventy-one, 1960. He was the ACLU's greatest Supreme Court litigator and one of the premier constitutional lawyers of all time. Beginning with *DeJonge v. Oregon* in 1937, Fraenkel made twenty-six separate arguments before the Supreme Court; the last occurred in 1974, one week before his eighty-fifth birthday. His name appeared on 103 briefs submitted to the court. (Photo courtesy of George Fraenkel)

Corliss Lamont, member of the ACLU board of directors, 1932 to 1954. Heir to a banking fortune, Lamont was a prominent leftist and persistent critic of the ACLU's policies during the cold war. He is shown here in July 1958, announcing his willingness to run for either governor or senator in New York on the United Socialist party ticket. Lamont successfully challenged attempts by both the House Un-American Activities Committee and Senator Joseph McCarthy to investigate him for his political beliefs. In the landmark case, *Lamont v. Postmaster General* (1965), the Supreme Court struck down a federal statute restricting the right of a citizen to receive Communist-oriented mail from abroad. (UPI/Bettmann Newsphotos)

Roger Baldwin (left), still vigorous at age eighty-two, with Jack Pemberton, ACLU executive director (1962–1970), in 1966. Pemberton supervised the transformation of the ACLU into a genuinely national organization, including the 1964 decision to open a Southern Regional Office in Atlanta. (Mudd Library, Princeton University)

Eleanor Holmes Norton became ACLU assistant legal director in 1964. One of her first cases involved representing George Wallace's right to hold a political rally in Shea Stadium that had been banned by liberal New York City Mayor John V. Lindsay. Norton later served as chair of the New York City Commission on Human Rights and of the U.S. Equal Employment Opportunity Commission. Currently professor of law at Georgetown University, she was appointed chair of the ACLU National Advisory Council in 1984. (AP/Wide World)

Charles B. Morgan, Jr., on the steps of the U.S. Supreme Court, early 1970s. Morgan directed the ACLU Southern Regional Office, 1964 to 1972, arguing and winning several landmark Supreme Court cases. His clients included Julian Bond and Muhammad Ali. From 1973 to 1976 he directed the ACLU Washington office and was a leader in the campaign to impeach President Richard Nixon because of the Watergate scandal. (Photo courtesy of Charles B. Morgan, Jr.)

Left page

Top. Aryeh Neier, executive director of the New York Civil Liberties Union, announces formation of a coalition to support civilian review of the New York City police, 1966. Also in attendance, left to right: Mayor John V. Lindsay, Senator Robert F. Kennedy, and civil rights attorney Morris B. Abram. Neier served as NYCLU executive director from 1965 to 1970 and then ACLU executive director from 1970 to 1978. (Photo courtesy of Aryeh Neier)

Bottom. Left to right: Alan Levine, Mel Wulf, and Ramsey Clark, in private law practice together, early 1970s. Wulf served as ACLU legal director from 1962 to 1977 and was instrumental in leading the ACLU into the forefront of the southern civil rights movement and to the defense of anti-Vietnam War protesters. Levine was one of many ACLU activists who went to Mississippi as civil rights volunteers in the summer of 1964 and, transformed by the experience, devoted the rest of their careers to civil liberties. As attorney general from 1965 to 1969, Clark authorized many assaults on civil liberties, but after leaving the Justice Department in 1969, he became an active civil libertarian and served as chair of the ACLU National Advisory Council from 1970 to 1984. (*New York Times*)

Frank Collin (center), leader of the National Socialist party, addresses a crowd in Marquette Park, Chicago, July 9, 1978. The ACLU's defense of Collin's right to hold a rally in the heavily Jewish village of Skokie, Illinois, was one of the most famous controversies in ACLU history. Thousands of members quit the ACLU in protest, precipitating a financial crisis. (AP/Wide World)

Left page

Top. New York Civil Liberties Union attorney Norman Siegel (right), with Supreme Court Justice William O. Douglas (center) and ACLU affiliate staff member Bob Free (left), on the porch of Justice Douglas's cabin in Goose Prairie, Washington, August 1973. The NYCLU attorneys successfully persuaded Douglas to order an end to the American bombing of Cambodia; the full court lifted Douglas's order hours later. Siegel served with Charles Morgan in the ACLU Southern Regional Office in the 1960s; as director of the New York Civil Liberties Union in the mid-1980s, he was a prominent champion of the rights of homeless people. (*Oregon Journal*/Photo: Dana Olsen)

Bottom. Eason Monroe, retiring director of the ACLU of Southern California, and Ramona Ripston, his successor, July 1972. Monroe refused to sign the California loyalty oath in 1952 and was subsequently fired from his teaching job at San Francisco State University. That year he was appointed executive director of the ACLU's then largest affiliate, Southern California. Ripston was a civil rights worker in Mississippi in 1964 and worked for the ACLU and the New York Civil Liberties Union in the 1960s; except for a one-year period in the mid-1980s, she has directed the ACLU of Southern California since 1972. (ACLU of Southern California Foundation)

Norman Dorsen, president of the ACLU, leads an ACLU contingent in the massive pro-choice march on Washington, April 9, 1989. Dorsen began working with the ACLU in 1961, served as general counsel from 1969 to 1976 and as president of the board of directors from 1976 to the present. He argued and won several landmark cases before the Supreme Court, including *In Re Gault* (1967); he also argued the first abortion case before the court, *Vuitch v. United States,* in 1971. (Photo courtesy of the ACLU)

Ira Glasser, ACLU executive director (left) and John A. Powell, ACLU legal director, discuss how to respond to the anti-civil libertarian trends in the Supreme Court, June 1989. Glasser succeeded Aryeh Neier as director of the New York Civil Liberties Union in 1970. In 1978, he became ACLU executive director when the organization was in the depths of the financial crisis caused by the Skokie episode, but he soon put the ACLU on the soundest financial footing it had ever known. As legal director since 1986, Powell confronted an increasingly anti-civil libertarian Supreme Court, coordinating the work of the more than seventy full-time ACLU attorneys in his office, the special projects, and the larger affiliates. (Photo: Tom Tyburski)

V

The Great Years,
1954-1964

Ten

The First Amendment
As an Absolute

The Warren Court's Constitutional Law Revolution

"It is an occasion for dancing in the streets." Alexander Meikeljohn's joy was prompted by the Supreme Court's 1964 decision in *New York Times v. Sullivan.* Overturning a libel suit against the *Times,* the Court found the "central meaning of the First Amendment" in the right of the people to criticize the government freely. The Court held that under the First Amendment "debate on public issues should be uninhibited, robust, and wide open."[1]

The *Times* decision was not the only reason for civil libertarians to celebrate in 1964. The decade between the 1954 *Brown v. Board of Education* decision and *Times* encompassed the greatest advances in civil liberties in American history. In a series of landmark decisions, the Supreme Court led the attack on racial segregation, banished religious exercises from public schools, dismantled the machinery of censorship, protected freedom of association, forced legislative redistricting, and introduced constitutional standards of due process in criminal justice.[2]

These were great years for the ACLU, as it played a leading role in virtually every major Court decision and, in several, directly influenced the Court's thinking. The ACLU's critics recognized the organization's influence. The old charges that the ACLU was Communist influenced were now joined by complaints that it was "Godless," "anti-Christian," an advocate of pornography, and the friend of criminals.

The ACLU's membership rose from thirty thousand in 1955 to eighty thousand in 1965, and by then it had staffed affiliates in seventeen states.[3] The ACLU's growth was symptomatic of the changing public attitudes. A new sense of freedom was in the air: An increasingly educated public expected the freedom to read without restrictions imposed by religious moralists. The sexual revolution challenged censorship in the arts and restrictions on birth control, eventually leading to a new concept of privacy. And in 1960 the sit-ins gave political participation a new personal dimension.

The rising tempo of civil liberties gains created its own dynamic, as each breakthrough raised expectations about individual liberty. An activist, civil libertarian Supreme Court called forth a burst of creative litigation by the ACLU. The 1954 *Brown v. Board of Education* decision spurred the civil rights movement; the 1952 *Miracle* decision, holding that films were a form of expression protected by the First Amendment, fostered an attack on movie censorship; and the first Court decisions limiting anti-Communist measures in 1957 encouraged further challenges.

On the front lines of the struggle, ACLU leaders often failed to see the general trend of expanding liberties. Instead, ACLU press releases habitually sounded the alarm over new threats. In his 1965 *Annual Report,* Executive Director Jack Pemberton warned of "the fears and anxieties that [could] lead to contraction" of recent civil liberties gains.[4] The sky, it seemed, was always falling for the ACLU. This lack of perspective was a product of the ACLU's restless activism. Always pointing out that the glass of liberty was half full, it tended to ignore the half that was full and did not see that the glass itself had changed. Indeed, the pace of change was so rapid that by the time of the 1964 Biennial Conference, the new generation of activists looked upon some of the veterans as stodgy "conservatives." Osmond Fraenkel, who had argued many landmark cases in the Court since 1937, suddenly found himself a moderate voice. Civil Rights lawyers William Kunstler and Phil Hirschkop arrived at ACLU board meetings in overalls, the uniform of the southern struggle, and expressed contempt for the older ACLU veterans. It was a bizarre experience for the older generation. Only a few years before, ACLU critics had reviled them as "Communists" and "God haters."[5]

As civil liberties values spread, the ACLU was no longer always a lonely voice. On a number of issues, other powerful groups joined the battle. For example, publishers and film distributors took on censorship cases, and powerful urban political interests fought for legislative reapportionment. The ACLU, however, still had to carry on its traditional defense of unpopular groups, including the Communists and the Ku Klux Klan. In the Supreme Court, the ACLU gradually moved toward an "absolutist" position on the First Amendment, eventually insisting, for example, on an end to all censorship and a complete separation of church and state. Then a new form of criticism of the ACLU arose: Many liberals accepted the basic civil liberties principles but criticized the ACLU for pressing them too far. The annual controversy over ACLU objections to Christmas displays on public property became the most common form of these attacks. At the same time, the affiliates assumed more of a watchdog role, ensuring the implementation of decisions that embodied civil liberties principles.

"A Wall of Separation": The Church–State Controversy

Everson *and Its Impact*

"The First Amendment has erected a wall between church and state," wrote Justice Hugo Black. "That wall must be kept high and impregnable. We would not approve the slightest breach."[6] In the 1947 *Everson* decision, the Supreme Court gave new meaning to the establishment clause of the First Amendment. Over the next forty years, the question of the "wall of separation" between church and state became one of the most hotly contested political issues in America. On the one side stood the forces of organized religion that sought to maintain their traditional prerogative of using the state's machinery—particularly the schools—to advance their religious doctrines. On the other side stood the ACLU and other separationist groups, insisting that in a pluralist society, government had to be neutral in religious matters.

At issue in *Everson* was a New Jersey law providing public funds for busing parochial school children, one of many laws providing public support for religious educational activities that began to appear in 1938. Others required students to participate in religious exercises or granted them released time for religious instruction. Despite the rhetoric of Justice Black's majority opinion, the Court sustained the New Jersey law in *Everson*. But this decision, instead of settling the issue, galvanized the partisans on both sides. Catholics stepped up their campaign for direct public support for parochial schools—a new goal they had adopted only in 1945.[7] Liberal Democrats welcomed Catholic support for federal aid to education. On the other side, *Everson* called forth a well-organized movement for separation of church and state.

The ACLU, which had sponsored the *Everson* case, was one of the three leading members of the separationist coalition. As the battle intensified, ACLU policy regarding the establishment clause evolved toward a more absolutist position. Since the 1920s it had regarded with horror the militant atheist Joseph Lewis, who brought several suits challenging state-supported religious practices. By the mid-1940s, however, a more aggressive attitude began to prevail in the ACLU.[8]

The second important separationist group—Protestants and other Americans United for Separation of Church and State (later changed to Americans United)—was organized in early 1948 as a direct result of Protestant alarm over *Everson*. The American Jewish Congress was the third major separationist group. Its Commission of Law and Social Action, directed by Will Maslow, had a broad civil libertarian agenda and cooperated with the ACLU on many issues. Staff member Leo Pfeffer soon emerged as the foremost authority on church and state, writing a number of Supreme Court briefs and several influential books. The American Jewish Committee and the Anti-Defamation League were always more cautious and at times joined cases only because they did not want to break ranks publicly with Pfeffer.[9]

The Jewish groups and many ACLU leaders were acutely sensitive to charges that the separationist position was "anti-Christian." Leo Pfeffer was virtually smuggled into Minneapolis in 1949 for a talk at a local synagogue on the separation of church and state.[10] In 1962 the Catholic magazine *America* editorially warned "our Jewish friends" that they were risking an anti-Semitic backlash on the church–state issue.[11] Concern about public image occasionally led to absurd results. The American Jewish Committee insisted on a non-Jewish plaintiff and attorney in the New York released-time case. But many people probably assumed anyway that plaintiff Tessim Zorach and attorney Kenneth Greenawalt were Jewish.[12] The ACLU shared these worries and made "every effort" to find "a Protestant plaintiff" in *Zorach*. For the school prayer case, the New York Civil Liberties Union insisted on non-Jews for both the plaintiff and the lead attorney, thereby assigning the case to William J. Butler, son-in-law of Arthur Garfield Hays, a Catholic and the only non-Jew on its lawyers' committee.[13]

Religion and the Court in American Life

The church–state issue involved the larger question of the place of religion in American life. The separationist position challenged the status of Protestantism as the country's unofficial religion. The "accommodationists," as church–state moderates came to be called, argued that the United States was essentially a Christian nation, that democracy would crumble without a religious foundation. The First Amendment, they observed, forbade only the establishment of an official state religion. Some reasoned that the free exercise clause of the First Amendment allowed the government to support some religious practices, such as parochial schools. Alexander Meikeljohn, a leading First Amendment authority and leader of the Northern California ACLU, argued that completely removing religion from the educational process would rob education of a necessary spiritual ingredient.[14]

The separationists replied that the two religion clauses of the First Amendment offered the only reasonable framework for mutual tolerance in a richly pluralistic society. The free exercise clause commanded respect for even the most obnoxious sects, whereas the establishment clause meant that politically powerful groups could not use government resources to advance their particular view. Separationist briefs cited the extent to which children of Jews and/or nonbelievers were subjected to Protestant dogma. Vashti McCollum, the plaintiff in the landmark 1948 Supreme Court case, told how her son Jim came home from school in tears after being forced to sit out in the hall alone because he did not participate in the "voluntary" religion classes.[15] In *Zorach,* Leah Cunn testified how her refusal to participate in released-time education classes resulted in comments about her being Jewish, including taunts that as a Jew she was a "Christ killer."[16]

From the 1940s through the 1950s, Catholics rather than Protestants were the focal point of the church–state controversy. Their new demand for public funds for parochial schools marked a new confidence in their social and political status in America. Many Protestants and Jews, however, were disturbed by the Catholics' assertiveness with respect to birth control, censorship, and school aid. In 1948 Walter Gellhorn suggested that the ACLU write to Catholics, expressing "our belief that the Church is throwing its weight around in a fashion which may ultimately make more difficult the preservation of religious and other liberties." Subsequently, Paul Blanshard's comprehensive attack on the Catholic role in politics, *American Freedom and Catholic Power,* sold several hundred thousand copies.[17]

The Court's intervention in the church–state question raised questions about the role of the Court itself, an issue that would arise in all the major civil liberties areas. Civil libertarians applauded the Court's growing activism, but conservatives argued for judicial restraint. Constitutional scholar Edward S. Corwin, quoting Justice Robert Jackson, warned that the Court should not assume the role of "a national school board." It could not and should not attempt to resolve every question of educational policy.[18] Ultimately, the Court did intervene in a broad range of social issues, concerning not just the schools, recasting them in civil liberties terms. In the long run, the ACLU's role in helping the Court "constitutionalize" so many public controversies represented perhaps its greatest impact on American life. The process of "constitutionalization," in turn, was one of the most important trends in American society.

Released Time and Other Issues

A year after *Everson,* the Court ruled on the question of released time for religious instruction. The Champaign, Illinois, program challenged in *McCollum* was designed as a compromise, allowing students to take religion classes taught by privately paid clergy. The classes were, however, held in the school building. Similar programs existed in as many as thirty-three states and enrolled anywhere from 1.2 to 3 million schoolchildren. In an eight-to-one decision, the Court declared the program unconstitutional, as use of the school building was an indirect form of assistance. Far more serious, Black argued, was the "use of the State's compulsory public school machinery. This is not the separation of Church and State."[19]

McCollum encouraged the separationists, but over the next few years the Court zigged and zagged in a confusing pattern. In 1952 it refused to hear an ACLU challenge to in-school Bible reading[20] and upheld a New York released-time program that excused students from school to attend religion classes off school property. By a six-to-three majority the Court ruled that this did not violate the establishment clause because it involved neither public funds nor the use of public buildings. In a passage that years later came back to haunt him and other separationists, Justice William O. Douglas wrote that "we find no constitutional requirement which makes it necessary for government to be hostile to religion and to throw its weight against efforts to widen the effective scope of religious influence."[21]

The national church–state controversy exposed a number of entrenched practices in which church and state had merged. For example, in some predominantly Catholic rural areas, parochial schools had been converted into public schools, but without dropping their religious character. One survey estimated that there were 340 of these "captive schools" around the country. Twenty New Mexico schools were simultaneously listed as public and Catholic schools. In Michigan, 19 parochial schools regularly received public funds. The ACLU brought a case in rural New Mexico, where 134 nuns and priests taught in public schools wearing religious garb, church officials selected and assigned teachers, crucifixes hung in the classrooms, and children were required to recite "Hail Mary."[22] The ACLU supported Lydia Zellers, a Presbyterian parent, on her claim that teachers should not wear religious garb in the classroom, but it refused to support her attempt to ban clergy from teaching in public schools altogether. The New Mexico Supreme Court upheld the ACLU on both points.[23]

Sunday closing laws were another long-established tradition. The NYCLU and the American Jewish Congress brought a 1949 suit on behalf of Orthodox Jews, arguing that the law violated the establishment clause as a state-sanctioned religious observance and the free exercise clause by denying Sabbatarians the right to close their businesses on Saturday and to open them on Sunday. The Supreme Court refused to hear the case but in 1961 eventually ruled on four related cases (with the ACLU involved in two). The Court rejected the separationist position in a six-to-three decision and upheld the closing laws, but in any event, the decision soon became irrelevant: Commercial pressures eliminated the Sunday closing far more effectively than any court could. The practice of Sunday closing thus quietly disappeared from American life without further controversy.[24]

The ACLU and the Catholic Church

Through the 1950s, the church–state controversy focused primarily on the Catholic church and was closely related to the church's position on censorship and birth control. Conflict between the ACLU and the church flared on several occasions. Father Robert Drinan, dean of the Boston College Law School, delivered the most articulate attack, accusing the ACLU of having "so magnified the establishment clause" that it ignored "the religious liberty section of the First Amendment." Catholic schools were entitled to public support, and the failure to provide it in the form of either transportation or textbooks inhibited the religious freedom of individual Catholics. Drinan did not feel that the ACLU was "antireligious," but he could not resist pointing out the absence of practicing Catholics on the ACLU board and staff. Drinan emerged as a strong civil libertarian in the 1960s and, as a member of Congress, was a leading opponent of the Vietnam War. He eventually joined the ACLU's National Advisory Council.[25]

The charge that it was antireligious stung the ACLU leadership, and in response, the national office quietly downplayed church–state issues in the mid-1950s. The ACLU's Religion Committee disappeared. Already facing repeated attacks from the American Legion and other professional anti-

Communists that the ACLU was pro-Communist, Malin and the board apparently decided to avoid alienating the politically powerful Catholics. When the board created a new Church–State Committee in 1959, it included a number of prominent clergy who supported the accommodationist position.[26]

The Pace Quickens

By the late 1950s, public attitudes toward church–state questions began to change markedly. In the ACLU, the new mood was felt in the affiliates. For instance, in 1957 the Greater Philadelphia ACLU reported "an increasing number of complaints regarding church–state problems." The new generation of ACLU activists were impatient with the remaining religious practices in the schools, particularly Bible reading and compulsory prayers. A 1960 survey found Bible reading in 42 percent of all American schools and in 77 percent of southern schools. A Pennsylvania law required the reading of ten verses from the Bible every day. Eleven other states required Bible reading, and thirty more legally permitted it.[27]

Challenges to these practices profoundly altered the politics of church and state because they offended the huge Protestant majority. Protestant fundamentalists replaced Catholics as the ACLU's primary antagonists. Several prominent Catholic theologians, notably John Courtney Murray, urged the church to drop its aggressive positions on aid to schools and censorship, to recognize the pluralism of American society, and not to attempt to impose its morality on others.[28]

With its members demanding action on Bible reading and prayer, the Philadelphia ACLU asked the national office for guidance.[29] The Church–State Committee, heavily weighted with accommodationist theologians, did not object to Christmas observances. Some members even argued that "it would seem the better part of wisdom to devote our energies to violations which constitute a major threat to civil liberties."[30] Others contended that the religious composition of the community should be a deciding factor. Protestant majorities could maintain their observances if there were no serious Jewish or atheist opponents. Rev. John C. Bennett, dean of Union Theological Seminary, summed up the accommodationist position: "Separation is not so much a solution as it is a problem." Pressing it too far would only aggravate religious conflict. Accordingly, Leo Pfeffer angrily resigned from the committee, stating that he was "shocked" by the proposed compromises.[31] The Church–State Committee was out of step with the ACLU membership; the board of directors quickly rejected its proposal and embraced an absolutist position. In 1962 the ACLU formulated its strongest statement yet, opposing in-school prayers, Bible reading, and the observance of Christmas, Hanukkah, or Easter as religious holidays. Although teaching about religion did not violate the separationist principle, teachers should be careful not "to *foster* a religious view in the classroom."[32]

In 1961 the ACLU won a case abolishing a Maryland requirement that all public officials swear an oath that they believe in God, with the Court holding that the government cannot "aid all religions as against nonbelievers."[33] Meanwhile, two other explosive cases were on their way to the Court: an NYCLU challenge to compulsory prayer and a Philadelphia challenge to in-school Bible reading. Both reflected the shifting balance of power within the ACLU: By the late 1950s the affiliates were not only initiating more cases but, on this and many other issues, also took more absolutist positions than did the national office. Between 1951 and 1957 the ACLU's national office handled all four of the major church–state cases reaching the Supreme Court in which there was any ACLU involvement; between 1958 and 1964, the affiliates initiated six of the seven cases with ACLU involvement; and between 1965 and 1971, the affiliates initiated eighteen out of nineteen.[34]

The Prayer and Bible Cases

The official New York Regents prayer read, "Almighty God, we acknowledge our dependence upon Thee, and we beg thy blessings upon us, our parents, our teachers, and our country." It had been composed in 1958 as a consequence of the ACLU's protests of the use of the Lord's Prayer in the schools. Officials hoped that this "nondenominational" prayer would satisfy both sides and that local school districts could use it at their discretion.[35] Then the NYCLU decided to challenge the law, much to the dismay of the ACLU's national office, which feared that the Supreme Court would uphold a nondenominational prayer and so preferred the seemingly stronger Philadelphia ACLU challenge to in-school Bible reading.[36]

The 1962 *Engel v. Vitale* decision declaring the New York prayer to be unconstitutional was a bombshell. The Court found the nondenominational prayer a religious activity "wholly inconsistent" with the First Amendment. Justice Hugo Black said, "It is no part of the business of goverment to compose official prayers." Anticipating adverse public reaction, he added that the decision did not imply hostility to religion and that it specifically exempted from the decision references to God in government ceremonies. The eight-to-one vote surprised even many Court watchers, by the extent to which the Court had moved toward a stricter interpretation of the separation of church and state.[37]

The Court dropped another bombshell a year later when it ruled that in-school Bible reading was unconstitutional. Two cases reached the Court: a Philadelphia ACLU challenge to the Pennsylvania Bible-reading law (*School District v. Schempp*) and a Maryland case brought by Madalyn Murray O'Hair, successor to Joseph Lewis as the country's most famous atheist. In an eight-to-one decision, the Court reaffirmed its view that government should neither promote nor inhibit religious activity. For the majority, Justice Tom Clark wrote, "In the relationship between man and religion, the State is firmly committed to a position of neutrality."[38] With these two decisions, the Court completed most of the process of disestablishing Protestantism as the nation's unofficial religion. The reaction was predictably ferocious.

Storm over the Court

Anger over *Engel* was both bitter and national in scope. Cardinal Francis Spellman was "shocked and frightened." North Carolina Senator Sam Ervin remarked that the Court had "made God unconstitutional." An Alabama congressman linked *Engel* to the earlier *Brown* decision, saying that the Court "put the Negroes in the schools and now they've driven God out." Conservatives were more convinced than ever that the Court was hell-bent on imposing integration, Communism, atheism, and pornography on the country.[39] Seventy-five members of Congress introduced 147 separate bills to allow prayer in school by statute or constitutional amendment. They reported being "flooded" with mail from angry constituents. Unlike other Court decisions on church and state, the prayer and Bible-reading decisions stimulated the Protestant fundamentalist community, particularly in the South. A Florida congressman even proposed buying a Bible "for the personal use of each [Supreme Court] justice."[40] The lead bill in Congress became New York Republican Frank J. Becker's amendment reading, "Nothing in this Constitution shall be deemed to prohibit the offering, reading from or listening to prayers or Biblical Scriptures, if participation therein is on a voluntary basis, in any governmental or public school, institution, or place." A disclaimer added, "Nothing in this Article shall constitute an establishment of religion."[41] Republican presidential candidate Barry Goldwater endorsed the amendment in 1964, and GOP Senate leader Everett Dirksen made it a personal issue in 1966.[42]

Alarmed by the prospect of a constitutional amendment, the ACLU and other separationist groups organized in 1964 an aggressive public education and lobbying campaign. The key strategy was mobilizing prominent clergy to reassure undecided members of Congress that voting against an amendment was not antireligious. The strategy worked. Hearings before the House Judiciary Committee became a platform for the separationists. The National Council of Churches and all of the major Jewish groups argued against the Becker amendment. Catholic opinion, meanwhile, was divided. Father Drinan called for a "cooperative separatism" on church–state issues. The church backed away from the prayer amendment but continued to press for financial aid to parochial schools.[43] Legal scholars, meanwhile, raised doubts about the wisdom of overturning a Supreme Court decision by means of a constitutional amendment.

The prayer amendment never passed, falling short of the needed two-thirds majority in the first Senate floor vote in 1966 by a vote of forty-nine to thirty-seven. A House bill failed by a similar margin, and the movement gradually lost steam, its failure revealing important changes in public attitudes toward church and state. Elite opinion makers were increasingly reconciled to the separationist principle. Although many might prefer some kind of prayer in the schools, they could see the logic behind the Court's decision. Southern resistance to school integration had discredited attacks on the Supreme Court in the eyes of many northerners. The majority of active Protestants and

Catholics, meanwhile, did not see religion in the schools as a fighting issue. But the outcome only accelerated the drift of people who sought a more vibrant and personal form of religious expression into the fundamentalist sects. In fact, by the 1970s they emerged as key members of a broad-based conservative and anti–civil libertarian movement.

Law and Social Change

The school prayer and Bible-reading decisions stimulated social scientists' interest in civil liberties issues and related questions about American government. What effect do Supreme Court decisions have? How do they affect public attitudes and behavior? What is the role of law in general, and the Bill of Rights in particular, in American society?[44]

In a study of the school prayer decision, political scientist William K. Muir asked, "Can legislation promote racial or religious tolerance or a democratic spirit? Can law affect the hearts of men: their feelings about themselves, their reactions toward others, their ideas about the world in which they live?" While examining the impact of *Schempp* in a midwestern community, Muir found good news for civil libertarians: Local officials generally complied with the Court's decision. Several adopted a separationist view, and only one moved in the opposite direction. Several factors accounted for this compliance. The decision was the law, after all, and school officials felt constrained to obey it, regardless of their personal feelings. Moreover, as additional school-related issues came under court scrutiny, local school officials relied more heavily on the school board attorney, who inevitably advised compliance. In short, civil liberties principles penetrated the fabric of daily life across the country.[45]

The Court's decisions also encouraged more activity by the ACLU and its allies. The steady growth of ACLU affiliates meant that schools in rural areas might get a call—and a threatened suit—over in-school religious practices. In this way, the ACLU carried the fight into areas long untouched by civil liberties principles. In a subtle but important shift, the ACLU's role increasingly became that of a watchdog fighting for implementation of civil liberties principles that were now a matter of law.

Compliance was far from universal, of course. A study of another midwestern state found absolutely no compliance with either the prayer or the Bible-reading decision. Because the local school officials did not like the decisions, they simply ignored them. The ACLU affiliate in this state (apparently Indiana) was extremely weak and so was absorbed by the problem of merely surviving. The state had a very small Jewish population, and neither the Anti-Defamation League nor the National Council of Christians and Jews was able to force compliance.[46] A third study, however, found local compliance with the Court's decisions in a rural Illinois community where the critical factor was a school superintendent who, though a very religious person himself, disliked in-school religious exercises and welcomed the Court's mandate.

Other community leaders followed his initiative and accepted the elimination of prayer and Bible reading.[47]

There were other ramifications of the Supreme Court's activism. By disestablishing Protestantism, the Court fostered a realignment of religious politics in America. The mainstream denominations largely accepted the idea of government neutrality on religion, while fundamentalist denominations grew in strength and became a potent political force. In the mid-1970s, school prayer again emerged as a powerful political issue. The ACLU thus had to defend its earlier victories, discovering the wisdom of Roger Baldwin's old saying that "no victory ever stays won."

Expanding Boundaries of Freedom of Expression

"The freedom to read . . . is under attack," charged the American Book Publishers Council.[48] The publishers' cry of alarm in 1953 represented the view from the trenches. But in fact, censorship was in full-scale retreat. What alarmed the publishers was a rearguard action against the swelling public demand for freer expression in books, movies, and the theater. Between the end of World War II and the mid-1960s, the entire apparatus of censorship collapsed.

No one in the ACLU could foresee how successful its anticensorship crusade would be. When it began an all-out campaign against censorship in 1945, the organization faced a formidable array of repressive measures.[49] For example, the U.S. Postal Service and the U.S. Customs Service prevented Americans from reading innumerable literary classics. Indeed, Customs inadvertently let ACLU board member Daniel Bell see its list of banned books in 1958 when he returned from Europe with a copy of Jean Genêt's underground classic, *Our Lady of the Flowers.* In 1953 Ernest Besig, director of the Northern California ACLU, lost a suit challenging the Customs ban on Henry Miller's *Tropic of Cancer* and *Tropic of Capricorn.*[50]

State and local officials were equally set on suppressing good books. In 1945 the Massachusetts Supreme Court sustained an obscenity conviction against Lillian Smith's antisegregationist *Strange Fruit.* New York Mayor Fiorello La Guardia shut down the play *Trio* because of its lesbian theme. In 1953 the Milwaukee district attorney banned Norman Mailer's *The Naked and the Dead* and James Jones's *From Here to Eternity.* In 1955 the Shreveport, Louisiana, school board removed all the back issues of *Time, Life,* and *Look* from its libraries because of their "biased and distorted views on the institution of segregation." The ACLU supported the New York City School Board against Jewish pressure to ban *Oliver Twist.* The Northern California ACLU represented Lawrence Ferlinghetti, poet and owner of the City Lights Book Store, prosecuted in 1957 for selling Allen Ginsberg's poem *Howl.*[51] The Hollywood Production Code continued to quash any treatment of sex, drugs, and crime and the irreverent treatment of religion. The power of the southern market restricted films presenting blacks in a dignified manner.

The ACLU revived the old National Council on Freedom from Censorship for its national campaign. Twenty-six organizations signed up in 1948, including CBS, *Reader's Digest, Mademoiselle,* the Children's Book Council, the Screen Publicists Guild, and the Radio Directors Guild.[52] The participation of established media added clout to the ACLU's effort and indicated how much public attitudes had changed in just ten years. Popular and commercial pressures were at that point ahead of the law on the question of the freedom to read. The spread of education created a significant market for books and movies dealing with mature themes, and the sexual revolution added a demand for the open treatment of sexuality.

The ACLU and the Scope of the First Amendment

Contrary to its own subsequent mythology, at this point the ACLU did not take an "absolutist" position on freedom of expression. It still placed libel and obscenity outside the scope of First Amendment protection. And most ACLU leaders accepted Alexander Meikeljohn's distinction between political speech, which enjoyed full protection, and other forms of expression, which were entitled to less protection.[53] A 1948 restatement of ACLU policy asserted that the First Amendment protected "with equal force . . . all forms of verbal and graphic expression, irrespective of subject matter." Yet it added that "charges of alleged indecency, obscenity, or immorality [must] be substantiated by objective proof that the publication . . . clearly violated existing law." This implicitly accepted the validity of such vague terms as *indecency* and *immorality.* Prosecutors should provide an "exact definition" of the harm done, in order to suppress a publication—implying that it was possible to arrive at a workable definition of obscenity. The ACLU's primary goal had not changed since the late 1920s: Censorship powers should be transferred from government bureaucrats to the courts for a judicial hearing—a principal upheld in the *Esquire* case, in which a lower federal court restricted the postmaster general's power to arbitrarily ban magazines.[54]

Morris Ernst, always in the vanguard of ACLU thinking on obscenity, complained that the "danger point" "always seems to the [ACLU] to be much nearer at hand through the use of obscene words than through the use of words which might disturb the peace, riot, etc." He reminded staff counsel Clifford Forster that "the Union has always been sqeamish with respect to matters sexual."[55] He was right. The ACLU took a much stronger position in defense of offensive or even potentially disruptive forms of expression when they involved political speech.

Offensive Political Speech

In the post–World War II years, the ACLU eagerly joined all of the important Supreme Court cases dealing with offensive political speech. Two of the first involved challenges to restrictions on loudspeakers. In *Saia v. New York*

(1948), one of the last of the long series of Jehovah's Witnesses cases, the Court found unconstitutional a Lockport, New York, ordinance limiting the use of sound amplification devices. A year later, however, the Court upheld a Trenton, New Jersey, ordinance prohibiting from public streets those vehicles with loudspeakers that emitted "loud and raucous noises" (*Kovacs v. Cooper*), its decision reflecting concern for the sensibilities of unwilling listeners.[56]

Three years later, the "forced listening" question briefly raised the issue of a right to privacy, when the Court narrowly upheld the right of the Washington, D.C., transit system to broadcast an FM radio station on its buses. It rejected the argument, supported by the ACLU, that this invaded the privacy of the bus riders. In dissent, Justice Douglas argued that "the right to be let alone" was "the beginning of all freedom." The ACLU found this "relatively unexplored legal area of the 'right to privacy'" somewhat "puzzling," but its *amicus* brief condemned forced listening as "viciously repugnant to the spiritual and intellectual assumptions of American life" and akin to "totalitarianism."[57] Neither the Court nor the ACLU pursued the privacy issue further at this time.

The ACLU vigorously defended offensive political speech in a case involving Arthur Terminello, a suspended Catholic priest and follower of Gerald L. K. Smith, the most notorious right-wing anti-Semite of the day. A 1946 Chicago speech denouncing "Communistic Zionistic Jews" provoked a wild confrontation, as a crowd of protesters threw rocks through the windows and tried to break into the auditorium. Convicted of disturbing the peace, Terminello was supported in his appeal by the Illinois ACLU. The normally libertarian American Jewish Congress supported the prosecution, while the Communist party organized a national campaign to ban Terminello's patron, Gerald L. K. Smith, from speaking.[58] In an important First Amendment decision, the Supreme Court overturned Terminello's conviction. Justice Douglas wrote that the "function of free speech under our system of government is to invite dispute. It may indeed best serve its high purpose when it invites a condition of unrest, creates dissatisfaction with conditions as they are, or even stirs people to anger."[59]

Two years later, in an NYCLU case argued by Osmond Fraenkel, the Court overturned the conviction of the anti-Catholic and anti-Semitic Carl Jacob Kunz, convicted for speaking without a police permit. The Court ruled that "New York cannot vest restraining control over the right to speak on religious subjects in an administrative official where there are no appropriate standards to guide his action." The same day, however, the Court upheld the conviction of Irving Feiner, arrested to prevent a breach of the peace. Also represented by NYCLU, Feiner had denounced President Truman as a "bum," called the American Legion "a Nazi Gestapo," and urged black Americans to "rise up in arms."[60]

The Court's position on political speech was uncertain and ambiguous in the early 1950s. In most cases it extended First Amendment protection to offensive and even deliberately provocative speech. At the same time, however, it upheld the conviction of the Communist party leaders in *Dennis,* casting a chill over certain forms of political activity.

Libel

The ACLU parted company with many of its allies over the Illinois "group libel" law. Joseph Beauharnais had organized the White Circle League to fight racial integration in Chicago and was arrested for distributing a pamphlet warning of "the white race . . . becoming mongrelized by the Negro." The 1917 law prohibited any speech or publication that "portrays depravity, criminality, unchastity, or lack of virtue of a class of citizens of any race, color, creed or religion" or exposes members of any racial or religious group to "contempt, derision, or obloquy or which is productive of breach of the peace or riots." The ACLU filed a brief for Beauharnais, but the American Jewish Congress supported the law. The Supreme Court upheld the Illinois law, with Justice Felix Frankfurter arguing that libelous attacks on groups were no different from the criminal libel of individuals. Although Frankfurter exempted attacks on strictly political groups, the decision had ominous implications for all political speech.[61] The ACLU confronted the issue of group libel in Illinois again: The state repealed the little-used law in 1962, but in 1977 the village of Skokie tried to ban a Nazi demonstration under a similar rationale. The Skokie affair became one of the most famous cases in ACLU history.[62]

The ACLU began to rethink its position on the libel of individuals. In 1948 Morris Ernst reminded his colleagues that the ACLU "is in favor of limiting free speech by libel laws" and suggested that the Hollywood Ten reply with libel suits to charges that they were Communists.[63] A special ACLU committee reviewed the entire subject, recommending that all comments about public officials should enjoy First Amendment protection, but not those about private individuals. Calling someone "antilabor," "prolabor," or "anti-Semitic" might be injurious but not libelous. Accusing someone of being a Communist, however, was a different matter. Because "Communists are in fact exposed to legal disabilities," such an accusation was far more serious than calling someone a "Nazi" or a "Fascist." Thus, falsely accused persons should be able to sue for libel. After a long debate, the ACLU board tabled the committee report. It also decided not to sue the American Legion for calling board member Rev. G. Bromley Oxnam a Communist sympathizer.[64] This marked the first step in a gradual evolution of ACLU policy toward opposition to virtually all libel actions as restrictions on free speech, except in cases of reckless disregard for the truth.[65]

Morris Ernst reflected the crosscurrents of ACLU thinking on the First Amendment in these years. He was opposed to all restrictions on artistic expression but supported measures to restrict Communist political activity. He continued to push his idea for a federal disclosure law, and the ACLU continued to reject it on grounds that it would inhibit the freedom of unpopular groups. On the issue of the mass media Ernst argued that increased monopoly control threatened freedom of expression. The ACLU initially accepted his argument and filed *amicus* briefs in two important cases, supporting the Federal Communications Commission's (FCC) antimonopoly regulations in a suit against NBC and joining the Justice Department's successful antitrust action against the motion picture industry. By the early 1950s, however, the ACLU concluded that communications monopolies were not a civil liberties issue and so dropped it from its agenda.[66]

Movies: The Collapse of the Code

Cardinal Spellman denounced the film from the pulpit as "sacrilegious and blasphemous." The 1950 confrontation over the otherwise unremarkable film, *The Miracle,* marked the beginning of the end of film censorship. Two years later in *The Miracle* case, the Supreme Court held that movies were a form of expression protected by the First Amendment.

Roberto Rossellini's film involved the story of a peasant woman who is seduced by a man she believes is St. Joseph and then bears a child she thinks is Jesus. The New York State censors granted it a license, and it opened in December 1950. The New York City commissioner of licenses immediately threatened to revoke the Paris Theater's license because the movie was "officially and personally blasphemous." The theater withdrew the film, but distributor Joseph Burstyn, assisted by the ACLU, won an injunction allowing it to be shown. Cardinal Spellman then condemned the film from the pulpit and ordered all Catholics to boycott it. Demonstrators picketed the theater with signs reading "This is a Communist Picture!" and "Buy American." Under heavy political pressure, the New York Board of Regents revoked *The Miracle*'s license and declared it to be "sacrilegious." Burstyn took his case to the Supreme Court and won a stunning unanimous verdict that reversed the thirty-seven-year-old *Mutual* decision.[67]

The fate of the ACLU *amicus* brief in *Burstyn* revealed the contentious state of religious politics in New York. The state attorney general first granted and then withdrew permission to file a brief. After protracted negotiations he permitted the ACLU to file, along with the Committee of Catholics for Cultural Action supporting the ACLU, and another Catholic *amicus* on the other side.[68]

Burstyn spelled doom for the prior restraints imposed by existing state and local licensing systems, and the courts steadily clipped the wings of the censors in a series of ACLU-supported cases. The Supreme Court ruled that Ohio could not deny the classic film *M* a license because it was allegedly "harmful"; nor could the New York ban *La Ronde* on the grounds that it was "immoral." In the nine years after the *Miracle* decision the Chicago Board of Censors had lost all seven of its court cases. In one, it had denied a license to show *Anatomy of a Murder* simply because the words *rape* and *contraceptive* were used.[69]

Commercial pressures were at least as important as litigation in the demise of censorship. A small but significant "art theater" circuit catered to sophisticated tastes. In fact, the term *foreign film* became a synonym for the freer treatment of sexual themes and the depiction of female nudity. Hollywood producers eventually sensed an opportunity to challenge the Production Code. Otto Preminger released *The Moon Is Blue* without a seal of approval in 1953, declaring the code to be "antiquated." And two years later he released *The Man with the Golden Arm,* denied a seal because of its explicit treatment of drug addiction. The days of the Production Code were clearly numbered.[70]

Private Pressure Groups: The ACLU and the Catholics

The *Miracle* episode was only one of many confrontations between the ACLU and the Catholic church in the fifties. In 1959, Boston's Cardinal Richard Cushing called the ACLU a "Communist Front."[71] The aggressive efforts of the National Organization for Decent Literature (NODL), the Legion of Decency (LOD), and the new Citizens for Decent Literature (CDL), organized in 1958, forced the ACLU to restate its position on the line between right to protest and censorship. An ACLU statement in 1958 held that the NODL's tactics violated "the principle of freedom" and restricted "what the American people may read." Some of the most eminent literary and political figures signed the ACLU statement: publishers Alfred A. Knopf and N. Lincoln Schuster (of Simon & Schuster); critics Lionel Trilling and Van Wyck Brooks; historians Allan Nevins and Richard Hofstadter; theologian Reinhold Niebuhr; and Eleanor Roosevelt. The ACLU argued that Catholics had a First Amendment right to protest, boycott, and "inform the general public of its opinion that certain writings are immoral." Using its political pressure to force local police and prosecutors into suppressing books, however, constituted censorship.[72] In the face of adverse public reaction, liberal Catholics such as theologian John Courtney Murray and law school dean Robert Drinan advised the Church to moderate its position on social issues.[73]

The Turning Point

In the mid-1950s there was a noticeable shift in public opinion regarding censorship as well as church–state issues. It was less a matter of law than a popular upsurge of free expression itself.

The new mood was dramatized by the 1957 prosecution of Allen Ginsburg's poem *Howl.* Now an American classic, *Howl* marked the advent of a new literary, cultural, and political generation in American life. The life-style of the apolitical "Beat generation" was in many respects more disturbing to middle-class Americans than was left-wing radicalism. San Francisco authorities prosecuted, on obscenity charges, Ginsberg's publisher, Lawrence Ferlinghetti, himself a prominent Beat poet. Northern California ACLU lawyers Lawrence Speiser and Al Bendich joined private attorney Jake Ehrlich in a celebrated trial that resulted in an acquittal. Citing the "clear and present danger" standard raised by the ACLU, the judge ruled that *Howl* posed no threat.[74]

Speiser moved to Washington to head the ACLU's legislative office and immediately found himself again defending beatniks, when the police revoked the license of the *Coffee 'n Confusion* cafe because its customers disturbed the "peace and quiet" of the neighborhood. An ACLU *amicus* conceded that "it is unusual, if not unprecedented, for civil liberties issues to be involved in a proceeding for the revocation of a restaurant license," but the police action was clearly an attempt to suppress a particular life-style. The captain of the Second Precinct had declared the Beats "unwelcome" in his area. The ACLU brief claimed that its "central purpose [was] to plead for tolerance of the unorthodox."[75] The case was a harbinger of the 1960s when the ACLU repeatedly defended unconventional life-styles, such as wearing long hair, on grounds of the right to personal freedom of expression.

Joining the Beats in challenging conventional life-styles was the commercially potent force of rock 'n roll, whose driving beat and sexual energy offended adult listening tastes and produced the inevitable attempts at censorship. When the American Legion hall in El Monte, California, refused to permit a rock 'n roll concert, the Southern California ACLU intervened. Staff counsel A. L. Wirin called himself "strictly a Beethoven man" but denounced the ban as "a monstrous denial of freedom of expression." In the end there were relatively few rock 'n roll cases.[76] The music won over the public by the sheer force of its commercial success and in the process extended the range of what was considered acceptable by the mass media. Hollywood producers, meanwhile, continued to stretch the limits of the Production Code, displaying more flesh, using more explicit language, and exploring previously forbidden themes. In 1956 the ACLU called on the film industry to abolish the Production Code and to let individuals decide what they wanted to produce and see.[77]

The Question of Obscenity

The growing openness of sexually explicit material finally forced a Supreme Court test of the constitutionality of obscenity, a question the Court had avoided until then. The ACLU had also tiptoed around the issue, but its hand was forced by the Court's decision to hear the *Roth* and *Alberts* cases in late 1956. Amid great uncertainty, the Censorship Committee hurriedly met to consider the ACLU's position on the two cases. Although most committee members opposed obscenity prosecutions, they were still reluctant to take an absolutist position. Harriet Pilpel, Morris Ernst's protégé and colleague, argued that children should be protected from materials depicting sexual perversity. Writer Dan Lacy warned that the real problem was private vigilante action. If the ACLU successfully eliminated government censorship through litigation, "we may encourage such vigilante action."[78] Lacy's position was similar to that of other ACLU moderates who, on a variety of issues, worried that an extreme position would provoke adverse reactions. Accommodationists, for example, took such a position on the separation of church and state; civil rights moderates were hesitant about directly challenging southern segregation; and cold war liberals were reluctant to oppose all restraints on Communists. On all of these issues, the more aggressive ACLU absolutists triumphed over the cautious moderates between the mid-1950s and the early 1960s.

The ACLU finally concluded that "the constitutional guarantees of free speech and press apply to all expression and there is no special category of obscenity or pornography to which different constitutional tests apply." The new policy was not quite as absolutist as it appeared: It added that any restriction on expression had to meet a test of definiteness and that "it must be established beyond a reasonable doubt that the material presents a clear and present danger of normally inducing behavior which validly has been made criminal by statute." The test was impossible for any prosecutor to meet, but the ACLU did not state its opposition to censorship in absolutist terms. In the *Roth* case, the ACLU *amicus* contended that there was no evidence that the publications in question "will probably and immediately cause anti-social conduct."

Roth featured the country's most notorious "literary outlaw." Over a long publishing career, Samuel Roth had been jailed many times and held the dubious distinction of publishing the first pirated American edition of James Joyce's *Ulysses*. His Supreme Court case involved a federal prosecution for sending through the mails, among other things, his *Good Times* magazine which contained photographs of nudes with the intimate body parts discreetly airbrushed out.[79] The ACLU was moderately optimistic about Roth's Supreme Court appeal. In early 1957 the Court unanimously struck down a Michigan law forbidding the sale to the general public of material "containing obscene language [tending] to incite minors to violence or depraved acts." Reducing all literature to a level safe for children was, in Justice Frankfurter's famous comment, "to burn the house to roast the pig."[80]

In what seemed to be a devastating defeat for freedom of expression, the Court upheld Roth's conviction. "Obscenity," Justice William Brennan wrote, "is not within the area of constitutionally protected speech or press." In the first of many attempts to define obscenity, Brennan held that the test was "whether to the average person, applying contemporary community standards, the dominant theme of the material taken as a whole appeals to prurient interest." The ACLU was particularly distressed at the Court's rejection of both the clear and present danger test and the argument that prevailing obscenity laws were too vague. It accordingly warned that the anticensorship fight faced "a strenuous legal re-thinking."[81]

There was more to *Roth* than first met the eye, however. Brennan's definition was a swamp of ambiguity. Who was this "average person"? What were "community standards"? How could they be determined? What constituted "prurient interest"? Brennan's conclusion that sex and obscenity are not synonymous suggested that candid discussions of sexuality were constitutionally protected. Even more important he wrote that "ideas having even the slightest redeeming social importance—unorthodox ideas, controversial ideas, even ideas hateful to the prevailing climate of opinion—have the full protection" of the First Amendment. The only exception was expression "utterly without redeeming social importance." Indeed, attorney Charles Rembar saw in this passage a loophole that might doom all obscenity prosecutions.[82]

The Aftermath of Roth: *The End of Obscenity?*

Roth settled nothing but instead opened a decade of obscenity litigation. In the context of rapidly changing public attitudes and case law, the ACLU again reexamined its position on obscenity. After three years of debate, in 1962 it embraced an absolutist stand, holding that the First Amendment protects "all expression" and that "limitations of expression on the grounds of obscenity are unconstitutional."[83]

The law of obscenity changed so rapidly after 1957 that by the time Samuel Roth was finishing his prison term, he would not have been convicted for distributing the publications that sent him to prison. The two most important post-*Roth* cases centered on D. H. Lawrence's long-suppressed novel *Lady Chatterley's Lover.* New York banned a film version, but the Court held that the film expressed an idea—"that adultery under circumstances may be proper behavior." Although the ruling dealt a serious blow to film censorship, only Justices Black and Douglas agreed with the ACLU's argument that all prior restraints on movies were unconstitutional.[84] That same year, 1959, Grove Press decided to publish an unexpurgated edition of *Lady Chatterley.* Postmaster General Arthur Summerfield pronounced it an "obscene and filthy book" and prosecuted under the old Comstock Act. The federal district court ruled the book not obscene, and after the court of appeals upheld that decision, the Postal Service gave up. Meanwhile, *Lady Chatterley* sold over six million copies. By 1960 the entire edifice of official censorship was crumbling.[85]

In 1964 the Supreme Court overturned a conviction involving the Louis Malle film *The Lovers,* in a case brought by the Ohio ACLU. The movie contained a love scene that would be considered laughingly innocent only a few years later. The Court in the *Jacobellis* decision was hopelessly divided in its effort to define obscenity. Brennan argued for a national standard, which would doom state and local censorship. Justice Potter Stewart offered his famous but evasive definition of obscenity: "I know it when I see it."[86] The Court's dilemma lent support to the ACLU argument, which Morris Ernst had formulated in the late 1920s, that no workable definition was possible and, as a consequence, that all prosecutions were inevitably arbitrary.

A year later, in a case joined by the Maryland ACLU, the Court severely restricted the power of the state licensing boards. Although it rejected the ACLU argument that all such arrangements were fundamentally unconstitutional, *Freedman v. Maryland* spurred a final wave of suits against the remaining forms of precensorship. Hollywood finally gave up the ghost and scrapped its production code. It was the end of an era in American movies.[87]

Although the Supreme Court still could not reach a consensus on the meaning of obscenity, it effectively ended successful prosecutions between 1967 and 1971, reversing thirty-one obscenity convictions. Attorney Charles Rembar called it the "end of obscenity" and the end of an era in censorship.[88] The new freedom of expression resulted in a flood of sexually explicit books and movies in the early 1970s, a development that generated a new anti-pornography movement in the following decade.

"Uninhibited, Robust, and Wide-Open": The Central Meaning of the First Amendment

The Warren Court's defense of free speech reached its apex in *New York Times v. Sullivan*. Like so many civil liberties advances, this 1964 decision was a product of the civil rights movement. It originated in 1960 in civil rights protests in Birmingham, Alabama. A full-page ad in the *Times* charged local officials with "an unprecedented wave of terror" against civil rights activists. The Birmingham police and fire commissioner sued for libel and won a $500,000 judgment against the *Times*. But on appeal, the Supreme Court overturned the judgment, ruling that public officials could recover damages only when they could prove "actual malice." The most important aspect of the decision was Brennan's ringing affirmation of the role of the First Amendment: "We consider this case against the background of a profound national commitment to the principle that debate on public issues should be uninhibited, robust, and wide-open." Further, "the constitutional protection does not turn upon the truth, popularity, or social utility of the ideas and beliefs which are offered."[89] The opinion was a vindication of the line of thinking that began with Oliver Wendell Holmes's *Abrams* dissent and the principle that had guided the ACLU throughout its history.

The ACLU at Its Apex

The last day of the Supreme Court's 1963–1964 term marked the apex of the ACLU's influence over American law and public policy. As ACLU members met in Boulder, Colorado, for its Biennial Conference, the Court handed them victories in seven of eight cases, including landmark decisions in the areas of freedom of expression (*Jacobellis*, a film censorship case), equal protection (*Reynolds*, the "one man–one vote" reapportionment case), and due process (*Escobedo*, guaranteeing a criminal suspect in custody the right to consult an attorney). These were only the most noteworthy of a broad range of cases in which the ACLU had helped the Court rewrite American constitutional law. The Biennial delegates, preoccupied with the urgent struggles of the moment—particularly the civil rights crisis in the South—paused only briefly to celebrate their victories before the Court. Indeed, many were too young to have a strong sense of how far American freedoms had grown in the past ten years or a sense of the ACLU's own role in that achievement.[90]

Eleven

Revolution in Equality and Due Process

The Civil Rights Revolution and Its Consequences

The "separate but equal doctrine" should be overruled. Four years before the historic *Brown v. Board of Education* decision, and before even the NAACP made this argument before the Court, the ACLU urged the Supreme Court to overturn the 1896 *Plessy* decision. The case involved black federal employee Elmer Henderson, who took a train trip from Washington, D.C., to Birmingham, Alabama, to investigate race discrimination in the war industries. He was unable to eat dinner because an overflow of white passengers had filled the two tables set aside for blacks. Henderson thereupon filed a complaint with the Interstate Commerce Commission, which the ACLU joined.[1]

The tempo of the civil rights movement quickened each year after World War II, with the creation of President Harry S. Truman's Civil Rights Committee in 1947 being a pivotal event. The following year, Truman desegregated the armed services. The Supreme Court's unanimous decision in 1954 declaring segregated public schools to be unconstitutional was, arguably, the most important Court decision of the entire postwar era. Two years later, the Montgomery, Alabama, bus boycott introduced a new militant style of protest and launched the career of Martin Luther King, Jr. Passage of the 1957 Civil Rights Act, although the law was admittedly weak, signaled the beginning of the end of the southern domination of Congress.[2]

The civil rights movement spilled over into innumerable other areas and had a profound effect on American society. It ended institutionalized segregation and brought black Americans into the center of national politics. The Supreme Court forged new constitutional doctrine on equal protection, the First Amendment, and due process. A series of cases involving the NAACP produced a new concept of freedom of association, and the fate of black suspects in the hands of the police spurred a revolution in due process of law

237

that reshaped the entire criminal justice system. And in 1960, the sit-ins defined a new style of political activism.

The postwar years were a time of both optimism and pessimism for civil rights activists. The steady progress of Supreme Court breakthroughs pointed toward a new era of racial equality, but Congress dragged its feet. Worse, antiblack vigilante violence erupted in both the North and the South. In 1946 and 1947 seven blacks were lynched in four separate incidents in the South. The ACLU offered a $500 reward for information leading to a conviction in the South Carolina lynching. It attracted worldwide publicity when twenty-eight admitted members of the lynch mob were acquitted of the crime. But the South had no monopoly on violence: The Southern California ACLU offered a $500 reward following a wave of cross burnings in Los Angeles, and the Northern California affiliate offered a similar reward for the conviction of the arsonists who burned down the home of a black resident in the Bay area. And Chicago in the early 1950s was the scene of a near civil war as white residents fought integration with vigilante violence on a neighborhood-by-neighborhood basis.[3]

General Counsel Morris Ernst was an influential member of Truman's Civil Rights Committee—whose call for an end to all forms of discrimination based on "race, color, creed or national origin" helped establish a national consensus on racial equality. The committee recommended a federal antilynching law, abolition of the poll tax, integration of the armed services, and more effective federal civil rights enforcement. Ernst lobbied to eliminate any criticism of the FBI's performance. Roger Baldwin convened the National Emergency Civil Rights Mobilization Committee to lobby for the Truman committee's recommendations.[4]

The ACLU carved out a special niche as a member of the civil rights coalition at both the national and local levels. While the NAACP took primary responsibility for Supreme Court litigation, the ACLU, the American Jewish Congress, and other national organizations joined with *amicus* briefs. The ACLU took the leading role on the issue of police misconduct. On others, it had to remind its allies that even racists had constitutional rights.

In the Supreme Court, the key issue was the separate but equal doctrine. Despite the Court's evident sympathy for racial equality, the NAACP's Thurgood Marshall agonized over whether the time was ripe to challenge it directly, for a premature case producing an adverse decision could set back the civil rights movement for decades. The *Henderson* decision in 1950 was the turning point. Even the Justice Department, the nominal defendant in the case, filed a brief urging the Court to overturn *Plessy*. In three decisions announced on the same day, the Court ended segregation in interstate travel (*Henderson*) and declared segregation by the Oklahoma and Texas law schools to be unconstitutional (*Sweatt* and *McLaurin*). At long last, the time appeared ripe for a challenge to public school segregation in the South. Marshall thus convened a meeting of the top civil rights and civil liberties lawyers and began planning the strategy that led to *Brown v. Board of Education*.[5]

The ACLU filed an *amicus* brief in *Brown,* as it did in all of the leading civil rights cases in these years. As ACLU staff counsel Herbert Monte Levy explained, "The lead is usually taken by the NAACP [and we] cooperate with them either in planning of strategy and/or filing of *amicus* briefs."[6] A collaborative atmosphere prevailed, and the legal strategy often emerged from meetings with lawyers from the NAACP, the ACLU, the American Jewish Congress, the Anti-Defamation League, and other groups. The names on a particular brief did not necessarily reflect who contributed to it. ACLU and American Jewish Congress lawyers, for example, wrote major sections of the NAACP brief in the crucial *NAACP v. Alabama* (1958) case, although without formal credit. Many court watchers felt that the *amicus* briefs had a significant impact on the Court—at times by their mere presence; at other times because of the specific ideas advanced. Some thought that the presence of eighteen separate *amicus* briefs representing over forty organizations played a key role in producing the unanimous 1947 *Shelley v. Kraemer* decision striking down restrictive covenants in the sale of private housing.[7]

The ACLU affiliates were well placed to wage the civil rights struggle at the local level. The Southern California ACLU, with A. L. Wirin as counsel, maintained a docket almost as large as that of the ACLU national office. In 1946–1947 alone the affiliate successfully challenged school segregation of Mexican-Americans in four rural school districts, ended segregation by the Pasadena Housing Authority, challenged segregated schools in the Imperial Valley, and joined with the NAACP in a suit against discrimination by Bullock's department store. Two years later it successfully overturned a California miscegenation law in the state supreme court.[8]

The fight for equal opportunity in housing was primarily a local struggle. After a white-led riot at the Fernwood Housing Project in 1947, the Chicago ACLU offered a $250 reward for information leading to the perpetrators' arrest. In July 1951 Illinois Governor Adlai Stevenson mobilized the National Guard to quell a riot in Cicero that erupted when a black veteran and his family moved into an all-white neighborhood. The Chicago ACLU cosponsored a report on the Cicero riot and protested when, incredibly, a grand jury indicted the apartment owner, his attorney, the rental agent, and the attorney for the Clark family that had rented the apartment. In 1956 one hundred police provided daily protection to twenty-seven black families in the Trumbull Park housing project. Most of this anti-integrationist violence went unreported, as civic leaders decided that publicity would inflame the vigilantes and damage Chicago's reputation.[9] The NYCLU–American Jewish Congress suit against the segregated Stuyvesant Town housing project failed, but the civil rights coalition won passage of a city ordinance barring discrimination in all future publicly supported housing.[10]

The Rights of Racists: Defending a Principle

The ACLU again clashed with its allies over the rights of racists. When the NAACP demanded removal of the "Amos 'n' Andy" radio program in 1947, the ACLU warned it of the dangers in coercive boycotts; the South, for example, had vetoed the dignified treatment of blacks in films. In 1956 segregation-ist agitator John Kasper was convicted of violating an injunction against his activities. The ACLU protested the injunction, arguing that it was a violation of free speech "to the extent that it enjoins speech in opposition to or advo-cating ignoring the order, or peaceful picketing for these purposes."[11]

The 1960 Civil Rights Act posed a difficult due process issue. The law did not allow southern election officials accused of discrimination to confront their accusors in hearings before the U.S. Civil Rights Commission. Yet blacks who testified in regard to voter discrimination faced retaliatory Ku Klux Klan (KKK) violence. The ACLU compromised a bit on the issue, ap-proving anonymous complaints in initial administrative hearings but insisting on confrontation with accusers in subsequent judicial proceedings. Indeed, for fifteen years the ACLU had been arguing for the right of people to con-front their accusers in investigations by the House Un-American Activities Committee (HUAC).[12]

Attack on the NAACP and a New Freedom of Association

Few cases better confirmed the wisdom of the ACLU's principle of the non-partisan defense of civil liberties than did those involving the NAACP. After the 1954 school desegregation decision, southern states enacted a series of laws designed to harass the civil rights organization.[13] Alabama began with a law requiring the state chapter to disclose its members' names and addresses, thereby exposing them to retaliation by employers or KKK violence. The NAACP refused to comply, and Alabama sued to enjoin it from operating in the state. In 1958 the Supreme Court unanimously upheld the NAACP, hold-ing that the "effective advocacy of both public and private points of view, par-ticulary controversial ones, is undeniably enhanced by group association." In the context of the South, "compelled disclosure of affiliation with groups engaged in advocacy" was a restraint on freedom of association.[14]

NAACP v. Alabama accorded to the NAACP the protections that the Court had consistently denied the Communist party, reflecting a double stan-dard for political groups. As ACLU legal director Mel Wulf put it, "There were red cases and black cases."[15] The decision also dealt a death blow to Morris Ernst's idea of disclosure. The attempt to force disclosure of the NAACP's membership lists dramatized the fact that the definition of an "unpopular" group depended on the context and that political freedom was best protected by the defense of all groups.[16]

Succeeding NAACP cases extended the freedom of association doctrine. Little Rock, Arkansas, amended an occupational license tax ordinance to re-quire disclosure of sources of "dues and contributions." This amendment had the legitimate goal of preventing businesses from using a nonprofit guise to evade the license tax and did not strike directly at political groups. But the local NAACP challenged the requirement, and in 1960 the Court ruled that even indirect threats to freedom of association were unconstitutional.[17]

Ten months later, in an Arkansas disclosure case, the Court enunciated a new legal principle with even broader ramifications. A state law required all public school teachers to report which organizations they belonged to or had contributed to in the past five years. Here again, the law had a seemingly legitimate purpose—to determine the fitness of public school teachers. The Court struck down the law on the grounds that the state could not pursue its interests in a way that would "broadly stifle fundamental liberties." The First Amendment rights of the individual required the state to use "less drastic means" to determine a candidate's suitability for a job. The concept of the "least restrictive alternative," first spelled out in *Shelton v. Tucker,* later became a crucial principle in the ACLU's subsequent campaigns on behalf of the rights of prisoners and mental hospital patients.[18]

Virginia tried a more subtle device against the NAACP, charging it with "improper solicitation" of legal cases. The Court again upheld the NAACP on the grounds that freedom of speech included "vigorous advocacy, certainly of lawful ends." Litigation was not merely "a technique for resolving private differences." The ability of groups to seek social change was "a form of political expression." And for the politically powerless, "litigation may be the most effective form of political association." *NAACP v. Button* was a resounding endorsement of the role of the NAACP and the ACLU.[19]

Southern legislatures then resorted to HUAC-style investigations to harass the NAACP. The Florida Legislative Investigation Committee ordered the NAACP's Miami chapter to produce its membership list, in an attempt to determine whether it was Communist influenced. The chapter president refused and was cited for contempt. The Supreme Court overturned his conviction in 1963, holding that "it is not alleged Communists who are the witnesses before the Committee . . . it is the NAACP itself which is the subject of the investigation." The Court asserted that there was "no suggestion that the Miami branch of the NAACP or the national organization . . . were, or are, themselves subversive organizations." Compelling "such an organization" to divulge its membership list was "wholly different from compelling the Communist Party to disclose its own membership."[20] Given the many cases involving suspected Communists, the Court's logic was tortured. As Justice John Marshall Harlan wrote in dissent, the decision forced investigators "to prove in advance the very things it is trying to find out." *Gibson* was the clearest indication of the extent to which the Court granted to the NAACP the protections it had refused to extend to the Communists.

The NAACP cases dramatized perhaps better than any other the central role of the First Amendment in preserving the democratic process and facilitating social change. The NAACP could not have survived in the South, and the civil rights movement would have been set back for years, without the new freedom of association protections. Moreover, after 1960, the sit-ins and other forms of increasingly militant protest depended on new definitions of First Amendment rights. Just as the initial reproductive rights issues involved freedom of expression, so the early civil rights movement depended on the First Amendment. As Georgetown University Law School professor Eleanor Holmes Norton later put it, "There was always the First."[21]

Norton carried on the ACLU tradition of defending one's enemy in the name of principle. After graduating from law school, she joined the ACLU as assistant legal director. In one of her very first cases she defended George Wallace's right to hold a meeting in New York's Shea Stadium. Liberal New York City Mayor John Lindsay had banned the meeting under pressure from civil rights groups. The Wallace people had no advance warning but did not blink when Norton walked into Court. In later speeches to the black community, she was introduced amid great cheers as "the sister George Wallace needed!"[22]

Dismantling the Cold War

Despite the advances in First Amendment law in the NAACP cases, the Supreme Court remained uncertain in Communist-related cases. The ACLU stepped up its attack on cold war restraints after its internal upheaval of 1954. The New York Civil Liberties Union accepted Harry Slochower's Fifth Amendment case in 1952 (while the ACLU argued on inconclusively), winning a 1956 Supreme Court decision that Slochower could not be fired for using the Fifth Amendment without a hearing. Although limited in its impact, the decision was a sign that the Court might strike down other cold war measures.[23] The Court also invalidated a Pennsylvania sedition law in 1956 on the grounds that federal law preempted the field.[24] One state sedition case involved Carl Braden who, with his wife Anne, had sold to a black family their Louisville, Kentucky, home in an all-white neighborhood. The house was bombed, the Bradens were indicted, and then Carl and seven others were separately indicted for advocating the violent overthrow of the government. The ACLU entered the case on appeal, providing an attorney and raising funds. The case raised a host of civil liberties issues, including the vagueness of the indictment, the penalty for mere possession of Communist party literature, the advocacy of political change, and the barring of the defense from examining documents used by FBI witnesses. The Kentucky Supreme Court overturned the original conviction, and subsequent indictments were dropped when the judge excluded much of the evidence. The *Braden* case provided another example of use of the Communist bogey to harass civil rights activists.[25]

In 1957 the Supreme Court struck at a broad range of cold war measures. Two ACLU cases involved lawyers denied admission to the bar because of their alleged left-wing associations. The Court unanimously held that Rudolf Schware's past membership in the Communist party did not "justify an inference that he presently has bad moral character." Rafael Konigsberg, represented by the Southern California ACLU, won a rehearing on the question of whether his refusal to answer questions about his political associations was sufficient grounds for denying him admission to the bar. The Court then turned its attention to the FBI's "faceless informers," overturning the perjury conviction of Clinton Jencks on the grounds that he had not been able to examine the FBI reports on which his case had been based.[26]

Next came "Red Monday," a set of decisions on June 17 that outraged conservatives. In *Yates,* the Court drastically limited the Smith Act by overturning the convictions of the "second tier" of the Communist party leadership. The conservative Justice Harlan drew a sharp distinction between advocacy leading to the overthrow of the government and teaching such a course of action as an "abstract doctrine." Although *Yates* did not overturn *Dennis,* it halted further Smith Act prosecutions. Harlan's opinion moved close to the traditional ACLU position that the advocacy of ideas, in the absence of direct incitement, was protected by the First Amendment.[27]

In the second controversial decision, the Court overturned HUAC's contempt conviction of United Automobile Workers (UAW) official John T. Watkins, who had testified freely about his own Communist associations but refused to answer questions about other people. Rather than take the Fifth, he claimed that questions about his political activity were "outside the scope of" the committee's mandate, on First Amendment grounds. The Court held that congressional investigative power was not unlimited, that HUAC's mandate was "loosely worded." "Who can define the meaning of 'Un-American'?" it asked. Watkins could not know the subject of the investigation and, therefore, could not determine whether or not he was within his rights in refusing to answer. His conviction was an unconstitutional violation of the due process clause of the Fifth Amendment. In a resounding rebuke to HUAC, the Court held that "there is no congressional power to expose for the sake of exposure."[28]

The 1957 decisions were cause for jubilation among civil libertarians. The ACLU had participated in all of the cases, and its *Annual Report* commented that the national mood was "in sharp contrast to the hysteria and near-terror of only a few years ago."[29]

Congressional conservatives were outraged, however, and Indiana Senator William Jenner introduced a sweeping "court-stripping" bill to overturn *Nelson, Yates,* and *Watkins.* It would bar the Court from hearing appeals in all cases involving congressional investigating committees, the federal loyalty program, state antisubversive laws, and the acts of state courts, school boards, and bar admission controversies involving alleged subversives. Southerners, already furious over *Brown,* welcomed their new allies. The anti-Court movement gained additional impetus because of the 1957 *Mallory* decision, in which the Court overturned a conviction because the defendant had been detained in police custody for over seven hours. Conservatives also introduced separate court-stripping bills to overturn the Court's examination of police procedures. Despite the intensity of reaction, none passed. The key player in Congress was Senate Majority Leader Lyndon B. Johnson. Because of his presidential aspirations, he shifted his loyalty from the southern bloc to the northern liberal Democrats, steering the 1957 Civil Rights Act through Congress and helping defeat the court-stripping bills. Although the latter indicated a decline in the cold war fever, the Supreme Court was evidently shaken by the threat of congressional retaliation. On several key issues over the next five years, therefore, it backed away from the promises of the 1957 decisions.[30]

The ACLU scored several important victories in the Supreme Court's 1957–1958 term. It joined the successful appeal of Rockwell Kent, who was denied a passport because of "a consistent and prolonged adherence to the Communist Party line." In *Kent v. Dulles,* the Court held that freedom of travel was one of the liberties guaranteed by the due process clause of the Fifth Amendment. In *Trop v. Dulles,* the Court held that Albert Trop could not be stripped of his citizenship because he had deserted the military during wartime. The ACLU's Osmond Fraenkel persuaded the Court that taking away Trop's citizenship violated the Eighth Amendment's prohibition on cruel and unusual punishment.[31]

The Court then backtracked on both HUAC and the Smith Act. The 1959 decision in *Barenblatt* surprised even some Justice Department lawyers who expected to lose the case. Vassar College professor Lloyd Barenblatt had refused on First Amendment grounds to answer HUAC's questions. The Court upheld his conviction on the grounds that the First Amendment did not "afford a witness the right to resist inquiry in all circumstances." HUAC's hunting license, seemingly restricted in *Watkins,* was again unleashed.[32]

The Meaning of the Bill of Rights: Absolutists Versus Balancers

Harlan's "balancing test" formula in *Barenblatt* touched off a scholarly debate over the scope of the First Amendment. Conservatives and moderates accepted his view that "the balance between the individual and the governmental interests here at stake must be struck in favor of the latter." In *Barenblatt,* for example, Harlan held that the government had a right of self-preservation in the face of a serious menace, that is, Communist subversion. Justice Hugo Black replied with a more forceful statement of his absolutist view of the First Amendment: "There are 'absolutes' in our Bill of Rights, . . . put there on purpose by men who knew what words meant, and meant their prohibitions to be 'absolutes'!"[33]

The debate between the "balancers" and the "absolutists" influenced the ACLU, helping it move, between 1959 and 1962, toward an absolutist position on the separation of church and state, obscenity, and most cold war issues. Three factors were at work. The initial successes before the Court raised everyone's expectations, and the new generation of activists was more willing to press civil liberties to the utmost. Finally, as the cold war waned, more people could see the damage that had been done by failing to adhere to stronger protections of First Amendment and due process rights.

HUAC: "Operation Abolition"

Watkins stimulated a renewed effort to abolish HUAC, a goal that the ACLU had essentially abandoned in 1939. Only two members of the House voted against its appropriation in 1953. Then Frank Wilkinson led the first serious anti-HUAC movement in Los Angeles. Fired from his job with the Los Angeles Housing Authority and then blacklisted in 1952, Wilkinson formed the Citizens Committee to Preserve American Freedoms, which worked closely with the Southern California ACLU in assisting people called before HUAC. In 1957 the Emergency Civil Liberties Committee (ECLC) hired him to coordinate a national "Operation Abolition" campaign,[34] an approach that made the national ACLU uneasy. Executive Director Patrick Malin called it a "waste of time" and preferred an effort to make HUAC a subcommittee of the Judiciary Committee.[35]

The Southern California and New York ACLU affiliates eagerly joined the abolition campaign. When Wilkinson left the ECLC in 1958, unhappy with its cliquishness, he and the Southern California ACLU organized a national petition drive, aimed at California Representative James Roosevelt. The strategy worked, and on April 25, 1960, Roosevelt delivered the first speech on the floor of the House calling for the abolition of HUAC. This breakthrough convinced the ACLU, and a month later the board voted to make abolition a "prime order of business." That same month nearly a thousand college students in San Francisco protested HUAC hearings, in a confrontation that launched the abolition drive in earnest.[36]

Roosevelt's "Dragonslayers" speech was partly written by Lawrence Speiser, the new director of the ACLU's Washington office, who had already made Supreme Court history by arguing and winning his own case before the Supreme Court two years before. Then legal director for the Northern California ACLU and a Korean War veteran, Speiser challenged a California law requiring veterans to take a loyalty oath to qualify for a property tax exemption. The Court upheld Speiser, holding that the law placed an impermissible burden of proof on the person claiming the tax exemption. For the state to restrict his freedom of speech it had the burden of coming forward with "sufficient proof to justify its inhibition." (Chief Justice Earl Warren abstained from the seven-to-one decision, having signed the law into effect as governor.) The Northern and Southern California ACLU affiliates also challenged a law requiring loyalty oaths of churches seeking a tax-exempt status, contending that it violated the free exercise of religion. The Court struck down the law on grounds similar to those it used in *Speiser,* but it did not address the religious freedom issue.[37]

To the surprise of most observers, the Court ruled in 1961 against Wilkinson's and Carl Braden's challenges to HUAC. Braden had been subpoenaed by HUAC as part of its investigation of alleged Communist influence in the southern labor movement. Wilkinson flew to Atlanta to organize protests against the HUAC hearings and was himself subpoenaed the minute he arrived—an obvious attempt by HUAC to harass its leading critic. Both Braden and Wilkinson refused to answer questions on First Amendment grounds and so were convicted of contempt. The ACLU represented Wilkinson, and the ECLC handled Braden's case. But the Court rejected their appeals and let stand their one-year prison terms.[38]

An Uncertain Court

Equivocal on cold war issues, the Court also gave the Smith Act new life in 1961 when it upheld its membership clause, sustaining the conviction of Junius Scales on the basis of his "knowing" membership in the Communist party, while at the same time it overturned the conviction in a different case on the basis of "passive" membership. The Court pursued an uneven course for several years. The registration requirement of the McCarran Act raised serious Fifth Amendment problems, for to register was to expose oneself to other liabilities. In 1961 the Court, by a five-to-four vote, sustained the requirement that the Communist party register with the Subversive Activities Control Board (SACB). Eleven years after the McCarran Act had become law, the battle was still not over. The SACB ordered specific individuals to register, and in 1965, the Court finally upheld their Fifth Amendment claims.[39] Fifteen years after the McCarran Act had become law, it was finally a dead letter.

By 1965 the composition of the Court had changed significantly, and it began invalidating virtually all restrictions on political activity. The conservative Frankfurter was gone, and the Warren Court was now dominated by a solid activist majority. In 1965 the Court struck down a federal law restricting the mailing of "communist political propaganda" from abroad. The plaintiff was Corliss Lamont, still a vigorous civil liberties activist. The Court also invalidated a Louisiana antisubversive law in a case involving civil rights activist James A. Dombrowski.[40] The cold war was not completely dead, but much of the apparatus of repression had been dismantled.

Police Misconduct and the Due Process Revolution

The ACLU made one of its most significant contributions to the civil rights movement in the area of police misconduct. In a burst of creativity, the ACLU and its affiliates developed the first civilian review board, published the first documented report on illegal detention by the police, opened the first storefront offices offering assistance to the victims of police abuse, and provided the arguments the Supreme Court used in its trio of landmark decisions on police procedures: *Mapp* (1961), *Escobedo* (1964), and *Miranda* (1966).

Since Walter Pollak's pioneering work in the 1932 *Powell* decision, the ACLU had been in the forefront of the movement to establish constitutional standards in criminal justice. It unsuccessfully urged the court to extend the Sixth Amendment right to counsel to all criminal defendants in a 1942 case, *Betts v. Brady*. The Southern California ACLU brought the 1951 *Rochin* case, in which the Court overturned the conviction because evidence had been obtained from the defendant through a stomach pump—a method that the conservative Justice Felix Frankfurter held "shocks the conscience." Beginning in 1961, the Court systematically refashioned the law of criminal justice.

The ACLU's network of affiliates was especially important to its attack on police misconduct. Police problems were inherently elusive to the national office, which in 1948 established the Committee on Police Practices with an ambitious agenda of eliminating wiretapping, the "third degree," protracted detention of suspects, excessive bail, and illegal searches and seizures. But the attempt to identify cases around the country was a complete failure. "So far we have drawn a blank," reported one staff member after a few months.[41] Unlike many other civil liberties issues that involved a statute or established practice (a released-time law, a loyalty oath), incidents of police abuse required time-consuming and often frustrating fact-finding. The affiliates, closer to the scene and able to mobilize local volunteers, could respond much more effectively than could the national office. By 1947 the Chicago and Southern California ACLUs had standing committees on police problems, and by 1951 New York and Philadelphia had followed suit.[42]

Civilian Review in Philadelphia

The new Philadelphia ACLU named police misconduct as one of its three priorities in 1951 and found a particularly favorable political climate. The reform administration of Mayor Joe Clark included five members of the affiliate's executive committee; affiliate president Henry Sawyer also was a member of the city council. Adopting the slogan "Cooperate While You Conflict," the affiliate established a close working relationship with the new police commissioner, Thomas Gibbons.[43]

Led by law professor Louis Schwartz and attorney (and later judge and author) Lois Forer, the Philadelphia ACLU Police Committee pursued several avenues of reform.[44] With Gibbons's approval they revised the police's duty manual. Traditionally, police manuals had extensive rules for grooming and the care of uniforms but said nothing about the critical questions of arrest, search and seizure, or deadly force. With few Supreme Court rulings on police conduct, American police were therefore essentially lawless.[45] The new Philadelphia duty manual spelled out a few elementary principles of due process, instructing police officers to inform an arrested person "(1) of the charge against him; (2) of his right to the aid and advice of counsel before and during his questioning and (3) of his constitutional privilege against self-incrimination." Written more than a decade before *Escobedo* and *Miranda,* the manual was an important first step toward the meaningful supervision of police officers.[46]

Forer also suggested a citizen's version of the police manual, in plain language, to educate the public about police powers. This was a logical counterpart to the affiliate's proposed pamphlet on FBI investigations.[47] The New York Civil Liberties Union, however, beat them to it in 1955 with a brochure *If You Are Arrested,* which informed people of their rights to "not say anything that may be used against you later" and "to the aid and advice of a lawyer at all times." It was an instant success. The NYCLU quickly distributed over forty thousand copies without even touching Brooklyn and Queens. Philadelphia, Chicago, and other affiliates reprinted it, and over the next ten years, it became one of the staples of local ACLU activity. Together with related major Supreme Court decisions, *If You Are Arrested* played a major role in educating the public about the scope of police powers.[48]

Despite Commissioner Gibbons's good intentions, the problem of police misconduct in Philadelphia persisted. Complaints about the police steadily increased, as civil rights activism grew, and black leaders pointed to the lack of adequate procedures for reviewing complaints. An internal board of inquiry, created by Gibbons, was dominated by police officers and proved to be inadequate. Finally, despairing of internal reform, the Philadelphia ACLU in 1957 began lobbying for a civilian review board.[49] When the city council refused to act, Mayor Richardson Dilworth created the Police Review Board by executive order in September 1958. It was a major precedent: the first independent agency empowered to review police actions. (New York City, under the threat of a federal investigation, had established a Civilian Complaint Review Board a few years earlier, but it was composed entirely of police department employees.) The five unpaid citizens on the board included black attorney William T. Coleman, the noted criminologist Thorsten Sellin, a Quaker, a Catholic school official, and a labor leader.[50]

Experience quickly exposed the weaknesses of the Police Review Board. With no staff other than a volunteer law student the first year, it had to rely on the police department's internal affairs unit for the crucial fact-finding. It had no independent disciplinary power and could only make recommendations to the commissioner, who did impose sanctions in the first eight cases recommended by the board.[51]

The board's creation by executive order proved to be a fatal weakness. When the old-machine Democrats replaced the reformist Republicans, it was doomed. As black complaints about the police escalated in the 1960s, the police union retaliated by successfully lobbying Mayor James Tate to abolish the board in 1967. Tate also promoted Frank Rizzo to police commissioner in a political move to placate the Italian-American community, at which point the cordial relations between the ACLU and city hall evaporated. The ACLU turned to litigation and brought a number of suits against the police. In one notable though unsuccessful case, after the police had violently dispersed a demonstration by black public school students, the ACLU sued to have the police department placed in receivership. But none of these suits—nor a U.S. Justice Department action—brought about any lasting change in the Philadelphia police department. By the 1980s, after thirty years of persistent effort, the ACLU had produced only marginal improvements in Philadelphia policing.[52]

Secret Detention by the Chicago Police

The Illinois ACLU took a different and more fruitful approach to police problems. After winning a $100,000 damage award in 1954 for a man shot by the police, it enthusiastically reported that "suits against the police for brutality and for illegal detention have proved effective."[53] It eventually became apparent, however, that damage awards produced no lasting changes. Embarking on a different course of action, therefore, the affiliate sponsored an empirical study of illegal detention by the police.

Published in 1959, *Secret Detention by the Chicago Police* was "the first systematic study ever made of the frequency of lengthy secret detentions by a municipal police force." Directed by attorney Bernard Weisberg, it examined a random sample of 2,038 municipal court cases from 1956. Although it covered only the period between arrest and formal booking, it confirmed everyone's worst suspicions. Only 20 percent of those persons arrested were booked within seventeen hours of arrest; 50 percent were held more than seventeen hours without any formal charge being filed. In fact, 10 percent of the suspects were held for forty-eight hours, and 5 percent were held for sixty hours or longer. Even these shocking figures understated the problem, as complete records did not exist for 30 percent of all arrests, and in fact Chicago police routinely failed to record "time and date booked." Based on this sample, the ACLU estimated that twenty thousand people a year were held for seventeen hours or longer. Illegal detention was "a regular police practice."[54]

Secret Detention concluded with a series of bold recommendations: a state law requiring the police to advise suspects of their right to remain silent while in custody and another excluding confessions made while a suspect was illegally detained.[55] The Illinois legislature refused to act, but the report had an enormous national impact. Requests for copies of *Secret Detention* poured into the Chicago ACLU office. Supreme Court Justices William O. Douglas and Tom Clark both asked for copies, and Douglas promptly cited it in a widely reported speech in St. Louis. The *New York Herald Tribune* praised it editorially, and the New York Police Academy quietly requested a copy. Locally, the *Chicago Sun-Times* praised it, and ACLU officials began negotiating with city officials to implement the recommendations. At a May 1959 meeting, Chicago Mayor Richard Daley conceded the accuracy of the report, and an assistant to Police Commissioner O. W. Wilson told Weisberg, "You have no idea how influential the ACLU *Secret Detention* report has been."[56]

Secret Detention threw the national spotlight on the hidden world of police station behavior. As it pointed out, "This problem is invisible to the great majority of law abiding citizens who rarely have any direct contact with the police." In a climate of rising concern about due process issues, heightened by the civil rights movement, *Secret Detention* embodied an idea whose time had come. The primary victims of this hidden pattern of abuse were, in the words of the report, "the poor, and racial and ethnic minorities."[57]

The Exclusionary Rule and Miranda

The ACLU had a direct influence on the three most controversial Supreme Court cases dealing with the police in the 1960s. The first case, *Mapp v. Ohio,* involved a characteristically outrageous abuse of police authority: Cleveland officers forced their way into Dollie Mapp's home and, after failing to find the suspect they wanted, arrested her for possessing obscene literature. Mapp appealed on the grounds that the search was illegal. The police were never able to produce the original search warrant or even a copy. The Supreme Court agreed and reversed her conviction, holding that evidence seized in violation of the Fourth Amendment could not be used against a suspect. The majority opinion was written by Justice Tom Clark, whose understanding of police lawlessness was undoubtedly enriched by his reading of *Secret Detention.*[58]

The significant doctrinal aspect of *Mapp* was the incorporation of the Fourth Amendment into the due process clause of the Fourteenth Amendment, a step that the Court had refused to take in the 1949 *Wolf* case brought by the ACLU. Significantly, Mapp's own attorney did not ask the Court to overturn *Wolf;* only the Ohio Civil Liberties Union's *amicus* brief urged it to do so. Application of the exclusionary rule to state and local police had the effect of creating national standards for police behavior. Such a rule was not new in 1961, as the Court had already applied it to federal cases in 1914 (*Weeks*), and it was in effect in half of the states.[59]

Mapp set off a storm of protest, with the police accusing the Court of "handcuffing" them in the fight against crime. The exclusionary rule became a focal point of charges, repeated by conservative political candidates through the 1988 presidential election, that the ACLU was the "friend" of criminals.[60]

The next major police case to reach the Court drew directly on the ACLU's *Secret Detention* report and concerned murder suspect Danny Escobedo, questioned by the police while they refused to let him see his lawyer. He confessed and was convicted. His appeal reached the Supreme Court a year after the *Gideon* decision held that felony defendants had a right to an attorney at trial. *Escobedo* raised the question of exactly when the Sixth Amendment's right to counsel began. The Illinois ACLU's Bernard Weisberg, who argued Escobedo's case before the Court, conceived the brilliant strategy of documenting police interrogation practices by citing extensively from the leading police textbooks. Ruling in Escobedo's favor, the Court held that suspects had a right to an attorney when in custody and when the questioning became accusatory, thereby bringing standards of due process into the previously hidden world of the police station.[61]

Court watchers realized that the next big case would address on-the-street police handling of suspects. That case was *Miranda v. Arizona,* decided in 1966, and once again the ACLU played a creative role in forging new constitutional doctrine. *Miranda* reached the Court as a Sixth Amendment right to counsel case. The ACLU's *amicus* brief, fashioned largely by Anthony Amsterdam, linked the Sixth with the Fifth Amendment: A suspect in custody had not only a right to a lawyer but also a more fundamental right not to incriminate himself or herself. The *Miranda* decision enunciated the now-famous "Miranda warning": Police were required to advise suspects of their right to remain silent and their right to an attorney. In one of his most passionate opinions, Chief Justice Earl Warren denounced police misconduct, quoted extensively from the police textbooks cited in the ACLU brief, and referred to *Secret Detention.* The five-to-four decision was even more controversial than those for *Mapp* and *Escobedo* were and, coming as it did in the

midst of urban riots and dramatically rising crime rates, intensified the controversies surrounding the Court, the police, and crime.[62]

Weisberg and Amsterdam represented the best of ACLU lawyering in this
period. From very different backgrounds, each brought fresh perspectives to
the problem of police misconduct. A Chicago corporate attorney, Weisberg
had no background in criminal procedure, which law professor Yale Kamisar
suggests gave him "the advantages of the amateur—'the freedom from traditional limitations and perspectives, the ability to raise fundamental questions
which professionals in the field have long forgotten to consider.' "[63]

In contrast, Amsterdam was a constitutional law scholar, brilliant and im-
perious. Indeed, many of his colleagues regarded his as one of the most creative minds of his generation. In addition to the *Miranda* brief, Amsterdam
devised the legal strategy for the NAACP's Legal Defense Fund's campaign
against the death penalty. His "last aid kits" helped lawyers block executions,
a strategy that brought a de facto moratorium on the death penalty between
1967 and 1976.[64]

The combination of an activist Court and the popular pressure of the civil
rights movement created a unique moment in the history of civil liberties.
Lawyers responded with fresh ideas and found in the ACLU a channel for
their energies. The result was the greatest burst of new civil liberties law in
American history. The two strands of ACLU thinking that had been present
since the early 1920s fused in this special environment. The strand of gut-
level identification with the oppressed reinforced the tradition of high legal
craftsmanship to generate new horizons of individual liberty. In later years,
many ACLU veterans looked back wistfully to the great days when it appeared that the Warren Court would set all things right.

Law and Social Change Revisited

Mapp, Escobedo, and *Miranda* had a lasting effect on the police that went far
beyond the decisions themselves, for the rulings stimulated police reform. Departments raised recruitment standards, improved training, and tightened supervision. Many police received the first meaningful training in the law of
criminal procedure. Scholars attempting to measure the impact of the exclusionary rule found that it did not actually hinder the police's crime-fighting
capacity. But the various court decisions did significantly alter the working environment of policing, by introducing the principle of accountability to the
law. Officers learned that they indeed could live with the exclusionary rule
and the *Miranda* warning. A study of Chicago narcotics detectives in 1987
found that most of them even thought the exclusionary rule was a good
thing.[65] The Court's rulings also affected public attitudes, educating people
about police powers. One survey in the 1970s found that over 90 percent of
all high school students knew that a suspect had the right to an attorney. As
was the case with the church–state decisions, the Court's rulings on the police penetrated deep into the fabric of American society, altering public expectations and reshaping the behavior of public officials.[66]

But not unexpectedly, the police reacted angrily to the Court's decisions affirming the rights of suspects—and the ACLU for its role in attacking police misconduct. Police officers claimed they were being "handcuffed" in their effort to fight crime. Through the late 1980s, politicians accused the ACLU of being the "criminals' lobby." Yet police officers turned to the ACLU when their own rights were violated. For instance, the ACLU defended the right of officers to belong to the John Birch Society, and in the Knapp Commission's investigation of police corruption in New York, NYCLU attorney Jerry Gutman successfully defended the Sergeants Benevolent Association against unreasonable searches and seizures of their lockers.[67]

The Court's decisions on police conduct had an equally important effect on national politics. Coinciding with an increase in serious crime, they became the target for conservatives who blamed the Court for being "soft" on criminals. In the 1968 presidential election, "law and order" was a principal issue, and Richard Nixon eventually fulfilled his promise to appoint conservative justices to the Supreme Court.[68] The Burger Court, with four Nixon appointees, whittled away at *Mapp* and *Miranda,* although it never overturned them completely. Ronald Reagan, also promising to abolish the exclusionary rule, appointed even more conservative justices to the Court. By the mid-1980s, the Court had little sympathy for the rights of suspects and was hostile to civil liberties in many other areas as well. It is a cliché in American politics that the Court follows the election returns. Nonetheless, the response to the Warren Court's police decisions suggests that the elections follow the Court, with a lasting effect on the Court itself.[69]

The Due Process Revolution Continued

The question of the Sixth Amendment right to counsel reached the Court in 1963 in the celebrated *Gideon* case. *Powell* (1932) had mandated counsel only in capital cases, and in the 1942 *Betts v. Brady* case, the Court had refused to extend it to all felony defendants. By the time of Clarence Gideon's appeal, however, the temper of both the Court and the nation had changed dramatically. A penniless drifter, Gideon was charged with burglarizing a poolroom. Denied an appointed attorney, he handled his own trial and appeal—and was sentenced to five years in prison. The Supreme Court, evidently ready to overturn *Betts,* assigned Abe Fortas as Gideon's attorney, undoubtedly knowing that Fortas, a prominent Washington lawyer and civil libertarian, would urge overturning *Betts.* Equally significant was the *amicus* brief filed by twenty-three state attorneys general supporting the right to counsel in all cases (they included Walter Mondale of Minnesota and Tom Eagleton of Missouri). Only Alabama and North Carolina supported Florida's position.[70]

Eager to handle the case, the ACLU continually ran into difficulties with the irascible Gideon. After an initial agreement, he disavowed their help. The ACLU cooperating attorney, Tobias Simon, angry over the rejection, fired off a memo to the ACLU in New York complaining of having wasted $300 and "an otherwise perfectly enjoyable July Fourth weekend." The ACLU salvaged some role through the new Arthur Garfield Hays Program at the New York University Law School, directed by Norman Dorsen, who supervised an ACLU *amicus*. The brief was "an exhaustive survey" of right-to-counsel cases in state courts that suggested there were many miscarriages of justice owing to lack of counsel. After this initial case, Dorsen went on to become a major figure in the ACLU, as general counsel from 1969 to 1976 and as president after 1976.[71]

The Court unanimously overturned Gideon's conviction, Justice Hugo Black writing that "in our adversary system of criminal justice, any person haled into court, who is too poor to hire a lawyer, cannot be assured a fair trial unless counsel is provided for him." Black's observation that "this seems to us to be an obvious truth" accurately gauged public attitudes: *Gideon* aroused none of the ferocious opposition that *Mapp, Escobedo,* or *Miranda* had provoked. The idea of a defendant's going to trial without a lawyer offended the new expectations of justice. The difference in public reaction involved the symbolism of the criminal process. The public expected trials (what Yale Kamisar called the "mansion" of the criminal process) to be surrounded with the full panoply of constitutional protections. The police, however, invoked the symbol of the "thin blue line" against crime. Here, a fearful public was more concerned about its own safety than the rights of suspects.[72]

Gideon also had a lasting impact on American criminal justice. Until 1963 criminal defendants across the country had been provided legal counsel in a patchwork fashion. Some cities maintained public defender or legal aid systems. In other areas, however, a defendant was assigned counsel, some of whom had no criminal law experience. *Gideon* thus forced the states to develop comprehensive public defender systems that within just a few years became a basic part of American criminal justice. Although there were frequent complaints about the quality of representation (as in the joke, "Did you have a lawyer?" "No, I had a public defender."),[73] the major problem was not the quality or commitment of individual public defenders but the sheer volume of cases, which often meant that public defenders saw their clients only briefly before appearing in court. Nonetheless, the institutionalized presence of public defenders undoubtedly served to check the worst abuses of defendants' rights.

Juvenile Justice and the Ghost of Roger Baldwin

In 1967 the Supreme Court turned to the juvenile court. Brought by the ACLU, *In re Gault* struck at the very foundations of the juvenile justice system, a foundation that had been laid, ironically, by Roger Baldwin over a half a century before. Gerald Gault's case was a classic horror story. At age fifteen he was accused of making an obscene phone call to a neighbor. Neither he nor his parents ever received written notice of the charges brought against him, and the judge "didn't feel it was necessary" for the complaining neighbor to appear in court. Gault never had the assistance of an attorney and was primarily convicted on the basis of his own statements. The judge sentenced him to the Arizona State Industrial School "for the period of his minority"—up to six years for a crime that would have brought a maximum $50 fine and two months in jail for adults. The Supreme Court overturned Gault's conviction and held that standards of due process were required in juvenile courts. That is, Gault had been denied written notice of charges, an opportunity to cross-examine his accuser, and assistance of counsel.[74]

The procedures that the Court ruled unconstitutional had been articulated fifty years earlier by ACLU founder Roger Baldwin. Now eighty-three years old, Baldwin grumbled and complained to the ACLU's Norman Dorsen, who argued the case, that the ACLU really should not be challenging juvenile court procedures. The case was a measure of how much the ACLU's own vision of civil liberties had grown. In fact, in the 1960s it developed a strong critique of most of the liberal social welfare programs that had originated in the Progressive Era. Good intentions were not enough. Indeed, Ira Glasser, future director of the ACLU, remarked that many of the clients of social welfare programs were "prisoners of benevolence." The vast discretionary power wielded by social welfare professionals was an invitation to abuse—as Gault's case clearly indicated.[75]

Gault was simultaneously one of the milestones in the evolving due process revolution in criminal justice and a harbinger of an entirely new set of civil liberties issues involving the rights of young people and of persons confined in public institutions. The ACLU played a leading role in this "rights revolution" of the 1960s.

The Rights of Labor Union Members

Almost lost amidst the great battles over Communism, censorship, civil rights, and due process during the 1940s and 1950s was the ACLU's interest in union democracy. It kept the issue alive virtually alone, as liberal Democrats did not wish to offend their AFL–CIO allies, and Republicans sought to curb the power of unions, not to protect the rights of individual members. Public concern finally came into play in the mid-1950s when Arkansas Senator John McClellan conducted highly publicized investigations of union corruption. The hearings employed all the HUAC tactics: scapegoating, conspiracy mongering, and exposure for the sake of exposure. Although corruption made the headlines—particularly in the Teamsters Union—union autocracy was at least as serious. Union bureaucrats no more respected the rights of the rank and file than management had in the years before the Wagner Act. Indeed, most unions were private enclaves of oppression in which the promises of the Bill of Rights had no practical meaning.

Law professor Clyde Summers (plaintiff in the *In re Summers* conscientious objector case) drafted an ACLU policy urging union self-regulation.

Warning that "rights of individuals cannot wait," the statement asked organized labor to clean up its own house in order to avoid federal legislation. Arthur Goldberg, counsel for the United Steelworkers, replied that free speech
for union members was a dangerous idea. In the face of antiunion attacks by
management, union leaders were analogous "to a political government which
may simultaneously face a revolution, and which is periodically at war." His
argument resembled the government's position in the free speech cases during
the World War I period. After he was appointed to the Supreme Court in
1962, however, Goldberg became a vigorous supporter of free speech.[76]

By 1958 it was clear that the unions would not clean up their own houses,
and so the ACLU reversed itself and endorsed federal legislation that established procedures for internal union democracy. The end result was the 1959
Landrum–Griffin Act (officially the Labor Management Reporting and Disclosure Act) which was largely based on ACLU recommendations. The law
asserted that rank-and-file union members had rights of free speech, press,
and assembly on internal union matters. They were entitled to fair access to
official union publications and could circulate or publish statements of their
own. No member could be disciplined (fined or expelled from the union)
without due process, including notice of charges, the right to an attorney, and
a right to a formal hearing. Other provisions required union officials to disclose their financial dealings with their own organization.[77]

The Landrum–Griffin Act was a flawed accomplishment. Although it affirmed the principle of union democracy, thirty years later many unions were
nearly as undemocratic as ever. The Teamsters were still corrupt and autocratic, despite the efforts of a dissident faction, Teamsters for a Democratic
Union. Dissidents in the other major unions also found they were no match
for the vast resources at the command of the entrenched leadership. Nonetheless, Herman Benson argued that "despite the law's built-in weaknesses,
despite feeble enforcement, despite the erratic quality of court decisions, the
law has made a decisive difference." The law established basic principles of
union members' rights and accountability. An active member of the NYCLU,
Benson valiantly carried on the fight through the 1980s as editor of *Union
Democracy Review*.[78]

Redrawing the Political Map: The Apportionment Revolution

"Legislators," Chief Justice Warren declared in *Reynolds v. Sims*, "represent
people, not trees or acres." The 1964 Supreme Court decision held that state
legislative districts had to be apportioned on the basis of one person–one
vote. *Reynolds* was the culmination of an ACLU campaign that had begun
in the 1940s to impose a constitutional standard of equal protection to legislative apportionment. In the end, this campaign rewrote the map of American
politics.

The ACLU first took up the issue during World War II in a challenge to
the Illinois legislature, which had not been reapportioned since 1901. By the

1940s the largest legislative district in Cook County was then nine times larger than the smallest rural district. When the legislature refused to redistrict, Northwestern University political science professor Kenneth W. Colegrove, with ACLU assistance, filed a suit challenging congressional district apportionment, claiming denial of equal protection under the Fourteenth Amendment. There was some optimism regarding a favorable decision in the Supreme Court: The 1944 decision invalidating the white election primaries in the South (*Smith v. Allwright*) suggested that the Court was willing to examine issues that involved the political process.[79]

These hopes were dashed, however, when the Court ruled in *Colegrove v. Green* (1946) that it should not enter what Justice Felix Frankfurter called a "political thicket." In one of his classic statements on judicial self-restraint, Frankfurter wrote, "It is hostile to a democratic system to involve the judiciary in the politics of the people."[80] In the face of this judicial impasse, the apportionment problem became steadily more serious through the 1950s, as cities and suburbs continued to grow and the rural population dwindled. With each passing year, the disparity between the political power of urban and rural areas increased. By 1960, voters in the least populous counties in the country had more than twice the voting power of those living in the sixty-four counties with populations greater than 500,000. In California, the largest state senate district had a population of 6 million, whereas the smallest had only 14,000 people—a ratio of 422 to 1. In Vermont, the difference between the largest and smallest lower house districts was 872 to 1. New York had a mere 12 to 1 disparity in lower house districts. The dilution of the urban vote had enormous ramifications, as rural legislators took little interest in the pressing needs of the urban communities: schools, housing, crime, medical care, and other social services. The victims of vote dilution included both blacks in the inner city and Republicans in the suburbs.

Unlike most civil liberties issues, reapportionment engaged the self-interest of wealthy and politically powerful urban interests. As the struggle turned back to the state courts and legislatures, ACLU affiliates played a crucial role. Under the threat of a Minnesota ACLU suit, for example, the legislature hastily reapportioned. Lawyers in other states requested the Minnesota brief, including those in Tennessee who in 1962 brought the landmark Supreme Court case of *Baker v. Carr*.

In *Baker*, the activist majority on the Warren Court overturned *Colegrove* and ruled that legislative apportionment was indeed a justiciable issue. That is, the plaintiffs had been denied equal protection of the laws through grossly inequitable legislative districts. The decision established the principle of judicial oversight but left unanswered the question of what standard should apply to apportioning legislative districts.[81]

The Court answered this question two years later in a set of cases from six different states. The lead case, *Reynolds v. Sims*, had been initiated by a group of civic leaders in Birmingham, Alabama, which included attorney Charles B. Morgan, who, nine months earlier, had become a national celebrity for daring to criticize KKK violence. Morgan soon became the director of a new ACLU Southern Regional Office. The ACLU filed an *amicus,* in cooperation with the American Jewish Congress, the NAACP, and other groups, which one scholar described as "perhaps the most important *amicus* brief" before the Court. It emphasized the impact of unequal representation on racial minorities, citing the obvious fact that minorities "tend to concentrate in the more populous areas" and arguing that there was no justification "for allowing any minority interest group, whether rural voters or any other, to gain absolute control of a state legislature."[82]

Reynolds held that legislative districts had to be apportioned on the basis of population. Chief Justice Warren held that "diluting the weight of votes because of place of residence impairs basic constitutional rights under the Fourteenth Amendment just as much as invidious discriminations based on factors such as race, or economic status." Predictably, conservatives responded with a proposed constitutional amendment to overturn the decision. The campaign failed, as did the other attempts to overrule the historic decisions of the Warren Court. Over the next few years the state legislatures realigned their districts in accord with the *Reynolds* principle. Urban voters, including the growing black communities, benefited immediately. Ironically, the long-term beneficiaries were the very conservatives who viewed the Warren Court's activism with horror: By the 1980s, reapportionment had swelled the influence of Republican voters in the suburbs.

The ACLU played a central role in voting rights in the South over the next twenty-five years. First under Chuck Morgan (from 1964 to 1972) and then Laughlin McDonald (from 1972 to the present) the ACLU Southern Regional Office challenged election procedures all across the South and helped elect hundreds of black officials.

June 1964: A Civil Liberties Watershed

The week of the 1964 ACLU Biennial Conference was framed by two Supreme Court decision days, June 15 and June 22, that confirmed the ACLU's impact on American law and policy. The Court's decisions in *Jacobellis, Escobedo,* and *Reynolds* marked the end of a great decade for the organization. Yet even then, the ACLU was entering new and often more controversial areas that would result in still greater changes in American life. For example, it was at the conference that the ACLU's Southern Regional Office was created, a decision that took the ACLU deeper into the civil rights struggle, with consequences that no one could foresee. Meanwhile, Harriet Pilpel delivered a paper placing the issues of abortion and gay rights on the ACLU agenda. Instead of looking back on a remarkable achievement in the great years between 1954 and 1964, the ACLU plunged forward, pushing back the frontier of individual liberty.

VI

The Rights Revolution,
1964-1974

Twelve

The Civil Rights Revolution

"A Generation No One Knew Was There"

On February 1, 1960, four black students from North Carolina A & T University sat in at the segregated Woolworth's lunch counter in Greensboro, North Carolina, and asked to be served. This quiet protest by Franklin McClain, Joseph McNeil, David Richmond, and Exell Blair sparked a wave of sit-ins across the South. Three months later a thousand college students protested hearings by the House Un-American Activities Committee (HUAC) in San Francisco. Police tried to clear them away, and a violent confrontation broke out.[1]

These two events opened one of the most turbulent eras in American history. The civil rights movement exploded out of the South and challenged every institution in American society. White college students embraced the militant style and tactics of the southern civil rights movement to protest the war in Vietnam. In 1964 the northern black ghettos exploded in the first of four "long hot summers" of riots. By 1968 the country was deeply polarized between militant radicals and conservatives demanding "law and order." Many thoughtful Americans even wondered whether the democratic process would survive the deepening crisis.[2]

Young people were on the cutting edge of political change. After the HUAC demonstration, one observer called them "an American generation nobody knew was there."[3] In 1967, as he was being arrested for distributing contraceptives to women at Boston University, Bill Baird cried out, "History is being made in Massachusetts today, and you, the students, are part of it."[4]

Militant protests created a new body of free speech law, and the civil rights movement inspired a host of new protest movements—for students' rights, women's rights, prisoners' rights, gay rights, and others. Underlying these movements was a new expectation of personal freedom which, for middle- and upper-middle-class Americans, expressed itself in a new expectation of privacy. The war and the Watergate scandal exposed a pattern of secret government and created a new civil liberties issue under the heading of national security. The end result was a "rights revolution," a broad range of new law and public attitudes that were the enduring legacy of the 1960s.

The ACLU and the Rights Revolution

The ACLU was in the forefront of all the crises of the sixties. It rushed to the aid of the first wave of sit-ins and provided lawyers for the HUAC witnesses in San Francisco.[5] The era transformed the ACLU as well, by resurrecting the direct-action spirit of the 1920s. NYCLU director Aryeh Neier and Southern California ACLU director Eason Monroe were arrested in demonstrations. Al Bronstein was assaulted in front of a Mississippi courthouse. Direct involvement in the Deep South and the northern ghettos forced ACLU activists to rethink the meaning of civil liberties. Millions of people were denied the most basic rights at the hands of the police, the public schools, the prisons, and the mental institutions. The shock of this discovery spurred creative thinking about how to fulfill the promise of the Bill of Rights.[6]

The ACLU began the decade with 52,000 members and ended it with twice that number.[7] In 1960 it had seven staffed affiliates, but with no presence in the Deep South, the Great Plains, and most small states. But by 1974 the ACLU had an affiliate in all but four states. ACLU lawyers abandoned their traditional reliance on *amicus* briefs in favor of direct representation, and foundation grants supported special ACLU projects devoted to prisoners' rights and other new civil liberties areas.[8]

This exhilarating expansion brought with it, however, great perils. The identification with protest movements took some ACLU activists to the brink of partisanship, provoking bitter internal disputes that resembled those over the ACLU's relationship to the labor movement in the late 1930s. Some critics charged that the ACLU had abandoned its traditional nonpartisan stand. Others thought that many of its new issues—abortion, the death penalty, the rights of the poor—were simply not civil liberties issues. The turbulent era, in short, raised the most fundamental questions about the meaning of the Bill of Rights and the role of the ACLU.[9]

The Cutting Edge: The Southern Civil Rights Movement

William Kunstler's phone rang at 6:00 A.M. on June 15, 1961. It was ACLU legal director Rowland Watts to tell him, "All hell is breaking loose in Jackson, Mississippi." The Freedom Riders were being arrested en masse. Could Kunstler go to Jackson for the ACLU? "Just introduce yourself to [Jack] Young and tell him that the American Civil Liberties Union is ready to help in any way it can." Kunstler left immediately. The decision, he recalled, "was to alter my life radically."[10]

As the sit-ins spread in early 1960, Rowland Watts and assistant ACLU legal director Mel Wulf desperately tried to arrange legal assistance. The ACLU represented forty-one black students arrested for demonstrating in front of Woolworth's in Raleigh, North Carolina. The state attorney general told the ACLU to "lump it," but the state supreme court overturned the convictions. The Florida ACLU represented eleven students arrested for a sit-in in Tallahassee, and in New Orleans the ACLU represented sixteen students expelled from Southern University for off-campus sit-ins. By 1961 the ACLU was involved in appeals in Virginia, Alabama, Kentucky, and Texas.[11]

An estimated 70,000 people, most of them black college students, participated in sit-ins in that first year. Over 3,600 were arrested. The Southern Regional Council estimated that "at least 141 students and 58 faculty members were dismissed by southern colleges and universities.[12] Nor were such problems confined to the South. The Michigan ACLU intervened when Wayne State University tried to prevent students from engaging in sympathy demonstrations. The Northern California ACLU fought restrictions on political activities at Berkeley, setting the stage for the 1964 Free Speech Movement.[13]

The sit-ins posed new questions about the boundaries of freedom of speech and assembly. Were sit-ins protected by the First Amendment, or were they simple trespass? Osmond Fraenkel, who had participated in the ACLU debates over the sit-down strikes of the 1930s, felt on "strong ground in challenging [sit-in] arrests for disorderly conduct" but was not sure about defending sit-ins per se on First Amendment grounds. The ACLU concluded that sit-ins were legal under a public accommodations rationale: "Once a person has been invited into a place of business, the storeowner cannot pick and choose what wares he will sell to customers; his place of business becomes at the very least a quasi-public facility and he must sell to all people who want to buy." This represented an important step in the ACLU's identification with militant sixties protests.[14]

How Americans Protest

Each year brought a new confrontation: the 1961 freedom rides and the 1962 integration of the University of Mississippi. The televised images of the 1963 protests in Birmingham, Alabama, where police attacked demonstrators with dogs and firehoses, were a turning point, arousing the conscience of millions of whites and inspiring militant demonstrations by blacks in the North. In an effort to contain protests, President John F. Kennedy went on national television and proposed a comprehensive civil rights bill.[15]

The ACLU responded with a major statement on the nature and limits of protest. *How Americans Protest* was a pivotal document in the organization's history, marking the watershed between its disengaged and elitist style of the 1950s and a new, emotionally engaged style.[16]

How Americans Protest strongly endorsed militant protest, citing a long American tradition that reached back to the Boston Tea Party. Disorder was an inescapable consequence of protest, but "disorder is less to be dreaded than suppression of the right to protest." But there were limits; for instance, the ACLU condemned obstructive demonstrations. A year later it criticized a planned "stall-in" intended to disrupt the opening of the 1964 World's Fair. But the right to protest could not be "abridged by the violent threats of lawless individuals opposed to the objectives of the demonstrators." The most significant aspect of *How Americans Protest* was its disillusionment with established political processes. Nine years after *Brown v. Board of Education,* only "a small proportion of Negro students in biracial districts attend integrated schools." The 1957 and 1960 civil rights acts had "made only a small dent" in winning southern blacks the right to vote. These facts indicated the "inadequacy of the forums in which . . . grievances have previously been heard." These criticisms of the conventional political process shaped the ACLU's response to the upheavals ahead.[17]

In the Supreme Court, the NAACP handled the principal sit-in cases, scoring an almost unbroken string of victories that overturned breach-of-the-peace and trespassing convictions between 1961 and 1964, at which point the new civil rights law outlawed segregation in public accommodations. Supreme Court decisions meant little in the backwoods of the Deep South, however, and the entire state of Mississippi was in the grip of a reign of terror. University of Mississippi professor James W. Silver called the state a "closed society" and was driven out by threats on his life.[18] With few lawyers available to handle the huge number of civil rights cases, there was a serious crisis in legal representation. In responding to this crisis, the ACLU made perhaps its greatest contribution to the entire civil rights movement.

The Crisis in Legal Representation

"All you read about is true," Mel Wulf told the ACLU board in 1962. "Those working for civil rights do so in an underground atmosphere."[19] The organization's new legal director, Wulf had just returned from a trip through the South in a search for cooperating attorneys. He had had fruitful discussions with Chuck Morgan in Birmingham and Bill Higgs in Jackson but found only a few others. The situation worsened drastically in 1963 when both Morgan and Higgs were driven out by threats. In Virginia, black attorney Len Holt faced a possible ten-year prison term on an incitement charge. White New Orleans lawyers Ben Smith and Bruce Waltzer were indicted under the state's "Little McCarran Act." Wulf and leaders from the NAACP, the Congress of Racial Equality (CORE), and the Southern Christian Leadership Conference (SCLC) met with Attorney General Robert Kennedy in August 1962 but found him distracted and uninterested in any vigorous federal effort to protect civil rights activists.[20]

The National Lawyers Guild acted first, establishing the Committee to Assist Southern Lawyers (CASL) in 1962, with commitments from eighty-five northern lawyers.[21] Decimated in the cold war, the Guild's resources were very slim. President Kennedy urged the American Bar Association (ABA) to create the Lawyers Committee for Civil Rights Under Law. But ACLU executive director Jack Pemberton soon concluded that the committee would do little and so decided that the ACLU should act. Citing the success of the Southern California ACLU in forming a civil rights coalition in Los Angeles, he argued that the ACLU could be "enormously effective" in a coordinating role.[22] After attending an emergency meeting of southern civil rights lawyers in New Orleans (the first interracial meeting of lawyers in anyone's memory), he organized a coalition of all the major civil rights groups: the ACLU, CORE, NAACP, the American Jewish Congress, and others. With Leo Pfeffer as chair and Henry Schwarzschild as director, the Lawyers Constitutional Defense Committee (LCDC) became the main instrument of the ACLU's activity.[23]

Wulf gave Schwarzschild a desk at the ACLU office, and they began recruiting lawyers and raising funds, in an atmosphere of emergency.[24] The Student Nonviolent Coordinating Committee (SNCC) planned to bring a thousand white college student volunteers to Mississippi. Hundreds of arrests were certain, and many feared violence and possible deaths. LCDC's call for volunteers brought an extraordinary response from across the country. Lawyers from the most prestigious firms signed up: Ralph Temple and Richard Sobol from Arnold, Fortas and Porter; Armand Derfner from Covington and Burling; and several from Millbank, Tweed. Public officials volunteered as well: an assistant county attorney from St. Paul, two assistant attorneys general from Washington State, and a legal officer with the U.S. Coast Guard. Even the future New York congressman and mayor Edward Koch enlisted.[25] Law student Phil Hirschkop organized the Law Students Civil Rights Research Council (LSCRRC, or "Liss-crick") and recruited over a hundred law students.[26]

The LCDC coalition provoked one final cold war crisis: Jack Greenberg of the Legal Defense Fund (LDF) refused to participate with the National Lawyers Guild because HUAC had labeled it the "legal bulwark" of the Communist party. That is, to him, the Guild's early commitment to the southern crisis counted for nothing. Civil rights lawyer Joe Rauh went even further and pressured Pemberton to fire Mel Wulf for cooperating with the Guild. Rauh was a power to be reckoned with, as his word was the key to some potential funding. But Pemberton brushed aside Rauh's objections and told him that LCDC would go ahead with or without him. With that, he laid to rest the lingering ghost of anti-Communism within the ACLU.[27]

The Mississippi summer was even more violent than anyone had expected. Klansmen led by Deputy Sheriff Cecil Price murdered civil rights workers James Chaney, Andrew Goodman, and Michael Schwerner. In the end there had been nearly one thousand arrests and thirty-five shooting incidents (with three people injured); thirty homes or churches had been bombed and another thirty-five burned; and eighty civil rights workers had been attacked and beaten. In addition, LCDC volunteers had their hands full with arrests for disorderly conduct, vagrancy, and other trumped-up charges. In a typical case in Madison, Mississippi, a civil rights worker was charged with improper parking. When he objected, a police officer said, "Don't keep talking to me or

I'll drag you out of that car and beat your damn brains out." Al Bronstein was beaten by the town constable and jailer in Magnolia, Mississippi, as he sought bail for forty-two people arrested for a voter registration demonstration.[28] By late 1965 the LCDC docket in Jackson listed 238 cases, with 150 still active. LCDC maintained offices in New Orleans, Tallahassee, and Atlanta. The Southern California ACLU office in the Los Angeles Watts ghetto was also under LCDC's auspices.

The ACLU provided more than a third of LCDC's initial 1964 budget of $50,000. A year later it "adopted" LCDC and assumed responsibility for $75,000 of its $130,000 budget. Private foundations—Field, Taconic, and New World—provided the rest, which supported five full-time lawyers, with Bronstein as the chief staff counsel.[29] LCDC was an important precedent for the ACLU, providing a model for the grant-funded projects that became one of the organizations' essential ingredients in the 1970s.

The LCDC experience transformed the lives of many volunteers who, after this firsthand contact with the depth of racism and poverty in Mississippi, dropped their conventional law careers and became full-time civil rights lawyers. As Schwarzschild put it, many of them "went south for two weeks and never returned." Alan Levine recalled that "I left Wall Street and worked as a volunteer for [LCDC] . . . I think that was one of the two or three best times in the ACLU's history." He returned to join the staff of NYCLU and worked on some of the key Vietnam War cases. Paul Chevigny returned from Mississippi to head the NYCLU police practices project. Ramona Ripston joined the NYCLU staff and later became the enormously effective director of the Southern California ACLU. Al Bronstein dropped his law practice (he had done some volunteer civil rights work on the side) and became a full-time LCDC attorney. He then became director of the ACLU's National Prison Project in 1972, and Schwarzschild later directed the ACLU's Capital Punishment Project.[30]

Turning Point in the ACLU

The impending Mississippi crisis was on everyone's mind at the June 1964 ACLU Biennial Conference. An emotional debate erupted over the ACLU's relationship to militant civil rights protest, with New Orleans attorney Ben Smith asking the ACLU to "endorse and support" all forms of demonstrations, protests, and civil disobedience. George Papcun from Arizona urged the ACLU to "support the Negro revolution totally." Another activist called for "all aid short of war." Moderate voices advised the ACLU to "keep to its traditional and central role of protecting civil liberties." It should assist all demonstrators whose rights have been violated, but the ACLU should not "endorse all the tactics of civil rights protesters." The integrity of the ACLU was at stake. Eighty-one-year-old Osmond Fraenkel rose to remind everyone "that a similar problem of identification with the objectives of a movement had occurred in the 30's in connection with labor." He tried to tell the younger activists that the ACLU should focus on neutral civil liberties principles, without reference to any particular cause.[31]

The issue remained unsettled, and a Biennial resolution simply reaffirmed the ACLU's "support of the ends and aspirations of the civil rights movement." On occasion it might defend "those arrested for civil disobedience," but this would be decided "on a case by case basis." The question of the ACLU's policy toward militant civil disobedience later resurfaced in relation to antiwar protests.[32]

In its most important action, the Biennial voted to create a Southern Regional Office in Atlanta, which would require a whopping 31 percent increase in the ACLU budget, to $1 million. The affiliates would provide $40,000 through a 10 percent "tax" on their normal share of dues income. The decision was not reckless, though, as the ACLU was riding a wave of growth. Membership had increased by 11 percent in 1964, and contributions, spurred by the ACLU's prominent civil rights activity, had risen by 27 percent.[33]

The Biennial also created the framework for a truly national organizational structure, with Aryeh Neier, Leonard Schroeter, and Eason Monroe emerging as the visionaries in this regard. Neier thought the ACLU could have 200,000 members by 1980, and Monroe saw 250,000 in 1975. At a time when membership had just reached 70,000, such projections were breathtaking and representative of a generation of leaders who did not inherit the traditional ACLU pessimism about potential membership.[34]

Expansion forced a showdown on the touchy question of internal governance. The self-perpetuating power of the New York–based board of directors was a contradiction for activists committed to "participatory democracy." Associate director Alan Reitman prepared a long memo, *The ACLU—Today and Tomorrow,* reviewing the ACLU's history and recommending democratization. Pemberton played an important role, by quietly lobbying reluctant board members to concede their monopoly power. Elitist to the end, Roger Baldwin warned that too much democracy could "water down our principles." But the board finally gave in, and the ACLU took a step toward genuine internal democracy. The result, however, was a cumbersome two-tiered structure. Affiliate representatives would attend two plenary meetings a year, and the old board would meet in the interim. It was inherently unstable and, not surprisingly, came apart three years later.[35]

Growth also raised new problems in coordination; in forty-four years the ACLU had never codified all of its policies, which were scattered about in press releases, position papers, and board decisions on particular cases. Washington office director Larry Speiser later admitted that he often just used his best judgment in deciding what the ACLU position was on a particular issue. The days of such informality had passed, and the Biennial authorized the preparation of an official ACLU policy guide which appeared in 1966.[36]

One other event pointed the ACLU in a new direction. At a panel, Civil Liberties and the War on Crime, Harriet Pilpel argued that current laws criminalizing abortion and consensual adult homosexuality were civil liberties issues, infringing on individual privacy. The Supreme Court's decision in

Griswold, affirming the constitutional right of privacy, was a year away, but public attitudes were changing rapidly. Pilpel thrust the ACLU into what became one of the most contentious civil liberties issues during the next twenty years.[37]

The 1964 Biennial marked the last period of relatively harmonious relations between the ACLU and liberal Democratic presidents. President Lyndon B. Johnson sent the organization a warm tribute: "Please express my warmest greetings to all participants at the Biennial Conference." The ACLU "has an essential role at this critical time." Although he sent another tribute two years later ("All fair-minded Americans stand in your debt"),[38] a parting of the ways was imminent: When Johnson escalated the war in Vietnam in early 1965, the ACLU rushed to the defense of antiwar protesters.

The war brought to the surface the latent tensions between the ACLU and mainstream liberalism. Already at odds with Attorney General Robert Kennedy over his enthusiasm for wiretapping as a law enforcement technique and the administration's failure to protect civil rights workers in the South, many in the ACLU viewed the Kennedy style as simultaneously too vigorous and not active enough. Mel Wulf met with Bobby Kennedy in 1962 to urge federal intervention on behalf of Martin Luther King, Jr.'s Albany, Georgia, campaign.[39] Instead, Kennedy later authorized an FBI wiretap on King. The Kennedys, in fact, had little concern for civil liberties. The president pressured the *New York Times* into downplaying coverage of the planned 1962 invasion of Cuba. Just as the civil rights movement exposed entrenched civil liberties violations in public institutions, the war exposed the established pattern of secret government. These would be the new civil liberties issues in the decade after 1964.

Chuck Morgan and the Southern Regional Office

"We sent a man south in the 1930's," Roger Baldwin told Chuck Morgan. "He lasted about six weeks."[40] Morgan stayed. In his eight years as director of the ACLU's Southern Regional Office, he became an imposing figure in American politics. He left a lasting impact on the South and on constitutional law, desegregating the juries in three states, outlawing segregation in prisons, and reforming the ancient election system in Georgia. His clients included Julian Bond, Muhammed Ali, and Dr. Howard Levy, whose trial was the first to raise the issue of American war crimes. In the end he was the only other charismatic figure in ACLU history besides Roger Baldwin.

Morgan was already a celebrity when Pemberton hired him in 1964, having come into national prominence the year before when he publicly condemned the bombing of a Birmingham, Alabama, church that killed four black children. In a courageous speech to the Young Men's Business Club he blamed the entire community: "Birmingham is not a dying city, it is dead." His law practice evaporated overnight, and there were threats against his life, with one caller asking, "Is the mortician there yet?" He and his family fled to

Washington, D.C., jobless and in debt. After working briefly for the Legal Defense Fund (LDF) and the American Association of University Professors (AAUP), he took the ACLU job.[41]

Morgan had just won the historic *Reynolds v. Sims* case and brought several civil rights suits with him, including a challenge to the exclusion of blacks from Alabama juries. *Reynolds* was a preview of Morgan's approach. He disdained the traditional ACLU *amicus* role in favor of direct representation. "We may have filed an *amicus* brief in my time at the ACLU," he laughingly recalled, "[but] I tried diligently not to." Morgan was not alone. In the most active ACLU affiliates—New York, New Jersey, and Northern and Southern California—60 percent to 80 percent of the cases now involved direct representation. Pemberton explained in 1966 that "the big thing that we're becoming aware of is the need for greater depth in our work. We're no longer satisfied to win a few test cases which establish a matter of principle. We're finding that we have to . . . take a lot of cases at lower court levels—to make the principle work."[42]

A complex and contradictory figure, Morgan was, in certain respects, a throwback to the ACLU of the 1920s. Like Baldwin, Arthur Garfield Hays, and Norman Thomas, he had a passionate sense of justice and identified with the poor and the outcast. At heart, he was a southern populist, with a deep faith in the people and a romanticized view of the South. "Free the South and you free the nation," he said. This belief spurred his attack on segregated juries and discriminatory voting systems. Give power to ordinary people, and they will do the right thing.[43] Few other ACLU leaders shared his populist vision. Rather they were deeply skeptical of majority rule; curbing the majority, after all, was the purpose of the Bill of Rights. And at times, Morgan's romantic view of the South shaded into a bias against northern liberals and New Yorkers in particular, which some saw as a latent anti-Semitism. Finally, his freewheeling style led to conflict with the ACLU office in New York. If a case struck him as a just cause, he would throw himself into it and worry about the formalities of ACLU policy later.[44]

"Operation Southern Justice"

Morgan's attack on racial discrimination in Alabama jury selection had begun in 1962. The issue acquired a new dimension after the murder of black civil rights worker Jonathan Daniels in August 1965. There was almost no chance that Daniels's murderers would be convicted by an all-white jury, and so Morgan brought a new suit (*White v. Crook*) challenging the exclusion of women as well as blacks from juries. The Justice Department entered the case on his side, and in 1966 a federal court ruled that both forms of discrimination were unconstitutional. With characteristic hyperbole, Morgan announced they had "killed Southern Justice." In truth, the ruling was a major step toward dismantling institutionalized segregation. One of the plaintiffs in *White v. Crook,* John Hulett, made history as the first black sheriff in Lowndes County, Alabama.[45] The attack on sex discrimination in *White v. Crook* was a secondary aspect of the case, but the civil rights movement was, in the mid-1960s, already revitalizing the women's movement.[46] Even before the Alabama victory, Morgan joined Al Bronstein in an LCDC case (*Bailey v. Wharton*) that eventually ended racial discrimination in the selection of federal juries in Mississippi.[47] Morgan then turned to Georgia and carried a challenge to jury discrimination (*Whitus v. Georgia*) to the Supreme Court where he argued and won another victory.[48]

By 1965 the ACLU had two legal teams in the South: the LCDC and Morgan's Southern Regional Office. They had more than enough business. The LCDC generally concentrated on defending civil rights workers, and Morgan launched affirmative suits attacking institutionalized segregation.[49]

Morgan had a particularly busy week at the Supreme Court in December 1966. Two days before arguing *Whitus,* he argued a challenge to the Georgia election law, ending a series of actions that had thrown the Georgia gubernatorial election into chaos. Earlier, he had gotten a federal court to throw out a state law forbidding anyone from assisting more than one illiterate person at the polls—a pertinent issue in a state in which 25 percent of the voters were illiterate.[50] In a series of suits challenging Alabama's election procedures, Morgan helped elect the first black officials in Sumter, Marengo, and Greene counties. Another of his Supreme Court cases ordered black candidates in Sumter and Marengo counties to "be treated as duly elected" and ordered new elections in Greene County. In July the black majority of Greene County elected its candidates and assumed control of the county commission and the school board. Across the South, voting rights suits were paving the way for a political revolution.

In 1968 Morgan argued and won a Supreme Court case ending segregation in the Alabama prison system. *Lee v. Washington* had broad ramifications, as the Court defined class actions "in a manner which authorized integration of every county, city, and town facility as well as state institutions in a single suit." The case also encouraged the new prisoners' rights movement. By 1969 Morgan's office was handling over six hundred requests from prisoners for assistance. In northern Virginia, LSCRRC veteran Phil Hirschkop, then in private practice, took a case on behalf of one prisoner and suddenly found himself flooded with letters from other prisoners, signaling the arrival of a comprehensive legal challenge to inhumane prison conditions.[51]

The War Protester Cases

Morgan's most celebrated cases involved Vietnam War protesters. After being elected to the Georgia legislature in fall of 1965, Julian Bond delivered a speech supporting draft resisters: "We are in sympathy with, and support, the men in this country who are unwilling to respond to a military draft which would compel them to contribute their lives to United States aggression in Vietnam in the name of the freedom we find so false in this country."[52] Outraged members of the legislature retaliated by refusing to seat him. Morgan immediately agreed to represent Bond for the ACLU. He was at the Supreme Court, waiting to argue his Georgia election case on December 5, 1966, when the Court ordered Bond seated.[53]

Bond v. Floyd had important freedom of speech implications, with the Court holding that "legislators have an obligation to take positions on controversial questions so that their constituents can be fully informed by them." The decision limited the application of oaths of office; criticizing U.S. foreign policy was not the same as violating an oath to uphold the constitution, and the Court rejected the idea of a higher standard of loyalty for legislators than for ordinary citizens.[54]

Even more sensational was Morgan's defense of Dr. Howard Levy. A dermatologist stationed at Fort Jackson, South Carolina, Levy refused to train Green Berets because they were "killers of peasants and murderers of women and children." After being court-martialed, he called Morgan, who agreed to help.[55] The trial began on May 10, 1967, before a jury of ten officers, focusing initially on Levy's character, his loyalty to the United States, and whether he had caused disaffection among military personnel. It was clear that the military officials were upset with Levy's off-duty civil rights activity. The basic issue, however, was the lawfulness of the order to train Special Forces, and the trial took a dramatic turn when presiding judge Colonel Earl V. Brown noted that Morgan had "intimated" that Green Berets were committing war crimes in Vietnam. Morgan thought to himself, "Intimated, hell! I'd shouted it." The issue could exonerate Levy, as a doctor was morally bound not to train people for war crimes.[56]

As surprised as anyone, Morgan found himself with an unprecedented opportunity for a court hearing on the United States' conduct in Vietnam. He asked for additional time: "It might take me an extra day to prove that." Brown gave him a day. The trial suddenly turned into an international event. Jean-Paul Sartre telegraphed from Paris. Bertrand Russell's office offered its files. Seymour Melman of Columbia University sent four thousand clippings on the war. Morgan drew on Special Forces training manuals and the army's *The Law of Land Warfare*. Witnesses included Robin Moore, author of *The Green Berets,* and Dr. Benjamin Spock. Judge Brown rejected the allegations of torture and murder by the Green Berets, found "no evidence" of war crimes, and pronounced Levy guilty, sentencing him to three years in prison. The appeals dragged on for another seven years, and Levy eventually served two years in prison.[57]

The Levy trial provoked a controversy in the ACLU and was a preview of further conflicts ahead. Pemberton, a Quaker with a deep aversion to war, supported Morgan. Some members of the ACLU board, however, thought the case was more a political attack on the war than a genuine civil liberties issue. ACLU general counsel and future president Ed Ennis flew to Fort Jackson to "advise" Morgan. Morgan told Ennis to "head north." The case recalled the conflict between the ACLU office and Clarence Darrow in the 1925 *Scopes* trial. The current division of opinion in the ACLU became evident when the New York Civil Liberties Union dispatched four staff members—Ira Glasser, Ramona Ripston, Alan Levine, and Eleanor Holmes Norton—to assist Morgan.[58]

Morgan next agreed to represent heavyweight boxing champion Muhammad Ali in his conscientious objection case. When Ali claimed CO status as a Black Muslim minister, boxing officials immediately stripped him of his title. The Justice Department ruled that Ali's objections were selective, being based on racial and political grounds. Ali first retained Hayden Covington, who had won so many landmark Supreme Court cases for the Jehovah's Witnesses. But when he wanted $200,000 for the appeal, Ali fired him and retained Morgan. Morgan refused to accept a $35,000 fee as a private attorney and took it as an ACLU case. As in the Levy case, some members of the ACLU executive committee complained that it was not a genuine civil liberties case. Although Morgan did not argue the Supreme Court appeal, the Court unanimously reversed Ali's conviction in 1971.[59]

Morgan and the ACLU

In his eight years as director of the Atlanta office, Morgan was a whirlwind of activity. By agreement with Pemberton, he spent half his time speaking around the country for the ACLU.[60] A cross between Clarence Darrow (by the mid-1980s his face actually resembled Darrow's) and an old-style southern politician, he was enormously popular, regaling audiences with tales of the Old South and then offering firsthand accounts of his historic cases. Through him, members of a fledgling midwestern ACLU affiliate could feel they were in direct touch with momentous events. He was everything his northern liberal audiences wanted: a southerner who believed in racial justice and had the courage to fight for it. Between 1964 and 1969 he spoke in thirty-five states for the ACLU, and many of his speeches helped launch new ACLU affiliates.

Morgan disrupted some ACLU financial traditions. When Pemberton offered him $12,000, Morgan said he needed $16,000, and Pemberton subsequently raised other staff salaries by 30 percent to keep them in line.[61] This ended the ACLU's traditional "church-basement" mentality, one of Roger Baldwin's legacies, and moved the ACLU in the direction of a truly professional organization, with appropriate salaries. The steady flow of new members financed the raises.[62]

In 1969 Morgan offered a five-year report of his activities. Assisted by Reber Boult, Norman Siegel, and Laughlin McDonald, his office was a madhouse. "No secretary has been physically able to work here for more than two years," he reported. They had taken 168 cases, won 69, lost 34, with 65 still pending. "The lesson of the Deep South is simply stamina." Morgan sneered at the U.S. Justice Department which, with its vast resources, had initiated only ninety-four civil rights cases in the 1967–1968 fiscal year. The situation then worsened. Richard M. Nixon had just been elected president on the basis of an anti–civil rights "southern strategy." Morgan also had criticized the policies of "some civil rights organizations" for their failure "to recognize the value of county-by-county and state-by-state suits to alter the structure of southern justice." The jibe was probably directed at the NAACP Legal Defense Fund, but Morgan conceded that they were coming around to his point of view.[63]

The ACLU packaged Morgan's work as "Operation Southern Justice" and sought foundation funding to continue it. But the foundations approached the ACLU first. At one point Leslie Dunbar of the Field Foundation commented that "the person we're most interested in [Morgan] won't apply." Foundation grants sustained the ACLU's Voting Rights Project through the 1980s.[64]

Morgan also contributed significantly to the integration of the legal profession, carrying the civil liberties message to southern law schools and encouraging private foundations to fund scholarships for black law students at southern law schools. Soon there were thirty-one black law students at the University of Mississippi under a Ford Foundation grant and twenty-eight at Emory University under a Field Foundation grant. This was another reflection of his faith in the South. In the long run, Morgan believed, the South could not depend on outside help but had to find its own resources for the cause of racial justice.[65]

Impact of the Civil Rights Movement

The southern civil rights movement also had a profound effect on civil liberties outside the South. The first sit-ins led to political action by white students in the North, who picketed chain stores that maintained segregated outlets in the South. This turned into confrontations over the students' own political rights, the main battle being the 1964 Berkeley Free Speech Movement (FSM).

University of California (UC) administrators had imposed restrictions on student political activity in the mid-1950s, and by 1959 the Northern California ACLU was helping students challenge a ban on campus meetings concerning off-campus issues. The great First Amendment theoretician, Alexander Meikeljohn, a member of the affiliate's executive committee, contended that the students did not have a constitutional right to bring political issues onto the campus, as that would undermine the university as a nonpartisan center for the search for truth. Meikeljohn was out of step with ACLU thinking, however, and the affiliate agreed to help the Berkeley students.[66]

In the spring of 1964, Berkeley students participated in sit-ins at major San Francisco hotels that were thought to be discriminatory. Business interests pressured UC Chancellor Clark Kerr to enforce the old university restrictions in the fall. Several students, including Mario Savio, who became the Free Speech Movement leader, had spent the summer in Mississippi. Thus when they returned to campus after confronting the Klan, they were hardly intimidated by university authorities. Kerr's restrictions sparked a student revolt that paralyzed the campus. The Free Speech Movement produced no landmark court cases but freed student political life through direct action. The administration was powerless in the face of a massive student assertion of their right to political action. Their example inspired students across the country, and the entire network of controls over student life, including the regulation of dormitory hours, collapsed.[67] And just as the FSM was winding down, President Johnson escalated American involvement in Vietnam, causing student political action to take an even more serious turn.

The ACLU in the Ghetto

The southern civil rights movement took the ACLU into the northern ghettos as well. Aryeh Neier first proposed ACLU storefront offices in 1964, "to make it easy for people to come off the street and report complaints of civil liberties violations."[68] The burning issue was police brutality, and black community leaders demanded civilian review boards, similar to the one in Philadelphia. NYCLU joined the campaign for a similar process in New York. When Mayor John Lindsay finally reorganized the existing Civilian Complaint Review Board (CCRB) in 1966 to give civilian appointees a majority, the effect was dramatic. The CCRB had been averaging two hundred complaints a year, but now one hundred complaints a month poured in.[69]

In response to Lindsay's move, the police union forced a referendum regarding the CCRB. The NYCLU received a $25,000 grant from the ACLU National Development Council and campaigned to keep the review board. In a bitter, racially polarized election the voters abolished the review board by a two-to-one margin. A year later Philadelphia Mayor James Tate abolished the police review board. These crushing political defeats heightened the importance of Supreme Court rulings as a means of controlling police behavior.

The NYCLU responded by strengthening Paul Chevigny's police practices project. Neier obtained a private foundation grant to hire Chevigny full time, with additional staff. Chevigny's prior experience had taught him that the key to effective action was legwork. Individual complaints of police abuse had to be carefully documented, an expensive and time-consuming process. Typically, citizen complaints were met with charges of resisting arrest or assaulting an officer against the complaining party ("cover charges"). Two years later, Chevigny reported mixed results. Between March 1966 and July 1967 the project received 441 complaints, accepted 123, and authenticated 71. This illustrated the problem of bringing potentially successful complaints against the police. A pessimistic Chevigny concluded that it was "a tale offering but faint hopes." The Southern California ACLU reported a similar lack of success in winning complaints against police officers; people seeking help through its storefront office won less than 10 percent of their complaints.[70]

The Southern California ACLU opened its first ghetto storefront offices after the 1965 Watts riot, with law student volunteers assisting people in filing formal complaints against the police department.[71] The New Jersey Civil Liberties Union established a ghetto office in Newark after the devastating 1967 riot. Directed by Nadine Taub, fresh from Yale Law School, the Community Legal Action Workshop (CLAW) preferred suits to bring about systemic change and assisted, for example, community groups seeking to reform welfare policies. In one notable case it represented a welfare recipient nominated to serve on the county welfare board. Officials leaked her welfare record to the public, and the chairman of the board ordered an investigation of possible welfare fraud. CLAW took her case, arguing invasion of privacy and denial of the right to hold office. A CLAW police brutality suit asked the court to appoint a special master to reform the department. Lois Forer organized a similar suit by the Philadelphia ACLU. Although the special master approach was used in prison and mental institution suits, it was never adopted as a remedy for police problems.[72]

The ACLU ghetto projects spun off in a dozen different directions, intellectually and organizationally. The firsthand experience in the heart of the ghettos spurred ACLU activity on behalf of the poor, welfare recipients, tenants, and other victimized groups. The "rights revolution" had its origins in the Deep South and the big-city ghettos.[73]

Community Control: The New York City Schoolteachers' Strike

Perhaps the most controversial ACLU civil rights action in the 1960s was NYCLU's prominent role in the controversial 1968 schoolteachers' strike, which polarized the city and ruptured relations between the black and Jewish communities and nearly tore apart the NYCLU in the process. The crisis originated with a plan for community control of neighborhood public schools, a reflection of broader discontent with the failure of public bureaucracies to respond to the people they served. Civilian review of the police sprang from the same criticism. The Ford Foundation provided a $44,000 planning grant in 1966 for an experimental program in the Ocean Hill–Brownsville neighborhood of Brooklyn. The plan envisioned control of the neighborhood schools by local boards answering to the superintendent of schools and the state commissioner of education, bypassing the board of education. The 1967 school year approached amidst great uncertainty over who actually controlled the Ocean Hill–Brownsville schools, and black community leaders accused the board of education of sabotaging the plan.[74]

The teachers' union then called a strike at the start of the school year. Because the union was predominantly white and Jewish, this added an explosive racial dimension to the crisis. Black leaders saw racism in the union's demand for power to expel disruptive students from classes. The Ford Foundation, meanwhile, said it would not make a previously discussed $250,000 grant for substantive programs. Community leaders felt that all the promises of autonomy were being broken. When the Ocean Hill–Brownsville board ordered the transfer of thirteen teachers and six administrators in May 1968, the teachers' union dug in its heels on the issue of transfers; there were no provisions in the existing union contract or school district bylaws regarding transfer (as opposed to dismissal). On September 9, 1968, the union staged the first of three separate strikes against the entire city school system.

The NYCLU joined the battle in October. Initially it had sided with the union over the question of due process in transfers. Now it dramatically reversed itself with a strongly worded report entitled *The Burden of Blame*. Written by associate director Ira Glasser, it condemned the board of education for sabotaging decentralization and attacked the union's analysis of the due process issue. Glasser did not mince his words: *"The chaos was not a result of local community control . . . the chaos resulted from efforts to undermine local community control."* Union leader Albert Shanker had deliberately distorted the issue by confusing transfers with dismissals. The union had used the due process issue as a "smokescreen" for other issues on its agenda. The essence of the report was a strong identification with the efforts of the black community.[75]

The Burden of Blame put the union on the defensive and, according to two observers, "exerted a major influence over public opinion." The controversy deeply divided New York liberals and radicals, with writers Nat Hentoff and Dwight MacDonald defending community control and Michael Harrington taking the side of the teachers. The enduring legacy of the strike was deep hostility between black and Jewish communities and neoconservative hostility to social experimentation.

NYCLU moderates who sided with the teachers opposed publication of *The Burden of Blame,* seeing due process problems in teacher transfers and a threat to academic freedom from politically influenced community school boards. Led by Herman Benson, a national leader of the union democracy movement, the moderates challenged Neier's and Glasser's leadership of the NYCLU, accusing them of "failing the test of civil liberties" by allowing their commitment to the black community to override basic civil liberties principles. Benson cited Glasser's own statement that *The Burden of Blame* "was a political pamphlet which attacked a political position." Benson challenged the Neier–Glasser argument that "transfers" were not "discharges." They replied that there had been no due process guarantees regarding transfers before the decentralization crisis. Prompted by the criticisms, Neier and Glasser called on the school board to develop new procedures and agreed to represent several teachers transferred punitively after the strike.

As black militancy increased across the country, the ACLU faced other difficult questions. In one episode, black students at Antioch College obtained a separate black dormitory, which whites were not allowed to visit. The one student to protest was himself black—Michael Meyers, a protégé of the noted psychologist Kenneth Clark and later an ACLU board member. Meyers contacted the Ohio Civil Liberties Union about challenging Antioch's "separate but equal" policy, but it begged off, as did the NAACP. The U.S. Department of Health, Education and Welfare (HEW) finally threatened to cut off federal funds, and Antioch abolished the segregated dorm. When the issue arose at the 1968 ACLU Biennial Conference, the delegates, reluctant to criticize militant blacks in the heat of the national racial crisis, ducked the matter by referring it to a special committee "to examine the possibilities and limits for civil liberties of self-determination by sub-communities, with special emphasis on the problems of the black community." Upon reflection, the ACLU reaffirmed its opposition to all forms of segregation and opposed separate black facilities.[76]

In the aftermath of the New York school strike, the moderates forced a public meeting over the direction of the NYCLU, which over one thousand people attended—a rare occasion when an immediate civil liberties issue was debated by the general membership. While there appeared at first to be some support for the teachers' union, the mood shifted noticeably in favor of Neier and Glasser. Rev. Howard Moody led a spirited defense, asking "why 'political' has suddenly become a dirty word." Summing up the new activist mood, he declared, to thunderous applause, that the NYCLU could "win cases till hell freezes over . . . but if the principles for which we stand are not translated into legislative change . . . the Union will be remembered as a relic of immense irrelevancy." A straw vote supported the NYCLU actions, 386 to 117. The moderates then lost a referendum on whether *The Burden of Blame* should be repudiated and ran an unsuccessful slate of candidates for the NYCLU board of directors.[77]

The moderates were defeated largely because of the NYCLU's immensely impressive record under Neier. "Let the record speak for itself," proclaimed his allies. They cited the NYCLU's new programs: repeal of criminal abortion laws, opposition to capital punishment, constitutional challenges to the draft, the students' rights campaign, application of the Bill of Rights to military personnel, and support for federally funded legal services for the poor. In addition, there were the "special projects": Chevigny's Police Practices Project and Bruce Ennis's Mental Health Commitment Project. In the 1967–1968 term, the NYCLU had ten cases before the U.S. Supreme Court, including *Miller* (a defense of a war protester who had burned his draft card), *Street,* and *Keyishian* (which overturned the loyalty oath for teachers). Supported by a large bequest, the NYCLU legal staff dwarfed the national ACLU staff uptairs at 156 Fifth Avenue.[78]

The NYCLU moderates simply could not compete with this record. No other national or local organization matched the ACLU's organizational strength and comprehensive activity. Despite the bitter internal controversies, the organization managed to avoid the self-destructiveness that plagued so many activist groups in the 1960s. Asked to explain how this had been accomplished, ACLU leaders in later years argued that dissidents simply had nowhere else to go. The ACLU's long history of defense of civil liberties was a powerful bond that overcame even the worst feuds.[79]

The bitter fight over the New York City schools, along with the controversies arising from black militancy across the country, obscured how much the racial situation had changed in just a few short years. At the beginning of the decade, institutionalized segregation reigned supreme; black citizens in the South were almost entirely disenfranchised. In 1964 a reign of terror existed in Mississippi as civil rights groups and their white allies were denied the most fundamental right to engage in political action. By the end of the decade, a new era of freedom had arrived in the South, under the impact of the 1964 Civil Rights Act, Supreme Court decisions, and, perhaps most important, the sheer courage and determination of civil rights activists to assert their rights. The ACLU could proudly claim to have played a significant role in those historic events. At the same time, however, racism was far from dead and more civil rights battles lay ahead.

Thirteen

From Vietnam to Watergate: Civil Liberties and National Security, 1965-1974

"Fuck the Draft." The message on Paul Cohen's jacket symbolized the impact of the Vietnam War on civil liberties. The most unpopular war in American history polarized the country, arousing militant protests that raised new First Amendment issues. The ACLU stood at the center of this turbulent period, defending antiwar protesters, eventually challenging the constitutionality of the war itself, and leading the campaign to impeach President Richard Nixon. The Vietnam Era also added a new issue to the ACLU agenda, one that outlasted the war itself: national security.

War, Dissent, and the First Amendment

When President Lyndon Johnson escalated the United States' involvement in Vietnam in early 1965, student protests followed almost immediately. An April 17 march on Washington drew a surprising twenty thousand people, and even the very first protests raised First Amendment issues.

When sixteen University of Michigan students had their draft deferments canceled after a sit-in at the Ann Arbor draft board, the ACLU protested this punitive use of the draft and provided them with legal assistance. Eight had their deferments reinstated, but the others were forced to appeal further. Selective Service Director Lewis B. Hershey said it was the prerogative of each local board to grant student deferments. These cases were the first of thousands that ultimately became a massive legal assault on the selective service system. By 1971 the NYCLU's Selective Service and Millitary Law Panel had 269 active cases. They won 90 percent of them, and lawyers in other areas were nearly as successful, the key to their success being the archaic and lawless selective service system. ACLU lawyers convinced prosecutors and judges that officials had violated their own procedures. The end result was a legal revolution that created a new body of law, marked by the appearance of the *Selective Service Law Reporter* in 1968, which introduced principles of constitutional law into a bureaucratic apparatus previously untouched by law.[1]

The first year of the war, 1965, brought a series of important First Amendment cases. David J. Miller burned his draft card on the steps of the New York City induction center, in defiance of a six-week-old law prohibiting such acts. NYCLU lawyers Osmond K. Fraenkel and Marvin Karpatkin argued that burning a draft card was a form of symbolic speech protected by the First Amendment. But the court found Miller guilty, ruling that the law was a valid criminal statute.[2] The Supreme Court refused to hear Miller's appeal but took up the issue two years later in the case of David O'Brien, who had burned his card on the steps of the South Boston courthouse. The Civil Liberties Union of Massachusetts took his appeal to the Supreme Court. In a serious setback for free speech, the Court upheld O'Brien's conviction. Chief Justice Earl Warren held that the law "no more abridges Free Speech on its face than a motor vehicle law prohibiting the destruction of drivers' licenses."[3]

Other ACLU cases, however, helped establish a significant new body of First Amendment law. The Court had unanimously held that the Georgia legislature violated Julian Bond's rights by refusing to seat him. The decision was an important affirmation of judicial protection for both antiwar and civil rights protests.[4]

Mary Beth Tinker's case set an even more important precedent. The thirteen-year-old Des Moines junior high school student wore a black armband to school on December 16, 1965, to protest the war. Refusing to take it off, she was suspended from school the next day, the principal explaining that "schools are no place for demonstrations." The ACLU took her case to the Supreme Court and, in *Tinker v. Des Moines,* won a victory with sweeping ramifications. Justice Abe Fortas held that "it can hardly be argued that either students or teachers shed their constitutional rights to freedom of speech or expression at the schoolhouse gate." Fortas wrote that schools ought not be "enclaves of totalitarianism," and *Tinker* opened up a new body of constitutional law involving the rights of students.[5]

Other antiwar protests extended the range of symbolic speech. The NYCLU successfully represented Sidney Street, who burned an American flag after hearing that a sniper had shot black civil rights leader James Meredith. Conservative Justice John Harlan held that Street "did not urge anyone to do anything unlawful." His "excited public advocacy of the idea that the United States should abandon, at least temporarily, one of its national symbols" was constitutionally protected. In a Washington ACLU case, the Court overturned the conviction of Harold Spence, who had been convicted of displaying the American flag with a peace symbol attached to it. Harlan also wrote the majority opinion upholding Cohen's right to walk through the Los Angeles courthouse with "Fuck the Draft" on the back of his jacket. The very vulgarity of Cohen's language was a vital part of "the overall message" he sought to communicate.[6]

The Court laid to rest the clear and present danger test in a KKK case when an Ohio Klan member was convicted under a 1919 criminal syndicalism law for a speech declaring that "if our President, our Congress, our Supreme Court, continues to suppress the white, Caucasian race, it's possible that there might have to be some revengance [*sic*] taken." An Ohio ACLU brief helped the Court overturn the 1927 *Whitney* precedent. The Court held that the First Amendment protected advocacy, even of the necessity of violent action. Only incitement to imminent lawless action could be punished. *Brandenburg* effectively abolished the clear and present danger test, invalidating the Smith Act and all state sedition laws restricting radical political groups. After a fifty-year struggle, the ACLU had finally persuaded the Court to accept its view of the First Amendment.[7]

In draft cases, the ACLU's record in the Supreme Court was mixed. It was most successful on due process issues. Representing James Oestereich, it persuaded the Court that he was entitled to a court hearing over his draft reclassification, which apparently was punishment for his antiwar activity. Two years later the Court ruled that student deferments had been established by Congress and so could not be arbitrarily revoked by local draft boards.[8]

The ACLU pressed the right of conscientious objection to new limits, with some success. The most important victory actually preceded the escalation of the war when, in the 1965 *Seeger* decision, the Court extended the right of conscientious objection to people who did not necessarily believe in a "supreme being" but whose beliefes paralleled those of conventional religion. The decision brought to fruition the ACLU's efforts to broaden the meaning of "religious training and belief" that had begun with the 1940 selective service act.[9] Because the Vietnam War was so repellent to many people, there were many claims of selective conscientious objection. ACLU executive director Jack Pemberton, a pacifist, regarded this as a particularly important ACLU issue. When the ACLU took the case of Dale Noyd, seeking release from the air force on selective objection grounds, Pemberton went to Clovis, New Mexico, to try the case himself.[10] The ACLU did not succeed on the selective objection issue, however.

Limits of Protest?

As the war escalated, the protests became increasingly radical, often taking on a bitter, anti-American tone. By 1968, fringe groups romanticized Third World revolutionaries and urged violent revolution in America. There was much talk about American "Fascism," and many radicals concluded that constitutional principles of free speech were nothing more than a mask for repression. The ACLU thus faced serious challenges to free speech principles from the New Left.[11]

The December 1967 "battle of Whitehall Street" in which protestors tried to close down the New York City induction center forced the ACLU again to reconsider the limits of peaceful protest. As in so many demonstrations, police discipline collapsed, and officers indiscriminantly beat and arrested demonstrators and bystanders alike. NYCLU offered to represent the more than five hundred persons arrested on grounds of false arrest and violation of their First Amendment rights. The NYCLU did not, however, defend the demonstrators' right per se to shut down the induction center.[12] This distinction was often lost on the media, much of the public, and even some ACLU members.

In response to public and internal misunderstanding, the ACLU restated its policy on civil disobedience. The issue brought to the surface a deep split between the new ACLU activists and moderates. The latter were concerned that the activists had allowed their commitment to the antiwar movement to cloud their judgment and had lost sight of basic civil liberties principles. The ACLU board drafted a statement distinguishing between two different types of civil disobedience. It reaffirmed its commitment to "defend individuals who violate laws which, either in themselves or as applied in the circumstances, the ACLU believes to be unconstitutional or to interfere with the exercise of constitutional right, whether or not the courts have previously ruled otherwise." The ACLU would not, however, defend someone who "violates a valid law with which [he or she] has no quarrel but does so to protest or call attention to some other evil." This included disruptive antiwar demonstrations. That is, the ACLU would not help people avoid the law's consequences simply because "they acted out of conscience or deeply felt convictions." It would defend them only with respect to due process violations in their arrest or prosecution.[13]

Although activist staff members at the ACLU and the NYCLU agreed with the statement in principle, they feared that the media would emphasize the criticisms of protest. Pemberton was inclined to agree and so delayed releasing the statement. Moderates responded angrily. Board member David Isbell asserted that this was "letting the P.R. tail wag the policy dog." The ACLU had an obligation to state the civil liberties principles involved. George Soll was convinced that the activists were leading the ACLU astray. Someone leaked the internal controversy to the press, adding more fuel to the fire, and the dispute became increasingly personal. Marvin Karpatkin even accused his former co-counsel Osmond Fraenkel of supporting the war.[14]

At the bottom of the dispute was the question of the war itself. In 1965 some antiwar activists argued that it was unconstitutional in the absence of a congressional declaration of war. The ACLU debated the issue and in January 1966 concluded that the war "does not, in and of itself, represent a civil liberties question." The only possible exception would be a prosecution for treason.[15] Over the next few years, as the war divided the country even more, the ACLU rethought the issue of the power to make war.

By 1969 the ACLU was increasingly disturbed about the intolerant spirit among antiwar activists. On a number of campuses, they shouted down speakers defending the war. San Francisco State University Professor John H.

Bunzel was drowned out in his own classroom. Arthur Goldberg was shouted down at a conference, and a pig's head was placed in front of him. The ACLU warned that protesters "have no right to deprive others of the opportunity to speak or be heard, take hostages, physically obstruct movement of others, or otherwise disrupt the educational or institutional processes in a way that interferes with the freedom and safety of others."[16]

Antiwar activists also tried to ban the military and certain defense contractors from recruiting on campus. The favorite target was Dow Chemical ("Dow Shall Not Kill"), a manufacturer of napalm, a symbol of the war's barbarity. Boston University professor Howard Zinn argued that the "civil liberties of Dow Chemical are not in question." Recruiting employees was action, not speech. The ACLU replied that all organizations had a right of access to campuses and that colleges could either admit or ban all recruiters. By judging the political aspects of an organization's activities, radical student protesters were betraying the principle of an open campus that they had won in the 1964 Berkeley Free Speech Movement.[17]

The NYCLU staff, a hotbed of antiwar activism, publicly attacked the ACLU statement in a letter to the *New York Times:* "Where the democratic process has been unresponsive, we believe it far more important to emphasize these conditions than to focus on the militant response which they have bred." This was essentially a restatement of the ACLU's 1963 *How Americans Protest.* The internal ACLU dispute turned on a question of emphasis: The activists felt that the ACLU should focus on the social and political problems that caused extreme protest, and the moderates were alarmed that the activists were ready to countenance anti–civil libertarian tactics.[18]

Split over Spock

The ACLU's dispute came to a head in January 1968 when the Justice Department indicted Dr. Benjamin Spock and four other antiwar activists, who had organized Stop the Draft Week in October, which the government called "a nationwide program of resistance to the functions and operations of the Selective Service System." The case proved to be a disaster for the Justice Department. Spock was the most well-known pediatrician in the country and immediately became a martyr in the eyes of the public. Also, the trial was held in Boston, a center of antiwar activity. Finally, the conspiracy charge was highly questionable. The defendants proudly proclaimed that there was nothing secret about their activities. The "Call to Resist Illegitimate Authority" praised draft resistance as a "courageous and justified" act and openly called for a "confrontation with immoral authority."[19]

The ACLU's legal director, Mel Wulf, attacking the case as "a major escalation in the administration's war against dissent," announced that the ACLU would represent the Boston Five. It was an instinctive response by Wulf, who passionately opposed the war. Other ACLU leaders had reservations. In a hastily called meeting, Osmond Fraenkel opposed taking the case. The defendants planned to raise questions about the legality of the war, which was not itself a civil liberties issue. Wulf was "appalled" that the ACLU might not take "the most important free speech case of our time."[20] But a week later the board of directors overruled Wulf and voted eleven to four not to take the case.[21]

The issue was in part a matter of legal ethics. A defense attorney had an obligation to represent the client fully and faithfully. Although Spock's case raised obvious First Amendment questions, ACLU lawyers could not raise issues that were outside the scope of ACLU policy, notably the legality of the war and possible American war crimes. Chuck Morgan had taken the ACLU into these areas in the Howard Levy trial only six months before, and the moderates were now determined to rein in the activists.[22]

The board's decision sparked a revolt by the staff and the activist affiliates, who began lobbying for reconsideration. The Massachusetts ACLU announced that it would represent any of the defendants who wanted ACLU assistance. The controversy exposed the cumbersome ACLU decision-making process. The 1964–1965 restructuring had produced a two-tiered board: The expanded board with affiliate representatives met twice a year, whereas the smaller, or "New York," board met in the interim. The latter had overruled Wulf in January, and everyone mobilized for a climactic struggle at the March meeting. Fraenkel grumbled darkly that NYCLU executive director Aryeh Neier "would undoubtedly try to get the richer affiliates to send delegates at their own expense."[23]

The March 2 meeting was one of the most acrimonious in ACLU history, filled with angry denunciations on both sides. The activists accused the moderates of supporting the war, and the moderates replied that the activists had thrown civil liberties principles overboard and that staff members had improperly lobbied wavering affiliates. Moderate board members were attacked because of their age. There was also the underlying question of direct legal representation. For both sides, the integrity of the ACLU was at stake. When it was over, the ACLU had reversed itself a second time. By a narrow twenty-six-to-twenty vote it approved Ed Ennis's motion to "provide direct legal representation to any defendant . . . who wishes our counsel." This motion included a disclaimer, however, that the ACLU would take no stand on whether the war itself was unconstitutional or whether American troops had committed war crimes. The positions taken by counsel, however, "must be shaped by the necessities of the defendants they represent regardless of what positions the ACLU may or may not have taken on these questions." In short, lawyers acting on behalf of the ACLU had a free hand to represent their clients fully, even on questions outside the scope of ACLU policy.[24]

The ACLU's reversals were conducted in full and embarrassing public view, and the final decision was largely irrelevant, as the Boston Five arranged their own legal representation. Michael Ferber and Mitchell Goodman took up the Massachusetts ACLU offer; Spock retained the noted radical lawyer Leonard Boudin; and William Sloane Coffin hired James D. St. Clair (later famous as one of President Nixon's many Watergate attorneys). Four of the defendants were convicted, but the First Circuit Court of Appeals overturned the convictions. The Justice Department finally dropped the case.

An ACLU Turning Point

The Spock case continued to reverberate within the ACLU. One of the moderates, Louis Lusky, wondered "whether the national Board is any longer in control of the Union" and saw "a deep sickness in the organization."[25] A number of moderates quit, and in later years, neoconservative critics saw the Spock case as the point at which the ACLU abandoned civil liberties for a "political" agenda. The ACLU then abolished the two-tiered board and created a new eighty-member board of directors with representatives from all the affiliates and thirty at-large members.

The case also forced the ACLU to confront the question of its legal role. In a formed debate, Norman Dorsen and Emil Oxfeld argued for direct representation. Dorsen saw litigation as a tool for social change that would allow the ACLU to shape cases at the trial level and introduce issues that might otherwise be ignored. The ACLU also had an obligation to provide representation for people who needed assistance. Finally, direct representation would "enhance" the ACLU's "standing as a vigorous and engaged organization" and sustain the morale of staff and cooperating attorneys. Unstated was the fear that the ACLU might lose many of its most talented and energetic lawyers to other organizations. Dorsen felt that critics had "exaggerated" the potential problems of direct representation.[26]

David Isbell, an attorney with the prestigious Washington, D.C., law firm of Covington and Burling, and law professor Larry Herman spoke for the ACLU's traditional *amicus* role. Both, however, conceded the benefits of direct representation. Isbell found "risks on both sides" and asserted that "no flat rule" should govern the ACLU's legal role. Herman, admitting that his views had changed, was also no longer completely opposed to direct representation. Oxfeld delivered the coup de grâce to the moderates by pointing out that it was a moot question: "Today about 90 per cent of our work . . . is direct." Experience rather than logic had settled the issue. Although the ACLU usually made a fetish of formal policy, in this instance it had made a major change in legal strategy without any formal discussion, having been propelled into a new role by the urgency of the civil rights and war issues.

An Unconstitutional War?

As the dispute over the Spock case indicated, the war itself increasingly dominated the minds of ACLU members. As the number of American troops in Vietnam reached 500,000, some ACLU activists began to consider a constitutional challenge. The New York and Southern California affiliates acted first, in 1967 calling the war unconstitutional on the grounds that Congress had not formally declared war. The turning point was the invasion of Cambodia and the Kent State University shootings in April and May 1970. After four Kent State students were killed by the Ohio National Guard, a wave of protests swept college campuses nationwide. Mel Wulf told the Executive Committee that "the time has come for the ACLU to acknowledge publicly that the war in Vietnam . . . is the immediate cause of the wholesale denial of civil liberties." The attacks on freedom of speech and press could no longer be separated from the war itself. Therefore, "the ACLU should finally declare that the war in Vietnam and Cambodia violates the Constitution."[27] The Ohio Civil Liberties Union, meanwhile, sprang to the aid of the families of the students killed at Kent State. Eight years later it won a settlement of $675,000 and an official apology from Ohio Governor James Rhodes and twenty-seven national guardsmen.[28]

The moderate opposition collapsed after Kent State. On June 2 the ACLU board took the fateful step and declared that the war "fostered an atmosphere of violence which resulted in the slaying of college students and black people, violent attacks on and by demonstrators both for and against the war, and a climate of repression in which attempts have been made to stifle criticism of the war." The violations of civil liberties included continuation of the draft, curbs on nonobstructive dissent, prosecutions for peaceful symbolic expression of opposition to the war, and numerous threats to academic freedom. Also criticizing the actions of some protesters, the ACLU noted that the war had created an "atmosphere" in which "academic freedom cannot be preserved." The war had drained national resources and caused a neglect of urgent urban problems. Finally, it violated the war powers clause of the Constitution. The power to declare war rested with the people, acting through Congress. The war was a "Presidential usurpation" of the "people's sovereignty."[29]

The ACLU plan of action included continued litigation in draft and First Amendment protest cases, lobbying for an end to the war, and abolition of the draft. It would also file an *amicus* brief in a state of Massachusetts suit challenging the constitutionality of the war. But the suit lost in the lower courts, and the Supreme Court refused to hear an appeal in late 1970.[30]

Meanwhile, in New York, Malcolm Berk filed a suit challenging the legality of an order sending him to Vietnam. The NYCLU's Burt Neuborne assisted his lead attorney, Ted Sorenson, former aide to President Kennedy. Neuborne eventually handled all of the major war cases. The federal district court refused to enjoin Berk's order, but on appeal, Supreme Court Justice Byron White issued a temporary stay. A second case, involving Salvatore Orlando, appeared. Citing Justice White's stay in *Berk,* the district court stayed the order sending him to Vietnam. The two rulings set the stage for trials on the merits of the issue. In both cases, however, the trial judges upheld the government. In *Orlando,* Judge John Dooling ruled that the repeated acts of Congress supporting the war effort constituted congressional approval. The judge in *Berk* also held that "Congress repeatedly and unmistakably authorized the use of armed forces . . . to fight in Vietnam." The second circuit court upheld the government in both cases, and the Supreme Court denied cert. For the moment, the legal challenge to the war was dead.[31]

One final and more dramatic challenge occurred in 1973 when New York Representative Elizabeth Holtzman sued to halt the bombing of Cambodia on the grounds that it was illegal. To everyone's surprise, Judge Orrin Judd, who had ruled against Berk only two years before, ordered the bombing stopped. The second circuit court stayed his order, and Neuborne and the NYCLU staff turned to the Supreme Court. When Justice Thurgood Marshall refused to overturn the second circuit court's ruling, one final option remained: Supreme Court rules permitted appeal to another justice.

Justice William O. Douglas appeared to be the best hope, and NYCLU attorney Norman Siegel flew to Goose Prairie, Washington, where Douglas was vacationing in an isolated cabin with no phone. Accompanied by a local affiliate staff member, Siegel arrived at the cabin early in the morning. The appeal was urgent, but they worried about waking him too early. After an attempt to "accidentally" wake him by racing the engine, Siegel finally knocked on the door. A receptive Douglas told him to arrange a hearing the following day. Neuborne flew out from New York, and on August 4, Douglas vacated the second circuit court's stay. But it was only a brief reprieve. Within hours, Marshall arranged a conference call of the other justices and overruled him. The *Holtzman* case ended there. For a few hours, at any rate, the ACLU had won a court order stopping the bombing.[32]

Years later NYCLU director Aryeh Neier felt that trying to stop the war through litigation was "a futile effort." The outcome of all the cases proved that "the direct exercise of the war powers is not susceptible to judicial limitation." The ACLU had been seduced by the belief that litigation could solve all problems. Neuborne had a different assessment. Although unsuccessful, the challenges were worth the effort, as they had established the fundamental principle of judicial review of presidential war-making power. Moreover, he argued, the ACLU had an obligation to raise fundamental issues, however futile. No one else would raise them. Finally, he commented that the cases had had a positive effect on the ACLU, stiffening its resolve to take even the boldest challenges to the highest authority and projecting the organization into the forefront of national attention. The war issues certainly benefited the ACLU in attracting new members. While critics complained and some members resigned, tens of thousands of new members poured in. In the two years after the ACLU declared the Vietnam War unconstitutional, its membership doubled.[33]

The Nixon Years: From the Pentagon Papers to Watergate

The election of Richard Nixon as president sent a shiver through the civil rights and antiwar movements—and the ACLU. A symbol of the cold war of the 1950s, Nixon appeared hostile to civil rights and to virtually all the recent gains in civil liberties.[34] Chuck Morgan feared the Supreme Court would be "lost to us during the next four years."[35] When ACLU executive director Neier asked him to head the Washington office in 1972, he eagerly accepted. "We loved Atlanta," Morgan said, "but the defense against Nixon's Southern Strategy required that the struggle be removed from the courts, carried to the people, and by them transformed into political action. To be in that fight, I needed to be in Washington."[36] The minute he arrived in Washington, Morgan plunged headlong into the Watergate affair.

Although not apparent immediately, the ACLU's decision to strengthen its Washington office in response to Nixon's election was an extremely important shift in strategy. In the heyday of the Warren Court, Neier explained, the ACLU was always certain the Court "would put all things right."[37] With Warren now retired and Nixon appointing conservative justices, the ACLU rediscovered the possibilities for the legislative protection of civil liberties. First under Morgan, and then more systematically under John Shattuck after 1976, the ACLU beefed up its Washington office. It also reduced the number of cases it took to the Court, from ninety-five cases in the 1976 term to forty-five in the 1978 term.[38]

The Nixon administration wasted no time fulfilling its critics' worst fears. In the fall of 1969, Vice President Spiro Agnew led a concerted attack on the news media. In a belligerent Des Moines speech he accused the news media of a liberal bias, reminding them that they enjoyed "a monopoly sanctioned and licensed by government." A week later he cited the local monopoly status of most daily newspapers. Even in the depths of the cold war, no administration had directly threatened the media. Frank Stanton, president of CBS, called Agnew's comments "shocking."[39] Action soon followed. The Federal Communications Commission (FCC) requested transcripts of the networks' commentary on Nixon's November 3 speech on the Vietnam War. Federal prosecutors began subpoenaing the files of *Time, Life,* and *Newsweek* for information on the radical Students for a Democratic Society (SDS). Media watchers criticized the television networks for providing only "spotty" coverage of the November march on Washington, the largest in American history, with over 500,000 demonstrators.[40]

More ominously, the administration launched a covert attack on news leaks. The pivotal event—and the origins of Watergate—was a May 8, 1969, *New York Times* article on the secret American bombing of Cambodia. National Security Advisor Henry Kissinger approved wiretaps on four government officials, including one of his own staff, Morton Halperin.

Halperin's growing doubts about the war set him on a course that led to the directorship of the ACLU Washington office. His transit from Nixon's National Security Council to the ACLU exemplified the emergence of national security as a civil liberties issue. He had begun his career as the consummate defense intellectual: a Ph.D. from Yale, a Harvard faculty appointment where he worked with Kissinger, and the author of numerous articles on books on foreign policy. Years later, when asked what caused him to change, he replied, "There are things I know now that I didn't know then." The steady revelations of secret government after 1965 thus made national security a civil liberties issue.[41]

The Pentagon Papers

The Sunday *New York Times* of June 13, 1971, carried a long front-page story headlined "Vietnam Archive." Prepared in great secrecy, the story was based on the so-called Pentagon Papers, a forty-seven-volume, seven thousand-page history and analysis of the United States' involvement in Vietnam. Commissioned by Secretary of Defense Robert McNamara in 1967, it had been largely forgotten, and only fifteen copies still existed. The *Times* got its copy from Daniel Ellsberg, a former Rand Corporation consultant for the Pentagon who had turned into a passionate opponent of the war.[42]

Though at first it was slow to respond, the White House then attacked the *Times* in what became the greatest freedom of the press confrontation in American history. After the second installment appeared, Attorney General John Mitchell asked the *Times* to stop the series. The *Times* refused, against the advice of its lawyers. The next day the Justice Department, citing the Espionage Act, won a restraining order against the paper. It was the first time in American history that the federal government had gotten a prior restraint ruling against the press. Then when Ellsberg gave four thousand pages of the Papers to the *Washington Post,* which began publishing its own series, the Justice Department immediately enjoined the *Post*.

The confrontation between the Nixon administration and two of the leading newspapers in the country forced a First Amendment test. Many legal scholars worried that freedom of the press would lose, as the 1931 *Near* decision had held "that a government might prevent . . . publication of the sailing dates of transports or the number or location of troops."[43] This did not fit the Pentagon Papers case exactly, but the country was in the midst of a shooting war, and the Papers were stolen top secret documents. Federal judges in New York and Washington upheld the *Times* and the *Post* but extended the restraining order to allow the government to appeal. The Supreme Court agreed to hear an appeal in an emergency Saturday morning session.

Better than any other case, *Times v. United States* illuminated how the ACLU now saw its role. Its *amicus* brief took a far more uncompromising stand than Alexander Bickel's main brief did for the *Times*. A Frankfurter disciple, Bickel thought his job was to win the case, and he criticized the ACLU for its "absolutist" stand. "If you go into these cases with an ideological interest, like the American Civil Liberties Union, you've got nothing to gain but your ideology. . . . I had to win a case." To take "an absolutist position would have been foolish to the point of being almost unprofessional." His brief argued against prior restraints but conceded their use "when publication could be held to lead directly and almost unavoidably to a disastrous event," which, he held, would not happen in this instance. The ACLU's brief warned that "if the Government's vague and broad test of 'information detrimental to the national security' is accepted, there would be virtually no limit to" possible prior restraints. The basic premise of " 'national security' is a political concept" that could be easily misused by future administrations. The ACLU's job was not to win the case immediately at hand but, rather, to frame the civil liberties issues in absolute terms, to make the points that other parties would not—the point that Neuborne argued with respect to the suits challenging the war.

On Wednesday afternoon, June 30, the Court handed the *Times* and the *Post* a great victory. By a six-to-three vote it overruled the government and allowed the papers to continue publishing their stories. Justice Douglas wrote that "the dominant purpose of the First Amendment was to prohibit the widespread practice of governmental suppression of embarrassing information." Black, accepting the ACLU argument, held that "the word 'security' is a broad, vague generality whose contours should not be invoked to abrogate the fundamental law embodied in the First Amendment." The decision was the occasion for jubilation among the news media and the antiwar community. It seemed a great victory for the First Amendment and a stinging rebuke to the Nixon administration.[44]

The ACLU was not so certain. The opinion suggested that the president and the Congress had the inherent power to restrain the press in national security matters, which went even further than the wartime exception defined in *Near*. John Shattuck later observed that *Times* "set in motion the development of a formal law of national security secrecy."[45] Indeed it did: In the next few years the Court upheld the government in several important censorship cases involving national security claims. For example, it upheld the right of the Central Intelligence Agency (CIA) to force deletions in Victor Marchetti's memoirs, *The CIA and the Cult of Intelligence*,[46] and to claim all of Frank Snepp's royalties for his memoirs, *Decent Interval*. An even more serious test of the First Amendment loomed when *The Progressive* magazine published an article allegedly revealing the "secret" of the H-bomb. When the government enjoined *The Progressive,* the ACLU rushed to its defense. Many observers, however, feared the First Amendment would lose. The case was mooted, however, when another newspaper published "the secret."[47]

National Security As a Civil Liberties Issue

The Pentagon Papers case was an alarm in the night for the ACLU, dramatizing the entire problem of secret government under the national security rationale. Setting ACLU priorities for 1972, Aryeh Neier urged "major efforts" in areas "that might come under the rubric of 'secret government.' "[48] To this end, he adopted the Committee for Public Justice, recently organized by Norman Dorsen and the noted playwright Lillian Hellman in 1970 (out of dissatisfaction with the ACLU national office under Pemberton).[49] The committee's first big project was an October 1971 conference on the FBI, the first serious academic inquiry into the bureau's activities. Some of the FBI's old critics appeared. Yale law professor Tom Emerson discussed the FBI's role as "a political police," and journalist Robert Sherrill analyzed its self-serving publicity machinery. These were familiar criticisms in left-wing circles, but Vietnam and the Pentagon Papers case had created a broader audience. The FBI was no longer untouchable.[50]

Predictably, J. Edgar Hoover refused to participate, accusing the planners of finding the FBI "guilty" before they began. No inquiry was needed because "the basic facts on how the FBI is organized and how it discharges its duties . . . are obvious to all."[51] Nothing could have been further from the truth. Few of the bureau's critics at the Princeton conference, in fact, had any idea of the full scope of illegal FBI activity.

The next Committee for Public Justice project was a 1973 conference on government secrecy. Neier was now the ACLU's executive director and had brought the committee under the ACLU's wing. Jointly sponsored by Dorsen's Hays Program at New York University, the conference met in the midst of the rapidly unfolding Watergate scandal, when revelations of illegal administration actions were practically a daily occurrence. Dorsen and Shattuck questioned the concept of executive privilege; journalist David Wise summarized the attacks on the news media (in 1964 the CIA had tried to suppress his book on the agency); ACLU client Ernest Fitzgerald discussed his career as the nation's most celebrated "whistle-blower" (he had been punished for exposing Pentagon waste); and Mort Halperin examined covert CIA operations.[52]

The conference made it clear that the problem was far deeper than Nixon, the liberals' favorite whipping boy. A secret government had evolved over the past thirty-five years, and liberal Democratic presidents were as guilty as conservative Republicans. Halperin emerged as the ACLU's expert on national security issues. Then at the Brookings Institution, he made his complete break with the government in the trial of Daniel Ellsberg, whom the Nixon administration prosecuted, along with his colleague Anthony Russo, for the theft of secret government documents. Halperin served as "the chief strategist for the defense [and] its key witness."[53] As a former National Security Council staff member, he had uniquely valuable insights into government thinking and decision making. The crucial aspect of the Pentagon Papers case, he contended, was the difference between what the government knew and what it wanted the public to know. This was the heart of the national security issue for the ACLU. Secrecy and covert action violated the basic premise of democracy: Public control over government policy required access to information and open debate.[54]

National security introduced a new element into First Amendment theory. The traditional view, first articulated in Oliver Wendell Holmes's 1919 *Abrams* dissent, held that free speech was essential to the democratic process. The people could make informed political choices only if they had heard all ideas. The idea of free speech as a means of personal fulfillment developed later.[55] National security added a new dimension which law professor Vincent Blasi formulated as a "checking" function. The freedoms of speech, press, and assembly served to check "the abuse of power by public officials." The Pentagon Papers case clearly demonstrated that "control over information" was the heart of the problem.[56]

Attacking Political Surveillance

The ACLU also launched suits attacking political spying, the most important one challenging surveillance by the United States Army. Asked to help quell urban riots, Army Intelligence at Fort Holabird, Maryland, began collecting information on individuals and groups that it believed might be involved in civil disorders, which inevitably included numerous civil rights and antiwar groups. The ACLU suit sought to abolish the program because it "exercises a present inhibiting effect on . . . the full expression [of] First Amendment rights." The district court agreed and ordered the Army to stop. On appeal, however, both the circuit court and the Supreme Court sustained the government. The crucial point in *Laird v. Tatum* was that the plaintiffs cited no specific harm to themselves. Rather, the purpose of the suit was entirely prospective: to stop potentially damaging surveillance in the future. The Court found that the army had done nothing more than what any competent journalist would do in terms of attending public meetings and taking notes.[57] In other suits, the Southern California ACLU represented actress Jane Fonda in an effort to collect damages for FBI spying against her. Meanwhile, Halperin pursued a suit seeking damages for having been wiretapped.[58]

Watergate: The Greatest Constitutional Crisis in American History

"Why it is necessary to impeach President Nixon. And how it can be done." With this headline on a full page ad in the *New York Times* on October 14, 1973, the ACLU emerged as the first national organization to call for Nixon's impeachment. The Watergate crisis was the most serious constitutional crisis in American history, turning on the fundamental question of whether the president of the United States was accountable to the rule of law.[59]

Chuck Morgan had already made up his mind that Nixon had to go when he took over the ACLU Washington office in late 1972. At that point there was some evidence about the Watergate burglars' ties to the White House, but no solid proof. But Morgan was convinced that the upcoming trial of the seven burglars was fixed, as part of a cover-up. Trying a long-shot strategy, he filed a motion with the court in January 1973 to suppress wiretap evidence crucial to the prosecution's case, hoping this would force the incriminating evidence out in the open. Although he won this legal point, it did not expose any cover-up.[60]

But Morgan's motion did open a conflict between him and the ACLU New York office, as his action was not clearly authorized by ACLU policy. Chairman Ed Ennis had regarded Morgan as a loose cannon ever since the Howard Levy trial, and now he moved to rein him in. Morgan had allies, however, among those who thought Nixon should be impeached. The Southern California ACLU called for Nixon's impeachment in 1971, over his conduct of the war. The ACLU board itself was deadlocked, twenty-three to twenty-three, on the California resolution.[61]

The Watergate cover-up began to unravel in March 1973, when convicted burglar James McCord told Judge John Sirica that there had been perjury in the trial. Morgan took another step on June 18, 1973, when he handed special prosecutor Archibald Cox a 106-page report entitled "Certain Aspects of the Watergate Affair." Three days later Morgan filed an ACLU motion to set aside the burglars' convictions on the grounds that they were "tainted by . . . perjured testimony." Ennis read about it in the *New York Times* and sent Morgan an "outraged protest" that the ACLU had not authorized the motion. He was only partly correct. Executive director Neier agreed with Morgan about Watergate and had quietly told him to proceed. Not sure that the ACLU Executive Committee or board would agree, however, Neier had tried to finesse the problem by not fully disclosing what Morgan was doing.[62]

In the end, Neier and Morgan were spared a confrontation by the rapidly unfolding scandal and the slow pace of ACLU procedures. The Executive Committee did not meet until July. By then, Judge Sirica had refused to accept Morgan's motion, leaving that issue moot, but presidential aide Alexander Butterfield had disclosed the secret White House taping system. By the time the ACLU board met in September, the overriding issue had become Nixon's refusal to turn over certain tapes to Congress and the special prosecutor. Watergate was now no longer a "third-rate burglary"; rather, it was a major constitutional crisis over the power of the president.

Calls for impeachment began to appear, with Representative Father Robert Drinan introducing a resolution on July 31; the old ACLU critic from the late 1950s was now a staunch ally and a member of its National Advisory Committee.[63] One by one, the ACLU affiliates added their voices, Southern California first, with Michigan and New York following suit. The NYCLU's executive director, Ira Glasser, framed the issue in terms of the fundamental constitutional principle of "limitations upon power." Nixon "has systematically sought to erode those limitations upon presidential power which define our rights." Nor was it just Nixon. The slow accretion of presidential power had begun decades before. In addition, there were specific violations of the law: surveillance of political groups and withholding sensitive information from the press. Nixon's claim of executive privilege, like national security, had no limit.[64]

Not everyone in the ACLU joined the rush to impeachment. For instance, the Ohio Civil Liberties Union felt that the ACLU had ignored a number of other civil liberties issues in Watergate. The harsh sentences that Judge Sirica gave the original seven Watergate defendants, together with his statement that he would "weigh" their cooperation "in appraising what sentence will finally be imposed," were blatantly coercive and probably violated due process standards. The televised Watergate hearings in the summer of 1973 bore an ominous resemblance to the old HUAC procedures—"unfriendly" witnesses had a guilty label hung on them. Ohio Civil Liberties Union Director Benson Wolman was deeply disturbed that the ACLU had not vigorously challenged these abuses: "I fear that we are not applying with equal fervor to the Watergate committee our traditional hostility to every aspect of witch hunting."[65]

Many critics were convinced that the ACLU had taken the final plunge into political partisanship,[66] seeing the impeachment campaign as simply an anti-Nixon move. Some remained unconvinced that Nixon had committed any impeachable offenses and that, even if he had, they were not a civil liberties matter. The board met on September 29 to debate his impeachment. In six hours of debate, the few remaining moderates vainly argued against an ACLU call for impeachment. Former Washington office director Larry Speiser argued that it should be left to the courts. David Isbell, always a voice of caution, said the ACLU should not delude itself into thinking it could bring about impeachment and that an acquittal in the Senate would leave Nixon even stronger than before. The board finally voted fifty-one to five for impeachment; the five dissidents subsequently abstained to make it officially unanimous.[67]

The staff wasted no time in acting. Neier and Glasser prepared a full-page ad to appear in the *New York Times*. Costing $12,500, it was a risky venture, but philanthropist Stewart Mott promised to cover any financial loss, and on Sunday, October 14, the ad appeared. In alarmist terms, it charged that "Richard Nixon has not left us in doubt. He means to function above the law. If he is allowed to continue, then the destruction of the Bill of Rights could follow." The ad asked readers to write their representatives in Congress, make a contribution to the ACLU, and join if not already a member. The response was overwhelming. Contributions and membership applications poured in. Across the country affiliates organized lobbying efforts. By December, several ads, costing $107,000, had raised $138,000. Over 25,000 new members joined in 1973 alone, driving the ACLU's membership to an all-time high of 275,000 (based on 205,000 paid memberships, of which 30 percent were married couples, by the ACLU's estimate).[68]

On October 20, Nixon sealed his own fate by firing special prosecutor Archibald Cox. The "Saturday Night Massacre" set off yet another firestorm of public protest. Impeachment became a respectable issue, and Nixon appointed a new special prosecutor. Discontent in the ACLU continued, however, with some dispute over exactly what the board had authorized. The resolution called on the House of Representatives to investigate whether there were sufficient grounds for articles of impeachment. Yet the *Times* ad clearly said it was "necessary to impeach President Nixon." Once again there were allegations that the staff had imposed its own views on official ACLU policy. Howard Besser, chair of the Ohio Civil Liberties Union, called the entire impeachment campaign "a drastic and uncalled-for departure from our general policy, one which is likely to haunt us in the future."[69]

The Watergate crisis headed for its denouement through 1974. Nixon refused to hand over crucial tapes to special prosecutor Leon Jaworski. When Jaworski sued, the question of the extent of presidential power reached the Supreme Court. The ACLU filed the only *amicus* brief in the case. Written by general counsel Norman Dorsen, it argued that "the fundamental issue raised in this case is whether the President, acting in his sole discretion, can disregard an obligation imposed on all other citizens to produce evidence demonstrably material to the trial of criminal charges of obstruction of justice in a federal court." In short, is the president of the United States, Dorsen asked, accountable to the rule of law? "There is no proposition more dangerous to the health of a constitutional democracy," Dorsen wrote, spelling out the central civil liberties issue in Watergate, "than the notion that an elected head of state is above the law and beyond the reach of judicial review."[70]

In a stunning, unanimous decision on July 24, the Supreme Court ordered Nixon to hand over the tapes, with even the conservative justices he had appointed voting against him. The Court rejected his argument that claims of executive privilege were immune to judicial review. It then held that "an absolute, unqualified [executive] privilege would "plainly conflict with the functions of the courts" in conducting criminal prosecutions. The president had to turn over the subpoenaed tapes; he was not above the law.[71] The tapes included the much-discussed "smoking gun" indicating Nixon's direct involvement in the Watergate cover-up. The Court's decision destroyed Nixon's last hopes. On July 27, the House Judiciary Committee approved the first article of impeachment. At 9:00 P.M. on August 8, Nixon announced his resignation. The Watergate crisis was over.

Aftermath: From Watergate to Contragate

Nixon was gone, but the national security issue remained. The next two years were a period of euphoria for civil libertarians, as the country seemed ready for real reforms in the area of national security. The 1973 War Powers Act reasserted congressional authority over war making. The sensational Church Committee investigation (1975–1976) exposed the long history of abuses by the FBI and the CIA and created a climate for reform. The ACLU established the Project on National Security and Civil Liberties, jointly sponsored by the Center for National Security Studies, with Mort Halperin as its director.

The optimism faded quickly. The political winds shifted in a conservative direction, and public concern about national security issues dissipated. The danger signals reached the ACLU almost immediately, although few read them correctly. In November 1974, only three months after Nixon's resignation, Neier reported an imminent financial crisis in the ACLU.[72] Many of the thousands of new ACLU members were single-issue (Watergate) people; most were not interested in the full range of civil liberties issues. The collapse of liberal energy, following Nixon's resignation and the United States' withdrawal from Vietnam, and a potent new conservative movement framed the ACLU's efforts over the next decade.

Controlling the Intelligence Agencies

Revelations of illegal activity by both the FBI and the CIA were one of the most important consequences of Watergate. In November 1974 Congress overrode President Gerald R. Ford's veto and created a right of access to intelligence agency files under the Freedom of Information Act (FOIA). FOIA became an institutionalized check on government power, and revelations of FBI and CIA misconduct poured forth. In 1981 the Center for National Security Studies listed seventeen books and eleven articles based on FOIA-obtained documents.

In early 1975 the Senate established a bipartisan, select committee to investigate the intelligence agencies. The Church Committee found a massive pattern of FBI spying on political groups, including wiretapping, burglaries, and the opening of mail. Under the COINTELPRO (Counter Intelligence Program), created in 1956, the bureau had disrupted dissident political groups. The most insidious episode was the attack on Dr. Martin Luther King, Jr., in which the FBI had created a tape recording of King's alleged sexual activities and mailed it to his wife. And the CIA, under Operation CHAOS, had spied on as many as seven thousand Americans in violation of its statutory charter.[73]

The Church Committee recommended statutory charters for both agencies to define and limit their powers: "Clear legal standards and effective oversight and controls are necessary to ensure that domestic intelligence activity does not itself undermine the democratic system it is intended to protect." The Senate promptly created the permanent Select Committee on Intelligence to oversee the CIA and the FBI. In February 1976 President Ford issued Executive Order 11905, restricting intelligence gathering by the CIA, and in March, Attorney General Edward Levi issued new guidelines limiting FBI investigations in domestic security cases.

The ACLU's Halperin, Jerry Berman, and John Shattuck offered a bill with additional controls over the FBI. The so-called Levi guidelines were an important step forward, but they were not enough. They did not cover criminal investigations but did maintain the executive branch's "inherent power" to conduct intelligence investigations. The ACLU proposed abolishing domestic political intelligence altogether, limiting intrusive FBI investigations to cases in which there was a reasonable suspicion of criminal activity and requiring judicial warrants for the use of informants and undercover agents. But the bill never received serious consideration, and efforts to control the CIA met a similar fate.[74]

It was a sobering lesson for the ACLU, as it discovered that the public was highly susceptible to media coverage of scandals. Watergate had provoked a surge of outrage, but the mood did not last, and public attention soon turned to other issues. Ten years later John Shattuck concluded that the lessons of Watergate were "all but forgotten as soon as the crisis of August 1974 was over."[75]

Controlling Police Spying

The ACLU was more successful in a new campaign to end spying by local police. In New York a group of black and antiwar groups filed a class action suit charging the police with infiltrating their ranks. Under a 1980 consent decree, the city agreed that only the police Public Security Section (PSS) could investigate political activity and only if it respected constitutionally guaranteed rights. Investigations required evidence of criminal activity and had to be terminated after thirty days unless written authorization was obtained. A new board, consisting of two deputy police commissioners and a civilian, would oversee the PSS.[76]

The settlement was sharply criticized by some left-wing groups, and the resulting controversy dramatized the dilemmas inherent in direct litigation. Most ACLU leaders agreed that direct representation afforded great opportunities. As Dorsen had argued earlier, it allowed ACLU lawyers to create the record at trial and raise issues that might otherwise be ignored. But it also put the ACLU in the same position that Bickel had found himself in the Pentagon Papers case: It had to think about winning the case, or at least about obtaining a reasonable settlement for the plaintiffs. It could not afford the luxury of the intellectual high ground that an *amicus* offered—a dilemma Glasser called the "dirty hands" problem. The settlement in the New York police-spying case was admittedly far from perfect, as it accepted the principle of the police's investigating political groups. But it was a decent settlement for the clients and an important precedent in controlling police spying.[77]

Far more creative was the outcome of the Seattle police-spying scandal. The Seattle police had intelligence files on an estimated 750 people, including prominent Republicans. The ACLU joined the National Lawyers Guild and the American Friends Service Committee in a coalition to attack the spying. Led by Kathleen Taylor, who later became the ACLU affiliate director, it won the enactment in 1979 of an extremely innovative ordinance. The law explicitly affirmed the constitutional right of citizens to engage in political, religious, and private sexual activity without police interference. That is, it restricted rather than outlawed police intelligence activity. The police could gather information on political, religious, or private sexual activity only with written authorization. Infiltration of any organization had to be authorized by the chief of police, and paid informants were prohibited from engaging in any criminal acts. Finally, disclosure of information was restricted to a few narrowly defined categories. Taylor's coalition sought criminal penalties for violating the law but had to accept civil penalties. The law's compliance mechanism authorized the city council to hire an auditor to review all police files (with a few enumerated exceptions). Thus the principle of accountability was established; for the first time anywhere, police investigations would be regularly scrutinized by an outsider.[78] Whether the ordinance achieved its objectives was not clear. As the Iran–*contra* scandal later revealed, a determined official could easily circumvent the formal controls. But despite this inherent limitation, the Seattle ordinance was a significant step forward.

End of the Vietnam–Watergate Era

The decade that began with the escalation of the Vietnam War and ended with Watergate left a lasting imprint on American society. The scars left by the war had still not healed fifteen years after the humiliating withdrawal of American troops from Vietnam. Amidst the lingering controversies, historians had difficulty putting this extraordinary period in perspective. Civil liberties had been changed irrevocably. The war not only produced an important new body of First Amendment law, but it also stripped away the veil surrounding a pattern of secret government: covert action abroad and political spying at home. The war was over, but the new issue of national security remained, raising difficult questions about the right of citizens to know what their government was doing and the power of Congress to control decisions committing the country to military action abroad.

Fourteen

The New Civil Liberties, 1965-1974

Enclaves and Victim Groups

"There are only two public institutions in the United States which steadfastly deny that the Bill of Rights applies to them," charged Ira Glasser—the military and the public schools. Six months later he found "four public institutions [that] have traditionally ignored the Bill of Rights: the military, the schools, mental 'hospitals,' and prisons."[1]

The rapid change in Glasser's thinking was an index of the explosive effect of the 1960s on civil liberties. He had just returned from the Howard Levy trial which exposed the archaic military justice system. Back at the NYCLU he threw himself into the issue of students' rights. Public school principals had unlimited authority to suspend students for wearing "improper" haircuts, conducting off-campus political activities, or challenging school procedures. Glasser and his NYCLU colleagues saw both the military and the public schools as "enclaves" of bureaucratic power untouched by the Bill of Rights. The NYCLU staff—Aryeh Neier, Ira Glasser, Burt Neuborne, Alan Levine, and Bruce Ennis—was a remarkable center of intellectual vitality in the late 1960s. Lunch at a nearby delicatessen was a floating seminar on constitutional law; one day the group sketched its "enclave theory" on a napkin. Its counterpart was the "victim groups" theory. Society was filled with groups systematically denied basic individual rights: women, the poor, homosexuals, and others. The ACLU's task, they argued, was to bring promises of the Bill of Rights to all of these previously neglected areas of American life. Fueled by the energy of the civil rights movement and the ground-breaking work of the Warren Court, Neier recalled, "Nothing seemed beyond the reach of litigation."[2]

The NYCLU staff were hardly the only ones thinking in these terms. The rights revolution reached across the country, to the schools, the new neighborhood law clinics, the new public-interest law centers, and the private foundations that supported many of these projects.[3] For example, the Southern California ACLU filed suit against oil-drilling permits off Santa Barbara, arguing that the public had the right to be free of a polluted environment.[4] In 1966, the Northern California affiliate began pressing due process issues in the welfare system, the mental health system, and the juvenile court.[5] The NYCLU activists developed perhaps the most comprehensive vision of civil liberties as a force for transforming American institutions; they represented the future of the ACLU. Neier and Glasser each eventually became the ACLU's executive director, and Ennis first and then Neuborne served as the ACLU's legal director.

The rights revolution was the longest-lasting legacy of the 1960s. Even long after the more exotic aspects of the "sixties" had faded, a new "rights consciousness" remained. Millions of ordinary people—students, prisoners, women, the poor, gays and lesbians, the handicapped, the mentally retarded, and others—discovered their own voices and demanded fair treatment and personal dignity. The empowerment of these previously silent groups was a political development of enormous significance, and the contribution of the ACLU was to shape these expectations into new principles of constitutional law. Nor was the rights revolution confined to victim groups. Most ordinary Americans had developed new expectations of personal freedom, generally expressed in terms of a right to privacy.

The Privacy Revolution

The idea of a right to privacy spread with astonishing speed in the early 1960s. Justice Louis Brandeis's 1928 dictum that "the right to be let alone [was] the most comprehensive of rights" had stimulated little response. In the late 1950s, however, a new concern about computers and the prospects of national data files on citizens provoked some of the first serious discussions of privacy. In a 1958 symposium, journalist Richard Rovere expressed the growing unease: "My behavior affects my neighbor in a hundred ways undreamed of a century ago . . . I may build a high fence, bolt the doors, draw the blinds and insist that my time to myself is mine alone, but his devices for intrusion are limitless."[6] As late as 1960, privacy was still discussed primarily as a Fourth Amendment search and seizure question.[7]

A constitutional right of privacy emerged out of the long fight over the Connecticut birth control law. Morris Ernst brought the first legal challenge in 1940, but the 1961 *Poe v. Ullman* case was the turning point. The ACLU *amicus* argued that prohibition of the sale and distribution of contraceptives violated the due process clause of the Fourteenth Amendment and restricted the free speech of ministers, inhibiting their ability to counsel on sexual matters.[8] The Court declined to rule on the merits of the law, but in a thirty-three-page dissent, conservative Justice John Marshall Harlan argued that the law was "an intolerable and unjustifiable invasion of privacy in the conduct of the most intimate concerns of an individual's personal life."[9] Privacy was no longer a question of search and seizure but a civil liberties issue that directly touched the lives of millions of middle- and upper-middle-class Americans.

The Connecticut law returned to the Court in 1965, when an activist civil libertarian majority was in command. In *Griswold,* Justice William O. Douglas found a constitutional right of privacy in what he termed the "penumbras" and "emanations" of the Bill of Rights: The First Amendment freedom of association; the Third Amendment prohibition on quartering soldiers; the Fourth Amendment protection against unreasonable searches and seizures; the Fifth Amendment protection against self-incrimination; and finally, the Ninth Amendment declaration that the people retained rights not spelled out in the Constitution.[10]

The sweeping assertion of a right to privacy in *Griswold* surprised even many in the ACLU. Law scholars hastily tried to assess its full impact. On one side *Griswold* gave constitutional affirmation to the rapidly rising expectation of privacy, and it laid the foundation for a constitutional attack on existing criminal abortion laws. At the same time, the decision provoked a powerful, although delayed, backlash. Legal scholars such as Robert Bork were deeply disturbed over what they saw as its shaky constitutional foundation. And the abortion rights movement, which it encouraged and ultimately sustained, led to a conservative political backlash that dominated American politics from the mid-1970s onward.[11]

Abortion Rights

"Abortion is the dread secret of our society,"[12] wrote Lawrence Lader, accurately describing public silence on the issue in the early 1960s. His pioneering 1966 book, *Abortion,* was turned down by twelve publishers. Under the impact of the sexual revolution, however, attitudes changed rapidly. The 1962 Sherri Finkbine case brought it to national attention. Afraid that her fetus was deformed because she had taken the drug Thalidomide (which had produced five thousand deformed children in West Germany and one thousand in England), she obtained permission for an abortion in Arizona, where state law permitted the operation only to save the life of the mother. Protests from religious groups and the local prosecutor forced the hospital to cancel the abortion, and so Finkbine flew to Sweden to have it performed. The publicity over her plight broke the silence on abortion. Women with unwanted pregnancies now loomed as victims of the archaic criminal abortion laws.[13]

Harriet Pilpel put the abortion issue on the ACLU's agenda at the 1964 Biennial Conference, attacking laws criminalizing both abortion and consensual adult homosexuality. They were "a dagger aimed at the heart of some of our most fundamental freedoms." Pilpel was a protégé of Morris Ernst and had inherited both his concern with sexual freedom and his dual role as general counsel for both the ACLU and Planned Parenthood. Framing the issue in constitutional terms, she argued that it was a deprivation of liberty for the state to "compel a husband and wife to have a baby when the medical testimony is that the baby may well be deformed."[14]

Many ACLU members were hesitant about embracing the abortion rights issue, as the legal foundation was uncertain, with *Griswold* still a year away in 1964. Others thought it was outside the scope of the ACLU's agenda. Some feared it would offend valuable allies. But events quickly swept aside these reservations. Even before *Griswold,* NYCLU Aryeh Neier and Pilpel helped organize the first campaign to repeal the New York abortion law. The Association for the Study of Abortion was in 1965 a group of genuine radicals—much like the birth control radicals fifty years earlier. They introduced the first abortion reform bill in New York in 1966.[15] Rev. Howard Moody's Clergy Consultation Service on Abortion had the air of the southern civil rights movement, operating under the constant threat of prosecution.

The ACLU board took up the issue in 1967. Support for abortion rights had grown considerably in three years, and after a long debate, the ACLU affirmed "the right of a woman to have an abortion, and the right of a physician to perform, or refuse to perform, an abortion, without the threat of criminal sanctions." ACLU policy went further than did that of any other national group; both the year-old National Organization for Women (NOW) and Planned Parenthood were deeply divided over whether to call for repeal of the abortion laws. The ACLU policy left several troubling questions unanswered. Was the right to an abortion completely unlimited? "Last minute" abortions raised the specter of infanticide. In January 1968 the ACLU revised its policy to support the right to an abortion "prior to the viability of the fetus."[16]

Meanwhile, seventeen states revised their abortion laws between 1967 and 1971. Colorado acted first, allowing abortions to be performed in order to protect the physical or mental health of the mother. North Carolina and California followed. The abortion rights movement was primarily a legislative effort, drawing on the network of civil rights and antiwar groups and sharing their moral fervor. Opponents of abortion were caught off guard and were hardly organized. But public opinion was changing quickly: A 1968 Gallup Poll found that 15 percent of Americans favored liberalizing abortion laws; by November 1969, 40 percent did; and by 1972, 64 percent did.[17]

Events in New York prefigured the abortion rights struggle of the next twenty years, as reformers mobilized a broad-based coalition and the anti-abortion forces, recovering quickly, fought back and attacked implementation of the New York law, thereby forcing state health officials to impose a series of crippling requirements. Abortion rights forces threatened to ignore them and, after a year's struggle, won the right to operate low-cost abortion clinics.[18]

Abortion Rights in the Courts

The abortion rights activists also attacked the existing laws in the courts. The first cases involved the prosecution of doctors who performed abortions. In

California, when Dr. Leon Belous was convicted of referring a patient to an abortionist, the Southern California ACLU assisted his defense, and the state supreme court eventually overturned his conviction on the grounds that the state law was unconstitutional.[19] In an even more important case, Dr. Milan Vuitch was arrested in Washington, D.C., for performing an abortion, when police entered his office while a patient was lying on the table. The District's law permitted abortions only to preserve a woman's life, but Vuitch claimed that only he, as a physician, could make that judgment. With the ACLU's Norman Dorsen making the oral argument, *Vuitch* was the first abortion case to appear before the Supreme Court. The Court's 1971 decision in *Vuitch* enlarged the concept of health to include psychological well-being and thus empowered doctors to judge when abortions were necessary.[20]

By the time *Vuitch* was settled, seventeen other abortion rights cases were headed for the Court. The lead case involved a Texas woman known pseudonymously as Jane Roe. Joining other abortion rights groups, the ACLU mobilized its top legal talent to work on the briefs.

Roe v. Wade *and Its Consequences*

It was destined to become one of the most controversial decisions in the history of the Supreme Court, rivaling *Dred Scott* and *Brown v. Board of Education*. *Roe v. Wade* swept aside existing criminal abortion laws, with Justice Harry Blackmun holding that the right to privacy included a woman's right to an abortion in consultation with her physician. This right was not absolute, however, and Blackmun divided the term of pregnancy into three trimesters. The interest of the state in protecting potential life increased as the pregnancy advanced. Sorting his way through the complex moral and medical considerations, Blackmun rejected the antiabortion argument that the fetus was a person entitled to protection of the Fourteenth Amendment.[21]

Blackmun's opinion went even further than did ACLU policy in affirming a right to abortion after viability, and *Roe* became the focal point of a new politics of morality over the next two decades. For many, the decision signified the collapse of traditional values. Conservatives were more convinced than ever that the Supreme Court was engaged in rootless, "results-oriented" lawmaking, even though the *Roe* decision was rendered by the conservative Burger Court.

A month after the decision, Neier congratulated ACLU board member Marjorie Pitts Hames, who had argued the companion *Doe v. Bolton* case, but urged "continued vigilance to assure implementation" of abortion rights. It was the understatement of the decade. *Roe* hardly brought the abortion rights movement to "a swift and satisfactory end," as he suggested: If anything, it intensified the battle.[22] The politics of abortion rights changed overnight. After this smashing court victory, the abortion rights legislative movement evaporated, and abortion opponents filled the void with a powerful political movement of their own. By 1980 they had enacted a number of federal and state laws restricting access to abortions and had claimed credit for defeating a number of prominent liberal legislators.[23] To defend *Roe,* therefore, the ACLU created the Reproductive Freedom Project in 1974.[24]

The Supreme Court delivered the coup de grâce for the old laws restricting birth control in 1972 when it struck down a Massachusetts law limiting the distribution of contraceptives to married couples by licensed physicians. Reproductive rights activist Bill Baird was arrested at Boston University for publicly distributing them to unmarried women students. In the first of two important cases involving Baird, the Supreme Court struck down the law under the equal protection clause: The right of privacy extended to married and unmarried alike.[25] Baird managed to offend just about everyone in the abortion rights movement—the ACLU, NOW, and Planned Parenthood—with his self-righteous posturing, but no one could question his pioneering efforts. He won a second landmark Supreme Court case in 1979 upholding the right of an unmarried minor to obtain an abortion without parental consent. *Bellotti v. Baird* affirmed and extended the earlier *Danforth* decision striking down a more restrictive Missouri law.[26]

Women's Rights

The feminist movement, after fading away in the 1950s, reappeared in the mid-1960s, its primary goal being the enactment of an equal rights amendment (ERA) to the U.S. Constitution. The publication of Betty Friedan's *The Feminine Mystique* in 1963 revitalized the movement, and in 1966, Friedan helped organize the National Organization for Women (NOW). The southern civil rights movement also played an extremely important role in raising the consciousness of women who chafed at being relegated to a subordinate role in the movement.

The ACLU did an about-face on the ERA, having led the opposition to it since the 1940s and even restating its position as late as 1963.[27] In 1970 ACLU board members Dorothy Kenyon and Pauli Murray argued that "there comes a time when you cannot wait any longer, when you must find new tools for the tools that have failed you." They called on the ACLU to abandon its emphasis on the Fourteenth Amendment as the best hope for women's rights and to endorse the ERA.[28] The organization did so by an overwhelming majority and the next year defined women's rights as its "top priority," creating the Women's Rights Project.[29]

The key figure in the ACLU's campaign was law professor Ruth Bader Ginsburg, who, as one of three general counsels, shaped the ACLU brief in *Reed v. Reed,* the breakthrough women's rights case in the Supreme Court. *Reed* challenged the automatic preference for men over women as administrators of estates, with Ginsburg contending that this violated the equal protection clause of the Fourteenth Amendment. The Court, however, did not go as far as the ACLU and women's groups wanted, holding that gender was not a "suspect classification" demanding the same "strict scrutiny" by the courts as race did.[30]

But *Reed* opened the way for a systematic program of women's rights litigation. Ginsburg followed it up with *Frontiero v. Richardson,* in which the Court ended a U.S. military policy that gave the husbands of servicewomen an automatic dependency, whereas the wives of servicemen had to meet a dependency test.[31] In a 1975 ACLU case, *Taylor v. Louisiana,* the Court ruled that a Louisiana law exempting women from juries violated a woman's Sixth Amendment right to a jury representative of the community. Kenyon and Murray had prepared a brief in *White v. Crook* ten years earlier, but Mississippi did not appeal the case to the Supreme Court.[32]

The ACLU Women's Rights Project quickly dominated the field, entering far more cases than any of the women's rights organizations. By 1974 the project and the ACLU affiliates had over three hundred sex discrimination cases. Between 1969 and 1980, the ACLU participated in 66 percent of the gender discrimination cases decided by the Supreme Court. This was more than twice as many as NOW, and the disparity was even greater in terms of direct representation. Two political scientists labeled the ACLU " 'the' representative of women before the Court."[33] The Women's Rights Project shared the same strengths as other ACLU special projects: The network of affiliates allowed them to develop cases that might otherwise not reach the courts, and the ACLU's prestige secured foundation grants that supported a cadre of full-time attorneys.[34]

The Affirmative Action Controversy

When the ACLU endorsed the ERA, there were only five women on the sixty-six-member ACLU board; the ACLU was a male bastion, as were other major organizations. But the rise of the women's movement challenged this dominance. Some of the older board members, stuffy and pompous when dealing with any of their colleagues, were even more condescending to the women members. Phil Hirschkop, who attend meetings in overalls, found the long-winded orations by "the law professors" insufferable. Dorothy Kenyon, who had been with the ACLU since the late 1930s, confessed to one of the younger women members that she had always adopted stereotypically "feminine" behavior in order to ingratiate herself.[35]

The concept of affirmative action proved to be a divisive issue both in national politics and within the ACLU. The ACLU endorsed in principle the use of employment goals and timetables to remedy discrimination against women and racial minorities. The national civil rights coalition later came apart over this issue in the contentious *Bakke* case. The ACLU sided with racial minority groups in its *amicus* brief, endorsing a racial quota for the University of California medical school, whereas all of the Jewish groups opposed it. Neoconservatives, disaffected from the ACLU on many other issues as well, were especially upset with the ACLU's stand on affirmative action.[36] They argued that the use of a racial classification, for whatever purpose, represented an unconstitutional form of reverse discrimination.[37]

Implementing affirmative action within the ACLU led to even more controversy. An ACLU women's caucus appeared in 1970 and won adoption of an official ACLU affirmative action plan in 1977. By then, there were nearly thirty women on the now eighty-member board. The plan set goals of 50 percent representation for women and 20 percent for racial minorities in paid staff positions and on the board itself. By the 1980s some of the most acrimonious disputes within the organization involved appointments to top staff positions and the question of whether the ACLU was complying with its own policy.[38]

Legal Assault on the Enclaves

The Rights of Students

Ira Glasser's main assignment as the new NYCLU associate director in 1967 was to become an expert on students' rights, a mission characteristic of Aryeh Neier's strategy: Identify a problem and frame it in civil liberties terms. Glasser quickly found that the New York City schools were a bastion of bureaucratic arrogance, racism, and hostility to the new youth counterculture. Thus the ACLU's approach to a solution centered on procedural due process in disciplinary actions, the First Amendment right to political activity in and out of school, and freedom of personal expression, including the right to wear long hair.[39]

Hair was a volatile political and cultural issue in the 1960s. Students, parents, and school authorities alike saw it as a symbol of rebellion, and ACLU affiliates handled hundreds of hair-related cases. The very first case taken by the new Nebraska affiliate in 1966 involved a student suspended for wearing his hair long. The Philadelphia ACLU defended fifteen-year-old David Harris, suspended by Haverford Junior High School because his Prince Valiant hairstyle "would tend to be a threat against reasonable discipline."[40]

In New York, the most dramatic students' rights case arose from the expulsion of 670 mostly black and Hispanic students from Franklin K. Lane High School in 1969. School officials sent a letter informing the students' parents that they had a week to challenge the action but then expelled the students three days later anyway. Glasser could not resist pointing out that the same school officials who had demanded due process for themselves in the teachers' strike the year before had just perpetrated "the single most stunning denial of due process ever to have occurred in the New York City school system." He cited the cases of Marcine Chestnut and Oscar Gonzalus, students in good academic standing who had simply missed classes because of the flu. Neither had had a chance to challenge their expulsion. The High School Principals Association attacked the NYCLU as "professional agitators."[41] To NYCLU activists who had been in the South, the charge sounded familiar. Federal judge Jack B. Weinstein (a former NYCLU cooperating attorney) ordered all 670 students reinstated on the grounds that their due process rights had been violated. The New York legislature then passed a new law guaranteeing notice, hearings, a right to counsel, confrontation of witnesses, and a right to appeal for students suspended for more than five days. The students, in short, gained all the rights enjoyed by the most dangerous criminal suspects.[42]

The Supreme Court, meanwhile, had begun to create a body of constitutional law on the rights of students. In the 1969 *Tinker* decision, Justice Abe Fortas embraced the enclave theory, writing that "in our system, state operated schools may not be enclaves of totalitarianism."[43] In 1975 the Court took up the question of students' due process rights in *Goss v. Lopez,* which arose out of racial unrest at three schools in Columbus, Ohio, in the spring of 1971. With the ACLU filing an *amicus* brief in support of the NAACP's suit, the Court established minimal due process rights for public school students. It held that even in the case of a temporary suspension (ten days or less), students had a right to oral or written notice of the charges, an explanation of the evidence against them, and an opportunity to rebut the charges. "Total exclusions from the educational process for more than a trivial period," the Court held, "is a serious event in the life of the suspended child." Further, students had a "legitimate entitlement to a public education as a property interest which is protected by the Due Process Clause."[44]

In the aftermath of *Goss,* twelve states passed legislation conforming to the Court's mandate or extending due process protections even further. The law of students' rights, however, seemed to stall at that point. Students had won an important degree of due process protection, but some skeptics wondered whether it amounted to anything more than "empty proceduralism." ACLU lawyers replied that as in the case of the police and the prisons, the introduction of constitutional principles in these previously neglected areas was a worthy achievement.[45] The neoconservatives, on the other hand, argued that Court rulings inhibited school discipline and encouraged disruptive behavior. By the late 1960s, school officials began to sound very much like police chiefs earlier in the decade, blaming all their problems on the Supreme Court.[46]

As in every other area of the rights revolution, sustained litigation by the ACLU and other advocacy groups reshaped the law. In January 1975 a new law reporter, *The School Student and the Courts,* appeared. Reporters also appeared in the areas of selective service law, mental health law, prisoners' rights, and women's rights. The creation of a reporter was an important index of social change, indicating that there was now a substantial body of law on a new subject. And behind the growing court opinions stood a new "rights consciousness" on the part of judges, the lawyers, plaintiffs, and millions of other Americans. This consciousness was the enduring monument to the creative legal work by the ACLU.

The Dossier Society: Student and Other Records

The students' rights movement opened up the question of access to student records. Often filled with derogatory comments by teachers and administrators, such records were routintely released to prospective employers but were withheld from students and their parents. Neier cited one instance in which a teacher described a student as "A real sickie . . . Have fun!"[47] The problem of secret dossiers was not confined to the schools: "Raw" FBI files traditionally contained wild allegations and were selectively leaked by the bureau, and credit bureaus collected unverified derogatory information of peoples' private lives. Neier warned of a growing "Dossier Society," and rising public concern led to a wave of remedial legislation. In 1974 Congress passed the Buckley amendment, guaranteeing parents and students access to "any and all" records and allowing them to challenge any derogatory information. New York Senator James Buckley was a prominent conservative, and accordingly the law indicated the extent to which privacy had strong support among conservatives.[48]

Other dossier systems came under attack. Although the computer was a convenient symbol, Neier argued that it was "not the villain," pointing out that the two largest systems, the FBI and retail credit files, both were manually operated.[49] The real problem was the data collection itself: that agencies kept such information in the first place, that much of it was unverified gossip, and that individuals had no access to their files.[50]

The 1970 Fair Credit Reporting Act of 1970 required private credit bureaus to disclose to an individual all the information contained in their files. The 1974 federal Privacy Act restricted the disclosure of information about an individual in federal government files to a few specific circumstances. Several states enacted their own fair credit and privacy laws.[51]

Given the considerable public support for the general principle of privacy, the ACLU's primary task became balancing it against other civil liberties principles. Access to criminal records presented a difficult problem. Holding police and other agencies accountable required detailed information about their activities (such as arrest patterns). Restricting access undercut accountability and threatened freedom of the press as well. By the same token, some criminal defendants' efforts to close court proceedings on privacy grounds violated the Sixth Amendment guarantee of public trials. Indeed, the 1970 Bank Secrecy Act could be more accurately described as a bank records disclosure law, as it gave federal authorities access to a broad range of individual financial records.[52]

The right to privacy was in a constant—and some said losing—race with technology. Ever-more sophisticated listening devices facilitated eavesdropping by police and private investigators. Powerful computers not only enhanced the capacity of data banks but made possible the sharing of information among different agencies. By the end of the 1980s the ACLU's Washington, D.C., office had scored some significant victories in the area of privacy. Although it could not persuade Congress to outlaw the "computer matching" of files in different federal agencies, it did secure some important procedural protections in such matching. The ACLU's greatest worry was that surveillance had become such a pervasive aspect of contemporary society—electronic detectors at airports, frisks at rock concerts (even Amnesty International frisked the audience at its 1988 benefit concerts)—that it threatened to legitimize all government claims of a right to intrude on privacy without probable cause. The expectation of privacy was, simultaneously, the most widely accepted civil liberties principle and the most systematically threatened.

Rights of the Mentally Retarded and Mentally Ill

The issue of the rights of the mentally ill was the first major ACLU project under the enclave theory. In 1968, while directing the NYCLU, Neier created the Mental Health Law Project after receiving an unexpected $500,000 bequest, and named Bruce Ennis as the director. Ennis was another in a long line of ACLU attorneys who had left corporate law for the exciting and often ground-breaking field of civil liberties law. Indeed, Ennis said he "got tired of saving millions of dollars for people I'd never met."[53]

The ACLU's position on mental health law evolved quickly under the impact of the 1960s rights consciousness. Roger Baldwin had taken an interest in the due process aspects of mental health commitment procedures in the 1940s. The ACLU had established the Committee on the Rights of the Mentally Ill in 1945 and had drafted a model commitment statute.[54] In 1945 the ACLU also opposed, on grounds of "medical liberty," laws requiring prostitutes to undergo compulsory health examinations and/or vaccinations.[55] The political and legal climate changed quickly by the 1960s. The ACLU was prodded by radical psychiatrist Thomas Szasz who challenged the whole concept of mental illness, believing it to be a "myth." Though not going as far as Szasz urged, the ACLU did oppose involuntary commitments except when the individual was clearly a danger to himself or herself or society. Even then, it pressed for more formal hearings to determine this dangerousness.[56]

Ennis's project was part of a broad assault on coercive institutions in American society that included the proposal of such theories as the "right to treatment." The ACLU was particularly concerned about institutionalization as a way to control people who were different or merely troublesome (Ennis estimated that 60 percent of all mental health patients were over the age of sixty).[57] To wit, the ACLU's most important Supreme Court case involved Kenneth Donaldson, who had been confined in the Florida State Hospital for fifteen years. He was not dangerous and had received no medical treatment. In 1975 the Supreme Court ordered Donaldson released and awarded him $20,000 in damages, establishing the principle that nondangerous persons could not be confined against their will.[58]

An even more sensational case involved the New York state school for the retarded at Willowbrook. Broadcast journalist Geraldo Rivera became a national celebrity through his surprise visit to Willowbrook on January 6, 1972. In ten minutes, he recorded shocking pictures of retarded children, many of them naked and on the floor, lying in their own feces. Ennis joined the suit on behalf of the 5,400 residents, and the ensuing "Willowbrook Wars" dramatized both the opportunities and limits of litigation designed to reform institutions. The case dragged on for nearly fifteen years. The initial

1975 consent decree ordering the state to improve conditions (such as hiring eighty-five additional nurses) came relatively easily, but as Al Bronstein was discovering as director of the prisoners' rights project, securing compliance with the order was an enormous task. Administrators dragged their feet, while at the same time the legislature balked at providing the necessary funds.[59]

Litigation achieved at least one notable result: The population of Willowbrook dropped from 5,400 to 1,500 by 1981. The deinstitutionalization of hospitals for the mentally retarded and the mentally ill had become a national movement. It had begun in the early 1960s, long before the concerted ACLU attack, and was motivated by cost-saving considerations and the discovery of psychotropic drugs. By the 1980s a backlash had set in, with critics blaming deinstitutionalization for the problem of homelessness. In one of his last speeches in late 1988, President Ronald Reagan specifically blamed the ACLU for creating the homeless. The ACLU thereupon replied that homelessness was a product of the economic conditions of the 1980s and that, as a result of its litigation, tens of thousands of confined people had actually been spared harm.[60]

Prisoners' Rights Movement

Prisons were the ultimate enclave, not only "out of sight and out of mind," but also beyond the purview of the courts. Until the early 1960s the courts took a hands-off attitude, accepting the idea that prisoners had suffered a "civil death."[61] The campaign for prisoners' rights was another outgrowth of the civil rights movement. In the late 1950s the ACLU took several cases involving black inmates who were Muslims. Wardens, terrified by black assertiveness, had banned reading the Koran and other religious practices. The ACLU defended the prisoners on free speech and religious freedom grounds.[62]

These cases established the principle that the Constitution also applied to prisoners and laid the foundation for more comprehensive challenges to prison conditions in later years. In 1968, Chuck Morgan won the Supreme Court case desegregating the Alabama prison system,[63] and in 1969 Buffalo, New York, law professor Herman Schwartz began representing prisoners in the state penitentiary at Attica. He approached Neier at the NYCLU, who eagerly adopted Schwartz's work as an affiliate project.[64] Meanwhile, in northern Virginia, LSCRRC (Law Students Civil Rights Research Council) founder Phil Hirschkop, now in private practice, began representing a few inmates. Word quickly spread in the prisons, and he was suddenly flooded with letters from inmates. "We were running a mom and pop operation in my living room," Hirschkop recalled.[65]

Hirschkop is credited with winning in 1971 the first significant case (*Landman v. Royster*) challenging a broad range of prison conditions. The case began when Hirschkop received a letter that was smuggled out of the state penitentiary describing the brutal conditions there: The prison was locked down after an inmate strike; all communication with the outside, including legal visits, was banned; inmates were confined in cells for weeks, even during

120-degree weather, and if they complained, they were teargassed in their cells; and jailhouse lawyer Robert Landman had been given 266 days in solitary for his complaint.[66] Hirschkop had to get a court order allowing him to visit the prison. Along with Schwartz he began to realize that the problems they faced extended far beyond discrete violations of individual rights. That is, the denial of civil liberties was systemic, and so any attempts at meaningful reform had to address the prison as an institution. Hirschkop coauthored the first law review article, arguing that prison life itself was unconstitutional. In it he pointed to due process violations in disciplinary proceedings, cruel and unusual punishment (often in the form of extended sentences to solitary confinement), denial of First Amendment rights to communicate with the outside world, discrimination against minorities, and the lack of minimal standards of food, sanitation, and medical care.[67]

By 1972, prison litigation was exploding across the country, and the ACLU consolidated Schwartz's and Hirschkop's work into the National Prison Project, directed by Al Bronstein.[68] The ACLU organized the first national conference of prisoners' rights lawyers, and the first law casebook appeared in 1973.[69] The key case was a challenge to conditions in the Alabama prison sytem in which Judge Frank Johnson condemned the prison's "rampant violence and jungle atmosphere." Johnson ordered sweeping changes throughout the Alabama prisons, encouraging the hope that the federal courts would become the primary instrument for bringing about even more fundamental changes in the prisons.[70]

A map in Al Bronstein's office offers a graphic testimony to the impact of the National Prison Project. Pins mark project suits in forty-five states; he had challenged the entire prison system in ten states and closed the state penitentiary in Vermont. A familiar figure in prisons across the country, Bronstein developed a curious love/hate relationship with many officials. Guards at the Rhode Island prison thanked him for making it a safer place to work and informally named the new fire escape, built as a result of the ACLU suit, after him. Some prison officials welcomed, if not invited, Prison Project suits, discovering that it was their best hope for getting needed money from their state legislatures. As in the area of policing, litigation spurred other reforms, including an accreditation movement for correctional facilities.[71]

But once the drama of the breakthrough suits passed, Bronstein's project faced the difficult task of implementation. This was difficult, time-consuming (often lasting many years), and unglamorous. A significant body of prisoners' rights law had developed by the mid-1970s, but prison life remained dangerous and debilitating in many institutions. The most serious problem was the extraordinary boom in prison populations in the 1980s. Most prison project suits challenged prison overcrowding, but Bronstein confessed that gains were often offset by subsequent increases.

Neoconservative critics blamed prisoners' rights litigation—and the ACLU in particular—for creating new problems in the prisons. Litigation, they charged, undermined the authority of prison officials and led to an increase in violence. There was no question that by the late 1970s, the prisons in the largest states were polarized along racial lines and often controlled by gangs.

Critics cited the case of Texas, where a serious increase in violence followed a sweeping court order on prisoners' rights. Bronstein replied that less crowding reduced prison violence by creating a more habitable environment. But Texas was a special case: The court order had created a condition of anarchy, in the sense of no law, as the prisons made the transition from one system of rule to another. Radical prison reformers, who wanted to abolish imprisonment altogether, criticized the ACLU for legitimizing prisons by eliminating the barbaric conditions. The organization replied that as long as prisons existed, the ACLU had an obligation to see that they were subject to the rule of law.

The complex work of litigating prison conditions—documenting existing conditions, pursuing implementation—required a large full-time staff. The National Prison Project was sustained by grants from the Edna McConnell Clark Foundation, as general ACLU revenues could not sustain Bronstein's project, and no other foundations seemed interested. The ACLU had set out to bring the rule of law to institutions such as the prisons. Although it achieved much, creating a new body of law, the task proved to be far more daunting than anyone had imagined. A prison was not changed by a simple lawsuit but required a sustained and expensive effort. Nor was this just a problem for the ACLU. It was a general problem for society and the legal system: How could the now-established principles of law be made a living reality?

Gay Rights

Homosexuals were another "victim group" added to the ACLU's new agenda. Harriet Pilpel raised the issue of gay rights in the ACLU in 1964, along with abortion rights. Seven years before, the ACLU had concluded that it was "not within the province of the Union to evaluate the social validity of laws" criminalizing homosexuality. It denounced police entrapment of homosexuals but saw this as a due process question. It also opposed proposals for the compulsory registration of homosexuals. Yet it conceded that homosexuality was a valid risk factor in determining security clearances.[72]

In the atmosphere of rising rights consciousness, however, the issue looked entirely different in 1964. Pilpel cited the pattern of arbitrary and discriminatory law enforcement, concluding that the prohibition of private consensual sex "inevitably involves violations of . . . privacy—of every kind." Although gay rights were an even more controversial issue than abortion was, the ACLU had "never been afraid to take stands in favor of unpopular causes. We consistently defend the rights of Communists and Nazis." The ACLU should not shrink from "attacking repressive laws and practices in the field of sex."[73]

The ACLU formally endorsed the principle of gay rights in 1966 and, in 1973, created the Sexual Privacy Project to fight discrimination against homosexuals. When the AIDS (acquired immune deficiency syndrome) crisis in the

1980s brought new forms of discrimination, the organization's Nan Hunter moved over from the Reproductive Freedom Project to head the Gay and Lesbian Rights Project, involving the ACLU in every major AIDS-related discrimination case.[74]

The Rights of the Poor

From the vantage point of the back roads of Mississippi and the ghetto storefront offices, the Bill of Rights looked very different to the well-educated ACLU lawyers and volunteers. The glittering promises of free speech, due process, and equal protection they had studied in college and law school had little practical meaning for the ordinary lives of the people they met. The experience set them thinking about the scope of civil liberties. Did the poor have rights? One line of thinking pursued the "enclave theory" and raised due process and equal protection issues in the operations of social welfare bureaucracies. Another raised a more fundamental question of whether poverty itself was a civil liberties issue. Was there a constitutional right to the necessities of life, to food, shelter, and a job?[75]

The development of a substantial body of poverty law was another product of concern about the poor in the 1960s. Much of the important work was done by lawyers associated with the war on poverty or private advocacy litigation groups.[76] The ACLU made its greatest contributions at the Supreme Court in the areas of due process and equal protection. Martin Garbus, director of the Roger Baldwin Foundation, won *King v. Smith,* which invalidated the traditional "man in the house" rule that denied Aid for Dependent Children (AFDC) benefits to children whose mother was living with someone to whom she was not married. The decision made AFDC benefits available to an estimated 500,000 previously ineligible children across the country.[77] In 1965 Norman Dorsen's Hays Program at New York University sponsored an early symposium on poverty and civil liberties, in conjunction with the Office of Economic Opportunity (OEO). Dorsen then argued and won *Levy v. Louisiana* which overturned a state law denying children the right to bring a wrongful death action on behalf of their mother because they were illegitimate.[78]

Due process and equal protection issues fit comfortably into the ACLU's larger civil liberties program. The activists first raised the economic rights issue at the 1966 ACLU Biennial Conference, with a resolution calling for the elimination of the current welfare system. It was rejected by a vote of thirty-six to forty-nine. But two years later, the complexion of ACLU membership had changed significantly under the impact of the Vietnam War, four straight summers of urban riots, and the recent assassinations of Martin Luther King, Jr., and Robert Kennedy. A mood of national emergency was in the air at the Biennial. The New York Civil Liberties Union had just called for a guaranteed annual income, and the Biennial adopted a similar proposal. Ironically, it was discussed in terms of a constitutional "right to life," the slogan appropriated by the antiabortion movement only a few years later. The board, however, rejected the resolution.[79]

The economic rights issue provided a glimpse into the ACLU's complex policymaking procedure. A Biennial resolution automatically became official ACLU policy unless the board rejected it within eighteen months. If the board did reject it, the resolution was submitted to a referendum, with the members of the affiliate boards of directors as the electorate. The Biennial had been created in the 1950s as a forum for lay member participation in the face of a self-perpetuating, New York–based board, and it was the principal forum for the more activist ACLU members. After the board itself was restructured to give the affiliates representation, the differences between the board and the membership lessened. Nonetheless, the Biennial remained the focal point of the more activist members. Through the 1970s and 1980s they repeatedly passed resolutions on economic rights and the civil liberties aspects of nuclear war, which the board and the electorate rejected.[80]

Moderates argued that an ACLU policy asserting a right to an income or shelter would take the ACLU into the realm of social and economic policy; the Constitution provided no guarantees in this area. The ACLU already had its hands full with traditional First Amendment, due process, and equal protection issues and could best serve poor people by fighting those issues. The activists replied that the ACLU was bound by no fixed agenda. As many of them put it, the scope of civil liberties is what we say it ought to be, not what the Supreme Court says it is at this moment. True, the Bill of Rights did not mention economic rights, but the word *privacy* did not appear either, and the ACLU was vigorously pursuing privacy rights. The ACLU had always taken an expansive view of the meaning of civil liberties. The "liberty" clause of the Fourteenth Amendment provided a sufficient constitutional anchor. Most important, the activists contended, was the fact that freedom of speech and press meant nothing to someone who had nothing to eat and no place to sleep. Were civil liberties simply playthings for the middle class and the rich? How could anyone claim that the poorest of the nation's poor were free?[81]

The debate went on for twenty years, with each side wrapping itself in the mantle of the Bill of Rights and posing as the guardian of the ACLU's historic mission. There was no definitive answer to the question, any more than there was a definitive answer to the question of what "free speech" or "due process" meant. The ACLU had gone into new and controversial areas before, however, raising issues that no one had thought were civil liberties concerns. The economic rights issue was one of the frontier issues of the 1970s and 1980s.

The New ACLU and Its Critics

The Advent of Aryeh Neier

Aryeh Neier's appointment in 1970 as the ACLU's executive director marked the advent of the "new" ACLU. Neier consolidated what had been developing over the past five years: the new civil liberties issues, direct legal representation, and grant-funded special projects. He became director in a virtual coup by his fellow directors of the large affiliates. He and Eason Monroe of Southern California, Jay Miller of Illinois, and Emil Mazey of Michigan (known as "the Barons") were becoming increasingly dissatisfied with Jack Pemberton's leadership. By temperament Pemberton was not an administrator and was overwhelmed by the problems created by the ACLU's growth. He yearned to practice law (he was the only lawyer ever to serve as the ACLU's executive director) and in 1967 jumped at the chance to try the Dale Noyd CO case. Neier was appalled that he would drop his administrative responsibilities for a trial in Clovis, New Mexico. As Pemberton lost his grip on the organization, associate director Alan Reitman, who eventually served the ACLU for 40 years, moved into the void to keep the ACLU's administrative machinery operating.[82]

The fate of the Roger Baldwin Foundation dramatized the disarray in the national office. Despite the evident success of the NAACP Legal Defense Fund, the ACLU did not create a tax-deductible litigation arm until the mid-1960s. The traditional system of volunteer cooperating attorneys seemed to work well enough. Neier had proposed creating a foundation in 1964, but Pemberton was slow to get it incorporated. Neier already had his own foundation at the NYCLU in 1968 when a $500,000 bequest arrived. With it, he assembled a legal staff that dwarfed the ACLU's staff upstairs.[83] Furthermore, the ACLU's Roger Baldwin Foundation had problems once it began. Director Martin Garbus was a brilliant civil liberties lawyer (winning the *Smith v. King* case) but not an effective administrator. And he did not pursue foundation grants outside his own areas of interest.

Unhappy and beset by family problems, Pemberton announced that he would retire in 1972, after straightening out the ACLU's administrative problems. Instead, the Barons and the executive committee forced him out immediately. It was a sad ending for the career of the man who had played a pivotal role in developing the ACLU as a national organization, putting the ACLU in the forefront of the civil rights movement, and ending the ACLU's lingering anti-Communism.[84]

Eason Monroe, director of the Southern California ACLU, wanted to succeed Pemberton and, to enhance his chances, volunteered to codirect the ACLU's fiftieth anniversary celebration in 1970. The result was a disaster all around. Spending half of his time in New York, Monroe thus neglected his affiliate, which ran into serious financial difficulties. The ACLU anniversary celebration was a failure and actually lost money. Monroe then resigned his affiliate position and returned to his teaching position at San Francisco State University, which he had just won back because of a suit over the old loyalty oath.[85]

Creating the New ACLU

Neier wasted no time transforming the ACLU. On his first day as executive director he informed the staff that many of them would be gone by the end of next week—and kept his word. A month later he organized an elaborate presentation for the major foundations: Carnegie, Field, Kaplan, the Rockefeller Brothers, Stern, and Norman (Ford received a separate presentation). ACLU lawyers and staff spent the day proposing eleven separate projects, with combined budgets of $2.478 million. All were in the forefront of the rights revolution: prisoners' rights, mental health patients' rights, military justice, gay rights, migrant workers' rights, and so on. The occasion was eloquent testimony to the ACLU's place on the frontier of social change.[86]

All of the proposals were eventually funded and incorporated into the renamed ACLU Foundation. Reliance on grant-funded "special projects" became a major element of the new ACLU under Neier. The Prisoners' Rights Project, the Reproductive Freedom Project, and the Voter Rights Project became the centers of legal expertise on their respective subjects. Conservatives paid the ACLU the highest tribute by creating their own network of grant-funded litigation centers.[87]

Especially concerned about public education, Neier created a series of ACLU handbooks. With Norman Dorsen as the general editor, each volume summarized a civil liberties issue in plain language for the layperson. The first volumes appeared in 1972: *The Rights of Servicemen, The Rights of Prisoners, The Rights of the Poor,* and *The Rights of Students.*[88] None of the subjects had been on the ACLU's agenda a few years earlier, but by the 1980s there were more than thirty-five titles in the series. Neier also established *The Civil Liberties Review* for serious discussions of civil liberties issues. The ACLU had never had a well-organized education program for its members, and with so many new issues developing, the *Review* filled a major void. It was canceled in 1978, however, because of a financial crisis in the ACLU.[89] All of Neier's expanded program was supported by the tremendous growth in ACLU membership, which peaked at 275,000 in mid-1974.

While the ACLU's litigation program expanded, the conservative drift of the Burger Court was a source of great anxiety. In March 1973 the ACLU brought one hundred staff and volunteer lawyers to Chicago to plan an effective response, the first such conference in ACLU history. Although the ACLU's success rate had declined from the heyday of the Warren Court years, it was still better than most civil libertarians had expected, falling from an extraordinary 90 percent in the 1968–1969 term to only 52 percent in 1970–1971. The Burger Court trimmed individual rights in a number of areas, particularly those of criminal suspects, but also handed down the *Roe v. Wade* abortion rights decision. ACLU leaders agreed that the Court could not be counted on as it had been in the past and that it thus was important to strengthen the organization's legislative efforts.[90]

The Agony of Success

The enormous ACLU expansion under Neier brought with it a number of serious problems. The ACLU now had a staffed affiliate in all but four states, an array of grant-funded special projects, a growing presence in Washington,

D.C., and an eighty-member board of directors that insisted on its policy making prerogatives. It was national in scope but loosely federated in structure. The affiliates jealously guarded their own independence. The expanded civil liberties agenda raised thorny policy questions. Privacy considerations, for example, often conflicted with other civil liberties principles: Did access to criminal records intrude on the privacy of arrested persons? Where exactly did the rights of parents raising religious free exercise claims end and the rights of children begin?[91]

The intellectually energetic Neier was uncomfortable with the bureaucratic apparatus he had helped create. He liked to rush into new areas and worry about formal ACLU policy later. In 1971 he conceded that "we are engaged in a great deal of action in defense of prisoners rights and the rights of mental patients but with very sketchy policy underpinnings."[92] Like Roger Baldwin, Neier had an autocratic streak and did not like being bound by a policy guide or an assertive board of directors (*New York Times* reporter J. Anthony Lukas remarked that his "substance is left, but his style is right").[93] Yet, formal policy statements were increasingly necessary to maintain some degree of consistency among the many ACLU units—the affiliates, the lobbyists in Washington, the special projects. In the past, the ACLU had often operated in an ad hoc, seat-of-the-pants style.

For the moment, however, these problems were hidden by the flood of new members and income. The ACLU had projected itself into the forefront of the most dramatic issues of the day and was forging new constitutional doctrine. But the day of reckoning lay just ahead: Part of the Watergate-induced boom in membership was an aberration, and once Nixon resigned, a serious financial crisis began. The ACLU entered a four-year time of troubles as it wrestled with the administrative burdens imposed by its own success.

New Criticisms of a New ACLU

Predictably, the ACLU's expanded activities evoked serious criticism. The traditional charges that the ACLU was a "Communist front" or "antireligion" were joined by new attacks from neoconservative intellectuals. Knowledgeable about constitutional law and social policy and with several former ACLU members in their midst, the neoconservatives raised basic questions not just about the ACLU but also about the role of the Constitution and the Supreme Court in American life.

One of the first of the new critics was Yale law professor Joseph W. Bishop, who conceded that the ACLU had an "impact and influence far out of proportion to its size and its tangible resources." As a law professor, he recognized the ACLU's sustained impact on the law. "It would be hard to name another private organization which comes close to matching this record," he allowed. His primary complaint was that the ACLU had abandoned its traditional role and had embarked on a purely partisan campaign, citing the ACLU's defense of Dr. Spock as the turning point. Bishop saw it not as a free speech case, but as a political attack on the war. His charge that the

ACLU adopted a "political agenda" in the late 1960s—that there was a distinction between a "good" old ACLU and a "bad" new one—became a standard neoconservative criticism. Like many neoconservatives, Bishop was repelled by the anti-Americanism of student protesters—and linked their views with those of the ACLU. He quoted legal director Mel Wulf's statement that "we are not yet a fascist state in general." Bishop advised that "a more dispassionate appraisal would be that the Bill of Rights . . . is at least in better shape than ever before in our history" and that "the government of the United States is, in fact, one of that small minority among the earth's governments which *does* provide for change by democratic and constitutional means."[94] Wulf was not the only one in the ACLU guilty of hyperbole in the face of attacks on antiwar dissent. And yet, compared with other self-styled "radical" lawyers of the 1960s, the ACLU was unwaveringly committed to established legal procedures and the idea of constitutional government. Nonetheless, neoconservatives stuck to their charge that the ACLU had abandoned the reasonable defense of civil liberties for a radical political agenda.

A second line of criticism focused primarily on the Supreme Court. A number of legal scholars had serious doubts about the *Griswold–Roe* line of decisions. Robert Bork, then a professor at the Yale law school, felt that the Court's rationale for the right to privacy was untenable. Because the word *privacy* did not appear in the Bill of Rights, Bork argued, there was no principled basis for the Court's decision in *Griswold*. Instead, the justices in the majority had simply imposed their own values on the country. Although this attack focused on the Court, the ACLU was obviously implicated for having supported not only the rationale in *Griswold* and *Roe* but also judicial activism in all areas.[95]

In reaction to *Griswold* and *Roe,* conservative legal scholars challenged judicial activism with a new theory of judicial restraint, "original intent." That is, the only principled basis for constitutional decision making was the framers' intent. This approach would invalidate most of the civil libertarian activism of the past several decades. But although the neoconservatives accused the Court—and by implication, the ACLU—of being "result oriented," they were just as concerned with results. Disliking what the Court had done over the past few decades, they developed a theory that would invalidate those results. The ACLU replied that the Constitution was a living document that had to be interpreted in the light of new circumstances. History clearly indicated that judicial enforcement was an important, though not necessarily the only, means of giving practical meaning to the promises of the Bill of Rights.

Another line of criticism held that the ACLU had pressed traditional civil liberties too far. Excessive individualism, the critics noted, undermined the civility and order required by a healthy society. The issue of pornography illuminated the disagreement between the ACLU and its critics. In large part because of the ACLU's long crusade against censorship, virtually all the old restraints collapsed in the late 1960s. Books, magazines, and movies depicting explicit sex—including "hard-core" pornography—circulated as never before. Adult theater marquees openly advertised "Live, Nude, Girls." Neoconservatives expressed a moral revulsion at the collapse of restraints and now argued that excessive liberty itself was the problem.

Political scientist Walter Berns framed the issue in terms of a choice between "pornography and democracy." Admitting that censorship had been discredited by its own absurdities—the long history of suppression of literary classics by small-minded bureaucrats and priggish moralists—he decried the liberal faith in progress. The long attack on censorship had often rested on the comfortable assumption that truth and beauty would prevail. With great delight, Berns quoted the ACLU's own Morris Ernst, now retired, that he "would hate to live in a world with utter freedom." Instead of truth and beauty, the "lowest common denominator" prevailed. Berns fashioned a new defense of censorship resting on the importance of shame. Shame implied self-restraint, a recognition that some things, such as the open circulation of pornography, were wrong in a healthy society. Democracy relied on self-restraint and could not survive unbridled self-indulgence, which Berns equated with the ACLU's position on absolute individual freedom.[96]

Reiterating the point first formulated by Ernst in the late 1920s, the ACLU replied that the advocates of censorship could not formulate a workable definition that would distinguish violent hard-core pornography from erotic works of art. The censorship Berns desired would only empower the most moralistic elements of the community and result in selective prosecutions, as it had in the past. In the changing cultural politics of the 1970s, the neoconservatives were so repelled by the consequences of freedom of expression that they swung far to the right and allied themselves with groups they had even less in common with than the ACLU—fundamentalists in the Moral Majority and similar groups.

The ACLU's policy on pornography left it in a very vulnerable position in the political arena, and in the 1988 presidential election campaign, GOP candidate George Bush made the most of it, tarring his opponent, Michael Dukakis, an ACLU member, with advocating child pornography. Bush also attacked the ACLU's opposition to tax exemptions for churches, a policy it adopted in 1970 and which further illustrated the dominance of absolutist thinking in the ACLU. The issue arose in *Walz,* a non-ACLU case. When it reached the Supreme Court, the ACLU debated what position to take. The staunch separationists insisted on a brief opposing tax exemptions for religious organizations, while others felt that denying exemptions would inhibit the legitimate free exercise of religion. Some worried that the case was certain to lose and would only alienate many people, including many ACLU members. Several ACLU Executive Committee members proposed a two-pronged brief that tried to have it both ways: arguing against tax exemptions on establishment clause grounds, while suggesting that if the Court rejected that argument, it could support them under a free exercise rationale. Leo Pfeffer denounced this as an unprincipled approach and persuaded the ACLU to draft a brief opposing tax exemptions. The Supreme Court rejected this argument, in any event, but *Walz* marked the dominance of absolutist thinking in the ACLU.[97]

In years to come, critics would cite *Walz* and the defense of child pornography as evidence of the ACLU's utter lack of reasonableness. The absolutist approach, they charged, had taken on a degree of fanaticism, with no concern about the social consequences. For its own part, the ACLU had no apologies. Its critics, it replied, could not formulate rational and objective standards to distinguish art from pornography or to define how much state aid to religion was reasonable. The commands of the Bill of Rights were absolutes. It had taken the ACLU over forty years to come to grips with the ramifications of that idea, but in the decade of the 1960s it moved from a hesitant to an unashamed embrace of the absolutist position.

The Rights Revolution and American Life

The rights revolution crested in the mid-1970s, at which point the ACLU could look back on its part in an extraordinary accomplishment. A "rights consciousness" permeated society, and social science research confirmed the spread of civil libertarian values.[98] The creation of entire new areas of constitutional law—abortion rights, women's rights, students' rights, prisoners' rights, privacy—represented a new demand for freedom and equality by millions of Americans. As one observer pointed out, the growth of public interest law since the mid-1960s—of which the ACLU was only a part—created "a new administrative atmosphere" in the agencies challenged and helped to educate citizen groups through their participation in lawsuits.[99] These were permanent changes, surviving as the sixties faded into the mists of nostalgia. While the moral energy and commitment to freedom had trouble surviving the seventies, much of it found an institutional home in the ACLU's special projects. Finally, the rights revolution defined the politics of the decade and a half that lay ahead. To a great extent the conservative revolt that began in the mid-1970s was a reaction against the civil liberties gains of the previous decade, particularly the collapse of official censorship and the new right to abortion. If the ACLU found itself besieged from the mid-1970s onward, it was largely because its successes had reshaped law and public policy.

VII

Holding the Line,
1975-1990

Fifteen

Skokie:
Crisis and Recovery,
1977-1979

Skokie: "A Classic First Amendment Case"

All hell broke loose in the Chicago ACLU office on April 28, 1977. Staff attorney David Goldberger appeared in Cook County Chancery Court to defend the right of American Nazi Frank Collin to demonstrate in Skokie, Illinois.[1] He thought it was a routine First Amendment case. The ACLU had long defended Nazis and had always faced protests from angry Jews and others; in fact, a number of members had resigned when the ACLU represented Nazi leader George Lincoln Rockwell in 1960.[2] But Skokie was different. Within hours it was a national media event. "Nazis to march through Skokie," screamed the headlines. Angry phone calls began pouring into the Illinois ACLU offices. Many were from members calling to say they were dropping their ACLU membership. Many attacked the ACLU leaders in the most vicious language. One threatened the life of David Hamlin, director of the Illinois ACLU. Another said, "I *spit* on you." ACLU executive director Aryeh Neier repeatedly faced the question, "How can you, a Jew, defend freedom for Nazis?"

Skokie was a classic ACLU First Amendment case: a defense of the rights of an unpopular group, in this case one espousing the most universally despised ideology in the country. But the response was unlike anything the ACLU had ever faced. Never before had it faced such hostility from within. The ACLU lost thousands of members, and the resulting financial crisis threatened its very existence.

Background of the Crisis

Skokie was no ordinary community. Nearly half of the seventy thousand residents of this suburban Chicago community were Jewish. Between eight hun-

323

dred and twelve hundred were survivors of the Nazi Holocaust, making it perhaps the largest concentration of survivors in the country, and many viewed the planned Nazi march as a direct affront to the memory of the six million Holocaust victims.

The confrontation in Skokie was an outgrowth of an earlier conflict between Frank Collin's National Socialist Party of America (NSPA) and the city of Chicago. Collin's pathetically small, ragtag group had its headquarters near Marquette Park on Chicago's southwest side. Racial conflict had escalated as black families began to move into this previously all-white neighborhood. Collin had led a series of antiblack demonstrations in Marquette Park during the summer of 1976 which attracted unemployed and restless white kids. The NSPA office displayed a sign reading "Nigger Go Home." To stop the growing violence, the city banned all demonstrations in the park. As David Hamlin put it, "In the offices of the City of Chicago . . . the First Amendment to the United States Constitution is thought to be an unverified rumor."[3] When Collin tried to march again, the park district adopted a new policy, requiring groups to post a bond or insurance of $250,000. This was impossible for small groups, including Collin's Nazi party, and so he turned to the ACLU for help. David Goldberger filed suit in federal court in the fall of 1976 challenging the requirement as an unreasonable infringement on the First Amendment. *Collin v. O'Malley* attracted little attention; it was still a routine ACLU case.

But Collin was not content to wait for the courts to decide. Noisy demonstrations were his organization's only activity. Casting about for alternatives, he decided to demonstrate in the suburbs where the park district's requirement did not apply. In February 1977 he sent letters to more than a dozen suburban towns seeking demonstration permits. The Skokie Park District, the only one to respond, informed him that he would have to post $350,000 in insurance. If they had ignored his request, as nearby Evanston did, there would probably never have been a confrontation. Sensing a chance for more publicity, Collin bypassed the Skokie Park District and informed the village council that he would hold a thirty-minute demonstration in front of the village hall on Sunday, May 1, 1977. He expected perhaps fifty demonstrators, some in neo-Nazi uniforms, but planned no speeches. Hoping to avoid a confrontation, the mayor and village attorney granted his request and planned to urge people to ignore the Nazis.

The Holocaust survivors, however, screamed in protest. The 1967 Six-Day War in the Mideast had sparked a revival of Jewish self-consciousness,[4] and the memory of the Holocaust, support for Soviet Jews, and support for Israel became important political rallying cries. In this atmosphere, Jewish community leaders felt constrained to defend the survivors. The militant Jewish Defense League (JDL), although an embarrassment to the Jewish establishment, upped the ante with its slogan of "Never Again." The JDL thus forced community leaders to take a more militant anti-Nazi position than they might otherwise have done. Responding to this pressure, village officials in Skokie obtained an injunction banning Collin's demonstration completely. Collin again contacted the Illinois ACLU, which agreed to represent him in a second case.

The next day, David Goldberger told the Cook County Chancery Court, "This is a classic First Amendment case, your honor." The village of Skokie's case was based on the argument that the neo-Nazi march would incite a breach of the peace. The ACLU had always argued that this represented a "heckler's veto." That is, it would allow any angry group of people to abrogate the free speech and assembly rights of unpopular organizations simply by threatening to be disruptive. Judge Wosik rejected Goldberger's argument and enjoined the May 1 demonstration.

Collin, seeing a loophole in Wosik's order, then announced a demonstration for April 30. The village of Skokie went back to court and, in an extraordinary emergency proceeding in which Collin was not represented, obtained a permanent ban "until further notice of the Court." On May 2, Skokie passed three ordinances aimed at Collin. The first required thirty days' advance notice and insurance of $350,000 for a permit to hold demonstrations. The second outlawed the public display of "symbols offensive to the community" and parades by political organizations wearing "military style" uniforms. The third outlawed the "dissemination of any material . . . which promotes and incites hatred against persons by reason of their race, national origin, or religion."

These three ordinances were virtually identical to the 1917 Illinois law upheld by the U.S. Supreme Court in the 1952 *Beauharnais* decision. Illinois, however, had repealed the law in 1964. Together, the three ordinances were an assault on the First Amendment, matching, if not exceeding, the various measures passed in the South to suppress the civil rights movement. That is, the ban on vaguely defined "symbols offensive to the community" had unlimited application and could be used to ban all radical political groups, or, in certain communities, advocacy of abortion, homosexuality, or even birth control. The group libel concept, which the ACLU had opposed since it first appeared in the late 1930s, was equally ill defined and could be directed against radical black groups or demonstrators protesting the policies of the Catholic church—to cite only the most obvious examples. As ACLU leaders pointed out, the Skokie ordinances could have been used to stop Martin Luther King, Jr.'s confrontational march into Cicero, Illinois, in 1968.

As media coverage of the Skokie crisis continued, the ACLU offices in Chicago and New York City were hit with angry calls and letters. Neier, already battered by a series of organizational problems, was shell-shocked. In a damage control effort, he and Norman Dorsen spoke to the leaders of the major Jewish organizations but received a generally frosty reception.[5] All the organizations opposed allowing the Nazis the right to demonstrate in Skokie. The Anti-Defamation League (ADL) had clashed with the ACLU on several occasions over the First Amendment rights of Nazis and racists, in 1966 attacking Neier for defending the right of New York City police officers to belong to the John Birch Society.[6] Most distressing to the ACLU was the opposition of the American Jewish Congress (AJC), the most consistently civil libertarian of the major Jewish groups and a longtime ACLU ally.

Under pressure to take a strong anti-Nazi position, the AJC announced in January 1978 that "the courts may and should prohibit" the Nazis "from marching through Skokie, Illinois."[7] The militant JDL, meanwhile, staged sit-ins at the ACLU offices in New York, Florida, and Los Angeles. Another group occupied the Illinois ACLU offices for thirty minutes. The NYCLU responded by defending the right of the JDL to picket in front of the Soviet mission in New York.[8]

The National Lawyers Guild also supported Skokie, accusing the ACLU of a "poisonous evenhandedness" that encouraged racism. In an interview, the Guild's Alexander Meikeljohn, despite his belief in the First Amendment as an "absolute," said he would ban the Nazis from demonstrating in Skokie.[9] The Guild had apparently forgotten that it had suffered during the cold war under a similar rationale that justified denying First Amendment rights to allegedly dangerous organizations. Once again the ACLU had to remind many liberal and left-wing groups of the long-range importance of a nonpartisan defense of free speech. In the face of this mounting hostility, the ACLU held firm. The Illinois affiliate voted unanimously to challenge the Skokie ordinances, and the ACLU's national board endorsed this stand.[10]

The litigation dragged on through 1977 and into 1978. When the Illinois Supreme Court ducked the issue on a technicality, the ACLU filed an emergency petition with Supreme Court Justice John Paul Stevens, who not only accepted the petition but also treated it as a full petition for certoriari. On June 14, 1977, the Supreme Court ruled that anyone subject to a prior restraint of speech was entitled to an immediate hearing and ordered the Illinois Supreme Court to hold an expedited hearing. But the Illinois courts continued to delay, perhaps intentionally. A three-judge appellate court left the injunction in place and sent it back to the lower court for another hearing. Because this violated the spirit, if not the letter, of the Supreme Court's decision, attorney David Goldberger filed another appeal with the Illinois Supreme Court. In late January 1978 the Illinois high court ruled that the injunction against Collin and the display of the swastika—a new element added by Skokie on appeal—was unconstitutional.

Meanwhile, the Chicago ADL filed a bizarre "menticide" suit against Collin, arguing that the display of Nazi flags and regalia constituted an extreme form of mental cruelty against Holocaust victims. Carried to its logical extreme, "menticide" would justify the suppression of all historical treatment of the Holocaust (and, for that matter, an undetermined number of distressing historical events, such as slavery)—a ludicrous solution in light of the Jewish community's campaign to keep alive the memory of the Holocaust. At that very moment, in fact, NBC was running a miniseries on the Holocaust, an event the ADL did not challenge. The Illinois court dismissed the menticide suit.

In February 1978, the federal district court ruled the three Skokie ordinances to be unconstitutional. Judge Bernard Decker ruled that "the Supreme Court has held that, above all else, the First Amendment means that government has no power to restrict expression because of its message, its ideas, its subject matter, or its content." The village of Skokie appealed but, on May 22, the U.S. Seventh Circuit Court of Appeals ordered the village to issue Frank Collin a permit. Three weeks later, by a seven-to-two vote, the U.S. Supreme Court refused to stay the seventh circuit order. Collin and the ACLU had won a great First Amendment victory.[11]

Having won, Collin was suddenly no longer a martyr and so had to produce his long-sought demonstration. Although armed with a permit for a demonstration in Skokie on June 25, 1978, he never used it. In fact, the Nazis never appeared in Skokie. Collin told the media that his real goal all along had been to demonstrate in Marquette Park. While the Skokie case dominated the news coverage, he and the ACLU won their challenge to the Chicago Park District's insurance requirement, a second great victory for the rights of small and unpopular groups that spring.[12]

But Collin did not immediately demonstrate in Marquette Park either. In a compromise negotiated through the U.S. Justice Department's Community Relations Service, he agreed instead to demonstrate at Federal Plaza in downtown Chicago. On June 24, 1978, a heavy contingent of Chicago police escorted Collin and his followers by a circuitous route to the site, where they were greeted by several thousand screaming counterdemonstrators. The confrontation lasted fifteen minutes. Two weeks later Collin held his first demonstration in Marquette Park in over two years. The battle over the First Amendment—in Skokie and Marquette Park—was over. The ACLU, however, was deep in crisis.

Aftermath: The ACLU in Crisis

Skokie was a struggle in keeping with the highest traditions of the ACLU. As its president, Norman Dorsen, explained, the ACLU had preserved its honor by "keeping faith with our principles."[13] In the face of ferocious public hostility, it had defended the First Amendment rights of the unpopular. The victory for the First Amendment had extracted an enormous price, however, as the loss of members and contributions plunged the ACLU into debt—nearly $500,000 by 1978. The ACLU national office, at first paralyzed by the financial crisis, did not know how to respond. A battered Aryeh Neier announced he would resign as executive director that summer. His replacement, Ira Glasser, looked at the books during his first week on the job and asked, only half jokingly, if public-interest groups could declare bankruptcy. But ultimately, Skokie was a blessing in disguise, exposing a host of organizational problems and forcing the ACLU to overhaul its operations. The changes quickly restored the ACLU's health and, just in the nick of time, put it in strong shape to fight the conservative, anti–civil libertarian backlash of the 1980s. "Thank God for Skokie," Glasser later commented.[14]

Neier had warned of a financial problem as early as November 1974. The

ACLU's income for that year was $240,000 below expectations, and the ACLU ended the year with a deficit of over $100,000. It thus had to scale down its budget each year (from a projected $1.9 million for 1974 to an actual income of $1.5 million in 1977). The ongoing problem led to trouble between Neier and the board of directors, with one board member accusing him of refusing to face reality and proposing budgets that were "not fiscally responsible." It was a wrenching experience for Neier personally. In his ten years with NYCLU and ACLU he had known nothing but a rapidly rising membership and income and an expanding program, and he seemed unable to adjust to a new political environment. In the fall of 1977, "the roof fell in," as membership renewals indicated a 15 percent drop from the year before. Income fell $300,000 short of expenditures. In late 1977 the board ordered a $200,000 cut in expenditures, laid off ten staff members, and killed the *Civil Liberties Review*.[15]

The financial crisis hit the affiliates particularly hard. Under the ACLU's sharing formula they received about 70 percent of each member's dues and as membership dropped many of the new small affiliates in the Midwest and South had difficulty paying their directors' salaries. The resulting turnover among directors disrupted their programs.

The ACLU's membership problem was twofold. Membership began dropping in late 1974, the downturn probably beginning the day Richard Nixon resigned as president. Many of the new members proved to be single-issue people. Once Nixon was gone and the Watergate crisis was over, they found they were little interested in the ACLU's other issues. The membership losses attributed to Skokie were, and still are, a matter of some confusion. Between late 1974 and 1978 the ACLU membership fell by 25 percent, from 275,000 to about 200,000. Two political scientists who studied the Skokie crisis concluded, however, that, at most, only half of all these people quit because of Skokie.[16] Some of the confusion arose from the distinction between "members" and "memberships." The ACLU based its 275,000 "member" figure on the basis of about 200,000 paid "memberships," assuming that approximately one-third of these memberships represented couples. For public consumption, then, it always used the higher figure. This was not entirely unjustified, as both household members probably supported the ACLU; both would be likely to attend a meeting, serve on a committee, or write a letter to a legislator on a civil liberties issue.[17]

The other half of the membership problem was sheer inefficiency in the national office. The membership department was in chaos, and some insiders later claimed that the consulting firm handling the ACLU's mailings temporarily lost about 20 percent of the files. Although they were later reconstructed, those members never received a renewal notice in the critical months of 1978. Also, after twenty-four years of virtually uninterrupted growth, the ACLU had grown lazy about recruitment, with members joining at their own initiative because of the ACLU's highly visible stand on the issues. As Florence Isbell sardonically put it, in the heady days of the 1960s the ACLU could send out a letter saying "Dear Charley, Fuck You" and get a check in the return mail. Isbell said the ACLU always regarded the membership operation as "an encumbrance, rather like an eccentric relative kept in the attic." Neier in particular disdained the membership operation, resembling Roger Baldwin in his preference for substantive issues and his boredom with mundane administrative tasks.[18]

Such a casual approach was inadequate to the new environment of the 1970s. Competition between public-interest groups for members and funds became ferocious. The key to organizational survival was direct mail. Conservative groups were the first to exploit these new techniques and did so with great success. The ACLU, along with many other groups, played catch-up in an environment of "direct mail or die." Mailings were effective but expensive and frought with danger. For example, an overly expensive or misdirected mailing (sending the wrong message to a particular target audience) could spell financial disaster.

Recovery

Skokie finally galvanized the ACLU into action. Faced with imminent financial collapse, the board appointed Jay Miller to head an emergency development campaign. Miller was an old ACLU hand as former director of the Illinois and Northern California affiliates and staff member of the Washington office since 1975. The development program included a major gifts campaign, a First Amendment convocation in New York, and a membership recruitment drive.[19] Almost to the ACLU's own surprise, the effort was an immediate success, uncovering a substantial reservoir of support.

The turning point was a fund-raising letter signed by David Goldberger. As the staff attorney for the Illinois affiliate, he had handled the Skokie litigation and suffered vicious personal attacks. In a four-page letter he briefly reviewed the facts of the case in an unemotional manner, asking readers to think of the implications for free speech if the Skokie ordinances had been upheld: "Think of such power in the hands of a racist sheriff, or a local police department hostile to antiwar demonstrations, or the wrong kind of president." Goldberger then turned to the financial crisis. The ACLU was "on the edge of a precipice." Additional cuts in staff and programs at the national office were imminent. He asked thirty thousand "staunch friends of civil liberties" to contribute $20 "right now."[20]

The Goldberger letter, as it came to be known, was a spectacular success; over 25,000 people contributed $550,000, whereas until then the most successful appeal had produced only $200,000. Particularly heartening for the organization were the many applications for membership, accompanied by letters expressing admiration for the ACLU's courage in standing by its principles. One Jewish couple wrote that they didn't support the ACLU on Skokie but sent a check "for your many other valuable contributions to life in America." A former staff member with the American Israeli Political Action Committee sent $50, fondly recalling his association with Roger Baldwin in 1934.[21]

The ACLU gained between 4,000 and 6,000 new members by mid-September 1978. By one estimate, perhaps half of them joined *because* of the ACLU's defense of the Nazis' right to demonstrate in Skokie.[22] One of the new members was the noted sociologist David Riesman who, thirty-five years earlier, had written an articulate defense of the very kind of laws restricting antidemocratic organizations that the ACLU had challenged in Skokie.[23]

The response suggested that the hostility to the ACLU had been greatly exaggerated by the media and the ACLU's own leaders in New York. Although the mood of the country was becoming more conservative, a bedrock of support for civil liberties still existed. The rising threat to abortion rights and the prominent role of the ACLU's Reproductive Rights Project in fighting it were particularly important to rallying support. Clearly, many ACLU members realized that the Nazi march in Skokie was a minor incident—though admittedly one with enormous symbolic significance—but that reproductive freedom was a daily and personal reality. Once the ACLU put its house in order, membership stabilized at a plateau of about 240,000 (based on 180,000 paid memberships). In the long run, the remarkable fact was not that 70,000 people quit the ACLU but that between 1970 and 1981 about 120,000 joined and stayed. As it braced for the challenge of the New Right in the early 1980s, the ACLU was twice as large as it had been a decade before.

The evident support for the ACLU in this time of crisis also contradicted the notion that Skokie signaled an anti–civil libertarian backlash within the Jewish community. A survey by the American Jewish Community found that American Jews were still far more liberal than the general population was and, in particular, were far more committed to the goals of the civil rights movement. The only exception was the issue of affirmative action, a sore point among many Jews who had traditionally been the victims of restrictive quotas. The attacks on the ACLU came from a small and very vocal conservative segment of the Jewish community, notably the group of neoconservative intellectuals led by Norman Podhoretz, editor of *Commentary*.[24] In short, the Jewish community resembled both the Protestant and Catholic communities in the 1970s and 1980s. All three contained vocal and well-organized conservative and anti–civil libertarian elements. The values of the majority of all three, however, were strongly, perhaps permanently, influenced by the rights revolution and remained committed to upholding most (although not all) civil liberties principles.

The ACLU turned the corner in terms of media coverage with a free speech convocation in June 1978. Organized largely by President Dorsen, it featured a glittering array of prominent public figures: Senators Ted Kennedy and Jacob Javits, publisher John Cowles and cartoonist Jules Feiffer. At a reception, the ACLU presented awards to writers James Baldwin, E. L. Doctorow, Jerzy Kosinski, Norman Mailer, Arthur Miller, and William Styron. The sessions featured sharp debates over civil liberties issues. Former CIA Director William Colby defended the government's right to keep secrets; Morton Halperin, future director of the ACLU's Washington, D.C., office, challenged him, arguing for the people's right to know about the operations of their government. Although Ted Kennedy was a featured speaker, the ACLU opposed his current bill to revise the federal criminal code. Inevitably, the question of Skokie came up. Neier presented the ACLU's case that even Nazis had a right to free speech. Radical attorney William Kunstler, no longer on the ACLU board, reluctantly agreed in principle but contended that the ACLU should not actively defend their right. The response to Kunstler's call for a selective and partisan defense of free speech came from ACLU founder Roger Baldwin. Now ninety-four years old, he looked back over fifty-eight years of free speech fights and concluded that the ACLU had "survived because of its integrity."[25]

The most thoughtful ACLU critics framed the Skokie issue in terms of communitarian values. Notre Dame University professor Donald Alexander Downs argued that First Amendment law had carried individual rights to a dangerous extreme. "But man is a political, communal animal in addition to being an individual," he continued. To preserve the sense of community, a "prudent jurisprudence should *balance* individualism and community." Attempting to revive the balancing-test debate that had flourished in the late 1950s, Down held that speech could and should be restricted when it pertains "to matters of race or ethnic origin [and] is accompanied by the advocacy of death or violence against members of that race or ethnic group, and is targeted at such members."[26] The criticism of extreme libertarianism—which represented an inadvertent tribute to the ACLU's success in shaping constitutional law—was shared by many neoconservatives in the mid-1970s. The most persuasive reply to Downs was offered by law professor Lee Bollinger. In a broad-ranging discussion of the First Amendment, he cast it in positive rather than negative terms. The commitment to free speech did not mean that American society was, in his words, "enslaved to freedom." Defending the rights of hateful ideas should not be seen as an unpleasant but "necessary price of our own liberty" but, rather, as affirming a positive value "that we should be proud of." That value was a "capacity for toleration" that expressed a deeper confidence in the enduring strength of democracy.[27] By provoking such a far-reaching debate over the meaning of the First Amendment, if not the nature of American society, the ACLU's defense of the Nazis in Skokie performed an enormous educational service to the nation. Years later, ACLU leader Gara LaMarche concluded that Skokie was "the best thing that happened to the ACLU in years," by defining the free speech issues in "stark, clear-cut terms." "If the ACLU did nothing else," LaMarche said, "it should take cases like Skokie."[28]

More Troubles: The ACLU "Tested"

"The year 1977 was a year of testing for the American Civil Liberties Union."[29] Neier began his 1977 *Annual Report* on a somber note. Skokie was not the only crisis facing the ACLU. Two cases involving the rights of KKK members had led to internal disputes. In May 1977 New York City radio talk show host Bob Grant had urged people to picket the ACLU office for not defending crime victims. ACLU staff handed the picketers a brochure entitled "Your Rights on the Street."[30] But there were deeper problems. The ACLU was beginning to come to grips with the consequences of its own success over the past decade. Long gone was the informal style that had prevailed through the late 1960s. Now, simply managing the ACLU enterprise was an enormous task. On top of this, the rising conservative mood in the mid-1970s—the right-to-life movement, the emerging power of the fundamentalists—had forced the ACLU into a defensive posture. The task at hand thus became preserving its newly won rights, and many ACLU veterans of the 1960s found it difficult to adjust. The combined effect of these changes took its toll on the leadership, and between 1976 and 1978 all four of the top officials departed.

The Rights of the Klan

The first KKK episode occurred at Camp Pendleton, California, in late 1976. Rising tensions between white and black marines erupted when black marines attacked and injured several white marines that they believed were members of the KKK. The camp commander then indicted the black marines on criminal charges and transferred the suspected KKK members to other bases. The San Diego ACLU chapter announced that it would defend the white marines on the grounds that they were being punished for their political associations. But the parent Southern California affiliate did not approve of the chapter's action, and so Neier flew to California to resolve the conflict. He found that the Marine Corps "had been impartial in its insensitivity to civil liberties"; it was not clear that the Marine Corps had arrested the black marines who participated in the assault. Moreover, they were charged with conspiracy, held in pretrial confinement for a month, were not allowed to see attorneys for several days, and were pressured to make incriminating statements.[31]

The conflict between the San Diego chapter, which represented the white marines, and the parent Southern California affiliate, which took the case of the black marines, was symptomatic of a larger conflict within the ACLU, which had made a strong commitment to a decentralized structure, placing a premium on affiliate autonomy. The independent-minded civil libertarians in some affiliates inevitably saw things differently from the national board. In particular, the differences between the Southern California ACLU and the national office became legendary within ACLU circles. These conflicts were often publicly embarrassing and internally debilitating.[32]

Meanwhile, a second controversy arose in Mississippi when the Harrison County Board of Education refused to allow the Klan to hold a rally at a local elementary school, then under a court order to desegregate. The Klan turned to the ACLU, and the Mississippi affiliate voted eight to seven to represent it. The losing faction demanded reconsideration, and Neier flew to Jackson for its next board meeting, at which he made a strong case for the ACLU's commitment to defending the rights of all groups, no matter how

unpopular. Some Mississippi ACLU members viewed his presence as interference in affiliate autonomy. The affiliate then reaffirmed its decision to
represent the Klan, but ten of the twenty-one board members resigned in
protest. It was a devastating blow to the small and struggling affiliate, especially as the ten included all seven black members and two officers. Dorsen
insisted that the matter be presented to the national board, which endorsed
the affiliate's decision to represent the Klan by a twenty-nine-to-nineteen
vote, the nineteen negative votes an indication of the willingness of a significant minority to compromise on a clear-cut First Amendment issue.[33] Like
the Camp Pendleton controversy, the Mississippi incident simultaneously
alienated the black community and exposed the difficult problems of national–
affiliate relations.

The FBI Files

Equally troublesome was the release in 1977 of the FBI's files on the ACLU.
The 41,728 pages of documents revealed the massive program of FBI spying
since 1917, but the public's attention, particularly in the liberal and left-wing
media, focused more on the relations between several ACLU leaders and the
FBI during the 1940s and 1950s. The files revived the old criticisms that the
ACLU had not done enough to defend civil liberties during the worst of
the cold war.[34]

A special ACLU commission appointed to review the FBI files did not
shrink from the unpleasant truth. Several ACLU leaders had sought information about ACLU members from the FBI and, worse, had given the FBI
information about the organization and individuals. The report denounced
these actions as "wrong" and charged that at least one staff member had
"betrayed the ACLU" by engaging in "a form of spying."[35]

The report singled out Irving Ferman, director of the Washington, D.C.,
office from 1952 to 1959, for the strongest criticism. His relationship with the
FBI was "the most intensive and extensive and most secretive . . . of any
ACLU staff or official reported in the FBI files."[36] He had given drafts of
official ACLU correspondence to the FBI and had even conceded that "perhaps he was violating his trust with the organization." In addition, Ferman
had sent the bureau minutes of the Massachusetts and Oregon affiliates,
prompting the FBI to establish files on all the people mentioned therein. The
FBI's associate director, Louis Nichols, once even praised Ferman for being
"as much a soldier as those of us serving in the Bureau."

Ferman angrily denied that he had been an "informer." His actions, he
argued, were consistent with ACLU policy and the actions of other top officials. The 1940 antitotalitarian Resolution had established anti-Communism
as official ACLU policy, while Roger Baldwin cultivated close ties with top
government officials, including Hoover. Finally, Ferman claimed that his contacts had protected the ACLU: He took credit for getting the FBI to help
quash a HUAC report critical of the ACLU.[37]

The report also charged that Morris Ernst had "maintained a friendly and somewhat clubby relationship with the FBI" and had provided Hoover with ACLU documents and information on ACLU activities. The commission's report was based exclusively on material in the ACLU files. A 1984 article by journalist Harrison Salisbury, drawing on Ernst's own FBI files, provided further details about the former ACLU general counsel's close relationship with Hoover.[38]

The ACLU commission pulled its punches on one point, characterizing Roger Baldwin's relationship with the bureau as "adversarial, otherwise cordial but distant."[39] Yet, the evidence from the files made it clear that Baldwin had cultivated a friendly relationship with Hoover. Material in the ACLU archives, in fact, indicates that Baldwin actually identified someone to the Justice Department as a "fellow traveler." In short, he did "name names." The ACLU report simply glossed over the fact that his actions were not all that different from those of the other ACLU figures it discussed. Baldwin was alive and still feisty at age ninety-five, and there was evident concern about offending him.[40]

The revelations from the FBI files were a ghost from the past, a relic of an era and an ACLU that were long gone. If anything, the ACLU's attitude had swung radically in the opposite direction. In the post-Watergate era, even the slightest contact with the FBI or the CIA was regarded with immediate suspicion by ACLU members. Nonetheless, the revelations compounded the ACLU's difficulties in the mid-1970s.[41]

The ACLU Reorganizes

Between 1976 and 1978 all four of the top ACLU officials—chairman, executive director, legal director, and Washington office director—resigned. Although personality clashes were partly responsible, the underlying cause was the changes in the national political climate and the transformation of the ACLU itself.

Discontent with the management of the ACLU finally surfaced at the 1976 Biennial Conference. The immediate causes were persistent complaints about Neier's autocratic style, Ed Ennis's handling of the board, and Mel Wulf's leadership of the legal program. The board thereupon created the Special Organizational Review Committee (SORC as it became known) to review all of the ACLU's operations. In open meetings at the Biennial, members took advantage of the opportunity to "vent a spleen, or merely gripe" about organizational problems.[42]

In one of its most pointed recommendations, the SORC report concluded that the chairperson of the board "should play a more active, stronger and more visible role" than in the past—a clear criticism of Ed Ennis, who resigned even before the report was completed, though he remained on the board through the 1980s.

Ed Ennis had a remarkable civil liberties career: He met Roger Baldwin during the Japanese-American internment crisis, fought from within the very program he was assigned to carry out, and joined the board as soon as he left the Justice Department in 1947. As the ACLU's general counsel from 1954 through 1969, Ennis wrote many of the ACLU briefs challenging cold war measures; and as chairman from 1969 through 1976, he led the ACLU's challenges to the constitutionality of the Vietnam War and the campaign to impeach President Nixon. Yet, many felt he had not run the new eighty-member board with a firm hand.

Norman Dorsen, elected ACLU president in late 1976 (SORC recommended the new title), took the SORC report to heart and began to play a very active role in day-to-day affairs. He had little choice; Skokie erupted a few months later, and when Neier became overwhelmed by the mounting problems, Dorsen set up a desk at the ACLU office. Over the next decade his ACLU role changed significantly, as he gave up the highly public role of Supreme Court litigator, where reputations are to be made, for the behind-the-scenes work of keeping the ACLU on an even keel. *New York Times* reporter J. Anthony Lukas found that Dorsen had a "genius" for peacemaking, a quality that the contentious and far-flung ACLU sorely needed.[43]

The first top staff member to go was Washington office director Chuck Morgan, in a characteristically noisy fashion. The precipitating event was a March 17, 1976, *New York Times* article about the Democratic presidential nomination, quoting him as saying that party leaders opposed Jimmy Carter because they did not control him.[44] The comment reflected Morgan's deep-seated southern populism. Although he personally supported Fred Harris for president, the comments about Carter caught everyone's attention. Executive Director Neier, citing the ACLU's strict policy of nonpartisanship, fired off a letter asking Morgan what steps he planned to take to correct the impression that he was speaking for the ACLU when he endorsed political candidates. It was a provocative request that reflected Neier's own conflicts with the ever-independent Morgan. It was all Morgan needed. He replied, "The step I am taking is to resign."[45]

The person the *New York Times* described as "one of the most successful and best known—most loved and hated" figures in the ACLU thus departed. Despite Morgan's great contributions to civil liberties, many in the ACLU were glad to see him go, regarding him as a loose cannon who jumped into cases without regard to ACLU policy. For his own part, Morgan was growing bored and restless. He seemed unable to adapt to the new political climate. Ten years later he commented that since early 1977, "American politics has been very boring." That he regarded as "boring" a period during which the rise of the New Right, the Moral Majority, and the Reagan administration posed the greatest threat to civil liberties since the cold war revealed a great deal about his political outlook. He had thrived in the period between 1964 and 1974, when he was on the front lines of the great battles of the day: the civil rights and antiwar movements and Watergate. Temperamentally, Morgan was unsuited for the defensive posture the ACLU now had to assume; therefore his departure marked the transition between two eras in American political history.[46]

After resigning, Morgan was elected to the board, where he fought and won a few battles over policy questions. But his heart wasn't in it. He faded away, drawn by the excitement of a growing private law practice, and left the board in 1978. He remained a controversial figure, however. In the late 1970s Morgan agreed to represent Sears, Roebuck's defense against a highly publicized affirmative action suit brought by the Equal Opportunity Commission. Pundits could not resist pointing out that the great civil rights advocate was now opposing one of the most important such suits in the country.

When Dorsen became president in late 1976, one of his first steps was to engineer the ouster of Legal Director Mel Wulf. Wulf was another casualty of the new environment of the 1970s. In fifteen years as legal director, he had taken the ACLU into the forefront of the civil rights and antiwar movements. His commitment and personal presence in the South were instrumental in drawing the ACLU deeper into the struggle. The 1970s, however, demanded a different style. Figuratively speaking, the civil liberties struggle was no longer in the streets. Faced with a conservative Supreme Court, many (Dorsen in particular) thought that the ACLU needed to develop a more sophisticated litigation strategy. Briefs and oral arguments needed more careful preparation. Some people suggested that the ACLU should consider not taking some appeals to the Burger Court at all, in order to avoid an anti–civil libertarian decision. And after Wulf's departure, the ACLU's presence before the Court declined from ninety-five cases in the 1976–1977 term to forty-five in 1978–1979 (although this also reflected the effect of the transition to a new legal director and the ACLU's financial problems).[47] The ACLU's litigation program demanded managerial talents. Burt Neuborne, who eventually became legal director in 1983, was fond of calling the ACLU the nation's largest law firm. It needed someone who could coordinate the work of the affiliates, which handled 80 percent of all ACLU cases, the special projects, and the nominal ACLU legal staff. Wulf was temperamentally unsuited for this role. Still others thought he was not interested in some major ACLU issues: church–state, abortion, and women's rights. Finally, Wulf's abrasive personal style offended many people. One incident that helped trigger his ouster was a pointedly offensive letter to a prominent New York City attorney.[48]

Accordingly, in early 1977 Dorsen and Neier forced him to resign after a tense confrontation. His allies thought his ouster represented a conservative reaction in the ACLU. At a stormy Executive Committee meeting over the issue, Alan Levine charged that "the 'passion people' [Morgan and Wulf] have been purged."[49] It was not a purge but a pivotal moment in the ACLU's history. Passion alone was no longer sufficient, as the ACLU had taken on an enormous role for itself in national affairs. Being a major player—in the Supreme Court, in Congress, and in all fifty states—required maintaining a large bureaucratic structure. Many of the "passion people" of the 1960s shuddered at the mere mention of the word *bureaucracy,* and a lot of them drifted away. But bureaucracy was the price of the ACLU's success.

The last to go was Executive Director Neier, who announced his resignation in the spring of 1978.[50] There was an element of tragedy in his demise:

He was unable to adapt to the demands of running the complex ACLU bureaucracy he had done so much to create. Like Morgan, he thrived on the sense of being on the frontier of new civil liberties issues. He was at his best during the great period of growth and so was not suited for the defensive posture of the 1970s. Battered by the Skokie crisis, he resigned in the spring of 1978. A few years later he joined and then led Americas Watch, which established an outstanding record in monitoring human rights abuses overseas. He was both happier and effective in a smaller organization in which, as he explained when describing his earlier role in the ACLU, he could put his "personal stamp on civil liberties."[51]

New Leaders

New ACLU Executive Director Ira Glasser was one of the veterans of the 1960s who did adapt to the demands of the 1970s. Taking office in September 1978, he immersed himself in the ACLU's administrative morass. On his first day on the job he found the ACLU on the verge of bankruptcy. When the Goldberger letter and a bequest of $400,000 averted immediate disaster, Glasser turned his attention to the underlying administrative problems. He brought in longtime ACLU staffer Florence Isbell to straighten out the membership department. In the 1940s Isbell had gone to work as a secretary for Roger Baldwin at age nineteen, and since then she had served as director of the Georgia and National Capital Area affiliates.[52]

A major part of the membership problem was purely administrative: straightening out the mess with the computer and staffing the department with a sufficient number of skilled professionals. Beyond this, however, the ACLU faced a problem common to all public-interest groups in the 1970s. Even under normal conditions, an organization loses each year at least 10 percent to 15 percent of its members. Some quit over a particular issue; others simply lose interest; and many just put aside the renewal letter and then forget about it. In the ACLU's case, this meant recruiting 25,000 to 30,000 new members annually just to maintain the status quo. This in turn required an expensive direct mail operation. Given a normal response rate of 0.75 percent, the ACLU therefore had to mail 4 million solicitations just to stay even. It was a crushing financial burden, aggravated by steadily rising postal rates. Direct mail solicitation was actually a money-losing operation, as the dues paid by each year's crop of new members did not pay for the mailing that recruited them. But the ACLU had no choice. If it failed to replace the normal attrition, the resulting loss of revenue would set in motion debilitating cuts in staff and programs. Such was the environment for public-interest groups by the late 1970s. Glasser was the first ACLU executive director who had to master the arcane details of "test mailings," "targeting," and "response rates."

The Goldberger letter suggested an untapped source of support. Glasser then brought in Carol Pitchersky, an experienced fund-raiser, as development director to create an ongoing program of soliciting tax-deductible contributions. Her operation was a phenomenal success. Contributions rose from less than $300,000 in 1977 to over $3 million in 1988,[53] which wiped out the debt and allowed the ACLU to strengthen its programs, particularly in the Washington office.

Glasser and Pitchersky threw out the normal rules for direct mail solicitations. Instead of emotional pitches with eye-catching graphics, they sent out rather long letters discussing civil liberties issues and reviewing the ACLU's work. With the advent of the Reagan administration in 1981 there was adequate justification for the sometimes hyperbolic rhetoric ("the most massive assault on civil liberties since the Cold War"). Consequently the ACLU faced the challenge of the Reagan years in better financial health than at any time in its history, having broadened its base of financial support and reduced its dependence on a few large contributors. Dorsen solidified their support in any event, by establishing the ACLU President's Club in 1978 for those who gave $25,000 or more.

The ACLU in a Time of Transition

Despite the many internal troubles in the mid-seventies, the ACLU's program remained vigorous. Neier's 1977 *Annual Report,* issued as the Skokie crisis reached its peak, showed no sign of the organization's slacking off. The Reproductive Rights Project and the National Prison Project had established themselves as the primary centers of litigation expertise in their respective areas. The Women's Rights project was responsible for virtually all of the initial Supreme Court cases in that area. In Atlanta, Laughlin MacDonald carried on Chuck Morgan's voting rights work and, with at least thirty or forty active cases at any moment, was directly responsible for the election of hundreds of local black elected officials. In 1977 alone it was involved in seventeen cases regarding discrimination in jury selection. The Mental Health Law Project won the landmark *Donaldson* case in 1977, establishing that nondangerous persons could not be confined against their will.[54]

In the Supreme Court, the ACLU was a major presence, appearing in more cases than any other organization did, except the federal government—and this even after the decision to decrease the number of filings. The ACLU continued to enjoy surprising success before the conservative Burger Court. It lost 65 percent of its cases in the 1973–1974 term but won 62 percent in 1978–1979.[55] The backbone of the ACLU's work was in the affiliates. The New York, Illinois, Tennessee, Washington, and Southern California affiliates all handled lengthy and complex suits against local police spying. All ended with at least partially successful settlements.

The Seattle police-spying ordinance, enacted in a campaign supported by the Washington affiliate and led by future affiliate director Kathleen Taylor, was but one example of the creativity and vigor of the local ACLU units. In addition, the affiliates handled a steady stream of routine freedom of speech and assembly cases, most involving the same issues as the Skokie case but without attracting national attention. In his 1977 *Annual Report,* Neier esti-mated a total of six thousand separate cases during the year. A true account-ing was difficult, if not impossible, to make. The ACLU affiliates settled many free speech and church–state cases with a single phone call or a meeting be-tween a cooperating attorney and a government official. With civil liberties principles deeply embedded in the law, the mere threat of an ACLU suit was often enough.

In one particularly important case, the NYCLU challenged one of the major liberal reforms of the Watergate era, political campaign financing re-form. The public-interest group Common Cause almost single-handedly won passage of the 1971 Federal Election Campaign Act and the very restrictive 1974 amendments, the latter a product of public outrage over financial irregu-larities by the 1972 Nixon campaign. The ACLU had not opposed either law, seeing no free speech problems in them.

In early 1972 a group advocating Nixon's impeachment had placed an ad in the *New York Times.* The government held that because it was an election year, this was a partisan political ad and so took action against the National Committee for Impeachment. NYCLU Executive Director Glasser, seeing a classic example of government harassment of an unpopular group, agreed to assist. The case was still pending when the *Buckley* case arose. Shortly after Congress passed the 1974 amendments, conservative New York Senator James Buckley asked Glasser to join him in a suit challenging its restrictions on campaign spending. The final list of plaintiffs was one of the strangest collec-tions of bedfellows in ACLU history: Buckley, the ACLU, liberal political activist Stewart Mott, liberal Minnesota Senator Eugene McCarthy, the Mis-sissippi Republican party, the American Conservative Union, and the New York Conservative party.[56]

In a complex decision, the Supreme Court accepted most of the NYCLU's arguments in *Buckley v. Valeo.* It agreed that the restrictions on spending "relative to a candidate" infringed on freedom of speech. The Court also agreed with the NYCLU that the compulsory disclosure of political contributions over $100 exposed members of minority parties to potential harassment (and in 1979 the ACLU won the right of the Socialist Workers party to not dis-close the names of its contributors). But the Court rejected the NYCLU's arguments that the law's formula for the public funding of presidential candi-dates discriminated against third parties. Glasser hailed *Buckley* as "a tri-umph, though not a complete one, for the First Amendment."[57]

Not everyone in the ACLU was happy with the NYCLU's role in the case. Some thought the affiliate had used bad judgment in rushing to challenge a federal law while the ACLU board was still debating. This was symptomatic of the tensions between the affiliates and the national ACLU. A significant minority, meanwhile, concerned about the impact of money on American politics, thought that civil liberties were best protected by more stringent restrictions on campaign spending, and it continued to press for a revision of ACLU policy through the 1980s.[58]

The ACLU's "Magna Carta"

At the depth of the Skokie crisis, the ACLU won a special victory in the Supreme Court. The case began in 1973 with the discovery that South Carolina officials were sterilizing women on public assistance, or were threatening to sterilize them as a condition of receiving Medicaid. ACLU cooperating attorney Edna Smith Primus—the daughter of sharecroppers and the first black woman to graduate from the University of South Carolina Law School—advised a group of women of their rights and suggested a possible lawsuit. In response to a subsequent inquiry from one woman, Primus sent a letter saying the ACLU "would like to file a lawsuit on your behalf for money against the doctor who performed the operation."[59]

The South Carolina Supreme Court publicly reprimanded Primus for improper solicitation. She appealed, and the ACLU carried her case to the U.S. Supreme Court. At issue was the ability of civil liberties and civil rights attorneys to advise people that their rights had been violated, that a suit was possible, and that the ACLU, the NAACP, or whoever could handle the case.

In a decision that was hailed as the "magna carta" for the ACLU and other public-interest law groups, the Supreme Court ruled that Primus's actions did not constitute unethical, in-person solicitation. The Court distinguished between lawyers who solicit cases "for pecuniary gain" and those who solicit to "further political and ideological goals through associational activity." The six-to-one decision acknowledged the special role of the ACLU "in the defense of unpopular causes and unpopular defendants."[60] It was a vindication of the ACLU's fifty-eight years of defending the unpopular.

Sixteen

The Reagan Era's Assault
on Civil Liberties

The Conservative Revolt

"I feel like we're fighting a twelve-front war," said ACLU Director Ira Glasser.[1] It *was* a twelve-front war. The Reagan administration, swept into power on a conservative political tide, was more hostile to civil liberties than any administration in memory had been. The New Right's "social agenda" included outlawing abortion, putting prayer back in the schools, banning pornography, stopping the ERA, and fighting gay rights. On crime issues, President Reagan wanted to eliminate the exclusionary rule and the Miranda warning. In the area of national security he promised to remove the new restraints on the FBI and the CIA.

Prospects for civil liberties looked very bad in Congress and the courts. Many of the ACLU's strongest supporters in Congress were defeated. Gone were Senators Gaylord Nelson (a 93 percent pro-ACLU voting record), George McGovern (87 percent), John Culver (87 percent), and Representative John Brademas (87 percent). Senator Strom Thurmond replaced Ted Kennedy as chair of the crucial Senate Judiciary Committee. John Shattuck, director of the ACLU's Washington, D.C., office, called the election results "a crisis of major proportions for civil liberties" and the next session of Congress a "state of siege" on the Constitution.[2] On the Supreme Court, Reagan stood to appoint anywhere from three to five Supreme Court justices. The remaining civil libertarians were the oldest: William J. Brennan was seventy-four, and Thurgood Marshall was seventy-two.

The conservative coalition included traditional economic conservatives, a well-organized antiabortion movement, the newly politicized religious fundamentalists, and a middle class worried about inflation. Televangelists led by Jerry Falwell carried their moralistic, anti–civil libertarian message into millions of homes every week. Ninety-seven-year-old Roger Baldwin, who had just received the Medal of Freedom from President Jimmy Carter, remarked that "these were the most dangerous times for civil liberties he had seen."[3]

The ACLU was a special target for New Right attacks. Attorney General William French Smith called the ACLU the "criminal's lobby." Falwell denounced it as "the single most destructive threat to our traditional American way of life." Daniel Popeo, of the Washington Legal Foundation, called it the "American Criminal Liberties Union." And President Reagan said he wore the ACLU hostility "like a badge of honor."[4]

The ACLU greeted the New Right in 1981 with a poster depicting a militant evangelical sallying forth on a horse: "If the Moral Majority gets its way, you better start praying." The conservative upsurge alarmed many lukewarm civil libertarians, and the ACLU's membership increased by 35,000 in 1981 alone.[5] The strength of support for civil liberties principles was evident in the fact that a new organization, People for the American Way, whose program was similar to the ACLU's, enrolled over 200,000 members without draining any support from the ACLU. In the end, the ACLU was far more successful in stopping the New Right's social agenda than anyone had expected on election night 1981. Shattuck said that even he was surprised at the support the ACLU was able to muster.[6] The ensuing battle over the social agenda revealed the extent to which civil liberties principles had permeated American society.

Religion and the Schools

Scopes Revisited: Scientific Creationism

For the ACLU, it seemed like déjà vu. Fifty-six years after the great Scopes "monkey trial," the ACLU was back in a southern courtroom defending evolution.

Fundamentalists—convinced that the Supreme Court had "kicked Christ out of the schools" and spawned a generation of crime, sexual promiscuity, abortion, and homosexuality—now advocated "creation science," that claimed scientific support for the biblical view of creation. Rather than ban the teaching of evolution, they sought a "balanced treatment" of evolution and creationism, which had the appeal of fairness and respect for academic freedom. Accordingly, balanced treatment bills were introduced in twenty-three state legislatures in 1980 and 1981.[7]

Arkansas was the scene of the ACLU's first confrontation with creationism. The state passed a balanced treatment law in March 1981, which the state senate had approved by a vote of sixteen to two after only fifteen minutes of debate. Roger Baldwin, five months away from death, phoned Ira Glasser: "Did you read about that Arkansas law?" he rasped. "What are you going to do about it?" Glasser patiently explained that a large New York law firm had promised to handle the case for the ACLU. "We needed only two lawyers in our day," Baldwin harrumphed (in fact, the ACLU had used five).[8]

The ACLU lined up twenty-three plaintiffs, representing parents, teachers,

and national religious organizations. Balanced treatment, the
violated the establishment clause because it advanced a par
creed. Local teachers and school administrators testified that
implement the law without teaching religious doctrine. As in
the ACLU called in noted scientists as expert witnesses, inc
selling author and scientist Carl Sagan of Cornell University ... ...
paleontologist Stephen Jay Gould of Harvard University.[9]

Reporters from over seventy-five news media around the world who flocked
to Little Rock expecting a replay of the theatrical Darrow–Bryan confrontation were disappointed. The trial was an orderly though spirited contest over
the issues. On January 5, 1982, the court ruled the balanced treatment law
unconstitutional, accepting the ACLU's argument that the law's primary
purpose was to advance religious doctrine: "It was simply and purely an
effort to introduce the Biblical version of creation into the public school curricula."[10]

The ACLU had little time to savor the victory. Louisiana had passed a law
scheduled to take effect in 1983. Because it lacked the worst features of the
Arkansas law—the findings of fact about creationism and the biblical definition of creation—it would be more difficult to challenge. The ACLU again
assembled a large group of plaintiffs, representing twenty-six organizations
and individuals. In June 1987 the Supreme Court handed the ACLU a particularly sweet victory, declaring the law unconstitutional in a seven-to-two
decision. Justice William Brennan held that "the preeminent purpose" of the
law "was clearly to advance the religious viewpoint that a supernatural being
created humankind." The decision indicated that the Court, even under the
new chief justice, William Rehnquist, was not going to overturn established
principles of separation of church and state.[11]

A reporter asked the ACLU executive director, "How long have you been
fighting this case?" Thinking back to Scopes, Glasser replied, "Sixty-two
years."

The Battle over Prayer in the Schools

The ACLU regarded prayer in the schools as far more serious a threat than
creationism was because it seemed to enjoy greater public support. Indeed,
President Reagan had personally endorsed a constitutional amendment permitting vocal, government-sponsored prayer in public schools. Yet, as on
several other issues, the New Right had less power than it first appeared. The
ACLU again mobilized a coalition of separationist groups which succeeded
in delaying a vote until March 1984 and then keeping it eleven votes short of
the necessary two-thirds majority (fifty-six to forty-four). The vote marked
twenty-two years of failure for the prayer amendment forces. Despite the
sound and fury of the Moral Majority, Americans were not quite ready to put
Protestant fundamentalism back into the schools.[12]

The prayer forces quickly responded with a proposal for "equal access."
Oregon Senator Mark Hatfield introduced a bill requiring school districts

eiving federal funds to grant all student groups access to school facilities. That is, if a school allowed any student group to use the building during non-instructional hours, it had to grant the same privilege to all, without discrimination "on the basis of the content of their speech."

John Swomley, chair of the ACLU's Church–State Committee, saw the equal access bill as an opening for religion in the schools; evangelical groups, he argued, had trained 4,500 youth ministers to proselytize in the schools.[13] Others saw equal access as advancing the free speech rights of students, as being able to protect the rights of groups advocating a nuclear freeze or gay rights. Caught in the midst of its own debate, therefore, the ACLU took no position on the equal access bill, although the Washington office lobbied to strengthen protection for unpopular groups. The separationists finally prevailed, and the ACLU opposed the law, passed in August 1984, as "a flagrant violation of the Establishment Clause" and called on Congress to repeal it.[14]

Opposition to the equal access law revived the old charges that the ACLU was antireligion. Falwell and the Moral Majority, of course, thought the ACLU was evil incarnate. But even moderate Protestant leaders were upset. Rev. Dean Kelley of the National Council of Churches accused the ACLU of being "almost exclusively concerned with establishment problems and hardly at all with free exercise."[15] In fact, though, the most important religious controversies of the 1980s involved the establishment clause rather than the free exercise clause: In one noteworthy free exercise case, the ACLU defended the right of an Orthodox Jewish rabbi in the air force to wear a yarmulke. The Supreme Court's decision upholding the air force in *Goldman v. Weinberger* was part of the Court's general pattern of deferring to the interests of institutional authorities (in the military, public schools, prisons) at the expense of the individual.[16]

While Congress debated the school prayer issue, several states passed laws permitting prayers or a "moment of silence." For instance, Alabama passed three laws between 1978 and 1981, permitting a one-minute period of silence for meditation, a period of "meditation or voluntary prayer," and one allowing teachers to lead "willing students" in a prescribed prayer to "almighty God . . . the Creator and Supreme Judge of the world." The ACLU and People for the American Way challenged the laws in a joint suit and convinced the Supreme Court that the prayer law violated the establishment clause.[17] The 1985 decision, however, left unresolved the question of whether a moment of silence was constitutional. The ACLU challenged this practice in a New Jersey case, winning lower court decisions. The Supreme Court, however, dismissed an appeal on procedural grounds, thus leaving the issue still unresolved.[18]

The Secular Humanism Controversy

In the wake of the Alabama prayer decision, District Court Judge Brevar Hand took the extraordinary step of reorganizing the original case on his own initiative. A militant fundamentalist, he had earlier held that Alabama had the power to establish an official religion if it wanted to and now argued that if prayer were unconstitutional, then all religion must be removed from the schools. This included the "religion of secular humanism," and in the most direct assault on the freedom to teach since Scopes, Hand ordered forty-four books removed from the Alabama schools. Conservatives who had long denounced judicial activism now enthusiastically supported the direct intrusion of a federal judge into curricular decisions. ACLU staff counsel Jack Novik called the judge "unlearned Hand," and "Hand without a head."[19]

The trial in Hand's court was a direct confrontation between the ACLU and the New Right. Televangelist Pat Robertson, who was planning to run for the Republican presidential nomination, rallied to the judge's defense. The secular humanism controversy turned on the question of what constituted a religion, and Robertson accused the ACLU of promoting atheism: "They're saying we don't want God in the schools. . . . We are going to drill children in atheism, which is what secular humanism is." The ACLU replied that a secular education involved neutrality on the question of religion and did not itself represent a religion. Judge Hand ordered the books out of the Mobile schools, as expected, but he was overruled by the circuit court of appeals.[20] The decision and the Louisiana creationism decision just a few weeks earlier were devastating blows to the New Right. The ACLU's Ira Glasser pointed out that they didn't "end the fight," but at least they confirmed that "the law is on our side, and [that] makes the fight easier to win."[21]

Meanwhile, another secular humanism controversy arose in Tennessee when a group of fundamentalist parents sued to remove certain books from the Hawkins County schools, on the grounds that exposing their children to them violated their free exercise of religion. The books in question included a widely used reading series published by Holt, Rinehart and Winston. The case raised a difficult free exercise question for the ACLU, recalling the Jehovah's Witnesses' objections to compulsory flag salutes. Were the children being compelled to participate in an exercise offensive to their religious views? ACLU board member Nadine Strossen cited the 1963 *Sherbert* case, holding that government benefits should not place a burden on the exercise of one's religious beliefs. She argued that the schools should be required to provide an alternative reading program or at least should allow students to choose not to read religiously offensive materials. The ACLU board, however, held that "mere exposure" to different points of view did not constitute indoctrination or forced participation in a religious exercise.[22] The trial court upheld the parents in *Mozert,* awarding them over $50,000 in damages. But when the Sixth Circuit Court of Appeals overturned the verdict, it dealt the third major defeat for the Christian Right in the summer of 1987.[23]

Religion and the Burger–Rehnquist Court

Despite these victories, the ACLU suffered some notable losses in the Supreme Court on church–state issues. The annual Christmastime battle over religious displays on public property was one of the ACLU's most publicized issues, with pundits attacking the ACLU as "the grinch that stole Christmas." In a case from Rhode Island, the Court ruled that a crèche on public property did not violate the establishment clause. The opinion in *Lynch v. Donnelly* left many issues unsettled. Chief Justice Warren Burger held that a crèche was permissible as long as a reasonable observer would not think it was promoting a religious point of view. In other words, it was all right if it were not really religious. ACLU Legal Director Burt Neuborne thus felt the decision was not a total defeat, as Burger's opinion suggested that a cross or a crèche standing by itself would not pass constitutional muster.[24]

The ACLU suffered a major defeat in a challenge to the federal "chastity act." One of the key New Right initiatives, the Adolescent Family Life Act of 1981, provided federal grants to programs promoting "self-discipline and chastity" among teenagers, thereby mandating grants to religious organizations. Janet Benshoof, director of the ACLU's Reproductive Freedom Project, argued that the law promoted religious doctrine and restricted free speech by prohibiting any discussion of abortion as a medical option.[25] But the Court ruled that the law did not violate the establishment clause on its face and remanded it for hearings on whether particular programs promoted religious doctrine.[26] The Rehnquist Court upheld the ACLU's position on creationism but was clearly more willing to accommodate government support for religion in other ways.

The Fight for Abortion Rights

Abortion was the great civil liberties battlefield of the 1980s, the issue that brought thousands of demonstrators into the streets. The stakes involved more than just abortion. It was a symbolic issue touching on the legally complex and emotionally charged issues of changing sex roles, sexual morality, and the question of when life begins.

The right-to-life movement was at flood tide in early 1981, claiming credit for electing Reagan and defeating prominent liberal senators. The Hyde amendment had already eliminated federal funding for abortions, and so the movement's primary goal was a constitutional amendment outlawing abortion. Short of that, the antiabortion movement sought a variety of restrictions on access to abortions, such as waiting periods and requirements of parental notification. Finally, militant demonstrators harassed abortion clinics through constant picketing. On the fringe, a criminal element resorted to terrorist bombings of abortion clinics.[27]

The abortion rights struggle brought out the best of both the old and the new ACLU. While Janet Benshoof's Reproductive Freedom Project became involved in every important court case and the Washington office led the fight in Congress against a constitutional amendment,[28] the ACLU honored its historic commitment to defend the rights of even its enemies. The ultimate test came in January 1985 when three antiabortion activists were arrested for bombing the ACLU's Washington office. When they were held without bail, the ACLU National Capital Area affiliate called on federal officials to set "reasonable bail." Legal Director Art Spitzer said that although "we are no more eager than anyone else to have our offices bombed, . . . we do not wish to be protected against that threat at the expense of the constitutional rights of any citizens."[29]

The Constitutional Amendment Battle

In early 1981 it appeared that a constitutional amendment outlawing abortion might sail through Congress. President Reagan gave it his support by declaring that human life "begins at the moment of conception." Antiabortion leaders took a variety of positions: North Carolina Senator Jesse Helms offered an "absolutist" constitutional amendment declaring that human life began at the moment of conception. This could outlaw some forms of birth control that are abortifacient. An alternative amendment would outlaw abortions except when "required to prevent the death of the mother." A third proposal was a federal statute declaring that "human life shall be deemed to exist from conception."[30]

As was the case with school prayer, the antiabortion forces were surprised to find that they had great difficulty bringing their proposals to a vote. Despite the seeming power of the right-to-life movement, the majority of Americans favored keeping abortion legal: Public opinion polls consistently indicated that 60 percent of the public took that position, with 20 percent favoring an unlimited right to abortion and 20 percent opposing all abortions. Working with the other prochoice groups, the ACLU Washington office mobilized this support for abortion rights, beginning with a series of 1981 conferences in Los Angeles, Chicago, Boston, Philadelphia, St. Louis, Seattle, New York, and Atlanta.[31] The first Senate vote did not come until September 1982, when the Senate tabled a human life statute bill by forty-seven to forty-six, thereby dispelling the myth of the all-powerful right-to-life movement. The ACLU called it "an astounding defeat for the New Right and President Reagan." A year later, Utah Senator Orrin Hatch's constitutional amendment ("a right to abortion is not secured by this Constitution") lost fifty to forty-nine. From that point on, the right-to-life movement began to unravel in an acrimonious feud beween hard-liners, who wanted to ban all abortions, and pragmatists, who were willing to accept an exception for rape and incest victims.[32]

Congress, however, continued to enact the Hyde amendment, prohibiting federal funds for abortions. Court challenges brought by the ACLU and other abortions rights groups, alleging discrimination against the poor, failed.[33] Many states also banned public funds for abortions; California did so eight years in a row, but with the two ACLU affiliates successfully enjoining the law each year.[34] The contrast between the failure of the constitutional amendment banning all abortions and the success of laws restricting public funds illuminated the complex public attitudes toward abortion. Legislators readily punished the poor by denying them public funds, while preserving access to abortions for most Americans. This essentially self-centered approach to civil liberties had a long history.

Abortion Rights in the Supreme Court

On top of the defeat of the Hatch amendment in 1983, the Supreme Court struck down an Akron, Ohio, ordinance restricting access to abortions. The law required a twenty-four-hour waiting period, compelled doctors to inform patients that "the unborn child is a human life from the moment of conception," and required that all second trimester abortions be conducted in hospitals rather than clinics. Fifteen states and a number of cities adopted similar restrictions. In a sweeping victory for the ACLU Reproductive Freedom Project, the Court rejected each of the law's provisions. Informed consent was "designed not to promote informed consent, but rather to withhold it altogether"; the waiting period was an "arbitrary and inflexible" requirement; and the second trimester provision imposed a "heavy and unnecessary burden on women's access to a relatively inexpensive . . . and safe abortion procedure."[35]

The legal challenges to abortion rights continued unabated after *Akron*. The Reproductive Freedom Project's 1987 docket listed 167 active cases, 25 percent of which were filed in the previous year.[36] By the end of the 1980s the lower federal courts, now dominated by Reagan appointees, became increasingly hostile to abortion rights. Particularly important was the eighth circuit court decision in *Hodgson v. Minnesota,* upholding a state law requiring minors seeking abortions to notify both parents. Benshoof introduced testimony from doctors, psychiatrists, nurses, and counselors on the extent to which parental notification, in practice, inhibited the choice to seek an abortion. The district court upheld the ACLU, ruling that the law offered pregnant minors "a choice between trauma in the courthouse, crisis at home or unwanted motherhood." In a decision that had far-reaching implications beyond abortion rights, the eighth circuit court reversed and upheld the law. Six of the seven judges in the majority were Reagan appointees, and all the three dissenters were Lyndon Johnson appointees. The vote was an indication of probable hard times ahead for civil liberties before the lower federal courts in which, by 1989, half of all judges had been appointed by President Reagan.[37]

In one curious footnote, the ACLU awoke in 1985 to discover that its abortion policy had never been revised since 1968 and did not go as far as *Roe v. Wade* in upholding the right to third trimester abortions. In the heat of the abortion rights struggle, no one had noticed. One board member pointed out that under existing policy, the ACLU could not enter pending abortion cases from Illinois and Pennsylvania. It was a curious oversight in an organization normally obsessed with the fine points of formal policy. The ACLU hurriedly authorized participation in the two cases and set out to overhaul its policy.[38]

Free Speech for Abortion Protesters

Although it played a leading role in the prochoice coalition in Congress and the courts, the ACLU parted company with many of its allies over free speech for antiabortion demonstrators. At clinics across the country, angry demonstrators accused patients and staff of "murder" and tried to block entrance to the clinics. Their tactics raised basic questions about the scope of First Amendment rights. The cries of "murderer" and "baby killer" constituted offensive speech, and many prochoice activists argued that the massive demonstrations interfered with a woman's constitutional right of access to abortion. By early 1989, Operation Rescue represented an even more aggressive effort to shut down abortion clinics.[39]

A Tacoma, Washington, case dramatized the conflict between the ACLU and its allies. A local clinic won an injunction limiting antiabortion picketing to a sidewalk along the side of the building and prohibiting picketers from making any reference to "murderers" or "killers." The ACLU filed an *amicus* on behalf of Tacoma Stands Up for Life (TSUFL), while Planned Parenthood, the National Organization of Women (NOW), the Religious Coalition for Abortion Rights (RCAR), and the National Lawyers Guild filed briefs supporting the clinic. The ACLU argued that both the place and content restrictions represented an unconstitutional restraint. The words *murderer* and *killer* were indeed offensive but did not incite violence. The clinic's lawyers contended, on the other hand, that the state had a compelling interest in protecting the delivery of health care services. The Michigan ACLU, meanwhile, represented right-to-life demonstrators in Livonia, Michigan, where an abortion clinic had obtained a restraining order prohibiting "harassing, annoying, photographing," or otherwise interfering with clinic patients. The order prohibited picketing and distributing written material within five hundred feet of the clinic. The Michigan Supreme Court agreed with the ACLU and threw out the restraining order.[40]

The legitimate First Amendment rights of antiabortion activists were tainted by the criminal activities of the lunatic fringe. In the winter of 1984–1985 there was a rash of bombings of abortion clinics, and the Justice Department rebuffed prochoice demands for an investigation. The ACLU remained leery of efforts by other prochoice groups to seek court injunctions against the more radical antiabortion activists.

Failing to deliver on a constitutional amendment, the Reagan administration tried to appease the right-to-life movement by cutting off funds for family-planning services. In August 1987 the Department of Health and Human Services (HHS) issued new regulations denying federal funds to any program that provided "counselling and referral for abortion services." Thus, a doctor could not even mention the option of abortion, much less refer the woman to another clinic, even in cases in which the pregnancy threatened her life. Title X of the Public Health Services Act supported more than five thousand family-planning clinics serving five million women, 80 percent of whom had low incomes. The ACLU's Benshoof immediately tried to enjoin the regulations, which, she held, violated the intent of the statute and threatened a doctor's ability to conform to medical ethics. It was a basic free speech issue involving the right of a doctor to discuss with a patient the full range of medical services available.[41]

The Censorship Wars

Faced with complaints from parents who called the books "anti-American, anti-Christian, anti-Semitic and just plain filthy," the Island Trees, New York, board of education removed Kurt Vonnegut's *Slaughterhouse Five,* Bernard Malamud's *The Fixer,* a collection of *Best Short Stories by Negro Writers,* and eight other books from the school library. Seventeen-year-old senior Steven Pico thought book banning occurred only in totalitarian countries and called the New York Civil Liberties Union. It took his case to the Supreme Court, which ruled that school boards could not remove books "simply because they dislike the ideas contained in those books."[42]

The censorship wars were fought on several fronts during the Reagan years: The Moral Majority waged a holy war against pornography; Attorney General Edwin Meese appointed a federal commission to study it; a group of feminists developed a novel antipornography ordinance; and Tennessee Senator Albert Gore's wife Tipper organized a national campaign against alleged "indecency" in rock music. In the realm of political speech, meanwhile, the Reagan administration engaged in a systematic effort to restrict speakers who opposed administration policy. In all, it was the most concerted attack on freedom of expression in decades.

The War on the Schools and Libraries

Steve Pico's case resembled other battles in schools and libraries: Kurt Vonnegut competing with Judy Blume for the status of the most frequently banned author. Another frequent target was the popular *Our Bodies, Ourselves.* Conservative moralists objected to its frank discussion of female sexuality, including masturbation, abortion, and lesbianism. The Georgia ACLU surveyed libraries in four southern states and found that almost half had faced challenges to books on their shelves. In 63 percent of the cases, the library yielded to the pressure, either removing the book or restricting access to it. Surveys by the Minnesota and Nebraska ACLU affiliates found similar pressures. Schools and libraries had always faced such efforts, however, and it was not clear whether there was an increase during the 1980s.[43]

The Feminist Antipornography Crusade

The newest censorship force was a group of antipornography feminists who distinguished pornography from obscenity or erotica, defining it as physical and psychological violence degrading to women. They were divided over how to deal with pornography, and many, recognizing the dangers to the women's movement in censorship, stressed public education through demonstrations and boycotts.[44]

The feminist campaign took a dramatic new turn in 1983 when author Andrea Dworkin and law professor Catherine MacKinnon entered the debate over a Minneapolis proposal to restrict the location of adult book stores and theaters. They offered a novel legal theory defining pornography as discrimination against women and giving individuals a cause of action to sue the producers and distributors of pornography. They defined pornography as anything presenting women as dehumanized sexual objects, particularly where they appeared to enjoy pain or humiliation. This included the presentation of body parts—breasts, vaginas, buttocks—"such that women are reduced to those parts." Women could seek personal damages and/or injunctions against the material.[45]

The Minneapolis Civil Liberties Union fought the Dworkin-MacKinnon proposal, calling it "censorship of ideas and images based on a disagreement with the content." The link between pornography and violence had not been established, and the proposal offered "no workable" definition of pornography. The city council passed the ordinance, but Mayor Donald Fraser vetoed it on the grounds that "the remedy sought . . . is neither appropriate nor enforceable within our cherished tradition and constitutionally protected right of free speech."[46]

The battle quickly shifted to Indianapolis. MacKinnon began advising city–county council member Beulah Coughenour—also leader of an anti-pornography campaign and an ally of Phyllis Schlafly in the Stop ERA crusade—over the objections of other feminists. Dworkin, meanwhile, blithely admitted in an Omaha speech that some of her own books could be suppressed under her and MacKinnon's proposal. Indianapolis enacted a revised version of the ordinance that authorized government censorship.

The ACLU responded to MacKinnon and Dworkin by organizing the Feminist Anti-Censorship Task Force. FACT mobilized an impressive array of feminist writers and legal scholars to fight the Indianapolis ordinance. Those signing the FACT *amicus* included writers Rita Mae Brown, Betty Friedan, Vivian Gornick, Kate Millett, Adrienne Rich, and Alix Kates Shulman. Friedan's was a voice to be reckoned with, as her 1963 book, *The Feminist Mystique,* had launched the modern feminist movement. The FACT *amicus* written by the ACLU's Nan Hunter and New York University law professor Sylvia Law, argued that the ordinance actually harmed women's rights by accepting traditional sexual stereotypes: "Good" women were either not interested in sex or had to be protected from it. The key terms, "graphic sexually explicit" and "subordinating," were impermissibly vague.[47]

The Indianapolis ordinance met a crushing defeat in the federal courts, with both the district and circuit courts declaring it unconstitutional. The Seventh Circuit Court of Appeals ruled that "the state may not ordain preferred viewpoints. The Constitution forbids the state to declare one perspective right and silence opponents."[48] The steam quickly went out of the feminist antipornography movement, with the wholly unanticipated consequence of forcing feminists to confront the question of sexually explicit material. The ensuing debate legitimized women's interest in sexually explicit material, and FACT produced *Caught Looking,* a collection of serious articles on feminism and censorship surrounded by graphic sexual images.[49]

Ed Meese's Pornography Commission

The Reagan administration entered the antipornography fray in 1985 when Attorney General Edwin Meese established a federal commission on pornography. Stacked with antipornography activists and hampered by a limited budget, it planned no new research and was designed primarily as a public relations effort.

The Meese Commission, as it was known, was a complete fiasco, largely because of the ACLU's Barry Lynn. In perhaps one of the ACLU's most brilliantly conceived and executed campaigns, Lynn seized the initiative and hounded the commission from the start. Following the commission to Chicago, Los Angeles, Houston, and Miami, he kept up a steady drumbeat of publicity about its bias and shoddy research methods, publicizing its visits to adult bookstores and exposing the bias of the hearings. Of the 208 witnesses who eventually testified, 160 (77 percent) were procensorship. The anticensorship witnesses were often badgered. The commission singled out Isabelle Katz Pinzler, director of the ACLU Women's Rights Project, for having once accepted a small Playboy Foundation grant. Playboy publisher Hugh Hefner, meanwhile, was smeared (with charges of sexual harassment, job discrimination, drug use, prostitution, rape, and even murder) in a manner reminiscent of the old HUAC anti-Communist crusade. Psychologist Edward Donnerstein publicly repudiated the commission's misuse of his research on the relationship between pornography and violence. The ACLU exposed the commission's tactics at a January 1986 conference, with Betty Friedan reminding everyone that *The Feminine Mystique* had been suppressed as pornographic and warning again of the dangers of censorship.[50]

In his most aggressive move, Lynn won access to the commission's working papers through a joint ACLU–Public Citizen suit, enabling him to see the commission's recommendations before they were officially released. This allowed the ACLU to greet the report with a detailed rebuttal. By keeping the commission continuously on the defensive, Lynn successfully blunted its impact. Political commentators treated the commission with derision. To wit: Announcing the report's release, Meese stood beneath a statue of a bare-breasted statue of Justice. *Esquire* labeled the picture "tits and ass."[51]

The Meese Commission report dodged the basic question of a workable definition of pornography but hinted at an extremely broad standard ("material [that] is predominantly sexually explicit and intended primarily for the purpose of sexual arousal"). It recommended federal laws to ease the prosecution of pornography in interstate commerce, to ban pornography on cable television, to outlaw sexually explicit "dial-a-porn" services, and to use federal racketeering statutes against producers of pornography. The last recommendation proved to be the most effective, and the Justice Department won an important Supreme Court case in 1989 upholding use of the Racketeer Influenced and Corrupt Organizations law ("RICO") against an Indiana "adult bookstore." The ACLU saw ominous threats to free speech, and other rights, in the RICO law.[52]

Tipper Gore's War on Rock Music

Another new censorship crusade appeared in 1985 when Tipper Gore, wife of a Democratic senator and presidential aspirant Albert Gore, launched an attack on rock music. Expressing outrage at the explicit sex, violence, and satanic cultism portrayed in popular music, she organized the Parent's Music Resource Center (PMRC) and campaigned for the labeling of rock music albums. The ACLU responded by organizing the Musical Majority with record industry executive Danny Goldberg, enlisting the support of top recording stars Tina Turner, John Cougar Mellencamp, Prince (whose album had set Gore into action in the first place), and the Pointer Sisters. Ira Glasser denounced scheduled Senate hearings on the grounds that "the government has absolutely no business conducting an inquiry into the content of published materials."[53] Musician Frank Zappa emerged as Gore's leading opponent in the media battle that ensued, testifying at the Senate hearings and making it his personal crusade over the next few years.

The Senate hearings revealed the extent to which free speech principles had permeated society: Even Tipper Gore had disavowed outright censorship in favor of warning labels on albums. Senator Ernest Hollings of South Carolina denounced the "outrageous filth" in "porn rock," and declared that "if I could find some way constitutionally to do away with it, I would." It was political bombast, and he proposed no action. When Gore said she did not seek federal legislation, Senator James J. Exon of Nebraska, a confessed Glenn Miller fan, asked, "What is the reason [then] for these hearings?" He accurately described them as a media event. The danger was not government censorship itself, however, but industry cowardice in the face of well-organized pressure.[54]

The media battle over rock music dramatized another of the ACLU's problems in the 1980s: The difficulty in reaching a rock music audience which was too young to have experienced the government censorship that prevailed through the mid-1960s. Heavy metal rock fans, after all, were not regular readers of the *New York Times* op-ed page. In the other arts, countless young poets, novelists and filmmakers took freedom of expression for granted (although the death threats against novelist Salman Rushdie in 1989 were a rude reminder of the censorial power of religious fanaticism). With respect to abortion, by 1988 there was an entire generation under the age of thirty-five that had had no experience with criminal abortion laws. The ACLU and its prochoice allies thus had trouble convincing them of the threat to abortion rights—and to the sexual freedom that they were busily enjoying.

In the end, there was only one notable rock music censorship prosecution: Those associated with the punk rock group The Dead Kennedys were charged with distributing material harmful to minors. The offending item was a poster included in the album *Frankenchrist* that depicted disembodied sex acts by various animals (the painting by H. R. Giger had been publicly displayed long before being issued with the album). The prosecution came when a four-teen-year-old San Fernando Valley (California) girl bought the album for her younger brother and their parents complained, bringing charges against the lead singer of the group, the record store that sold it, and the record company. The Southern California ACLU assisted the defense, and the trial ended in a verdict of not guilty. Like the feminist antipornography crusade, Tipper Gore's campaign had faded away by the end of the decade.[55]

Free Speech in Oregon: A New Avenue for Protecting Civil Liberties?

For civil libertarians, the most hopeful free speech event was a January 1987 decision by the Oregon Supreme Court overturning the conviction of an "adult" bookstore owner. The Court based its unanimous decision on the state constitution which provided that "no law shall be passed restraining the free expression of opinion, or restricting the right to speak, write, or print freely on any subject whatever." In certain respects, the wording offered stronger protection for free speech than did the First Amendment of the U.S. Constitution. The Oregon court held that "speech, writing or equivalent forms of communication" involving alleged obscenity "are 'speech' nonetheless." It left the door open for regulations to protect "unwilling viewers . . . minors, and beleaguered neighbors" but held that "no law can prohibit or censor communication itself." Writer Nat Hentoff hailed Oregon as "the first state to abolish obscenity."[56]

The decision pointed in the direction of a neglected avenue for protecting civil liberties: state constitutions. This had been discussed since the advent of the Burger Court in the 1970s but had never been explored systematically. Yet, there were important developments in this area that escaped the attention of most civil libertarians. One scholar found more than 350 state court decisions after 1970 that provided stronger protection for civil liberties than Supreme Court interpretations of the federal Constitution. Jim Harrington, legal director of the Texas Civil Liberties Union, found several parts of the Texas Constitution that provided broader protections than did the U.S. Constitution. One Texas judge ruled that the free speech clause of the state constitution was an affirmative grant of freedom to the people, rather than a neg-ative limit on government action. Accordingly, the state Equal Rights Amendment, enacted in 1972, was used to prohibit the discriminatory exclusion of migratory farm workers from workers' compensation and unemployment insurance benefits. The Texas due process clause went further than the Fifth or Fourteenth amendments. The state courts, for example, held that people who had a "pecuniary interest" in an organization could not be terminated without a due process hearing.[57] Justice William Brennan, one of the two remaining civil libertarians on the Court, argued that "rediscovery by state courts of the broader protections afforded their own citizens by the state constitutions is probably the most important jurisprudence of our times."[58]

With the advent of the Rehnquist Court in 1986, ACLU lawyers began giving more serious attention to state constitutions, and the subject was a major topic at a July 1986 conference of affiliate lawyers. The conference itself was a significant step in the direction of coordinating the work of the ACLU's highly independent affiliate litigation programs, and it led to the creation of the *State Constitutional Law Newsletter,* published with the assistance of the Southern California ACLU in June 1987.[59]

The Assault on Civil Rights

The Reagan administration, the ACLU charged, was "at war with Congress and the courts." Its failure to enforce existing civil rights laws represented a "radical and shameful assault on law enforcement."[60] Reagan was committed to reversing many of the gains of the civil rights movement, opposed to renewal of the Voting Rights Act, and hostile to affirmative action. A 1984 ACLU report, entitled *In Contempt of Congress and the Courts,* concluded that in four years, the administration had achieved many of its goals, primarily by gutting civil rights laws from within, through nonenforcement.[61]

The civil rights coalition fought back, led by the Leadership Conference on Civil Rights and with the ACLU's Washington office as the largest single lobbying presence. It scored a number of important victories, proving that the commitment to civil rights was still alive in Congress.

One of the ACLU's most important victories was the 1988 Civil Rights Restoration Act, which overturned the Supreme Court's 1984 *Grove City* decision. To retrace its history: Title IX of the 1972 Education Act prohibited sex discrimination in federally funded education programs. Between 1971 and 1979 the number of girls participating in high school athletics increased from 300,000 to over 2,000,000. Many sports commentators even thought that the law contributed directly to the outstanding performance of American women in the 1984 Olympics. Then in *Grove City College v. Bell,* the Court held that federal funds could be withheld only from the particular program found to be discriminating, rather than from the entire institution. The impact on sex discrimination enforcement was immediate: Two years later a joint ACLU–NAACP Legal Defense Fund report, *Justice Denied,* found that sixty-four discrimination investigations had been dropped. For example, the Pickens County, South Carolina, Department of Education had been found guilty of sex discrimination in its athletic programs, but the Reagan administration had dropped its suit.[62] Finally Congress passed the 1988 law overturning *Grove*

City over Reagan's veto, thereby signaling strong congressional support for civil rights.[63]

Voting Rights

The ACLU project with the greatest impact on civil rights was also probably the least well known. The Voting Rights Project was directly responsible for the election of countless black officials in the South and, as a result, had had a profound impact on local, state, and national politics. Laughlin McDonald inherited the project from Chuck Morgan in 1972, and the contrast between Morgan's flamboyant style and McDonald's low-key work was emblematic of the difference between two political eras. Morgan broke new ground; McDonald cultivated it.

McDonald was another of the lawyers who had fled the boredom of corporate law practice in the 1960s for the turbulent world of the ACLU. Scion of an established South Carolina family with close ties to Senator Strom Thurmond, he grew up with racist views. But after one year of corporate law practice, he quit and joined Chuck Morgan in the ACLU Atlanta office. Almost immediately he was in the midst of the Howard Levy trial and the question of American war crimes in Vietnam.[64]

From the passage of the 1965 Voting Rights Act through the late 1980s, the ACLU Voting Rights Project "shouldered most of the burden of private voting rights enforcement." By 1988, McDonald estimated that he had filed a total of 157 suits against 180 jurisdictions. At any given moment he had 15 or 20 active suits, as the Justice Department under Reagan had virtually abandoned its voting rights enforcement responsibilities under the law.[65]

The day of the breakthrough cases had passed, and instead the ACLU faced the task of securing voting rights in small towns and rural counties across the South. Some suits took ten years or more. The project's successful challenge to the at-large system of electing the county council in Edgefield, South Carolina, illustrated what McDonald—and black southern voters— were up against. Although the county was almost 50 percent black in the early 1970s, no black official had ever been elected to the council. McDonald originally filed suit in 1974, won a favorable district court decision in 1980, but then had it vacated after the Supreme Court's decision in *City of Mobile,* which required proof of intent to discriminate. The decision was a serious blow, as intent was often difficult to prove. Two years later, however, Congress strengthened Section 2 of the Voting Rights Act, eliminating the intent requirement, and the Supreme Court reversed itself, restoring the results test. These two developments revitalized the Voting Rights Project's suit in Edgefield, and the Supreme Court finally sustained it in 1984 (*McCain v. Lybrand*). That October, black candidates won three of the five seats on the county council. Nineteen years after passage of the Voting Rights Act and ten years after the litigation began, black political power finally came to Edgefield County, South Carolina.[66] This story was repeated all across the South, and by 1982 there were over 2,400 black elected officials in the region, up from fewer than 300 in 1965.[67]

The civil rights coalition's first great legislative victory over the Reagan administration was the reenactment of the Voting Rights Act in 1982. McDonald testified at both Senate and House hearings, offering a fine-grained analysis of "vote dilution" in the South. Congress not only reenacted the law but also strengthened it: Section 2 overturned *City of Mobile,* reinstating the effects test in voting discrimination cases. This enormously strengthened the Voting Rights Project's hand, and McDonald estimated that over the next five years forty-one Georgia counties scrapped their at-large voting arrangements.[68]

By the late 1980s, McDonald was more optimistic about the pace of litigation. An increasing number of towns and counties began to settle quickly. The original Edgefield suit had taken ten years and went all the way to the Supreme Court. But a second suit, challenging the school board elections in the same county, took only two years. A third, against the Edgefield town council, took only six months. Small towns and counties then decided they could not bear the cost of complex voting rights suits that they now appeared certain to lose.[69]

The quiet voting rights litigation in the South had national political ramifications. Indeed, one of the decisive factors in the 1987 fight over the nomination of Robert Bork for the Supreme Court was the opposition of southern Democratic senators, who were now necessarily responsive to their black constituents. Thus, to the extent that several decades of ACLU voting rights litigation had strengthened southern black political activity, it played a key role in Bork's defeat.

Despite its great success, the Voting Rights Project was little known, even among ACLU members, a problem that illustrated another of the ACLU's dilemmas in the 1980s. That is, some of the most important work—particularly by the Voting Rights Project and the National Prison Project—required patient, low-visibility litigation, much of it focusing on implementation. Such work was difficult to publicize, but it also depended on the continued support of foundation grants to underwrite the enormous cost of maintaining a large professional staff. Yet, the ACLU had little choice. The day of the dramatic victory had passed, and the civil liberties fight in many areas now required painstaking and costly litigation to achieve implementation of established principles. Such was the price of the ACLU's own success.

The War on Crime

Perhaps the greatest civil liberties setbacks occurred in the area of criminal justice. As fear of crime gripped the public, all three branches of the federal government, along with state governments, responded with measures designed to "get tough" with criminals. Attitudes toward the death penalty offered the most concrete evidence of the public's mood. By 1986, 83 percent of the public supported capital punishment, an all-time high. The ACLU found itself in a lonely position defending the rights of suspects. In 1984 the Washington office director, John Shattuck, reported that the ACLU was the only organization opposing a package of anti–civil libertarian crime bills: Many staunch civil libertarians in the House had caved in to election-year pressure and supported legislation curbing individual rights. Four years later the ACLU was again alone in opposing the several hundred bills designed to crack down on drugs.[70]

Weakening or eliminating due process protections for criminal suspects was one of the top items on the Reagan administration's agenda. The Attorney General's Task Force on Violent Crime recommended preventive detention for dangerous suspects, a "good-faith" exception to the exclusionary rule, a three-year statute of limitations on prisoners' habeas corpus petitions, and abolition of the insanity defense. The Task Force Report on the Rights of Crime Victims made similar recommendations. Neither the administration nor the public was swayed by the substantial research indicating that protecting the rights of suspects did not limit the capacity of the police to fight crime.[71]

The anticrime hysteria peaked in 1984. Congress enacted a federal preventive detention law allowing judges to deny bail to defendants they deemed a "danger to the community." Although the law included some procedural protections, it did not define the key concept of "dangerousness." Another law restricted the use of the insanity defense, shifting the burden of proof to the defendant. Meanwhile, by the mid-1980s over thirty states had adopted some version of preventive detention. The Supreme Court upheld preventive detention for both juveniles and adults. Chief Justice William Rehnquist reflected the prevailing mood by arguing that preventive detention was simply a "regulatory" measure and not punishment.[72]

The Court also continued to nibble away at both the exclusionary rule and *Miranda*. In 1984, a disastrous term for the ACLU, the Court created a good-faith exception to the exclusionary rule and a "public safety" exception to *Miranda*. Nonetheless, the Court did not overturn directly either *Mapp* or *Miranda*.

The ACLU tried to influence public opinion on the crime issue with a national conference jointly sponsored by the NAACP and the city of Atlanta.[73] But it had little noticeable effect, and the public's fear of crime took an even more ominous turn by 1988 with the advent of well-organized and highly armed gangs dealing in the drug called *crack*. Gangs simply took over black neighborhoods in Los Angeles, Washington, and New York. "Drive-by" shootings of rival gangs became routine and often resulted in the deaths of innocent bystanders. Public pressure on the police to "do something," or at least to appear to be doing something, encouraged massive "sweep" arrests and threatened to erode much of the police reforms of the past twenty years. The Los Angeles police conducted several such sweeps in 1988, arresting over one thousand people on the first weekend alone. But the results clearly demonstrated the futility of the tactic. Most of the suspects were quickly released, and the arrests had no remarkable effect on the gang problem. The Southern

California ACLU challenged the indiscriminate police arrests of people without probable cause. As the drug problem worsened, however, the pressure on all criminal justice officials to take extreme measures increased.[74]

Lonely Vigil on the Death Penalty

Of all the ACLU positions, Henry Schwarzschild's most closely resembled the lonely role of ACLU leaders during the 1920s. As director of the Capital Punishment Project he faced overwhelmingly hostile public opinion and found little support in the courts. Nor was any private foundation willing to support his project.

Each year the number of prisoners on death row increased, reaching nineteen hundred by early 1988. The ACLU engaged in some extraordinary efforts to block executions: In 1977 it filed last-minute appeals on behalf of and against the wishes of Gary Gilmore, the first person executed in the United States in ten years. Once Gilmore's execution broke the de facto "moratorium," the pace of executions steadily increased: two in 1979, five in 1983, and more than one hundred in 1988.

The mounting backlog of death row cases created a serious crisis in legal representation, overwhelming the resources of the ACLU and the NAACP LDF, the only two organizations providing any regular assistance. The American Bar Association (ABA) belatedly organized a campaign to provide volunteer lawyers for prisoners on death row. In response to the crisis, the 1985 ACLU Biennial Conference mandated the creation of two litigation backup centers, in the fifth and eleventh circuits.[75] But at best it was a holding action, designed to delay each execution as long as possible and to overturn the sentence in a few cases. No other area of the ACLU's program seemed to offer so little hope.

Reagan and the National Security State

President Reagan revived McCarthy era rhetoric about an omnipresent Communist threat and, under the rubric of protecting national security, set out to remove controls over the intelligence agencies. Relying on a Heritage Foundation report charging that "clergymen, students, businessmen, entertainers, labor officials, journalists and government workers all may engage in subversive activities without being fully aware of the extent, purpose, or control of their activities," Reagan issued an executive order in December 1981 authorizing the CIA to collect information on citizens within the United States. Then in 1983 the Justice Department revised its guidelines on FBI domestic security investigation, allowing the bureau to open investigations of any person or group it believed "advocate[d] criminal activity."

These steps exposed the limits of the earlier reforms: Executive orders and administrative guidelines could be changed or abolished by a president with a different political outlook. The ACLU's National Center for Security Studies (CNSS), which was gradually merged into the Washington office, fought the administration's policies, but with little success. Congress and the public were swayed by the administration's argument that the threat of terrorism required greater surveillance.[76]

FBI Director William Webster, a respected former judge, reassured Congress that the bureau would not abuse its power. The public and the media were inclined to trust him, until 1987 when there were revelations of the FBI's spying on the Committee in Solidarity with the People of El Salvador (CISPES). There was no evidence of terrorist or other criminal activity by CISPES; the reason for the surveillance was solely CISPES's opposition to U.S. foreign policy. There were additional allegations of the FBI's harassment of Americans visiting Nicaragua. Finally, the FBI Library Awareness Program was exposed in 1988, in which the bureau asked certain libraries to keep track of foreigners suspected of being Soviet agents. The American Library Association denounced the program as "an unconscionable and unconstitutional invasion of privacy of library users."[77]

Another ominous development was the conviction of former naval intelligence employee Samuel Loring Morison for giving government documents to *Jane's Defence Weekly*. The British military journal was not a foreign government, and furthermore, "leaking" important information was a routine activity in Washington. ACLU Washington office director Morton Halperin argued that Morison's conviction created a de facto "official secrets act," in reference to the English law that posed a serious restriction on the free flow of information in that country.[78]

Free Trade in Ideas: The ACLU Counterattacks

The featured speakers at the 1984 ACLU Conference on Free Trade in Ideas could not appear in person. Hortensia Allende therefore addressed the audience on videotape: "I am not an extremist, I am not going to throw a bomb." The only "bomb" she had was speaking the truth about the American role in the 1973 coup that had deposed her husband as president of Chile. Playwright Dario Fo spoke by satellite from Toronto. His play, *Accidental Death of an Anarchist,* was opening in New York later that year, but he was barred from entering the country. Nobel Prize–winning novelist Gabriel Garcia Marquez also spoke by videotape. The conference was the ACLU's counterattack to the Reagan administration's assault on the free flow of ideas, advancing the argument that the issue was not a Communist threat, as the Reagan administration maintained, but the right of Americans to discuss freely all relevant ideas concerning foreign policy matters. Ira Glasser opened the conference by suggesting that "if America stands for anything, it stands for the commitment to open and robust debate about public policy." This was "the first administration in American history that sees restrictions on information as a central strategy of government."[79]

The administration's assault included excluding foreign nationals who criticized American policy, restricting the travel of Americans overseas, and restricting both the import and export of certain goods. The featured speakers at the ACLU conference had been excluded under the 1952 Immigration Act, which allowed the government to deny visas to any foreign national it believed might engage in activities "prejudicial to the public interest." The administration had even barred certain right-wingers, such as Roberto d'Aubuisson of El Salvador, whose views did not coincide with current American policy. The State Department also had the power to deny or revoke passports to Americans whose travel it deemed a threat to the national security. Indeed, the Supreme Court had upheld revocation of the passport of Philip Agee, a former CIA agent who had published several books critical of the agency. New Treasury Department regulations in 1982 prohibited Americans from paying for "transportation-related" expenses in Cuba. Ostensibly, this was to prevent U.S. currency from entering Cuba, but the practical effect was to restrict travel to Cuba.

In an effort to prevent the Soviet Union from obtaining advanced scientific information, the Reagan administration threatened the freedom of scientific research in the United States: In 1982 the Defense Department prevented the presentation of one hundred papers at an international symposium on photo-optics. The Pentagon held that the papers, representing work done under federal grants or contracts, contained information requiring a license under the International Traffic in Arms regulations. In 1981 the administration warned the Massachusetts Institute of Technology (MIT) and several other universities about allowing certain foreign nationals to enroll in advanced science courses. Given the critical role of federal grants and contracts to scientific research, scientists were easily intimidated. Finally, in one of its most outrageous actions, the administration ruled that three Canadian documentary films had to be labeled *propaganda* under the terms of the Foreign Agents Registration Act. One of the films, *If You Love This Planet,* examined the medical effects of nuclear war.

Cosponsored by thirty-nine other organizations (Americans for Democratic Action, American Friends Service Committee, PEN American Center) the ACLU Free Trade in Ideas conference developed a specific legislative agenda that began to show "significant progress" within two years. In 1987 Congress temporarily repealed provisions of the 1952 McCarran–Walter Act that allowed the State Department to deny visas or to deport foreigners because of their political beliefs. It was a sign that the ACLU Washington office could persuade Congress to put aside the traditional anti-Communist rhetoric. The State Department's legal adviser, in fact, indicated that the administration would not oppose the bill. Then in late 1988, a federal judge ruled the original law to be unconstitutional in an ACLU-sponsored case involving the administration's attempt to deport a group of Palestinians who it claimed were associated with the Palestine Liberation Organization.[80] These developments were straws in the wind but important first steps in an ACLU campaign against the government's attempt to restrict "dangerous foreign ideas" that reached back to the 1920s. Other cases included a suit on behalf of Hortensia

Allende's request for a visa, a State Department denial of visas to two Palestinian representatives invited to speak at Harvard, and a challenge to the labeling of the three Canadian films.[81]

The Reagan Years: A Civil Liberties Balance Sheet

As the Reagan era came to an end, the ACLU could say that the status of civil liberties, though precarious, was far better than what it had expected on election night 1980. On the positive side, the ACLU could claim credit for defeating much of the New Right's social agenda: the constitutional amendments to outlaw abortion and to require school prayer, the effort to require teaching creation science, and the attempt to abolish or weaken the Voting Rights Act. The antipornography campaign had achieved little of substance, and the administration had been soundly defeated on several items by Congress and the Supreme Court. At the same time, however, there were serious setbacks to civil liberties in the areas of criminal justice and national security. Although abortion remained legal, it was everywhere under attack. But the future of the Supreme Court worried civil libertarians the most. It had rejected the ACLU's position on a strict separation of church and state on a number of issues and was willing to limit individual rights in certain "special environments," such as public schools, prisons, and the military.

The mixed record was an index of ambivalent public attitudes toward civil liberties. The ACLU was able to mobilize broad public support on privacy issues, which directly touched the broad middle and upper-middle classes. Self-interest was a double-edged sword, however. The personal fear of crime underpinned the erosion of the rights of suspects and support for the death penalty, and not many Americans felt threatened by the loosening of restraints on the FBI or the CIA. On some of the church–state issues, the ACLU was able to mobilize support for its position by portraying the Moral Majority and other fundamentalists as fanatics, out of step with the American mainstream. But idealism was not entirely dead, as congressional support for civil rights enforcement triumphed over the Reagan administration's attempts to weaken it. Yet at the same time, racism underlay much of the public hysteria over crime. As had been the case in the past, American attitudes toward civil liberties remained profoundly ambivalent.

Seventeen

The Bicentennial, Bork, and Bush, 1987-1988

The Bicentennial Year

The ACLU approached its seventieth anniversary where it had begun, at the center of national controversy. In the 1988 presidential election campaign, Republican candidate George Bush attacked his opponent, Michael Dukakis, as a "card-carrying member" of the ACLU. The ACLU's values, he charged, were out of the "mainstream" of American life. The Bush attacks followed two controversies in 1987 that raised similar questions about the place of civil liberties in American life: the Bicentennial celebration of the Constitution, which focused attention on the country's basic governing document, and the nomination of Robert Bork for the U.S. Supreme Court, which provoked a bitter fight that turned on the question of the role of the Court in protecting individual rights.

The Debate over the Constitution

Attorney General Edwin Meese opened the debate over the Constitution in 1985 when, in a speech to the American Bar Association (ABA), he attacked a wide range of Supreme Court decisions as "bizarre." Application of the Bill of Rights to the states was on "intellectually shaky" ground. The Court was guilty of making "policy choices [rather] than articulations of constitutional principle." The text of the Constitution itself was the only valid foundation, and Meese called for a return to "a jurisprudence of Original Intention."[1] A year later he suggested that particular Court decisions were binding only on the parties in that case and did "not establish a 'supreme law of the Land' that is binding on all persons." He singled out the 1958 *Cooper v. Aaron* decision in which the Court sternly rebuked resistance to its 1954 school desegregation decision.

Constitutional scholars were aghast. The idea that everyone was not bound by Court decisions threatened the entire structure of constitutional government, and accordingly the ACLU denounced Meese's idea as an "invitation to lawlessness." Ira Glasser called Meese "the most radical and dangerous Attorney General in this century."[2] In December 1985 Glasser sent Meese a tongue-in-cheek letter offering to "buy" the Justice Department. "We are only the principals in a broadly based group of investors and would be pleased to meet with you to discuss the details of our proposal."[3] Sensing an opportunity, Glasser organized a "Stop Meese" public-education and fund-raising campaign. The effort revealed a great deal about the dynamics of public attitudes toward civil liberties, as well as the dynamics of direct mail techniques in the 1980s.

Glasser's staff prepared a mock legal document: "IN THE UNITED STATES COURT OF PUBLIC OPINION. The American People v. Edwin Meese, III, United States Attorney General." The indictment listed six separate "counts" against Meese. Count 1 cited his "attacks on freedom of speech and the First Amendment," including his efforts to weaken the Freedom of Information Act and his recent pornography commission. Count 2 accused him of "undermining the integrity and independence of the federal courts," by supporting court-stripping proposals. Count 3 accused him of violating the principle of separation of church and state. The remaining counts attacked Meese for his attack on abortion rights, his efforts to repeal the exclusionary rule and *Miranda,* and his failure to enforce civil rights laws. Calling for his "removal," the ACLU asked people to sign the petition, which would be delivered to the Justice Department, to contribute to the Stop Meese campaign, and, if they were not members, to join the ACLU.[4]

The petition was a brilliant production, with an eye-catching design and a text providing a succinct summary of Meese's record. It clearly touched a sensitive nerve, and the test mailings produced spectacular results. The initial response rate was 2.6 percent, compared with a normal rate of 0.7 percent for ACLU mailings. In the direct mail world of the 1980s, different "packages" were test mailed to specially "targeted" audiences. If the response rate held up, the ACLU might recruit as many as 75,000 new members, an undreamed-of 30 percent increase.[5]

But the Stop Meese campaign immediately ran into problems. Several board members objected on the grounds that they had not approved it. Did removal mean impeachment? The Executive Committee met in a hastily called telephone conference call to decide whether the petition violated ACLU Policy 529 on political nonpartisanship. The issue exacerbated the old tensions between those board members who thought the staff might be a little too freewheeling in making policy and those staff who sometimes felt hamstrung by a meddlesome board. But the board finally approved the campaign, and the mass mailing proceeded.[6]

All went well at first. The petition generated about thirty thousand new members and then died in its tracks, as the Iran–*contra* scandal broke in early November 1986 and the Reagan administration became embroiled in a morass of illegal actions, evasions, and lies. Meese himself was sinking under the weight of several scandals regarding his ethics. He now looked politically wounded and, with less than two years left in office, no longer seemed a threat. Responses to the ACLU petitions dwindled to a trickle. The ACLU staff had gambled on a very expensive package, and in the end, the campaign ran up a large deficit.[7]

The affair dramatized the problems of organizational survival for public-interest groups in the 1980s. As conservative groups first demonstrated, sophisticated direct mail programs could mobilize significant public support and raise large amounts of money. Indeed, public-interest groups had to play the game just to survive, and under Glasser's leadership, the ACLU had played the game very well in the 1980s. But it was a hazardous enterprise. For instance, environmental groups used Interior Secretary James Watt as a foil in the early 1980s, but contributions and membership declined after he resigned. The National Organization for Women (NOW) raised large sums to support the equal rights amendment (ERA), only to experience a precipitous decline when the ERA died in 1983. The ACLU's experience with the Stop Meese campaign likewise demonstrated that the public response to certain issues was often fickle.

The Bicentennial, 1987

The Bicentennial celebration of the Constitution did avoid the cheap commercialism of the 1976 celebration of the Revolution, but it failed to stimulate much serious public education about the document. As always, the public had little interest in history and so participated halfheartedly in the ceremonies. The debate over original intent, because it had such immediate ramifications for the Supreme Court and administration policy, was a far more vigorous and intellectually serious affair.

The Bicentennial coincided with the ACLU's de facto seventieth birthday, the founding of the Civil Liberties Bureau in the summer of 1917. The changes in American law and attitudes since the day that Crystal Eastman and Roger Baldwin took up the free speech fight had been enormous. The *New York Times* found among the ACLU members "a feeling that during the last generation or so, the nation's system of values has veered fundamentally in a libertarian direction." ACLU President Norman Dorsen felt that "the ideas of equality and due process and privacy have permeated the society." Civil liberties, though always under attack, were nonetheless firmly entrenched in the law. Then the Supreme Court handed the ACLU a birthday present in the form of the decision striking down the Louisiana creationism law.[8]

The Battle over Bork

The Robert Bork nomination electrified civil rights and civil liberties activists and quickly became the most heated political issue of 1987. Far more than the Bicentennial, it prompted a national debate over the Court and the Constitution in American life. Bork was a true radical, in the sense that his views pertained to root issues. The anti-Bork forces called his judicial philosophy "frightening." ACLU President Dorsen called Bork "more radical than conservative . . . [and] certainly well outside the mainstream of conservative judicial philosophy."

Bork offered the fullest statement of his views in a 1971 *Indiana Law Journal* article entitled "Neutral Principles and Some First Amendment Problems." Joining a long-running debate over constitutional decision making, he criticized the main thrust of Supreme Court decisions over the past half-century. As an undemocratic institution in a democratic society, he argued, the Court could sustain its legitimacy only by adhering to "certain enduring principles," which could be found only in the language of the Constitution. Judges thus erred when they strayed beyond the text and imposed their own "value choices." Bork focused on the 1965 *Griswold* decision. Why did the Court offer greater judicial protection for sexuality than, say, economic gratification? *Griswold* was "result oriented" and, therefore, unprincipled. In 1971, Bork could not know that *Griswold* would be the cornerstone of *Roe v. Wade* or that abortion would be the most controversial social issue of the 1980s. But his opposition to a constitutionally protected right of privacy became one of the two focal points of the attack on his nomination.[9]

Other points in the 1971 article caused Bork just as much trouble. His criticism of the 1947 *Shelley v. Kraemer* decision outlawing restrictive covenants in the sale of private housing seemed, by implication, to question the entire line of civil rights decisions. Critics also cited his initial opposition to the 1964 Civil Rights Act. On the subject of free speech, he advanced an extreme version of the old Meikeljohn argument that the First Amendment protected only "speech that is explicitly political," which apparently left literary and artistic forms of expression unprotected.

Bork complained that his critics distorted his views—some called him anti-woman, antiabortion, or racist. Although he was not personally prejudiced, the core of his philosophy was opposition to the judicial protection of women's rights, abortion, and civil rights. Indeed, he meant what he wrote in 1971: The Court had gone off in the wrong direction. The anti-Bork movement therefore capitalized on the broad public support for the judicial enforcement of civil rights and the constitutional protection of women and a right to privacy.

The nomination provoked a major crisis in the ACLU, which had jealously guarded its policy of nonpartisanship prohibiting the support of or opposition to candidates for elected or appointed office. The ACLU had deviated from this policy only once, when it opposed the nomination of William Rehnquist to the Supreme Court, the thirty-to-twenty-six board vote revealing the sharp division of opinion. Many in the ACLU were later embarrassed by this deviation from a fundamental organizational policy (the ACLU did not oppose Rehnquist's elevation to chief justice in 1986).[10] Nonetheless, many members urged opposition to the appointments of Griffin Bell (1977) and Ed Meese (1984) as attorney general. The board modified the ACLU's policy slightly in 1986, allowing the staff to publish the civil liberties records of nominees for four offices—Supreme Court, attorney general, solicitor general, and assistant attorney general for civil rights—but without taking a stand on the nominations.[11]

The Bork nomination, however, reopened the issue. As a national anti-Bork coalition formed in the summer of 1987, the ACLU was conspicuously absent. Then board member Frank Askin took the lead and called for an emergency Executive Committee meeting to reconsider the ACLU's policy. This triggered an intense internal debate, conducted under crushing time pressure. The crucial Senate Judiciary Committee hearings were scheduled for September, but the ACLU board would not meet again until mid-October, too late for any meaningful action. At Askin's prodding, the Executive Committee called a special board meeting for August 29 and 30.[12]

The meeting proved anticlimactic; by the time the board members arrived for it, most had been convinced that the ACLU should oppose Bork. A staff report on Bork's philosophy swung many of the uncertain. Larry Herman led a last-ditch effort by those opposing any change in policy, invoking the "slippery slope" argument on the dangers of partisanship and arguing that the staff report had distorted Bork's views. But he persuaded few, if any. On the issue of basic ACLU policy, the board voted forty-seven to sixteen to permit the ACLU to oppose a Supreme Court nominee "whose record demonstrates a judicial philosophy that would fundamentally jeopardize the Supreme Court's critical and unique role in protecting civil liberties." To satisfy uneasy moderates, the policy was hedged with conditions, applying only to Supreme Court nominees and requiring a vote of 60 percent of the board to apply it to a particular nominee. On Sunday, the board voted sixty-one to three to oppose Bork.[13]

By Sunday evening, staff members in New York began phoning affiliates across the country. The campaign dramatized the ACLU's considerable strengths. No other civil rights, civil liberties, or feminist organization had the same combination of a national network of affiliates and a large Washington staff (only the National Education Association and the AFL–CIO had comparable organizational strength). In Texas, Nebraska, and other states, the ACLU affiliate organized the statewide anti-Bork coalition. Texas and Nebraska were critical, as their conservative Democratic senators—Lloyd Bentsen and James Exon—were swing votes.

By early September, Bork was on the defensive. In the Senate Judiciary Committee hearings, his opponents hammered away at his opposition to the judicial enforcement of civil rights and privacy. Few mentioned the word *abortion,* but it was clearly implied in the incessant questioning over *Griswold* and birth control. The debate over Bork was the closest thing the country had had to a national referendum on civil liberties, and it indicated that a significant majority supported judicial activism on behalf of civil rights and privacy. There were some serious distortions. Bork was not a racist, as some critics suggested, but the hearings also ignored his bias toward the government over the individual and toward private business over the government, as reflected in his judicial opinions. Then on October 23, the Senate rejected his nomination by a fifty-eight-to-forty-two vote.[14]

Reagan's next nominee, Douglas Ginsburg, withdrew following revelations of marijuana smoking. The third nominee, Anthony Kennedy, was confirmed rather quickly. The ACLU took no position on either nominee. Although very conservative, Kennedy did not articulate the same kind of extreme philosophy as Bork did, but his confirmation did raise grave concern about the future of civil liberties before the Court. Many thought he would be the fifth vote to overturn *Roe v. Wade*. The battle over abortion rights, which had dominated American politics for fifteen years, was not over.

"A Card-Carrying Member of the ACLU"

"My opponent is a card-carrying member of the ACLU." With that, Republican candidate George Bush introduced the ACLU into the 1988 presidential election campaign. It was an unprecedented event. Never before had a candidate's membership in a single organization been a prominent issue in a campaign.

The Democratic party candidate, Michael Dukakis, was indeed an ACLU member. Through market research techniques, Bush strategists had discovered that the ACLU's name evoked strong negative reactions among voters. They thus devised an aggressive strategy of labeling Dukakis a *liberal,* attacking his veto of a flag salute bill, accusing him of letting dangerous criminals out on weekend furloughs—and of being an ACLU member. The connections were clear: The liberal Dukakis lacked patriotism, was soft on crime, and belonged to an organization that endorsed child pornography. Both Dukakis and the ACLU, Bush implied, were out of the "mainstream."

Bush's strategy worked: Dukakis's early lead evaporated, and he lost badly in November, in part because of his ineffective responses. That is, he responded quickly and angrily to the implications about his patriotism, late in the campaign finally identified himself as a liberal, and replied to the furlough criticism by finding similar horror stories in programs under Reagan and Bush. But Dukakis never said anything about the ACLU.

The 1988 campaign was remarkable for the prominence of current and former ACLU members. Dukakis's campaign manager, Susan Estrich, was a former president of the Civil Liberties Union of Massachusetts and a former member of the ACLU board (from 1984 to 1987). Unsuccessful Democratic candidate Paul Simon, senator from Illinois, was also an ACLU member. Finally, Attorney General Richard Thornburgh, appointed to replace Meese in the summer of 1988, had been an active member of the Pittsburgh ACLU chapter. But when this came to light, Thornburg claimed that he had resigned over disagreement with the ACLU's "political" agenda, but in fact, he resigned because he was taking a state government position and wanted to avoid any conflict of interest. The ACLU produced affiliate members who were present the night he resigned.[15]

The immediate effect of Bush's singling out the ACLU was a rush of publicity and membership applications. Political columnists mentioned the ACLU regularly, with most of the liberal and moderate pundits accusing Bush of engaging in the guilt-by-association techniques reminiscent of the cold war. Conservative columnists—James J. Kilpatrick, Pat Buchanan, Norman Podhoretz—reiterated the charge that the ACLU had deviated from its original course and now had a "political agenda."[16] Initially, the ACLU was not sure how to respond. Replies to Bush might easily be construed as an endorsement of Dukakis and, thereby, create the impression that the ACLU was indeed an ally of the Democratic party. But by September, when it was clear that Bush had no intention of letting up, the ACLU responded with its own media blitz. Ira Glasser gave a speech on October 6 explaining the ACLU to the National Press Club. Broadcast live over National Public Radio, it generated several thousand membership applications in the next few days. Glasser joked that if Bush lost the election, the ACLU might appoint him as director of memberships. Bush might also have a full-time job resigning from the ACLU, as inevitably, many people had sent in memberships in the name of "George Bush."[17] Staff members spent much of their time in October talking with reporters, usually correcting misunderstandings about the organization. Some favorable coverage resulted: a *New York Times* article highlighted the extent to which almost all of the clients in the ACLU's Long Island suburban chapter were Republicans. But an ACLU ad in the Sunday *New York Times,* however, was disappointing and did not pay for itself.[18]

Even before the ACLU launched its response, new members began spontaneously flocking in. In the end, it added nearly 70,000 new members, perhaps half as a direct result of the campaign, and membership passed 275,000, exceeding even the peak of the Watergate years. Many longtime members called their affiliate offices demanding their "card." Many of the new members were people who had let their membership lapse or who might be described as "lukewarm" civil libertarians, individuals who agreed with most of the ACLU program but never felt motivated to actually join.[19]

ACLU leaders, however, worried about the long-term effect of the Bush attacks on civil liberties. By not replying to the attacks on his ACLU membership, Dukakis seemed to let stand the implication that there was something shameful about belonging to the ACLU. Some members, furious at his silence, felt that he should have more strongly affirmed his support for judicial enforcement of civil rights, freedom of speech, and the right to privacy. He could have distanced himself from the ACLU, they pointed out, by citing the many times the Massachusetts affiliate had sued his administration over civil liberties violations.[20] Dorsen also worried about the impact of the campaign on the many people who did not know much about the ACLU, those he described as being "not for us, but not against us either." He and others were concerned, for example, that many law students and young lawyers with political aspirations would decline to take an ACLU case, afraid that it might come back later to haunt them.[21]

Bush's success in using the ACLU as a weapon against Dukakis was the result of several factors, including the organization's controversial stand on issues such as pornography and Dukakis's failure to respond effectively. But it was also true that the ACLU had never told its own story very well. Glasser and other leaders had to spend hours with reporters clearing up misunderstandings. The organization had recently expanded its public education department—and then only after a long internal debate—but the impact of this had yet to be felt. Over the years the ACLU had been extremely successful in fighting particular issues—from free speech to abortion to voting rights—but it had failed to educate the larger public about the role of the Bill of Rights as a positive good, as the foundation for the values of tolerance, fairness, and equality. The always-controversial First Amendment cases—defense of Nazis, for example—were usually cast in negative terms: We must defend them lest worse things happen. Lost was the idea that defense of the unpopular was an affirmation of the strengths of a democratic society, particularly the value of tolerance.[22]

Nor had the ACLU done a good job in publicizing its own history. Few people knew that the ACLU had been the only organization to defend in court the Japanese-Americans during World War II; and despite the enormous literature on the exclusionary rule and the *Miranda* warning, there was almost no mention that the Supreme Court's opinions in both the *Mapp* and *Miranda* cases were based on the ACLU *amici* briefs. Even many ACLU leaders were under the impression that the organization had never done much in the areas of civil rights. These failures were especially curious for an organization that had always attracted a large number of writers. Part of the explanation lay in the fact that the ACLU shared a trait common to all Americans, a lack of historical consciousness. Indeed, the ACLU's strength over the years was a result of its restless present-mindedness, its preoccuption with today's crisis rather than yesterday's accomplishment.

The Bork nomination only a year before offered an instructive contrast with the presidential race. In that campaign, the ACLU and its allies had successfully portrayed Bork as the one who was outside the "mainstream," focusing on his opposition to a constitutional right of privacy and the judicial enforcement of civil rights. The two events highlighted the majority of Americans' ambivalent attitudes toward civil liberties. George Bush could discredit the ACLU by identifying it with child pornography. Yet Americans supported certain civil liberties principles, especially when presented in the most favorable light, as in the Bork campaign.

The ACLU's record in Congress in 1988 offered further evidence of this ambivalence: The report of the ACLU's Washington office indicated that the ACLU's position prevailed in half of thirty key votes, an extraordinary record for an organization that defended "unpopular" ideas. The ACLU's victories had occurred most consistently in the areas of civil rights and privacy. The ACLU had helped win enactment of the Japanese-American Redress Act, which atoned for the World War II internment and vindicated the ACLU's position in that event; the Civil Rights Restoration Act, which overturned the Supreme Court's 1984 *Grove City* decision and strengthened federal efforts to fight sex discrimination; amendments to the Fair Housing Act that prohibited discrimination against handicapped persons and families with children; and a law that banned the use of lie detectors by private employers. All of these laws represented positive advances for civil liberties principles and were indications of a deep reservoir of public support, at least on certain issues. The ACLU, however, suffered continued defeats in the area of criminal justice. Caught up in public hysteria over an epidemic of drug-related gang violence, Congress enacted a new law with many anti–civil liberties provisions.[23]

Worried about the effects of the Bush attacks, in early 1989 the ACLU commissioned a public opinion survey of attitudes toward the organization. The results were surprisingly positive. Of the 1,003 adults interviewed, 47 percent had a favorable attitude toward the ACLU; 18 percent expressed an unfavorable attitude; 22 percent had no opinion; and 13 percent had never heard of the organization. The ACLU had an overall net positive rating of +29, compared with +67 for Planned Parenthood, +50 for the National Organization for Women, +35 for Amnesty International, only +9 for the seemingly powerful National Rifle Association, and −28 for the John Birch Society. One surprising finding was that only 25 percent of those interviewed were even aware of the Bush attacks. Only 15 percent thought the ACLU was antireligious, and only 7 percent felt it was "a left-wing organization"; 50 percent agreed that the ACLU "performs an important service by safeguarding the rights of everyone." The results were heartening for ACLU leaders and suggested that the storm of the 1988 presidential election may have been a significant boon, in regard to raising membership and revenues, and had not done any long-term damage.[24]

The ACLU at Seventy

As the ACLU celebrated its seventieth anniversary in 1990, it surveyed the status of civil liberties with mixed feelings. It could look back on an extraordinary record of accomplishment but, at the same time, see civil liberties under serious attack. The threats came, in roughly equal measure, from the longstanding pressures of intolerance and public fear, threats to individual liberty posed by new technology, and by the evident retreat by the Supreme Court on a number of civil liberties issues. On the positive side, civil liberties principles that in 1920 were regarded as dangerous, radical, and "un-American" were now deeply embedded in American law. The ACLU had been involved in 80 percent of the post-1920 "landmark" cases regularly cited in constitutional law texts. In some of the most important ones, such as *Gitlow* (1925), the

ACLU brief helped persuade the Supreme Court to establish a principle that became the foundation for a vast body of law protecting individual rights.

Changes in the law had subsequently affected public opinion. Surveys repeatedly showed broad support for freedom of speech, tolerance of unpopular views, equality, and privacy. The most thorough study, *The Dimensions of Tolerance,* undertaken in the aftermath of Skokie, found that support for civil liberties was strongest among society's elite—civic leaders and opinion makers. Among the general public, the responses varied, depending on the wording of the questions. Over half (58 percent) agreed that free speech should be granted "to everyone regardless of how intolerant they are of other people's opinions," but 66 percent would deny the Nazis use of a town hall for a meeting. In addition, 67 percent felt that it would be all right to violate a suspect's rights in order to "make the streets safe." At the same time, however, 58 percent felt that the "right to remain silent" was necessary to protect people from forced confessions, and even half of the police officials surveyed agreed. The 1989 survey of attitudes toward the ACLU found similar differences: People tended to agree strongly with the ACLU on issues of privacy (including abortion) and civil rights but to disagree with it strongly on issues related to crime.[25]

Despite indications of ambivalent support for civil liberties, the data in *The Dimensions of Tolerance* had to be viewed from the perspective of history. At the very least, they reflected far more support for civil liberties than did the Stouffer survey conducted thirty years earlier in the depths of the McCarthy era.[26] Even more significant, the degree of support for civil liberties represented a sea change since the terrible days during World War I when the public had applauded the government's wholesale suppression of dissent.

The growth of constitutional law, the expansion of individual rights, and the consequent change in public attitudes and behavior had permanently altered the fabric of American life. What historians and political scientists referred to as *constitutionalism,* the public sense of the Constitution and its place in American society, was not fixed.[27] Rather, it had changed and acquired new meaning over the years: The concept of privacy, to cite the most obvious example, was a new and still evolving principle. The ACLU could legitimately claim to have played a leading role in that process of change. If nothing else, the organization's history was eloquent testimony to the power of ideas and, more specifically, the power of the Constitution and the Bill of Rights as symbols of the nation's highest ideals. By championing the idea of freedom of speech, even for unpopular groups—in the courts and in the arena of public opinion—the ACLU had over the course of seventy years persuaded a substantial number of Americans that it was a worthy idea.

The ACLU had little time to bask in the glory of its substantial achievements, however, as threats to civil liberties arose from many directions. Events of the late 1980s seemed, to the ACLU, to reaffirm the three "lessons" of its history: that "no battle ever stays won"; that it is important to adhere to principle, including defending one's enemy; and that the ACLU's own role was to continue to push forward the frontiers of freedom.

The fight to preserve abortion rights was the clearest example of a battle that would not stay won. The battle escalated in 1989, both in the streets and in the Supreme Court. Antiabortion forces, under the rubric of Operation Rescue, staged massive demonstrations designed to shut down abortion clinics. Hundreds of arrests did not seem to deter them. Even more ominous from the standpoint of the ACLU and its prochoice allies was the posture of the Supreme Court. Following the appointment of Justice Anthony Kennedy, it appeared that there might be five votes to overturn *Roe v. Wade,* and national attention was riveted on the April 25, 1989, oral arguments in a Missouri case in which the Bush administration had urged the Court to take that step. This prospect galvanized the prochoice forces, and between 300,000 and 600,000 of their supporters converged on Washington on April 9 for one of the largest demonstrations on any issue in the nation's capital. On July 3 the Supreme Court sharply cut back on abortion rights and returned the abortion battle to the states.[28]

ACLU leaders had reason to believe that the abortion issue was the key to an untapped reservoir of support. A full-page ad in the *New York Times* in January 1989 drew over 25,000 letters and $50,000 in contributions. It was a striking contrast with the disappointing response to the ACLU's *Times* ad during the 1988 presidential election campaign, again suggesting that people responded more to specific issues, particularly those that affected them directly, than to abstract statements about civil liberties.

Innumerable other cases illustrated the extent to which the ACLU had to fight to preserve free speech for unpopular views. In Chicago, it sprang to the defense of an artist whose painting was physically seized by local politicians because it portrayed the late Mayor Harold Washington in an unfavorable light. In Kansas City the ACLU affiliate waged a long and controversial fight for the Ku Klux Klan's right to use a public access cable television channel. Finally, the ACLU defended the rights of people associated with the Palestine Liberation Organization (PLO), perhaps the most unpopular group in American society today: It challenged the State Department's attempt to shut down the Palestine Information Office on the grounds that it was a "terrorist" organization and protested the department's refusal to grant PLO leader Yasir Arafat a visa allowing him to speak at the United Nations in late 1988. Dorsen's and Glasser's letter to Secretary of State George Shultz, reflecting the ACLU's long fight against restrictions on foreign ideas, argued that "the principle of free speech . . . protects us all [and] the First Amendment rights of Americans are damaged by your action."[29]

Protecting established principles included, as it had since the World War I years, the ACLU's speaking out against public hysteria. The AIDS and drug crises in the later 1980s also threatened to erode Fourth Amendment protections against searches and seizures and the broader principle of privacy. On AIDS-related issues the ACLU was remarkably successful in preventing the country from being stampeded by extreme fear mongers who proposed such measures as mandatory testing for the entire population or even quarantine persons with AIDS. Nan Hunter, director of the Gay and Lesbian Rights Project, was involved in every major AIDS-related court case in the country.

In the most important case, brought by the Florida affiliate, the ACLU won job reinstatement for Todd Shuttleworth, an AIDS victim fired by Broward County. The settlement in federal district court helped established that AIDS was a handicap under the 1973 Rehabilitation Act and so Shuttleworth's firing constituted discrimination. It was the third straight win for the Lesbian and Gay Rights Project. Previous suits had won reinstatement for a Massachusetts telephone employee under a state handicap discrimination law, and in a Southern California ACLU case, a federal judge ruled that the San Luis Obispo schools could not bar five-year-old Ryan Thomas from school because he had AIDS.[30]

The ACLU was much less successful in fighting the rising public fears of drugs, a situation that became even worse with the rise of the crack, gang, and murder epidemic by 1988. Congress and the Supreme Court had already eroded the rights of suspects since the 1970s because of the public mood. By July 1988, with an election ahead, members of Congress introduced 245 bills purporting to get tough with drug traffickers. Proposals included narrowing the exclusionary rule and denying passports and eligibility for various federal benefits to persons convicted of drug offenses. The Washington office succeeded in preventing the enactment of most of the worst provisions. When the Supreme Court upheld the constitutionality of drug testing of federal transportation workers in early 1989, however, it was an indication that the Court would probably continue to weaken individual rights in favor of drug and crime control measures.[31]

The ACLU's success on these different issues was dependent on the crosscurrents of public opinion. As long as it could define issues in terms of intrusions on the privacy of the vast majority of Americans, it was able to mobilize considerable support—witness its success in the AIDS cases and the new federal ban on polygraphs. But when the issue was perceived in terms of the rights of criminals versus public safety, the ACLU steadily lost ground. The erosion of Fourth and Fifth amendment rights, in state legislatures and in the Supreme Court, along with public support for the death penalty, reflected the strong majority feeling that the rights of criminal suspects threatened their well-being. Perceived self-interest could provide both a solid base of support for civil liberties and a rationale for disregarding them. As Nat Hentoff put it, "saving the exclusionary rule does not bring people to their feet—as when the cry goes up that the First Amendment is being mugged."[32]

The ACLU faced a particularly serious threat in the Supreme Court. Although the increasingly conservative Court had sustained the ACLU on a number of important issues—notably "creationism"—it had also dealt civil liberties several serious defeats. One of the worst, from the ACLU's perspective, was the 1987 *Hazlewood* decision affirming the right of school principals to censor school newspapers.[33] The case involved student articles on sexuality and divorce and seemed to portend further restrictions on the rights of students, if not all individuals in large public bureaucracies. Also alarming was the *Hardwick v. Bowers* decision in which the Court upheld a Georgia sodomy statute. A serious setback for gay rights, the decision was all the more alarming as the facts of the case indicated a pattern of harassment against Michael Hardwick by a police officer, including an outrageous intrusion into his bedroom.[34] A 1989 decision upholding the drug testing of transportation workers eroded Fourth Amendment privacy rights even further, by virtually abandoning the principle of individualized suspicion.[35]

The trend in the Supreme Court forced the ACLU again to reevaluate its strategy and tactics. Veterans wistfully recalled the days when the Warren Court stood not just as a bulwark of civil liberties but was in the vanguard of expanding individual liberties. It was clear to many ACLU leaders that more attention would have to be given to the legislative protection of civil liberties. The Washington office already had a sizable staff and a considerable record of success. But the fifty state legislatures posed an even more serious challenge, and so each ACLU affiliate would have to mobilize its own independent lobbying effort. From a purely organizational standpoint, this would be a far more difficult task than, for example, sponsoring a test case in the courts. After the 1989 abortion decision, the ensuing battle required a state-by-state effort. The ACLU found not only that no battle stayed won but also that the battleground itself continually changed.

The ACLU also honored its commitment to defend even its enemies. Former Attorney General Edwin Meese had attacked the ACLU as the "criminals' lobby." By the late 1980s, however, he was himself under investigation for numerous charges of misconduct. When one of Meese's supporters complained about the rush to convict him, ACLU Director Ira Glasser replied in a letter to the *New York Times* that Meese himself had "derided the rights of suspects by saying that 'you don't have many suspects who are innocent.' " If Meese now felt he was being prejudged, Glasser pointed out, "it is a tendency he himself has labored hard to create."[36]

Then, in an action that disconcerted even many of its members, the ACLU filed an *amicus* brief on behalf of Lt. Col. Oliver North, arguing that the federal criminal case against him, for perjury and other crimes, violated his Fifth Amendment protection against self-incrimination. The prosecution's case against North, the ACLU argued, relied on compelled testimony he had given before a congressional investigating committee. Few people, including North himself, recalled that in the early 1950s fanatic anti-Communists, such as North, attempted to gut the Fifth Amendment. North's trial was a reminder of the ACLU adage that "sooner or later, everyone needs the Bill of Rights."[37] Finally, even George Bush needed the ACLU. In the midst of the 1988 campaign, as he was attacking his opponent for being an ACLU member, the Michigan ACLU affiliate took the case of a homeowner who had a Bush/Quayle sign in her front yard. The Wayne, Michigan, ordinance prohibiting yard signs, the ACLU argued, infringed on her First Amendment rights.[38]

Defending your enemy often meant alienating your friends. By 1989 some abortion rights groups had succeeded in using the federal Racketeering and Corrupt Organizations Act (the "RICO" law) against antiabortion groups, charging them with conspiracy to violate the rights of abortion clinic operators and clinic patients. The ACLU, already opposed to the RICO law because it threatened freedom of the press (as a result of an important pornography case), was deeply worried that this tactic could be used against other political groups.

Tension between the ACLU and some of the militant civil rights and feminist groups continued. In response to an upsurge in racist incidents on college campuses, several elite universities—including Stanford and Wisconsin—adopted rules restricting racist or sexist speech. But Ira Glasser warned that this was the wrong way to attack racism "because it doesn't work and because it's incompatible with freedom of speech and religion."[39] The attempt by some black and women students to suppress offensive speech recalled another melancholy aspect of the ACLU's history: Since the early 1920s many of its clients, themselves the victims of systematic repression, often tried to deny freedom of speech to their opponents.

The ACLU also continued to explore the frontiers of civil liberties, including complex new issues such as surrogate parenting and the question of whether the Constitution had secured economic rights.

Surrogate parenting burst on the country in 1987. The practice of paying a woman to bear the child of a man married to someone else touched on the most basic question of human dignity. Some regarded it as baby selling, and others saw it as the economic exploitation of poor women. The ACLU resolved the complex legal and moral issues by emphasizing the right of parents to make decisions involving their own reproduction. Dividing the surrogate parenting process into two stages, the ACLU held that parents could avail themselves of new reproductive technology and enter into contracts to bear children but that questions about the custody of the child had to be determined on a nondiscriminatory basis, taking into account the best interests of the child. Most important, the ACLU held that a woman could not agree to waive her fundamental parental rights in advance of the birth; in short, the sperm donor could not "buy" the baby. The Michigan affiliate took the first imtant case, winning a decision that sustained the key elements of the ACLU's position.[40]

The ACLU took the first tentative step into the area of economic rights, evidently influenced by the national scandal of homelessness. The New York Civil Liberties Union captured national headlines when it defended Joyce Brown in a celebrated case. In October 1987 Mayor Ed Koch announced that New York City would pick up homeless people who appeared seriously mentally ill and force them to accept medical and psychiatric care. The basic issue was whether such individuals could make informed decisions about their own welfare. The first person picked up under the new policy was forty-year-old Joyce Brown, sometimes known as Billie Boggs. Despite her protests, the city held her for twelve weeks in Bellevue Hospital. An NYCLU suit finally won her release but was overturned on appeal. Brown was then released when Bellevue doctors decided they could not treat her. NYCLU Director Norman Siegel promptly hired her as an NYCLU receptionist, and she became an instant celebrity, appearing on "60 Minutes" and the Phil Donahue show, and lecturing at the Harvard and New York University law schools. Mayor Koch responded by angrily attacking Siegel and the NYCLU.[41]

The homelessness crisis had an evident effect on the ACLU's thinking about economic rights, which it had been debating since 1966. It had defended poor people in a broad range of cases, involving equal protection and due process issues. In perhaps its most far-reaching victory, it had enjoined the Social Security Administration from terminating benefits without due process. In Washington, D.C., it had fought and won the right of homeless people to register to vote (one of the defendants was District of Columbia official Ed Norton, husband of Eleanor Holmes Norton, chair of the ACLU's National Advisory Committee). In addition, the ACLU helped preserve access to legal services for poor people by joining the coalition that defeated the Reagan administration's attempt to eliminate the Legal Services Corporation.[42]

The Southern California ACLU, long the leading advocate of a more affirmative ACLU stance on economic rights, also won a series of cases on behalf of the poor. It successfully challenged the practice of denying shelter to people who lacked "proper identification," succeeded in forcing the city to raise the $8.00-per-day housing voucher to $16.00, forced Los Angeles County to modify its "sixty-day rule," which allowed it to suspend all general relief for two months for minor eligibility-rule violations, and challenged the inadequacy of existing shelter and forced the county to add an additional one thousand beds. The Southern California ACLU had its own "right to employment" policy, adopted in 1983, declaring that "every person in the United States who desires to work and is capable of working should be assured of a safe, meaningful, and socially useful job that pays a fair living wage." The second half of its "Economic Bill of Rights" declared that "every person in the United States should be assured of a basic standard of living."[43]

In April 1988 the ACLU adopted a policy asserting that "housing is a basic necessity of life" and that "government policies and actions which result in deprivation of housing for those poor or near poor constitute a deprivation of life and liberty." Predictably, moderates on the board objected to this new initiative and promptly moved for reconsideration. But a year later, in somewhat revised language, the ACLU reaffirmed its stand and, citing equal protection and due process concerns, held that "the ACLU opposes government policies that deprive people of the availability of permanent housing and believes that government has an affirmative obligation to reform its housing policies."[44]

"An Experiment, As All Life Is an Experiment"

The ACLU's policy on housing was a tentative step into uncharted and controversial waters. But such steps were an organizational habit. At issue were fundamental questions about the scope of civil liberties, the meaning of the Bill of Rights, and the role of the ACLU. Did the Constitution guarantee a right to the essentials of life? What did the "liberty" clause of the Fourteenth Amendment encompass? There was no definitive answer to these questions. As Oliver Wendell Holmes argued in his 1919 *Abrams* dissent, the Constitution was "an experiment, as all life is an experiment."

The ACLU had played a leading role in that experiment since 1920, continually pressing for an expansion of individual rights. Indeed, the ACLU was itself an experiment. Who was to say with any degree of finality that the Constitution did not secure economic rights? In the summer of 1917 the courts and most Americans thought the Civil Liberties Bureau was wrong when it set out to defend both conscientious objectors and critics of the government's war policy. When they founded the ACLU in 1920, neither Roger Baldwin nor any of his colleagues could have imagined how the idea of freedom of speech would develop in the years ahead. When Walter Pollak argued *Gitlow* before the Supreme Court in 1925, few agreed that the Fourteenth Amendment extended the protections of the Bill of Rights to the states. Nor could Pollak have imagined in 1932, when he successfully argued the *Powell* case, how the concept of due process would evolve. And during World War II, almost no one outside the ACLU agreed with its legal challenge to the evacuation and internment of the Japanese-Americans. In each of these instances— and the list could be extended—the ACLU had taken an unpopular or at least a novel stand on behalf of individual rights. And in each of these instances it eventually prevailed, convincing not just the courts but also millions of Americans that its position, controversial in the first instance, represented an important and worthy principle.

In his oft-quoted 1944 speech, "The Spirit of Liberty," Judge Learned Hand argued that "liberty lies in the hearts of men and women; when it dies there, no constitution, no law, no court can save it." The ACLU's history suggests otherwise. Respect for civil liberties is not a natural impulse, certainly not in American society with its seething religious, ethnic, and racial tensions. Rather, respect is molded by the very constitutions, laws, and courts that Hand seemed to dismiss as unimportant. It also is evident that the Constitution is not self-enforcing and that legal principles do not arise spontaneously. The ACLU's history is eloquent testimony to the fact that the principles in the Bill of Rights acquire flesh and blood only when someone fights for them. These fights, moreover, are never easy ones, often requiring the defense of an unpopular and, at times, seemingly "dangerous" idea. Defense of the unpopular has been the ACLU's contribution to the United States' continuing experiment in constitutional government.[45]

Notes

Abbreviations

ACLU–Chi   ACLU–Chicago Division/Illinois Affiliate Papers, University of Chicago

ACLU/FBI   FBI Files on ACLU. (Document numbers are those on copies of files in the ACLU National Office)

ACLU–GrPh   ACLU Greater Philadelphia Branch Papers, Temple University

ACLU–NC   ACLU–Northern California Papers, California Historical Society

ACLU–NY   ACLU Papers; storage, ACLU office, New York City

ACLUP   American Civil Liberties Union Papers, Mudd Library, Princeton University

ACLU–SC   ACLU–Southern California Papers, UCLA

ACLU–StL   ACLU–St. Louis Affiliate Papers, Washington University

AFPS   American Fund for Public Service Papers, New York Public Library

AGHP   Arthur Garfield Hays Papers, Mudd Library, Princeton University

ANP   Aryeh Neier Papers; storage, ACLU office, New York City

AUAMP   American Union Against Militarism Papers, Swarthmore College

BOIF   Bureau of Investigation Files, National Archives, Record Group 65

COHC   Columbia Oral History Collection, Columbia University

FFP/HLS   Felix Frankfurter Papers, Harvard University Law School

FFP/LC   Felix Frankfurter Papers, Library of Congress

JHHP   John Haynes Holmes Papers, Library of Congress

MVKP   Mary Van Kleeck Papers, Smith College

NAACP   National Association for the Advancement of Colored People Papers, Library of Congress. (Code numbers refer to series and box classification system)

NCARLP   National Committee Against Repressive Legislation Papers, Wisconsin Historical Society

NCCOP   National Committee on Conscientious Objectors Papers, Swarthmore College

NDP   Norman Dorsen Papers, New York University Law School

NTP   Norman Thomas Papers, New York Public Library

NYBLFA   New York Bureau of Legal First Aid, Bobst Library, New York University

NYPL   New York Public Library
RNB/FBI   Roger Baldwin FBI file, author's possession
RNBP   Roger Nash Baldwin Papers, Mudd Library, Princeton University
Wald/CU   Lillian Wald Papers, Columbia University
Wald/NYPL   Lillian Wald Papers, New York Public Library
WHS   Wisconsin Historical Society

Persons Interviewed

Janet Benshoof	Barry Lynn
Vivian Berger	Laughlin McDonald
Ernest Besig	Nancy MacDonald
Reber Boult	Will Maslow
Al Bronstein	Michael Meyers
Ralph Brown	Jay Miller
Leroy Clark	Laura Monroe
Spencer Coxe	Charles Morgan
Dorothy Davidson	Aryeh Neier
Jack Day	Burt Neuborne
Norman Dorsen	Herbert Northrup
Hope Eastman	Eleanor Holmes Norton
Edward Ennis	William L. Nunn
Ellen Feingold	Frank Haiman
Irving Ferman	Rollo O'Hare
Clifford Forster	Fred Okrand
Walter Gellhorn	Jack Pemberton
Ira Glasser	Leo Pfeffer
Alex Gottfried	Gerard Piel
Jeremiah Gutman	Harriet Pilpel
Morton Halperin	Louis Pollak
David Hamlin	Dan Pollitt
Nat Hentoff	Suzy Post
Phil Hirschkop	Norman Redlich
Jeanette Hopkins	Alan Reitman
Charles Horsky	Ramona Ripston
Nan Hunter	Catherine Rorabach
Florence Isbell	Dorothy Samuels
Maurice Isserman	Trudi Schutz
Art Kobler	Herman Schwartz
Gara LaMarche	Henry Schwarzchild
Corliss Lamont	John Shattuck
Alan Levine	Norman Siegel

George Slaff   Nancy Wechsler
Carol Sobel   Alan Westin
Lawrence Speiser   Frank Wilkinson
Matthew Stark   Mel Wulf
John Swomley

Introduction

1. Norman Dorsen, "Civil Liberties," in Leonard Levy, ed., *Encyclopedia of the Constitution* (New York: Macmillan, 1986), pp. 263–270.

Chapter 1

1. *New York Times,* July 4, 1917.

2. Paul L. Murphy, *World War I and the Origin of Civil Liberties in the United States* (New York: Norton, 1979).

3. Wilson, letter to Rep. E. Y. Webb, May 22, 1917, in Wilson, *Life and Letters* (New York: Greenwood Press, 1968), vol. 7, p. 81; Wilson, letter to Eastman, September 18, 1917, *Life and Letters,* p. 273.

4. Norman Thomas, "War's Heretics," *The Survey,* August 4, 1917, pp. 391–394; reprinted by American Union Against Militarism (AUAM), August 1917. On its being banned, see Baldwin, letter to Keppel, September 5, 1917, ACLUP, 1917, vol. 15.

5. *American Socialist,* April 21, 1917. David A. Shannon, *The Socialist Party of America* (Chicago: Quadrangle Books, 1967).

6. Max Eastman, in *The Masses* 9 (July 1917): 18. H. C. Peterson and Gilbert C. Fite, *Opponents of War, 1917–1918* (Seattle: University of Washington Press, 1968).

7. Wilson, War Message, April 2, 1917, in *The Papers of Woodrow Wilson* (Princeton: Princeton University Press, 1983), vol. 41, pp. 519–527. Theodore Roosevelt, *The Foes of Our Own Household* (New York, 1917), pp. 293–295.

8. Roosevelt, *The Foes of Our Own Household,* pp. 293–295. Murphy, *World War I.* William Preston, *Aliens and Dissenters, Federal Suppression of Radicals, 1903–1933* (New York: Harper & Row, 1966).

9. *Mother Earth* 12 (June 1917): 112–114; (July 1917): 129–162. Emma Goldman, *Living My Life* (New York: Dover, 1970), vol. 2, pp. 598–599.

10. Zechariah Chafee, Jr., *Freedom of Speech* (1920), revised and expanded, *Free Speech in the United States* (Cambridge, Mass.: Harvard University Press, 1941). Richard Polenberg, *Fighting Faiths: The Abrams Case, The Supreme Court, and Free Speech* (New York: Viking, 1987), pp. 27–36.

11. Polenberg, *Fighting Faiths,* pp. 154–160. Preston, *Aliens and Dissenters.*

12. Burleson: Murphy, *World War I,* p. 98. Huebsch, COHC, pp. 423–424.

13. *The Masses* 9 (April 1917).

14. *Masses v. Patten,* 245 Fed 102 (C.C.A. 2d, 1917). Chafee, *Free Speech,* pp. 42–51. Max Eastman, *Love and Revolution* (New York: Random House, 1964), pp. 58–59.

15. Joan M. Jensen, *The Price of Vigilance* (Chicago: Rand McNally, 1968). National Civil Liberties Bureau, *The Outrage on Rev. Herbert S. Bigelow* (March 1918).

16. Walter P. Metzger, *Academic Freedom in the Age of the University* (New York: Columbia University Press, 1961), pp. 225–230. American Association of University

Professors (AAUP), Committee on Academic Freedom in Wartime, *AAUP Bulletin* 4 (February–March 1918).

17. See the discussion in Murphy, *World War I*, pp. 15–31. Polenberg, *Fighting Faiths*, pp. 154–196.

18. Athan Theoharis and John Stuart Cox, *The Boss: J. Edgar Hoover and the Great American Inquisition* (Philadelphia: Temple University Press, 1988). Richard Gid Powers, *Secrecy and Power: The Life of J. Edgar Hoover* (New York: Free Press, 1987), pp. 36–55. Donald L. Smith, *Zechariah Chafee: Defender of Liberty and Law* (Cambridge, Mass.: Harvard University Press, 1986), pp. 36–57. Robert K. Murray, *Red Scare: A Study in National Hysteria, 1919–1920* (New York: McGraw-Hill, 1964).

19. New York (State) Senate, Joint Legislative Committee Investigating Seditious Activities, *Revolutionary Radicalism*, 4 vols. (Albany: J. B. Lyon, 1920).

20. David M. Kennedy, *Over Here: The First World War and American Society* (New York: Oxford University Press, 1980).

21. AUAM, Pamphlet, ca. 1916; Wald, letter to Wilson, February 28, 1917, Wald Papers, NYPL, Reel 28. John Haynes Holmes, "Where Are the Prewar Radicals?" *The Survey*, February 1, 1926, p. 564. M. Eastman, Statement, February 28, 1917, Wald Papers, CU, Box 88. Huebsch, COHC, p. 168.

22. AUAM, Past Programs of the American Union Against Militarism, ca. 1917, AUAMP, Reel 1. C. Roland Marchand, *The American Peace Movement and Social Reform, 1898–1918* (Princeton, N.J.: Princeton University Press, 1972), pp. 240–258.

23. Crystal Eastman, *Work Accidents and the Law* [1910] (New York: Arno Press, 1969). Bernard Flexner and Roger N. Baldwin, *Juvenile Courts and Probation* (New York: Century, 1916).

24. Charles Chatfield, *For Peace and Justice: Pacifism in America, 1914–1941* (Knoxville: University of Tennessee Press, 1971). Norman Thomas, *The Conscientious Objector* (New York: B. W. Huebsch, 1923).

25. Wilson, cited in Eastman, letter to AUAM, June 14, 1917, AUAM Papers, Reel 1. AUAM, *Concerning Conscription* (April 1917), RNBP, Box 3. AUAM, Letter to President Wilson, April 17, 1917, ACLUP, 1917, vol. 26. AUAM, *Constitutional Rights in War Time*, 2nd ed. (July 1917), RNBP, Box 3.

26. Baldwin, letter to Baker, June 15, 1917; Baldwin, letter to Keppel, June 2, 1917, ACLUP, 1917, vol. 15.

27. Baldwin, memo, June 22, 1917, ACLUP, 1917, vol. 15. Baldwin, letter to Baker, June 30, 1917, ACLUP, 1917, vol. 15; AUAM, "Conscription and the 'Conscientious Objector' " (July 1917), RNBP, Box 3.

28. AUAM, *Some Aspects of the Constitutional Questions Involved in the Draft Act of May 18, 1917 (Extracts from Attorneys' Briefs)*, 1917, RNBP, Box 3. Nelles, *amicus* brief, *Ruthenberg v. United States*, RNBP, Box 3. *Selective Draft Cases*, 245 U.S. 366 (1918). Polenberg, *Fighting Faiths*, pp. 79–81. The AUAM eventually evolved into the Foreign Policy Association.

29. AUAM, letter to Wilson, April 17, 1917, ACLUP, 1917–1919, vol. 26.

30. Baldwin, letter to Weinberger, May 3, 1917, RNBP, Box 3. AUAM, Executive Committee, Minutes, May 28, 1917, AUAMP, Reel 1.

31. AUAM, Executive Committee, Minutes, June 1, 1917, June 4, 1917, AUAMP, Reel 1.

32. C. Eastman, letter to AUAM, June 14, 1917; AUAM, Executive Committee, Minutes, June 15, 1917, AUAMP, Reel 1.

33. Wald, letter to C. Eastman, September 27, 1917; L. H. Wood, letter to Amos

Pinchot, Chair, AUAM, October 2, 1917; NCLB, Directing Committee, Minutes, December 3, 1917, AUAMP, Reel 1.

34. On the actions of other prewar pacifists, see Marchand, *The American Peace Movement.* Allen F. Davis, "Welfare, Reform and World War I," *American Quarterly* 19 (1967): 516–533. Kennedy, *Over Here.* "Mary Van Kleeck," *Notable American Women* (Cambridge, Mass.: Harvard University Press, 1980), vol. 4, pp. 707–709.

35. John Dewey, "Conscription of Thought," *New Republic,* September 1, 1917, pp. 128–130. John C. Farrell, "John Dewey and World War I: Armageddon Tests a Liberal's Faith," *Perspectives in American History* 9 (1975). Lippmann: Murphy, *World War I,* p. 108, n. 100.

36. Carl Resek, ed., *War and the Intellectuals: Essays by Randolph S. Bourne, 1915–1919* (New York: Harper & Row, 1964).

37. Blanche Wiesen Cook, ed., *Crystal Eastman: On Women and Revolution* (New York: Oxford University Press, 1978). On Baldwin, see Chapter Two.

38. W. A. Swanberg, *Norman Thomas: The Last Idealist* (New York: Scribner, 1976). Harry F. Ward, *The Social Creed of the Churches* (New York: Abingdon Press, 1917). John Haynes Holmes, *I Speak for Myself: The Autobiography of John Haynes Holmes* (New York: Harper Bros., 1959).

39. Walter Nelles, *A Liberal in Wartime: The Education of Albert DeSilver* (New York: Norton, 1940), p. 118.

40. David Rabban, "The First Amendment in Its Forgotten Years," *Yale Law Journal* 90 (1981): 514–597. David Brudnoy, "Theodore Schroeder and the Suppression of Vice," *Civil Liberties Review* 3 (June–July 1976): 48–56. David Rabban, "The Free Speech League and the Origins of the ACLU," unpublished ms.

41. Clippings and correspondence, Schroeder Papers, University of Southern Illinois. Lincoln Steffens, *The Autobiography of Lincoln Steffens* (New York: Harcourt, Brace, 1931), pp. 635–639.

42. Schroeder, letter to Baldwin, October 26, 1917, ACLUP, 1917–1919, vol. 3. Schroeder, letter to G. Roe, January 5, 1918, Schroeder Papers, Box 12.

43. NCLB, *War-Time Prosecutions and Mob Violence* (July 1918).

44. AUAM, Memo to Members, July 13, 1917; AUAM, Executive Committee, Minutes, July 24, 1917, AUAMP, Reel 1. Darrow interview: *American Socialist,* August 11, 1917.

45. AUAM, Executive Committee, Minutes, Emergency Meeting, July 24, 1917, AUAMP, Reel 1. Lamar, Memo to Bielaski, March 8, 1918, Bureau of Investigation, RG 65, Reel 436; Lamar, Memo to Postmaster, New York City, May 7, 1918, Bureau of Investigation, RG 65, Reel 614.

46. Baldwin and Eastman, letter to AUAM, August 31, 1917, Wald Papers, CU, Box 88. Smith, letter to Dennett, December 20, 1917, Shaw, letter to Dennett, December 19, 1917, Wise, letter to Wood, January 5, 1918, ACLUP, 1917, vol. 3.

47. Smith, *Zechariah Chafee,* p. 18.

48. NCLB, A Statement, November 1, 1917, ACLUP, 1917, vol. 18.

49. Civil Liberties Bureau, Memo, September 11–12, 1917; Baldwin, Memorandum Relating to Conscientious Objectors, September 18, 1917, ACLUP, 1917, vol. 15.

50. Thomas, *The Conscientious Objector.*

51. Frankfurter, letter to Baldwin, September 27, 1917; Baldwin, letter to Baker, October 20, 1917; Baldwin, letters to Keppel, October 12, 1917, October 16, 1917; Baldwin, letter to Keppel, September 6, 1917; Baldwin, letter to Baker, November 22, 1917, ACLUP, 1917, vol. 15.

52. Thomas, *The Conscientious Objector.*

53. Baldwin, letter to International Bible Students Association, February 14, 1918, ACLUP, 1918, vol. 18.

54. Jensen, *The Price of Vigilance.* Preston, *Aliens and Dissenters.*

55. Melvyn Dubofsky, *We Shall Be All: A History of the Industrial Workers of the World* (Chicago: Quadrangle Books, 1969), pp. 398–444.

56. Flynn, letter to Baldwin, March 19, 1918; Baldwin, letter to Frankfurter, January 5, 1918; Creel, letter to Baldwin, January 7, 1918; Baldwin, telegram to Tumulty, January 31, 1918; Baldwin letter to William B. Wilson, February 26, 1918; Baldwin, letter to President Wilson, January 27, 1918, ACLUP, 1918, vol. 26. NCLB, Defense Fund Account, ca. February, 1919, BLFAP, Box 3. Corliss Lamont, *The Trial of Elizabeth Gurley Flynn by the American Civil Liberties Union* (New York: Horizon Books, 1968).

57. Lamar, letter to Bielaski, March 8, 1918, Bureau of Investigation, Case Files, NA, RG 65, Reel 436.

58. Baldwin, letter to Haywood, March 27, 1918, ACLUP, 1918, vol. 26; Dumar [*New Republic*], letter to Baldwin, May 9, 1918, ACLUP, 1918, vol. 28. DeSilver, correspondence, April–May, 1919, ACLUP, 1919, vol. 108. Eastman, *Love and Revolution,* p. 70.

59. Chafee, *Free Speech in the United States.*

60. *Schenck v. United States,* 249 U.S. 47 (1919).

61. *Debs v. United States,* 249 U.S. 211 (1919). The speech and other documents are in Ronald Radosh, ed., *Debs* (Englewood Cliffs, N.J.: Prentice-Hall, 1971). Nick Salvatore, *Eugene V. Debs: Citizen and Socialist* (Urbana: University of Illinois Press, 1982), pp. 262–302.

62. *Abrams v. United States,* 250 U.S. 616 (1919). Polenberg, *Fighting Faiths.*

63. *Abrams v. United States,* 250 U.S. 616, 624 (1919).

64. John Henry Wigmore, "Abrams v. U.S.: Freedom of Speech and Freedom of Thuggery in War-Time and Peace-Time," *Illinois Law Review* 14 (March 1920): 554.

65. Fred Ragan, "Justice Oliver Wendell Holmes, Jr., Zechariah Chafee, Jr., and the Clear and Present Danger Test for Free Speech: The First Year," *Journal of American History* 58 (June 1971): 24–45. Peter Irons, " 'Fighting Fair': Zechariah Chafee, Jr., The Department of Justice, and the Trial at the Harvard Club," *Harvard Law Review* 94 (April 1981): 1205–1236. Polenberg, *Fighting Faiths,* pp. 218–228. But see Smith, *Zechariah Chafee,* p. 30.

66. Leonard M. Levy, *Legacy of Suppression: Freedom of Speech and Press in Early American History* (Cambridge, Mass.: Harvard University Press, 1960).

67. Chafee, *Freedom of Speech* (1920); Chafee, *Free Speech;* reprinted in 1942, 1946, 1948, 1954, 1964, and 1969. Smith, *Zechariah Chafee,* pp. 18, 36–57. Irons, " 'Fighting Fair.' "

68. David M. Rabban, "The Emergence of Modern First Amendment Doctrine," *University of Chicago Law Review* 50 (Fall 1983): 1205–1355. Rabban, "The First Amendment," pp. 514–597.

69. *Patterson v. Colorado,* 205 U.S. 454 (1907).

70. *Davis v. Massachusetts,* 167 U.S. 43 (1897). Rabban, "The First Amendment."

71. *Mutual Film Corp. v. Industrial Commission,* 236 U.S. 230 (1915). Rabban, "The First Amendment," p. 557.

72. John P. Roche, "American Liberty: An Examination of the 'Tradition' of Freedom," in Milton R. Konvitz and Clinton Rossiter, eds., *Aspects of Liberty* (Ithaca, N.Y.: Cornell University Press, 1958), p. 137. James Willard Hurst, *Law and the Conditions*

of Freedom in the Nineteenth Century United States (Madison: University of Wisconsin Press, 1956).

73. Roscoe Pound, "The Causes of Popular Dissatisfaction with the Administration of Justice," *Reports of the American Bar Association* 29 (1906): 395–417. Richard Maxwell Brown, "Lawful Lawfulness: Legal and Behavioral Perspectives on American Vigilantism," in Maxwell Brown, *Strain of Violence* (New York: Oxford University Press, 1975).

Chapter 2

1. Bureau of Legal First Aid Papers, New York University, Weinberger Papers, Yale University. Harry Weinberger, "A Rebel's Interrupted Autobiography," *American Journal of Economics and Sociology* 2 (October 1942): 111–122.

2. Peggy Lamson, *Roger Baldwin: Founder of the American Civil Liberties Union* (Boston: Houghton Mifflin, 1976).

3. Baldwin, remarks, January 20, 1964, cited in ACLU, *Weekly Bulletin*, March 23, 1964. Baldwin, Memo, "Recollections re Debs," ca. 1964, RNBP, Box 27. Norman Thomas, "Where Are the Pre-War Radicals?" *The Survey*, February 1, 1926, p. 563. Lamson, *Roger Baldwin*, p. 132. Forster, interview.

4. Lamson, *Roger Baldwin*, pp. 115–122. Isbell, interview. On an alleged affair with Elizabeth Gurley Flynn, see Rosalyn Fraad Baxandall, *Words on Fire: The Life and Writing of Elizabeth Gurley Flynn* (New Brunswick, N.J.: Rutgers University Press), p. 41.

5. Baldwin [on Brandeis], *The New Leader*, October 18, 1941; Baldwin, memo, Impressions of Judge Brandeis, April 24, 1942, RNBP, Box 8.

6. Lamson, *Roger Baldwin*, pp. 30–57. Baldwin, COHC, pp. 24, 51.

7. Anthony M. Platt, *The Child Savers: The Invention of Delinquency* (Chicago: University of Chicago Press, 1969). Samuel Walker, *Popular Justice* (New York: Oxford University Press, 1980).

8. Bernard Flexner and Roger Baldwin, *Juvenile Courts and Probation* (New York: Century, 1916), p. 64.

9. *In re Gault*, 387 U.S. 1 (1967). Dorsen, interview. Ira Glasser, "Prisoners of Benevolence: Power Versus Liberty in the Wefare State," in Willard Gaylin et al., eds., *Doing Good: The Limits of Benevolence* (New York: Pantheon, 1978), pp. 97–168.

10. Baldwin, COHC, pp. 35–36.

11. Baldwin, letter to Goldman, September 20, 1909, RNBP, Box 1.

12. Baldwin, letter to E. H. Wuerpel, January 12, 1910, RNBP, Box 1. Goldman's accounts of her 1911 and 1914 engagements in St. Louis do not mention Baldwin. See Emma Goldman, *Mother Earth* 6 (March 1911): 20–22; and *Mother Earth* 9 (January 1915): 364–365.

13. Baldwin, COHC, pp. 48–49. Baldwin, Westin interview, vol. 4, p. 11. On Goldman in St. Louis, see *Mother Earth* 6 (March 1911): 20–22.

14. Baldwin, letter to George W. Pieksen, ed., *Student Life*, Washington University, March 27, 1909; Baldwin, letter to Chancellor David F. Houston, Washington University, August 4, 1911; Houston, letter to Baldwin, August 26, 1911, RNBP, Box 1.

15. Committee for Social Service, "Statement," May 1912; Pamphlet, "The Legal Segregation of Negroes in St. Louis, January 1913; Baldwin, Summary of the Investigation of Industrial Conditions Among Negroes in St. Louis (1914), RNBP, Box 1.

16. Roger Baldwin, "Negro Segregation by Initiative Election in St. Louis," *American*

City 14 (April 1916): 356. *New York Times,* March 1, 1916. *Buchanan v. Warley,* 245 U.S. 60 (1917). Clement E. Vose, *Caucasians Only* (Berkeley and Los Angeles: University of California Press, 1959), pp. 50–54.

17. Baldwin, COHC, p. 33. On the social work profession, see Roy Lubove, *The Professional Altruist: The Emergence of Social Work As a Career, 1880–1930* (New York: Atheneum, 1971).

18. Baldwin, letter to Frank P. Walsh, June 16, 1915, RNBP, Box 1. Graham Adams, *The Age of Industrial Violence* (New York: Columbia University Press, 1966).

19. Emma Goldman, *Living My Life* (New York: Dover, 1970), vol. 1, p. 477, and vol. 2, p. 665.

20. Roger Baldwin, "An Industrial Program for After the War," National Conference of Social Work, *Proceedings* 5, no. 45 (1918): 426–429. Roger Baldwin, "Social Work and Radical Economic Movements," *Proceedings* 5, no. 45 (1918): 396–398.

21. Baldwin telegram to L. H. Wood, January 5, 1915. Baldwin letter to Wood, January 9, 1915, RNBP, Box 1.

22. AUAM, Executive Committee, Minutes, February 10, 1917, AUAM Papers, Reel 1. Baldwin, letter to C. Eastman, February 14, 1917, ACLU/FBI/21057; Baldwin, letter to C. Eastman, March 23, 1917, ACLU/FBI/21059.

23. Keppel, letters to Baldwin, February 26, 1918. March 11, 1917, March 22, 1918; Baldwin, letter to Keppel, March 13, 1918; Baldwin, letter to Major Nicholas Biddle, March 8, 1918, ACLUP, 1917, vol. 15.

24. Baldwin, letter to Wald, June 4, 1917, Wald Papers, CU, Box 88. Bureau of Investigation, Memo, November 22, 1917, April 1, 1918; Bureau of Investigation, Memo to Bielaski, April 22, 1918, BOICF, NA, RG 65, Reel 311. Bielaski, letter to Baldwin, February 9, 1918, ACLUP, 1918, vol. 107. Nelles, letter to Bielaski, September 20, 1918, NYBLFA, Box 3.

25. Bureau of Investigation, Memo to Bielaski, April 22, 1918, BOICF, NA, RG 65, Reel 934.

26. Keppel, letter to Baldwin, May 19, 1918; Wood, letter to Keppel, May 21, 1918; Keppel, letter to Wood, May 22, 1918, ACLUP, 1917, vol. 15.

27. Baldwin, letter to Keppel, August 3, 1918; Baldwin letter to Van Denman, August 17, 1918, ACLUP, 1917, vol. 15. Wood, Memo to NCLB, ca. August, 1918, AUAMP, Reel 1.

28. R. H. Finch, Bureau of Investigation, Memo, September 10, 1918, BOICF, NA, RG 65, Reel 934. John L. Spivak, *A Man and His Times* (New York: Horizon, 1967), p. 51.

29. Finch, memo, September 10, 1918, BOICF, NA, RG 65, Reel 934. Baldwin, letter to Department of Justice, September 6, 1918, ACLUP, 1919, vol. 107. Joan Jensen, *The Price of Vigilance* (Chicago: Rand McNally, 1968), pp. 203–218. "Civil Liberty Dead," *The Nation,* September 14, 1918, p. 382.

30. Nevin Sayre, telegram to Francis B. Sayre, ca. September 1918, ACLUP, 1919, vol. 107. Wood, letter, "To the Friends of the Bureau," September 17, 1918, ACLUP, 1917, vol. 44. James R. Mock, *Censorship 1917* (Princeton, N.J.: Princeton University Press, 1941), p. 140. *New York Times,* November 20, 1918.

31. NCLB, Directing Committee, Minutes, August 26, 1918, AUAMP, Reel 1. Baldwin, letter to District Attorney Caffey, October 9, 1918, RNBP, Box 2.

32. Baldwin, letter to Local Board 129; Baldwin, letter to U.S. Attorney Caffey, October 9, 1918, RNBP, Box 2.

33. Baldwin, letter to mother, October 10, 1918, November 3, 1918, RNBP, Box 3. Lamson, *Roger Baldwin,* pp. 84–91. New York Senate, Joint Legislative Committee In-

vestigating Seditious Activities, *Revolutionary Radicalism,* 4 vols. (Albany, N.Y.: J. B. Lyon, 1920).

34. Roger Baldwin, "The Individual and the State: The Problem As Presented by the Sentencing of Roger N. Baldwin" (November 1918), privately printed and circulated by Baldwin's friends; reprinted in *The Survey,* November 9, 1918, p. 253; *The Nation,* November 9, 1918, p. 54.

35. *New York Times,* October 31, 1918, and November 1, 1918.

36. Baldwin, letter to mother, October 31, 1918, RNBP, Box 2. C. Eastman, letter to Doty, cited in Madeline Z. Doty, unpublished autobiography, chap. 12, p. 3, Doty Papers. *New York Times,* October 31, 1918.

37. Baldwin, "The Individual and the State."

38. Roger Baldwin, "Recollections of Debs," typescript, March 1964, RNBP, Box 27. Ronald Radosh, ed., *Debs* (Englewood Cliffs, N.J.: Prentice-Hall, 1971), pp. 78–84. Robert L. Duffus, "The Legend of Roger Baldwin," *American Mercury,* August 1925, pp. 408–414.

39. Roger Baldwin, "My Vacation on the Government," RNBP, Box 2.

40. Baldwin, letter to mother, November 16, 1918; prison correspondence and papers, RNBP, Box 2.

41. Arthur I. Waskow, *From Race Riot to Sit-In: 1919 and the 1960's* (Garden City, N.Y.: Anchor Books, 1967).

42. Robert K. Murray, *Red Scare* (New York: McGraw-Hill, 1964), pp. 70–71.

43. Richard Gid Powers, *Secrecy and Power: The Life of J. Edgar Hoover* (New York: Free Press, 1986). David Williams, "The Bureau of Investigation and Its Critics, 1919–1921: The Origins of Federal Political Surveillance," *Journal of American History* 68 (December 1981): 560–579. Stanley Coben, *A. Mitchell Palmer: Politician* (New York: Columbia University Press, 1963), p. 207.

44. New York Senate, Joint Committee, *Revolutionary Radicalism,* p. 1982.

45. Zechariah Chafee, Jr., *Free Speech in the United States* (Cambridge, Mass.: Harvard University Press, 1941), pp. 141–195.

46. *Gitlow v. New York,* 268 U.S. 652 (1925). *Whitney v. California,* 274 U.S. 357 (1927). Chafee, *Free Speech in the United States,* pp. 141–195, 343–354.

47. Murray, *Red Scare,* p. 211.

48. Murray, *Red Scare.* National Popular Government League, *Report upon the Illegal Practices of the United States Department of Justice* (May 1920), reprinted by the ACLU.

49. Nelles, letter and telegram to Chafee, January 13, 1920, January 15, 1920, Chafee Papers, Box 29. Charles Evans Hughes, *New York Times,* January 10, 1920.

50. *Report upon the Illegal Practices,* p. 4.

51. *Colyer v. Skeffington,* 265 Fed. 17 (D. Mass. 1920). Chafee, *Free Speech in the United States,* pp. 205–215.

52. Flynn quoted in Nearing, letter to Baldwin, May 5, 1919, RNBP, Box 3.

53. Clippings, *New York Tribune,* July 20, 1919, St. Louis Post-Dispatch, July 24, 1919, RNBP, Box 3. Oswald Garrison Villard, "On Being in Jail," *The Nation,* August 2, 1919, pp. 142–143. Invoice, William Fowler, Caterer, July 21, 1919, ACLUP, 1919, vol. 108. L. S. Chumley, letter to Albert DeSilver, July 18, 1919, ACLUP, 1919, vol. 107.

54. Doty, unpublished autobiography, p. 31.

55. Madeline Z. Doty, "Maggie Martin" and "Maggie Martin's Friends," *The Century* 89 (October 1914): 843–857 and 875–883. On her prewar career, see Madeline Z. Doty,

"Treatment of Minor Cases of Juvenile Delinquency" (July 1911), in her *Reform of the Criminal Law and Procedure* (New York: Arno Press, 1974). Madeline Z. Doty, "The Feminist Movement," *The Intercollegiate Socialist* 7 (October–November 1918): 17–18; Madeline Z. Doty, "The German Revolution," *The Socialist Review* 8 (May 1920): 321–325; and Doty, unpublished autobiography.

56. Clipping, Doty Papers, Box 1. Lamson, *Roger Baldwin,* pp. 115–122.

57. Baldwin, letter "To My Friends," July 31, 1918, RNBP, Box 3.

58. Baldwin, letter to Doty, October 2, 1919, Doty Papers, Box 1. Baldwin, Westin interview, vol. 1, pp. 1–5. Baldwin, letter to Mother, October 26, 1919; Baldwin, letter to St. Louis Board of Police Commissioners, October 13, 1919; Baldwin, letter to Haywood, November 10, 1919, RNBP, Box 3.

59. DeSilver, letter to Wald, January 30, 1919, Wald Papers, CU, Box 17. Conference, The Anglo-American Tradition of Liberty, *Proceedings,* ACLUP, 1919, vol. 73.

60. NCSW, Clippings, May–June 1919; Scrapbook, RNBP, Box 4. Roger Baldwin, "Suggestions for Reorganization of the National Civil Liberties Bureau" (Nelles memo attached), ACLUP, 1919, vol. 112. Roger Baldwin, "Proposed Reorganization of the Work for Civil Liberty," ACLUP, 1919, vol. 44.

61. NCLB, Executive Committee, Minutes, January 12, 1919; ACLU, Executive Committee, Minutes, January 19, 1919. "A New Civil Liberties Union," *The Survey,* January 31, 1920, p. 480.

62. Paul Murphy, *World War I and the Origins of Civil Liberties in the United States* (New York: Norton, 1979).

Chapter 3

1. Clipping, *New York Call,* April 19, 1920, in ACLUP, 1920, vol. 151. Martha Glaser, "Paterson, 1924: The ACLU and Labor," *New Jersey History* 94 (Winter 1976): 156. ACLU, *Annual Report,* 1921, pp. 8–9.

2. Paul Murphy, "Sources and Nature of Intolerance in the 1920s," *Journal of American History* 51 (June 1964): 66. ACLU, *Annual Report,* 1928, pp. 28–29.

3. ACLU, "Report on Civil Liberty Situation for Week Ending August 15, 1921," NAACP, I, C-192.

4. ACLU, *Annual Report,* 1921, pp. 8–9.

5. Arthur Garfield Hays, *Let Freedom Ring* (New York: Boni & Liveright, 1928), pp. 102–109. Martin Zanger, "The Politics of Confrontation: Upton Sinclair and the Launching of the ACLU in Southern California," *Pacific Historical Review* 28 (November 1969): 383–406. ACLU, *Annual Report,* 1925, pp. 25–27. On the Sanger incident, see Robert Morss Lovett, *All Our Years* (New York: Viking, 1948), pp. 194–195; Clippings, ACLUP, 1923, vol. 239.

6. ACLU, *Annual Report,* 1921, p. 8.

7. National Popular Government League, *Report upon the Illegal Practices of the United States Department of Justice* (May 1920), reprinted by the ACLU.

8. Charles T. Hallinan in AUAM *Bulletin,* February 14, 1920, Wald Papers, CU, Box 88. ACLU, "Report on Civil Liberty Situation," August 15, 1921, August 29, 1921, NAACP/I/C-192.

9. ACLU, *Annual Report,* 1921, pp. 9–10.

10. Roger Baldwin, "What Shall We Do?," typescript, January 25, 1939, RNBP, Box 8.

11. Baldwin, letter to Ward, December 4, 1926, RNBP, Box 4.

12. Roger Baldwin, Tribute to Hays, December 16, 1954, RNBP, Box 20.

13. Hays, letter to Alexander Meikeljohn, October 5, 1949. Meikeljohn Papers, Box 16. Hays, *City Lawyer*. Hays, *Let Freedom Ring*.

14. Hays, *City Lawyer*, pp. 196–197. *New York Times*, December 15, 1954. Baldwin, Tribute to Hays, December 16, 1954, RNBP, Box 20.

15. Louis H. Pollak, "Advocating Civil Liberties: A Young Lawyer Before the Old Court," *Harvard Civil Rights–Civil Liberties Law Review* 17 (Spring 1982): 1–30. Pollak, interview.

16. On the place of constitutionalism in American life, see Michael Kammen, *A Machine That Would Go by Itself: The Constitution in American Culture* (New York: Knopf, 1987).

17. See the symposium "Where Are the Pre-War Radicals?" *The Survey*, February 1, 1926, pp. 556–566.

18. Paul L. Murphy, *The Meaning of Freedom of Speech: First Amendment Freedoms from Wilson to FDR* (Westport, Conn.: Greenwood Press, 1972). Murphy's account is a de facto history of the ACLU in the 1920s.

19. Norman Hapgood, *Professional Patriots* (New York: Albert and Charles Boni, 1927). Irving Bernstein, *The Lean Years: A History of the American Worker, 1920–1933* (Baltimore: Penguin, 1966).

20. *New York Times*, March 5, 1923. ACLU, *Annual Report*, 1923, p. 26. Winthrop D. Lane, *Civil War in West Virginia* (New York: B. W. Huebsch, 1921), pp. 15, 18. ACLU, *The Denial of Civil Liberties in the Coal Fields*, 1923. Hays, *Let Freedom Ring*, pp. 102–109, 128–129. John L. Spivak, *A Man and His Times* (New York: Horizon, 1967), pp. 51–95. Donald L. Smith, *Zechariah Chafee: Defender of Liberty and Law* (Cambridge, Mass.: Harvard University Press, 1986), p. 9.

21. Zanger, "The Politics of Confrontation," pp. 383–406. "They Who Save the Republic," *The Nation*, May 30, 1923, p. 618.

22. Felix Frankfurter and Nathan Greene, *The Labor Injunction* (New York: Macmillan, 1930), pp. 89–105. Bernstein, *The Lean Years*, pp. 190–243.

23. Baldwin, Ward, DeSilver, letter to Frankfurter, December 11, 1920, Frankfurter Papers, LC.

24. Frankfurter and Greene, *The Labor Injunction*. ACLU, *Annual Report*, 1931, p. 21. Bernstein, *The Lean Years*, pp. 412–414.

25. Dwight MacDonald, "The Defense of Everybody," *The New Yorker*, July 11, 1953, pp. 31 ff. and July 18, 1953, pp. 29 ff.

26. ACLU, letter to W. Hays, November 15, 1921; W. Hays, letter to DeSilver, November 19, 1921, ACLUP, 1921, vol. 167. Albert DeSilver, "Backward and Forward," *The World Tomorrow*, April 1921, pp. 117–118. Albert DeSilver, "On Civil Liberty: 1921," *The World Tomorrow*, December 1921, p. 361.

27. *New York Times*, January 30 through February 4, 1928. Hays, letter to Baldwin, March 26, 1928; Baldwin, letter to Chase, May 18, 1928, RNBP, Box 4. *Gomez v. Kieley* (1928). ACLU, *Annual Report*, 1929, p. 25.

28. Amnesty Meeting, Minutes, November 16, 1918, ACLUP, 1918, vol. 98. "Amnesty and the Civil Liberties Union," *The Nation*, March 26, 1924, p. 346. ACLU, *Annual Report*, 1923, pp. 9–16.

29. ACLU, Executive Committee, Minutes, November 29, 1920, April 18, 1921. ACLU, *Annual Report*, 1923, pp. 10–11.

30. Joint Amnesty Committee, Minutes, November 17, 1922, March 23, 1923, ACLUP, 1922, vol. 72. Baldwin, Memorandum to the Joint Amnesty Committee, March 9, 1923, ACLUP, 1922, vol. 72.

31. ACLU, *Annual Report*, 1933, pp. 10–11; 1934, p. 13.

32. Zechariah Chafee, Jr., *Free Speech in the United States* (Cambridge, Mass.: Harvard University Press, 1941), pp. 306–317.

33. Hapgood, *Professional Patriots.* Easley, letter to Hoover, September 16, 1925, ACLU/FBI.

34. *New York Times,* September 11, 1923, September 12, 1923. ACLU, *Who's Un-American?* (September 1935), pp. 21–25.

35. Hapgood, *Professional Patriots,* Edwin Layton, "The Better America Federation: A Case Study of Superpatriotism," *Pacific Historical Review* 30 (May 1961): 137–147.

36. ACLU, Executive Committee, Minutes, November 19, 1923. ACLU, *Annual Report,* 1924, pp. 19–20.

37. Bureau of Investigation, Memo, March 1, 1920; Bureau of Investigation, Los Angeles office, memo, May 2, 1924, ACLU/FBI/361. Bureau of Investigation, Pittsburgh office, memo, February 12, 1921, BOIF. Athan Theoharis and John Stuart Cox, *The Boss: J. Edgar Hoover and the Great American Inquisition* (Philadelphia: Temple University Press, 1988).

38. ACLU, *Annual Report,* 1927, pp. 21–22. "Eighty-Three Enforce It," *The Survey,* December 15, 1925. *Hamilton v. Regents,* 293 U.S. 245 (1934). Roger Baldwin, Memo, The California R.O.T.C. Cases in the Supreme Court, October 17, 1934, ACLUP, 1934, vol. 679.

39. ACLU, Executive Committee, Minutes, April 26, 1926, July 8, 1929. ACLU, Press Release, November 18, 1926.

40. Leon Whipple, *The Story of Civil Liberties in the United States* (New York: Vanguard Press and American Civil Liberties Union, 1927). ACLU, *Annual Report,* 1925, p. 27. Gara LaMarche, "Champion of the Public Interest: Highlights of the 50-Year Work of the Academic Freedom Committee," October 1, 1976, author's files. *America,* quoted in Edward De Grazia and Roger K. Newman, *Banned Films* (New York: Bowker, 1982), p. 45.

41. New York City, Board of Education, "Regulations Governing Forums," copy in ACLUP, 1926, vol. 307. Brief of Petitioner, *In re American Civil Liberties Union and New York City Board of Education, Before the Commissioner of Education,* copy in ACLUP, 1926, vol. 307. ACLU, *Annual Report,* 1928, pp. 28–29. ACLU, Executive Committee, Minutes, April 25, 1921. ACLU, *Annual Report,* 1928, pp. 28–29.

42. ACLU, *The National Council on Freedom from Censorship* (ca. 1930). NCFC, Executive Committee, Minutes, March 2, 1932. ACLU, *Annual Report,* 1958, p. 15.

43. ACLU, *Annual Report,* 1924, p. 10. Pethick-Lawrence, letter to Baldwin, February 25, 1927, RNBP, Box 6.

44. ACLU, *Annual Report,* 1921, p. 18. Milner, letter to Stanger, June 29, 1934, ACLUP, 1934, v. 684. Ovington, letter to Baldwin, May 8, 1920, NAACP/I/C-192. Charles Morgan, interview.

45. ACLU, *Black Justice* (1931).

46. ACLU, Executive Committee, Minutes, December 6, 1920.

47. *New York Times,* September 10, 1923. Clippings in ACLUP, 1923, vol. 228.

48. Curley, letter to Codman, October 4, 1923, Chafee Papers, Box 30.

49. ACLU, letter to Curley, October 11, 1923, Chafee Papers, Box 30. *New York Times,* September 10, 1923.

50. Curley, letter to Codman, March 23, 1925, Chafee Papers, Box 30.

51. Milner, letter to Mayor, Cudahy, Wisc., December 24, 1924, ACLUP, 1925, vol. 291. ACLU, Executive Committee, Minutes, August 25, 1924. ACLU, Press Release, December 6, 1928, ACLUP, 1928, vol. 339. *Bryant v. Zimmerman,* 278 U.S. 63 (1928).

52. ACLU, Executive Committee, Minutes, December 27, 1920, January 3, 1921. DeSilver, letter to Johnson, January 10, 1921, ACLUP, 1921, vol. 168. White, letter to Baldwin, March 5, 1931, NAACP/I/C-194. G. W. Moss, letter to Isserman, September 22, 1931, ACLUP, 1931, vol. 506.

53. Seymour Martin Lipset and Earl Raab, *The Politics of Unreason: Right-Wing Extremism in America, 1790–1977,* 2nd ed. (Chicago: University of Chicago Press, 1978), pp. 135–138.

54. Baldwin, letter to Holmes, March 30, 1921; ACLU, "Report on Civil Liberty Situation for the Week of March 28, 1921, April 18, 1921," NAACP Papers, I/C, Box 192.

55. Roger Baldwin, *Liberty Under the Soviets* (New York: Vanguard Press, 1928). J. P. Morray, *Project Kuzbas* (New York: International Publishers, 1983).

56. ACLU, Executive Committee, Minutes, March 9, 1925, May 25, 1925, April 15, 1929. ACLU, Statement, February 1930, ACLUP, 1930, vol. 417.

57. Taft, letter to Baldwin, July 25, 1924; Baldwin, letter to Taft, August 1, 1924, ACLUP, 1924, vol. 257. ACLU, Executive Committee, Minutes, May 2, 1921, May 16, 1921, May 23, 1921, June 6, 1921. ACLU, *The Communist Prosecutions* (ca. 1921), ACLUP, 1921, vol. 181.

58. Roger N. Baldwin, "Introduction," in Alexander Berkman, ed., *Letters from Russian Prisons* (New York: Albert and Charles Boni, 1925).

59. International Committee for Political Prisoners, Press Release, March 10, 1925, ACLUP, 1925, vol. 288. Baldwin, letter to unidentified, March 26, 1927. Baldwin, letter to Nehru, December 27, 1927, letter to Munzenberg, May 24, 1928; letter to Nehru, April 29, 1931, RNBP, Box 5.

60. MacDonald, "The Defense of Everybody."

61. Norman Thomas, R. M. Lovett, and Roger Baldwin, letter to Attorney General Daugherty, August 24, 1922, ACLUP, 1922, vol. 220. *New York Times,* August 25, 1922. ACLU, *The Nation-Wide Spy System Centering in the Department of Justice* (May 1924).

62. ACLU, *The Michigan Communist Trials* (October 1922). Foster, letter to "Dear Comrade," September 18, 1922, Flynn Papers, WHS. Baldwin, letter to Foster, October 17, 1922, ACLUP, 1922, vol. 219.

63. Baldwin, letter to George Maurer, May 26, 1924; Maurer, letter to Baldwin, September 9, 1924, ACLUP, 1924, vol. 261.

64. Theoharis and Cox, *The Boss*. Richard Gid Powers, *Secrecy and Power: The Life of J. Edgar Hoover* (New York: Free Press, 1987), pp. 142–155. A. T. Mason, *Harlan Fiske Stone* (New York: Viking, 1956), pp. 149–152.

65. Hoover, "Memorandum for the Attorney General," July 21, 1924, ACLU/FBI.

66. Baldwin, letters to Hoover, August 15, 1924, October 3, 1924, January 21, 1925; Baldwin, letter to Stone, August 7, 1924, August 11, 1924; Hoover, letter to Baldwin, September 30, 1924; Baldwin, Memorandum on the Department of Justice, October 17, 1924, ACLUP, 1924, vol. 271. ACLU, Executive Committee, Minutes, January 19, 1925.

67. C. D. McKean (special agent in charge, NYC FBI office), letter to Hoover, February 27, 1929, ACLU/FBI/6930.

68. Baldwin, letter to Doyle, August 17, 1933, ACLUP, 1933, vol. 608. Walsh, letter to Baldwin, September 22, 1924, ACLUP, 1924, vol. 274. Walsh, letter to Baldwin, September 25, 1924, ACLUP, 1924, vol. 261. David Williams, "Failed Reform: FBI Political Surveillance, 1924–1936," *First Principles* 7 (September–October 1981): 1–4.

69. Huebsch, COHC, p. 119.

70. Walter Nelles, *A Liberal in Wartime: The Education of Albert DeSilver* (New York: Norton, 1940).

71. Baldwin, *Memoir,* 1978, p. 33, ACLUP, 1978, vol. 11.

72. Hays, *City Lawyer,* pp. 224, 227. Huebsch, COHC. Elmer Rice, *Minority Report: An Autobiography* (New York: Simon & Schuster, 1963), p. 347.

73. Baldwin, *Memoir,* 1978, pp. 35–36, ACLUP, 1978, vol. 11.

74. Ibid., pp. 61–62.

75. ACLU, Memo, ca. 1935, Holmes Papers, LC.

76. ACLU, *Annual Report,* 1921. Charles Lam Markmann, *The Noblest Cry* (New York: St. Martin's Press, 1965), p. 32.

77. Baldwin, letter to Ward, December 4, 1926, RNBP, Box 4.

78. Baldwin, Westin interview, vol. 1, pp. 23–25. Reitman, interview. Isbell, interview.

79. Baldwin, letter to Ward, January 22, 1925, ACLUP, 1925, vol. 281. Baldwin, Westin interview, vol. 1, pp. 61–62.

80. Scott Nearing, *The Making of a Radical* (New York: Harper & Row, 1972), pp. 46–47. Roger Baldwin, "Working Outside," *The World Tomorrow* 7 (July 1924): 202–203.

81. Pemberton, interview. Isbell, interview.

82. American Fund for Public Service, *Report for the Three Years, 1925–1928* (February 1929), ACLUP, 1929, vol. 316. See also AFPS Papers, NYPL. *New York Times,* August 13, 1922. "Pope" quotation: Lovett, *All Our Years,* pp. 207–208. Merle Curti, "Subsidizing Radicalism: The American Fund for Public Service, 1921–1941," *Social Service Review* 33 (September 1959): 277–295. *New York Times,* August 13, 1922, p. 7. Roger Baldwin, Memo, "Garland's Millions," RNBP, Box 5. ACLU, Executive Committee, Minutes, May 8, 1922.

83. Baldwin, letter to Ward, January 22, 1925, ACLUP, 1925, vol. 281. ACLU, *Annual Report,* 1926, p. 3.

Chapter 4

1. Paul L. Murphy, *The Meaning of Freedom of Speech* (Westport, Conn.: Greenwood Press, 1972), argues the case for popular sources of tolerance.

2. Lucille Milner, *Education of an American Liberal: An Autobiography* (New York: Horizon, 1954), p. 161.

3. ACLU, *Annual Report,* 1925, p. 27.

4. The following account draws on Ray Ginger, *Six Days or Forever?* (Chicago: Quadrangle Paperbacks, 1969). John T. Scopes and James Presley, *Center of the Storm: Memoirs of John T. Scopes* (New York: Holt, Rinehart and Winston, 1967). Edward J. Larson, *Trial and Error: The American Controversy over Creation and Evolution* (New York: Oxford University Press, 1985). Martin E. Marty, *Pilgrims in Their Own Land: 500 Years of Religion in America* (New York: Penguin, 1985), pp. 373–401.

5. Arthur Weinberg, ed., *Attorney for the Damned* (New York: Simon & Schuster, 1957).

6. Baldwin, Westin interview, vol. 6, p. 5.

7. Baldwin, letter to R. Fosdick, Rockefeller Foundation, October 21, 1925; Hays, letter to Nelles, September 9, 1925, ACLUP, 1925, vol. 274.

8. Darrow quoted in Weinberg, *Attorney for the Damned,* pp. 187–188.

9. *New York Times,* July 18, 1925.

10. Ginger, *Six Days or Forever?*

11. Arthur Garfield Hays, "The Strategy of the Scopes Defense," *The Nation,* August 5, 1925, p. 332.

12. Arthur Garfield Hays, *City Lawyer* (New York: Simon & Schuster, 1942), pp. 208–210.

13. Ginger, *Six Days or Forever?*

14. Howard K. Beale, *Are American Teachers Free?* (New York: Scribner, 1936), pp. 238–240. ACLU, Press Release, March 20, 1926. ACLU, Executive Committee, Minutes, May 2, 1927.

15. Charles Evans Hughes, "Liberty and Law," *ABA Journal* 11 (September 1925): 563–569.

16. Editorial, *St. Louis Post-Dispatch*, June 13, 1926, copy in Hays Papers, Box 78.

17. ACLU, *Annual Report*, 1928, pp. 56–57.

18. Beale, *Are American Teachers Free?*, pp. 258–259. "From Dayton to New York," *The Nation*, June 2, 1926, p. 595.

19. Larson, *Trial and Error*. Langdon Gilkey, *Creationism on Trial: Evolution and God at Little Rock* (Minneapolis: Winston Press, 1985). On Texas, see *New York Times*, October 17, 1925.

20. *Epperson v. Arkansas*, 393 U.S. 97 (1968). Larson, *Trial and Error*, pp. 98–119. Glasser, interview, 1987.

21. Anson Phelps Stokes, *Church and State in the United States* (New York: Harper & Row, 1950).

22. ACLU–NC, Executive Committee, Minutes, August 31, 1926. ACLU, Executive Committee, Minutes, September 27, 1926. ACLU–NC, Executive Committee, Minutes, August 3, 1926. ACLU–NC, Memo, Citizens of California, ca. 1926. Thomas, letter to Bailey, September 7, 1926; Hillquit, letter to Bailey, September 10, 1926; Lovett, letter to Bailey, September 8, 1926; Ross, letter to Bailey, September 15, 1926, ACLUP, 1926, vol. 303.

23. ACLU–NC, Executive Committee, Minutes, March 2, 1927. Baldwin, letter to Hays, May 7, 1930; Hays, letter to Baldwin, June 11, 1930; Ernst, letter to Baldwin, August 27, 1930, ACLUP, 1930, vol. 424. ACLU, Press Release, October 28, 1932. ACLU, Executive Committee, Minutes, April 26, 1926. ACLU, *Annual Report*, 1927, pp. 21–22.

24. ACLU, *Annual Report*, 1927, pp. 21–22.

25. ACLU, *"Unlawful Assembly" in Paterson* (May 1925), ACLUP, 1927, vol. 327. ACLU, *The Victory in New Jersey* (June 1928), ACLUP, 1928, vol. 346. Martha Glaser, "Paterson, 1924: The ACLU and Labor," *New Jersey History* 94 (Winter 1976): 155–172.

26. Frankfurter, letter to Samuel D. Smoleff, January 26, 1926; Frankfurter, letter to Baldwin, March 24, 1926; Hays, letter to Baldwin, January 26, 1926, FFP/LC. Nelles, letter to Hays, January 26, 1926, ACLUP, 1924, vol. 159A.

27. Baldwin, letter to Nelles, January 27, 1926, FFP/LC. Baldwin, letter to Ernst, April 6, 1926, Ernst Papers, vol. 402.

28. Bailey, letter to Frankfurter, November 3, 1927; Untermyer, letter to Smoleff, November 23, 1927, ACLUP, 1927, vol. 327.

29. Baldwin, typescript, ca. 1928, RNBP, Box 4.

30. Baldwin, letter to Vanderbilt, April 16, 1928; Vanderbilt, letter to Baldwin, April 18, 1928, ACLUP, 1928, vol. 346.

31. *State v. Butterworth*, 142 A. 57 (May 14, 1928). *New York Times*, May 15, 1928.

32. *Gitlow v. New York*, 268 U.S. 652 (1925). Zechariah Chafee, Jr., *Free Speech in the United States* (Cambridge, Mass.: Harvard University Press, 1941), pp. 318–325.

33. Harold Josephson, "Political Justice During the Red Scare: The Trial of Benjamin Gitlow," in Michael Belknap, ed., *Political Trials* (Westport, Conn.: Greenwood Press,

1981), pp. 153–176. Louis H. Pollak, "Advocating Civil Liberties: A Young Lawyer Before the Old Court," *Harvard Civil Rights–Civil Liberties Law Review* 17 (Spring 1982): 1–30.

34. *Gitlow v. New York*, 268 U.S. 652 (1925).

35. Charles Warren, "The New 'Liberty' Under the Fourteenth Amendment," *Harvard Law Review* 39 (February 1926): 431–465. Chafee, *Free Speech in the United States*, pp. 318–325.

36. ACLU, *Annual Report*, 1926, p. 3.

37. Ibid., pp. 31–32. Pollak, "Advocating Civil Liberties."

38. *Whitney v. California*, 274 U.S. 357 (1927).

39. Ibid.

40. *Fiske v. Kansas*, 274 U.S. 380 (1927). Chafee, *Free Speech in the United States*, p. 352.

41. *Meyer v. Nebraska*, 262 U.S. 390 (1923). *Pierce v. Society of Sisters*, 268 U.S. 510 (1925).

42. [Felix Frankfurter], "Can the Supreme Court Guarantee Toleration?" *The New Republic*, June 17, 1925, pp. 85–87. The article was unsigned but was later published in a collection of Frankfurter's essays.

43. Pollak, "Advocating Civil Liberties." Zechariah Chafee, Jr., "Walter Heilprin Pollak," *The Nation*, October 12, 1940, pp. 318–319. *Powell v. Alabama*, 287 U.S. 45 (1932). *Norris v. Alabama*, 294 U.S. 587 (1935). Yale Kamisar, *Police Interrogations* (Ann Arbor: University of Michigan Press, 1980), pp. 95–112. Dan T. Carter, *Scottsboro: A Tragedy of the American South* (New York: Oxford University Press, 1969).

44. ACLU, *Annual Report*, 1930, p. 50. ACLU, Board of Directors, Minutes, January 22, 1934.

45. Herbert Asbury, "Hatrack," *American Mercury* 7 (April 1926): 479–483. *American Mercury v. Chase*, 13 F. (2d) 224 (1926). Arthur Garfield Hays, *Let Freedom Ring* (New York: Boni & Liveright, 1928), pp. 157–184. Carl Bode, ed., *The Editor, the Bluenose, and the Prostitute* (Boulder, Colo.: Robert Rinehart, 1988).

46. Paul Boyer, *Purity in Print* (New York: Scribner, 1968), Zechariah Chafee, Jr., *The Censorship in Boston* (Boston: Civil Liberties Union of Massachusetts, 1929). Casey quoted in Heywood Hale Broun, "It Seems to Me," *New York Telegram*, December 6, 1929.

47. Chafee, *Free Speech in the United States*, pp. 529–530, n. 15. Alexander Meikeljohn, *Free Speech and Its Relation to Self-Government* (New York: Harper Bros., 1948).

48. Holmes, quoted in Peggy Lamson, *Roger Baldwin: Founder of the American Civil Liberties Union* (Boston: Houghton Mifflin, 1976), p. 256. Thomas, letter to Baldwin, January 21, 1931, Ernst Papers, vol. 401. Bailey, letter to Wellman, March 31, 1927, ACLUP, 1927, vol. 327.

49. Hays, letter to ACLU, February 3, 1938, Ernst Papers, vol. 404. Arthur Garfield Hays, "New Morals for Old: Modern Marriage and Ancient Laws," *The Nation*, August 20, 1924, pp. 187–189. Arthur Garfield Hays, "Companionate Divorce," *The Nation*, April 10, 1929, pp. 420–421. Hays, *City Lawyer*.

50. Morris L. Ernst and William Seagle, *To the Pure . . . A Study of Obscenity and the Censor* (New York: Viking, 1928). Morris L. Ernst and Alexander Lindey, *The Censor Marches On* (New York: Doubleday, 1940). Morris L. Ernst and Alan U. Schwartz, *Censorship: The Search for the Obscene* (New York: Macmillan, 1964). On Ernst's influence, see Walter Kendrick, *The Secret Museum: Pornography in Modern Culture* (New York: Penguin, 1988), pp. 202–203.

51. Baldwin, letter to Gardner Jackson, February 16, 1929, ACLUP, 1929, vol. 373.

52. Clipping, *Boston Globe,* April 17, 1929, in ACLUP, 1929, vol. 373. CLUM, "Report of 1929–1930," ACLUP, 1930, vol. 423.

53. Chafee, *The Censorship in Boston,* pp. 17, 21–23. On the authorship, see Baldwin, letter to Codman, June 17, 1929, ACLUP, 1929, vol. 373. Chafee, *Free Speech in the United States,* pp. 517–555.

54. On the Brennan incident, see Edward De Grazia and Roger K. Newman, *Banned Films* (New York: Bowker, 1982), pp. 204–205. Richard S. Randall, *Censorship of the Movies* (Madison: University of Wisconsin Press, 1968).

55. ACLU, Press Release, January 24, 1929. ACLU, *Annual Report,* 1929, pp. 24–25. Morris Ernst and Pare Lorentz, *Censored: The Private Life of the Movie* (New York: Cape & H. Smith, 1930). ACLU, *What Shocked the Censors* (1933).

56. "Mary Ware Dennett," *Notable American Women* (Cambridge, Mass.: Harvard University Press, 1980), vol. 1, pp. 463–465. The pamphlet is reprinted in Mary Ware Dennett, *Who's Obscene?* (New York: Vanguard Press, 1930).

57. David Kennedy, *Birth Control in America: The Career of Margaret Sanger* (New Haven, Conn.: Yale University Press, 1970). Linda Gordon, *Woman's Body, Woman's Right* (Baltimore: Penguin, 1977), pp. 249–300.

58. Dewey, letter to Ernst, n.d., Ernst Papers, vol. 46. On the case, see Ernst papers, vols. 46, 47, 86. ACLU, *The Prosecution of Mary Ware Dennett for "Obscenity"* (June 1929). *U.S. v. Dennett,* 39 F. 2d 564 (1930).

59. Bailey, Memos to Dennett Defense Committee, May 24, 1929, October 31, 1930. Bailey (Committee Against Stage Censorship), form letter, April 4, 1931, ACLUP, vol. 516.

60. Hays, *City Lawyer,* pp. 154–182.

61. Morris L. Ernst, "Sex Wins in America," *The Nation,* August 10, 1932, pp. 122–124.

62. NCFC correspondence in ACLUP, 1933, vol. 603. Morris L. Ernst, "How We Nullify," *The Nation,* January 27, 1932, pp. 113–114.

63. *U.S. v. Married Love,* 48 F. (2d) 821 (1931). *U.S. v. One Book Called Ulysses,* 5 F. Supp. 182 (1933).

64. Baldwin, letters to Executive Committee and National Committee, January 12, 1929, February 7, 1929, ACLUP, 1930, vol. 384.

65. Baldwin, letters to the National Committee, February 7, 1929, February 14, 1929, ACLUP, 1930, vol. 384.

66. Frankfurter, letter to Baldwin, February 16, 1929; Baldwin, letter to Frankfurter, February 20, 1929, FFP/LC. Baldwin, interview, 1974, pp. 76–77, ACLUP, 1978, vol. 11.

67. Felix Frankfurter and Nathan Greene, *The Labor Injunction* (New York: Macmillan, 1930). Irving Bernstein, *The Lean Years: A History of the American Worker, 1920–1933* (Baltimore: Penguin, 1970), pp. 397–402. ACLU, *Annual Report,* 1931, pp. 21–22.

68. Ernst, letter to Bailey, March 1, 1928, Ernst Papers, vol. 401.

69. U.S. Commission on Law Enforcement and Observance, *Lawlessness in Law Enforcement* (Washington, D.C.: U.S. Government Printing Office, 1931). ACLU, Executive Committee, Minutes, January 11, 1926, May 13, 1929. Baldwin, letter to Pollak, October 21, 1929, ACLUP, 1929, vol. 360.

70. U.S. Commission, *Lawlessness in Law Enforcement.*

71. ACLU, Memo, Methods of Combatting the Third Degree (September 1935), AGHP, Box 78. Report of Subcommittee Which Investigated Disturbances of March 19th, 1935,

p. 19, AGHP, Box 21. Samuel Walker, *A Critical History of Police Reform* (Lexington, Mass.: Lexington Books, 1977).

72. ACLU, *Annual Report*, 1932, p. 35; 1934, p. 29. Wilcomb E. Washburn, *The Indian in America* (New York: Harper & Row, 1975), pp. 254–257.

73. ACLU, *Black Justice* (May 1931).

74. Richard Kluger, *Simple Justice* (New York: Vintage Books, 1977), pp. 132–138. Mark V. Tushnet, *The NAACP's Legal Strategy Against Segregated Education, 1925–1950* (Chapel Hill: University of North Carolina Press, 1987), pp. 1–21.

75. AFPS, Committee on Negro Work, Report, October 13, 1929, AFPS Papers, Box 7.

76. Ibid.

77. Baldwin, Memo, ca. 1929, AFPS Papers, Box 7. Roger N. Baldwin, "Negro Rights and the Class Struggle," *Opportunity* 12 (September 1934): 264–269.

78. Baldwin, letter to Ernst, November 11, 1929, Ernst Papers, vol. 401. Wood, letter to Baldwin, n.d., AFPS Papers, Box 7. Wood, letter to Walter White, September 9, 1930; Odum, letter to Walter White, September 10, 1930, Ernst Papers, vol. 477.

79. Frankfurter, letter to Ernst, June 5, 1930, Ernst Papers, vol. 477. Margold Report, ca. 1931, NAACP/I/C-200. Kluger, *Simple Justice*, pp. 132–138.

80. Beardsley, letter to Bailey, January 20, 1931; Bailey, letter to Beardsley, March 10, 1931, ACLUP, 1931, vol. 162. On the breach with the ILD, see ACLU, Executive Committee, Minutes, November 24, 1930.

81. *Stromberg v. California*, 283 U.S. 359 (1931).

82. Fred W. Friendly, *Minnesota Rag: The Dramatic Story of the Landmark Supreme Court Case That Gave New Meaning to Freedom of the Press* (New York: Vintage Books, 1982). ACLU, *Annual Report*, 1925, p. 31.

83. *Near v. Minnesota*, 283 U.S. 697 (1931).

84. Murphy, *The Meaning of Freedom of Speech*, esp. pp. 3–10, 270.

85. *Powell v. Alabama*, 287 U.S. 45 (1932). Dan T. Carter, *Scottsboro: A Tragedy of the American South* (New York: Oxford University Press, 1969). Morris Ernst, "Dissenting Opinion," *The Nation*, December 7, 1932, p. 559.

86. Murphy, *The Meaning of Freedom of Speech*, pp. 273–288.

Chapter 5

1. Holmes, letter to Ward, February 11, 1938, Holmes Papers, Box 7.

2. ACLU, *Annual Report*, 1930, p. 20; 1931, pp. 5, 19–20; 1932, pp. 21–22, 26–27; 1934, p. 33. ACLU–SC, Report, ca. 1933, Memo, July 7, 1933, ACLUP, 1933, vol. 648.

3. ACLU, *The Right of Asylum* (June 1935). Lamont, letter to Baldwin, September 23, 1932; Dombrowsky, letter to Customs, September 22, 1932, ACLUP, 1931, vol. 504.

4. Baldwin, "What Is the Truth About Constitution [*sic*] Rights?" December 14, 1936, ACLUP, 1936, vol. 904. Baldwin, "Whad'Ye Mean . . . ?" *Student Outlook*, March 1933, p. 6. Roger N. Baldwin, "Negro Rights and the Class Struggle," *Opportunity* 12 (September 1934): 264–269.

5. ACLU, *Annual Report*, 1931, pp. 3, 5; 1934, p. 3. William E. Leuchtenberg, "The New Deal and the Analogue of War," in John Braeman et al., eds., *Change and Continuity in Twentieth-Century America* (New York: Harper & Row, 1964), pp. 81–144. Arthur Garfield Hays, *Democracy Works* (New York: Random House, 1939).

6. Van Kleeck, "Labor's Rights in the NRA," February 19, 1934; ACLU, Conference on Civil Liberties Under the New Deal, Minutes, December 1934, p. 9, ACLUP, 1934, vol. 721.

7. ACLU, *Annual Report,* 1933, p. 4; 1934, p. 13. Morganthau quoted in Paul Boyer, *Purity in Print* (New York: Scribner, 1968), p. 237. Baldwin, Memo, March 16, 1933, Borchard Papers, Box 1. ACLU, *The Right of Asylum* (June 1935), p. 7.

8. ACLU, Board of Directors, Minutes, March 1, 1937. ACLU, *Annual Report,* 1937, p. 48. U.S. Office of Education, *Beacon Lights of Democracy* (Washington, D.C.: U.S. Government Printing Office, 1937).

9. Baldwin, Conference on Civil Liberties Under the New Deal, Minutes, ACLUP, 1934, vol. 721. Baldwin, quoted in Civil Liberties Committee of Massachusetts, Minutes, April 26, 1938, Luscomb Papers, Box 5. Baldwin, COHC, p. 197. Clipping and correspondence, ACLUP, 1934, vol. 715. Elizabeth Dilling, *The Roosevelt Red Record and Its Background* (Chicago: Published privately by the author, 1936), pp. 130–143.

10. ACLU, *Annual Report,* 1931, p. 21; 1933, p. 10. ACLU, Board of Directors, Minutes, November 5, 1934. Chicago Civil Liberties Committee, *Civil Liberties News,* April 1939.

11. ACLU, "Confidential" letter re criticisms of La Guardia, September 9, 1943, NAACP/II-B/Box 2. Baldwin, 1974 interview, p. 78, ACLUP, 1978, vol. 11. Morris L. Ernst, *The Best Is Yet . . .* (New York: Harper Bros., 1945), pp. 174–178. ACLU, "Local Civil Liberties Committee Reports 1940–1941" (June 1941), p. 21. Fraenkel, Diaries, 1943, n.d. *New York Times,* March 21, 1940.

12. ACLU, Conference on Civil Liberties Under the New Deal, 1934, Minutes, pp. 5–6. Baldwin, letter to Elmer Rice, January 3, 1935, Rice Papers, Box 69.

13. Garth Jowett, *Film: The Democratic Art: A Social History of American Film* (Boston: Focal Press, 1976), pp. 246–256.

14. Leaflet, March 4, 1923, AGHP, Box 78. ACLU, Board of Directors, Minutes, September 4, 1934. Frederick L. Broderick, *Right Reverend New Dealer, John A. Ryan* (New York: Macmillan, 1963). Ryan, *Declining Liberty* (New York: Macmillan, 1927), pp. 115–120, 307–314.

15. Norman E. Himes, "A Decade of Progress in Birth Control," *Annals of the American Academy of Social and Political Science* 212 (November 1940): 88–96. David Kennedy, *Birth Control in America* (New Haven, Conn.: Yale University Press, 1970), pp. 233–238. Linda Gordon, *Woman's Body, Woman's Right: A Social History of Birth Control in America* (New York: Penguin, 1977), pp. 301–340. Ernst, *The Best Is Yet,* pp. 251–257.

16. *U.S. v. One Package,* 86 F (2d) 737 (1936). Kennedy, *Birth Control in America,* pp. 248–252. *Commonwealth v. Gardner,* 15 N.E.2d 222 (1938). *State v. Nelson* 11 A2d 856 (1940). *Tileston v. Ullman* 26 A2d 582 (1942). Ernst, Memo, February 16, 1944, Ernst papers, vol. 267.

17. Michael Sherer, "The Birth of a Baby Photo Essay: Was It Obscenity or Censorship?" *Free Speech Yearbook,* 1983, pp. 185–198. ACLU, *Annual Report,* 1938, pp. 56–57; 1940, p. 38. Morris L. Ernst and Alexander Lindey, *The Censor Marches On* (New York: Doubleday, 1940), pp. 52–57.

18. Henry James Forman, *Our Movie Made Children* (New York: Macmillan, 1934), p. 281. Edward de Grazia and Roger K. Newman, *Banned Films* (New York: Bowker, 1982), pp. 37–38. Jowett, *Film,* pp. 210–259.

19. Harold C. Gardiner, S.J., *Catholic Viewpoint on Censorship* (Garden City, N.Y.: Image Books, 1961), pp. 94–95.

20. Richard S. Randall, *Censorship of the Movies* (Madison: University of Wisconsin Press, 1968). Jowett, *Film,* pp. 233–259.

21. Jowett, *Film,* pp. 233–259.

22. On the context of informal pressures, see Randall, *Censorship of the Movies,* pp. 147–178.

23. ACLU, Statement, ca. 1934, ACLUP, 1934, vol. 677.

24. ACLU, *Annual Report,* 1937, p. 68; 1938, pp. 52–54. Chicago Civil Liberties Committee, Memo on Film Censorship, ca. 1939, ACLUP, 1939, vol. 2059.

25. ACLU, Memo, ACLUP, 1939, vol. 2060. ACLU, *Annual Report,* 1939, pp. 42–43.

26. Jerold S. Auerbach, *Labor and Liberty: The La Follette Committee and the New Deal* (Indianapolis: Bobbs-Merrill, 1966). See also Cletus Daniel, *The ACLU and the Wagner Act* (Ithaca, N.Y.: Cornell University Press, 1980).

27. Irving Bernstein, *Turbulent Years: A History of the American Worker, 1933–1941* (Boston: Houghton Mifflin, 1971).

28. Baldwin, letters to Wagner, April 1, 1935, May 28, 1935; Hays, letter to ACLU, May 7, 1935, ACLUP, 1935, vol. 780.

29. New York Civil Liberties Committee, Statement October 21, 1936, ACLUP, 1936, vol. 884. ACLU, Board of Directors, Minutes, January 25, 1937, March 8, 1937, March 22, 1937. ACLU, *Annual Report,* 1937, pp. 14–15; 1938, p. 70.

30. Greene, Memo, The National Labor Relations Board on Freedom of Press, ACLUP, 1937, vol. 978.

31. *In the Matter of Ford Motor Co.,* 4 N.L.R.B. 621 (1937); set aside, 10 *N.L.R.B.* 1373 (1939).

32. ACLU, Committee on Labor's Rights, Majority Report, January 31, 1938, AGHP, Box 23. Bernstein, *Turbulent Years,* pp. 657–660.

33. Roger W. Riis, Minority Report, Committee on Labor's Rights, January 31, 1938, AGHP, Box 23.

34. Roger W. Riis, "Free Speech for Whom?" *Forum* 100 (December 1938): 312–316; abridged and reprinted in *Reader's Digest* 33 (December 1938): 32–37.

35. Holmes, letter to Ward, February 11, 1938, Holmes Papers, Box 7. Baldwin, letter to Holmes, March 27, 1936, Holmes Papers, Box 5.

36. Hays, letter to ACLU, February 3, 1938, Ernst Papers, vol. 404. Hays, Memorandum on the Ford Case, February 2, 1938, AGHP, Box 23. ACLU, Board of Directors, Minutes, March 2, 1938. *NLRB v. Ford Motor Co.,* 114 F.2d 905 (6th Cir. 1940).

37. Walter Gellhorn, *Individual Liberty and Governmental Restraints* (Baton Rouge: Louisiana State University Press, 1956), pp. 13–14.

38. Holmes, Hays, Baldwin, Memo, The ACLU on Labor Issues, March 1940, ACLUP, 1940, vol. 2142. Baldwin's new position on labor issues is in Roger N. Baldwin, "Union Administration and Civil Liberties," *The Annals* 248 (November 1946): 54–61.

39. *Lawyers Guild Review* 1 (October 1940): 26–28. ACLU, Board of Directors, Minutes, February 7, 1938.

40. Fred Rodell, "Morris Ernst: New York's Unlawyerlike Liberal Lawyer Is the Censor's Enemy, the President's Friend," *Life* 16 (February 21, 1944): 96–98. Ernst, Memo, Possible Methods of Defeating Legislation in Derogation of the Bill of Rights, October 27, 1939, ACLUP, 1939, vol. 2047. Ernst, Memo, October 9, 1941, ACLUP, 1940, vol. 2186. Ernst, letter to Holmes, April 14, 1942; Baldwin, letter to Holmes, April 20, 1942, ACLUP, 1942, vol. 2355.

41. Ernst, letter to Holmes, April 14, 1942, ACLUP, 1940, vol. 2186.

42. Paul L. Murphy, *The Constitution in Crisis Times, 1918–1969* (New York: Harper & Row, 1972), pp. 128–169. Norman Thomas, "A Socialist Looks at the Constitution," *Annals of the American Academy* 185 (May 1936): 92–101.

43. Murphy, *The Constitution in Crisis Times,* pp. 153–156.

44. ACLU, Board of Directors, Minutes, February 1, 1937, February 15, 1937, March 1, 1937. ACLU, Press Release, May 28, 1937, ACLUP, 1937, vol. 978. Gellhorn, in

ACLU, Preliminary Report on Supreme Court, 1937, Thomas Papers. Fraenkel, letter to Norman Thomas, March 1, 1937, Thomas Papers.

45. Osmond K. Fraenkel, "What Can Be Done About the Constitution and the Supreme Court?" *Columbia Law Review* 37 (February 1937): 212–226. Thomas, letter to Baldwin, February 25, 1937, ACLUP, 1937, vol. 969.

46. *West Coast Hotel v. Parrish,* 300 U.S. 379 (1937). *N.L.R.B. v. Jones and Laughlin Steel Co.,* 301 U.S.1 (1937). Murphy, *The Constitution in Crisis Times,* pp. 152–158.

47. *DeJonge v. Oregon,* 299 U.S. 353 (1937). Fraenkel, COHC, pp. 83–84.

48. Norman Dorsen, "An Appreciation of Osmond K. Fraenkel," *New York Law Journal,* June 14, 1983. Fraenkel, COHC.

49. *Herndon v. Georgia,* 301 U.S. 242 (1937). Charles H. Martin, *The Angelo Herndon Case and Southern Justice* (Baton Rouge: Louisiana State University Press, 1976).

50. ACLU, Press Release, March 20, 1936, ACLUP, 1936, vol. 877. Hugo Black, "Inside an Investigation," *Harpers* 172 (February 1936): 275–286. ACLU, Telegram to Senator Robert M. LaFollette, August 16, 1937, ACLUP, 1937, vol. 978.

51. *New York Times,* January 11, 1939; January 12, 1939. Baldwin, interview, 1974, pp. 76–77, ACLUP, 1978, vol. 11.

52. *Palko v. Connecticut,* 302 U.S. 319 (1937).

53. *United States v. Carolene Products Co.,* 304 U.S. 144 (1938). Louis Lusky, "Footnote Redux: A *Carolene Products* Reminiscence," *Columbia Law Review* 82 (October 1982): 1093–1105.

54. Supreme Court estimates in Henry J. Abraham, *Freedom and the Court,* 4th ed. (New York: Oxford University Press, 1982), p. 236; and M. James Penton, *Apocalypse Delayed: The Story of Jehovah's Witnesses* (Toronto: University of Toronto Press, 1985), p. 88. For Marshall's estimate, see Carl Rowan, *Thurgood Marshall: The Man* (PBS television broadcast, September 22, 1988).

55. *Lovell v. Griffin,* 303 U.S. 444 (1938).

56. *Schneider v. Irvington,* 308 U.S. 147 (1939).

57. *Martin v. Struthers,* 319 U.S. 141 (1943).

58. *Cox v. New Hampshire,* 312 U.S. 569 (1941). *Chaplinsky v. New Hampshire,* 315 U.S. 568 (1942).

59. *Cantwell v. Connecticut,* 310 U.S. 296 (1940).

60. David R. Manwaring, *Render unto Caesar: The Flag-Salute Controversy* (Chicago: University of Chicago Press, 1962). ACLU, Press Release, December 11, 1937; November 23, 1940. *New York Times,* April 25, 1940.

61. *Minersville School District v. Gobitis,* 310 U.S. 586 (1940).

62. ACLU, Board of Directors, Minutes, September 9, 1940. Manwaring, *Render unto Caesar,* pp. 164–166. ACLU, *Civil Liberties Quarterly,* September 1940, p. 1. J. Edgar Hoover, "Outlaw the Vigilante," *This Week Magazine,* August 17, 1940, copy in ACLUP, 1940, vol. 2161.

63. Manwaring, *Render upon Caesar,* pp. 188–190. *Jones v. Opelika,* 316 U.S. 584, 623 (1943).

64. *West Virginia State Board of Education v. Barnette,* 319 U.S. 624 (1943).

65. Dayton David McKean, *The Boss: The Hague Machine in Action* (Boston: Houghton Mifflin, 1940).

66. Lamont, transcript, ACLUP, 1934, vol. 749. Corliss Lamont, *Yes to Life* (New York: Horizon, 1981), pp. 104–105. Clippings, ACLUP, 1938, vol. 2021. Reitman, interview.

67. ACLU, "More Candid Views of Mayor Hague" (1938). Norman Thomas, *Haguism Is Fascism* (New York: Workers Defense League, 1938). *New York Times,* September 25, 1939.

68. Ernst, *The Best Is Yet,* pp. 188–190.

69. *Hague v. CIO,* 307 U.S. 496 (1939).

70. *Thornhill v. Alabama,* 310 U.S. 88 (1940). *Edwards v. California,* 314 U.S. 160 (1941).

71. Gellhorn, interview. Dorsen, "An Appreciation of Osmond K. Fraenkel." Fraenkel, COHC. Raymond L. Wise, "We Still Need a Bill of Rights, *The Nation,* March 11, 1939, pp. 291–293.

72. Stephen L. Wasby, "How Planned Is 'Planned Litigation'?" *American Bar Foundation Research Journal* 5 (Winter 1984): 83–138.

73. On the NAACP, see Richard Kluger, *Simple Justice* (New York: Vintage Books, 1977), p. 221. On the *amicus* brief, see Samuel Krislov, "The Amicus Curiae Brief: From Friendship to Advocacy," in Gottfried Dietze, ed., *Essays on the American Constitution* (Englewood Cliffs, N.J.: Prentice-Hall, 1964), pp. 77–98. Leo Pfeffer, "Amici in Church–State Litigation," *Law and Contemporary Problems* 44 (Winter 1981): 83–110. Gellhorn, interview. Maslow, interview. Charles R. Halpern, "The Public Interest Bar: An Audit," in Ralph Nader and Mark Green, eds., *Verdicts on Lawyers* (New York: Crowell, 1976), pp. 158–171.

74. Michael Kammen, *A Machine That Would Go of Itself: The Constitution in American Culture* (New York: Knopf, 1987), pp. 307–312. Virginius Dabney, "Civil Liberties in the South," *Virginia Quarterly Review* 16 (Winter 1940): 81–91.

75. *Hague v. CIO,* 25 F.Supp 127, 152 (1938).

76. ACLU, Press Release, August 11, 1938, ACLUP, 1938, vol. 1079. *New York Times,* June 12, 1938. Grenville Clark, "Conservatism and Civil Liberty," *American Bar Association Journal* 24 (August 1938): 640–644. Percival R. Bailey, "Progressive Lawyers: A History of the National Lawyers Guild, 1936–1958" (Ph.D. diss., Rutgers University, 1979).

77. William J. Donovan, "An Independent Supreme Court and the Protection of Minority Rights," *ABA Journal* 23 (April 1937): 254, 260, 295–296.

78. *ABA Journal* 24 (September 1938): 735, 774. Sub-Committee on Civil Rights of the Executive Council of the Junior Bar, Report, July 26, 1938, Clark Papers, vol. 8, p. 7. Ernst, letter to Clark, September 7, 1938, Clark Papers, vol. 8, p. 2. Clark, letter to Hays, September 1, 1938, ACLUP, 1938, vol. 1079. Baldwin, letter to Clark, November 17, 1938, Clark Papers, vol. 8, p. 1. ACLU, Board of Directors, October 3, 1938.

79. ABA, Bill of Rights Committee, Proceedings, January 9, 1940, pp. 19–20, Clark Papers, vol. 8, p. 7. *Bill of Rights Review* 1 (Summer 1940). Donald L. Smith, *Zechariah Chafee, Jr.: Defender of Liberty and Law* (Cambridge, Mass.: Harvard University Press, 1986), pp. 195–214.

80. Memo, Clark Papers, vol. 8, p. 7. *ABA Journal* 25 (January 1939): 1–2.

81. *Library Journal,* December 15, 1938, p. 965; July 1939, p. 549. David Berninghausen, "The Librarian's Commitment to the Library Bill of Rights," *Library Trends,* 19 (July 1970): 19–38.

82. Walter P. Metzger, *Academic Freedom in the Age of the University* (New York: Columbia University Press, 1955), pp. 206–216.

83. Robert K. Carr, *Federal Protection of Civil Rights: Quest for a Sword* (Ithaca, N.Y.: Cornell University Press, 1947), p. 25. Baldwin, COHC, pp. 202–203.

84. Learned Hand, *The Spirit of Liberty* (New York: Vintage Books, 1959), pp. 62, 143–145.

Chapter 6

1. Martha Glaser, "The German-American Bund in New Jersey," *New Jersey History* 92 (1974): 33–49.

2. Roger N. Baldwin, "Voting Red in Austria," *The Nation*, June 15, 1927, pp. 663–664. Arthur Garfield Hays, *City Lawyer* (New York: Simon & Schuster, 1942), pp. 337–388. Arthur Garfield Hays, "Men in the Shadow of Death," *Modern Monthly*, January 1934, pp. 708–712. Arthur Garfield Hays, "The Burning of the German Reichstag," *The Nation*, November 22, 1933, pp. 586–589.

3. Ronald Steel, *Walter Lippmann and the American Century* (Boston: Atlantic–Little, Brown, 1980), pp. 330–333.

4. Milner, letter to Alfred Wagenknecht, October 26, 1934, ACLUP, 1934, vol. 718.

5. M. DeSilver, letter to Ernst, ca. 1934, ACLUP, 1934, vol. 718.

6. Wirin, letter to House Committee Investigating Un-American Activities, July 13, 1934, ACLUP, 1934, vol. 718. Criticisms of ACLU in ACLUP, 1934, vol. 700.

7. Baldwin, letter to C. Burlingham, January 11, 1934, ACLUP, 1934, vol. 718. ACLU, Board of Directors, Minutes, April 30, 1934. ACLU, *Shall We Defend Free Speech for Nazis in America?* (October 1934).

8. ACLU, *Shall We Defend.*

9. Travis Hoke, *Shirts!* June 1934, p. 3, ACLUP, 1934, vol. 718.

10. ACLU, Memo, January 21, 1938, ACLUP, 1938, vol. 1079. Karl Loewenstein, "Militant Democracy and Fundamental Rights," *American Political Science Review* 31, June 1937, pp. 417–432; August 1937, pp. 638–658. Karl Loewenstein, "Legislative Control of Political Extremism in European Democracies I," *Columbia Law Review* 38 (April 1938): 591–622; II, 38 (May 1938): 725–774. Lucille Milner, "Fighting Fascism by Law," *The Nation*, January 15, 1938, pp. 65–67.

11. ACLU, Board of Directors, Minutes, April 25, 1938; June 27, 1938. ACLU, *Civil Liberties Quarterly*, June 1938, p. 1. ACLU, Memo, Legislation to Curb Fascist Activities, May 1939, p. 6, ACLUP, 1938, vol. 1079.

12. ACLU, *Annual Report*, 1935, p. 14.

13. ACLU, Press Release, November 13, 1935, ACLUP, 1935, vol. 845.

14. Carl J. Austrian, American Jewish Committee, letter to ACLU, March 1, 1937, ACLUP, 1937, vol. 1001. ACLU, Board of Directors, Minutes, October 28, 1940. Glaser, "The German-American Bund," pp. 33–49. *State of New Jersey v. Klapprott et al.*, 127 N.J.L. (1941). Memos, AGHP, Box 21.

15. See the essays commemorating the fiftieth anniversary of the NCCL in Peter Wallington, ed., *Civil Liberties 1984* (Oxford, England: Martin Robertson, 1984), especially the article by Norman Dorsen comparing the ACLU and the NCCL.

16. Harvey Klehr, *The Heyday of American Communism: The Depression Decade* (New York: Basic Books, 1984).

17. ACLU, Executive Committee, Minutes, November 24, 1930. ACLU, *Annual Report*, 1931, p. 39. See also the prior agreement in International Legal Defense (ILD), "To All Local and Language Section Secretaries," August 16, 1928, ACLUP, 1928, vol. 337. On Hays's and the ACLU's role in Gastonia, see Fred Beal, *Proletarian Journey* (New York: Hillman-Curl, 1937), pp. 185–186.

18. Baldwin, letter to Brodsky, February 18, 1938; March 25, 1938, ACLUP, 1938, vol. 1097. Baldwin, letter to R. W. Hale, July 21, 1937, ACLUP, 1937, vol. 990.

19. On the ILD agreement, see ACLU, Board of Directors, Minutes, October 14, 1935. ACLU, *Annual Report*, 1937, p. 75.

20. ACLU, *Annual Report,* 1938, pp. 90–95.

21. ACLU, *Local Civil Liberties Committees: Reports,* 1938, 1939, 1940, 1941.

22. Baldwin, Harvard Class Yearbook statement, June 1935, ACLUP, 1935, vol. 763. Baldwin, letter to C. E. Mason, September 23, 1937; Mason, letter to Baldwin, September 22, 1937, RNBP, Box 7. Roger N. Baldwin, "Freedom in the U.S.A. and the U.S.S.R.," *Soviet Russia Today* 3 (September 1934): 11. Peggy Lamson, *Roger Baldwin: Founder of the American Civil Liberties Union* (Boston: Houghton Mifflin, 1976). On the attacks based on Baldwin's Popular Front associations as late as the 1960s, see *Congressional Record,* May 25, 1961, pp. 8966–8967.

23. American League for Peace and Democracy, *A Program Against War and Fascism* (July 1936), in ALPD, Miscellaneous Pamphlets, Firestone Library, Princeton University.

24. ACLU, "Report of Commission of Inquiry to the Board of Directors," in ACLUP, 1934, vol. 712. ACLU, Statement (draft); Van Kleeck, letter to Baldwin, March 3, 1934, MVKP, Box 37. Thomas, letter to Lamont, April 4, 1934, ACLUP, 1934, vol. 712.

25. U.S. House of Representatives, Special Committee to Investigate Communist Activities in the United States, 71st Cong., 2nd and 3rd sess., *Hearings,* pp. 409–412. ACLU, *The Right to Advocate Violence* (March 1931).

26. ACLU, letter to Hon. John W. MacCormack, December 20, 1934, Thomas Papers. U.S. House of Representatives, Special Committee on Un-American Activities, 74th Cong., 1st sess., *Report,* H. Rep. 153, February 15, 1935. Walter Goodman, *The Committee* (New York: Farrar, Straus & Giroux, 1968), pp. 3–24.

27. Goodman, *The Committee,* pp. 25–61. See "Communizing the Indians," in Elizabeth Dilling, *The Roosevelt Red Record and Its Background* (Chicago: Published privately by the author, 1936), pp. 64–74.

28. Dies Committee Report, January 3, 1939, p. 82. Stuart Henderson Britt and Selden C. Menefee, "Did the Publicity of the Dies Committee in 1938 Influence Public Opinion?" *Public Opinion Quarterly* 3 (July 1939): 449–457.

29. Jerold Simmons, "The American Civil Liberties Union and the Dies Committee, 1938–1940," *Harvard Civil Rights–Civil Liberties Review* 17 (Spring 1982): 183–207.

30. Abraham Isserman, Memorandum on Power of Congressional Investigating Committee [*sic*], ca. 1939, ACLUP, 1939, vol. 2007. ACLU, Board of Directors, Minutes, February 20, 1939. Baldwin, letter to Isserman, June 6, 1939; Isserman, letter to Britchey, July 19, 1939, ACLUP, 1939, vol. 2077. National Federation for Constitutional Liberties, *Investigating Committees and Civil Rights* (1941).

31. ACLU, Memos and Correspondence, ACLUP, 1937, vol. 1005. Jerold S. Auerbach, *Labor and Liberty: The LaFollette Committee and the New Deal* (Indianapolis: Bobbs-Merrill, 1966), pp. 1–11. Telford Taylor, *Grand Inquest: The Story of Congressional Investigations* (New York: Simon & Schuster, 1955), pp. 58–88.

32. Felix Frankfurter, "Hands Off the Investigations," *The New Republic,* May 21, 1924, pp. 329–331. Hugo L. Black, "Inside a Senate Investigation," *Harper's* 172 (February 1936): 275–286.

33. ACLU, Press Release, March 20, 1936, ACLUP, 1936, vol. 877. ACLU, Board of Directors, Minutes, June 6, 1938. *New York Times,* January 23, 1940. ACLU, *Civil Liberties Quarterly* 36 (March 1940): 2.

34. Browder, telegram to ACLU, September 8, 1939, ACLUP, 1939, vol. 2076. *New York Times,* August 21, 1939; August 22, 1939. Goodman, *The Committee.* Simmons, "The American Civil Liberties Union and the Dies Committee."

35. ACLU, Press Release, November 9, 1939, ACLUP, 1939, vol. 2077. ACLU, letter

to Dies, April 9, 1940, Clark Papers, vol. 8. ACLU, Conference on Civil Liberties in the Present Emergency, *Proceedings,* October 1939. ACLU, letter to Latimer, May 19, 1941, ACLUP, 1941, vol. 2325.

36. Ernest Goodman, "The Spanish Loyalist Indictments: Skirmish in Detroit," *Guild Practitioner* 36 (Winter 1979): 1–13.

37. U.S. House, Judiciary Committee, Subcommittee no. 3, *Hearings on H.R. 5138,* April 12 and 13, 1939, 76th Cong., 1st sess., pp. 6–15. U.S. Senate, Judiciary Committee, Subcommittee on H.R. 5138, *Hearings,* May 17, 1940, 76th Cong., 3rd sess., pp. 44–52.

38. Baldwin, letter to "Friends," June 20, 1940, Clark Papers, vol. 8, p. 1. Zechariah Chafee, Jr., *Free Speech in the United States* (Cambridge, Mass.: Harvard University Press, 1941), pp. 439–490.

39. ACLU, memo, ca. 1932, ACLUP, 1932, vol. 619. ACLU, *Minority Parties on the Ballot* (August 1940).

40. ACLU, Board of Directors, Minutes, July 8, 1940, August 26, 1940.

41. ACLU, Board of Directors, Minutes, May 19, 1941. ACLU, Press Release, December 1942, ACLUP, 1942, vol. 2375. ACLU, *Minority Parties on the Ballot* (August 1940). Memos and briefs, AGHP, Box 28.

42. ACLU, Board of Directors, Minutes, February 10, 1941. Farquharson, letter to Baldwin, February 6, 1941, ACLUP, 1941, vol. 2345.

43. Ellen W. Schrecker, *No Ivory Tower: McCarthyism and the Universities* (New York: Oxford University Press, 1986), pp. 63–83. ACLU, *The Gag on Teaching* (1940). Milton Konvitz, *Fundamental Liberties of a Free People* (Ithaca, N.Y.: Cornell University Press, 1957), pp. 230–231.

44. Bertrand Russell, *Why I Am Not a Christian* (New York: Simon & Schuster, 1957), pp. 207–259. ACLU, *The Story of the Bertrand Russell Case* (1941). Fraenkel, Diaries, 1940, p. 2. ACLU, *Annual Report,* 1941, p. 35.

45. ACLU, Press Release, June 16, 1941, ACLUP, 1941, vol. 2293. Schrecker, *No Ivory Tower,* pp. 75–82.

46. O'Neill, "Credo in re Communists," May 23, 1941, ACLUP, 1941, vol. 2257.

47. ACLU, letter to Coudert, December 13, 1940, Holmes Papers, Box 20.

48. ACLU, Academic Freedom Committee, Minutes, May 20, 1941; ACLU, Academic Freedom Committee, Memo, April 1941 (approved by ACLU board of directors); Spofford, letter to Baldwin, March 29, 1941, ACLUP, 1941, vol. 2258.

49. Britchey, letter to Witt, July 22, 1941; ACLU, Press Release, July 19, 1941, ACLUP, 1941, vol. 2288. NYCLU, Board of Directors, Minutes, January 16, 1941, November 6, 1941, October 22, 1942. NYCLU, Press Release, December 27, 1940, ACLUP, 1941, v. 2293.

50. Hoover, letter, "To All Law Enforcement Officials," September 6, 1939, ACLUP, 1939, vol. 2063. *New York Herald Tribune,* September 9, 1939. Richard Gid Powers, *Secrecy and Power: The Life of J. Edgar Hoover* (New York: Free Press, 1987), pp. 228–274. Athan Theoharis, *Spying on Americans: Political Surveillance from Hoover to the Huston Plan* (Philadelphia: Temple University Press, 1978), pp. 65–93.

51. ACLU, Press Release, June 15, 1940. Norris, *Congressional Record,* March 7, 1940.

52. FBI, Memo, December 17, 1940, ACLU/FBI/12371. Hoover, Memo to SAC, Pittsburgh, April 28, 1941, ACLU/FBI/41905. P. E. Foxworth, letter to Director, FBI, January 29, 1942, ACLU/FBI/1584.

53. ACLU, letter to Senator Glass, Appropriations Committee, April 15, 1941, ACLU/FBI/41016.

54. FBI, San Francisco office, Memo, September 1, 1940, ACLU/FBI/37216. FBI, Card on Baldwin ("Communist"), October 12, 1940, RNB/FBI. On custodial detention, see FBI, Memo, October 21, 1941, RNB/FBI. U.S. Senate, Select Committee to Study Governmental Operations with Respect to Intelligence Activities, *Final Report,* Book 3, 94th Cong., 2nd sess., 1976, p. 423.

55. Baldwin, Memo to Reitman, December 21, 1951, RNBP. Baldwin, letter to Ward, July 12, 1938, RNBP, Box 8. American League for Peace and Democracy, *Proceedings,* January 6–8, 1939, Luscomb Papers, Box 5. Baldwin, letter to Claude Williams, November 28, 1938, RNBP, Box 8. Baldwin, letter to Ward, July 12, 1938, RNBP, Box 8. Seymour, letter to Baldwin, May 10, 1939, ACLUP, 1939, vol. 2063. Baldwin, letter re Nominating Committee, September 13, 1939, ACLUP, 1939, vol. 2064.

56. Harold Lord Varney, "The Civil Liberties Union: Liberalism à la Moscow," *The American Mercury* 39 (December 1936): 385–399. Hays, letter to Baldwin, January 22, 1937; Ernst, letter to Hays, January 26, 1937, AGHP. H. L. Mencken, "The American Civil Liberties Union," *The American Mercury* 45 (October 1938): 182–190; ACLU, "A Letter from the ACLU," *The American Mercury* 45 (October 1938): 190–193. ACLU, Memo, May 27, 1938, AGHP, Box 27. ACLU, Board of Directors, Minutes, June 27, 1938.

57. Finerty, Memo, Proposed Pamphlet, January 31, 1939, ACLUP, 1939, vol. 2063. Van Kleeck, letter to Rice, March 27, 1939; Rice, letter to Van Kleeck, March 28, 1939, MVKP, Box 36. ACLU, Board of Directors, Minutes, January 30, 1939, April 3, 1939. ACLU, *Why We Defend Free Speech for Nazis, Fascists—and Communists* (April 1939).

58. Baldwin, affidavit, December 31, 1938; Holmes, Huebsch, Baldwin, affidavit, December 31, 1938, RNBP, Box 8.

59. Wise, letter to Milner, July 20, 1939; Baldwin, letter to Wise, August 6, 1939, ACLUP, 1939, vol. 2076.

60. Hays, telegram to Dies, August 30, 1938, ACLUP, vol. 2076. Hays, Radio talk, January 19, 1939, typescript, AGHP. Hays, letter to Whitley, October 4, 1939, ACLUP, 1939, vol. 2076.

61. Lamson, *Roger Baldwin,* p. 201.

62. Jackson, Gellhorn et al., letter to ACLU, December 14, 1939, ACLUP, 1939, vol. 2077. *Daily Worker,* November 24, 1939, clipping in ACLUP, 1939, vol. 2077. *New York World Telegram,* December 4, 1939, clipping in ACLUP, 1939, vol. 2064.

63. Corliss Lamont, *Freedom Is As Freedom Does* (New York: Horizon, 1956), p. 269.

64. Simmons, "The American Civil Liberties Union."

65. The three versions of the report are dated December 14, 1939, December 29, 1939, ACLUP, 1939, vol. 2077; and January 8, 1940, ACLUP, 1948, Box 22.

66. See the controversy in Alan Reitman, *The Pulse of Liberty* (New York: Norton, 1968), pp. 70–71, regarding which, thirty-five years later, Baldwin went to extraordinary lengths to justify the actions in 1940.

67. ACLU, Board of Directors, January 23, 1939, March 6, 1939, March 27, 1939. Thomas, letter to Ward, October 10, 1939, ACLUP, 1939, vol. 2064.

68. Thomas, letter to Baldwin, November 27, 1939, ACLUP, 1939, vol. 2064. ACLU, Board of Directors, Minutes, December 18, 1939. Fraenkel, letter to Thomas, December 20, 1939, Thomas, letter to Fraenkel, December 21, 1939, ACLUP, 1939, vol. 2064.

69. Finerty, letter to Childs, December 19, 1939, Van Kleeck Papers, Box 36. Simmons, "The American Civil Liberties Union."

70. ACLU, Board of Directors, Minutes, February 5, 1940.

71. See the discussion and documents in Corliss Lamont, ed., *The Trial of Elizabeth Gurley Flynn by the American Civil Liberties Union* (New York: Horizon, 1968).

72. "Elizabeth Gurley Flynn," in *Notable American Women* (Cambridge, Mass.: Harvard University Press, 1980), vol. 4, pp. 243–246. Elizabeth Gurley Flynn, *The Rebel Girl: An Autobiography* (New York: International Publishers, 1973). Rosalyn Fraad Baxandall, ed., *Words on Fire: The Life and Writing of Elizabeth Gurley Flynn* (New Brunswick, N.J.: Rutgers University Press, 1987). ACLU, *Annual Report,* 1929, p. 32; 1937, p. 74.

73. ACLU, Board of Directors, Minutes, March 4, 1940. Elizabeth Gurley Flynn, "Why I Won't Resign from the ACLU," *New Masses,* March 19, 1940, p. 11. Elizabeth Gurley Flynn, "I Am Expelled from Civil Liberties!" *Sunday Worker,* March 17, 1940. Both articles are in Lamont, ed., *The Trial,* pp. 151–162.

74. Lamont, *The Trial.* Lamont, interview.

75. Altman, letter to Holmes, January 20, 1937, May 13, 1936, Holmes Papers, Box 7.

76. Lamont, ed., *The Trial,* p. 99. Lamont, interview.

77. Nunn, interview. Lamont, interview.

78. Lamont, ed., *The Trial.* See Victor Navasky, *Naming Names* (New York: Viking, 1980). Charles B. Morgan, *One Man, One Voice* (New York: Holt, Rinehart and Winston, 1979), pp. 260–263.

79. ACLU, Board of Directors, Minutes, June 8, 1964, April 20–21, 1974, April 10–11, 1976.

80. Chicago Civil Liberties Committee, Memo, 1939, CCLCP, Box 102. ACLU, Conference on Civil Liberties in the Present Emergency, 1939, *Proceedings,* ACLUP, 1939, vol. 2067.

81. Chicago Civil Liberties Committee, Pamphlet, ca. 1940, CCLCP, Box 102. ACLU, Weekly Bulletin, January 25, 1941, ACLUP, 1941, vol. 2256. Abram C. Joseph, in *Bill of Rights Review* 2 (Winter 1942): 145.

Chapter 7

1. Roosevelt, Speech, December 15, 1941, quoted in ACLU, *The Bill of Rights in War-Time* (January 1942).

2. Frank Murphy, "The Test of Patriotism," Conference on Civil Liberties in the Present Emergency, *Proceedings,* October 13, 1939, ACLUP, 1939, vol. 2067.

3. Lucille B. Milner and Groff Conklin, "Conscience in Wartime," *Harper's* 179 (October 1939): 503–509. Lucille B. Milner and Groff Conklin, "Wartime Censorship in the United States, *Harper's* 180 (January 1940): 187–195: Lucille B. Milner and Groff Conklin, "Teachers in Wartime," *American Mercury* 50 (June 1940): 162–167. Lucille B. Milner, "Freedom of Speech in Wartime," *The New Republic,* November 25, 1940, pp. 713–715. James R. Mock, *Censorship 1917* (Princeton, N.J.: Princeton University Press, 1941). Zechariah Chafee, Jr., *Free Speech in the United States* (Cambridge, Mass.: Harvard University Press, 1941).

4. Roosevelt, Biddle, Willkie quoted in ACLU, *The Bill of Rights in War-Time.* J. Edgar Hoover, "Outlaw the Vigilante," *This Week Magazine,* reprinted by ACLU, 1941.

5. Peter Irons, *Justice at War* (New York: Oxford University Press, 1983), p. 19. The following account is based on Irons; Morton Grodzins, *Americans Betrayed* (Chicago: University of Chicago Press, 1949); Jacobus ten Broek et al., *Prejudice, War and the Constitution* [1954] (Berkeley and Los Angeles: University of California Press, 1970); and Allan R. Bosworth, *America's Concentration Camps* (New York: Norton, 1967).

6. On Warren, see Grodzins, *Americans Betrayed,* pp. 92–100.

7. Irons, *Justice at War,* pp. 62–63. Ennis, interview.

8. Richard Drinnon, *Keeper of Concentration Camps: Dillon S. Myer and American Racism* (Berkeley and Los Angeles: University of California Press, 1987).

9. ACLU, Board of Directors, Minutes, March 2, 1942, March 19, 1942. Baldwin, Holmes, Ross et al., letter to Roosevelt, March 20, 1942, ACLUP, 1942, vol. 2363. Holmes, Dewey, Niebuhr et al., to Roosevelt, April 30, 1942, ACLUP, 1942, vol. 2394.

10. Carey McWilliams, *Prejudice* (Boston: Little, Brown, 1944), p. 113. Frank Chuman, *Bamboo People* (Del Mar, Calif.: Japanese American Citizens, 1976), pp. 168–171. Irons, *Justice at War,* pp. 75ff. Besig, letters to Baldwin, March 6, 1942, March 13, 1942, ACLUP, 1942, vol. 2363. Irons, *Justice at War,* p. 112.

11. Irons, *Justice at War,* pp. 75–103.

12. Baldwin, letter to Besig, February 8, 1943; Besig, letter to Forster, February 20, 1943, ACLUP, 1943, vol. 2466. ACLU, Board of Directors, Minutes, April 19, 1943.

13. Irons, *Justice at War,* pp. 114–116.

14. ACLU, Board of Directors, Minutes, March 23, 1942, March 30, 1942.

15. Fraenkel, Dairies, May 4, 1942, July 20, 1942. On the referendum, see ACLU, Memo, June 16, 1942, ACLUP, 1943, vol. 2444. Meikeljohn, letter to Baldwin, March 17, 1942, ACLUP, 1942, vol. 2363. ACLU–NC, Executive Committee, Minutes, April 2, 1942. Lamont, letter to Holmes, May 12, 1942, JHHP, Box 25.

16. E. Thomas, Statement, ca. 1942, Beale Papers, Box 1.

17. ACLU, Memo, May 22, 1942, ACLUP, 1942, vol. 2394. Dissenting view in ACLU, *Military Power and Civil Rights* (December 1942), p. 9.

18. ACLU, Memo, May 22, 1942, ACLUP, 1942, vol. 2394.

19. ACLU, Board of Directors, June 22, 1942. Although its vote did not count, the Northern California ACLU's Executive Committee favored Resolution 1, 6–4; ACLU–NC, Executive Committee, Minutes, June 4, 1942.

20. ACLU, *Military Power and Civil Rights.* For examples of misinterpretation, see Michi Weglyn, *Years of Infamy* (New York: Morrow, 1976); Drinnon, *Keeper of Concentration Camps.*

21. Farquharson, letter to Baldwin, June 29, 1942, ACLUP, 1943, vol. 2470. Besig, letter to Forster, July 10, 1942, ACLUP, 1942, vol. 2397. Besig, interview.

22. ACLU–NC, Executive Committee, Minutes, March 19, 1942, April 2, 1942. Besig, telegram to Baldwin, March 20, 1942, ACLUP, 1942, vol. 2363.

23. Besig, interview.

24. *Lawyers Guild Review* (July 1942): 37; (September 1942): 44; (March–April 1942): 4–16; (July–August 1943): 58–59.

25. Carey McWilliams, "Japanese Evacuation: Policy and Perspectives," *Common Ground* (Summer 1942): 1–8.

26. Eason Monroe, Oral History Interview, University of California at Los Angeles, p. 104. Pollitt, interview.

27. Irons, *Justice at War,* pp. 260–268.

28. C. Forster, letter to Wirin, March 19, 1943, ACLUP, 1943, vol. 2524. Baldwin, letter to Ennis, September 22, 1943, ACLUP, 1944, vol. 2629. *Duncan v. Kahanamoku,* 327 U.S. 304 (1946). ACLU, *Annual Report,* 1946, p. 44. ACLU, Board of Directors, Minutes, April 30, 1942. Baldwin, letter to E. Parsons, October 27, 1942, RNBP, Box 8.

29. ACLU, Board of Directors, Minutes, January 19, 1942, July 6, 1942, March 13, 1944. National Committee on Conscientious Objectors, Minutes, March 5, 1943, April 5,

1943, NCCOP. "Confidential Memoranda": July 1, 1942, August 26, 1942, ACLUP, 1943, vol. 2466.

30. Baldwin, Confidential Memorandum, August 26, 1942, ACLUP, vol. 2466. Meikeljohn, letter to ACLU Board, November 20, 1942, ACLU–NC. See the observations in Florence Isbell, "Carter's Civil Libertarians," *Civil Liberties Review* 4 (July–August 1977): 57–58.

31. ACLU, letter to DeWitt, November 3, 1932, ACLUP, 1943, vol. 2444. Thomas, letter to Baldwin, November 7, 1942, NT Papers.

32. Holmes, letter to Baldwin, December 14, 1942, RNBP, Box 8.

33. Thomas, letters to Baldwin, September 1, 1942, November 10, 1942, December 14, 1942; Thomas, letter to Holmes, November 14, 1942; Baldwin, letter to Holmes, November 16, 1942; Hays, letter to Thomas, November 16, 1942, ACLUP, 1942, vol. 2355. Fraenkel, Diary, November 20, 1942.

34. Drinnon, *Keeper of Concentration Camps,* pp. 144–147.

35. ACLU–NC, Executive Committee, Minutes, November 5, 1942. Wirin, letter to Forster, March 29, 1943, ACLUP, 1943, vol. 2463.

36. Irons, *Justice at War,* pp. 278–307.

37. Ernst, letter to Roosevelt, April 15, 1943; Roosevelt, letter to Ernst, April 24, 1943, Ernst Papers, vol. 98.

38. *Ex parte Milligan,* 71 U.S. 2 (1866).

39. *Hirabayashi v. United States,* 320 U.S. 81 (1943).

40. Irons, *Justice at War.*

41. ACLU, Board of Directors, Minutes, March 8, 1943. Besig, letter to Holmes, April 9, 1943; Baldwin, letter to Parsons, August 31, 1943; Forster, letter to Besig, November 12, 1943, ACLUP, 1943, vol. 2466. Baldwin, letter to Parsons, November 13, 1945, ACLUP, 1945, vol. 2669.

42. Chicago Civil Liberties Committee, Board of Directors, Minutes, October 19, 1943. ACLU, Board of Directors, Minutes, March 19, 1945, April 27, 1945.

43. Irons, *Justice at War,* pp. 182–183, 254, 263–268. Ennis denied the allegation that he breached legal ethics in advising the ACLU; Ennis, interview.

44. Chuman, *Bamboo People,* pp. 263–277.

45. *Korematsu v. United States,* 232 U.S. 214 (1944).

46. Irons, *Justice at War,* p. 19.

47. *Ex parte Endo,* 323 U.S. 283 (1944).

48. Eugene V. Rostow, "Our Worst Wartime Mistake," *Harper's* 191 (September 1945): 193–201. Eugene V. Rostow, "The Japanese-American Cases—A Disaster," *Yale Law Journal* 54 (June 1945): 489–533. Nanette Dembitz, "Racial Discrimination and the Military Judgement," *Columbia Law Review* 45 (March 1945): 175–239.

49. Besig, letter to Baldwin, March 18, 1946, ACLUP, 1946, vol. 2712.

50. Chuman, *Bamboo People,* pp. 270–278. ACLU–SC, *Open Forum,* October 4, 1947, May 29, 1948. ACLU, *Annual Report,* 1951, pp. 58–59.

51. *Oyama v. California,* 332 U.S. 633 (1948). *Takahashi v. Fish Commission,* 334 U.S. 410 (1948).

52. ACLU, *Annual Report,* 1937, p. 9. Baldwin, letter to Doty, October 18, 1937, Doty Papers, Box 1. ACLU, Board of Directors, Minutes, July 15, July 22, 1940. J. Garry Clifford and Samuel R. Spencer, Jr., *The First Peacetime Draft* (Lawrence: University of Kansas Press, 1986), pp. 124–125.

53. ACLU, Board of Directors, Minutes, July 15, 1940. ACLU, Statement in Regard to Provisions for Conscientious Objectors, July 26, 1940, ACLUP, 1940, vol. 2169.

54. Richard Seelye Jones, *A History of the American Legion* (Indianapolis: Bobbs-Merrill, 1946), p. 291. ACLU, *Annual Report*, 1941, p. 31.

55. Conference on Conscientious Objectors, Minutes, September 26, 1940, ACLUP, 1940, vol. 2168. ACLU, Board of Directors, Minutes, September 30, 1940, October 14, 1940, October 21, 1940, December 15, 1941. *New York Herald Tribune*, October 17, 1940. *New York Times*, October 3, 1940. David Dellinger, "Statement," in David Dellinger, *Revolutionary Nonviolence* (Indianapolis: Bobbs-Merrill, 1970), pp. 3, 14–15. Swomley, interview.

56. ACLU, *Annual Report*, 1942, p. 38. Maurice Isserman, *Which Side Were You On?* (Middletown, Conn.: Wesleyan University Press, 1982), pp. 87–100, 161–166.

57. ACLU, Board of Directors, September 30, 1940. Baldwin, letter to Dykstra, November 7, 1940, ACLUP, 1940, vol. 2168. Baldwin to Oxnam, December 18, 1941, ACLUP, 1941, vol. 2273. NCCO, Minutes, April 5, 1943, September 2, 1943, SPC. ACLU, Board of Directors, Minutes, March 13, 1944. Clifford and Spencer, *The First Peacetime Draft*, p. 221.

58. Lawrence S. Wittner, *Rebels Against War: The American Peace Movement, 1933–1983* (Philadelphia: Temple University Press, 1984), pp. 41–42.

59. Thomas, letter to Muste, February 3, 1943, NT Papers. Wittner, *Rebels Against War*.

60. Jim Peck, *We Who Would Not Kill* (New York: Lyle Stuart, 1958). August Meier and Elliott Rudwick, *CORE: A Study in the Civil Rights Movement, 1942–1968* (New York: Oxford University Press, 1973), pp. 3–39. Swomley, interview. Dellinger, *Revolutionary Nonviolence*, pp. 14–15.

61. ACLU, Board of Directors, October 7, 1946. ACLU–SC, *Open Forum*, January 11, 1947. *Berman v. United States*, 156 F.2d 377 (1946).

62. Muste, letter to Baldwin, January 24, 1941, ACLUP, 1941, vol. 2273. NCCO, Legal Memorandum 6, December 11, 1944, ACLUP, 1944, vol. 2557. ACLU, *Annual Report*, 1945, pp. 37–38.

63. ACLU, Board of Directors, Minutes, May 25, 1942. Fraenkel, Diary, May 4, 1942.

64. ACLU, Board of Directors, Minutes, December 11, 1944, January 22, 1945.

65. ACLU, Memorandum of Civil Rights in the Military Forces (August 1941), adopted, ACLU, Board of Directors, Minutes, September 8, 1941; sustained in referendum, October 20, 1941.

66. *In re Summers*, 325 U.S. 561 (1944). ACLU, Twenty-fifth Anniversary Conference, *Proceedings*, November 24, 1945, ACLUP, 1946, vol. 8. ACLU, *Annual Report*, 1945, p. 37. *Girouard v. United States*, 328 U.S. 61 (1946).

67. Patrick S. Washburn, *A Question of Sedition: The Federal Government's Investigation of the Black Press During World War II* (New York: Oxford University Press, 1986). Francis Biddle, *In Brief Authority* (Garden City, N.Y.: Doubleday, 1962), pp. 150–160, 233–251. Robert Cushman, "Civil Liberties," *American Political Science Review* 37 (February 1943): 49–56.

68. *Dunne v. United States*, 138 F.2d 137 (1943). ACLU, Board of Directors, Minutes, September 8, 1941, August 17, 1942. ACLU, *Sedition!* (October 1941). Fraenkel, COHC, p. 91. Correspondence and brief, Hays Papers, Box 28. Biddle, *In Brief Authority*, p. 151.

69. Washburn, *A Question of Sedition*, pp. 46–47.

70. ACLU, Memo, War-Time Prosecutions for Speech and Publication, typescript (April

1944). Leo P. Ribuffo, *"United States v. McWilliams:* The Roosevelt Administration and the Far Right," in Michael Belknap, *Political Trials* (Westport, Conn.: Greenwood Press, 1981), pp. 201–232. ACLU Board of Directors, Minutes, March 16, 1942.

71. Baldwin, Hays et al., letter to Biddle, April 4, 1942, ACLUP, 1943, vol. 2482.

72. Davis, letter to Baldwin, April 15, 1942. ACLU, Board of Directors, Minutes, April 20, 1942, May 11, 1942.

73. Rice, Memo, ca. August, 1942, Rice Papers, Box 69.

74. David Riesman, "Democracy and Defamation," *Columbia Law Review* 42 (1942): 729–780, 1085–1123, 1282–1318, especially pp. 779–780, 1318. David Riesman, "Civil Liberties in a Period of Transition," *Public Policy* 3 (1942): 33–96.

75. Lamont, letter to Holmes, May 12, 1942, Holmes Papers, Box 25, Fraenkel, Diary, July 20, 1942, September 28, 1942. ACLU, Board of Directors, Minutes, November 29, 1943. Holmes, letter to Lamont, May 11, 1942, RNBP. Ernst, letter to Lamont, June 4, 1943, Rice Papers, Box 69.

76. James N. Rosenberg, "Words Are Triggers: An Open Letter to Arthur Garfield Hays," *The Nation,* May 2, 1942, pp. 511–512. Freda Kirchwey, "Curb the Fascist Press!" *The Nation,* March 28, 1942, pp. 357–358. "Lock Them Up, Mr. Biddle," *New Masses,* April 14, 1942, p. 1. Minority statement in ACLU, *Military Power and Civil Rights* (December 1942). National Lawyers Guild, *The National Lawyers Guild Presents the Case for the Prosecution of "Social Justice"* (1942), copy, NYPL. Kirchwey: ACLU, Board of Directors, Minutes, April 13, 1942. Chicago Civil Liberties Committee, *Annual Report,* 1942.

77. Arthur Garfield Hays, "Indictments Pull the Triggers," *The Nation* 154 (May 9, 1942), pp. 543–545.

78. ACLU, Notes on the Special Meeting, October 12, 1942, ACLUP, 1942, vol. 2355. Fraenkel, Diary, October 12, 1942.

79. ACLU, Board of Directors, Minutes, October 19, 1942.

80. Fraenkel, Diary, January 4, 1943. Baldwin, letter to Holmes, August 12, 1942, Holmes Papers, Box 25. Ernst, letter to Holmes, February 25, 1943, Ernst Papers, vol. 134.

81. Wirin quoted in ACLU–NC, Executive Committee, Minutes, January 7, 1943. ACLU, Board of Directors, March 8, 1943.

82. Irons, *Justice at War,* pp. 128–134.

83. Baldwin, letter to signers of petition, May 21, 1943, ACLUP, 1946, Addendum 2. ACLU, Board of Directors, May 24, 1943.

84. ACLU, Sedition Committee, Minutes, February 17, 1943, ACLUP, 1943, vol. 2605.

85. ACLU, Board of Directors, Minutes, January 4, 1943, January 18, 1943, March 1, 1943. Seymour, Hays, Statements, Referendum Materials, January 28, 1943, ACLUP, 1943, vol. 2105. Ribuffo, *"United States v. McWilliams."*

86. ACLU, *Annual Report,* 1942, pp. 5, 29–30.

87. ACLU, Board of Directors, Minutes, January 25, 1943, March 8, 1943.

88. Washburn, *A Question of Sedition.*

89. *Hannegan v. Esquire,* 327 U.S. 146 (1946). ACLU, *Annual Report,* 1944, pp. 41–42.

90. Robert E. Summers, *Wartime Censorship of Press and Radio* (New York: H. W. Wilson, 1942).

91. Clayton R. Koppes, *Hollywood Goes to War: How Politics, Profits and Propaganda Shaped World War II Movies* (New York: Free Press, 1987).

92. Thomas, article cited in *Variety*, February 11, 1942; reprinted in Summers, *Wartime Censorship*, pp. 207–208.

93. Isserman, *Which Side Were You On?*

94. *United States v. Schneidermann*, 320 U.S. 118 (1943).

95. *Congressional Record*, September 24, 1942, pp. 7440–7458.

96. *U.S. v. Lovett*, 328 U.S. 303 (1946). Walter Goodman, *The Committee* (New York: Farrar, Straus & Giroux, 1968), pp. 152–159.

97. Baldwin, letter to Hoover, November 28, 1941, ACLU/FBI. Hoover, Memorandum for Mr. L. M. C. Smith, April 3, 1941, Hoover, Memo to SAC, New York City, October 21, 1941, RNB/FBI. Hoover, letter to Baldwin, October 29, 1942, ACLU/FBI/3022.

98. Baldwin, Memo for the Files, July 1943, attached to manuscript, "Civil Rights and the FBI," March 12, 1942, RNBP, Box 9.

99. Lee Finkel, *Forum for Protest: The Black Press During World War II* (Rutherford, N.J.: Fairleigh Dickinson, 1975).

100. Herbert Garfinkel, *When Negroes March* (Glencoe, Ill.: Free Press, 1959).

101. Alfred McClung Lee and Norman D. Humphrey, *Race Riot* (New York: Dryden Press, 1943).

102. Samuel Walker, "Origins of the Police–Community Relations Movement: The 1940's," in *Criminal Justice History*, vol. 1 (New York: John Jay Press, 1980), pp. 225–246.

103. ACLU, Board of Directors, Minutes, February 2, 1942, March 16, 1942. Milner, letter to Wilkins, February 5, 1942; Wilkins, letter to Milner, February 19, 1942; ACLU, memo, May 13, 1942, ACLUP, 1942, vol. 2357. ACLU, *Annual Report*, 1943, pp. 47–51. Ladd, Memorandum for the Director, November 2, 1943, ACLU/FBI/3096.

104. Whitney, letter to Holmes, May 4, 1943, ACLUP, 1946, Addendum 2. ACLU, Board of Directors, Minutes, May 10, 1943. ACLU, Press Release, July 3, 1944, ACLUP, 1944, vol. 2562. Herbert R. Northrup, "Race Discrimination in Unions," *American Mercury* 61 (August 1945): 90–95.

105. ACLU, Memorandum in Support of Draft of a State Civil Rights Law, December, 1944, ACLUP, 1944, vol. 2577. Maslow, letter to Forster, December 19, 1945, ACLUP, 1946, Addendum 2. ACLU, Board of Directors, Minutes, September 13, 1943. ACLU, *Supplemental Annual Report*, 1940, p. 10. Norman Redlich, "Private Attorneys General," *Yale Law Journal* 58 (1949): 574–598. Maslow, interview. Pfeffer, interview.

106. St. Louis Civil Liberties Committee, Executive Committee, Minutes, August 12, 1942, March 19, 1943, StLCLCP, Ser. I, Box 1.

107. *McNabb v. U.S.*, 318 U.S. 332 (1943). ACLU–Chicago Division, *Civil Liberties Brief*, May 8, 1947. ACLU–SC, *Open Forum*, December 27, 1947.

108. *Smith v. Allwright*, 321 U.S. 649 (1944). ACLU, Board of Directors, Minutes, November 15, 1943.

109. *United States v. Classic*, 313 U.S. 299 (1941). *Smith v. Allwright*, 321 U.S. 649 (1944); *Shelley v. Kraemer*, 334 U.S. 1 (1948). Genna Rae McNeil, *Groundwork: Charles Hamilton Houston and the Struggle for Civil Rights* (Philadelphia: University of Pennsylvania Press, 1983), p. 181. Clement E. Vose, *Caucasians Only: The Supreme Court, the NAACP, and the Restrictive Covenant Cases* (Berkeley and Los Angeles: University of California Press, 1959).

110. John L. Dower, *War Without Mercy* (New York: Pantheon, 1986).

111. On the NAACP debate, see Riis Papers, letter to Milner, February 17, 1942, RWRP, Box 2. ACLU–NAACP strategy session: Memo, March 26, 1942, NAACP/

II-A/Box 13. Baldwin, Memo re conference with Angell, September 2, 1942, ACLUP, 1942, vol. 2363. ACLU, *Annual Report,* 1945, p. 23.

112. Conrad Lynn, letter to Baldwin, September 23, 1942, Thomas Papers. Baldwin, Memo of conference with Angell, September 2, 1942, ACLUP, 1942, vol. 2363. Dwight MacDonald, "The Novel Case of Winfred Lynn," *The Nation,* February 20, 1943, pp. 268–270. Nancy MacDonald, interview.

113. Dwight MacDonald, "The Supreme Court's New Moot Suit," *The Nation,* July 1, 1944, pp. 13–14. ACLU, Press Release, June 5, 1944, ACLUP, 1945, vol. 2645.

114. Dwight MacDonald, "On the Conduct of the Lynn Case," *Politics* 1 (April 1944): 85–88. Arthur Garfield Hays, "Rejoinder," *Politics* 1 (April 1944): 88. On the NAACP brief, see Hays, letter to Marshall, May 12, 1944, NAACP/II-B/Box 147.

115. Roger N. Baldwin, "Union Administration and Civil Liberties," *The Annals* 248 (November 1946): 54–61.

116. Ibid.

117. ACLU, Board of Directors, Minutes, June 25, 1941, November 24, 1941. ACLU, *Labor's Civil Rights* (September 1945).

118. Thomas, memo, ca. 1933, ACLUP, 1933, vol. 618. Lindeman, Memo to Committee on Democracy in Trade Unions, May 2, 1942, ACLUP, 1959, vol. 70. ACLU, *Democracy in Trade Unions* (November 1944). ACLU, Board of Directors, Minutes, May 25, 1959. Michael Harrington, "Blue Collar Democracy," in Alan Reitman, ed., *The Price of Liberty* (New York: Norton, 1968), pp. 215–216.

119. Joan Hoff-Wilson, *Rites of Passage: The Past and Future of the ERA* (Bloomington: Indiana University Press, 1986).

120. ACLU, Board of Directors, Minutes, June 7, 1943, July 26, 1943. ACLU, *Annual Report,* 1946, p. 46; 1947, p. 45. "Dorothy Kenyon," *Notable American Women* (Cambridge, Mass.: Harvard University Press, 1980), vol. 4, pp. 395–397.

121. ACLU, Board of Directors, Minutes, March 21, 1938, April 4, 1938. Alonzo F. Myers, letter to Ellen Donohue, May 13, 1938, ACLUP, 1938, vol. 1068.

122. Hoff-Wilson, *Rites of Passage,* pp. 13–16.

123. ACLU, Twenty-fifth Anniversary Conference, "What's Ahead for American Liberties?" November 24, 1945, *Proceedings,* ACLUP, 1946, vol. 8.

124. Arthur Garfield Hays, *City Lawyer* (New York: Simon & Schuster, 1942), pp. 221–222.

125. ACLU, Twenty-fifth Anniversary Conference, *Proceedings,* pp. 15–16.

126. Ibid., p. 11.

Chapter 8

1. Theodore H. White, *In Search of History: A Personal Adventure* (New York: Warner Books, 1978), pp. 381–386.

2. Jessica Mitford, *A Fine Old Conflict* (New York: Pantheon, 1977), pp. 259–266.

3. David Caute, *The Great Fear* (New York: Simon & Schuster, 1978), p. 519. Dalton Trumbo, *The Time of the Toad* (New York: Harper & Row, 1972).

4. David J. Garrow, *The FBI and Martin Luther King, Jr.* (New York: Norton, 1981), pp. 60–61.

5. On Albert Canwell, see ACLU, *Annual Report,* 1949, p. 18.

6. Caute, *The Great Fear.* Clark quoted in Michael Kammen, *A Machine That Would Go of Itself: The Constitution in American Culture* (New York: Knopf, 1987), p. 344.

7. Athan Theoharis, *Seeds of Repression: Harry S. Truman and the Origins of McCarthyism* (New York: Quadrangle Books, 1971).

8. Ibid.

9. Arthur M. Schlesinger, Jr., *The Vital Center* (Boston: Houghton Mifflin, 1949). Christopher Lasch, *The Agony of the American Left* (New York: Vintage Books, 1969), pp. 61–114.

10. Mary S. McAuliffe, "The American Civil Liberties Union During the McCarthy Years," in Robert Griffith and Athan Theoharis, eds., *The Specter* (New York: New Viewpoints, 1974), pp. 152–170. Corliss Lamont, *Freedom Is As Freedom Does* (New York: Horizon, 1955), pp. 261–287.

11. C. Herman Pritchett, *Civil Liberties and the Vinson Court* (Chicago: University of Chicago Press, 1954).

12. Executive Order 9835, 12 *Fed. Reg.* 1935, March 21, 1947.

13. The ACLU was never officially labeled a Communist front organization by either the HUAC or the attorney general's list. But the California Fact-Finding Committee on Un-American Activities did list the ACLU as a Communist front in 1948. See Edward L. Barrett, Jr., *The Tenney Committee* (Ithaca, N.Y.: Cornell University Press, 1951), app. I, p. 255.

14. ACLU, Statement, April 7, 1947, ACLUP, 1947, Box 5.

15. ACLU, Board of Directors, Minutes, October 11, 1948, January 17, 1949. ACLU, Report of Committee on Clear and Present Danger Test, November 18, 1948, ACLUP, 1948, Box 16. ACLU, *Annual Report,* 1949, pp. 71–72.

16. Baldwin, letter to Nina Dexter, September 29, 1947; Besig, letter to Baldwin, October 16, 1947, ACLUP, 1947, vol. 11. Heist, letter to Robin, June 23, 1947, ACLUP, 1947, vol. 4. Robin, Memo to ACLU board, September 4, 1947, ACLUP, 1947, Box 5. ACLU–SC, Memo to members, October 13, 1947, ACLUP, 1947, vol. 11. Baldwin, Memo to National Committee, May 21, 1948, ACLUP, 1948, vol. 20. ACLU, *Annual Report,* 1948, pp. 80–81.

17. Clark, telegram to John Haynes Holmes, April 7, 1947, ACLUP, 1947, vol. 11; Nichols, Memo to Tolson, March 26, 1948, ACLU/FBI/3329.

18. David D. Lloyd, Memo to James Loeb, ADA, August 4, 1947, ACLUP, 1947, vol. 11. Forster, Memo, "Procedures for Handling Loyalty Cases Under Executive Order 9835," September 14, 1948, ACLUP, 1948, vol. 4. ACLU, *Annual Report,* 1949, p. 12. Thomas I. Emerson and David M. Helfeld, "Loyalty Among Government Employees," *Yale Law Journal* 58 (December 1948): 1–143.

19. *In re Abraham Chasanow,* U.S. Department of the Navy, Bureau of National Affairs, *Manual of Government Security-Loyalty* 19 (1953): 527–531. *New York Times,* April 16, 1954. Anthony Lewis, *Washington Daily News,* clipping in ACLUP, 1954, vol. 6. "See It Now," October 23, 1953, Museum of Broadcasting, New York City.

20. Berne file, Folder 872, ACLU–NCP, CHS. *San Francisco Chronicle,* March 12, 1954.

21. Attorney General's List, published, *Fed. Reg.* October 21, 1948. Caute, *The Great Fear,* p. 162.

22. ACLU, Board of Directors, Minutes, November 22, 1948, December 20, 1948. Wise, Fly, Fraenkel, Brief for the ACLU, as *amicus curiae, Joint Anti-Fascist Refugee Committee v. Clark,* 177 F.2d 79 (D.C. Cir. 1949).

23. *Joint Anti-Fascist Refugee Committee v. McGrath,* 341 U.S. 123 (1951).

24. James Kutcher, *The Case of the Legless Veteran* (New York: Monad Press, 1973). ACLU, Board of Directors, Minutes, June 20, 1949.

25. Kutcher, *Case of the Legless Veteran.* ACLU, *Annual Report,* 1953, pp. 42–43; 1958, p. 76.

26. Walter Goodman, *The Committee* (New York: Farrar, Straus & Giroux, 1968).

27. Caute, *The Great Fear,* pp. 487–520.

28. ACLU, Board of Directors, Minutes, January 19, 1948, March 1, 1948. *Barsky v. United States,* 167 F.2d 241 (D.C. Cir. 1948).

29. *Barsky v. U.S. Lawson v. U.S.,* 176 F.2d 49 (D.C. Cir. 1949). Caute, *The Great Fear,* pp. 177–178. Ring Lardner, Jr., "A Dark Anniversary," *Premier,* December 1987, p. 103. ACLU, *Annual Report,* 1948, p. 28. ACLU–SC, *Open Forum,* January 1957, March 1958.

30. Goodman, *The Committee,* pp. 213–237.

31. Barrett, *The Tenney Committee,* pp. 257–268. Walter Gellhorn, ed., *The States and Subversion* (Ithaca, N.Y.: Cornell University Press, 1952).

32. Victor Navasky, *Naming Names* (New York: Viking, 1980). Lillian Hellman, *Scoundrel Time* (New York: Bantam, 1977), pp. 89–91.

33. Richard H. Rovere, *Senator Joe McCarthy* (Cleveland: World Publishing, 1959), pp. 157–159.

34. Merle Miller, *The Judges and the Judged* (Garden City, N.Y.: Doubleday, 1952), pp. 35–46.

35. Kirkpatrick, American Business Consultants, letter to ACLU, January 5, 1949, ACLUP, 1948, vol. 32.

36. ACLU, Board of Directors, Minutes, August 28, 1950, September 11, 1950. Miller, *The Judges and the Judged.*

37. ACLU, Board of Directors, Minutes, May 12, 1952, May 15, 1952, June 23, 1952, July 21, 1952. For a misleading account of the ACLU's internal controversy, see William L. O'Neill, *A Better World* (New York: Simon & Schuster, 1982), pp. 228–234. John Cogley, *Report on Blacklisting,* vol. 1, *Movies,* and vol. 2, *Radio–Television* (New York: Fund for the Republic, 1956).

38. Ernst, letter to Nixon, January 19, 1948, Ernst Papers, vol. 65.

39. Holmes, letter to Nixon, October 5, 1948, ACLUP, 1948, Box 16. Ferman, interview. ACLU response to HUAC report: Malin, Memo to Rep. Walter, December 10, 1955, ACLUP, 1968, vol. 34. Ferman's justification in ACLU, Report of Special Commission on the FBI Files to ACLU Board of Directors, October 2, 1979, author's files. Virginia Gardner, "Roger Baldwin: What Are You Hiding?" *New Masses,* May 20, 1947, pp. 3–4.

40. President's Committee on Civil Rights, *To Secure These Rights* (New York: Simon & Schuster, 1947), p. 164. Arthur Garfield Hays, "Full Disclosure: Dangerous Precedent," *The Nation,* January 29, 1949, pp. 121–123.

41. ACLU, Board of Directors, Minutes, December 17, 1945. ACLU, *Annual Report,* 1946, p. 48. Baldwin, letter to "Friends," June 25, 1947, RNBP, Box 12. Malin, Memo to Rep. Walter, December 10, 1955, ACLUP, 1968, vol. 34.

42. ACLU, *Annual Report,* 1955, pp. 80–81.

43. Caute, *The Great Fear,* pp. 185–215.

44. ACLU, letter to Clark, July 21, 1948, ACLUP, 1951, Box 58. ACLU, Board of Directors, Minutes, August 9, 1948, September 27, 1948.

45. McWilliams, letter to Baldwin, January 22, 1946, ACLUP, 1946, vol. 2711. ACLU, *Annual Report,* 1946, pp. 45–46. Clippings, ca. October 1945, in ACLUP, 1945, vol. 2690.

46. Norman Dorsen and Leon Friedman, *Disorder in the Court* (New York: Pantheon, 1973), pp. 49–56. Stanley Kutler, *The American Inquisition* (New York: Hill and Wang, 1982), pp. 152–182.

47. Fraenkel, Diary, November 7, 1949. ACLU, Board of Directors, Minutes, November 7, 1949. Pollitt, interview. Terence C. Halliday, "Idiom of Legalism in Bar Politics: Lawyers, McCarthyism, and the Civil Rights Era," *American Bar Foundation Research Journal,* Fall 1982, pp. 911–988.

48. Levy, Memo to Committee on Freedom of Expression, July 3, 1951, ACLUP, 1951, vol. 1. Caute, *The Great Fear,* pp. 173–174.

49. ACLU, Board of Directors, Minutes, January 3, 1949, March 20, 1950, April 17, 1950. Wulf, interview.

50. ACLU, Memorandum, September 23, 1949, ACLUP, 1951, vol. 50.

51. ACLU, Board of Directors, April 3, 1950, June 26, 1950; H. M. Levy to C. C. Burlingham, October 31, 1950; Charles Cropley, Clerk, U.S. Supreme Court, letter to Fraenkel, November 27, 1950; ACLUP, 1951, Box 58.

52. Baldwin, letter to Malin, June 27, 1951, ACLUP, 1951, Box 58.

53. *Dennis v. United States,* 341 U.S. 494 (1951). Henry J. Abraham, *Freedom and the Court,* 4th ed. (New York: Oxford University Press, 1982), p. 214.

54. Malin, Memo to ACLU Board, June 20, 1951, ACLUP, 1951, Box 49. ACLU, *The Smith Act and the Supreme Court* (April 1952). Malin, Memo to Board, October 1, 1952, ACLUP, 1953, vol. 29. ACLU, Board of Directors, Minutes, June 25, 1951.

55. ACLU–SC, *Open Forum,* February 2, 1952; August 12, 1952. *Ohio CLU News,* February 1956, p. 1. Thielking to Watts, March 11, 1958, ACLUP, 1958, vol. 19. ACLU, Board of Directors, Minutes, October 8, 1956.

56. "On the History of the N.E.C.L.C.," *Bill of Rights Journal* (December 1976). Lamont, interview. Wilkinson, interview. Ripston, interview.

57. Generally, see Gellhorn, *The States and Subversion.*

58. Ibid., pp. 140–183. Maryland Civil Liberties Union, *Think,* ca. 1949, ACLUP, 1951, vol. 37.

59. On New York, see ACLU, Board of Directors, Minutes, July 25, 1949. On Illinois, see ACLU–Chicago Division, *"To Take a Copy from the Nazis . . ."* ca. 1951, ACLUP, 1951, vol. 37. On Dilworth, see ACLU–GrPh, Press Release, ca. 1952, ACLU–GrPh, 1952, vol. 3.

60. *American Communications Association v. Douds,* 339 U.S. 382 (1950). ACLU correspondence and brief in ACLUP, 1950, vol. 26.

61. *Garner v. Board of Public Works,* 341 U.S. 716 (1951). ACLU–SC, *Open Forum,* March 20, 1948, April 16, 1949, May 12, 1951.

62. *Wieman v. Updegraff,* 344 U.S. 183 (1952). On the ACLU *amicus,* see ACLU, *Annual Report,* 1953, p. 60.

63. ACLU, Board of Directors, Minutes, October 24, 1949. *Imbrie v. Marsh,* 3 N.J. 578 (1950).

64. ACLU–NC, *Crisis at the University of California* (December 1950); revised and reissued by ACLU, November 1951. Ellen W. Schrecker, *No Ivory Tower: McCarthyism and the Universities* (New York: Oxford University Press, 1986), pp. 117–125.

65. ACLU–NC, *ACLU News,* August 1953, p. 3. *Speiser v. Randall,* 357 U.S. 513 (1958). Speiser, interview.

66. ACLU, *Annual Report,* 1958, pp. 78–79; 1959, p. 87.

67. Schrecker, *No Ivory Tower,* pp. 111–112, 188. Walter P. Metzger, "Ralph F. Fuchs

and Ralph E. Himstead: A Note on the AAUP in the McCarthy Period," *Academe,* November–December 1986, pp. 29–35.

68. Thomas, Memo to ACLU Board of Directors, November 18, 1948, ACLUP, 1948, Box 16. M. DeSilver, letter to Baldwin, March 31, 1951, RNBP, Box 18. On the Catholic issue, see Malin, form letter, ca. 1957, ACLUP, 1957, Box 140.

69. ACLU, *Civil Liberties of Teachers and Students* (1949). ACLU, *Annual Report, 1949,* p. 71. On the referendum results, see Malin, Memo to the Corporation, November 30, 1951, RNBP, Box 18.

70. Athan G. Theoharis and John Stuart Cox, *The Boss: J. Edgar Hoover and the Great American Inquisition* (Philadelphia: Temple University Press, 1988). Richard Gid Powers, *Secrecy and Power: The Life of J. Edgar Hoover* (New York: Free Press, 1987).

71. ACLU, *Annual Report,* 1953, p. 82. J. Edgar Hoover, "Civil Liberties and Law Enforcement: The Role of the FBI," *Iowa Law Review* 37 (Winter 1952): 175–195. Levy, letter to Savelle, September 29, 1955, ACLUP, 1955, vol. 21. Harrison E. Salisbury, "The Strange Correspondence of Morris Ernst and John Edgar Hoover, 1939–1964," *The Nation* 239 (December 1, 1984): 575–589.

72. Emerson and Helfeld, "Loyalty Among Government Employees." For the Lowenthal incident, see Theoharis and Cox, *The Boss,* pp. 275–278. Max Lowenthal, *The Federal Bureau of Investigation* (New York: William Sloan, 1950).

73. Theoharis and Cox, *The Boss.*

74. Fly, letter to Rep. Cannon, Chair, House Appropriations Committee, January 16, 1950, Fly Papers, Box 41. James L. Fly, "The Wiretapping Outrage," *The New Republic,* February 6, 1950, pp. 14–15.

75. Ferman, testimony, House Judiciary Committee, May 20, 1953, Fly Papers, Box 41. ACLU, *Annual Report,* 1953, pp. 90–92.

76. Morris Ernst, "Why I No Longer Fear the FBI," *Reader's Digest* 57 (December 1950): 135–139. Salisbury, "The Strange Correspondence." ACLU, Report of ACLU Special Commission on the FBI Files, author's files.

77. On Malin, see Lamont, letter to Neier, May 2, 1978, ANP. Baldwin, letter to Rep. Sabath, April 3, 1947; Baldwin, letter to Asst. U.S. Attorney General Peyton Ford, November 10, 1947, ACLUP, 1947, vol. 5.

78. ACLU, Report of the Special Commission on the FBI Files.

79. ACLU–SC, *Open Forum,* September 16, 1950.

80. Savelle, letter to Levy, August 20, 1955, ACLUP, 1955, vol. 21.

81. Spencer Coxe, letter to Levy, November 12, 1954; William Allen Rahill, letter to Herbert M. Linsenberg, December 16, 1954; Pamphlet on FBI, typescript, n.d., ACLU–GrPh, Box 18.

82. Levy, Memo to Due Process Committee, March 22, 1955; ACLU, Due Process Committee, Minutes, March 31, 1955; Levy, letter to Coxe, September 24, 1954; Joughin, Memo to Due Process Committee, November 22, 1955, ACLU/FBI. Levy, letter to Coxe cited in ACLU–GrPh, Loyalty-Security Committee, Minutes, October 25, 1955, November 23, 1955, April 25, 1956, ACLU–GrPh, Box 18.

83. Samuel Walker, "Hysteria and Civil Liberties" (Paper delivered at the ACLU Biennial Conference, 1987).

84. Samuel A. Stouffer, *Communism, Conformity, and Civil Liberties* (Gloucester, Mass.: Peter Smith, 1963).

85. There is no adequate survey of public opinion on the full range of civil liberties questions in the cold war period: The conclusions here rest on the evidence and arguments in Chapters Eleven and Twelve.

86. Pritchett, *Civil Liberties and the Vinson Court*.

87. ACLU–SC, *Open Forum*, April 16, 1949. Glasser, interview.

88. Special Agent Dow, Memo to Boston FBI office, October 19, 1951, ACLU/FBI/40750.

89. Malin, memo to Rep. Walter, December 10, 1955, ACLUP, 1968, vol. 34. Ferman, interview. Reitman, interview.

90. Lamont, *Freedom Is As Freedom Does*, pp. 33–48.

91. ACLU, *Annual Report*, 1953, p. 27; 1954, p. 76. Reitman, Memo re Single Standard Defense of Civil Liberties, November 18, 1987, author's files.

92. "Argument in Indianapolis," "See It Now," November 24, 1953, Museum of Broadcasting, New York City. ACLU, *Annual Report*, 1954, pp. 18–19.

Chapter 9

1. This quotation is from Richard H. Rovere, *Senator Joe McCarthy* (Cleveland: World Publishing, 1960), p. 125; on the Kenyon incident, see p. 147. Also see Susan M. Hartmann, "Dorothy Kenyon," *Notable American Women* (Cambridge, Mass.: Harvard University Press, 1980), vol. 4, pp. 395–397.

2. *New York Times*, April 1, 1950, April 2, 1950, May 22, 1950. Gerard Piel, *Science in the Cause of Man*, 2nd ed. (New York: Knopf, 1962), pp. 3–20. *Scientific American*, April 1950. Piel, interview.

3. ACLU, Memorandum, April 27, 1950, ACLUP, 1950, Box 41. Piel, interview.

4. William R. Tanner and Robert Griffith, "Legislative Politics and 'McCarthyism': The Internal Security Act of 1950," in Robert Griffith and Athan Theoharis, eds., *The Specter* (New York: Franklin Watts, 1974), pp. 174–189.

5. Policy Committee, Majority and Minority Statements on Emergency Detention Provisions, ca. 1951, ACLUP, 1951, Box 49. ACLU, Board of Directors, Minutes, January 22, 1951. Fraenkel, Diary, January 22, 1951.

6. Forster, letter to Seymour, August 24, 1948; Forster, letter to Editor, *Commonweal*, June 24, 1948; Hays, letter to "Dear Senator," June 3, 1948, ACLUP, 1948, vol. 18.

7. Hays–Nixon exchange in Eric Bentley, *Thirty Years of Treason* (New York: Viking, 1971), p. 265. Ernst, letter to Levy, November 29, 1950; Malin, Angell, Hays, letter to Truman, September 14, 1950, October 3, 1950, ACLUP, 1950, vol. 22.

8. ACLU, Emergency Policy Committee, Minutes, August 15, 1950; ACLU, Board of Directors, Minutes, August 28, 1950. Stanley I. Kutler, "Government by Discretion: The Queendom of Passports," in Stanley I. Kutler, *The American Inquisition* (New York: Hill and Wang, 1982), pp. 89–117. Martin Bauml Duberman, *Paul Robeson* (New York: Knopf, 1988), pp. 388–390.

9. ACLU, Special Committee on Issuance of Passports, Report, November 23, 1951, ACLUP, 1951, Box 49. ACLU, Board of Directors, Minutes, January 21, 1952.

10. ACLU, Board of Directors, October 29, 1951. Pitzele, letter to Malin, November 19, 1951, Thomas Papers. David Caute, *The Great Fear* (New York: Simon & Schuster, 1978), pp. 247–248.

11. "U.S. Clearance Given to Roger N. Baldwin," *New York Times*, April 26, 1951. U.S. House of Representatives, Appropriations Committee, *Hearings*, April 3, 1951, pp. 1114–1136.

12. Baldwin, Correspondence and memos, RNBP, Boxes 11, 12.

13. *Kent v. Dulles*, 357 U.S. 116 (1958). ACLU, Board of Directors, August 8, 1955, January 7, 1957, November 18, 1957. ACLU, *Annual Report*, 1959, pp. 46–49.

14. G. Bromley Oxnam, *I Protest* (New York: Harper Bros., 1954). James Wechsler, *The Age of Suspicion* (New York: Random House, 1953), pp. 249–325. Victor Navasky, *Naming Names* (New York: Viking, 1980), pp. 58–66.

15. Herbert Brownell, "Remedy for Abuse of Constitutional Privilege Against Self-Incrimination," October 14, 1953, reported in *New York Times,* October 15, 1953.

16. NYCLU, *Civil Liberties in New York,* February 1957, March 1957, November 1958. ACLU, *Annual Report, 1955,* p. 36.

17. *ABA Journal* 36 (1950): 948; April 1953, p. 344.

18. Ralph S. Brown, Jr., "Lawyers and the Fifth Amendment: A Dissent," *ABA Journal* 40 (May 1954): 404–407. Association of the Bar of New York City, *Report,* November 4, 1953, in ACLUP, 1953, vol. 63. Jerold S. Auerbach, *Unequal Justice: Lawyers and Social Change in Modern America* (New York: Oxford University Press, 1976), pp. 231–262. Terence C. Halliday, "The Idiom of Legalism in Bar Politics: Lawyers, McCarthyism, and the Civil Rights Era," *American Bar Foundation Research Journal,* 1982 (No. 4), pp. 911–988. Jonathan D. Casper, *Lawyers Before the Warren Court* (Urbana: University of Illinois Press, 1972).

19. Sidney Hook, *Common Sense and the Fifth Amendment* (New York: Criterion Books, 1957), pp. 13, 44. Alan F. Westin, "Do Silent Witnesses Defend Civil Liberties?" *Commentary,* June 1953, pp. 537–546. Donald L. Smith, *Zechariah Chafee: Defender of Liberty and Law* (Cambridge, Mass.: Harvard University Press, 1986), p. 264.

20. C. Dickerman Williams, "Problems of the Fifth Amendment," *Fordham Law Review* 24 (1955–1956): 47. Fraenkel, Diary, April 15, 1953. *Slochower v. Board of Higher Education of New York,* 350 U.S. 551 (1956). ACLU, Board of Directors, Minutes, August 13, 1956.

21. ACLU, Referendum Materials, 1953, ACLUP, 1953, Box 84. ACLU, Policy Statements on National Security, July 21, 1954, ACLUP, 1954, Box 108.

22. ACLU, *Annual Report,* 1954, p. 59.

23. Erwin N. Griswold, *The Fifth Amendment Today* (Cambridge, Mass.: Harvard University Press, 1955), pp. 76–81.

24. Northrup, interview. Isbell, interview.

25. ACLU, Report of the Policy Planning Committee, March 14, 1949, RNBP, Box 18. Gellhorn, interview.

26. Baldwin, Memorandum on ACLU Program, December 27, 1948, ACLUP, 1948, vol. 4. Isbell, interview.

27. Norman Redlich, "Private Attorneys-General: Group Action in the Fight for Civil Liberties," *Yale Law Journal* 58 (1949): 574–598. Redlich, interview.

28. Correspondence in RNBP, Boxes 11 and 12.

29. Baldwin, Memo, "Shogun and Emperor," ca. 1947; Baldwin, Memo, June 1947, RNBP, Box 11.

30. Northrup, interview. *New York Times,* February 23, 1950.

31. Baldwin, Memo to Board, September 9, 1949; Gellhorn, Memo to Board, August 30, 1949, ACLUP, 1949, vol. 5. Day, interview. "Patrick Murphy Malin," *Current Biography 1950* (New York: H. H. Wilson, 1951), pp. 377–379.

32. Gellhorn, Memo to Board, November 30, 1949, ACLUP, 1949, Box 32.

33. Charles E. Silberman, *A Certain People* (New York: Summit Books, 1985), pp. 98–101.

34. ACLU, Committee on Membership and Affiliates, April 10, 1951; Malin, Memo to Board, June 4, 1951, ACLUP, 1951, vol. 1.

35. ACLU–NC, *Annual Report,* 1950, p. 18; 1956, p. 2. *Civil Liberties in New York*

(January 1954), p. 3. ACLU, Board of Directors, Minutes, February 5, 1951. ACLU, *Civil Liberties* (March 1955), p. 3.

36. ACLU, *Annual Report,* 1956, pp. 87–89.

37. ACLU, Constitution and By-Laws, Approved April 16, 1951, ACLUP, 1951, Box 49.

38. ACLU, Board of Directors, Minutes, March 17, 1953.

39. ACLU, Memo to Corporation Members, May 8, 1953, ACLUP, 1953, Box 84.

40. Beale, letter to Malin, June 27, 1953; Beale, letter to Baldwin, June 28, 1953, RNBP, Box 19. Emerson and Brown, Memo, June 9, 1953, ACLUP 1953, Box 84. Lamont, Memo to My Fellow Members of the A.C.L.U. Corporation, June 1953, ACLUP, 1954, Box 108. ACLU–NC, *ACLU News,* August 1953.

41. Angell, letter to corporation members, September 1, 1953; Lamont, telegram, September 11, 1953, ACLUP, 1953, Box 84. Corliss Lamont, *Freedom Is As Freedom Does* (New York: Horizon, 1956), pp. 261–287.

42. Fraenkel, Diaries, October 19, 1953. ACLU, Board of Directors, Minutes, November 2, 1953, November 30, 1953. *I. F. Stone's Weekly,* October 31, 1953.

43. ACLU, Board of Directors, Minutes, November 30, 1953. ACLU, Statement by Special Graham Committee, February 14, 1954, ACLUP, 1954, Box 108.

44. Fraenkel, Diary, March 13, 1954, March 15, 1954. ACLU, Board of Directors, Minutes, March 15, 1954. New Haven Civil Liberties Council, Resolution, March 18, 1954, ACLUP, 1954, Box 108.

45. ACLU, Policy Statements, July 21, 1954, ACLUP, 1954, Box 108. ACLU, Board of Directors, Minutes, August 2, 1954.

46. The anti-Communists' version appears in William H. McIlhany II, *The ACLU on Trial* (New Rochelle, N.Y.: Arlington House, 1976), pp. 152, 257, n. 50.

47. "Corliss Lamont's Inside Story After 21 Years," *I. F. Stone's Weekly,* March 1, 1954, pp. 4–6. Lamont, *Freedom Is As Freedom Does,* pp. 261–287. Lamont, interview.

48. Lamont, *Freedom Is As Freedom Does.* Lamont, interview.

49. Fraenkel, Diary, April 2, 1956. *New York Times,* December 15, 1954.

50. "See It Now," March 9, 1954, Museum of Broadcasting, New York City. Alexander Kendrick, *Prime Time: The Life of Edward R. Murrow* (New York: Avon Books, 1970), pp. 45–85.

51. Rovere, *Senator Joe McCarthy.*

52. *Denver Post,* "Faceless Informers and Our Schools" (reprint); original articles in *Denver Post,* September 19, 1954. Reitman, Memo to Malin, November 8, 1954, ACLUP, 1955, vol. 80.

53. Erwin N. Griswold, *The Fifth Amendment Today* (Cambridge: Harvard University Press, 1955), pp. 76–80.

54. Peter Pringle and James Spigelman, *The Nuclear Barons* (New York: Avon Books, 1983), pp. 243–246.

55. ACLU, *Annual Report,* 1946, p. 45; 1947, p. 11. Walter Gellhorn, *Security, Loyalty and Science* (Ithaca, N.Y.: Cornell University Press, 1950).

56. Allen Raymond, *The People's Right to Know: A Report on Government News Suppression* (ACLU Report) (December 1955).

57. ACLU, *Annual Report,* 1955, pp. 21–22.

Chapter 10

1. *New York Times Co. v. Sullivan,* 376 U.S. 255 (1964). Meikeljohn is quoted by Harry Kalven, in Philip B. Kurland, ed., *The Supreme Court and the Judicial Function* (Chicago: University of Chicago Press, 1975), p. 114, n. 125.

2. G. Theodore Mitau, *Decade of Decision: The Supreme Court and the Constitutional Revolution, 1954–1964* (New York: Scribner, 1967). Richard H. Sayler et al., eds., *The Warren Court: A Critical Analysis* (New York: Chelsea House, 1980).

3. ACLU, *Annual Report,* 1965, p. 9.

4. Ibid., p. 3.

5. Fraenkel, COHC, p. 60. Hirschkop, interview.

6. *Everson v. Board of Education,* 330 U.S. 1 (1947).

7. Paul Blanshard, *American Freedom and Catholic Power,* 2nd ed. (Boston: Beacon Press, 1958), p. 118.

8. ACLU, Informal Committee on Released Time, Minutes, May 10, 1948, ACLUP, 1948, vol. 4. Frank J. Souraf, *Wall of Separation: The Constitutional Politics of Church and State* (Princeton, N.J.: Princeton University Press, 1976), pp. 107–108. Leo Pfeffer, *Church, State, and Freedom,* rev. ed. (Boston: Beacon Press, 1967), pp. 165, 170, 173, 181, 182, 316, 353.

9. Blanshard, *American Freedom and Catholic Power,* p. 354. Souraf, *Wall of Separation.* Leo Pfeffer, "An Autobiographical Sketch," in James E. Wood, ed., *Religion and the State: Essays in Honor of Leo Pfeffer* (Waco, Tex.: Baylor University Press, 1985), pp. 487–534. Pfeffer, interview. Maslow, interview.

10. Pfeffer, interview.

11. *America,* 107, September 1, 1962, pp. 665–666. Pfeffer, "An Autobiographical Sketch," pp. 514–515.

12. Pfeffer, "An Autobiographical Sketch," p. 498–499.

13. ACLU, Informal Committee on Released Time, Minutes, May 10, 1948, ACLUP, 1948, vol. 4. On *Engel,* see Fred W. Friendly and Martha J. H. Elliott, *The Constitution: That Delicate Balance* (New York: Random House, 1984), pp. 118–119.

14. Alexander Meikeljohn, "Educational Cooperation Between Church and State," *Law and Contemporary Problems* 14 (Winter 1949): 61–72.

15. Vashti Cromwell McCollum, *One Woman's Fight* (Boston: Beacon Press, 1952), p. 23.

16. Cited in Pfeffer, *Church, State, and Freedom,* pp. 356–357.

17. Gellhorn, letter to Baldwin, January 13, 1948, ACLUP, 1948, vol. 4. Blanshard, *American Freedom and Catholic Power.*

18. Edward S. Corwin, "The Supreme Court As National School Board," *Law and Contemporary Problems* 14 (Winter 1949): 3–22.

19. *McCollum v. Board of Education,* 333 U.S. 203 (1948). McCollum's *One Woman's Fight.*

20. *Doremus v. Board of Education,* 342 U.S. 429 (1952). ACLU, *Annual Report,* 1953, pp. 69–70.

21. *Zorach v. Clauson,* 343 U.S. 306 (1952). Henry J. Abraham, *Freedom and the Court,* 4th ed. (New York: Oxford University Press, 1982), p. 276.

22. Blanshard, *American Freedom and Catholic Power,* pp. 125–127. Pfeffer, *Church, State, and Freedom,* pp. 447–464.

23. ACLU, Board of Directors, January 29, 1951, February 5, 1951. Souraf, *The Wall of Separation*, pp. 98–101. Pfeffer, *Church, State, and Freedom*, pp. 455–462.

24. NYCLU, Minutes, November 15, 1949, copy in Ernst Papers, vol. 402. ACLU, *Annual Report*, 1961, pp. 29–30.

25. Robert F. Drinan, "Religion and the ACLU," *America*, September 27, 1958, pp. 663–665. ACLU, Board of Directors, Minutes, October 20, 1958.

26. Souraf, *The Wall of Separation*, pp. 39–40. The list of committees is in Index to ACLUP, 1952, 1959.

27. Coxe, letter to Joughin, September 18, 1957, ACLU–GrPh, Box 10. R. D. Dierenfield, *Religion in American Public Schools* (Washington, D.C.: Public Affairs Press, 1962).

28. John Courtney Murray, S.J., *We Hold These Truths* (New York: Sheed and Ward, 1960).

29. Coxe, letter to Joughin, September 18, 1957, ACLU–GrPh, Box 10. The Philadelphia affiliate was unable to develop a comprehensive policy: See "Proposed Statement," October 3, 1957, ACLU–GrPh, Box 10.

30. ACLU, Church–State Committee, Minutes, June 28, 1961, ACLU–GrPh, Box 10.

31. ACLU, Church–State Committee, Minutes, January 25, 1961, ACLU–GrPh, Box 10. Pfeffer, letter to Malin, October 30, 1961, ACLU–GrPh, Box 10. Angell, letter to Pfeffer, November 7, 1961, ACLU, *Annual Report*, 1962, pp. 22–23. Pfeffer, interview.

32. ACLU, *Annual Report*, 1962, pp. 22–23.

33. *Torcaso v. Watkins*, 367 U.S. 488 (1961).

34. Sorauf, *The Wall of Separation*, p. 44.

35. ACLU, *Annual Report*, 1947, p. 50. Pfeffer, *Church, State, and Freedom*, pp. 460–469.

36. Bromley, for ACLU Church–State Committee, letter to Bouton, May 10, 1962, ACLU–GrPh, Box 10.

37. *Engel v. Vitale*, 370 U.S. 421 (1962).

38. *Abidington School District v. Schempp* and *Murray v. Curlett*, 374 U.S. 203 (1963).

39. Mitau, *Decade of Decision*, pp. 134–141.

40. William M. Beaney and Edward N. Beiser, "Prayer and Politics: The Impact of *Engel* and *Schempp* on the Political Process," *Journal of Public Law* 13, no. 2 (1964): 475–503.

41. Pfeffer, *Church, State, and Freedom*, pp. 466–478.

42. Mitau, *Decade of Decision*, pp. 134–141.

43. Robert F. Drinan, S.J., *Religion, the Courts, and Public Policy* (New York: McGraw-Hill, 1963).

44. Generally, see Theodore L. Becker and Malcolm M. Feeley, *The Impact of Supreme Court Decisions*, 2nd ed. (New York: Oxford University Press, 1973).

45. William K. Muir, *Law and Attitude Change* (Chicago: University of Chicago Press, 1973), p. 1.

46. Kenneth M. Dolbeare and Philip E. Hammond, *The School Prayer Decisions: From Court Policy to Local Practice* (Chicago: University of Chicago Press, 1971). The state, called *Midway* in the study, appears to be Indiana.

47. Richard M. Johnson, *The Dynamics of Compliance: Supreme Court Decision-Making from a New Perspective* (Evanston, Ill.: Northwestern University Press, 1967). Robert H. Birkby, "The Supreme Court and the Bible Belt: Tennessee Reaction to the

'Schempp' Decision," *Midwest Journal of Political Science* 10 (August 1966): 304–315. Dolbeare and Hammond, *The School Prayer Decisions,* p. 32.

48. American Book Publishers Council and the American Library Association, "The Freedom to Read," May 1953, reprinted in Robert B. Downs, ed., *The First Freedom* (Chicago: American Library Association, 1960).

49. ACLU, What's Ahead for American Liberties? Twenty-fifth Anniversary Conference, *Proceedings,* November 24, 1945, ACLUP, 1946, vol. 8.

50. ACLU, *Annual Report,* 1959, p. 15. Frank J. Delany, Solicitor, Post Office Department, letter to Forster, November 17, 1948, ACLUP, 1948, vol. 5. ACLU, *Annual Report,* 1953, p. 20; 1958, p. 15. Besig, interview.

51. ACLU, *Annual Report,* 1945, pp. 50–51; 1956, pp. 12–13; 1957, p. 44.

52. National Council on Freedom from Censorship, Minutes, April 2, 1948, Rice Papers, Box 69. ACLU, *Annual Report,* 1948, p. 51.

53. Alexander Meikeljohn, *Free Speech and Its Relation to Self-Government* (New York: Harper Bros., 1948).

54. ACLU, Board of Directors, Minutes, June 21, 1948. ACLU, *Annual Report,* 1949, pp. 71–72.

55. Ernst, letter to Forster, June 15, 1948, ACLUP, 1948, Box 24. Zechariah Chafee, Jr., *Free Speech in the United States* (Cambridge, Mass.: Harvard University Press, 1941), p. 530.

56. *Saia v. New York,* 334 U.S. 558 (1948). *Kovacs v. Cooper,* 336 U.S. 77 (1949).

57. *Public Utilities Commission v. Pollak,* 343 U.S. 451 (1952). ACLU, *Annual Report,* 1953, p. 38.

58. ACLU, *Annual Report,* 1949, p. 42.

59. *Terminello v. Chicago,* 337 U.S. 1 (1949). *Kunz v. New York,* 340 U.S. 290 (1951).

60. ACLU, Board of Directors, Minutes, October 23, 1950. *Feiner v. New York,* 340 U.S. 315 (1951); ACLU, Policy Committee, Minutes, August 15, 1950, ACLUP, 1951, vol. 50.

61. *Beauharnais v. Illinois,* 343 U.S. 250 (1952).

62. See Chapter Sixteen.

63. Ernst, Minority Report, Committee on Hollywood Writers, January 1948, Thomas Papers.

64. ACLU, "Report of the Committee on Libel per Se," April 17, 1947, ACLUP, 1947, vol. 10. ACLU, Board of Directors, Minutes, April 21, 1947. ACLU, Ad Hoc Committee on Libel, Minutes, December 19, 1951, ACLUP, 1952, vol. 1. ACLU, Board of Directors, Minutes, June 23, 1952.

65. ACLU, Board of Directors, Minutes, April 3, 1961. ACLU, *Annual Report,* 1965, p. 27.

66. Morris L. Ernst, *The First Freedom* (New York: Macmillan, 1946). ACLU, *Annual Report,* p. 54.

67. *Burstyn v. Wilson,* 343 U.S. 495 (1952). Garth Jowett, *Film: The Democratic Art* (Boston: Focal Press, 1976), pp. 404–408. Richard S. Randall, *Censorship of the Movies* (Madison: University of Wisconsin Press, 1976), pp. 28–32.

68. ACLU, Board of Directors, Minutes, March 3, 1952, March 17, 1952, March 31, 1952.

69. Jowett, *Film,* pp. 408–410. ACLU, *Annual Report,* 1954, pp. 14–16; 1955, pp. 14–16.

70. Jowett, *Film,* pp. 408–419.

71. ACLU, *Inside ACLU* (October 1959), ACLUP, 1959, Box 174.

72. ACLU, *Annual Report,* 1957, pp. 40–41.

73. Murray, *We Hold These Truths.* Drinan, *Religion, the Courts, and Public Policy.*

74. ACLU, *Annual Report,* 1958, p. 14. Speiser, interview. David Perlman, "How Captain Hanrahan Made 'Howl' a Best-Seller," *The Reporter,* December 12, 1957, pp. 37–39. *Life,* September 9, 1957.

75. Memos and Briefs, in ACLUP, 1962, Washington office files, Part C.

76. ACLU, *Annual Report,* 1957, p. 53.

77. ACLU, *Annual Report,* 1956, pp. 14–15.

78. ACLU, Censorship Panel, Minutes, November 28, 1956, December 18, 1956, ACLUP, 1957, Box 40. ACLU, *Annual Report,* 1957, p. 37.

79. A sketch of Roth's career appears in Gay Talese, *Thy Neighbor's Wife* (New York: Dell, 1981), pp. 112–131.

80. *Butler v. Michigan,* 352 U.S. 380 (1957).

81. *Roth v. United States,* 354 U.S. 476 (1957). ACLU, *Annual Report,* 1957, pp. 37–38.

82. Charles Rembar, *The End of Obscenity* (New York: Random House, 1968), pp. 55–58; see also his criticism of the ACLU's use of the clear and present danger standard as being too absolutist, on pp. 420–421.

83. ACLU, *Annual Report,* 1962, pp. 1–3.

84. *Kingsley International v. Regents,* 360 U.S. 684 (1959).

85. Rembar, *The End of Obscenity,* pp. 59–160.

86. *Jacobellis v. Ohio,* 378 U.S. 184 (1964). ACLU, *Annual Report,* 1964, p. 21.

87. *Freedman v. Maryland,* 380 U.S. 51 (1965).

88. *Redrup v. New York,* 386 U.S. 767 (1967). Rembar, *The End of Obscenity.*

89. *New York Times Co. v. Sullivan,* 376 U.S. 254 (1964). Harry Kalven, "The New York Times Case: A Note on the Central Meaning of the First Amendment," *Supreme Court Review 1964* (Chicago: University of Chicago Press, 1965).

90. Pemberton, interview.

Chapter 11

1. *Henderson v. United States,* 339 U.S. 816 (1950). ACLU, *Annual Report,* 1951, p. 50.

2. John Hope Franklin, *From Slavery to Freedom,* 3rd ed. (New York: Vintage Books, 1969). Loren Miller, *The Petitioners* (Cleveland: World Publishing, 1967).

3. ACLU, *Annual Report,* 1947, pp. 23–24.

4. President's Committee on Civil Rights, *To Secure These Rights* (New York: Simon & Schuster, 1947). On Morris Ernst's role, see Wechsler, interview (Nancy Wechsler, daughter of Osmond Fraenkel, served as staff counsel for the committee).

5. On *Henderson* and Marshall's uncertainty, see Richard Kluger, *Simple Justice* (New York: Vintage Books, 1977), pp. 275–284. ACLU, *Annual Report,* 1951, p. 50.

6. Levy, letter to Elliston, U.S. Information Service, May 1, 1951, ACLUP, 1951, vol. 47.

7. Clement E. Vose, *Caucasians Only: The Supreme Court, the NAACP, and the Re-*

strictive Covenant Cases (Berkeley and Los Angeles: University of California Press, 1959), pp. 193–197, 241–243. On the role of *amici* and the civil rights coalition by a major participant, see Leo Pfeffer, "Amici in Church–State Litigation," *Law and Contemporary Problems* 44 (Winter 1981): 83–110.

8. ACLU, *Annual Report,* 1947, p. 28; 1949, p. 29.

9. ACLU–Chicago Division, *The Brief,* October 1952, and February 1955. ACLU, *Annual Report,* 1956, p. 78.

10. ACLU, *Annual Report,* 1951, p. 54.

11. ACLU, *Annual Report,* 1957, pp. 80–81.

12. ACLU, *Annual Report,* 1960, pp. 44–45.

13. Harry Kalven, Jr., *The Negro and the First Amendment* (Chicago: University of Chicago Press, 1965), pp. 65–121.

14. *NAACP v. Alabama,* 357 U.S. 449 (1958). Pfeffer, "Amici," p. 106, n. 145.

15. Wulf, interview. Also see the discussion in Harry Kalven, Jr., *A Worthy Tradition* (New York: Harper & Row, 1988), pp. 258–263.

16. President's Committee, *To Secure These Rights,* pp. 164–165.

17. *Bates v. Little Rock,* 316 U.S. 516 (1960).

18. *Shelton v. Tucker,* 364 U.S. 479 (1960).

19. *NAACP v. Button,* 371 U.S. 415 (1963).

20. *Gibson v. Florida Legislative Investigating Comm.,* 372 U.S. 539 (1963).

21. Norton, interview.

22. Norton, interview. Eleanor Holmes Norton, "Defender of Unpopular Causes," *Ebony* 24 (January 1969): 37–38.

23. *Slochower v. Board of Education,* 350 U.S. 513 (1956). ACLU, Board of Directors, Minutes, December 1, 1952, August 13, 1956. Fraenkel, Diary, April 15, 1953. ACLU, *Annual Report,* 1956, p. 39.

24. *Pennsylvania v. Nelson,* 350 U.S. 497 (1956). ACLU, *Annual Report,* 1956, p. 25.

25. ACLU, *Annual Report,* 1955, pp. 33–34; 1956, p. 25. Anne Braden, *HUAC: Bulwark of Segregation* (National Committee to Abolish HUAC, 1963).

26. *Schware v. Board of Examiners,* 353 U.S. 232 (1957). *Konigsberg v. State Bar of California,* 353 U.S. 252 (1957). *Jencks v. U.S.,* 353 U.S. 657 (1957). ACLU, *Annual Report,* 1957, pp. 9–10, 21–22.

27. *Jencks v. U.S.,* 353 U.S. 657 (1957). *Yates v. U.S.,* 354 U.S. 298 (1957).

28. *Watkins v. U.S.,* 354 U.S. 178 (1957).

29. ACLU, *Annual Report,* 1957, p. 9.

30. C. Herman Pritchett, *Congress Versus the Supreme Court, 1957–1960* (Minneapolis: University of Minnesota Press, 1961).

31. *Kent v. Dulles,* 357 U.S. 116 (1958). *Trop v. Dulles,* 356 U.S. 86 (1958).

32. *Barenblatt v. United States,* 360 U.S. 109 (1959). *Uphaus v. Wyman,* 360 U.S. 72 (1959).

33. Hugo L. Black, "The Bill of Rights," *New York University Law Review* 35 (April 1960): 867.

34. Wilkinson, interview. Wilkinson was immediately disenchanted with the ECLC and returned to California as quickly as possible. He and others associated with the ECLC found it controlled by a small clique beholden to Corliss Lamont's money. It is largely for this reason that the ECLC never developed into a large national organization. See Wilkinson, letter to E. Monroe, March 25, 1958; John T. Gojak, letter to Wilkinson,

March 25, 1958; Eleanor F. Kirstein, letter to Lamont, May 29, 1958, NCARLP, Box 29.

35. Malin, Memo to Affiliates, July 18, 1957, ACLUP, 1961, vol. 57. ACLU, Board of Directors, Minutes, December 2, 1957. Wilkinson, interview. Fraenkel, Diary, April 2, 1957, November 17, 1957.

36. Wilkinson, interview. ACLU–SC, *Open Forum,* January 1959. ACLU, Board of Directors, Minutes, May 23, 1960. Walter Goodman, *The Committee* (New York: Farrar, Straus & Giroux, 1968), pp. 419–456.

37. *Speiser v. Randall,* 357 U.S. 513 (1958). Speiser, interview. *First Unitarian Church v. County of Los Angeles,* 357 U.S. 545 (1958).

38. *Wilkinson v. United States,* 365 U.S. 399 (1961). *Braden v. United States,* 365 U.S. 431 (1961) Wilkinson, interview. Goodman, *The Committee,* pp. 441–445.

39. *Albertson v. SACB,* 382 U.S. 70 (1965).

40. *Lamont v. Postmaster General,* 381 U.S. 301 (1965). *Dombrowski v. Pfister,* 380 U.S. 479 (1965).

41. ACLU, Memo to Affiliates, October 15, 1948, ACLUP, 1948, vol. 4, addendum; Rundquist, Memo to Affiliates, January 21, 1949, ACLUP, 1949, vol. 6.

42. ACLU–Chicago Division, *Civil Liberties Brief,* May 8, 1947. ACLU–SC, *Open Forum,* December 27, 1947, April 28, 1951.

43. ACLU–GrPh, *Civil Liberties Record* 7 (July 1958). Coxe, interview.

44. Rundquist, letter to Forer, September 8, 1952, ACLUP, 1952, vol. 3; Forer, Memo to Police Practices Committee, July 31, 1952, ACLU–GrPh, Box 25, Forer, interview.

45. Samuel Walker, *Popular Justice: A History of American Criminal Justice* (New York: Oxford University Press, 1980).

46. Manuscript, "Suggested Revisions Phila Police Manual," ACLU–GrPh, Box 25. Forer, interview. Coxe, interview.

47. Forer, Memo, October 24, 1952, ACLU–GrPh, Box 25.

48. NYCLU, "If You Are Arrested . . . What Are Your Rights?" originally published in NYCLU, *Civil Liberties in New York,* September, 1955; Josephine Scheiber to Coxe, June 12, 1956, ACLU–GrPh, Box 25.

49. Coxe, memo to ACLU–GrPh Board of Directors, May 29, 1957.

50. Coxe, letter to Ernst, November 24, 1958, ACLU–GrPh, Box 26.

51. Spencer Coxe, "The Police Review Board of the City of Philadelphia—A Description and Appraisal," October 2, 1959, ACLUP, 1959, Box 174.

52. Coxe, interview.

53. ACLU–Chicago Division, *The Brief,* May 8, 1947, May 1954. Memos, ACLU–ILDP.

54. ACLU–Illinois Division, *Secret Detention by the Chicago Police* (Glencoe, Ill.: Free Press, 1959), pp. 24–26, 28.

55. Ibid., pp. 32–33.

56. W. Douglas, letter to Sprayragen, March 17, 1959; Douty, letter to Dilliard, editor, *St. Louis Post-Dispatch,* March 19, 1959; Lt. Diamond, NYPD, letter to ACLU, March 3, 1959; *New York Herald Tribune,* February 27, 1959; *Chicago Sun-Times,* March 11, 1958, ACLU–Chi, Box 77. Memo, ca. 1959, ACLUP–Chi, Box 78. Police and Criminal Law Committee, Minutes, November 11, 1960; ACLU–Chi, Box 108.

57. ACLU–Illinois Division, *Secret Detention.*

58. *Mapp v. Ohio,* 367 U.S. 643 (1961).

59. Louis Lusky, *By What Right* (Charlottesville: Michie, 1975), p. 161. Fred W. Friendly and Martha J. H. Elliott, *The Constitution: That Delicate Balance* (New York: Random House, 1984), p. 139.

60. Walker, *Popular Justice,* pp. 221–239.

61. *Escobedo v. Illinois,* 378 U.S. 478 (1964). On Weisberg's career, see Yale Kamisar, *Police Interrogation and Confessions* (Ann Arbor: University of Michigan Press, 1980), pp. 107–110.

62. *Miranda v. Arizona,* 384 U.S. 436 (1966). Liva Baker, *Miranda: Crime, Law and Politics* (New York: Atheneum, 1983). Kamisar, *Police Interrogation.*

63. Kamisar, *Police Interrogation,* pp. 108–109.

64. Michael Meltsner, *Cruel and Unusual: The Supreme Court and Capital Punishment* (New York: Random House, 1973).

65. Note, "The Exclusionary Rule and Deterrence: An Empirical Study of Chicago Narcotics Officers," *University of Chicago Law Review* 54 (1987): 1016–1069. Samuel Walker, "Controlling the Cops: A Legislative Approach to Police Rulemaking," *University of Detroit Law Review* 63 (Spring 1986): 361–391.

66. Samuel Walker, *The Police in America: An Introduction* (New York: McGraw-Hill, 1983).

67. Theodore H. White, *The Making of the President 1968* (New York: Pocket Books, 1970).

68. James F. Simon, *In His Own Image: The Supreme Court in Richard Nixon's America* (New York: McKay, 1974). Vincent Blasi, *The Burger Court: The Counter-Revolution That Wasn't* (New Haven, Conn.: Yale University Press, 1983).

69. Anthony Lewis, *Gideon's Trumpet* (New York: Vintage Books, 1966).

70. Ibid., pp. 151–152. Norman Dorsen, *Frontiers of Civil Liberties* (New York: Pantheon, 1968), pp. 193–211.

71. Yale Kamisar, "Equal Justice in the Gatehouses and Mansions of American Criminal Procedure," in Kamisar, *Police Interrogation,* pp. 27–40.

72. The phrase comes from Jonathan Casper, *Criminal Justice: The Defendant's Perspective* (Englewood Cliffs, N.J.: Prentice-Hall, 1972).

73. *In re Gault,* 387 U.S. 1 (1967). Dorsen, *Frontiers,* pp. 213–232. Dorsen, interview. Sam Epstein and Beryl Epstein, *Kids in Court: The ACLU Defends Their Rights* (New York: Four Winds Press, 1982), pp. 29–38.

74. Dorsen, interview. Ira Glasser, "Prisoners of Benevolence: Power Versus Liberty in the Welfare State," in Willard Gaylin et al., eds., *Doing Good: The Limits of Benevolence* (New York: Pantheon, 1978), pp. 91–168. Bernard Flexner and Roger N. Baldwin, *Juvenile Courts and Probation* (New York: Century, 1916).

75. Glasser, "Prisoners of Benevolence."

76. Goldberg, quoted in Herman Benson, "The Fight for Union Democracy," in Seymour M. Lipset, ed., *Unions in Transition* (San Francisco: Institute for Contemporary Studies, 1986), p. 348.

77. ACLU, *Trade Union Democracy* (April 1952), ACLUP, 1952, Box 63. ACLU, *Statement on the Kennedy–Ives Bill,* September 1958, ACLUP, 1959, vol. 70.

78. ACLU, *Statement on the Kennedy–Ives Bill,* p. 351. Joseph L. Rauh, Jr., "Twenty-five Years of Landrum Griffin," *Union Democracy Review,* September 1984, pp. 1–4.

79. ACLU, *Annual Report,* 1947, p. 67.

80. *Colegrove v. Green,* 328 U.S. 549 (1946). Richard C. Cortner, *The Reapportionment Cases* (Knoxville: University of Tennessee Press, 1970), chap. 1.

81. *Baker v. Carr,* 369 U.S. 186 (1962). Pemberton, interview.

82. *Reynolds v. Sims,* 377 U.S. 533 (1964). Cortner, *The Reapportionment Cases,* p. 207.

Chapter 12

1. Anthony Lewis, *Portrait of a Decade* (New York: Bantam, 1965), pp. 72–87. Walter Goodman, *The Committee* (New York: Farrar, Straus & Giroux, 1968), pp. 450–456.

2. William L. O'Neill, *Coming Apart: An Informal History of America in the 1960's* (Chicago: Quadrangle Books, 1971). Todd Gitlin, *The Sixties: Years of Hope, Days of Rage* (New York: Bantam, 1987).

3. Ralph Tyler, "Why It Happened in San Francisco," *Frontier,* June 1960, pp. 5–9.

4. Quoted in Lawrence Lader, *Abortion II: Making the Revolution* (Boston: Beacon Press, 1973), p. 54.

5. ACLU, Board of Directors, Minutes, February 29, 1960. ACLU–NC, Board of Directors, Minutes, July 2, 1959, June 9, 1960.

6. Gertrude Samuels, "The Fight for Civil Liberties Never Stays Won," *New York Times Magazine,* June 19, 1966. Neier, interview. Glasser, interview. Schwarzschild, interview.

7. ACLU, *Annual Report,* 1960, pp. 4, 73–74.

8. For illuminating insights based on the NAACP and the NAACP–LDF experience, see Stephen L. Wasby, "How Planned Is 'Planned Litigation'?" *American Bar Foundation Research Journal* (Winter 1984): 83–138.

9. Joseph W. Bishop, Jr., *Obiter Dicta* (New York: Atheneum, 1971). Richard E. Morgan, *Disabling America: The "Rights Industry" in Our Time* (New York: Basic Books, 1984).

10. William Kunstler, *Deep in My Heart* (New York: Morrow, 1966), pp. 3–4.

11. ACLU, Board of Directors, Minutes, February 29, March 28, 1960. Fraenkel, Diary, March 28, 1960. ACLU, *Annual Report,* 1960, pp. 47–48.

12. Southern Regional Council, "Direct Action in the South," *New South* 18 (October–November 1963): 4.

13. ACLU, *Annual Report,* 1960, pp. 47–48. ACLU–NC, Board of Directors, Minutes, December 8, 1960, ACLU–NCP.

14. ACLU, *Annual Report,* 1960, p. 47; 1961, pp. 48–49.

15. Arthur M. Schlesinger, Jr., *A Thousand Days* (New York: Fawcett Crest, 1967), pp. 874–882.

16. See the illiminating comments on Justice Department lawyers in Victor Navasky, *Kennedy Justice* (New York: Atheneum, 1971), pp. 193–194.

17. ACLU, *How Americans Protest: A Statement on the Civil Rights Demonstrations* (August 1963).

18. James W. Silver, *The Closed Society* (New York: Harcourt Brace, 1964).

19. ACLU, Board of Directors, Minutes, September 24, 1962.

20. ACLU, Board of Directors, Minutes, August 13, 1962, February 4, 1963. Wulf, interview. Kunstler, *Deep in My Heart,* pp. 118–119.

21. National Lawyers Guild, Convention Report on the Committee to Assist Southern Lawyers, ca. 1964, in Arthur Kinoy, *Rights on Trial* (Cambridge, Mass.: Harvard University Press, 1983), p. 213.

22. Pemberton, Memo to Affiliates, July 5, 1963, ACLUP, 1965, Box 403. Pemberton,

Memo to ACLU National Development Council, March 30, 1965, ACLUP–NY. Pemberton, interview. Schwarzschild, interview.

23. Pemberton, interview. Schwarzschild, interview.

24. Charles Morgan, Jr., *A Time to Speak* (New York: Holt, Rinehart and Winston, 1964).

25. LCDC, Docket, September 7, 1965, ACLU–NY. See also accounts in Leon H. Friedman, ed., *Southern Justice* (Cleveland: World Publishing, 1967).

26. Hirschkop, interview.

27. Pemberton, interview. Wulf, interview.

28. Bronstein, LCDC Docket, April 1965, ACLUP–NY. Samuels, "The Fight for Civil Liberties."

29. ACLU, Board of Directors, Minutes, April 13, 1964. ACLU, *Policy Guide,* 1965, Policy 519. Schwarzschild, interview. ACLU, *Civil Liberties* (May 1965).

30. Schwarzschild, interview. Ripston, interview. Bronstein, interview. Levine quoted in ACLU, Executive Committee, Transcript of Minutes, January, 1977, ANP. Levine, interview.

31. Fraenkel, Diary, June 23, 1964. ACLU, Summary Report of the 1964 ACLU Biennial Conference, July 9, 1964, ACLUP, 1964, vol. 71.

32. ACLU, Summary Report.

33. Ibid., pp. 1–2. ACLU, *Annual Report,* 1963, p. 95; 1965, p. 101.

34. Neier, Memo to National Development Council Steering Committee, July 31, 1964, ACLUP, 1965, vol. 26. Monroe, Memo to National Planning Committee, January 26, 1965, ACLUP–NY. Neier, interview. Gottfried, interview.

35. ACLU, Summary Report of the 1964 ACLU Biennial Conference, pp. 1–8. Pemberton, interview. Baldwin, letter to Angell and Pemberton, June 4, 1964, ACLUP, 1964, Box 372.

36. ACLU, Summary Report of the 1964 Biennial Conference, p. 4.

37. Pilpel, paper, "Civil Liberties and the War on Crime," ACLU Biennial, ACLUP, 1964, vol. 71. Pilpel, interview.

38. Johnson, letter to ACLU, June 19, 1964, in Summary Report of the 1964 Biennial Conference. Johnson, letter to ACLU, in *Civil Liberties* (September 1966).

39. ACLU, Board of Directors, Minutes, August 13, 1962. Wulf, interview. On the Kennedy style, see Navasky, *Kennedy Justice,* pp. 193–194. For an apology for the Kennedys, see Arthur M. Schlesinger, Jr., *Robert Kennedy and His Times* (New York: Ballantine, 1979), pp. 307–340.

40. Charles Morgan, Jr., *One Man, One Voice* (New York: Holt, Rinehart and Winston, 1979), p. 3.

41. Morgan, *A Time to Speak.* The speech was published in *Current,* November 1963, pp. 32–33 (edited by Ira Glasser, later director of the NYCLU and then the ACLU).

42. Morgan, interview. Pemberton in Samuels, "The Fight for Civil Liberties." For an estimate of direct representation, see Emil Oxfeld in symposium, *Civil Liberties,* March–April 1968.

43. ACLU, Five Year Report of the Southern Regional Office, October 3, 1969, p. 12. ACLUP, 1969, vol. 34, p. 29. Morgan, *One Man, One Voice.* Morgan, interview.

44. ACLU, Five Year Report. Morgan, interview. Neier, interview.

45. *White v. Crook,* 251 F. Supp. 401 (M.D. Ala. 1966). Morgan, *One Man, One Voice,* pp. 24–47.

46. ACLU, Five Year Report, p. 13. Sarah Evans, *Personal Politics* (New York: Vintage Books, 1980).

47. Morgan, *One Man, One Voice,* pp. 29–30. See Gerald M. Stern, "Judge William Harold Cox and the Right to Vote in Clarke County, Mississippi," in Friedman, ed., *Southern Justice,* pp. 165–186.

48. *Whitus v. Georgia,* 385 U.S. 545 (1967). Morgan, *One Man, One Voice,* pp. 85, 87.

49. Schwarzschild, interview. Morgan, interview.

50. Morgan, *One Man, One Voice,* pp. 79–90.

51. *Lee v. Washington,* 390 U.S. 333 (1968). Morgan, interview. Hirschkop, interview. Philip J. Hirschkop, "The Rights of Prisoners," in Norman Dorsen, ed., *The Rights of Americans* (New York: Vintage Books, 1972), pp. 451–468.

52. Quoted in Morgan, *One Man, One Voice,* p. 150.

53. Ibid., pp. 150–161.

54. *Bond v. Floyd,* 385 U.S. 116 (1983).

55. Morgan, *One Man, One Voice,* pp. 114–149.

56. Ibid.

57. Ibid.

58. Ibid., pp. 139, 253. Morgan, interview. Glasser, interview.

59. Ibid., pp. 162–182.

60. ACLU, Five Year Report.

61. Morgan, interview. Pemberton, interview.

62. Pemberton, interview. Isbell, interview.

63. ACLU, Five Year Report.

64. Pemberton, interview.

65. ACLU, *Annual Report,* 1964, pp. 45–46.

66. ACLU–NC, Executive Committee, Minutes, March 5, 1959, September 17, 1959, February 2, 1960. Max Heirich and Sam Kaplan, "Yesterday's Discord," in Seymour M. Lipset and Sheldin Wolin, eds., *The Berkeley Student Revolt* (Garden City, N.Y.: Anchor Books, 1965), pp. 10–35.

67. Documents and analyses in Lipset and Wolin, *The Berkeley Student Revolt.*

68. Neier, memo to ACLU National Development Council, July 31, 1964, ACLUP, 1965, vol. 26. Paul G. Chevigny, "A Busy Spring in the Magnolia State," in Friedman, ed., *Southern Justice,* pp. 13–34.

69. Figures in ACLU, *Police Powers and Citizens' Rights: The Case for an Independent Police Review Board* (1966). Ronald Kahn, "Urban Reform and Police Accountability in New York City: 1950–1974," in Robert L. Lineberry and Louis H. Masotti, eds., *Urban Problems and Public Policy* (Lexington, Mass.: Lexington Books, 1975), pp. 107–127.

70. Paul Chevigny, *Police Power: Police Abuses in New York City* (New York: Vintage Books, 1969), statistical data, pp. 285–287; conclusions, pp. 248–275; quotation, p. 265. Paul Chevigny, *Cops and Rebels: A Study of Provocation* (New York: Curtis Books, 1972). ACLU of Southern California, *Law Enforcement: The Matter of Redress* (1969).

71. "The ACLU and the Urban Ghetto," *Civil Liberties,* September 1970, p. 6.

72. Ibid., pp. 3–6. For a critical view, see *Barron's,* September 9, 1968.

73. For reflections on this development, see Aryeh Neier, *Only Judgement: The Limits of Litigation in Social Change* (Middletown, Conn.: Wesleyan University Press, 1982).

74. For the documents and chronology, see Maurice R. Berube and Marilyn Gittell, eds., *Confrontation at Ocean Hill–Brownsville* (New York: Praeger, 1969).

75. NYCLU, *The Burden of Blame,* October 9, 1968, ACLUP, 1968, Box 486; reprinted in Berube and Gittell, eds., *Confrontation,* pp. 104–119. Glasser, interview. Neier, interview. Hentoff, interview.

76. Meyers, interview. ACLU, Memo to Board, November 5, 1969, ACLUP, vol. 11. *Civil Liberties* (April 1971).

77. Clark Whelton, "NYCLU's Trial from Within," *Village Voice,* March 27, 1969; reprinted in NYCLU, *Civil Liberties in New York* (May 1969).

78. Committee to Support the New York Civil Liberties Union, letter to NYCLU members, June 6, 1969, ACLUP, 1969, Box 534. NYCLU, *Civil Liberties in New York* (November 1967).

79. Hentoff, interview. Glasser, interview. Dorsen, interview.

Chapter 13

1. ACLU, *Annual Report,* 1971, p. 11. Public Law Education Institute, *Selective Service Law Reporter* 6 (April 1968). Steven E. Barkan, *Protesters on Trial: Criminal Justice in the Southern Civil Rights and Vietnam Antiwar Movements* (New Brunswick, N.J.: Rutgers University Press, 1985), pp. 87–104.

2. John F. Bannan and Rosemary S. Bannan, *Law, Morality and Vietnam: The Peace Militants and the Courts* (Bloomington: Indiana University Press, 1974), pp. 40–62. *David Miller v. United States,* 367 F.2d 72 (DCSDNY 1966). Fraenkel, Diary, October 25, 1965.

3. *United States v. O'Brien,* 391 U.S. 367 (1968). Dean Alfange, Jr., "Free Speech and Symbolic Conduct: The Draft Card Burning Case," in Philip B. Kurland, ed., *Free Speech and Association: The Supreme Court and the First Amendment* (Chicago: University of Chicago Press, 1975), pp. 250–301.

4. *Bond v. Floyd,* 385 U.S. 116 (1966).

5. *Tinker v. Des Moines School District,* 393 U.S. 503 (1969). Nat Hentoff, *The First Freedom* (New York: Delacorte, 1980), pp. 3–7.

6. *Street v. New York,* 394 U.S. 576 (1969). *Spence v. Washington,* 418 U.S. 405 (1974). Douglas Honig and Laura Breener, *On Freedom's Frontier: The First Fifty Years of the American Civil Liberties Union in Washington State* (Seattle: ACLU–W, 1987), p. 54. *Cohen v. California,* 403 U.S. 15 (1971).

7. *Brandenburg v. Ohio,* 395 U.S. 444 (1969).

8. ACLU, *Annual Report,* 1967, pp. 34–35. *Oestereich v. Selective Service Board,* 393 U.S. 233 (1968). *Breen v. Selective Service Board,* 396 U.S. 460 (1970).

9. *United States v. Seeger,* 380 U.S. 163 (1965). ACLU, *Annual Report,* 1965, p. 41.

10. *Civil Liberties* (April 1967). Pemberton, interview.

11. Todd Gitlin, *The Sixties* (New York: Bantam, 1987). Jim Miller, *Democracy Is in the Streets* (New York: Simon & Schuster, 1987).

12. *Civil Liberties in New York* (January 1968), (February 1968).

13. ACLU, Board of Directors, Minutes, October 5–6, 1968. ACLU, *Policy Guide,* Policy 40.

14. D. Isbell, letter to Angell, January 23, 1968, ACLUP, 1968, Box 486. Fraenkel, Diary, January 25, 1968, February 6, 1968.

15. ACLU, Board of Directors, Minutes, January 30, 1966.

16. ACLU, Board of Directors, Minutes, April 3, 1969, December 5–7, 1969, February 14–15, 1970. ACLU, *Policy Guide,* Policy 69.

17. I. Wallerstein, ed., *University Crisis Reader* (New York: Random House, 1971), vol. 1.

18. Fabricant, Chevigny, Neuborne, Levine, letter to Pemberton, *New York Times,* April 4, 1969; reprinted in *Civil Liberties in New York* (May 1969), p. 2.

19. Jessica Mitford, *The Trial of Dr. Spock* (New York: Knopf, 1969).

20. Fraenkel, Diary, January 10, 1968.

21. Ibid. ACLU, Board of Directors, Minutes, January 12, 1968. Wulf, interview.

22. Mitford, *The Trial of Dr. Spock,* especially app. 6, "The Role of the American Civil Liberties Union in the Case of the Boston Five."

23. Fraenkel, Diary, January 17, 1968.

24. ACLU, Board of Directors, Minutes, March 2, 1968.

25. ACLU, Board of Directors, Minutes, May 9, 1968; Neier, interview. Wulf, interview.

26. Symposium, ACLU: Friend of the Court or Counsel to the Accused? *Civil Liberties* (March–April 1968), pp. 6–8.

27. Wulf, memo to ACLU Executive Committee, May 26, 1970, ACLUP, 1970, vol. 10.

28. ACLU, *Civil Liberties* (February 1979), p. 1.

29. ACLU, Board of Directors, Minutes, June 2, 1970. ACLU, *Policy Guide,* Policy 116.

30. *Massachusetts v. Laird,* 451 F.2d (1st Cir. 1971).

31. *Berk v. Laird,* 429 F.Supp. 302 (2d Cir. 1970). *Orlando v. Laird,* 443 F.2d 1039 (2d Cir. 1971). Aryeh Neier, *Only Judgment: The Limits of Litigation in Social Change* (Middletown, Conn.: Wesleyan University Press, 1982), pp. 141–153. Leon Friedman and Burt Neuborne, *Unquestioning Obedience to the President* (New York: Norton, 1972).

32. *Holtzman v. Schlesinger,* 361 F. Supp. 553 (E.D. N.Y. 1973), rev'd, 484 F.2d 1307 (2d Cir. 1973). Neier, *Only Judgment,* p. 151. Neuborne, interview. Siegel, interview.

33. Neier, *Only Judgment.* Friedman and Neuborne, *Unquestioning Obedience.* Neuborne, interview.

34. Theodore H. White, *The Making of the President 1968* (New York: Pocket Books, 1970).

35. ACLU, Five Year Report of the Southern Regional Office, October 3, 1965, ACLUP, 1969, vol. 34, pp. 28–29.

36. Charles Morgan, Jr., *One Man, One Voice* (New York: Holt, Rinehart and Winston, 1979), p. 206.

37. Neier in ACLU, *Annual Report,* 1970–1971.

38. ACLU, *ACLU Lawyer,* December 1979, p. 2.

39. Fred Powledge, *The Engineering of Restraint: The Nixon Administration and the Press* (New York: ACLU, 1971).

40. Ibid., p. 31.

41. Halperin, interview.

42. Sanford J. Ungar, *The Papers and the Papers* (New York: Dutton, 1972).

43. *Near v. Minnesota,* 283 U.S. 697 (1931).

44. *New York Times Co. v. United States,* 403 U.S. 713 (1971).

45. John Shattuck, "National Security a Decade After Watergate," *democracy,* Winter 1983, p. 63.

46. Victor Marchetti and John D. Marks, *The CIA and the Cult of Intelligence* (New York: Dell, 1975), esp. "Introduction" by ACLU legal director Mel Wulf.

47. Howard Morland, *The Secret That Exploded* (New York: Random House, 1981). *Civil Liberties* (June 1979), (November 1979).

48. Neier, Memo to ACLU Executive Committee on Priorities, September 13, 1971, ACLUP, 1971, vol. 11.

49. Roger Wilkins, letter to Ennis, October 27, 1971, ACLUP, 1971, vol. 11. Neier, interview.

50. The conference proceedings in Pat Watters and Stephen Gillers, eds., *Investigating the FBI* (New York: Ballantine, 1973).

51. Hoover, letter to Duane Lockard, October 7, 1971, in ibid., pp. 415–423.

52. Conference proceedings in Norman Dorsen and Stephen Gillers, eds., *None of Your Business: Government Secrecy in America* (New York: Penguin, 1975).

53. Peter Schrag, *Test of Loyalty: Daniel Ellsberg and the Rituals of Secret Government* (New York: Simon & Schuster, 1974), pp. 294, 300.

54. Schrag, *Test of Loyalty*, p. 296.

55. Thomas I. Emerson, *The System of Freedom of Expression* (New York: Vintage Books, 1971).

56. Vincent Blasi, "The Checking Value in First Amendment Theory," *American Bar Foundation Research Journal*, Summer 1977, pp. 521–649.

57. *Laird v. Tatum*, 408 U.S. 1 (1972).

58. ACLU, *Annual Report*, 1972–1973.

59. The ad first appeared on the last page of Sec. 4 of the Sunday *New York Times*, October 14, 1973.

60. Morgan, *One Man, One Voice*.

61. Ibid. E. Monroe, letter to "Dear Congressman," April 9, 1971, ACLUP, 1971, vol. 9. ACLU, Board of Directors, Minutes, June 12–13, 1971.

62. Morgan, interview. Ennis, interview. Morgan, *One Man, One Voice*.

63. Drinan in *Civil Liberties Review* 1 (Fall 1973): 75–95.

64. ACLU–Michigan, Memo to ACLU Board, September 23, 1973; Glasser, Memo to ACLU Board, September 27, 1973, ACLUP, 1973, vol. 9.

65. Wolman, Memo to ACLU Board, September 21, 1973, ACLUP, 1973, vol. 9.

66. While spending the year at Berkeley, Dorsen was shocked at the prevailing view among the law faculty that the ACLU was too "political" and "too left wing." Dorsen, letter to Neier, September 5, 1974, ANP.

67. ACLU, Board of Directors, Minutes, September 29, 1973.

68. ACLU, *Annual Report*, 1972–1973.

69. Cleland to Ennis et al., October 22, 1973; Besser, letter to Ennis, October 31, 1973, ACLUP, 1973, vol. 9.

70. Brief *Amicus Curiae* of the American Civil Liberties Union, *United States v. Nixon*, 418 U.S. 683 (1974).

71. *United States v. Nixon*, 418 U.S. 683 (1974).

72. Neier, letter to ACLU members, in *Civil Liberties* (November 1974).

73. Morton Halperin et al., *The Lawless State: The Crimes of the U.S. Intelligence Agencies* (New York: Penguin, 1976). It is based on the Church Committee's work, officially *Hearings and Final Reports of the Select Committee to Study Governmental*

Operations with Respect to Intelligence Activities, U.S. Senate, 94th Cong., 1st and 2d sess., 1976.

74. Berman, Halperin, Shattuck, testimony, "Controlling the FBI, Senate Judiciary Committee," *Hearings,* April 25, 1978, reprinted as *ACLU Reports* (1978). The fate of intelligence agency reform can be traced in Center for National Security Studies, *First Principles,* from the late 1970s through the early 1980s.

75. Shattuck, "National Security," pp. 56–71.

76. *Handschu v. Special Services Division,* 349 F. Supp. 766 (S.D.N.Y. 1972).

77. Allan Adler and Jay Peterzell, "Courts Curtail Political Surveillance by Police Intelligence Units," *First Principles* 6 (March–April 1981).

78. Samuel Walker, "The Politics of Police Accountability: The Seattle Police Spying Ordinance As a Case Study," in Vincent Webb and Erika Fairchild, eds., *The Politics of Criminal Justice* (Beverly Hills, Calif.: Sage, 1985), pp. 144–157. Taylor, interview.

Chapter 14

1. Ira Glasser, "Schools for Scandal—The Bill of Rights and Public Education," *Phi Delta Kappan,* December 1969, pp. 190–194. Ira Glasser, "Repressive Institutions," *Trial Magazine,* June–July 1970, pp. 28–29.

2. Aryeh Neier, *Only Judgment: The Limits of Litigation in Social Change* (Middletown, Conn.: Wesleyan University Press, 1982), pp. 129–130. Neier, interview. Glasser, interview. Neuborne, interview.

3. On the "rights explosion," see the articles in *Yale Law Journal* 79 (1970); and Burton A. Weisbrod et al., eds., *Public Interest Law: An Economic and Institutional Analysis* (Berkeley and Los Angeles: University of California Press, 1978).

4. ACLU–SC, *Open Forum* (September 1969), p. 1.

5. ACLU–NC, Executive Committee, Minutes, December 8, 1966.

6. Richard Rovere, "The Invasion of Privacy: Technology and the Claims of Community," *American Scholar* 27 (1958): 416.

7. Alan F. Westin, *Privacy and Freedom* (New York: Atheneum, 1967).

8. ACLU, Board of Directors, Minutes, August 17, 1959. ACLU, *Annual Report,* 1960, pp. 30–31.

9. *Poe v. Ullman,* 367 U.S. 497 (1961).

10. *Griswold v. Connecticut,* 381 U.S. 479 (1965).

11. Robert Bork, "Neutral Principles and Some First Amendment Problems," *Indiana Law Journal* 47 (1971): 1.

12. Lawrence Lader, *Abortion* (Boston: Beacon Press, 1966), p. 1.

13. Ibid., pp. 10–16.

14. Harriet Pilpel, "Civil Liberties and the War on Crime" (paper delivered at the ACLU Biennial Conference, June 1964), ACLUP, 1964, vol. 71. Pilpel, interview.

15. Pilpel, testimony, New York State Assembly, Committee on Health, in NYCLU, *Civil Liberties in New York* (April 1966), p. 3. Neier, *Only Judgment,* pp. 114–116.

16. ACLU, Board of Directors, Minutes, June 16, 1967, January 25, 1968.

17. Lader, *Abortion.*

18. Lawrence Lader, *Abortion II: The Making of a Revolution* (Boston: Beacon Press, 1973).

19. Wulf, Memo re ACLU *amicus* in *Belous v. California*, February 13, 1969, ACLU–NY.

20. *United States v. Vuitch*, 402 U.S. 62 (1971). Dorsen, interview.

21. *Roe v. Wade*, 410 U.S. 113 (1973).

22. ACLU, Board of Directors, Minutes, February 17, 1973. *Doe v. Bolton*, 410 U.S. 179 (1973).

23. Frederick S. Jaffe et al., *Abortion Politics* (New York: McGraw-Hill, 1981). Lader, *Abortion II.*

24. ACLU, *Annual Report,* 1974, p. 6.

25. *Eisenstadt v. Baird*, 405 U.S. 438 (1972).

26. *Bellotti v. Baird*, 443 U.S. 622 (1979). *Planned Parenthood v. Danforth*, 428 U.S. 52 (1976). Robert H. Mnookin, "A Hard Case," in Robert H. Mnookin, ed., *In the Interest of Children* (New York: Freeman, 1985), pp. 149–264.

27. ACLU, Board of Directors, Minutes, April 1, 1963.

28. Kenyon and Murray, Memo to ACLU Board, September 24, 1970, ACLUP, 1970, vol. 10.

29. ACLU, Board of Directors, Minutes, September 26, 1970, October 1971. *Civil Liberties* (February 1972), p. 2.

30. *Reed v. Reed,* 404 U.S. 71 (1971).

31. *Frontiero v. Richardson*, 411 U.S. 677 (1973).

32. *Taylor v. Louisiana*, 419 U.S. 522 (1975). On *White v. Crook,* see Pauli Murray and Mary Eastwood, "Jane Crow," *George Washington Law Review,* 34 (December 1965): 232. Correspondence, Eastwood Papers, Box 1.

33. Ginsburg in *ACLU Women's Rights Report* 2 (Spring 1980): 5.

34. Karen O'Connor, *Women's Organizations' Use of the Courts* (Lexington: Lexington Books, 1980).

35. Kenyon apologizes for "temper tantrum": Kenyon, letter to ACLU Board, December 23, 1968, ACLUP–NY. Hirschkop, interview. Post, interview.

36. Aaron Wildavsky, "Foreword," in William A. Donohue, *The Politics of the American Civil Liberties Union* (New Brunswick, N.J.: Transaction Books, 1985).

37. Ira Glasser, "Affirmative Action and the Legacy of Racial Injustice," in Phyllis A. Katz and Dalmas A. Taylor, *Eliminating Racism* (New York: Plenum, 1988), pp. 341–357.

38. ACLU, Board of Directors, Minutes, September 24, 1977. ACLU, *1976 Biennial Conference Report,* June 10–13, 1976, ACLUP, 1976, vol. 5.

39. Glasser, "Schools for Scandal," pp. 190–194. Special supplement on students' rights, *Civil Liberties in New York* (March 1968), pp. 4–5, 7.

40. Spencer Coxe, "The Great Hair Problem," *Youth,* June 18, 1967; reprinted by ACLU (October 1967).

41. *Civil Liberties in New York* (April 1969), p. 4. Howard L. Hurwitz, "Student Rights: ACLU Formula for School Disruption," *Human Events,* September 13, 1975, pp. 8–9.

42. *Civil Liberties in New York* (June 1969), p. 5. Glasser, "Schools for Scandal," p. 191.

43. *Tinker v. Des Moines School District,* 393 U.S. 503 (1969).

44. *Goss v. Lopez,* 419 U.S. 565 (1975).

45. The most sophisticated reflections on ACLU litigation are found in Neier, *Only Judgment.*

46. Richard E. Morgan, *Disabling America: The "Rights Industry" in Our Time* (New York: Basic Books, 1984).

47. Aryeh Neier. *Dossier: The Secret Files They Keep on You* (New York: Stein & Day, 1975), p. 17.

48. Robert Ellis Smith, *Privacy: How to Protect What's Left of It* (Garden City, N.Y.: Anchor Books, 1979). Smith headed the short-lived ACLU Privacy Project in the early 1970s.

49. Neier, *Dossier,* p. 162.

50. Ibid. Stanton Wheeler, ed., *On Record: Files and Dossiers in American Life* (New York: Russell Sage Foundation, 1969).

51. Smith, *Privacy.*

52. Trudy Haden and Jack Novik, *Your Rights to Privacy* [ACLU Handbook] (New York: Avon Books, 1980).

53. Peter Andrews, "ACLU—Let There Be Law," *Playboy,* October 1971. Neier, *Only Judgment,* pp. 170–193. Bruce Ennis, *Prisoners of Psychiatry* (New York: Harcourt Brace Jovanovich, 1972).

54. Memos and correspondence, ACLUP, 1953, vol. 61.

55. ACLU, *Annual Report,* 1945, pp. 56–57.

56. Thomas Szasz, "The ACLU's 'Mental Illness' Cop-Out," *Reason,* January 1974, pp. 4–9.

57. On the conflicting objectives of reformers, see Neier, *Only Judgment,* pp. 179–183.

58. Thomas Szasz, *Psychiatric Slavery* (New York: Free Press, 1977).

59. David J. Rothman and Shelia M. Rothman, *The Willowbrook Wars* (New York: Harper & Row, 1984).

60. *New York Times,* January 22, 1989.

61. Note, "Beyond the Ken of the Courts: A Critique of Judicial Refusal to Review the Complaints of Convicts," *Yale Law Journal* 72 (1963): 506.

62. ACLU, *Annual Report,* 1962, p. 26.

63. *Lee v. Washington,* 390 U.S. 333 (1968).

64. Herman Schwartz, interview. Neier, interview. See the contributions to the fifteenth anniversary issue of the ACLU National Prison Project, in *National Prison Project Journal,* Fall 1987.

65. Hirschkop, interview.

66. Michael Millemann, "VA Prisoners Find Advocates in Early Prison Reformers," *National Prison Journal,* Fall 1987, pp. 3–4.

67. Phil Hirschkop and Michael Millemann, "The Unconstitutionality of Prison Life," *Virginia Law Review* 55 (1969): 795. Phil Hirschkop, "The Rights of Prisoners," in Norman Dorsen, ed., *The Rights We Have: What They Are—What They Should Be* (New York: Vintage Books, 1972), pp. 451–468.

68. Neier, interview. Bronstein, interview.

69. Sheldon Krantz, *The Law of Corrections* (St. Paul: West Publishing, 1973).

70. Matthew L. Myers, "12 Years After James v. Wallace," *National Prison Project Journal* 13 (Fall 1987): 8–12.

71. Bronstein, interview.

72. ACLU, Board of Directors, Minutes, January 7, 1957. Vern L. Bullough, "Lesbianism, Homosexuality, and the American Civil Liberties Union, *Journal of Homosexuality* 13 (Fall 1986): 23–33.

73. Pilpel, "Civil Liberties."

74. Nan Hunter, "Lesbian and Gay Rights" (Paper delivered at the ACLU Biennial, 1987), author's files. Hunter, interview.

75. See the first eight essays in Dorsen, ed., *The Rights of Americans.*

76. Jean Cahn and Edgar Cahn, "The War on Poverty: A Civilian Perspective," *Yale Law Journal* 73 (July 1964): 1317–1352.

77. *King v. Smith,* 392 U.S. 309 (1968). Martin Garbus, *Ready for the Defense* (New York: Avon Books, 1971), pp. 147–208.

78. Norman Dorsen, *Frontiers of Civil Liberties* (New York: Pantheon, 1968), pp. 295–316, 393–406.

79. Fraenkel, Diary, May 21, 1968. ACLU, *Annual Report,* 1969, p. 7.

80. On the history and impact of the Biennial, see Alan Reitman, Memo to Executive Committee, re Biennial Conference, May 20, 1980 (with supporting documents), author's files.

81. See papers and proceedings, ACLU Biennial Conferences, 1966, 1968, 1972, 1976, 1979, 1983, 1985. See the summary of Biennial and board actions in staff memo, "Economic Rights" (December 1985).

82. Pemberton, interview. Neier, interview. F. Isbell, interview.

83. Pemberton, interview. Neier, interview. ACLU, National Planning Committee–National Development Council, Joint Meeting, Minutes, February 13, 1965, ACLU–NY. ACLU, *Annual Report,* 1969, pp. 23–27. Garbus, *Ready For the Defense.*

84. Wulf, interview. Pemberton, interview. Morgan, interview. Isbell, interview.

85. L. Monroe, interview.

86. ACLU Foundation Project Proposals (December 1970), ACLUP, 1970, vol. 12. Neier, interview.

87. Lee Epstein, *Conservatives in Court* (Knoxville: University of Tennessee Press, 1985).

88. David Rudovsky, *The Rights of Prisoners* (New York: Avon Books, 1973). Robert S. Rivkin, *The Rights of Servicemen* (New York: Avon Books, 1972). Sylvia Law, *The Rights of the Poor* (New York: Avon Books, 1974). Joel M. Gora, *The Rights of Reporters* (New York: Avon Books, 1974).

89. *Civil Liberties Review* (1973–1978). Westin, interview.

90. Leon Friedman, "Up Against the Burger Court," *Civil Liberties Review* 1 (Fall 1973): 156–161. ACLU, Board of Directors, Minutes, October 9, 1961, February 17, 1964. NYCLU, *Civil Liberties in New York* (November 1967). ACLU, *Civil Liberties* (March–April 1968). ACLU, *Annual Report,* 1971, p. 1. ACLU, Activity Report, September, 1972, ACLUP, 1972, vol. 11.

91. See the debates, with supporting documents, on these and other issues in ACLU, Board of Directors, Minutes, 1983–present.

92. Neier, Memo to ACLU Executive Committee, September 13, 1971, ACLUP, 1971, vol. 11.

93. J. Anthony Lukas, "The ACLU Against Itself," *New York Times Magazine,* July 9, 1978, p. 18.

94. Joseph W. Bishop, Jr., "Politics and ACLU," *Commentary* 52 (December 1971): 50–58, reprinted in *Obiter Dicta* (New York: Atheneum, 1971).

95. Robert Bork, "Neutral Principles and Some First Amendment Problems," *Indiana Law Journal* 47 (Fall 1971): 1–35.

96. Walter Berns, "Pornography vs. Democracy: The Case for Censorship," *The Public Interest* 22 (Winter 1971): 3–24. Walter Berns, *The First Amendment and the Future of American Democracy* (New York: Basic Books, 1976).

97. ACLU, Memo to Board, September 23, 1969, ACLUP, 1969, v. 11. ACLU, Board of Directors, Minutes, October 1969. Leo Pfeffer, "An Autobiographical Sketch," in James E. Wood, ed., *Religion and the State: Essays in Honor of Leo Pfeffer* (Waco, Tex.: Baylor University Press, 1985), p. 519. Frank J. Souraf, *The Wall of Separation: The Constitutional Politics of Church and State* (Princeton, N.J.: Princeton University Press, 1976), pp. 38–39. *Walz v. Tax Commission*, 397 U.S. 664 (1970).

98. Herbert McClosky and Alida Brill, *Dimensions of Tolerance: What Americans Believe About Civil Liberties* (New York: Russell Sage Foundation, 1983).

99. Charles Halpern, "The Public Interest Bar," in Ralph Nader, ed., *Verdicts on Lawyers* (New York: Crowell, 1976), pp. 165–167.

Chapter 15

1. This account relies on David Hamlin, *The Nazi/Skokie Conflict: A Civil Liberties Battle* (Boston: Beacon Press, 1980). Aryeh Neier, *Defending My Enemy* (New York: Dutton, 1979). James L. Gibson and Richard D. Bingham, *Civil Liberties and Nazis: The Skokie Free-Speech Controversy* (New York: Praeger, 1985). Donald Alexander Downs, *Nazis in Skokie: Freedom, Community, and the First Amendment* (Notre Dame, Ind.: University of Notre Dame Press, 1985). Lee C. Bollinger, *The Tolerant Society: Freedom of Speech and Extremist Speech in America* (New York: Oxford University Press, 1986). Neier, interview. Dorsen, interview. Glasser, interview. Miller, interview. Hamlin, interview.

2. ACLU, *Annual Report,* 1960, p. 35. ACLU, Board of Directors, Minutes, March 28, 1960. Fraenkel, Diary, October 4, 1960.

3. Hamlin, *The Nazi/Skokie Conflict,* p. 11.

4. Charles Silberman, *A Certain People* (New York: Summit Books, 1985), pp. 181–185, 197–202, 205–207.

5. *New York Times,* December 17, 1977. Dorsen speech to the American Jewish Committee, January 19, 1978, cited in Neier–Dorsen correspondence, ca. 1977–1978, ANP.

6. Gertrude Samuels, "The Fight for Civil Liberties Never Stays Won," *New York Times,* June 19, 1966.

7. Neier, *Defending My Enemy,* p. 31.

8. NYCLU, Memo, May, 1978, ANP.

9. Neier, *Defending My Enemy,* pp. 69–104. Alexander Meikeljohn, "Meikeljohn on Skokie," *Guild Practitioner* 35 (Summer 1978): 84–96.

10. ACLU, Board of Directors, Minutes, September 24–25, 1977.

11. *Smith v. Collin,* 436 U.S. 953 (1978).

12. *Collin v. O'Malley,* 452 F.Supp. 577 (1978).

13. *Civil Liberties* (January 1978).

14. Glasser, interview.

15. Neier, letter to ACLU members, in *Civil Liberties* (November 1974). ACLU, Board of Directors, Minutes, December 6–7, 1975. ACLU, Board of Directors, Minutes, December 3–4, 1977. Glasser, Memo to Board, November 27, 1978, ACLUP, 1978, vol. 4.

16. Gibson and Bingham, *Civil Liberties and Nazis,* p. 85.

17. ACLU, Board of Directors, Minutes, March 5, 1977. Glasser, interview.

18. F. Isbell, Memo, ACLU Membership Operations, ca. April 1979, ACLUP, 1979, vol. 3. F. Isbell, interview. A bowdlerized version of the "Fuck You" letter story appears in J. Anthony Lukas, "The ACLU Against Itself," *New York Times Magazine,* July 9, 1978, pp. 9ff.

19. *Civil Liberties* (January 1978). Miller, interview.

20. Goldberger, letter, "My Dear Friend," ca. August 1978, author's files. See also David Goldberger, "Would You Defend an Unpopular Cause: On Defending Nazis," *Barrister* 5 (Winter 1977).

21. Voluminous correspondence, pro and con, ANP.

22. J. Miller, report in *Civil Liberties* (November 1978). Dorsen, letter to "Special" Members, September 20, 1978, ACLUP, 1978, vol. 4. Gibson and Bingham, *Civil Liberties and Nazis,* pp. 81–87.

23. Riesman, letter to Dorsen, September 1, 1978, Dorsen papers.

24. American Jewish Committee, *American Jewish Yearbook 1983* (New York: American Jewish Committee, 1982), pp. 89–110. Silberman, *A Certain People.* NYCLU, Tompkins County, Memo, May, 1978, ANP.

25. *Civil Liberties* (July 1978). Dorsen, interview. Schutz, interview.

26. Downs, *Nazis in Skokie,* p. 156.

27. Bollinger, *The Tolerant Society,* pp. 34–35, 240–241.

28. LaMarche, interview.

29. ACLU, *Annual Report,* 1977, p. 3.

30. T. Schutz, Memo to staff, April 29, 1977, Dorsen Papers.

31. ACLU, *Civil Liberties* (May 1977).

32. See, for example, the problems related to integrating fund-raising efforts and the dispute over ACLU policy on amendments to the Freedom of Information Act in 1982–1984. Keenen Peck, "Strange Bedfellows," *The Progressive,* November 1984, pp. 28–31. Ira Glasser, "The Case for the New F.O.I.A. Bill," *The Nation,* June 2, 1984.

33. ACLU, Board of Directors, Minutes, September 24, 1977. Neier, Memo to Dorsen, October 21, 1977, Dorsen Papers. Ed King, Letter to ACLU Board, in ACLU, Board of Directors, Minutes, December 3, 1977.

34. *Civil Liberties* (July 1977). The files are available, as are all documents released under the Freedom of Information Act, in the reading room at FBI Headquarters in Washington, D.C.

35. ACLU, Report of ACLU Special Commission on the FBI Files to the ACLU Board of Directors, October 2, 1979, author's files.

36. Ibid., pp. 64–65.

37. Ferman, interview. Response of Irving Ferman to Neier *Civil Liberties Review* article, in Appendix, ACLU, Report of ACLU Special Commission.

38. Ernst FBI file, author's possession. Harrison E. Salisbury, "The Strange Correspondence of Morris Ernst & John Edgar Hoover, 1939–1964," *The Nation,* December 1, 1984, pp. 575–589.

39. ACLU, Report of the ACLU Special Commission, p. 53.

40. Baldwin was still highly sensitive about the ACLU's role in the cold war and the 1940 resolution in particular. In 1975 he took exception to historian Jerold S. Auerbach's treatment of the 1940 events in an ACLU-sponsored collection of essays on

ACLU history. In an astounding and unprofessional move, he even managed to insert his own rebuttal in the middle of Auerbach's text. See Alan Reitman, ed., *The Pulse of Freedom: American Liberties: 1920–1970's* (New York: Mentor Books, 1976), pp. 70–71.

41. Charles Morgan, Jr., *One Man, One Voice* (New York: Holt, Rinehart and Winston, 1979), pp. ix–xi. Aryeh Neier, "Adhering to Principle: Lessons from the 1950's," *Civil Liberties Review* 4 (November–December 1977): 26–32.

42. Special Organizational Review Committee, Memo, Final SORC Report, June 1977, ACLUP, 1977, vol. 6. Feingold, interview. Dorsen, interview.

43. ACLU, Final SORC Report. Dorsen, interview. Lukas, "The ACLU Against Itself."

44. *New York Times,* March 17, 1976, p. 17.

45. Morgan, *One Man, One Voice,* pp. 336–337. *New York Times,* April 18, 1976.

46. Morgan, interview. *New York Times,* April 18, 1976.

47. ". . . in part from our strategy decision to take fewer cases to the Burger Court." *ACLU Lawyer,* December 1979.

48. ACLU, Committee on Legal Department, Memo, May 6, 1976, Dorsen Papers. Wulf, letter to ACLU friends, January 12, 1977, Dorsen Papers. Dorsen, interview. Wulf, interview. Neuborne, interview. Burt Neuborne, "The Structure of the ACLU Legal Program—Where Do We Want to Be in Five Years" (paper delivered to the ACLU Biennial Conference, 1983).

49. ACLU, Executive Committee, transcript of January 1977 meeting, ANP. Wulf, interview. Dorsen, interview.

50. *Civil Liberties* (July 1978).

51. Neier, interview. Dorsen, interview. Glasser, interview.

52. F. Isbell, interview. Glasser, interview.

53. Glasser, Budget Memo, January 13, 1988, author's files.

54. ACLU, *Annual Report,* 1977.

55. *Civil Liberties* (January 1975). *ACLU Lawyer,* October 15, 1978; December 1979, author's files.

56. "Inside the Great Campaign Finance Case of 1976: A Conversation with Ira Glasser," *Civil Liberties Review* 4 (September–October 1977): 8–19.

57. *Buckley v. Valeo,* 424 U.S. 1 (1976). *Civil Liberties* (February 1979).

58. ACLU, Board of Directors, Minutes, April 1988.

59. *Civil Liberties* (July 1978).

60. *In re Primus,* 436 U.S. 412 (1978).

Chapter 16

1. Quoted in *Civil Liberties* (Winter 1985).

2. Shattuck, in *Civil Liberties* (November 1980). *Civil Liberties Alert* 5 (November 1981).

3. Glasser quoting Baldwin in Colleen O'Connor, "Growing Watchdog of Liberty," *Bergen Sunday Record,* February 20, 1983.

4. Falwell quoted in Charles Silberman, *A Certain People* (New York: Summit Books, 1985), p. 350. Popeo quoted in *National Law Journal,* May 23, 1983, September 5, 1983.

5. For an overview, see Glasser, Memo to ACLU Board on proposed 1988 budget, January 13, 1988, author's files.

6. Shattuck, interview.

7. Edward J. Larson, *Trial and Error: The American Controversy over Creation and Evolution* (New York: Oxford, 1985), pp. 122–167. On the creation science organizations, see Langdon Gilkey, *Creationism on Trial: Evolution and God at Little Rock* (Minneapolis: Winston Press, 1985), p. 20.

8. Glasser, interview. The Skadden, Arps, Slate, Maegher, and Flom law firm handled the case for the ACLU.

9. *Civil Liberties* (June 1981), (February 1982). Gilkey, *Creationism on Trial.*

10. *McLean v. Arkansas Board of Education,* 663 F.2d 47 (8th Cir. 1981), aff'g No. LRC 81–322. (W.D. Ark. August 20, 1981).

11. *Edwards v. Aguillard,* 482 U.S. — (1987).

12. *Civil Liberties Alert* 7 (May 1984).

13. John Swomley, "Separation of Church and State Under Attack" (paper delivered at the ACLU Biennial Conference, 1987), p. 1, author's files.

14. ACLU, Board of Directors, Minutes, January 26–27, 1985, January 25–26, 1986.

15. Dean M. Kelley, "The Tension Between Establishment and Free Exercise of Religion" (paper and speech delivered at the ACLU Biennial Conference, 1985).

16. *Goldman v. Weinberger,* 106 S. Ct. 1310.

17. *Wallace v. Jaffree,* 472 U.S. 38 (1985).

18. *Karcher v. May,* 56 U.S. L.W. 4022 (1987). Jeffrey Fogel, Executive Director, New Jersey ACLU, statement, January 1983, author's files.

19. Novik, comments, ACLU Board of Directors, Minutes, October 19, 1986. On Hand, see *New York Times,* March 7, 1987.

20. *Smith v. Board of School Commissioners,* 827 F.2d 684 (1987).

21. *New York Times,* August 29, 1987.

22. ACLU, Board of Directors, Minutes, January 1987. Nadine Strossen, " 'Secular Humanism' and 'Scientific Creationism': Proposed Standards for Reviewing Curricular Decisions Affecting Students' Religious Freedom," *Ohio State Law Journal* 47 (1986): 333–407.

23. *Mozert v. Hawkins County Public Schools,* 827 F.2d 1058 (6th Cir. 1987). *New York Times,* August 29, 1987.

24. *Lynch v. Donnelly,* 465 U.S. 668 (1984). Neuborne, Memo to ACLU affiliates, March 8, 1984, author's files.

25. Janet Benshoof, "The Chastity Act: Government Manipulation of Abortion Information and the First Amendment," *Harvard Law Review* 101 (June 1988): 1916–1937.

26. *Bowen v. Kendrick,* 487 U.S. — (1988).

27. Frederick S. Jaffe et al., *Abortion Politics* (New York: McGraw-Hill, 1981).

28. ACLU, Reproductive Freedom Project, *Annual Report,* annual.

29. ACLU–NCA, Press Release, January 23, 1985, author's files.

30. *National Right to Life News,* passim.

31. On public opinion, see *New York Times,* April 26, 1989; *Newsweek,* April 24, 1989.

32. *Civil Liberties Alert* 6 (July 1983). Charlotte Low, "The Pro-Life Movement in Disarray," *The American Spectator* 20 (October 1987): 23–26.

33. *Harris v. McRae,* 448 U.S. 297 (1980).

34. ACLU–SC, *Annual Report,* 1985, pp. 13–14.

35. *City of Akron v. Akron Center for Reproductive Health,* 462 U.S. 416 (1983).

36. ACLU, Reproductive Freedom Project, *Annual Report 1987* (1988).

37. Quoted from ACLU, Reproductive Freedom Project, *Annual Report,* 1986, p. 12. *Hodgson v. Minnesota,* 853 F.2d 1452 (8th Cir. 1988). *New York Times,* August 9, 1988.

38. ACLU, Executive Committee, Minutes, June, 1985. ACLU, Board of Directors, Minutes, January, 1988.

39. ACLU, Reproductive Freedom Project, *Preserving the Right to Choose* (1986).

40. Nat Hentoff, "Abortion Protesters Have First Amendment Rights Too," *Washington Post,* February 7, 1986.

41. Benshoof, Memo to All Parties Interested in the Proposed Title X Regulations, September 17, 1987, author's files. *New York Times,* February 7, 1988.

42. *Pico v. Board of Education,* 102 S. Ct. 2799. National Coalition Against Censorship, *Censorship News* (January 1983).

43. Edward B. Jenkinson, *Censors in the Classroom: The Mind Benders* (New York: Avon Books, 1979). Minnesota Civil Liberties Union, *A Report on a Survey on Censorship* (1981). Nebraska Civil Liberties Union, *Censorship in Nebraska Public Schools and Public School Libraries* (1983).

44. Laura Lederer, ed., *Take Back the Night: Women on Pornography* (New York: Bantam Books, 1982).

45. Catherine MacKinnon, "Pornography, Civil Rights and Speech, *Harvard Civil Rights—Civil Liberties Review* 20 (1985): 1–70.

46. MCLU, Press Release, c. 1983, author's files. Fraser, letter to City Council, January 5, 1984.

47. Brief *Amici Curiae* of Feminist Anticensorship Task Force in *American Booksellers Association v. Hudnut,* 771 F.2d 323 (7th Cir. 1985).

48. *American Booksellers Association v. Hudnut,* 771 F.2d 323 (7th Cir. 1985).

49. F.A.C.T. Book Committee, *Caught Looking* (New York: Caught Looking, Inc., 1986).

50. National Coalition Against Censorship, *The Meese Commission Exposed,* Proceedings, January 16, 1986. Lynn, interview.

51. Attorney General's Commission on Pornography, *Final Report,* 2 vols. (1986). ACLU, *Polluting the Censorship Debate* (July 1986). Lynn, interview.

52. *Fort Wayne Books, Inc. v. Indiana,* 57 U.S.L.W. 4180 (1989). Gara La Marche, "Some Censorship Trends in Censorless America" (paper delivered to the ACLU Biennial Conference, 1989).

53. ACLU, Press Release, September 18, 1985, author's files.

54. *New York Times,* September 20, 1985.

55. Steven Wishnia, "Rockin' With the First Amendment," *The Nation,* October 24, 1987, pp. 444–446.

56. *State v. Henry,* 302 OR. 510, 732 P.2d 9 (1987). Nat Hentoff, "The First State to Abolish Obscenity," *The Village Voice,* May 12, 1987, p. 41.

57. James C. Harrington, "Yes, There Is a Texas Bill of Rights," *State Constitutional Law Newsletter* 1 (June 1987): 9–10. James C. Harrington, "The Texas Bill of Rights and Civil Liberties," *Texas Tech Law Review* 17 (1986): 1487.

58. William J. Brennan, Jr., "The Bill of Rights and the States: The Revival of State Constitutions As Guardians of Individual Rights," in Norman Dorsen, ed., *The Evolving Constitution* (Middletown, Conn.: Wesleyan University Press, 1987), pp. 254–270.

59. *State Constitutional Law Newsletter,* I (June 1987).

60. ACLU, *In Contempt of Congress and the Courts,* February 27, 1984. Glasser, Opening Remarks, 1985 ACLU Biennial.

61. ACLU, *In Contempt of Congress.* Glasser, Opening Remarks, 1987 ACLU Biennial.

62. ACLU and NAACP Legal Defense and Education Fund, Inc., *Justice Denied: The Loss of Civil Rights After the Grove City College Decision* (March 1986).

63. *Grove City College v. Bell,* 465 U.S. 555 (1984). ACLU and NAACP Legal Defense and Educational Fund, Inc., *Justice Denied: The Loss of Civil Rights After the Grove College Decision* (March 1986). ACLU, *Civil Liberties Alert* 11 (May 1988).

64. *The State* (Columbia, S.C.), January 31, 1988. McDonald, interview.

65. ACLU, *In Contempt of Congress and the Courts. New York Times,* May 30, 1984.

66. ACLU Voting Rights Project, Report to ACLU Board, October 7, 1985, author's files. *The State,* January 31, 1988.

67. ACLU, *Voting Rights in the South: Ten Years of Litigation Challenging Continuing Discrimination Against Minorities* (New York: ACLU, January 1982).

68. ACLU, Southern Regional Office, Memo to ACLU Foundation Board, October 7, 1985, p. 3, author's files.

69. McDonald, interview.

70. Shattuck, interview. Halperin, interview. *Civil Liberties Alert* 7 (November 1984).

71. U.S. Department of Justice, *Attorney General's Task Force on Violent Crime: Final Report* (Washington, D.C.: Government Printing Office, 1981). Samuel Walker, *Sense and Nonsense About Crime,* 2nd ed. (Monterey, Calif.: Brooks/Cole, 1989).

72. *Schall v. Martin,* 467 U.S. 253 (1984). *U.S. v. Salerno,* 481 U.S. 739 (1987).

73. Conference, *Redefining the Crime Debate,* March 6–8, 1986, Atlanta.

74. *Los Angeles Times,* March 3, 1988.

75. ACLU, *Report of the 1985 ACLU Biennial Conference* (1985), pp. 39–41; app. I, pp. 1–2, author's files.

76. Center for National Security Studies, *First Principles,* passim.

77. Diana Gordon, "Old FBI Tricks," *The Nation,* February 13, 1988, p. 185. *New York Times,* February 14, 1988. Natalie Robins, "The F.B.I.'s Invasion of Libraries," *The Nation,* April 9, 1988, p. 1.

78. Morton Halperin, "A U.S. 'Official Secrets Act'?" *Washington Post,* February 22, 1985. *New York Times,* October 20, 1985. *First Principles* 11 (May 1986): 1–2.

79. ACLU, *Free Trade in Ideas: A Constitutional Imperative* (May 1984).

80. ACLU, *Civil Liberties Alert* 11 (January 1988): 3. *American-Arab Anti-Discrimination Committee v. Meese,* Civ. No. 87–2107 (C.D. Cal May 21, 1987).

81. "Free Trade in Ideas—A Progress Report," CNSS, *First Principles* 11 (July 1986).

Chapter 17

1. Edwin Meese III, "The Law of the Constitution," October 21, 1986 (U.S. Department of Justice).

2. *New York Times,* October 24, 1986.

3. Glasser, letter to Meese, December 17, 1985, author's files. *New York Times,* December 18, 1985. *Newsweek,* December 30, 1985.

4. ACLU, Petition, "In the Court of Public Opinion," 1986, author's files.

5. Glasser, remarks to ACLU Board of Directors, October 1986.

6. Glasser, Memo, Campaign to Stop Ed Meese, October 18, 1986, author's files.

7. Glasser, Memo to ACLU Board, re 1988 Budget, January 13, 1988, author's files.

8. *New York Times,* June 22, 1987.

9. Robert H. Bork, "Neutral Principles and Some First Amendment Problems," *Indiana Law Journal* 47 (Fall 1971): 1–35.

10. ACLU, Board of Directors, Minutes, December 3–4, 1971. See the summary of debates and decisions from 1935 onward in Dorsen, Memo to Board, July 31, 1987, author's files.

11. ACLU, Board of Directors, Minutes, October 20–21, 1984.

12. Askin, Memo to ACLU Board, June 29, 1987; Dorsen, Memo to Board, July 31, 1987, author's files.

13. ACLU, Board of Directors, Minutes, August 29–30, 1987. ACLU, Memorandum to the Board on the Civil Liberties Record of Judge Robert H. Bork, 1987, author's files.

14. *New York Times,* October 24, 1987.

15. *New York Times,* September 23, 1988.

16. Norman Podhoretz, "Who Should Define the American Mainstream?" *Omaha World Herald,* October 15, 1988. James J. Kilpatrick, "ACLU's Causes Are Far Beyond Mainstream," *Omaha World Herald,* October 15, 1988.

17. Ira Glasser, Speech to the National Press Club, October 6, 1988, author's files.

18. Glasser, Comments, ACLU Board of Directors, December 3, 1988.

19. *New York Times,* September 27, 1988, January 27, 1989. James Ledbetter, "New Members, New Problems," *The Nation,* April 3, 1989, pp. 442–444.

20. Samuel Walker, "What Are Objections to ACLU?" *Omaha World Herald,* September 20, 1988.

21. Dorsen, Comments, ACLU Executive Committee Meeting, December 2, 1988.

22. Lee Bollinger, *The Tolerant Society* (New York: Oxford University Press, 1986).

23. ACLU, *Civil Liberties Alert* 11 (November 1988).

24. *National Attitudes Toward the American Civil Liberties Union* (March 1989), author's files. The 1,003 respondents appeared to be a representative cross-section of the electorate: 22 percent described themselves as "liberal," 36 percent as "moderate," and 35 percent as "conservative."

25. Herbert McClosky and Alida Brill, *Dimension of Tolerance: What Americans Believe About Civil Liberties* (New York: Russell Sage Foundation, 1983). *National Attitudes Toward the American Civil Liberties Union* (March 1989).

26. Samuel Stouffer, *Communism, Conformity, and Civil Liberties* (New York: Doubleday, 1955).

27. Michael Kammen, *A Machine That Would Go of Itself: The Constitution in American Culture* (New York: Knopf, 1986).

28. *New York Times,* April 10, 1989, April 26, 1989, July 4, 1989.

29. Dorsen and Glasser, letter to Schultz, December 1, 1988, reprinted in *First Principles* 13 (December 1988).

30. Hunter, Report to ACLU National Board, The ACLU's Work Against AIDS-related Discrimination, July 27, 1987, author's files. Hunter, interview.

31. *New York Times,* July 10, 1988. ACLU, *Civil Liberties Alert* 11 (November 1988). *National Treasury Employees Union v. Von Raab,* 489 U.S. — (1989).

32. Nat Hentoff, in *The Village Voice,* December 15, 1987.

33. *Hazlewood v. Kuhlmeier.* 107 S. Ct. 926 (1987).

34. *Bowers v. Hardwick,* 478 U.S. 186 (1986). See the account in Peter Irons, *The Courage of Their Convictions* (New York: Free Press, 1988), pp. 379–403.

35. *National Treasury Employees Union v. Von Raab,* 489 U.S. — (1989). Nat Hentoff, "The Supreme Court's Huge Dragnet," *The Village Voice,* April 25, 1989.

36. Glasser, letter to *New York Times,* February 25, 1988.

37. For the ACLU's role in the North case, see *First Principles* 13 (September 1988). Samuel Walker, "The ACLU Defended: A Response to Bill Donohue," *The World and I,* June 1987, pp. 633–640.

38. *Detroit Free Press,* November 2, 1988.

39. *New York Times,* April 25, 1989.

40. ACLU, Board of Directors, Minutes, April, 1988.

41. *New York Times,* October 29, 1987. *Newsweek,* November 9, 1987, March 28, 1988. Edward L. Koch, "Billie Boggs Proves the NYCLU Wrong," *Staten Island Advance,* March 26, 1989.

42. Glasser and Piven, Memo to ACLU Board of Directors, Implementation of Policy 318, March 31, 1987.

43. Ramona Ripston, "Implementation of Affiliate Policy on Poverty" (paper delivered to the ACLU Biennial Conference, 1985). ACLU–SC, Board of Directors, Minutes, May 14, 1983.

44. ACLU, Board of Directors, Minutes, April 17, 1988, April 9, 1989.

45. Learned Hand, *The Spirit of Liberty* (New York: Vintage Books, 1959), p. 144.

Manuscript Sources

ACLU Records

The ACLU archives, located in the Mudd Library at Princeton University, provide the primary source material for this book. This extremely rich collection is enormous, totaling nearly two thousand scrapbooks and two thousand cartons of files. It has been relatively neglected by historians working on issues in which the ACLU also had an interest. The material through the 1950s contains more personal correspondence and is, in many respects, more revealing than are the more bureaucratic records of the recent years. The World War I–era files, from 1917 to 1919, are very disorganized and need to be supplemented by research in the Peace Collection at Swarthmore College and the Lillian Wald Papers at Columbia University. Additional ACLU records for the last fifteen years are in storage in the ACLU's national office in New York. Norman Dorsen's papers are available in his office at the New York University Law School.

The ACLU files at Princeton also contain much material on the ACLU affiliates. In many cases there are complete sets of minutes and newsletters, along with correspondence with the national office. For this and other reasons, I read the official files of the affiliates selectively. The Philadelphia, Chicago, and Northern and Southern California affiliate records are carefully curated and useful. The New York Civil Liberties Union files are in various warehouses and not available.

In several instances, earlier documents were culled by the ACLU staff for purposes of review. Consequently, the dates of their location in the files do not conform to the dates of the documents themselves. Recent documents cited in the notes as "author's files" are official documents and will eventually be available in the ACLU archives.

Manuscript Collections

Individuals

The Mudd Library at Princeton also contains the Roger Baldwin Papers. It is a relatively small collection, and most of the material relates to Baldwin's ACLU activities. Additional material was added as this book was going to press. The most valuable interview with Baldwin is the one conducted by Alan Westin in the 1970s. The Columbia University Oral History Collection interview with Baldwin is very disappointing. The Arthur Garfield Hays Papers also are in the Mudd Library and contain primarily documents and legal briefs; correspondence revelant to his ACLU work is scattered throughout the ACLU files.

Finally, the Mudd Library contains typed copies of those portions of Osmond Fraenkel's diary that relate to the ACLU. This is an extremely valuable source but one that must be handled with some caution. The original diary is in the Harvard Law School Library and is closed to scholars until the year 2033. There thus is no way to check for possible errors that might have occurred in transcription, and also the omission of Fraenkel's other activities, particularly those with the National Lawyers Guild, leaves us with an incomplete portrait. A second Fraenkel "diary" is in the Harvard Law School Library, but it is a brief recollection, written many years after the fact and not very useful.

The Norman Thomas Papers at the New York Public Library are disappointing, as Thomas saved little before the late 1930s. The material from the 1940s and 1950s is, however, very useful. The Morris L. Ernst Papers at the University of Texas are also extremely useful and provide considerable insight into Ernst's wide-ranging activities outside the ACLU. The Felix Frankfurter Papers at the Library of Congress are disappointingly slim with respect to the ACLU, but there are a few important items.

The Sophie Smith Collection at Smith College contains several relevant collections, including the papers of Madeline Doty, Roger Baldwin's first wife, Mary Van Kleeck, an important member of the ACLU board in the 1930s, and Dorothy Kenyon, an important ACLU figure from the late 1930s through the late 1950s. The Schlesinger Library at Radcliffe College contains the papers of several women active in the ACLU.

The Library of Congress contains several important collections, as does the University of Wisconsin Historical Society. The interviews in the Columbia University Oral History Collection are, with one exception, extremely disappointing and, in some cases, unreliable because of poor editing. The exception is the Osmond Fraenkel interview.

A complete list of manuscript sources for individuals follows:
Jane Addams Papers, Swarthmore College
Emily G. Balch Papers, Swarthmore College
Roger Nash Baldwin Papers, Princeton University
Howard K. Beale Papers, Wisconsin Historical Society
Alfred M. Bingham Papers, Yale University
Edwin M. Borchard Papers, Yale University
Earl Browder Papers, Syracuse University (microfilm copy)
Zechariah Chafee Papers, Harvard University Law School
Grenville Clark Papers, Dartmouth College
Clarence Darrow Papers, Library of Congress
Norman Dorsen Papers, New York University
Madeline Z. Doty Papers, Smith College
Robert W. Dunn Papers, New York University
Mary Eastwood Papers, Radcliffe College
Morris Ernst Papers, University of Texas
Elizabeth Glendower Evans Papers, Radcliffe College
James L. Fly Papers, Columbia University
Elizabeth Gurley Flynn Papers, New York University
Elizabeth Gurley Flynn Papers, Wisconsin Historical Society
Osmond K. Fraenkel Diary, Princeton University
Osmond K. Fraenkel Papers, Harvard University Law School
Felix Frankfurter Papers, Harvard University Law School
Felix Frankfurter Papers, Library of Congress
Arthur Garfield Hays Papers, Princeton University

John Haynes Holmes Papers, Library of Congress
Ben Huebsch Papers, Library of Congress
Dorothy Kenyon Papers, Smith College
Corliss Lamont Papers, Columbia University
Florence Luscomb Papers, Radcliffe College
Dwight MacDonald Papers, Yale University
Alexander Meikeljohn Papers, Wisconsin Historical Society
Pauli Murray Papers, Radcliffe College
Aryeh Neier Papers, ACLU Office, New York City
G. Bromley Oxnam Papers, Library of Congress
Elmer Rice Papers, University of Texas
Roger W. Riis Papers, Library of Congress
Gilbert Roe Papers, in LaFollette Family Papers, Library of Congress
Margaret Sanger Papers, Library of Congress
Theodore Schroeder Papers, Southern Illinois University
Norman Thomas Papers, New York Public Library
Mary Van Kleeck Papers, Smith College
Lillian Wald Papers, Columbia University
Lillian Wald Papers, New York Public Library
Harry Weinberger Papers, Yale University
L. Hollingsworth Wood Papers, Columbia University

Organizations

The Peace Collection at Swarthmore College contains the records of the AUAM, the World War II–era National Committee on Conscientious Objectors, and other pacifist organizations relevant to ACLU history. The Papers of the American Fund for Public Service at the New York Public Library are extremely valuable for the 1920s. The NAACP Papers at the Library of Congress contain useful material. The Tamiment Institute Collection at New York University has small but useful collections of a number of organizations as well as individuals.

A complete list of manuscript sources for organizations follows:
ACLU-Greater Philadelphia Branch Papers, Temple University
ACLU-Illinois Division Papers, University of Chicago
ACLU-Northern California Papers, California Historical Society
ACLU-Southern California Papers, University of California at Los Angeles
American Civil Liberties Union Papers, Princeton University
American Fund for Public Service Papers, New York Public Library
American Union Against Militarism Papers, Swarthmore College
International Labor Defense Papers, Schomburg Collection, New York Public
    Library
National Association for the Advancement of Colored People Papers, Library
    of Congress
National Committee Against Repressive Legislation Papers, Wisconsin Histori-
    cal Society
National Committee on Conscientious Objectors Papers, Swarthmore College
New York Bureau of Legal First Aid Papers, New York University
Radical Pamphlet Collection, New York University
St. Louis Civil Liberties Committee Papers, Washington University
Wisconsin Civil Liberties Union Papers, Wisconsin Historical Society

FBI Files

The political surveillance by the Federal Bureau of Investigation, though deplorable, has left us with a valuable collection of source material. All FBI material must be handled with care, however. It is often a better measure of the bureau than of the individual or organization spied on. The Bureau of Investigation Case Files, 1908–1922 (available on microfilm) provides insight into the early years. The ACLU obtained over 40,000 pages of documents from FBI files on the organization under the Freedom of Information Act; one copy is in the ACLU national office, subject to certain restrictions, and another is available in the FBI Reading Room in Washington, D.C. Under the Freedom of Information Act, I obtained a copy of Roger Baldwin's FBI file. It contained a few interesting items but otherwise does not add anything significant to the ACLU files. A copy remains in my possession, and another is available in the FBI Reading Room. Professor Athan Theoharis has made available his copy of Morris Ernst's files.

Bibliographic Essay

Although there is a voluminous literature on many of the ACLU's cases and controversies, there is surprisingly little scholarship on the ACLU itself. Charles Lamm Markmann's *The Noblest Cry: A History of the American Civil Liberties Union* (New York: St. Martin's Press, 1965) suffers from inadequate research, an idiosyncratic viewpoint, and a topical rather than a chronological format. Peggy Lamson's *Roger Baldwin: Founder of the American Civil Liberties Union* (Boston: Houghton Mifflin, 1976) is essentially an annotated interview rather than a detailed biography. The best overview of civil liberties history is found in the various essays by professional historians in Alan Reitman, ed., *The Pulse of Freedom: American Liberties, 1920–1970's* (New York: Norton, 1975). Several important cases are covered in Peter Irons, *The Courage of Their Convictions* (New York: Free Press, 1988). William Donohue's *The Politics of the American Civil Liberties Union* (New Brunswick, N.J.: Transaction Books, 1985) is a conservative diatribe based on little research and less understanding of the issues. The best analysis of the ACLU is by Norman Dorsen, "The American Civil Liberties Union: An Institutional Analysis," *Tulane Lawyer,* Spring 1984, pp. 6–14. On the early years of the ACLU, see Paul L. Murphy, *World War I and the Origin of Civil Liberties in the United States* (New York: Norton, 1979), which far surpasses Donald Johnson's *The Challenge to American Freedoms: World War I and the Rise of the American Civil Liberties Union* (Lexington: University of Kentucky Press, 1963). Also on the early years, see Walter Nelles, *A Liberal in Wartime: The Education of Albert DeSilver* (New York: Norton, 1940); and Lucille Milner, *Education of an American Liberal: An Autobiography* (New York: Horizon, 1954). Paul L. Murphy, *The Meaning of Freedom of Speech: First Amendment Freedoms From Wilson to FDR* (Westport, Conn.: Greenwood Press, 1972) is a de facto history of the ACLU in the 1920s, although it focuses almost exclusively on labor and political speech issues.

On the suppression of civil liberties during World War I, I have relied on H. C. Peterson and Gilbert C. Fite, *Opponents of War, 1917–1918* (Seattle: University of Washington Press, 1968); William Preston, *Aliens and Dissenters: Federal Suppression of Radicals, 1903–1933* (New York: Harper & Row, 1966); Robert K. Murray, *Red Scare: A Study in National Hysteria, 1919–1920* (New York: McGraw-Hill, 1964); Joan M. Jensen, *The Price of Vigilance* (Chicago: Rand McNally, 1968). Roland Marchand's *The American Peace Movement and Social Reform, 1898–1918* (Princeton, N.J.: Princeton University Press, 1972) has a particularly valuable section on the social and political context from which the ACLU's founders emerged. On the constitutional issues raised by the war, Zechariah Chafee, Jr.'s *Free Speech in the United States* (Cambridge, Mass.: Harvard University Press, 1941) is the classic work. I have also learned much from David

Rabban's "The Emergence of Modern First Amendment Doctrine," *University of Chicago Law Review* 50 (Fall 1983): 1205–1355; "The First Amendment in Its Forgotten Years," *Yale Law Journal* 90 (1981): 514–597; and his unpublished manuscript on the Free Speech League and the ACLU.

For the 1920s, see Murphy, *The Meaning of Freedom of Speech.* Firsthand accounts of some important ACLU cases can be found in Arthur Garfield Hays, *Let Freedom Ring,* rev. ed. (New York: Liveright, 1937); and *City Lawyer* (New York: Simon & Schuster, 1942). The standard work on the Scopes case is by Ray Ginger, *Six Days or Forever?* (Chicago: Quadrangle Books, 1969). Edward J. Larson's *Trial and Error* (New York: Oxford University Press, 1985) brings the story down to the current "creationism" controversies.

The best treatment of the ACLU's philosophical reorientation in the 1930s is by Jerold S. Auerbach, *Labor and Liberty: The LaFollette Committee and the New Deal* (Indianapolis: Bobbs-Merrill, 1966), far surpassing Cletus Daniel, *The ACLU and the Wagner Act* (Ithaca, N.Y.: Cornell University Press, 1980). On the Popular Front, see Harvey Klehr, *The Heyday of American Communism* (New York: Basic Books, 1984). On the ACLU events of 1940, see Corliss Lamont, ed., *The Trial of Elizabeth Gurley Flynn by the American Civil Liberties Union;* Jerold Simmons, "The American Civil Liberties Union and the Dies Committee, 1938–1940," *Harvard Civil Rights–Civil Liberties Law Review* 17 (Spring 1982): 183–207. On HUAC, see Walter Goodman, *The Committee* (New York: Farrar, Straus & Giroux, 1968); on academic freedom issues in the 1930s, see Ellen Schrecker, *No Ivory Tower: McCarthyism and the Universities* (New York: Oxford University Press, 1986).

The best work on the Japanese-American internment is Peter Irons, *Justice at War* (New York: Oxford University Press, 1983). Also see Morton Grodzins, *Americans Betrayed* (Chicago: University of Chicago Press, 1949); and Jacobus ten Broek et al., *Prejudice, War and the Constitution* (Berkeley and Los Angeles: University of California Press, 1970).

The literature on the cold war is enormous. I have relied on David Caute, *The Great Fear* (New York: Simon & Schuster, 1978). The Cornell University series of books on the cold war is still extremely valuable; see, for example, Walter Gellhorn, ed., *The States and Subversion* (Ithaca, N.Y.: Cornell University Press, 1952). On J. Edgar Hoover, see Athan Theoharis and John Stuart Cox, *The Boss: J. Edgar Hoover and the Great American Inquisition* (Philadelphia: Temple University Press, 1988); and Athan Theoharis, *Spying on Americans: Political Surveillance from Hoover to the Huston Plan* (Philadelphia: Temple University Press, 1978). On HUAC, see Goodman, *The Committee;* and the excellent work by Victor Navasky, *Naming Names* (New York: Viking, 1980). On the ACLU in this period, see Corliss Lamont's opinionated *Freedom Is As Freedom Does* (New York: Horizon, 1956), which has shaped the reputation of the ACLU for this period; and Mary S. McAuliffe, "The American Civil Liberties Union During the McCarthy Years," in Robert Griffith and Athan Theoharis, eds., *The Specter* (New York: New Viewpoints, 1974), although both accounts ignore important aspects of the ACLU's activities.

The literature on the 1960s is growing rapidly, although no book examines the civil liberties issues in detail. But for a good account of the decade, see Todd Gitlin, *The Sixties: Years of Hope, Days of Rage* (New York: Bantam, 1987). On the ACLU's activities, Charles Morgan, Jr.'s memoir, *One Man, One Voice* (New York: Holt, Rinehart and Winston, 1979) is valuable but very opinionated and so must be read with care. Aryeh Neier's *Only Judgment: The Limits of Litigation in Social Change* (Middletown, Conn.: Wesleyan University Press, 1982) is an extremely thoughtful reconsideration of the ACLU's role in many of the new civil liberties issues of the 1960s and 1970s. The Skokie episode spawned a sizable literature. See the firsthand accounts: Aryeh Neier, *Defending My Enemy* (New York: Dutton, 1979); and David Hamlin, *The Nazi/Skokie Conflict* (Boston: Beacon Press, 1980). The impact on the ACLU is examined by James L. Gibson and Richard D. Bingham, *Civil Liberties and Nazis: The Skokie Free-Speech Controversy* (New York: Praeger, 1985). On the free speech issue, see the neoconservative Donald Alexander Downs, *Nazis and Skokie: Freedom Community, and the First Amendment* (Notre Dame, Ind.: Notre Dame University Press, 1985); and the extremely thoughtful Lee Bollinger, *The Tolerant Society* (New York: Oxford University Press, 1986).

On literary censorship, particularly during the 1920s, see Paul Boyer, *Purity in Print* (New York: Scribner, 1968). For the 1960s, see Charles Rembar, *The End of Obscenity* (New York: Random House, 1968). On film censorship, see Garth Jowett, *Film: The Democratic Art* (Boston: Focal Press, 1976); Richard S. Randall, *Censorship of the Movies* (Madison: University of Wisconsin Press, 1968). See also the voluminous writings of Morris Ernst.

On church and state issues, the most comprehensive survey is by Leo Pfeffer, *Church, State and Freedom*, rev. ed. (Boston: Beacon Press, 1967). A particularly insightful analysis of the role of the ACLU and other groups in church–state cases is by Frank Souraf, *The Wall of Separation: The Constitutional Politics of Church and State* (Princeton, N.J.: Princeton University Press, 1976).

On civil rights, Richard Kluger's *Simple Justice* (New York: Vintage Books, 1977) covers the litigation leading up to the 1954 *Brown* decision. On the ACLU's contribution in the sixties, see Morgan, *One Man, One Voice*. On criminal justice, see Samuel Walker, *Popular Justice: A History of American Criminal Justice* (New York: Oxford University Press, 1980). On abortion, see Lawrence Lader, *Abortion* (Boston: Beacon Press, 1966); and *Abortion II* (Boston: Beacon Press, 1973).

On the ACLU and the Vietnam War, see Neier, *Only Judgment;* on the Pentagon Papers case, see Sanford J. Ungar, *The Papers and the Papers* (New York: Dutton, 1972); and on the ACLU and Watergate, Morgan, *One Man, One Voice*.

The ACLU has periodically sponsored collections of essays on civil liberties issues which serve as useful benchmarks in the organization's development. See Alan Reitman, ed., *The Price of Liberty* (New York: Norton, 1968); the particularly valuable Norman Dorsen, ed., *The Rights of Americans: What They Are— What They Should Be* (New York: Vintage Books, 1972); and Norman Dorsen, ed., *Our Endangered Rights* (New York: Pantheon, 1984).

On the development of constitutional doctrine, I have relied on Chafee, *Free Speech in the United States;* Paul L. Murphy, *The Constitution in Crisis Times* (New York: Harper & Row, 1972); Henry J. Abraham, *Freedom and the Court*, 4th ed. (New York: Oxford University Press, 1982); Harry Kalven, Jr., *A Worthy Tradition: Freedom of Speech in America* (New York: Harper & Row, 1988). On constitutionalism, see Michael Kammen, *A Machine That Would Go of Itself: The Constitution in American Culture* (New York: Knopf, 1986). On conservative criticisms of civil liberties litigation, see Richard E. Morgan, *Disabling America: The "Rights Industry" in Our Time* (New York: Basic Books, 1984). On public-interest group litigation, see [Norman Redlich], "Private Attorneys General: Group

Action in the Fight for Civil Liberties," *Yale Law Journal* 58 (1949): 574–598; Leo Pfeffer, "Amici in Church–State Litigation," *Law and Contemporary Problems* 44 (Winter 1981): 83–110; Stephen Wasby, "How Planned Is 'Planned Litigation'?" *American Bar Foundation Research Journal* (Winter 1984): 83–138; Souraf, *Wall of Separation;* and Neier, *Only Judgment.*

There is no adequate biography of any major ACLU figure. Lamson's *Roger Baldwin* is an annotated interview, but see the insightful although uneven articles by Dwight MacDonald, "The Defense of Everybody," *The New Yorker,* July 11, 1953, and July 18, 1953. Baldwin's numerous articles in the political press are particularly revealing of his complex and often-changing views. After 1940, however, he rewrote his past out of embarrassment over his associations with Communists.

On the other founders of the ACLU, see Blanche Wiesen Cook, ed., *Crystal Eastman on Women and Revolution* (New York: Oxford University Press, 1978); and Rosalyn Fraad Baxandall, *Works on Fire: The Life and Writing of Elizabeth Gurley Flynn* (New Brunswick, N.J.: Rutgers University Press, 1987). None of the biographies of Norman Thomas adequately examines his civil liberties career. There is useful firsthand material in Hays, *Let Freedom Ring* and *City Lawyer.* Morris L. Ernst wrote several volumes of memoirs and many books on civil liberties issues. See especially his *The Best Is Yet . . .* (New York: Harper Bros., 1945); with William Seagle, *To the Pure: The Study of Obscenity and the Censor* (New York: Viking, 1928); with Alexander Lindey, *The Censor Marches On* (New York: Doubleday, 1940). Corliss Lamont's *Freedom Is As Freedom Does* has been extremely influential; see also his *Yes to Life* (New York: Horizon, 1981); and *Voice in the Wilderness* (Buffalo, N.Y.: Prometheus Books, 1974).

Index